A CONCISE HISTORY OF

America and Its People

VOLUME TWO SINCE 1865

James Kirby Martin
University of Houston

Randy Roberts
Purdue University

Steven Mintz
University of Houston

Linda O. McMurry
North Carolina State University

James H. Jones
University of Houston
and

Sam W. Haynes
University of Texas at Arlington

HarperCollins *CollegePublishers*

*F*or Our Students

Executive Editor: Bruce Borland
Director of Development: Betty Slack
Cover Design: Kay Petronio
Cover Illustration: Jane Sterrett
Photo Researcher: Judy Ladendorf/Ellen Berman
Electronic Production Manager: Angel Gonzalez Jr.
Publishing Services: Ruttle, Shaw & Wetherill, Inc.
Electronic Page Makeup: Ruttle Graphics, Inc.
Printer and Binder: RR Donnelley & Sons Company
Cover Printer: RR Donnelley & Sons Company

For permission to use copyrighted material, grateful acknowledgment is made to the copyright holders on pages C-1 and C-2, which are hereby made part of this copyright page.

A Concise History of America and Its People, Volume Two Since 1865

Library of Congress Cataloging-in-Publication Data
A concise history of America and its people/James Kirby Martin . . .
    [et al.].—Single vol. ed.
    p. cm.
    Includes bibliographical references (p.) and index.
    ISBN 0-673-46782-1
    1. United States—History. I. Martin, James Kirby
E178.1.C74 1995
973—dc20   94-20138
                                                    CIP

95 96 97 9 8 7 6 5 4 3 2

Brief Contents

Detailed Contents v

Maps, Charts, Figures, and Tables xi

Preface xiii

About the Authors xviii

Chapter 1   *The Peopling and Unpeopling of America   1*

Chapter 2   *Plantations and Cities upon a Hill, 1620–1700   27*

Chapter 3   *Provincial America in Upheaval, 1660–1760   52*

Chapter 4   *Breaking the Bonds of Empire, 1760–1775   78*

Chapter 5   *The Times That Tried Many Souls, 1775–1783   106*

Chapter 6   *Securing the Republic and Its Ideals, 1776–1789   132*

Chapter 7   *Shaping the New Nation, 1789–1800   159*

Chapter 8   *The Jeffersonians in Power, 1800–1815   180*

Chapter 9   *Nationalism, Economic Growth, and the Roots of Sectional Conflict, 1815–1824   201*

Chapter 10 *Power and Politics in Jackson's America   223*

Chapter 11 *Reforming American Society   250*

Chapter 12 *The Divided North, the Divided South   276*

Chapter 13 *Surge to the Pacific   303*

Chapter 14 *The House Divided   333*

Chapter 15 *A Nation Shattered by Civil War, 1860–1865   358*

VOLUME TWO BEGINS

Chapter 16 *The Nation Reconstructed: North, South, and the West, 1865–1877   386*

Chapter 17 *Emergence as an Economic Power   416*

Chapter 18 *Immigrants and Workers in Industrial America   445*

Chapter 19 *The Rise of an Urban Society and City People   471*

Chapter 20   *End of the Century Crisis*   498

Chapter 21   *Imperial America, 1870–1900*   524

Chapter 22   *The Progressive Struggle*   551

Chapter 23   *The United States and World War I*   580

Chapter 24   *Modern Times, the 1920s*   609

Chapter 25   *The Age of Roosevelt*   636

Chapter 26   *The End of Isolation: America Faces the World, 1920–1945*   662

Chapter 27   *Waging Peace and War*   694

Chapter 28   *Ike's America*   719

Chapter 29   *Vietnam and the Crisis of Authority*   744

Chapter 30   *The Struggle for a Just Society*   771

Chapter 31   *America in Our Time*   804

Appendix   A-1

Credits   C-1

Index   I-1

Detailed Contents

Maps, Charts, Figures, and Tables xi

Preface xiii

About the Authors xviii

Chapter 1 **The Peopling and Unpeopling of America** 1
The First Discovery of America 4
Preparing Europe for Westward Expansion 7
Explorers, Conquerors, and the Making of New Spain 10
Challengers for North America: France and England 15
Joining in the Invasion of America 19

Chapter 2 **Plantations and Cities upon a Hill, 1620–1700** 27
From Settlements to Societies in the South 29
Religious Dissenters Colonize New England 32
Surviving in Early America 39
Commercial Values and the Rise of Chattel Slavery 43

Chapter 3 **Provincial America in Upheaval, 1660–1760** 52
Designing England's North American Empire 54
Defying the Imperial Will: Provincial Convulsions and Rebellions 60
Maturing Colonial Societies in Unsettled Times 65

Chapter 4 **Breaking the Bonds of Empire, 1760–1775** 78
Provoking an Imperial Crisis 80
"Liberty, Property, and No Stamps" 86
A Second Crisis: The Townshend Duties 92
The Rupturing of Imperial Relations 96

*At the end of each chapter are a Chronology of Key Events, a Conclusion, and Suggestions for Further Reading.

Chapter 5   **The Times That Tried Many Souls, 1775–1783**   *106*

    Reconciliation or Independence   109
    Lord Dunmore's Proclamation of Emancipation   112
    Without Visible Allies: The War in the North   116
    Rescuing the Patriots: Toward Global Conflict   120
    The World Turned Upside Down   123

Chapter 6   **Securing the Republic and Its Ideals, 1776–1789**   *132*

    Establishing New Republican Governments   136
    Crises of the Confederation   138
    Human Rights and Social Change   144
    Second New Beginning, New National Government   150

Chapter 7   **Shaping the New Nation, 1789–1800**   *159*

    Putting the New National Government into
    Operation   161
    The Birth of Political Parties   167
    A New President and New Challenges   173
    The Revolution of 1800   176

Chapter 8   **The Jeffersonians in Power, 1800–1815**   *180*

    Jefferson Takes Command   182
    The Eagle, the Tiger, and the Shark   191

Chapter 9   **Nationalism, Economic Growth, and the Roots of
Sectional Conflict, 1815–1824**   *201*

    The Growth of American Nationalism   203
    The Roots of American Economic Growth   211
    *The Growth of Political Factionalism and
Sectionalism   218*

Chapter 10   **Power and Politics in Jackson's America**   *223*

    Political Democratization   225
    The Rebirth of Parties   228
    Andrew Jackson: The Politics of Egalitarianism   233
    Rise of a Political Opposition   245

Chapter 11   **Reforming American Society**   *250*

    The Reform Impulse   251
    Moral Reform   253
    Social Reform   255
    Radical Reform   259
    Artistic and Cultural Ferment   268

Chapter 12 **The Divided North, the Divided South** *276*

A Divided Culture *277*
The Emergence of a New Industrial Order in the North
279
Southern Distinctiveness *286*
Slavery *292*

Chapter 13 **Surge to the Pacific** *303*

Opening the West *305*
Spanish and Indian America *309*
Settling the Far West *312*
Manifest Destiny *314*
The Mexican War *321*

Chapter 14 **The House Divided** *333*

The Crisis of 1850 *335*
Disintegration of the Party System *341*
The Gathering Storm *346*
Crisis of the Union *352*

Chapter 15 **A Nation Shattered by Civil War, 1860–1865** *358*

From Secession to Full-Scale War *361*
"Forward to Richmond!" and "On to Washington!" *367*
To and From Emancipation: The War on the
Home Front *373*
Breaking Confederate Resistance, 1863–1865 *379*

VOLUME TWO BEGINS

Chapter 16 **The Nation Reconstructed: North, South, and the West,**
1865–1877 *386*

Postwar Conditions and Issues *388*
Presidential Reconstruction *392*
Congressional Reconstruction *395*
Reconstruction in the South *399*
Reconstruction in the North and West *407*

Chapter 17 **Emergence as an Economic Power** *416*

America: Land of Plenty *418*
A Favorable Climate: The Role of Ideology, Politics, and
Finance *424*
The Rise of Big Business *429*
Economic Modernization in the South and West *436*

Chapter 18 Immigrants and Workers in Industrial America 445

Huddled Masses at the Golden Door 447
Nativism: The Anti-Immigrant Reaction 453
Working in Industrial America 458

Chapter 19 The Rise of an Urban Society and City People 471

New Cities and New Problems 474
City Culture 482
Entertaining the Multitudes 488

Chapter 20 End of the Century Crisis 498

*Equilibrium and Inertia: The National Political
Scene 501*
Style over Substance: Government in the Gilded Age 506
The Farmers Revolt 513
Depression and Turbulence in the 1890s 517

Chapter 21 Imperial America, 1870–1900 524

*Congressional Control and the Reduction of American
Power 526*
The Spirit of American Greatness 528
*The Emergence of Aggression in American Foreign
Policy 533*
The War for Empire 538

Chapter 22 The Progressive Struggle 551

The Progressive Impulse 553
Progressives in Action 557
Progressivism Moves to the National Level 564
Progressivism in the International Arena 569
Progressive Accomplishments, Progressive Failures 573

Chapter 23 The United States and World War I 580

The Road to War 582
American Industry Goes to War 588
The American Public Goes to War 591
The War Front 596
Social Unrest After the War 598
The Treaty of Versailles 600

Chapter 24 Modern Times, the 1920s 609

The Clash of Values 611
The Revolt of the Traditionalists 616
The Rise of Urban Culture 621

The Republican Restoration   626
The Great Crash   629

Chapter 25   The Age of Roosevelt   636

Herbert Hoover and the Great Depression   638
Franklin Roosevelt and the First New Deal   641
The Second New Deal   652
The New Deal and Minorities   655
The New Deal in Decline   658

**Chapter 26   The End of Isolation: America Faces the World,
1920–1945   662**

Diplomacy Between the Wars   664
The Coming of World War II   666
America at War   673
Social Changes During the War   677
The War in Europe   681
The War in the Pacific   687

Chapter 27   Waging Peace and War   694

Containing the Russian Bear   697
The Containment Policy   702
The Cold War at Home   707
The Paranoid Style   713

Chapter 28   Ike's America   719

Quiet Changes   722
We Shall Overcome   731
The Sounds of Change   736

Chapter 29   Vietnam and the Crisis of Authority   744

The Illusion of Greatness   747
Vietnam: America's Longest War   752
The Tortuous Path Toward Peace   762

Chapter 30   The Struggle for a Just Society   771

The Struggle for Racial Justice   774
The Youth Revolt   789
Liberation Movements   792

Chapter 31   America in Our Time   804

Crisis of Political Leadership   807
Wrenching Economic Transformations   810
A New American Role in the World   814

The Reagan Revolution 819
The Bush Presidency 826

Appendix *A-1*
The Declaration of Independence *A-3*
The Constitution of the United States of America *A-7*
Amendments to the Constitution *A-18*
Presidential Elections *A-28*
Presidential Administrations *A-35*
Supreme Court Justices *A-54*
Admission of States to the Union *A-58*

Credits *C-1*

Index *I-1*

$\mathcal{M}$aps, Charts, Figures, and Tables

Voyages of Exploration   11
Chesapeake Settlements, 1650   22
New England Colonies, 1650   39
African Slave Trade   47
Middle Colonies, 1685   57
North America, 1763   82
Northern Theater of War, 1775–1778   119
Southern Theater of War, 1780–1781   127
Western Land Claims Ceded by the States   140
Slave Concentration, 1790   149
Barbary States   188
The Louisiana Purchase and Route of Lewis and Clark   190
Missouri Compromise   220
Extension of Male Suffrage   226
Election of 1828   233
Total Immigration, 1840–1860   285
Western Trails   308
Oregon Country, Pacific Northwest Boundary Dispute   319
Mexican War   326
Slave Concentration, 1860/The Cotton Kingdom   337
Compromise of 1850/Kansas-Nebraska Act   345
Election of 1860   363
Secession   365
Civil War, 1861–1862   368
Civil War, 1863–1865   380
Election of 1876   412

Immigration, 1880–1889 and 1900–1909   449

American Empire   546

Election of 1912   567

American Interventions in the Caribbean   571

Unemployment, 1929–1942   640

Depression Shopping List: 1932–1934   645

Legislation Enacted During the Hundred Days,
March 9–June 16, 1933   650

World War II, European Theater   682

World War II, Pacific Theater   688

Korean War   706

Vietnam Conflict, 1964–1975   757

U.S. Troop Levels in Vietnam, 1960–1972   765

U.S. Involvement in Central America and the Caribbean   823

Major Action in the Persian Gulf   831

Preface

A *Concise History of America and Its People*, a newly abridged version of the full-length *America and Its People* (2nd edition), has been designed with both instructors and students of the U.S. history survey in mind. It is hoped that this text will serve the needs of teachers who require a brief overview of American history, one which will allow them to develop particular themes and issues through the use of supplemental readings such as primary sources, monographs, novels, and the like. At the same time, the authors have not lost sight of the primary task of any textbook: to engage students and hold their interest. A history text which merely synopsizes the past does so at the risk of losing the richness, color, and drama of the American experience. The challenge of the authors in *A Concise History of America and Its People*, then, has been to streamline the full-length text without compromising its effectiveness as a pedagogical tool.

In addition to retaining the style and flavor of the original, *A Concise History of America and Its People* resembles its parent in terms of organization and structure. Although more than a third shorter than the full-length text, this abridgement contains many of the distinctive and popular features of *America and Its People*. The anecdotes that open each chapter, which frame the chapter's central themes and draw students into the material, have been retained with only minor revisions. Readers will find in the abridged text more than half of the original's maps and illustrations, as well as the useful Chronology of Events at the end of each chapter. Although the Special Features section has been dropped from the format in this brief edition, some material has been rewoven into the main text, albeit in abbreviated form.

As with all books there is always room for improvement, and we have worked hard to fine-tune this new version of *America and Its People*. A number of key events have been clarified, and every effort has been made to incorporate the findings of significant recent scholarship. To improve the narrative flow and emphasize the causative effects of national affairs on American foreign policy, the sequence of chapters covering the late nineteenth century has been changed. "Imperial America," a chapter which deals with such issues as the United States' search for markets and the Spanish-American War, now follows the chapter entitled "End of the Century Crisis," which covers politics in the Gilded Age, Populism and the Panic of 1893. Whereas the second edition of the full-length text ends with the election of 1992, the final chapter (Chapter 31) of the abridged text now includes a discussion of the Clinton administration. Bibliographies at the end of each chapter have also been updated.

Most important, this abridgement of the full-length text strives to remain true to the purpose of the original: to provide students with a "people-centered" approach to the American past. By focusing on people, both the great and the ordinary, the authors endeavor to highlight the dramatic conflict among individuals and groups that has so often produced meaningful change. Both the full-length and abridged versions of *America and Its People* attempt to go beyond the study of major historical figures and their impact on national affairs; both texts seek to show how ordinary people lived their lives, and to do so in ways that students will find meaningful and relevant to their own experience. It is the authors' belief that ethnicity, gender, and race should not be treated as adjunct information, tacked onto the end of a political narrative, but rather should be presented as an integral part of American history. It is our hope that this book has succeeded in presenting a compelling, balanced, and sensitive account of a nation and its people.

The Authors

Supplements

For Instructors

Instructors Resource Manual

This extensive resource by Mark Newman of the University of Illinois at Chicago, begins with essays on teaching history through maps, film, and primary sources. Each chapter contains a synopsis, sample discussion questions, lecture supplements called "Connections and Extensions," and instructional flowcharts. The manual includes a special reproducible set of map exercises by James Conrad of Nichols College, designed to teach basic geographic literacy.

America Through the Eyes of Its People: A Collection of Primary Sources

Prepared by Carol Brown, this one-volume collection of primary documents portraying the rich and varied tapestry of American life contains documents concerning women, Native Americans, African-Americans, Hispanics, and others who helped to shape the course of U.S. history. Designed to be duplicated by instructors for student use, the documents have accompanying student exercises.

A Guide to Teaching American History through Film

Created by Randy Roberts of Purdue University, this guide provides instructors with a creative and practical tool for stimulating classroom discussions. The sections include: "American Films: A Historian's Perspective," a listing of "Films for Specific Periods of American History," "Practical Suggestions," and "Bibliography." The film listing is in a narrative form, explaining the connection between each film and the topics being studied.

Video Lecture Launchers

Prepared by Mark Newman, University of Illinois at Chicago, these video lecture launchers (each 2 to 5 minutes in duration) cover key issues in American history from 1877 to the present. The launchers are accompanied by an Instructor's Manual.

American Impressions: A CD-ROM for U.S. History

This unique, ground-breaking product for the Introduction to U.S. History course is organized in a topical/thematic framework which allows an in-depth coverage for each topic with a media-centered focus. Hundreds of photos, maps, art, graphics, and historical film clips are organized into narrated vignettes and interactive activities to create a tool for both professors and students. This first volume of a series includes: When Three Cultures Meet, The Constitution, Labor and Reform, and Democracy and Diversity: The History of Civil Rights. Each topic is explored through three major themes, Politics, Culture and Society, and Science and Health. Available for Macintosh and Windows formats.

Visual Archives of American History, 2/e

This two-sided video laserdisc explores history from a meeting of three cultures to the present and is an encyclopedic chronology of U.S. History offering hundreds of photographs and illustrations, a variety of source and reference maps—several of which are animated—plus approximately 50 minutes of video clips. For ease in planning lectures, a manual listing barcodes for scanning and frame numbers for all the content will be provided.

Transparencies

A set of over 30 map transparencies drawn from the text of *America and Its People.*

Discovering American History Through Maps and Views

Created by Gerald Danzer of the University of Illinois at Chicago, the recipient of the AHA's 1990 James Harvey Robinson Prize for his work in the development of map transparencies—this set of 140 four-color acetates is a unique instructional tool. It contains an introduction on teaching history through maps and a detailed commentary on each transparency. The collection includes cartographic and pictorial maps, views and photos, urban plans, building diagrams, and works of art.

Test Bank

This *Test Bank,* prepared by Ken Weatherbie of Del Mar College, contains over 2,000 test items, including multiple-choice, true/false and essay questions, and map exercises. The questions are keyed to topic, difficulty level, cognitive type, and relevant text page.

TestMaster Computerized Testing System

This flexible, easy-to-master computer test bank includes all the test items in the printed test bank. The *TestMaster* software allows you to edit existing questions and add your own items. Tests can be printed in several different formats and can include figures such as graphs and tables. Available for IBM and Macintosh computers.

QuizMaster

This new program enables you to design *TestMaster* generated tests that your students can take on a computer rather than in printed form. *QuizMaster* is available separately from *TestMaster* and can be obtained free through your sales representative.

Grades

A grade-keeping and classroom management software program that maintains data for up to 200 students.

For Students

Study Guide and Practice Tests

This two-volume study guide, by Ken Chiaro of Pima Community College, is designed to provide students with a comprehensive review of text material and to encourage application and critical analysis of the material. Each chapter contains a student introduction, reading comprehension and geography exercises, true-false, completion, and multiple-choice "Practice Tests."

Learning to Think Critically: Films and Myths About American History

Randy Roberts and Robert May of Purdue University use well-known films such as *Gone with the Wind* and *Casablanca* to explore some common myths about America and its past. Many widely held assumptions about our country's past come from or are perpetuated by popular films. Which are true? Which are patently not true? And how does a student of history approach documents, sources, and textbooks with a critical and discerning eye? This short handbook subjects some popular beliefs to historical scrutiny in order to help students develop a method of inquiry for approaching the subject of history in general.

Mapping American History: Student Activities

Written by Gerald Danzer of the University of Illinois at Chicago, this free map workbook for students features exercises designed to teach students to interpret and analyze cartographic materials as historical documents. The instructor is entitled to a free copy of the workbook for each copy of the text purchased from HarperCollins.

TimeLink Computer Atlas of American History

This atlas, compiled by William Hamblin of Brigham Young University, is an introductory software tutorial and textbook companion. This Macintosh program presents the historical geography of the continental United States from colonial times to the settling of the West and the admission of the last continental state in 1912. The program covers territories in different time periods, provides quizzes, and includes a special Civil War module.

About the Authors

JAMES KIRBY MARTIN is a member of the Department of History at the University of Houston. A graduate of Hiram College in Ohio, he earned his Ph.D. degree at the University of Wisconsin in 1969, specializing in Early American history. His interests also include American social and military history. Among his publications are *Men in Rebellion* (1973), *In the Course of Human Events* (1979), *A Respectable Army* (1982), and *Drinking in America: A History*, rev. ed. (1987), the latter two volumes in collaboration with Mark E. Lender. Martin serves as general editor of the *American Social Experience* series, New York University Press. He recently was a senior fellow at the Philadelphia Center for Early American Studies, University of Pennsylvania, as well as scholar-in-residence at the David Library of the American Revolution, Washington Crossing, Pennsylvania. He is completing a biography of Benedict Arnold.

RANDY ROBERTS earned his Ph.D degree in 1978 from Louisiana State University. His areas of specialization include modern U.S. history and the history of American popular culture and sports. He is a member of the Department of History at Purdue University, where he recently won the Murphy Award for outstanding undergraduate teaching. His publications include *Jack Dempsey: The Manassa Mauler* (1979), *Papa Jack: Jack Johnson and the Era of White Hopes* (1983), and, in collaboration with James S. Olson, *Playing for Keeps: Sports and American Society, 1945 to the Present* (1989) and *Where the Domino Fell: America and Vietnam, 1945–1990* (1991). Roberts serves as co-editor of the *Studies in Sports and Society* series, University of Illinois Press, and is on the editorial board of the *Journal of Sports History*. His current research and writing interests include a biographical investigation of Hollywood actor John Wayne.

STEVEN MINTZ graduated from Oberlin College in Ohio before earning his Ph.D. degree at Yale University in 1979. His special interests include American social history with particular reference to families, women, children, and communities. Mintz is a member of the Department of History at the University of Houston. From 1989 to 1990 he was a visiting scholar at Harvard University's Center for European Studies, and has served as a consultant to the Smithsonian Institution's National Museum of American History. His books include *A Prison of Expectations: The Family in Victorian Culture* (1983), and, in collaboration with Susan Kellogg, *Domestic Revolutions: A Social History of American Family Life* (1988). Mintz is an editor of the *American Social Experience* series, New York University Press, and is completing a book on pre-Civil War American reform.

LINDA O. McMURRY is a member of the Department of History at North Carolina State University. She completed her undergraduate studies at Auburn University, where she also earned her Ph.D. degree in 1976. Her fields of specialization include nineteenth- and twentieth-century U.S. history with an emphasis on the African-American experience and the New South. A recipient of a Rockefeller Foundation Humanities fellowship, she has written *George Washington Carver: Scientist and Symbol* (1981), and *Recorder of the Black Experience: A Biography of Monroe Nathan Work* (1985). McMurry has been active as a consultant to public television stations and museums on topics relating to black history, and is currently completing a study of biracial organizations in the South from the Reconstruction era to World War II.

JAMES H. JONES earned his Ph.D. degree at Indiana University in 1972. His areas of specialization include modern U.S. history, the history of medical ethics and medicine, and the history of sexual behavior. A member of the Department of History at the University of Houston, Jones has been a senior fellow of the National Endowment for the Humanities, a Kennedy fellow at Harvard University, a senior research fellow at the Kennedy Institute of Ethics, Georgetown University, and a Rockefeller fellow at the University of Texas Medical Branch, Galveston. His published writings include *Bad Blood: The Tuskegee Syphilis Experiment* (1981), and he is currently finishing a book on Alfred C. Kinsey and the emergence of scientific research dealing with human sexual behavior.

SAM W. HAYNES received his B.A. from Columbia University and his Ph.D. from the University of Houston in 1988. He is the author of *Soldiers of Misfortune: The Somervell and Mier Expeditions* (1990) and the editor of Thomas Jefferson Green's memoir *Journal of the Texian Expedition Against Mier* (1993). In 1993 he received a Dobie-Paisano

Fellowship awarded by the Texas Institute of Letters. He is currently completing a biography of James K. Polk. His areas of specialization include nineteenth-century U.S. expansionism, early Texas history, and the American Southwest. He is a member of the history faculty at the University of Texas at Arlington, where he also serves as a Fellow at the Center for Greater Southwestern Studies.

Chapter **16**

The Nation Reconstructed: North, South, and the West, 1865–1877

Postwar Conditions and Issues
The War's Impact on Individuals
Unresolved Issues

Presidential Reconstruction
Lincoln's Plan
Johnson's Plan
Black Codes in the South

Congressional Reconstruction
"Radical" Reconstruction
Black Suffrage

Reconstruction in the South
Carpetbaggers, Scalawags, and Black Republicans
Character of Republican Rule
Black and White Adaptation
Violent White Resistance

Reconstruction in the North and West
Northern Shifts in Attitudes
Racism and American Indians
Final Retreat from Reconstruction

A s Thomas Pinckney approached El Dorado, his plantation in South Carolina, he felt a quiver of apprehension. Pinckney, a captain in the defeated Confederate army, had stayed the night with neighbors before going to reclaim his land. "Your negroes sacked your house," they reported. "They got it in their heads that the property of whites belongs to them." Pinckney remembered the days when he had been met with cheerful greetings from his slaves; now he was welcomed with an eerie silence. In the house, a single servant seemed genuinely glad to see him, but she pleaded ignorance as to the whereabouts of the other freed persons. He lingered about the house until after the dinner hour. Still no one appeared, so he informed the servant that he would return in the morning.

The next day Pinckney returned and summoned his former slaves. Their sullen faces reflected their defiant spirits. Pinckney told them, "I do not wish to interfere with your freedom. But I want my old hands to work my lands for me. I will pay wages." The freed persons remained silent as he gave further reassurances. Finally one responded. They would never again work for a white man, he told his former master. Pinckney seemed confused and asked how they expected to support themselves and where they would go. They quickly informed him that they intended to stay and work the land themselves.

Pinckney had no intention of allowing his former slaves to lay claim to his property. He joined with his neighbors in an appeal to the Union commander at Charleston, who sent a company of troops. The freed persons still refused to work under his terms, so Pinckney denied them access to food and supplies. Soon his head plowman begged food for his hungry family, claiming he wanted to work. Slowly, other former slaves drifted back. "They had suffered," he later recalled, "and their ex-master had suffered with them."

All over the South this scenario was acted out with variations, as former masters and slaves sought to define their new relationships. Whites tried to keep the freed persons a dependent labor source; African Americans struggled to win as much independence as possible. At the same time the other sections of the nation faced similar problems of determining the status of heterogeneous populations whose interests were sometimes in conflict with the majority. The war had reaped a costly harvest in lives and property, but at the same time it accelerated the modernization of the economy and society. Western expansion forced Americans to deal with the often hostile presence of the Plains Indians; the resumption of large-scale immigration raised issues of how to adapt to a society made up of many different ethnic and religious groups. Complicating these issues were unresolved questions about federal authority, widespread racial prejudice in both North and South, and strongly held beliefs in the sanctity of property rights.

Reconstruction offered an opportunity to balance conflicting interests with justice and fairness. In the end, however, the government was unwilling to establish ongoing programs and permanent mechanisms to protect the rights of minorities. As on Pinckney's plantation, economic power usually became the determining factor in establishing relationships. Authorities sacrificed the interests of both African Americans and the Indians of the West to the goals of national unity and economic growth. Yet in the ashes of failure were left two cornerstones on which the future could be built—the Fourteenth and Fifteenth Amendments to the Constitution.

Postwar Conditions and Issues

The war had exacted a heavy price on Americans, but its costs were not borne equally. Many segments of the Northern economy were stimulated by wartime demands and had benefited from federal programs enacted to aid industrial growth. Virtually exempt from the devastation of the battlefield, the North built railroads and industries and increased agricultural production. At the same time torn-up Southern rails were twisted around trees, Southern factories were put to the torch, and Southern farmland lay choked with weeds.

In 1865 Southerners were still reeling from the bitter legacy of total war. General Philip Sheridan announced that after his troops had finished in the Shenandoah Valley even a crow would have to carry rations to fly over the area. One year after the war Carl Schurz noted that along the path of Sherman's march the countryside still "looked for many miles like a broad black streak of ruin and desolation." Southern cities suffered the most. Much of what was not destroyed was confiscated, and emancipation divested Southerners of another $2 billion to $4 billion in assets. The decline of Southern wealth has been estimated at more than 40 percent during the four years of war.

The War's Impact on Individuals

Returning soldiers and their wives had to reconstruct relationships disrupted by separation—and the assumption of control by the women on farms and plantations. Southerners worried about how to meet their obligations, since Confederate currency and bonds were now worthless. Many white Southerners also feared that the end of slavery would bring a nightmare of black revenge, rape, and pillage unless whites retained social control.

For four million former slaves, emancipation had come piecemeal, following the course of the Northern armies. It was not finalized until the ratification of the Thirteenth Amendment in December 1865. By then most border states had voluntarily adopted emancipation, but the amendment destroyed the remnants of slavery in Delaware and Kentucky. Most slaves waited patiently for the day of freedom, continuing to work the plantations but speaking up more boldly. Sometimes the Yankees came, proclaimed them free, and then left them to the mercy of their masters. Most, therefore, reacted cautiously in testing the limits of their new freedom.

Many African Americans had to leave their plantations, at least for a short time, to feel liberated. A few were not sure about the meaning of freedom and thought they would never have to work again. Soon, most learned they had gained everything—and nothing. As Frederick Douglass noted, the freed person "was free from the individual master but a slave of society. He had neither money, property, nor friends. He was free from the old plantation, but he had nothing but the dusty road under his feet. . . . He was turned loose, naked, hungry, and destitute to the open sky."

The wartime plight of homeless and hungry blacks as well as whites impelled Congress to take unprecedented action, establishing on March 3, 1865, the Freedmen's Bureau within the War Department. The bureau was to provide "such issues of provisions, clothing, and fuel" as were needed to relieve "destitute and suffering refugees and their wives and children." Never before had the national government assumed responsibility for relief. Feeding and clothing the population had not been deemed its proper function. Considered a drastic measure warranted only by civil war, the bureau was to operate for only a year.

The bureau was more than a relief agency. It had its own courts to deal with land and labor disputes. Agents in every state provided rations and medical supplies and helped to negotiate labor contracts between former slaves and landowners. The quality of the service rendered to the freed persons depended on the ability and motivation of the individual agents. Some courageously championed the freed persons' cause; others sided with the former masters. One of the most lasting benefits of the Freedmen's Bureau was the schools it established, frequently in cooperation with such Northern agencies as the American Missionary Association. During and after the war, African Americans of all ages flocked to these schools. The freed persons shrewdly recognized the keys to the planters' power—land, literacy, and the vote. The white South legally denied all three to African Amerians in slavery, and many former slaves were determined to have them all.

During the war General Sherman had been plagued with swarms of freed persons following his army, and in January 1865 he issued an order setting aside a strip of abandoned coastal lands from Charleston, South Carolina, to Jacksonville, Florida, for the exclusive use of freed blacks who were to be given title to 40-acre lots. Three months later the bill establishing the Freedmen's Bureau gave the agency control of thousands of acres of abandoned and confiscated lands to be rented to former slaves for three-year periods with an option to buy at a later date. By June 1865, 40,000 African Americans were cultivating land. In the Sea Islands and elsewhere they proved they could succeed as independent farmers. Yet land reform was not a popular cause among whites. Although a few congressmen continued to advocate land confiscation and redistribution, most freed persons never realized the dream of "forty acres and a mule."

Unresolved Issues

At war's end many questions remained unanswered. The first of these concerned the status of the former slaves. They were indeed free, but were

Former slaves realized that education was one key to real freedom and flocked to schools opened by the Freedmen's Bureau, the American Missionary Association, and various religious and human rights groups.

they citizens? The Dred Scott decision had denied citizenship to all African Americans. Even if it were decided that they were citizens, what rights were conferred by that citizenship? Would they be segregated as free blacks in the antebellum North had often been? Also, citizenship did not automatically convey suffrage rights; women were proof of that. Were the freed persons to be given the ballot? Racial prejudice as well as constitutional and partisan questions complicated these weighty matters.

The Constitution had been severely tested by civil war, and many felt it had been twisted by the desire to save the Union. Once the emergency was over, how were constitutional balance and limits to be restored? Except during the terms of a few strong presidents, Congress had been the most powerful branch of government during the nation's first 70 years. Lincoln had assumed unprecedented powers, and Congress was determined to regain its ascendency. The ensuing battle directly influenced Reconstruction policies and their implementation.

Secession was dead, but what about states' rights? Almost everyone agreed that a division of power between the national and state governments was crucial to the maintenance of freedom. The fear of centralized tyranny remained strong. There was reluctance to enlarge federal power into areas traditionally controlled by the states, even though action in some of those areas was essential to craft the kind of peace many desired. Hesitation to reduce states' rights produced timid and compromised solutions to such issues as suffrage. Also of concern was federal action in the realm of social welfare, a new and controversial role for the national government.

Another constitutional question concerned the status of the former Confederate states and how they were to be readmitted to the Union. There was no constitutional provision for failed secession, and many people debated whether the South had actually left the Union. Southerners and their Democratic party sympathizers now argued that the states had never legally separated from the rest of the nation, thus denying validity to the Confederacy in order to quickly regain their place in the Union. Extremists on the other side—Radical Republicans—insisted that the South had reverted to the status of conquered territory, forfeiting all rights as states. Lincoln and others believed that the Confederate states had remained in the Union but had forfeited their rights. This constitutional hairsplitting grew out of a struggle between the executive and legislative branches to determine which had the power to readmit the states and on what terms. It also reflected the hostility of some Northerners toward the "traitorous rebels" and the unwillingness of some Southerners to accept the consequences of defeat.

Affecting all these questions was partisan politics. The Republican party had very few adherents in the South. Its continued existence was dubious in the face of the probable reunion of the Northern and Southern wings of the Democratic party. Paradoxically, the political power of the

South, and in turn the Democratic party, was increased by the abolition of slavery. As freed persons, all African Americans would be counted for representation; as slaves only three-fifths of them had been counted. Thus the Republican party's perceived need to make itself a national party also influenced the course of Reconstruction.

Presidential Reconstruction

Early in the conflict questions regarding the reconstruction of the nation were secondary to winning the war—without victory there would be no nation to reconstruct. Nonetheless, Lincoln had to take some action as Union forces pushed into the South. Authority had to be imposed in the reclaimed territory, so the president named military governors for Tennessee, Arkansas, and Louisiana in 1862 after federal armies occupied most of those states. Lincoln also began formulating plans for civilian governments for those states and for other Confederate areas once they came under the control of Union forces.

Lincoln's Plan

Called the 10 percent plan, Lincoln's provisions were incredibly lenient. Rebels could receive presidential pardon by merely swearing their future allegiance to the Union and their acceptance of the end of slavery. Only a few people were excluded from pardons: Confederate military and civilian officers; United States judges, congressmen, and military officers who had resigned their posts to serve the Confederacy. Nevertheless, Lincoln did not require the new state governments to bar such people from future voting or officeholding. Moreover, after only 10 percent of the number who had voted in 1860 had taken the oath of allegiance, a state could form a civilian government. When such states produced a constitution outlawing slavery, Lincoln promised to recognize them as reconstructed. He did not demand any provisions for protecting black rights or allowing black suffrage.

The president's generosity outraged Radical Republicans, such as Representative Thaddeus Stevens of Pennsylvania and Senator Charles Sumner of Massachusetts. They thought the provisions did not adequately punish Confederate treason, restructure Southern society, protect the rights of African Americans, or aid the Republican party. The Radicals were in a minority, but Lincoln's leniency also dismayed many moderate Republicans. They shared the Radical view that Reconstruction was a congressional, not a presidential, function.

Congress then drew up a plan of its own: the Wade-Davis Bill. Its terms were much more stringent, yet not unreasonable. A majority, rather than 10 percent, of each state's voters had to declare their allegiance to form a government. Only those taking "ironclad" oaths of their past Union loyalty were allowed to participate in the making of new state constitutions. Barely a handful of high-ranking Confederates, however, were to be permanently barred from political participation. The only additional requirement imposed by Congress was the repudiation of the Confederate debt; Northerners did not want Confederate bondholders to benefit from their "investment in treason" at the cost to northern taxpayers. Congress would determine when a state had met these requirements.

A constitutional collision was postponed by Lincoln's pocket veto of the bill and his assassination on April 14, 1865. His successor, Andrew Johnson, was a Tennessee Democrat and Unionist. Of humble origins and illiterate until adulthood, he was the only Southerner to remain in the Senate after his state seceded. As with the Radical wing of the Republican party Johnson hated the planter class, but it was their aristocratic domination of the South, not their slaveholding, that he disliked. He was a firm believer in black inferiority and did not support the Radical aim of black legal equality. He also advocated strict adherence to the Constitution and strongly supported states' rights.

Johnson's Plan

In the end Johnson did not reverse Lincoln's lenient policy. Congress was not in session when Johnson became president so he had about eight months to pursue policies without congressional interference. He issued his own proclamation of amnesty in May 1865 and issued about 13,000 pardons. The most important aspect of the pardons was Johnson's claim that they restored all rights, including property rights. Thus many freed persons with crops in the ground suddenly found their masters back in charge—a disillusioning first taste of freedom that foreclosed further attempts at widespread land redistribution.

Johnson also announced plans for the reconstruction of North Carolina—a plan that was to set the pattern for all Southern states. A native Unionist was named provisional governor with the power to call a constitutional convention elected by loyal voters. Omitting Lincoln's 10 percent provision, Johnson did eventually require ratification of the Thirteenth Amendment, repudiation of Confederate debts, and state constitutional provisions abolishing slavery and renouncing secession. He also recommended limited suffrage for African Americans, primarily to stave off congressional attempts to give the vote to all black males.

The presidential plan fell short of the Radicals' hopes, but many moderates might have accepted it had the South complied with the letter

Andrew Johnson was the only president of the United States to be impeached.
His successful defense centered on the legitimate uses of his executive powers.

and the spirit of Johnson's proposals. Instead, Southerners seemed determined to ignore their defeat. The state governments, for the most part,
met the minimum requirements, but their apparent acceptance grew out
of a belief that very little had actually changed. Thus Southerners proceeded to show almost total disregard for Northern sensibilities. Presenting themselves, like prodigal sons, for admission to Congress were four
Confederate generals, six Confederate cabinet officials, and as the crowning indignity, Confederate Vice President Alexander H. Stephens. Most
Northerners were not exceedingly vindictive. Still, the North wanted
signs of change and indications of repentence by the former rebels.

Black Codes in the South

At the very least, Northerners expected adherence to the abolition of slavery, but the South was blatantly forging new forms of bondage. African
Americans were to be technically free, but Southern whites expected them
to work and live as they had before emancipation. To accomplish this

purpose, the new state governments enacted a series of laws known as the Black Codes. This legislation granted certain rights denied to slaves. Freed persons had the right to marry, own property, sue and be sued, and testify in court. However, Black Codes in all states prohibited racial inter-marriage, and some forbade freed persons from owning certain types of property, such as alcoholic beverages and firearms. Most so tightly re-stricted black legal rights that they were practically nonexistent. Black Codes imposed curfews on African Americans, segregated them, and out-lawed their right to congregate in large groups.

The Black Codes also sought to fashion a labor system as close to slavery as possible. Some laws required that African Americans obtain spe-cial licenses for any job except agricultural labor or domestic service. Most mandated the signing of yearly labor contracts, which sometimes required African Americans to call the landowner "master" and allowed withhold-ing wages for minor infractions. Mississippi even prohibited black owner-ship or rental of land. Mandatory apprenticeship programs took children away from their parents, and vagrancy laws allowed authorities to arrest blacks and use them on chain gangs or rent them out to planters for as long as a year at a time.

Most Northerners would not have insisted on black equality or suf-frage, but the South had regressed too far. Some Black Codes were virtually identical to the old slave codes, with the word *negro* substituted for *slave*. At the same time, reports of white violence against blacks filtered back to Washington. As a result, Congress refused to seat the representatives and senators from the former Confederate states when it reconvened in De-cember 1865 and instead proceeded to investigate conditions in the South.

Congressional Reconstruction

To discover what was really happening in the South, Congress established the Joint Committee on Reconstruction, which conducted inquiries and interviews that provided graphic and chilling examples of white repres-sion and brutality toward African Americans. Prior to the committee's final report, even moderates came to believe that action was necessary. In early 1866 Congress passed a bill to extend the life of the Freedmen's Bu-reau, but Johnson vetoed it, claiming that the bureau was constitutional only as a wartime measure. Congress then passed the Civil Rights Act, granting citizenship to all persons born in the United States. Once again, Johnson used his veto power to kill a bill that he deemed both unconsti-tutional and unwise. This time, however, Congress overrode the veto. It then passed a slightly revised Freedmen's Bureau bill in July and enacted it over Johnson's veto. Even though the South had ignored much of Johnson's advice, such as granting limited suffrage to blacks, the president stubbornly held to his conviction that reconstruction was complete and labeled his congressional opponents as "traitors."

Johnson's language did not create a climate of cooperation. Congress did not care about the constitutional questions that he raised and his challenge to congressional authority. Determined to establish an alternate program of reconstruction, Congress drafted the Fourteenth Amendment. Undoubtedly the most significant legacy of Reconstruction, the first article of the amendment defined citizenship and its basic rights. Every person born in the United States and subject to its jurisdiction was declared a citizen. The amendment also forbade any state from abridging the rights of citizenship or from depriving any person of "due process of law." Although 100 years would pass before its provisions were enforced as intended, the amendment has been interpreted to mean that states as well as the federal government are bound by the Bill of Rights—an important constitutional change that paved the way for the civil rights decisions and laws of the twentieth century.

The amendment did not require black suffrage but reduced the "basis of representation" proportionately for those states not allowing it. Former Confederate leaders were also barred from holding office unless pardoned by Congress—not the president. Finally, neither Confederate war debts nor compensation to former slaveholders were ever to be paid. Congress adopted the amendment, in June 1866 and then sent it to the states for ratification.

President Johnson bristled at this assault on his perceived powers and urged the Southern states not to ratify the amendment. All but Tennessee decided to take his advice and wait for further congressional action. Johnson took to the campaign trail, urging voters to oust the Radicals in the 1866 congressional elections. He met with heckling and humiliation during his "swing around the circle." The campaign was vicious, characterized by appeals to racial prejudice by the Democrats and charges of Democratic treason by the Republicans. The Republicans won overwhelming victories, which they interpreted as a mandate for congressional reconstruction.

"Radical" Reconstruction

The election results along with Southern intransigence finally gave the Radicals the upper hand. In 1867 Congress passed the Military Reconstruction Act that raised the price of readmission. This act declared all existing "Johnson governments," except Tennessee's, void and divided the

South into five military districts headed by military governors who were to be granted broad powers. Following the ratification of a new state constitution that provided for black suffrage, elections were to be held and the state would be required to ratify the Fourteenth Amendment. When that amendment became part of the Constitution and Congress approved the new state constitutions, the states would be granted representation in Congress once again.

Obviously, Johnson disliked the congressional plan; he vetoed it, only to see his veto overridden. Nevertheless, as commander-in-chief he reluctantly appointed military governors, and by the end of 1867 elections had been held in every state except Texas. Because many white Southerners boycotted the elections, the South came under the control of Republicans supported by Union forces. In a way, however, Southerners had brought more radical measures upon themselves by their inflexibility.

Congress realized the plan it had enacted was unprecedented and subject to challenge by the other two branches of government. To check Johnson's power, Congress also passed the Tenure of Office Act, which required Senate consent for the removal of any official whose appointment had required the Senate's confirmation. It was meant in part to protect Secretary of War Edwin M. Stanton, who supported the Radicals.

When the president attempted to remove Stanton, the House of Representatives voted to impeach Johnson. In the Senate trial that followed radical prosecutors argued that Johnson had committed "high crimes and misdemeanors" and asserted that a president could be removed for political reasons, even without being found legally guilty of crimes—a position James Madison had supported during the drafting of the Constitution.

The vote for conviction fell one short of the required two-thirds majority, when seven Republicans broke ranks and voted against conviction. This action set the precedent that a president must be guilty of serious misdeeds to be removed from office. The outcome was a political blow to the Radicals, costing them some support. On the other hand, Johnson's brush with impeachment did make him more cooperative for the last months of his presidency.

Black Suffrage

In the 1868 presidential election the Republicans won with Ulysses S. Grant, whose Civil War victories made his name a household word. His slogan, "Let us have peace," was appealing, but his election was less than a ringing endorsement for Radical policies. The military hero who had seemed invincible barely won the popular vote in several key states.

While a few Radicals had long favored black suffrage, only after the Republicans' electoral close call in 1868 did the bulk of the party begin to consider a suffrage amendment. Many were swayed by the political certainty that the black vote would be theirs and might give them the margin of victory in future close elections. Others were embarrassed by the hypocrisy of forcing black suffrage on the South while only 7 percent of Northern African Americans could vote. Still others believed that granting African Americans the vote would relieve whites of any further responsibility to protect black rights.

Suffrage supporters faced many objections to such an amendment. One was based on the lack of popular support. At that time only seven Northern states granted blacks the right to vote, and, since 1865, referendum proposals for black suffrage in eight states had been voted down. The amendment was so unpopular that, ironically, it could never have won adoption without its ratification by the Southern states, where black suffrage already existed. A more serious challenge was the question of whether Congress could legislate suffrage at all. Before Reconstruction the national government had never taken any action regarding the right to vote; suffrage had been considered not a right but a privilege which only the states could confer.

The issue of an amendment guaranteeing black suffrage also raised the question of whether women should be granted the franchise. As leaders of the Women's Loyal League, Elizabeth Cady Stanton and Susan B. Anthony had both worked hard for the adoption of the Thirteenth Amendment, only to be rewarded by inclusion of the word *male* in the Fourteenth Amendment of the Constitution—the first time that word appears. Some women, such as Lucy Stone of the American Woman Suffrage Association, accepted the plea of longtime women's suffrage supporter Frederick Douglass that it was the "Negro's hour," and worked for ratification. Anthony, however, vowed to "cut off this right arm of mine before I will ever work for or demand the ballot for the Negro and not the woman." Such differences played a role in splitting the women's movement in 1869 between those working for a national suffrage amendment and those who concentrated their efforts on the state level. Anthony and Stanton founded the National Woman Suffrage Association to fight for a constitutional amendment and other feminist reforms. Others became disillusioned with that approach and established the American Woman Suffrage Association, which focused on obtaining suffrage on a state-by-state basis.

Actually, women did not lose much by not being included in the Fifteenth Amendment. To meet the various objections, compromise was necessary. The resulting amendment did not grant the vote to anyone. It merely stated that the vote could not be denied "on account of race, color, or previous condition of servitude." Suffrage was still essentially to be controlled by the states, and other bases of exclusion would not be deemed unconstitutional. These loopholes would eventually allow white Southerners to make a mockery of the amendment.

Although congressional reconstruction was labeled "radical," compromise and caution had prevailed. What Congress did *not* do is as important as what it did. It did not even guarantee the right to vote. There was only one execution for war crimes and only Jefferson Davis was imprisoned for more than a few months. For all but a handful, ex-Confederates were not permanently barred from voting or holding office. Most local Southern governments were undisturbed. Land as well as rights were restored to former rebels, eliminating the possibility of extensive land redistribution. The only attempt by the national government to meet the basic needs of African-American citizens was the temporary Freedmen's Bureau—justified only as an emergency measure. The cautious nature of Reconstruction doomed it as an opportunity to provide means for the protection of minority rights.

Such congressional moderation reflected the spirit of the age. Long-cherished beliefs in the need for strict construction of the Constitution and in states' rights presented formidable barriers to truly radical changes. Property rights were considered sacrosanct—even for "traitors." Cherished ideals of self-reliance and the conviction that a person determined his or her own destiny led many to believe that African Americans should take care of themselves.

Tainting every action was the widespread racist conviction that African Americans were not equal to whites. Many Northerners were more concerned with keeping blacks in the South than with abstract black rights. Even Radical Representative George Julian admitted to his Indiana constituents, "the real trouble is that *we hate the negro.* It is not his ignorance that offends us, but his color."

The plan for Reconstruction evolved fitfully, buffeted first one way and then another by the forces of the many unresolved issues at war's end. If permanent changes were very limited, nonetheless precedents had been set for later action, and for a brief time congressional reconstruction brought about the most democratic governments the South had ever seen—or would see for another hundred years.

Reconstruction in the South

Regardless of the specific details hammered out in Washington, any dictated peace would probably have been unpalatable to Southern whites. They were especially leery of any action that seemed to threaten white supremacy. Most Southerners condemned the Freedmen's Bureau, believing that its agents were partial to African Americans. Actually there was great diversity in the background and goals of bureau agents. Some were idealistic young New England men and women who came south to aid in the transition to freedom. Others were army officers whose first priority was to maintain order, often by siding with the landowners.

The results of bureau actions were mixed in regard to conditions for African Americans. The agents helped to negotiate labor contracts that African Americans had to sign to obtain rations. Frequently the wages were well below the rate at which slaves had been hired out by their owners before the war. Although money was scarce at the time, these contracts helped to keep African Americans on the farm—someone else's farm. On the other hand, between 1865 and 1869 the bureau issued over 21 million rations, of which about 5 million went to whites. The bureau also operated more than 40 hospitals, opened hundreds of schools, and accomplished the herculean task of resettling some 30,000 people displaced by the war. The agency showed that the federal government could establish and administer a massive relief program, as it would again do during the depression of the 1930s.

Carpetbaggers, Scalawags, and Black Republicans

After the passage of the Reconstruction Acts in 1867, Republican officeholders joined bureau agents in directing the course of Reconstruction. Northerners who came to the South during or after the war and became engaged in politics were called "carpetbaggers" by resentful Southerners. They supposedly arrived with a few meager belongings in their carpetbags, which they would fill with their ill-gotten gains from looting an already devastated South. Probably what most infuriated whites was the carpetbaggers' willingness to cooperate with African Americans. Native whites accused the carpetbaggers of cynically exploiting the freed persons for their own gain.

White Southerners who voted for Republicans were labeled "scalawags." The term had been used previously as a synonym for a loafer or rascal. Such men were said to have "sold themselves for office" and become a "subservient tool and accomplice" of the carpetbaggers. Some scalawags were members of the old commercial elite of bankers and merchants who, as former Whigs, favored the economic policies of the Republican party. The majority of Southern white Republican voters were yeoman farmers and poor whites from areas where slavery had been unimportant. They had long resented planter domination and had opposed secession.

Northerners who engaged in politics in the South before or after the war were called carpetbaggers. This cartoon shows Ulysses S. Grant and Union soldiers propping up carpetbag rule with bayonets, while the "Solid South" staggers under the weight.

Most detested by white Southerners were the black Republicans. They loathed the prospect of African Americans in authority. They feared that the former slaves would exact payment for their years of bondage. Democrats also knew that racism was their best rallying cry to regain power. Whites claimed that ignorant freed persons, incapable of managing their own affairs, were allowed to run the affairs of state with disastrous results.

Such myths persisted for a long time. Southern whites had determined even before Reconstruction began that it would be "the most galling tyranny and most stupendous system of organized robbery that is to be met with in history." The truth was, as black leader W. E. B. Du Bois later wrote, "There is one thing that the white South feared more than negro dishonesty, ignorance, and incompetency, and that was negro honesty, knowledge, and efficiency." To a surprising degree they got what they most feared.

Black voters were certainly as fit to vote as the millions of illiterate whites enfranchised by Jacksonian democracy. Black officials as a group were as qualified as their white counterparts. In South Carolina two-thirds of them were literate, and in all states most of the acknowledged leaders were well educated and articulate. They usually had been members of the Northern or Southern free black elite or part of the slave aristocracy of skilled artisans and household slaves. Hiram Revels, a U.S. senator from Mississippi, was the son of free blacks who had sent him to college in the North. James Walker Hood, the presiding officer of the North Carolina constitutional convention of 1867, was a Pennsylvania native and an African Methodist Episcopal missionary. Some, such as Francis Cardoza of South Carolina, were the privileged mulatto sons of white planters. Cardoza had been educated in Scottish and English universities. During Reconstruction 14 such men served in the U.S. House of Representatives and two in the Senate. By 1901, six others were elected to the House, before Southern black political power was effectively demolished.

In a historic first, seven African Americans were elected to the Forty-first and Forty-second Congresses. Between 1869 and 1901, two African Americans became senators and 20 served in the House.

Even if black Republicans had been incompetent, they could hardly be held responsible for the perceived abuses of so-called black reconstruction. Only in South Carolina did African Americans have a majority of the delegates to the constitutional convention provided for by the Reconstruction Acts. Neither did they dominate the new governments; only for a two-year period in South Carolina did blacks control both houses of the legislature. When the vote was restored to ex-Confederates, African Americans comprised only one-third of the voters of the South, and only in two states did they have a majority.

Actually, carpetbaggers dominated most Republican governments. They accounted for less than one percent of the party's voters but held a third of the offices. Their power was especially obvious in the higher offices. Over half of all Southern Republican governors and almost half of the Republican congressmen and senators were former Northerners. Although some carpetbaggers did resemble their stereotypes, most did not. Many had come south before black enfranchisement and could not have predicted political futures based on black votes. Most were Union veterans; some brought with them much-needed capital for local investments. A few came with a sense of mission to educate blacks and reform Southern society.

Since African Americans constituted only a third of the population and carpetbaggers less than one percent, those two groups had to depend on the votes of a sizable number of native white Southerners to obtain political offices in some regions of the South. To win the scalawags' vote (most of whom were poor whites) the Republicans appealed to class interests, playing on traditional lower-class resentment of the planter aristocracy. Many Southerners, won over by campaign promises of debtor relief, accepted such arguments and joined African Americans to put Republicans into office. The coalition, however, was always shaky, given the racism of poor whites. The scalawags actually represented a swing vote that finally moved toward the Democratic party of white supremacy later in the 1870s.

Character of Republican Rule

While the coalition lasted, the Republican governments became the most democratic that the South had ever had. More people could vote for more offices; all remaining property requirements for voting and officeholding were dropped; representation was made fairer through reapportionment; and more offices became elective rather than appointive. Salaries for public officials made it possible to serve without being wealthy. Most important, universal male suffrage was enacted with the support of black legislators. Ironically, by refusing to deny Southern whites what had been denied to them—the vote—African Americans sowed the seeds of their own destruction.

The Republican state constitutions, which brought the South firmly into the mainstream of national reform, often remained in effect years after the end of Reconstruction. Legislatures abolished automatic imprisonment for debt and reduced the use of the death penalty. More institutions for the care of the indigent, orphans, mentally ill, deaf, and blind were established. Tax structures were overhauled, reducing head taxes and increasing property taxes to relieve somewhat poorer taxpayers. At the same time, Southern railroads, harbors, and bridges were rebuilt.

Black legislators had the most success in laying the foundations for public education. Antebellum provisions for public schools below the Mason-Dixon line were meager to nonexistent. In every state African Americans were among the main proponents of state-supported schools, but most accepted segregated facilities as necessary compromises. Some black parents did not even desire integration; they believed their children could not flourish in environments tainted by white supremacy. By 1877 some 600,000 blacks were in schools, but only the University of South Carolina and the public schools of New Orleans were integrated.

As desirable as many of the new social services were, they required money and money was scarce. The war had destroyed not only railroads and bridges but also much of the Southern tax base. The necessary tax increases were unpopular, as were soaring state debts. Both were blamed on corruption, with some justification. Louisiana Governor Henry C. Warmouth netted some $100,000 during a year in which his salary was only $8,000. One black man was paid $9,000 to repair a bridge with an original cost of only $500. Contracts for rebuilding and expanding railroads, subsidies to industries, and bureaucracies for administering social services offered abundant opportunities for graft and bribery.

When these scandals came to light, Southern whites were quick to point an accusing finger at freed persons who, they claimed, were unfit for positions of authority. Actually, although African Americans received a large share of the blame, they received little of the profit. A smaller percentage of blacks than whites were involved in the scandals. Also the corruption that the Democrats denounced at every turn was rather meager in comparison to the shenanigans of some Democratic regimes in the North. In the aftermath of the war an orgy of national corruption seemed to infect both political parties.

Black and White Adaptation

The "tyranny" that so distressed Southern whites did not include wholesale disfranchisement or confiscation of their lands. Just as the ex-slaves on Thomas Pinckney's plantation had learned, freed persons everywhere soon realized that the economic power of whites had diminished little. If anything, land became more concentrated in the hands of a few. In one Alabama county the richest 10 percent of landowners increased their share of landed wealth from 55 to 63 percent between 1860 and 1870. Some African Americans, usually through hard work and incredible sacrifice, were able to obtain land. The percentage of blacks who owned property increased from less than 1 to 20 percent. Indeed, African Americans seemed to fare better than poor whites, for whom the percentage of land ownership dropped from 80 to 67 percent.

Most poor blacks and whites worked on someone else's land as sharecroppers. Under this system, landowners gave tenants a plot of land to work in return for a share of the crops. African Americans preferred the sharecropping system because working in gangs as contract and wage laborers under white supervision smacked too much of slavery. Anxious to obtain as much autonomy as possible, some freed persons hitched mule teams to their old slave cabins and carried them off to their assigned acres.

Sharecropping at first seemed to be a good bargain for African Americans. Receiving a half share of the crops they produced, they were making more for working less. Fewer family members worked and black men labored shorter hours; as a group African Americans worked one-third fewer hours than under slavery.

But sharecropping proved to be disastrous for most blacks and poor whites. They needed more than land to farm; they also required seeds, fertilizers, and provisions to live on until they harvested their crops. To obtain these necessities they often borrowed against their share of the crops. Falling crop prices, high credit rates, and, in later years, laws favoring creditors left many to harvest a growing burden of debt with each crop.

If most freedmen did not win economic freedom, they benefited from freedom in other ways. Since it was no longer illegal to learn to read and write, African Americans pursued education with much zeal. A growing number also sought higher education. Between 1860 and 1880 over 1,000 African Americans earned college degrees. Some went north to college, but most attended one of the 13 Southern colleges established by the American Missionary Association or by black and white churches with the assistance of the Freedmen's Bureau. Such schools as Howard University and Fisk University were a permanent legacy of Reconstruction.

African Americans were also able to enjoy and expand their rich cultural heritage. Religion was a central focus for most, just as it had been in slavery. Church membership in such antebellum denominations as the African Methodist Episcopal soared. In essence, black Christians declared their religious independence, and their churches became centers of political and social activities as well as religious ones.

The very changes that gave African Americans hope during Reconstruction distressed poor whites. Black political equality rankled them, but much more serious was their own declining economic status. As their land ownership decreased, more whites became dependent on sharecropping and low-wage jobs, primarily in the textile industry.

Ironically, although nearly everyone perceived poor whites as the group most hostile to blacks, the two shared many aspects of a rich Southern cultural heritage. In religion and recreation their experiences were similar. At camp meetings and revivals poor whites practiced a highly emotional religion, just as many black Southerners did. Both groups spun yarns and sang songs that reflected the perils of their existence and provided folk heroes. They also shared many superstitions as well as useful folk remedies. Race, however, was a potent wedge between them that upper-class whites frequently exploited for their own political and economic goals.

Planters no longer dominated the white elite; sharecropping turned them and others into absentee landlords. The sons of the old privileged families joined the growing ranks of lawyers, railroad entrepreneurs, bankers, industrialists, and merchants. In some ways, the upper and middle classes began to merge, but in many places the old elite and their children still enjoyed a degree of deference and political leadership. Their hostility toward African Americans was not as intense, largely because they possessed means of control. When their control slipped, however, they also became strident racists.

Violent White Resistance

Large numbers of whites of all classes engaged in massive resistance to Reconstruction. In 1866 some young men in Pulaski, Tennessee, organized the Ku Klux Klan, which began as a social club with all the trappings of fraternal orders—secret rituals, costumes, and practical jokes. They soon learned that their antics intimidated African Americans; thenceforth the Klan grew into a terrorist organization, copied all over the South under various names. A major goal of the Klan was to intimidate Republican voters and restore Democrats to office. In South Carolina, when blacks working for a scalawag began to vote, Klansmen visited the plantation and "whipped every nigger man they could lay their hands on." The group's increasing lawlessness alarmed many people and led to congressional action. The Klan was broken up by three Enforcement Acts that gave the president the right to suspend habeas corpus against "armed combinations" interfering with any citizen's right to vote. In 1871 Grant did so in nine South Carolina counties. Disbanding the Klan, however, did little to decrease Southern violence or the activities of similar terrorist groups.

Some black Southerners were probably never allowed to vote freely. At the peak of Reconstruction, fewer than 30,000 federal troops were stationed in the entire South, hardly enough to protect the rights of 4.5 million African Americans. As troops were being withdrawn, Democrats sought to regain control of their states. Without secret ballots landowners could threaten sharecroppers with eviction for "improper" voting. In addition to economic intimidation, violence against freed persons escalated in most states as the Democrats increased their political power. When victory seemed close, Democrats justified any means to "redeem" the South and rid it of Republican influence. In six heavily black counties in Mississippi such tactics proved highly successful, reducing Republican votes from more than 14,000 in 1873 to only 723 in 1876. Beginning with Virginia and Tennessee in 1869, by 1876 all but three states—Louisiana, Florida, and South Carolina—had Democratic "Redeemer" governments. The final collapse of Reconstruction became official the following year with the withdrawal of federal troops from the three unredeemed states.

Reconstruction in the North and West

In the end, the South could be said to have lost the war but won the peace. After 1877 Southern whites found little resistance to their efforts to forge new institutions to replace both the economic benefits and racial control of slavery. By 1910 they had devised a system of legalized repression that gave whites many of the benefits of slavery without all the responsibilities. Surely this pattern was not what the North had envisioned after Appomattox in 1865; nonetheless, as the years passed, civil rights for African Americans ceased to become a Northern priority. A shifting political climate, economic hard times, increasing preoccupation with other issues, and continued racism combined to make most Northerners retreat from any responsibility for the protection of black rights.

Northern Shifts in Attitudes

When Grant won the presidency in 1868, the voters had chosen a war hero who had no political record or experience. They voted not so much for a program, but for Grant's campaign slogan: "Let us have peace." The victorious general proved to be a poor choice. Politically inexperienced, haunted by a fear of failure, and socially insecure, Grant was too easily influenced by men of wealth and prestige. He made some dismal appointments and remained loyal to individuals who did not merit his trust. The result was a series of national political scandals. Grant was not personally involved, but his close association with the perpetrators blemished both his and his party's image. The first major scandal involved the Crédit Mobilier, a dummy construction company used to milk money from railroad investors in order to line the pockets of a few insiders, including Vice President Schuyler Colfax and a number of other prominent Republicans. Later, bribes and kickback schemes surfaced that involved Indian trading posts, post office contracts, and commissions for tax collection. Such revelations as well as the corruption in some Southern Republican governments did little to enhance the public image of the party, and Democrats were quick to make corruption a major issue in both the North and the South.

In the 1872 presidential election disenchantment with the Grant administration prompted a group calling themselves Liberal Republicans to form a separate party and nominate their own candidate, *New York Tribune* editor Horace Greeley. Among Greeley's campaign pledges was a more moderate Southern policy. Even with the Democrats also nominating Greeley, Grant easily won reelection, but Republican dominance was slipping. That year the Democrats captured the House and made gains in the Senate, following further revelations of Republican corruption.

At least as detrimental to Republican political fortunes was a depression that followed the panic of 1873, which resulted from overinvestment in railroads and risky financial deals. Lasting six years, the depression was the most serious economic downturn the nation had yet experienced. Whatever their cause, depressions usually result in "voting the rascals out." Yet economic distress had an even wider impact on Reconstruction. People's attention became focused on their pocketbooks rather than on abstract ideals of equality and justice. Economic scrutiny brought such issues as currency and tariffs to the forefront. As the depression deepened, many questioned Republican support for "sound money" backed by gold and the retirement of the legal-tender "greenback" paper money that had been issued during the war.

Those greenbacks had increased the money supply needed to finance postwar economic expansion. Yet many Republicans were suspicious of any money not backed by specie—that is, gold or silver. One of the last actions of the Republican-controlled Congress was to pass the Resumption Act of 1875. This bill provided for the gradual redemption of greenbacks in gold. The resulting deflation favored creditors over debtors because debtors were forced to repay loans with money that was worth more than when they borrowed it. Many Americans, especially farmers, were already in debt, and deflation coupled with a depression brought economic distress.

Actually, the panic of 1873 brought into clearer focus the vast changes occurring in the North during Reconstruction. The United States was experiencing the growing pains of economic modernization and westward expansion, the effects of which, such as the completion of the first transcontinental railroad in 1869, overshadowed Reconstruction-related issues. By the late 1870s the Republican party had foresaken its reformist past to become a protector of railroad and business interests rather than a guarantor of basic rights.

Racism and American Indians

The major reason for the decline of Reconstruction was the pervasive belief in white supremacy. There could be little determination to secure equal rights for those who were considered unequal in all other respects. Reconstruction represented a failed opportunity to resolve justly the status of one minority, and the climate of racism almost ensured failure for others as well. Westward expansion not only diverted attention from Reconstruction but also raised the question of what was to be done about the Plains Indians. They, too, were considered inferior to whites. Although Reconstruction at first offered hope to African Americans, for the American Indian hope was fading.

In the end, African Americans were oppressed; Native Americans were exterminated or pushed onto shrinking reservations. Because most Africans, like Europeans, depended on agriculture rather than hunting, they adapted more easily to agricultural slavery. Black labor was valuable, if controlled; Indians stood as barriers to expansion.

When settlers first began moving onto the Great Plains, they encountered about 250,000 Plains Indians and 13 million buffalo. Some tribes, including the Zuñi, Hopi, Navaho, and Pawnee, had fixed settlements and depended on gardening and farming. Such tribes as the Sioux, Apache, and Cheyenne, however, were nomadic hunters who followed the buffalo herds over vast tracts of land.

Cultural differences caused misunderstandings between settlers and Native Americans and ultimately led to conflict. Among Anglo-Americans capitalism fostered competition and frontier living promoted individualism. On the other hand, Plains Indians lived in tribes based on kinship ties. As members of an extended family that included distant cousins, Indians were taught to place the welfare of the group over the interests of the individual. The emphasis within a tribe was on cooperation rather than competition. Some tribes might be richer than others, but there was seldom a large gap between the rich and the poor within a tribe.

The two cultures' widely divergent forms of political organization also caused problems. Among the Indian tribes, power as well as wealth was usually shared. Chiefs seldom had much individual power, but were generally religious and ceremonial leaders. Whites incorrectly believed that an Indian chief could make decisions and sign treaties that would be considered legal and binding by fellow tribal members.

Another major cultural difference between the newly arriving settlers and the Plains tribes was their attitude toward the land. Most Indians had no concept of private property. They refused to draw property lines and borders because of how they viewed the place of people in the world. Whites tended to see land, plants, and animals as resources to be exploited. Indians, on the other hand, stressed the unity of all life. Most of the Plains Indians believed that land could be utilized, but never owned. The idea of owning land was as absurd as owning the air people breathed. As Chief Joseph of the Nez Percé tribe said, "The earth and myself are of one mind." Thus people were not meant to dominate the rest of nature; they were a part of it.

Although some tribes could coexist peacefully with settlers, nomadic Indians had a way of life that was incompatible with miners, railroad developers, cattle ranchers, and farmers. Most had no desire for assimilation; they merely wanted to be left alone. To Anglo-Americans the Indians were barriers to expansion. They agreed with Theodore Roosevelt that the West was not meant to be "a game reserve for squalid savages." Thus U.S. Indian policy focused on getting more territory for white settlement. Prior to Reconstruction the federal government signed treaties that divided land between Indians and settlers and restricted the movement of each on the lands of the other. Frequently Indian consent was fraudulently obtained, and white respect for Indian land depended on how desirable it was for settlement.

During the Civil War, Sioux, Cheyenne, and Arapaho warriors rejected the land cessions made by their chiefs. Violence against settlers erupted as frontier troop strength was reduced to fight the Confederacy. The war also provided an excuse to nullify previous treaties and pledges with the tribes resettled in Oklahoma by Andrew Jackson's Indian removal. Some Native Americans did support the Confederacy, but all suffered the consequences of Confederate defeat. Settlers moved into the most desirable land, pushing the Indians farther south and west. Some Indians began to resist.

In 1864 the territorial governor of Colorado persuaded most of the warring Cheyennes and Arapahoes to come to Fort Lyon on Sand Creek, promising them protection. Colonel J. M. Chivington's militia, however, attacked an Indian camp flying a white flag and the American flag and killed hundreds of Indian men, women, and children. The following year Congress established a committee to investigate the causes of conflict. Its final report in 1867 led to the creation of an Indian Peace Commission charged with negotiating settlements. At two conferences in 1867 and

1868 Indian chiefs were asked to restrict their tribes to reservations in the undesirable lands of Oklahoma and the Black Hills of the Dakotas in return for supplies and assistance from the government.

Most Indians did not consider the offer very generous, but those who refused to acquiesce soon found that resistance was futile. Railroads had penetrated the West, bringing in both settlers and federal troops more rapidly. The destruction of the buffalo herds by hunters was a particularly important factor in the subjugation of the Indian tribes. These herds played a crucial role in most Plains Indians' culture—providing almost all the basic necessities. Indians ate the buffalo meat, made clothing and tepees out of the hides, used the fats for cosmetics, fashioned the bones into tools, made thread from the sinews, and even burned dried buffalo droppings as fuel. Without the buffalo, most Indians became dependent on the federal government for food and clothing, and submitted peacefully to the new reservation policy.

In 1874 gold was discovered in the Black Hills Indian reservation in the present-day Dakotas. The area suddenly became tempting to whites, and miners began pouring into lands guaranteed to the Indians only five years before. In June 1876 federal troops were sent in to crush an uprising of Chief Sitting Bull's Sioux warriors and their Cheyenne allies. Instead, the warring tribes won their greatest victory against white encroachment when Indians overwhelmed and killed Lieutenant Colonel George A. Custer and 264 men at Little Bighorn. The battle had little long-term effect, however, except to strengthen white resolve in dealing with the "Indian problem."

The treatment of both Indians and African Americans would be justified by the increasingly virulent racism of whites, which was given "scientific" support by scholars of the late nineteenth century. One point was clear by 1876: Northerners who believed that the only good Indian was a dead Indian could hardly condemn Southern whites for their treatment of African Americans.

Final Retreat from Reconstruction

By 1876, fewer Americans championed black rights than had at the close of the Civil War. Some of the old abolitionist Radicals had grown tired of what had become a protracted and complex situation. Radical Republicans such as Thaddeus Stevens and Charles Sumner, who had labored to guarantee civil rights for African Americans, were dead. By 1876, all the elements were present for a national retreat on Reconstruction: the distraction of economic distress, a deep desire for unity among whites, the respectability of racism, a frustrated weariness with black problems by former allies, a growing conservatism on economic and social issues, a changing political climate featuring a resurgence of the Democratic party, and finally a general public disgust with the failure of Reconstruction.

The presidential election of that year sealed the fate of Reconstruction and brought this chapter in American history to a close.

Corruption was a major issue in the 1876 election. The Democrats chose Samuel J. Tilden, a New Yorker whose claim to fame was breaking up the notorious Boss Tweed Ring in New York City. The Republicans nominated Rutherford B. Hayes, a man who had offended few, largely by doing little. The election itself was so riddled with corruption and violence that no one can ever know what would have happened in a fair election. Tilden won the popular vote and led Hayes in undisputed electoral votes 184 to 165. However, 185 votes were needed for election, and 20 votes were disputed—19 of them from Louisiana, Florida, and South Carolina. These were the only Southern states still under Republican rule with the backing of federal troops. In each, rival election boards sent in different returns.

With no constitutional provision for such an occurrence, the Republican Senate and Democratic House established a special commission to decide which returns were valid. Composed of eight Republicans and seven Democrats, the Electoral Commission proceeded to vote along party lines, and gave all the disputed votes to Hayes. Democrats were outraged, and a constitutional crisis seemed in the making if a united Democratic front in the House voted to reject the commission's findings.

A series of agreements between Hayes's advisers and Southern Democratic congressmen averted the crisis. In what came to be called the "Compromise of 1877," Hayes agreed to support federal aid for Southern internal improvements, especially a transcontinental railroad. He also promised to appoint a Southern Democrat to his cabinet and to allow Southern Democrats a say in the allocation of federal offices in their region. Most important, however, was his pledge to remove the remaining federal troops from the South. In return, Southern Democrats promised to protect black rights and to support the findings of the Electoral Commission. On March 2 the House declared Hayes the presidential winner by an electoral vote of 185 to 184. After taking office, Hayes removed the

Table 16.1

Election of 1876

Candidate	Party	Uncontested Electoral Vote	Popular Vote	Electoral Vote
Ruthford B. Hayes	Republican	165	4,034,311	185
Samuel J. Tilden	Democratic	184	4,288,546	184
Peter Cooper	Greenback	—	75,973	—

troops, and the remaining Republican governments in the South soon collapsed.

Scholars once considered the Compromise of 1877 an important factor in the end of Reconstruction. Actually, its role was more symbolic than real; it merely buried the corpse. The battle for the Republican party's soul had been lost by its abolitionist faction well before the election of 1876. The Democratic party had never sought to extend or protect black rights. The Supreme Court began to interpret the Fourteenth and Fifteenth Amendments very narrowly, stripping them of their strength. Thus one by one many African-American rights were lost during the next four decades.

Conclusion

As the Civil War ended, many unresolved issues remained. The most crucial involved the status of former slaves and of the former Confederate states. The destinies of both were inextricably intertwined. Anything

*C*hronology of Key Events

1863	Lincoln proposes 10 percent plan for Reconstruction
1864	Lincoln vetoes Wade-Davis Bill; Sand Creek Massacre
1865	Freedmen's Bureau established; Lincoln assassinated; Andrew Johnson becomes seventeenth president; Thirteenth Amendment ratified, abolishing slavery
1866	Civil Rights Act
1867	Reconstruction Act divides South into five military districts
1868	President Johnson impeached; Fourteenth Amendment, guarenteeing citizenship to African Americans, ratified; Ulysses S. Grant elected eighteenth president
1870	Fifteenth Amendment ratified, outlaws exclusion from voting on basis of race
1870–71	Ku Klux Klan Acts passed
1876	Custer defeated at Little Bighorn
1877	Compromise of 1877; Rutherford B. Hayes becomes nineteenth president

affecting the status of one influenced the fate of the other. Quick read-mission of the states with little change would doom black rights. Enforced equality of African Americans under the law would create turbulence and drastic change in the South. This difficult problem was further complicated by constitutional, economic, and political considerations, ensuring that the course of Reconstruction would be chaotic and contradictory.

Presidential Reconstruction under both Lincoln and Johnson favored rapid reunification and white unity more than changes in the racial structure of the South. The South, however, refused to accept a meaningful end to slavery, as the Black Codes blatantly demonstrated. Congressional desire to reestablish legislative supremacy and the Republican need to build a national party combined with this Southern intransigence to unite Radical and moderate Republicans in the need to protect black rights and to restructure the South. What emerged from congressional reconstruction were Republican governments that expanded democracy and enacted needed reforms which many Southern whites deeply resented. At the core of that resentment was not disgust over incompetence or corruption but hostility to black political power in any form.

Given the pervasiveness of racial prejudice, what was remarkable was not that the Freedmen's Bureau, the constitutional amendments, and the civil rights legislation failed to produce permanent change but that these actions were taken at all. Cherished ideas of property rights, limited government, and self-reliance, as well as an almost universal belief in black inferiority, virtually guaranteed that the experiment would fail. The first national attempt to resolve fairly and justly the question of minority rights in a pluralistic society was abandoned in less than a decade. Indians, blacks, and women saw the truth of the Alabama planter's words of 1865: "Poor elk—poor buffaloe—poor Indian—poor Nigger—this is indeed a white man country." Nevertheless, less than a century later, seeds planted by the Reconstruction era amendments would finally germinate, flower, and be harvested.

Suggestions for Further Reading

Effective overviews of the Reconstruction period are Eric Foner, *Reconstruction: America's Unfinished Revolution* (1988); Leon Litwack, *Been in the Storm So Long* (1979); James McPherson, *Ordeal by Fire* (1982); Kenneth M. Stampp, *The Era of Reconstruction* (1965).

For information on the Johnson and Grant presidencies see Michael Les Benedict, *The Impeachment of Andrew Johnson* (1973); William S. McFeely, *Grant: A Biography* (1981); Eric McKitrick, *Andrew Johnson and Reconstruction* (1960).

Conditions in the South during Reconstruction are examined in Stephen J. DeCanio, *Agriculture in the Postbellum South* (1974); Herbert G. Gutman, *The Black Family in Slavery and Freedom* (1976); Thomas Holt, *Black over White* (1977); Jay R. Mandle, *The Roots of Black Poverty* (1978); Michael Perman, *The Road to Redemption: Southern Politics, 1869–1879* (1984); George C. Rable, *But There Was No Peace* (1984); James Roark, *Masters Without Slaves* (1977).

On the West during the Reconstruction period see Robert F. Berkhofer, *The White Man's Indian* (1978); Eugene H. Berwanger, *The West and Reconstruction* (1981); Francis Paul Prucha, *American Indian Policy in Crisis* (1975); Wilcomb E. Washburn, *The Indian in America* (1975).

Chapter *17*

Emergence as an Economic Power

America: Land of Plenty
Mineral and Geographic Possibilities
Technological Change
Population Patterns and the New Industrial Work Force
An Expanding Railroad Network

A Favorable Climate: The Role of Ideology, Politics, and Finance
Social Darwinism and the Gospel of Wealth
Laissez-Faire in Theory and Practice
Corporations and Capital Formation

The Rise of Big Business
Controlling Competition
New Managerial Styles and an Expanding Middle Class
Mass Marketing, Assembly Lines, and Mass Production
The Power of Bigness

Economic Modernization in the South and West
Western Expansion
The Changing Nature of Farming
The New South

On a cold winter's night in December 1900, 75 of the richest, most influential American businessmen gathered in New York for a dinner to honor Charles Schwab, president of Carnegie Steel Company. Seated to the honoree's right was J. P. Morgan, the powerful investment banker and consolidator of industry. In his after-dinner speech, Schwab predicted a bright future of low prices and stability for the steel industry, to be ushered in by the formation of a scientifically integrated firm—one that combined all phases of the industry from the production of raw steel to the manufacture of finished products.

Morgan did not miss the point of the speech. Previously, Carnegie Steel had limited its operations to making raw steel, while Morgan and others had been busily creating trusts among the producers of such finished steel products as tubes and wire. Trusts were attempts to unite smaller competing firms in order to control the market and raise prices. Trusts often used their combined power to put remaining competitors out of business. The steel products trusts, however, had a problem. Andrew Carnegie, whose company was the largest supplier of raw steel, hated trusts. Deciding to beat the the trusts at their own game, he joined several informal arrangements to fix prices, known as "pools," only to sabotage them from within. Morgan and his cohorts soon realized that depending on Carnegie for raw steel would doom their consolidation schemes. Consequently, in July 1900 three steel products companies canceled all their contracts with Carnegie, determined to produce their own steel or buy it from others—and put Carnegie out of business.

Carnegie, however, refused to surrender. By continuing his policy of spending money to make money, Carnegie knew he could produce superior products at cheaper prices. He decided to pay no dividends on common stock and began plans to build a $12 million tube plant.

The antiquated and scattered plants of his competitors would have been no match for Carnegie's new ones. Few promoters doubted one steel executive's assertion that Carnegie could "have driven entirely out of business every steel company in the United States." Carnegie, however, wanted to retire. Schwab's speech was aimed at producing a bargain, not a war. After the dinner and into the night Morgan fired questions at Schwab. Finally, in the early hours of the next day Morgan said, "Well, if Andy wants to sell, I'll buy. Go find his price."

When Schwab approached Carnegie about selling his steel empire, Carnegie listened. The following day they met again, at which time Carnegie handed him a slip of paper with his asking price of $480 million written in pencil. When Schwab gave Morgan the offer, he replied, "I accept the price." A few days later Morgan stopped by Carnegie's office to congratulate him "on being the richest man in the world."

The transaction was a good deal for both men. Carnegie had his millions to endow libraries and anything else that struck his fancy. Morgan founded United States Steel Corporation. A colossus even among the existing giants of American industry, it was capitalized at $1.4 billion, a figure three times larger than the annual budget of the federal government.

The fates of Carnegie and Morgan reflected the momentous changes that took place after the Civil War. Moving from the ranks of second-rate industrial powers, by 1900 the nation was the leader—with a manufacturing output exceeding the combined total of Great Britain, France, and Germany. As Andrew Carnegie exclaimed in 1886, "The old nations of the earth creep on at a snail's pace; the Republic thunders past with the rush of an express."

Many yardsticks supported his assertion. Between 1870 and 1914 railroad mileage increased from 53,000 to 250,000—more than the combined mileage of the rest of the world. Land under agricultural production doubled; the gross national product was six times larger; the amount of manufactured goods per person tripled.

The rapidity of change produced chaotic conditions, which led to new managerial styles and finally to economic consolidation and the rise of supercorporations like United States Steel. The forces of economic modernization swept through all sections and all segments of the economy. The results were profound alterations of the social order that touched virtually every aspect of American life.

America: Land of Plenty

The phenomenal growth which the American economy experienced during the last quarter of the nineteenth century was built on the foundations laid during the antebellum period. Industrial development, the abundance of land and people, technological breakthroughs, and a favorable business climate had all been characteristic of the United States on the eve of the Civil War.

Mineral and Geographic Possibilities

Explorers and early settlers in what would become the United States were disappointed not to find the same abundance of gold and silver that had enriched their Spanish neighbors to the south. Only in the nineteenth century did Americans begin to realize the vast wealth that their expansion had brought. Most spectacular was the discovery of gold in California in the late 1840s. It sparked frenzied prospecting all through the West.

Each new discovery led to "rushes," creating mining towns almost overnight. Between 1850 and the 1880s thousands of men and women of almost every ethnic background helped create makeshift social institutions whenever and wherever strikes were made.

After living weeks or months at subsistence level, many miners went home poorer than when they had started. While a few did strike it rich, inefficient mining methods quickly exhausted the easily obtainable supplies of precious metals. Extracting ore from beneath the ground and in veins of quartz was expensive. It required large capital investments best raised by mining syndicates, frequently financed by eastern and European investors, which bought prospectors' claims for a fraction of their value.

As mining became an organized business, its focus moved to less exotic but more useful minerals such as copper, lead, talc, zinc, quartz, and oil, which fed the growing demands of the industrializing East. By the 1880s mining no longer represented easy riches for pioneering individuals; it had become an integrated part of the nation's modern, industrial economy. Emerging basic industries such as steel, petroleum, and electric power depended on large supplies of various minerals, which seemed to become available as needed. Sometimes new deposits were found; other times new uses for minerals spurred the mining of known deposits.

Iron, which had been widely used prior to the war for plows and other implements, was limited by its lack of durability. Then Andrew Carnegie and others employed new technology to produce large quantities of relatively cheap and durable steel. The availability of steel opened new manufacturing vistas, and between 1870 and 1900 the output of steel grew from 850,000 tons to over 10.5 million tons.

The same pattern characterized the mining of other minerals. Copper, at first mainly used for household products, became a key ingredient in such new fields as oil refining, electrical generation and conduction, and telephone communications. Most went into the miles and miles of wiring that electrified the cities. Similarly, the spectacular rise of the coal industry was generated by the increased use of coal-burning steam engines to power machinery and locomotives. As late as 1869 almost half of all power used in manufacturing came from waterwheels; by 1900 coal-burning steam engines supplied 80 percent of such power.

Even more dramatic was the rise of the petroleum industry. Many people were aware of large oil reserves in Pennsylvania, which seeped into streams and springs. Early demand was mainly limited to such uses as patent medicines of dubious value. Encouraged by reports that petroleum could be developed as a lighting source and lubricating oil, Pennsylvania businessman George Bissell funded drilling efforts, and in 1859 his employee, Edwin L. Drake, tapped the first oil well in Titusville, Pennsylvania. Oil was soon being used to lubricate machine parts, and by the 1870s about 20 million barrels were being produced annually. When refined into kerosene, it could also be used for illumination and cooking. During the late nineteenth century kerosene lamps and stoves were common features in American homes.

Growing demand led to the search for "liquid gold" in the Southwest. In 1901 a well shot a 160-foot stream of oil into the air at Spindletop, Texas. New sources thus became available for the development of the gasoline engine in the twentieth century. Abundant natural resources and technology often interacted—each shaping the evolution of the other.

Technological Change

Seldom has a single generation experienced such rapid change as in the late nineteenth century. Technology dramatically transformed much of people's lives. Bewildering as the changes sometimes were, the public generally welcomed new inventions with wide-eyed wonder. Across the country, thousands greeted the completion of the first transcontinental railway at Promontory Point, Utah, in 1869. Awed sightseers crammed expositions celebrating "progress," such as the 1876 Philadelphia Centennial Exposition, where visitors saw for the first time the Corliss engine, bicycles, the typewriter, the elevator, Alexander Graham Bell's telephone, and even the "floor covering of the future"—linoleum. At the 1893 World's Columbian Exposition in Chicago everything was powered by electricity, and many of the miracles of 1876 had become commonplace "necessities."

The impact of new inventions was enormous. Whereas only 276 inventions had been recorded during the Patent Office's first decade in the 1790s, during the single year of the Columbian Exposition 22,000 patents were issued. Offices became mechanized with the invention of the typewriter in 1867 and the development of a practical adding machine in 1888. Numerous inventions such as George Westinghouse's airbrake, which made longer, faster trains possible, revolutionized railroad transportation. Later, electric streetcars profoundly changed the character of urban development by accelerating the move to the suburbs.

Along with transportation changes, communications innovations welded a collection of communities into a unified nation. Links with the rest of the world also increased when an Atlantic telegraphic cable was completed in 1866. New inventions in the field of printing made popular newspapers with wide circulations a reality—along with mass advertising. Photographic advances culminated in George Eastman's hand-held Kodak camera in 1888. However, few, if any, inventions rivaled the importance of the telephone—more than one and one-half million were installed by 1900.

Increasingly, new inventions such as the telephone relied on cheap and efficient sources of electricity. Here the name of Thomas Edison stands above the rest. Beginning his career at an early age by peddling candy and newspapers on trains, Edison soon became a telegrapher and invented various improvements. The success of his ideas convinced him to go into the "invention business." Establishing a research lab at Menlo Park, New Jersey, in 1876, he invented the phonograph, the incandescent light bulb, as well as hundreds of other devices such as a better telephone, the dictaphone, the mimeograph, the dynamo, motion pictures, and electric transmission. With backing from banker J. P. Morgan, he created the first electric company in 1882 in New York City and formed the Edison General Electric Company in 1888 to produce light bulbs.

As in all research, Edison followed a number of blind alleys, but his only serious mistake was the choice of direct electrical current. This decision limited the range of transmission to a radius of about two miles. George Westinghouse's development of an alternating current system in 1886 soon supplanted direct current, forcing even Edison's companies to make the switch.

While a handful of inventors struck it rich, inventions often paved the way to vast fortunes for such entrepreneurs as Carnegie. The success of most of the captains of industry came from their effective exploitation of new technology. Carnegie utilized such advances as the Bessemer and open-hearth processes to produce cheap and plentiful steel. In like manner,

In his Menlo Park, New Jersey, laboratory, Thomas Edison aimed at practicality in his inventions. He eventually obtained over 1,000 patents. Here he is listening to his phonograph in 1888.

John D. Rockefeller built his industrial empire on new oil refining methods, and Gustavus Swift's meat-packing operation depended on the invention of the refrigerated railroad car. Eventually machine-made, interchangeable parts revolutionized every industry engaged in mass production.

Population Patterns and the New Industrial Work Force

Population changes and growth played an important role in the expanding economy. By the 1890s farmers became a minority for the first time, and by 1900 six out of every ten Americans made their living outside of agriculture. Although technology produced machines that displaced many skilled craftspeople and farmers, employment rose. For example, despite a tremendous increase in agricultural productivity, the needs of a rapidly expanding population created so many new markets that the agricultural work force still grew by 50 percent.

At the same time, nonagricultural employment rose 300 percent. Those not engaged in farming increasingly concentrated in the cities. Between 1860 and 1900 urban residents increased from 6 million to 24 million. This growing urbanization was essential to the expansion of industry—both feeding it and being fed by it.

Some economic historians contend that of all the factors spurring industrial growth none was more important than the rise of an American mass market. The urban population boom and the transportation revolution made mass consumerism possible by creating markets unparalleled in vastness and accessibility.

Mass markets would not have inevitably led to mass production without the public's acceptance of standardized goods. Several factors made Americans more receptive than Europeans to such products. Class distinctions, though not absent, were more blurred and became increasingly so with the availability of ready-made clothing. Also, physical mobility broke down many of the local loyalties so prevalent in Europe. Such factors created opportunities that modern mass advertising exploited. By 1900, $90 million was being spent annually to convince Americans of the advantages of specific brand names; modern advertising had embarked on its unending mission to shape the tastes of the public.

Advertising increased demand for many products, creating more industrial jobs for urban consumers. The dramatic expansion of this industrial work force was fed mainly by massive migration to the cities, rather than by the natural increase of the urban population. Four-fifths of the 18 million new city residents moved there; approximately half of them were migrants from rural America. They came to cities for a variety of reasons.

One was an increasing surplus of young men and women in the countryside. Rural birthrates remained high while mechanization decreased the number of hands needed to produce a crop. Such surpluses naturally "pushed" people from rural areas, but the cities also "pulled" them with the promise of more excitement, variety, and modern conveniences. Urban jobs also paid more; in 1890 clerical workers averaged $848 a year, more than three times as much as farm laborers.

Internal migration alone could not supply the enormous demand for industrial labor. Even before the Civil War native-born Americans could no longer be lured in sufficient numbers to work in factories. Rural white Americans more frequently joined the growing ranks of white-collar workers. Because of the persistent notions of black inferiority, rural African Americans, who would have gladly worked in factories, were passed over in favor of foreign workers. Thus, in 1890 only seven percent of black males held factory jobs, and as late as 1900 about 90 percent of African Americans remained in the South—the least urbanized section of the nation.

Unlike industrializing European nations, therefore, the United States did not rely primarily on its own population to produce its industrial work force. Instead, large numbers of immigrants manned the factories. The "pull" of job opportunities combined with factors "pushing" Europeans out of their native countries to produce a virtual flood of immigration (see Chapter 18). These large numbers facilitated industrialization but eventually produced a backlash from native-born Americans.

An Expanding Railroad Network

Americans developed a love/hate relationship with the railroads. The same locomotive that inspired Walt Whitman's rhapsody to its "fierce throated beauty" was described as "the leviathan, with tentacles of steel clutching into the soil" by Frank Norris in 1901. Despite these differing visions, no one doubted the importance of the railroads.

The railroads provoked strong emotions because of their crucial role in forging a new society. More than anything else, railroads helped to create an interdependent national economy. Rails brought raw materials to population centers, making possible large factories that mass-produced goods. Those goods could then be shipped to national markets over the same rails. Changes were required, however, before railroads could meet the needs of an expanding economy.

The early railroads were strictly local affairs. By 1865 there were already 35,000 miles of rails, but few linked up in any rational way. Eleven different gauges of rail caused both goods and passengers to be unloaded from one set of cars and reloaded on another set—sometimes at a depot on the opposite side of town. Between New York and Chicago, cargoes had to be unloaded and reloaded as many as six times. In some cases the inefficiency was intentional. Many small antebellum roads purposely adopted different gauges and conflicting schedules to prevent being swallowed up by larger, powerful competitors.

Unlike many European rail systems, American railroads grew with little advance planning or regulation by government, sprouting like weeds in areas where immediate profits could be made. Especially in the South, where too many small lines serviced the same places, four hundred companies sprang up, each with an average track length of a mere 40 miles.

While too many railroads served some sections in the East, prior to 1869 no transcontinental lines linked the East and West coasts. Financing their construction was the major problem. The construction of the railroads of the East required large amounts of capital, but a return on the investment came quickly. This was not true in the West, where railroads often preceded settlement and, therefore, demand for their lines. Because of the need for transcontinental routes, land grants became the solution. Many analysts have questioned the size of those grants, but they undoubtedly had the desired effect. By the turn of the century five transcontinental routes had been established.

At the same time, after some fierce competitive battles, a few eastern railroad companies gained control of many of the numerous local lines. When the dust settled, seven major groups controlled over two-thirds of the nation's railroad mileage; the average track length of a railroad grew from a mere 100 miles in 1865 to over 1,000 in two decades; gauges were standardized; and a more efficient rail system emerged.

A Favorable Climate: The Role of Ideology, Politics, and Finance

People, materials, and machinery were the "seeds" of industrialization. For an abundant harvest, however, good soil, favorable climatic conditions, and adequate fertilization were required. The bountiful economic harvest of the late nineteenth century depended on the "good soil" of popular support fostered by intellectual and cultural justifications. Favorable governmental policies created a desirable climate, while legal and financial developments provided the needed "fertilizer." This combination produced not only more industries but also larger industries.

Social Darwinism and the Gospel of Wealth

Expanding economic opportunities fostered cutthroat competition from which fewer and fewer winners emerged. The road to wealth taken by the new captains of industry was strewn with ruined competitors and broken labor movements. Ruthlessness not only became increasingly necessary, it was also transformed into a virtue by the twin ideologies of Social Darwinism and the Gospel of Wealth.

For men like Andrew Carnegie, the writings of Social Darwinists Herbert Spencer and William Graham Sumner helped to relieve any unwelcome guilt. Spencer and his followers applied the evolutionary concepts of Charles Darwin to society. A process of natural selection was said to cause the fittest individuals to survive and flourish in the marketplace. Survival of the fittest supposedly enriched not only the winners but also society as a whole, since human evolution would produce what Spencer called "the ultimate and inevitable development of the ideal man."

According to the Social Darwinists, poverty and slums were as inevitable as the concentration of wealth in the hands of the "fittest." Spencer and Sumner argued that governmental or charitable intervention to improve the conditions of the poor would only interfere with the functioning of natural law and prolong the life of "defective gene pools" to the detriment of society as a whole.

The so-called fittest naturally greeted "scientific" endorsement of their elite positions with eagerness. But even many businessmen found the ruthlessness of Social Darwinism an unpalatable justification for their actions. They sought their solace in religious rationales for the accumulation of great wealth. Since colonial times, the Protestant work ethic had denounced idleness and viewed success as evidence of being among the "elect"—God's chosen people. Building upon this base, apologists constructed the "Gospel of Wealth." John D. Rockefeller asserted, "God gave me my riches." Not surprisingly, Carnegie was the one to produce a written, logically argued rationale which asserted that the "fittest" at the top were better able to decide what people needed than the people themselves. In Carnegie's case, he took that responsibility seriously, distributing some $300 million to such philanthropic causes as founding libraries.

Among the most effective apologists for the wealthy, however, were religious leaders of the era. In 1901 Bishop William Lawrence proclaimed, "Godliness is in league with riches." Not only did the elite deserve their riches, but the poor also were responsible for their status. Perhaps the most popular evangelist for the Gospel of Wealth was Russell Conwell, who delivered his celebrated "Acres of Diamonds" speech, in which he declared that anyone could get rich, approximately 6,000 times between 1861 and 1925.

Thus the maldistribution of wealth was not only inevitable but also desirable according to both scientific and religious thought. Probably more important was the support provided by popular culture. *McGuffey Readers* continued to stress the virtue of hard work and its inevitable rewards in poems such as "Try, Try Again." Novelist Horatio Alger penned many stories whose heroes rose from poverty to comfortable middle-class status through a combination of diligence and good luck. Thus popular literature reinforced the idea that success always came to those who deserved it in America, the land of opportunity.

Laissez-Faire in Theory and Practice

Economic theory also lent respectability to greed and to the idea that government should not intervene in the economy. In 1776 Adam Smith's *The Wealth of Nations* presented arguments that would long be used to explain the workings of a free economy and to proscribe government's role in that economy. Smith asserted that the market was directed and controlled by an "invisible hand" composed of a multitude of individual choices. If government did not meddle, and everyone was left free to act according to self-interest, competition engendered by an unregulated market would naturally lead to the production of desired goods and services at reasonable prices—an economy best suited to meet the needs of society in general.

Acceptance of the "invisible hand" of supply-and-demand economic theory naturally led to a policy called "laissez-faire." Government's proper role was to leave the economy alone, so as not to disrupt the operation of the natural forces that ordered the economy. Business leaders naturally endorsed the theory's rejection of governmental regulation, yet saw no contradiction in asking for government aid and subsidies to foster industrialization. To a large extent the industrialists got what they wanted—a laissez-faire policy that left them alone, except when they needed help. Ironically, this distortion of theory helped to produce an economy in which business consolidation wreaked havoc upon the very competition needed for natural regulation of the economy.

Absolute free enterprise never really existed. There was plenty of governmental activity—just not in the area of regulation. No laws protected the consumer from adulterated foods, spurious claims for ineffective or even dangerous patent medicines, the sale of stock in nonexistent companies, or unsafe and overpriced transportation services. No national regulating agency existed prior to the establishment of the Interstate Commerce Commission in 1887.

While denying support and protection to consumers or workers, government at all levels aided businesspeople. Alexander Hamilton's vision of an industrializing nation fostered by favorable governmental action never entirely died and was rejuvenated by the Republican party. Among the party's many promises in 1860 were pledges to enact higher tariffs, to subsidize the completion of a transcontinental railroad, and to establish a stable national banking system. The victory of Republican ideology undoubtedly helped to create a favorable environment for rapid industrialization.

Tariffs had a long history. Two days before Lincoln took office, Democratic President Buchanan signed the Morrill Tariff, which marked the first tariff increase since 1842, and initiated an upward, practically uninterrupted, rise in tariff rates for the remainder of the century. At first, such American industries as steel needed to be protected from European competition to survive. Yet even after the cost of steel production was greatly reduced, the tariff remained—allowing higher profits at the expense of consumers. Without foreign competition, businesspeople were able to charge more for goods. Consumers came to resent these higher prices. Such bonanzas should not, however, obscure the fact that tariffs were widely viewed as serving the national interest by fostering economic independence from the British and other industrial competitors.

Additional forms of subsidy were also meant to serve the public good. Dwarfing all others were government land grants to railroads. Only the scale of these grants was new; prior to the war railroads had already received nearly 20 million acres of federal land. During the 1860s Congress granted 20 square miles of public land in alternating sections for each mile of track laid by the Union Pacific and Central Pacific railroads in order to speed the completion of a transcontinental route. By the time the grants ended, a total of 130 million acres of federal land and 51 million acres of state land went to various railroads. Nevertheless, even that incredible number of acres constituted less than 7 percent of the national domain in the West. Although the land grants were later subject to severe public criticism, the federal government did receive certain benefits, paying only half fare to move troops and supplies. In addition, the value of the remaining land increased, and the uniting of the East and West spurred the entire economy.

Business also benefited from favorable labor and financial legislation as well as low-interest loans. Individuals exploited these policies for personal gain, and the results were not uniformly positive. Aid to business, however, was never unlimited or unrestricted, and enjoyed wide public support at first. Indeed nationalism and patriotism accompanied the process of industrialization. Many Americans took pride in the nation's growing economic power. Only after the problems of industrialization became more apparent did the public begin to cry "foul."

Corporations and Capital Formation

Such governmental aid as high tariffs, land grants, low interest loans, and lack of regulation provided rich fertilizer for economic expansion, which brought both blessings and problems. The same was true for the rise of the modern corporation and decline of individual ownership and partnerships.

There were many advantages to incorporation for large-scale enterprises, including selling "shares" to a multitude of individual investors, so that the great sums of capital needed by modern industry could be amassed. Furthermore, corporations did not risk the disruption of operation due to death of a partner or arguments between partners, and individuals could hedge their bets by investing their capital in several ventures.

Although corporations had a long history, their postwar domination of the economy was due in part to legal changes that had taken place during the Jacksonian period. Businesspeople had once been required to apply to a state legislature for a charter; by the 1830s, however, they could incorporate on their own, provided they met certain standards. Following the Civil War, courts also began to affirm the principle of "limited liability." Previously, bankruptcy could bring not only the loss of one's investment but also seizure of personal property by creditors. A corporation's liability finally became limited to its assets, making investment a safer and more desirable venture.

In *Santa Clara County* v. *The Southern Pacific Railroad* (1886) the Supreme Court perverted the Fourteenth Amendment, ruling that a corporation was a legal "person" and therefore entitled to all the protections granted by the amendment. States could not deny corporations "equal protection of the law" or deprive them of their rights or property without "due process" of the law. Corporations were also later granted the "right" to "reasonable" profits—to be determined by the courts, not the government.

Instead of receiving "equal protection," corporations actually became privileged members of society. Real people whose rights were protected by the Constitution were held personally responsible for illegal activities, whereas corporate directors and corporations were not. Such advantages helped to spur the growth of corporations; by 1904 almost 70 percent of all manufacturing employees worked for corporations.

Perhaps the greatest advantage of corporations remained the ability to raise large amounts of capital. The expansion of industry in the late nineteenth century required big infusions of money. Every sector of the economy demanded capital: farmers needed new machinery to increase productivity; manufacturers needed new plants to utilize the latest technology; cities needed new construction to service the needs of the urban population.

From where was all this money to come? Some, of course, was generated by the rising gross national product—the total value of goods and services produced in one year—which grew from $225 per person in 1870 to nearly $500 in 1900. New technology increased productivity and put more money into the hands of people—"extra money" not required to meet physical needs. This disposable income was often reinvested rather than spent for personal consumption, thus laying the foundations of the modern American economy.

Increasing amounts of this capital were invested in manufacturing partly because investment bankers like J. P. Morgan marketed corporate stocks and bonds. Foreign investment was also important; by 1900 Europeans had invested approximately one-third of the almost $10 billion used to finance manufacturing in the United States.

The net result of the favorable conditions of the late nineteenth century was industrial supremacy. Americans reveled in their nation's transformation to a colossus outproducing the entire world. Vast mineral wealth, technological breakthroughs, population changes, railroads, popular support, beneficial government policies, liberal corporation laws, and the availability of capital fostered this transformation. At first, favorable conditions worked like overfertilized land—producing too many plants for the available space and resources. In this overgrown industrial garden competition created chaos until such entrepreneurs as Andrew Carnegie found ways to prune away their rivals.

The Rise of Big Business

"You might as well endeavor to stay the formation of clouds, the falling of rains, the flowing of streams, as to attempt . . . to prevent the organization of industry." These words of John D. Rockefeller's attorney described what he considered to be the inevitable domination of entire industries by large corporations. In industry after industry, men like Rockefeller, Morgan, and Carnegie eliminated competitors and controlled markets. The impact of this consolidation of industry was enormous. As companies grew larger, new management styles and more white-collar workers were needed. Mass production began to rise—profoundly changing the nature of work for industrial laborers. Also giant corporations amassed great power over production, people, and politics.

Controlling Competition

Most business leaders did not really advocate free enterprise fueled by competition. To them competition meant chaos, and they sought to eliminate it. Men like J. P. Morgan believed that too many companies glutted the markets—producing instability and cutthroat competition.

As America's first big business, the railroad industry was the first to confront the problems of competition. Railroads desperately sought to woo shippers to their lines by giving lower rates for bulk shipments and long hauls. To some preferred customers they also gave "rebates"—secret kickbacks below their published prices. They sought to make up for the lost revenue by overcharging smaller shippers. Such tactics did not really solve the railroads' problems, especially when rate wars broke out. In the 1870s some railroad managers tried cooperation as a cure for competition. They formed "pools," regional federations to divide traffic equitably and to raise rates to increase profits. However, pools were difficult to enforce, and greed frequently doomed many such agreements.

For the railroads, consolidation—accompanied by ruthless tactics— became the key to controlling competition. The former shipping magnate Cornelius Vanderbilt gained control of the New York Central Railroad in 1867 by buying two key lines that connected with it, and then refusing to accept any rail cars going to or from the Central. In response to criticism, Vanderbilt replied: "Can't I do what I want with my own?" Elsewhere buyouts and mergers eventually reduced the number of competitors, especially after depressions in the 1870s and 1890s.

After a period of intense competition in the railroad industry, a few rail barons consolidated lines by often using unscrupulous methods, seemingly carving up the nation at will.

Like the railroads, the oil industry also suffered from the proliferation of so many small companies and dramatically fluctuating prices. John D. Rockefeller, founder of the Standard Oil Company, first tried a combination of pooling and rebates to deal with these problems. In 1872 he organized the South Improvement Company. This venture represented a combination of oil refiners and railroad directors aimed at dividing the oil carriage trade among the railroads. In return for a guaranteed share of the shipments, Rockefeller convinced the railroads to give rebates. Eventually Rockefeller was able to obtain rebates not only on the oil he shipped but also on the shipments of his competitors. Thus Rockefeller could undersell his competitors, whom he often bought out during bad economic times.

Such techniques allowed Rockefeller to control 90 percent of the oil business, but legal problems arose from Standard Oil's far-flung holdings. His solution was the "trust." In 1882 he convinced the major stockholders in a number of refineries to surrender their stock to a board of nine trustees. In return they received trust certificates that entitled them to a share of the joint profits of all the refineries. The benefits of this device were readily apparent. Pools had no legal standing and could be manipulated by some members to the detriment of other members. In a trust, however, competitive actions were of no benefit. Everyone shared all losses and gains.

John D. Rockefeller used ruthless techniques to eliminate competition and consolidate the oil-refining industry.

Andrew Carnegie disliked pools and trusts, but found other ways to gain a competitive edge. One of these was "vertical integration." Buying the sources of his raw materials—iron ore and coke—he both lowered their cost to him and controlled his supplies. Carnegie also acquired many of the transportation facilities needed to distribute his steel. This vertical integration lowered final prices by cutting out profit-taking by suppliers and shippers.

The key to Carnegie's success was his ability to cut costs without lowering quality. He used such traditional measures as wage cuts and increased hours for workers, but he also constantly explored new methods to increase productivity. By not focusing on short-term profits, he was willing to invest in expensive new technology to lower long-term costs of production.

Carnegie often boasted that he knew almost nothing about steel. He hired experts to do that. What he did know was how to run a company and make money. Carnegie effectively used all the economies of scale available to large firms. Soon he was able to undersell and destroy most of the steel companies that had blossomed in response to the increased demand by railroads and industry. He also was a master at exploiting downturns in business cycles. Most of his acquisitions were made during depressions, when prices were lower. Competitors and labor movements suffered from Carnegie's actions, but the result was better steel at cheaper prices. Such cheap steel aided the expansion of the railroads and the rise of other industries.

The role of bankers was also an important factor in the trend toward greater consolidation. J. P. Morgan and other bankers often stepped in during economic panics to reorganize bankrupt companies, forming them into single supercorporations. The result was a more orderly economy, but at the price of centralizing vast economic power into the hands of a few unelected individuals.

Andrew Carnegie rose from an immigrant textile mill worker to control the U.S. steel industry.

New Managerial Styles and an Expanding Middle Class

The consolidation of companies into giant corporations created the need for new management techniques. Again, the railroads served as pioneers. As railroad companies grew larger, their activities covered hundreds of miles and employed thousands of workers. Safety and market conditions also required the entire system to operate as a single unit under a tight schedule. These conditions caused managerial problems, since railroad management required a level of coordination previously unknown in business.

To deal with these problems, railroads established sophisticated administrative structures, defining the responsibilities of all employees, from local train agents to the president and board of directors. Better accounting procedures were also needed to keep track of the monies collected and paid out. Management and accounting of funds became the function of controllers' offices, and a cost-accounting system was adopted to provide accurate data to judge the performance of their lines.

Other large-scale businesses began to adopt these accounting methods, hierarchical administrative structures, and divisions of responsibilities pioneered by the railroads. The result was the creation of "middle management," which coordinated the operations of far-flung local plants and reported to the top executives. Big businesses were now run by bureaucracies staffed by white-collar workers.

A profound consequence of the new economic order was the expansion of the middle class. Corporations needed accountants, middle managers, clerical workers, and sales representatives. The urban growth that accompanied industrialization also created demands for the services of professionals, shopkeepers, and government employees. The earnings of the middle class rose nearly 30 percent between the Civil War and the 1890s. By 1900 more than a third of urban families owned their homes. Although its members were sometimes dissatisfied, the middle class clearly derived benefits from and had a stake in the new economic order.

Mass Marketing, Assembly Lines, and Mass Production

Drastic transformations occurred in consumer industries as well as basic industry, as can be seen in the meat-packing business. There the interplay of new technology and new organization also ushered in new marketing techniques. Once again, the railroads played a key role by providing access to the grazing ranges of the Great Plains. Because of its rail network, Chicago quickly became the major funnel through which cattle were distributed from the Union Stock Yards to slaughterhouses on the outskirts of eastern cities. The meat was then distributed through local butchers to city residents.

There were several problems with such a distribution system, chief of which was the deterioration of the stock during long train journeys. Until the development of the refrigerated car, the only alternative was pickling or curing meat. Cattle dealer Gustavus Swift realized the possibilities opened up by refrigerated cars. Not only could fresh beef and pork be shipped more safely, but by centralizing slaughtering, waste products could be utilized. Profits were increased by making horns into buttons and hooves into glue. Eventually Swift formed glue, fertilizer, soap, and glycerine factories. People said that Swift used every part of a pig except the squeal.

Local butchers and wholesalers usually lacked refrigerated storage facilities, so Swift established his own warehouses, bypassing wholesale distributors and their cut of the profits. Swift overcame consumer resistance to the idea of buying meat weeks after the animal was slaughtered in a distant city with a major advertising campaign that stressed the superiority of Western beef. His mass-marketing tactics proved successful. By the late 1890s six packers supplied almost 90 percent of all meat shipped in interstate commerce. Swift was also a pioneer in mass production, employing assembly lines that subdivided the slaughtering and packing process into numerous distinct jobs.

Engineer Frederick W. Taylor laid the foundations of "scientific management" with his time-and-motion studies. Stopwatch in hand, Taylor observed the workers and then divided the manufacturing process into units that allowed for little wasted motion. He believed his ideas would benefit labor as well as management. Instead, his aim "to induce men to act as nearly like machines as possible" promoted monotony and displaced workers—especially higher-paid, skilled ones.

In meat packing, machinery did not replace workers; their work was merely subdivided to increase efficiency. In other industries, after the work had been broken down into simple, repetitive tasks, machines were created to replace hand labor. Mass production by machine worked best on products made from standardized, interchangeable parts. The ingredients were now in place to mass produce large numbers of standardized goods.

The Power of Bigness

The creation of the gigantic U.S. Steel Corporation was not an isolated occurrence. By 1904 a single firm in each of 50 different industries accounted for 60 percent or more of the total output. Such concentrations of economic power alarmed many Americans. Competition was never entirely eliminated, however, and consolidation did bring such benefits as lower prices and higher standards of living. Nevertheless, the transition from local, independently owned shops and factories to giant national corporations with impersonal boards of directors dramatically altered the work and leisure time of the American people. However, the transition was often painful for individuals. The economy experienced a frightening cycle of boom and bust, and periodic depressions caused widespread unemployment and business failures.

Big business also created a class of millionaires who flaunted ostentatious homes and lavish life-styles. When one realizes that in 1890 about 11 million of the 12.5 million families in the United States averaged less than $380 a year in income, it is obvious that all did not share equally in the economic expansion of the era. Wealth had always been concentrated and industrialization continued the trend.

Many people resented or envied the life-styles such wealth provided, but they feared the power it produced. Big business grew while government and organized labor remained relatively small. Thus business leaders wielded enormous power over many phases of American life. Some actions benefited the nation but were taken in a high-handed manner. For example, to simplify train schedules, in 1883 railroad owners established four time zones—without consulting any branch of government. Such arbitrary power alarmed the American public, and popular outcries would eventually force government action to curb the excesses that the new industrial order had produced.

This portrait of the family of William Astor illustrates the lavish life-style of the rich. Parties of the wealthy were especially ostentatious; at one, guests smoked cigarettes rolled in one hundred dollar bills after drinking coffee.

Economic Modernization in the South and West

Although most industrialization occurred in the industrial Northeast, farming regions also experienced profound changes as a national, interdependent economy emerged, and a world based on personal relationships was displaced by a more impersonal world based on contractual relationships. The largely self-sufficient farmer gave way to the cash-crop farmer whose produce went to feed urban masses hundreds of miles away. Rural population kept growing, although not as rapidly as urban population. While the benefits of economic modernization were not shared equally— the South lagged far behind other regions of the country—the demand by the urban masses for food sparked a farming revolution based on mechanization and scientific agriculture.

Western Expansion

The transcontinental railroads were not originally meant to "open up" the West. They were laid across what was called the "Great American Desert" in order to link the East and West coasts. The perceived worthlessness of the Great Plains was reflected in the willingness to give much of it away— to the Indians and later to the railroads. The mining frontier first altered perceptions of the region's value. In addition to mineral wealth, the region had two other plentiful resources: grass and cattle. Railroads provided the means to get the cattle to eastern cities, where urban residents wanted more meat to eat. The result was the birth of western ranching.

At first, ranching did not require much capital. Both the cattle and the grass were free. By 1860 some five million head of wild Texas longhorns had descended from cattle imported by Spanish colonists. Joseph G. McCoy realized the potential for profit and established the first "cow town" at Abilene, Kansas, where he built stock pens and loading chutes. Cowboys drove cattle there for shipment by rail to Chicago, where they sold for $30 to $50 a head. Other cow towns arose as some six million head of cattle endured the "long drive" to those sites between 1866 and 1888.

The heyday of the cowboy was rather brief, since ranching, like mining, soon became an organized business. Profits from a successful drive were very good—about 40 percent. This naturally attracted eastern investors, and soon the long drives gave way to more efficient methods. The rounding up of stray, lean, rangy longhorns ended as the rail network expanded into Texas and ranchers began raising and breeding the longhorns with superior imported stock to improve the quality of the beef.

The cattle breeders needed large tracts of grassland for grazing and usually just appropriated land from the public domain. During this open-range era, high profits attracted even more investors. Eventually the ranchers joined other segments of the economy that were outproducing demand. Beef prices dropped from $30 to $10 a head in 1885 and 1886. Poorer producers were driven out by these low prices, challenges to their land claims by sheepherders and farmers, and bad weather. A winter of terrible blizzards following the scorching summer in 1886 led to the death of 90 percent of western cattle.

After sometimes bloody battles for supremacy between these economic competitors, the "Wild West" was largely tamed by the 1890s. Ranchers who remained established legal title to their grazing lands, fenced them in with barbed wire, and practiced scientific breeding and feeding of their stock. The forces of economic consolidation had reached ranching—making it a business requiring large amounts of capital.

Land legislation of the era aided the monopolization of ranching by a relatively few "cattle barons." Large tracts of public lands were given away or sold cheaply through such acts as the Homestead Act of 1862, the Timber Culture Act of 1873, and the Desert Land Act of 1877. Enacted to promote socially desirable goals, all had large loopholes that were exploited by cattlemen and land speculators. To promote settlement, the Homestead Act offered 160 free acres to those who would cultivate it for five years. The Desert Land Act granted 640 acres at $1.25 an acre to anyone who would irrigate the land. The Timber Culture Act, based on the theory that the trees increased rainfall, awarded 160 acres to anyone who would plant trees on a quarter of the land. Cattlemen and speculators fraudulently claimed to have met the terms of the grants or hired dummy entrymen to stake claims for them. A bucket of water was sometimes the only basis for claims of irrigation. Lumber barons in the Pacific Northwest similarly utilized other land-granting laws. Thus much of the newly discovered wealth of the West ended up in the hands of a few winners in the great land lottery.

While the mining, cattle, and lumber frontiers offered some quick, easy riches before being transformed into capital-intensive businesses, the farming frontier required more patience to make profits. By the time farmers arrived in the new West, much of the best land had already been appropriated. Most of the 274 million acres distributed under the terms of the Homestead Act were eventually purchased by bona fide settlers from speculators and cattlemen. Other farmers bought land from the railroads, which promoted settlement to increase traffic in isolated areas. To lure settlers, railroad companies often provided easy credit terms and extolled western opportunities in flyers and speeches.

Many farming pioneers soon learned that railroad propaganda sometimes overstated the promise of the West. When they arrived, they discovered a shortage of wood and water but an overabundance of severe weather, insects, and social isolation. The houses they built of "bricks" cut from thick prairie sod were functional but bleak. At first, many farmers managed only to eke out a bare subsistence. Eventually, however, western farmers were caught up in the forces of change that transformed agriculture as dramatically as other sectors of the economy.

The Changing Nature of Farming

When Congress passed the Homestead Act in 1862, most of the arable land east of the Mississippi was already taken. The established farmers of the old Northeast adapted fairly well to the changing economy and were generally prosperous, supplying rapidly growing urban areas with vegetables, dairy products, poultry, and pigs. They also profited from rising land values by selling extra acres to residential and industrial developers at high prices.

The challenges of farming were much greater in the West, and when they were finally met, overproduction depressed prices. Cultivation of the West required new agricultural techniques and adaptations to the environment. The scarcity of trees not only dictated the building of sod-houses, but also made the cost of fencing prohibitive. Until the develop-

Because of the scarcity of trees on the Plains, settlers built homes from "bricks" of sod. With walls 2 to 3 feet thick, the houses were gloomy but provided cozy and solid protection from the elements.

ment of barbed wire in 1874, crops were not easily protected from the millions of roaming cattle.

A more serious problem was the lack of water. Farmers tried to alleviate water shortages by using new varieties of seed, pumping water from far below the ground surface with windmills, and using cultivation techniques known as "dry farming." During good times, optimism flourished; but then came the droughts. By 1900 two-thirds of the homesteaders had failed, and farmers returned east with signs saying, "In God We Trusted; in Kansas We Busted."

In the South, at the very time the rest of the economy was consolidating, agriculture was marching off in the opposite, less efficient direction. The devastation caused by the Civil War had destroyed half the region's farm equipment and killed one-third of its draft animals. Productivity declined as large plantations were subdivided for use by sharecroppers. Another problem was a shortage of cash, which forced Southern farmers to borrow against future crops. Crop liens and high credit costs kept both black and white farmers trapped in a cycle of debt and poverty.

Many Plains and Southern farmers became losers in the economic modernization of agriculture. Nevertheless, both the winners and the losers were playing essentially the same game, the commercialization of farming. Most of the rules were the same as those for manufacturers: specialization, new technology, mechanization, expanded markets, heavier capital investment, and reliance on interstate transportation. Many farmers of that generation wholeheartedly embraced these changes until they fell behind their industrial cousins in the expanding economy.

Specialization became apparent in the decline of subsistence farming and the growing importance of cash crops. Although general farming continued, most farmers planted more of their acreage in the single crop best suited for their land and market. Cash crops were usually supplemented by small gardens and stock raising, except in the South, where landowners often forced debt-ridden tenant farmers to plant all available acreage with cotton.

Technology and mechanization revolutionized agriculture and increased productivity dramatically. After the mechanization of wheat farming, the hours required to farm an acre dropped from 61 to 3, and the per acre cost of production fell from $3.65 to $0.66. Machines entered every phase of agriculture, and included such items as hay loaders, cord binders, seeders, rotary plows, mowers, and combines. Farmers began to learn "scientific agriculture" at land-grant colleges that Congress had provided for under the Morrill Land Grant Act of 1862. Agricultural researchers explored ways to increase production and found new uses for overabundant crops at agricultural experiment stations funded by the Hatch Act of 1887. Obviously, farmers were not opposed to all government aid to the economy.

Although the average farm remained about 150 acres, the farms of the West were usually much larger because dry-farming techniques produced low yields per acre. To succeed, a western farmer needed more acres and more machines; both cost money. Thus, like businesspeople, farmers needed access to capital. Most obtained personal loans using their land, machinery, and crops as collateral. Unfortunately, as production increased, prices fell, and to counteract lower profits farmers further expanded production in a self-defeating downward spiral.

One solution to overproduction was to expand markets, which required cheap and reliable transportation facilities. Railroads, therefore, had as much impact on agriculture as on industry.

Most farmers realized and, at first, even celebrated their status as businesspeople. Agricultural expansion was as dramatic as that of industry, yet farmers began to lose ground in terms of wealth, status, and percentage of the total population. When they discovered that they could not adapt as well as industrialists to the new economic order, they began to assert the superiority of rural culture. They stressed farmers' ties to the soil and heralded individualism and self-sufficiency as truly American characteristics.

The New South

Many Southerners wholeheartedly endorsed the new economic order at first. Some even saw the South's salvation in the destruction of slavery and proclaimed the emergence of "a New South." Henry W. Grady, the editor of the *Atlanta Constitution,* wrote and traveled extensively to promote the region's unlimited opportunities. Grady envisioned three major changes from the Old South: diversified farming, industrialization, and racial accommodation and cooperation.

Many shared Grady's vision. At the Cotton States Exposition of 1895 in Atlanta, a black spokesman for the New South emerged. Booker T. Washington, principal of Tuskegee Normal and Industrial Institute in Alabama, was asked by the exposition's white organizers to give an address. His speech, known as the "Atlanta Compromise," offered an optimistic appraisal of Southern potential and outlined a basis for racial cooperation. Washington urged blacks to make themselves economically indispensable to whites and forego agitation for political and social rights in return for educational and economic opportunities. Their economic importance would bring them white acceptance—and the rights they desired. Washington practiced what he preached. Tuskegee was a model New South institution, focusing on industrial education and promoting diversified farming.

The New South optimism was based on dramatic changes taking place in the region. Railroad development increased at a rate greater than in the nation at large. The textile, timber, and tobacco industries boomed. Birmingham, Alabama grew into a major producer of raw steel, and by 1890 Southern steel and iron made up almost 20 percent of the national total. At the same time Southern agriculture was recovering. Cotton production exceeded prewar records by the 1870s.

The tobacco and textile industries especially seemed to bring the dream to life. Both were based on major Southern crops. In the 1880s James B. Duke introduced the cigarette industry to the region. By 1890 he had created a trust through which he controlled 150 companies in an almost perfect monopoly until 1911 federal antitrust actions disbanded the trust.

Textile mills were seen as the key to Southern economic salvation. Although profitable, these mills were not run according to the New South guidelines advocated by Grady. Workers, often whole families of poor whites—by custom African Americans were denied employment—labored an average of 12 hours a day. Wages were as low as 50 cents a day and were usually not paid in cash, but in "trade checks." These trade checks were accepted to pay rent on company houses or buy goods in company stores. Elsewhere merchants and landlords would not accept the checks at face value. Thus some mill workers never saw any cash, merely turning their trade checks back over to the mill owners in return for supplies and housing. It is no wonder that profits were high for mill owners. Those high profits caused a textile boom in the South, and the number of mills grew from 161 in 1880 to 400 in 1900.

Despite all the signs of progress, major obstacles prevented the South's economy from keeping pace with the rest of the nation. Southern agriculture remained trapped in the inefficient sharecropping system and single-crop agriculture. Increased cotton production was accompanied by falling crop prices. By 1900 over half of the region's white farmers and three-quarters of black farmers were tenants. Most barely made enough to feed and clothe their families; few had the money to improve farming techniques or try new crops. By 1880 the South was not growing enough food to feed its people. Poor nutrition added bad health and disease to the region's problems.

The persistent ideology of white supremacy also helped keep the South mired in poverty. Race relations actually worsened in the 1890s as white Southerners struggled to keep black Southerners "in their place." In 1896 the Supreme Court ruled in the *Plessy* v. *Ferguson* decision that separate accommodations for African Americans did not violate the Fourteenth Amendment if the facilities were substantially equal in quality. The effect was to legalize segregation—a disaster for both black and white Southerners. Accommodations were never really equal, and African Americans suffered from inferior schools and services. At the same time, keeping most of the black third of the Southern population in ignorance and poverty depressed wage scales and the tax base needed to support public education and other services.

Another key to the South's relative poverty was its shortage of capital, which was rooted in the slave system and the Civil War. Reliance on slavery and cotton had enriched the Old South but helped to impoverish the New South. While the antebellum North employed its capital to build canals, railroads, cities, and factories, the South used its profits to buy more slaves. Emancipation meant that as much as $4 billion that had been invested in slaves was lost. In addition, the war was largely fought on Southern soil. Railroads had been torn up, factories and cities were burned down. Before the Civil War the South had seen little reason to use its capital to build factories and cities. After the war, the region no longer had the capital to do those things.

In the late nineteenth century Northern dollars did flow south. In the 1880s Northerners increased their investments in the cotton industry sevenfold. They also provided most of the capital to rebuild and expand Southern railroads and to start the region's steel industry. However, the use of Northern capital in most industries also meant that the profits went to Northerners as well. For the most part, the region supplied unfinished raw materials, such as lumber, for which prices were rather low. After these products were converted into manufactured goods in the North, the South had to buy those goods at higher prices than it had received for the raw materials.

For all these reasons the South remained at the bottom of the economic ladder. As happened in the West, the South's reliance on Northern capital kept the majority of profits going elsewhere. By the late 1880s farmers in both regions would unite to oppose the changes brought by industrial capitalism.

Conclusion

In one generation the United States became the economic colossus of the world. There were many positive benefits of this economic expansion and consolidation. In some cases people were able to buy superior goods at cheaper prices. Although some skilled artisans slipped downward on the social ladder, upward social mobility did increase for large segments of the population. Of course, not all shared equally in the nation's newfound

Chronology of Key Events

1856	Bessemer steelmaking process invented
1859	Edwin Drake drills first commercial oil well
1861	Morrill Tariff, first in series of high protective tariffs, passed
1862	Homestead Act gives 160 acres of public land to those who will cultivate it for five years; Morrill Land Grant Act establishes many technical and agricultural colleges
1866	First trans-Atlantic telegraph cable laid
1869	First transcontinental railroad completed
1870	John D. Rockefeller founds Standard Oil Company
1873	Timber Culture Act awards 160 acres of public land to those who would plant trees on a quarter of the land
1876	Alexander Graham Bell invents telephone
1877	Thomas Edison invents phonograph; Desert Land Act grants 640 acres to those who would irrigate the land
1879	Edison invents incandescent light bulb
1883	Country divided into time zones
1886	*Santa Clara County* v. *Southern Pacific Railroad* rules that a corporation is entitled to constitutional protection
1888	George Eastman produces the first hand-held camera
1895	Booker T. Washington's "Atlanta Compromise" speech
1896	*Plessy* v. *Ferguson* rules that "separate but equal" facilities are unconstitutional
1901	Carnegie Steel company sold to J. P. Morgan

wealth, and few made the transition from rags to riches that Carnegie accomplished. Most industrial leaders instead came from rather privileged backgrounds. The majority were relatively well educated Protestants of native birth. Average annual incomes rose steadily for almost all classes of workers. On the other hand, those wage increases rarely equaled the rising cost of living. Nevertheless, most families' standard of living improved because more members of the family worked for wages.

At the same time, individuals paid huge social costs for these advances. Some people paid a disproportionate share of these costs. Patterns of working and living dramatically changed. Many workers found themselves in a new status that imperiled their independence. Personal relationships were being replaced by impersonal, contractual arrangements. Shady corporate practices corrupted public morality. In short, all aspects of life underwent profound transformation, and the story of the late nineteenth century is the story of adaptation and adjustment to the new social and economic order.

Suggestions for Further Reading

Valuable overviews of industrialization and the rise of big business include Alfred D. Chandler, *The Visible Hand: The Managerial Revolution in American Business* (1977); Carl N. Degler, ed., *The Age of the Economic Revolution* (1977); Glenn Porter, *The Rise of Big Business, 1865–1920,* 2d ed. (1992).

For more on ideology, culture, and public opinion consult Robert Bannister, *Social Darwinism* (1979); Louis Galambos, *The Public Image of Big Business in America* (1975); T. Jackson Lears, *No Place of Grace: Antimodernism and the Transformation of American Culture* (1981); Alan Trachtenberg, *The Incorporation of America: Culture and Society in the Gilded Age* (1982).

Issues regarding the modernization of the West are examined in Gunther Barth, *Instant Cities: Urbanization and the Rise of San Francisco and Denver* (1975); Edward E. Dale, *The Range Cattle Industry, 1865 to 1925,* rev. ed. (1969); Robert V. Hine, *The American West,* 2d ed. (1984); Patricia Nelson Limerick, *Legacy of Conquest* (1987); Rodman W. Paul, *Mining Frontiers of the Far West, 1848–1880* (1963). On the New South see Peter Daniel, *Breaking the Land* (1985); Paul Gaston, *The New South Creed* (1964).

Good biographies on the captains of industry include Maury Klein, *The Life and Legend of Jay Gould* (1986); Harold C. Livesay, *Andrew Carnegie and the Rise of Big Business* (1975); Andrew Sinclair, *Corsair: The Life of J. Pierpont Morgan* (1981).

Chapter *18*

Immigrants and Workers in Industrial America

Huddled Masses at the Golden Door
"Birds of Passage"
In Search of a New Home

Nativism: The Anti-Immigrant Reaction
Sources of Conflict
Closing the Golden Door
Nativism and Native Americans

Working in Industrial America
Wages, Hours, and Standard of Living
The Lost Crafts
Worker Discontent
Early Labor Violence
Employers Gain Power
Unorganized and Organized Labor

In 1862, while the nation was locked in the grip of a terrible Civil War, Congress authorized the most ambitious building project that the country had ever contemplated: construction of a transcontinental railroad. The price tag was staggering: $136 million, more than twice the federal budget of 1861. The challenge was enormous: 1,800 miles across arid plains and desert and the rugged granite walls of the Sierra Nevada and the Rocky Mountains.

Two companies undertook the actual construction. The Union Pacific began laying track westward from Omaha, Nebraska, and the Central Pacific commenced eastward from Sacramento, California. Of the two companies, the Central Pacific faced the more arduous task. It had to carve a rail bed through the high Sierra Nevada. It also faced the more severe labor shortages.

In early 1865 the Central Pacific decided to dip into a new labor pool: Chinese immigrants. Within two years, 12,000 of the Central Pacific's 13,500 employees were Chinese immigrants. Earning reputations as tireless and extraordinarily reliable employees, they labored high in the mountains and inside tunnels. Explosions, avalanches, and other accidents left an estimated 1,200 Chinese workers dead.

Despite their heroic labors, California's Chinese immigrants faced discrimination and racial violence. White Americans criticized their attachment to their homeland and questioned their loyalty to the United States.

Since most Chinese immigrants never intended to stay in the United States, many may not have developed any emotional attachment to America or its institutions. In America they sought the opportunity to work— not voting rights, education, or assimilation—and no form of labor was beneath them. They resignedly accepted the most menial jobs in the mines, on the railroad construction gangs, and in the booming western cities.

Because they only came to America to accumulate money, the Chinese immigrants lived as inexpensively as possible. Sleeping in huge halls on matted floors, and sometimes sharing one mat by sleeping in eight-hour shifts, they were able to reduce lodging expenses to ten cents a month. Chinese workers sent most of their earnings back to their families in China, to whom they intended to return someday.

Immigration, then, could in no way be interpreted as a rejection of China. In reality, it was a defense of the Chinese way of life, for the money sent home helped preserve the traditional order. America was not a sacred idea, but a means to an end and, of course, sometimes a very lonely country.

Americans failed to understand the mind of the Chinese immigrant. To them, the Chinese were just non-Western, non-Christian, and non-white aliens. Although railroad builders and mine owners regarded the Chinese as good, inexpensive laborers, native-born American workers believed they brought down wages for all workers. Every major American labor organizer of the period called for federal action to restrict Chinese immigration. Some leaders charged that the "coolies" so depressed wages that women in white working families had to resort to prostitution to avoid starvation.

Labor leaders were joined by Irish-American politicians, the Catholic church, eastern editorialists, and California workers in their crusade against Chinese laborers. All agreed, the Chinese should—*must*—be excluded from the United States as undesirable, unassimilable aliens. In 1882 Congress responded with the Chinese Exclusion Act, which suspended Chinese immigration. It was the first time that the United States closed its doors to any immigrants for ethnocultural reasons.

Later, other immigrant groups shared experiences similar to the Chinese. Native-born Americans saw other ethnic groups as beyond reform, as not having the "right stuff" to become Americans. Again and again labor leaders, religious authorities, and old-line Americans joined forces in opposition to certain groups of immigrants. The entire movement toward restriction culminated in 1924 with the passage of the National Origins Act.

Yet immigrants contributed greatly to the growth of industrial America. They and their fellow workers—native-born white and black Americans—built the railroads that crisscrossed the country; mined the gold and silver that made other men rich; and labored in the oilfields, steel mills, coal pits, packing plants, and factories that made such names as Rockefeller, Carnegie, Swift, and Westinghouse famous. Without these men and their companions, there would have been no industrialization. In the process they made the United States an ethnically rich nation.

Huddled Masses at the Golden Door

On October 28, 1886, President Grover Cleveland traveled to New York Harbor to watch the unveiling of the Statue of Liberty. A gift from France, Frederic Auguste Bartholdi's grand statue was meant to symbolize solidarity between the two republics, but that was not how Americans and incoming immigrants interpreted the sculpture. For them it was a simple symbol of welcome, with the statue's torch lighting the path to a better future. A poem, written by Emma Lazarus and eventually placed at the base of the statue, emphasized the promise of America:

Most of the miners from Pennsylvania to California were immigrants from Europe and Asia. Anxious to improve their standard of living in their homeland, these immigrants would accept dangerous, but high-paying jobs.

Give me your tired, your poor,
Your huddled masses yearning to breathe free,
The wretched refuse of your teeming shore.
Send these, the homeless, tempest-tossed to me,
I lift my lamp beside the golden door!

In popular theory, the promise of America exerted a powerful pull on Europe and Asia. The United States stood for political freedom, social mobility, and economic opportunity. Since the first settlers landed in Jamestown, millions of immigrants had responded to the American magnet. At no time was immigration as great as in the late nineteenth and early twentieth centuries; between 1860 and 1920 more than 25 million more people arrived.

The United States was not the only country to lure immigrants from Europe. Millions more immigrated to Australia, New Zealand, South Africa, Canada, Brazil, Argentina, and other underpopulated areas of the globe. In truth, seen in its worldwide context, the United States' pull was less powerful than Europe's push. During the nineteenth century almost every European country experienced a dramatic population increase due to advances in medicine and improved public health standards. Available land and food, however, could not increase sufficiently to meet the new population demands. Thus emigration increased sharply.

Historians have divided immigration to the United States into two categories: old and new. The source of the old immigration was northern and western Europe—England, Ireland, France, Germany, and Scandinavia. The immigrants were mostly Protestants (except for the Irish Catholics) and always white; a majority were literate and had lived under constitutional forms of government. Assimilation for them was a relatively easy process. The new immigration came from eastern and southern Europe. Greeks, Poles, Russians, Italians, Slavs, Turks—these people found assimilation more difficult. Politically, religiously, and culturally, they differed greatly from both the earlier immigrants and native-born Americans.

The shift from "old" to "new" occurred during the 1880s. For example, in 1882, 87 percent of the immigrants to the United States came from northern and western Europe. By 1907 this pattern had changed;

Immigration, 1880–1889 and 1900–1909

The source of old immigration was primarily northern and western Europe— England, Ireland, Germany, and Scandinavia. By the late 1890s a wave of new immigrants began to arrive from eastern and southern Europe.

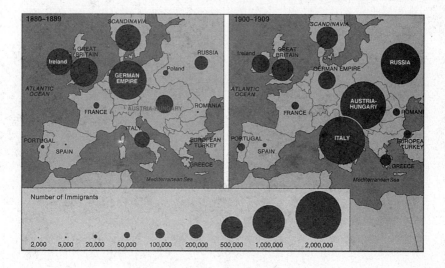

more than 80 percent were from southern and eastern Europe. Certainly, a geographic shift in origin of immigration to the United States took place, but more than geography differentiated the old and the new immigrants. Their reasons for leaving Europe, visions of America, settlement patterns, and occupational choices varied greatly.

By the late nineteenth century the motives and the opportunity to migrate to America were present in southern and eastern Europe. With the abolition of serfdom, peasants were free to emigrate; and with the rise in population, young men faced job, land, and food shortages. Finally, railroads and steamships made travel faster and less expensive. During the 1880s steamships carried immigrants across the Atlantic for as little as $8, and by the turn of the century the trip took only five and a half days. In short, the conditions were right for the push to America.

"Birds of Passage"

Essentially two types of immigrants came to America. Permanent immigrants formed one group; migrant workers comprised the other. The people in the second group, often called birds of passage, were like the Chinese. They never intended to make the United States their home, but simply came to America to work, save, and then returned to their homeland. Most were young men in their teens and twenties. They left behind their parents, young wives, and children, indications that their absence would not be too long. Before 1900 an estimated 78 percent of Italian immigrants and 95 percent of Greek immigrants were men. Some immigrants came to America fully intending to return home, but for one reason or another—love, hardship, early death—did not. Overall, 20 to 30 percent of all immigrants returned to their native land.

The activity of the birds of passage can be clearly seen in Italian immigration patterns of the late nineteenth century. Starting in the 1870s Italian birthrates began to rise and mortality rates fell. Heavily taxed and hurt by high protective tariffs on northern industrial goods, southern Italians sank deeper into poverty. Soon nature also joined the opposition. Natural disasters rocked southern Italy during the first decade of the twentieth century. Earthquakes and volcanic eruptions caused untold devastation. The most cruel blow came in 1908 when an earthquake and tidal wave swept through the Strait of Messina between Sicily and the Italian mainland. The disaster destroyed hundreds of villages and killed hundreds of thousands of people.

The kinds of jobs that Italian men sought reflected their attitude toward America. They did not look for careers. Occupations that provided opportunity for upward economic mobility were alien to them. Unlike most of the earlier immigrants to America, they did not want to farm or even own land, both of which implied a permanence that did not figure in their plans. Instead, Italians headed for the cities, where many found work in the construction industry. Few jobs were beneath them. Native-born Americans commented that the Italian birds of passage readily accepted "work no white man could stand." Expecting their stay in America to be short, they lived as inexpensively as possible under conditions that native-born families considered intolerable.

Italians were not the only birds of passage. The same forces—population pressure, unemployment, hunger, and the breakdown of agrarian societies—sent Greeks, Slavs, Chinese, Japanese, Mexicans, French Canadians, and inhabitants of scores of other nations to the United States. Seeking neither permanent homes nor citizenship, they desired only an opportunity to work for a living, hoping to save enough money to return to a better life in the country of their birth.

Slavs, and especially Poles, dramatized this pattern of temporary migration—the desire to use America as a means of improving their lot in their home country. Strong and determined, they preferred the work that paid the best, usually the most dangerous and physically exhausting. After disembarking at East Coast ports, Slavs generally headed directly to the mill and mining towns of Pennsylvania and the Midwest. Unlike the Italians who preferred to work in sociable gangs and above ground, Poles readily accepted the hard lonely labor of the mines and steel mills. The extra money was enough compensation for the danger of underground or indoor work. Employers quickly noted this Slavic inclination and solicited the labor of hardy Slavs in search of good wages and the fast route home.

In Search of a New Home

In contrast to the birds of passage, several million other immigrants came to America with no intention of ever returning to the land of their birth. These were the permanent immigrants, for whom America offered political and religious freedom as well as economic opportunity. The promise of America was especially appealing to members of ethnic and religious minorities who were persecuted, abused, and despised in their homelands.

The Jews were the prototypical true immigrants. Like the Irish Catholics a generation before, they fled nearly unbearable hardships. For millions of Russian Jews, for whom life was difficult in the best of times, conditions deteriorated rapidly following the assassination of the liberal

Czar Alexander II. Laws restricted Jewish businesses, prevented Jewish land ownership, and limited Jewish education. Pogroms, a form of legally sanctioned mob attack against Jews, killed and injured thousands of persons. Sometimes at the whim of authorities, Russian Cossacks burned Jewish houses and destroyed Jewish possessions.

Because they came to the United States to stay, the form of Jewish immigration differed substantially from that of the birds of passage. For them, immigration was not simply a young man's alternative. Jews, as all other permanent immigrants, tended to come to America in family units. Men and women, young and old—they were all represented. They brought their life savings and most valuable possessions with them, never expecting to see again what they left behind. As a result, the move to

In 1882 Congress passed the Chinese Exclusion Act, which barred Chinese laborers from entering the United States for ten years.

America was financially and physically taxing. And once in America, whole families had more expenses than the young male birds of passage.

Since America was now their home, Jewish men looked for jobs offering future opportunities rather than simply the opportunity to work for wages. They were not drawn to the steel mills and mines or even to jobs in construction. They desired skilled, not unskilled, labor. Many Jews were artisans, and in America they put these skills to use as tailors and seamstresses, cigar makers and toy makers, tanners and butchers, carpenters, joiners, roofers, and masons, coppersmiths and blacksmiths. They had the knowledge and ability to perform the thousands of skilled tasks needed in an urban environment.

Nativism: The Anti-Immigrant Reaction

Sometimes an isolated event, by itself not historically important, can illuminate like a flash of lightning the social landscape and beliefs of a particular time. Certainly this is true with the Hennessy case. In 1890 a feud between gangs on the New Orleans docks turned violent. The following year David Hennessy, the New Orleans superintendent of police, asserted that he had evidence that a secret Sicilian organization known as the Mafia was involved in the affair. Shortly after Hennessy made his bold charges, five armed men gunned him down.

The crime raised a hue and cry against Sicilians, and local police arrested scores, urged on by Mayor Joseph Shakespeare's instructions to "arrest every Italian you come across, if necessary." The mayor told the public, "We must teach these people a lesson that they will not forget for all time." Eleven Sicilians were brought to trial, but a jury failed to convict them. Undaunted, a local mob promptly took matters into its own hands and shot or clubbed to death nine and hanged two of the suspects. As far as most natives of New Orleans were concerned, justice had been done. Many Americans seemed to agree.

The Hennessy case soon faded from the front pages of American newspapers, but the emotions it revealed were very real. Native-born Americans harbored deep resentment toward immigrants, especially those from southern and eastern Europe. If American industrialists saw in the immigrants a bottomless pool of dependable inexpensive labor, American workers saw competition. Protestants saw Catholics and Jews. Educators saw illiterate hordes. Politicians saw peasants, unfamiliar with the workings of democracy. Social Darwinists saw a mass of dark-skinned people who were far "below" northern and western Europeans on the evolutionary ladder. In short, native-born Americans, heirs of a different culture, religion, and complexion, saw something alien and inferior, perhaps even dangerous.

This atmosphere of hostility often spilled over into open violence. In 1891 in a New Jersey mill town 500 tending boys in a glassworks rioted when the management hired 14 young Russian Jews. During an 1895 labor conflict in the southern Colorado coal fields, a group of American miners killed six Italians. When Slavic coal miners went on strike in 1897 in eastern Pennsylvania, local citizens massacred 21 Polish and Hungarian workers. On the West Coast, Chinese workers were subject to regular and vicious attacks. Especially during economic hard times, native-born Americans lashed out against the new immigrants.

Sources of Conflict

Nativism, as this anti-immigrant backlash was called, took many forms. Racial nativism decried the new immigrants as biologically less advanced than the Americans who traced their ancestry back to northern and western Europe. Some scholars gathered data on complexion, size of cranium, length of forehead, and slope of shoulders in an effort to demonstrate the inferiority of immigrants. Popular writers readily accepted these stereotypes. Jacob Riis, a Danish immigrant who became an urban reformer in America and wrote the popular book *How the Other Half Lives* (1890), characterized Italians as "born gamblers" who lived destitute and disorderly lives; Chinese as secretive and addicted to every vice; and Jews as "enslaved" by their pursuit of gold and living amid filth.

Religious differences reinforced ethnic variations. Overwhelmingly Catholic and Jewish, the new immigrants challenged the Protestant orthodoxy of the United States. Many Americans regarded the pope as the anti-Christ and Catholics as his evil minions. Native-born Americans viewed Jews with even greater suspicion. "Money is their God," wrote leading journalist and social critic Jacob Riis. Eventually many social clubs, country clubs, hotels, and universities excluded Jews, arguing that money alone could not purchase respectability.

The Leo Frank case painfully demonstrated the ubiquitous anti-Semitism in American society. Frank, the son of a wealthy New York merchant, managed an Atlanta pencil factory. In 1914 one of the factory hands, Mary Phagan, was found murdered on the premises. Frank was tried and convicted on flimsy evidence, but after reviewing the case the governor of Georgia commuted Frank's death sentence to life imprisonment. The decision outraged native Georgian whites. They boycotted Jewish merchants and clamored for Frank's blood. Finally, a group of citizens from Mary Phagan's hometown took Leo Frank from a state prison, transported him 175 miles across the state, and coldly hanged him. In the 1980s new evidence in the Phagan case proved Frank innocent, and Georgia's Board of Pardons granted him a posthumous pardon.

The wave of immigrants sparked political fears as well as racial and religious ones. Many Americans tended to equate immigration with radicalism and suspected that every boat that docked at Ellis Island contained a swarm of revolutionaries. As unfounded as their fears were, isolated cases of radicalism among immigrants did occur. They drew attention, for example, to Leon Czolgosz, born of eastern European immigrant parents and a convert to revolutionary anarchism. On September 6, 1901, Czolgosz shot and killed President William McKinley at the Pan-American Conference in Buffalo, New York. Such actions seemed to confirm the worst fears of antiradical nativists.

The strongest resentments against the new immigrants, however, were purely economic. American workers, particularly the unskilled, believed that the immigrants depressed wages by their willingness to "work cheap." Even skilled workers maintained that birds of passage were unwilling to support any union efforts to improve working conditions in America. Samuel Gompers, head of the American Federation of Labor, believed that the immigrants from eastern and southern Europe and from Asia were ignorant, unskilled, and unassimilable. Calling for strong restrictive legislation, he said, "Some way must be found to safeguard America."

In short, by the 1890s, when a terrible depression had disrupted the normal economic and social course of America, the new immigrants became a convenient scapegoat for the nation's ills. It was a time when people elevated racial prejudice and rumors to universal truths. Swept along by a wave of xenophobic fear, nativists claimed that the social ills of America's expanding cities—corruption, poor sanitation, violence, crime, disease, pollution—were the fault of the new immigrants. And they looked to the federal government for relief and protection.

Closing the Golden Door

The first immigrants attacked were those who were the most different from native-born Americans and the most unskilled—the Chinese. Between 1868 and 1882, more than 160,000 Chinese entered the United States. They laid down railroad tracks and mined for gold, silver, and coal. During the depression of the mid-1870s the Chinese came under increasingly bitter and violent attack. At the forefront of the nativistic onslaught were the Irish, themselves recent immigrants, who competed with the Chinese for unskilled jobs. Irish political leaders in America demanded an end to Chinese immigration into the United States.

Eventually Congress responded to the pressure for restriction. In 1880 China gave the United States the right "to regulate, limit, or suspend," though not to prohibit, the immigration of workers. Quickly the golden door slammed shut. In 1882 the Chinese Exclusion Act suspended Chinese immigration for ten years and drastically restricted the rights of the Chinese already in the United States. In 1892 Congress extended the act for another ten years, and then in 1902 extended it indefinitely. The legislation established a precedent for the future exclusion of other immigrants. By the 1890s most Americans agreed that the country should restrict "undesirable" immigrants.

In 1896 Congress passed a literacy test bill, which would have excluded any adult immigrant unable to read 40 words in his language. President Grover Cleveland vetoed the measure, arguing that it tested prior circumstances and America stood for open opportunities. The demand for restrictive legislation continued, however, and in 1917 Congress passed a literacy test bill, overriding the veto of Woodrow Wilson.

Hester Street, 1907, on New York City's Lower East Side was home to thousands of Jewish immigrants from Russia and eastern Europe. The immigrants crowded into the tenements lining the street, which bustled with peddlers and pedestrians.

World War I and the Bolshevik Revolution in Russia in 1917 chilled an already cold climate for immigrants from southern and eastern Europe. Once again American authorities regarded Jews from Russia as potential revolutionaries. Responding to this fear, in 1918 and 1920 Congress passed legislation to exclude or deport anarchists and other "dangerous radicals."

The generation-long battle over restriction ended with a clear victory for nativism, when Congress in 1921 passed the Emergency Quota Act, which limited immigration to a nation-based quota system. It provided that no more than 3 percent of any given nationality in America in 1910 could annually immigrate to the United States. In 1924 the National Origins Act lowered the quota to 2 percent of each nationality residing in America in 1890. The act was clearly aimed at restricting eastern and southern Europeans, and although modified in 1927 it achieved its desired result. The golden door was no longer fully open to eastern and southern Europeans, and it was completely closed to Asians. An important era in American history had ended.

Nativism and Native Americans

Immigrants were not the only people affected by nativist impulses. In a cruel irony, American Indians also felt the impact of nativist theories and prejudices. During the 1860s, 1870s, and 1880s Indians were forced onto reservations by the federal government. The process was not peaceful. At almost every step Indian tribes resisted, often clashing with federal troops.

The last major bloody confrontation occurred during the cold December of 1890 on the Pine Ridge Reservation (Sioux) in South Dakota. Poorly fed and supplied on the reservation and longing for the glories of their past, members of the Teton Sioux took up the "Ghost Dance," a ritual that promised the faithful the mystical disappearance of the whites and the return of their tribal lands. Troops were called in to suppress the Ghost Dance and arrest the Sioux leader Sitting Bull, who the government considered the focal point of Indian resistance. Sitting Bull was killed, and some Sioux took up arms and left the reservation. Near Wounded Knee Creek, U.S. soldiers, armed with rapid-fire Hotchkiss guns, attempted to disarm the Indians. When one Indian resisted, soldiers opened fire, killing more than 300 men, women, and children. The Battle of Wounded Knee, which resembled more a slaughter than a battle, ended the violent era of Indian and white relations.

By the time of Wounded Knee, however, the U.S. government had embarked on a new solution to the Indian problem. At the heart of this new policy was the destruction of the reservation system. Reservations encouraged tribal unity, and, as such, distinctiveness from white American society. Congress believed that the solution was to treat Indians less like members of individual tribes and more like autonomous individuals. In 1887 Congress passed the Dawes Severalty Act, which authorized the president to divide tribal lands and redistribute the lands among tribal members, giving 160 acres to each head of a family and lesser amounts to bachelors, women, and children. Although the plots would be held in trust for 25 years to prevent Indians from immediately selling the land, the object of the legislation was to make Indians individual landowners. In addition, all Indians receiving land grants were also made citizens of the United States.

Henry Dawes, a U.S. senator from Massachusetts, was motivated by what he believed were the best interests of the Indians. Like other reformers, he believed that the most effective solution to the Indian problem was to assimilate Indians into mainstream white American culture. Other reformers opened Indian schools to teach Indian children to be mechanics and farmers and to train them for citizenship. More than two dozen eastern boarding schools were established on the premise that the fastest and surest way to achieve assimilation was to remove children from their Indian way of life. Even more boarding schools were established on reservations to serve the same ends. However, the schools failed to break tribal loyalties or destroy Native-American culture.

While the reformers opened schools, Congress continued its efforts to break up the reservations. The Curtis Act of 1898 ended tribal sovereignty in Indian Territory, voiding tribal control of mineral rights, abolishing tribal laws and courts, and imposing the laws and courts of the United States on the Indians. Finally, in 1924 Congress enacted the Snyder Act, which granted all Indians born in the United States full citizenship. As far as Congress was concerned, the United States had now assimilated its true natives.

Reformers believed that these acts would end the tribal system and lead to assimilation. The legislation, however, served only the land interests of white Americans. By 1932 the allotment program had taken 90 million acres of land away from tribal control, and as late as 1981 a U.S. district court decision branded the program "probably one of the best-intended grievous errors in the history of American policy-making." Far from being assimilated, Indians saw their own culture attacked and partially destroyed, while at the same time they were never fully accepted into the dominant American culture.

Working in Industrial America

If during the 1920s advocates of immigration restrictions and Indian assimilation won an important battle, they lost their self-proclaimed war. They longed for a rural, white, Protestant, ethnically homogeneous

America, but the war they waged took the form more of a rearguard action than an offensive. Between 1870 and 1920 America had changed dramatically. It became a richly complex, ethnically diverse, industrial country. In 1880 more than 87 percent of the inhabitants of Chicago were immigrants and their children. In other major American cities the statistics were similar: Milwaukee and Detroit, 84 percent; New York and Cleveland, 80 percent; St. Louis and San Francisco, 78 percent.

These new immigrants provided the muscle for America's spectacular industrial growth. Indeed, without immigrant labor American industrialization would have moved forward at a far slower pace.

Wages, Hours, and Standard of Living

Was the price paid by native-born and immigrant labor for industrialization worth the benefits they received? This is not a simple question to answer; in fact, each laborer might have answered it differently, although their answers would have contained common themes. Unquestionably, industrialization extracted a heavy toll from the laborers, who suffered psychologically and emotionally in industrial America. It changed not only how, when, and where they worked but also how they regarded work and how they perceived themselves. Equally unquestionably, however, industrialization transformed the United States into the most prosperous country in the world. To some degree, laborers shared in that prosperity and increase in material comfort.

Wages played an important role in a laborer's attitude toward work. In general, wages rose and prices fell during the late nineteenth and early twentieth centuries. Exactly how much is a question of heated historical debate, but it is clear that the pace of wages and earnings lagged well behind the spectacular growth in the American economy. And even with modest improvements in wages, laborers fought a continual battle with poverty.

The most important factor in determining the economic well-being of a working-class family was how many members of the family had jobs. Fathers and sons, mothers and daughters, and often aunts, uncles, and grandparents—all contributed to the "family economy." To be sure, the nature of the family economy caused concern. Carroll D. Wright in the United States Census of 1880 warned, "the factory system necessitates the employment of women and children to an injurious extent, and consequently its tendency is to destroy family life and ties and domestic habits, and ultimately the home."

In truth, the opposite was probably true. Without the income earned by wives and children, families faced greater threats to their unity. Economically, families worked as a single entity; the desires of any particular individual often had to be sacrificed for the good of the family. This meant that women and children worked, families took in boarders, and all earnings were used for a common end. Far from destroying the family, the family economy often strengthened it.

During the first decade of the twentieth century social workers conducted numerous studies to determine how much a family or a single individual needed to sustain a typical working-class existence for a year. Estimates for New York City ranged between $800 and $876 for a family of four, $505 for a single man, and $466 for a working woman. Many of New York's laborers fell painfully below the recommended minimum. Single women lived particularly difficult lives. A New York study concluded that women earned about half as much as men, and that the majority made less than $300 per year. What was true for women was equally valid for blacks, Asians, and Mexicans in America. They were given the most exhausting and dangerous work, paid the least, and were fired first during economic hard times.

There were clear divisions even among workers. At the top ranks were the highly skilled laborers. Mostly English-speaking, generally Protestant, and almost exclusively white, they were paid well, had good job security, and considered themselves elite craftsmen. Below them were the semiskilled and unskilled workers. Most were immigrants from southern and eastern Europe, spoke halting if any English, and were Catholics or Jews. They lacked job security and had to struggle for a decent existence. At the bottom of the semiskilled and unskilled category were the nonwhite and women workers, for whom even a decent existence was normally out of reach.

Like wages, hours varied widely. Long hours were not a new phenomenon tied to industrial America. Farm workers and artisans often labored from sunup to sundown, but the tempo and quality of their labor was different. Farm work was governed by the season and the weather. The rhythms of the preindustrial workshop similarly mixed work with fellowship. If the work days were long, they were also sociable. Moreover, punctuality was not the golden virtue it became during industrialization. The idea of punching a time clock was alien to the preindustrial worker, who might think in terms of hours but not in terms of minutes.

Preindustrial labor, then, had a more relaxed atmosphere. Farm work and shop labor could be hard and dangerous, but there were not sharp lines between labor and leisure. Thrift, regularity, sobriety, orderliness, punctuality—hallmarks of an industrial society—were virtues not rigorously observed.

Given this new standard of work and time demanded by factory owners, laborers were reluctant to work the preindustrial dawn-to-dusk day. In 1889 hundreds of trade unionists paraded through the streets of

Worcester, Massachusetts, behind a banner which read: "Eight Hours for Work, Eight Hours for Rest, Eight Hours for What We Will." The reality, however, fell far short of the ideal. It is difficult to generalize about hours because they varied considerably from occupation to occupation. In 1890, for example, bakers averaged over 65 hours a week, steelworkers over 66, and canners nearly 77. Working in a steel mill blast furnace was a 12-hour-a-day, 7-day-a-week job, including one 24-hour continuous shift and one day off every two weeks.

For women, the new ideals of industrial America created even more work. The increased emphasis on cleanliness and greater demand for tidy homes resulted in more time devoted to cleaning, dusting, and scrubbing. In addition, the growing availability of washable cotton fabrics increased the amount of laundering housewives performed. Finally, more varied diets meant that women spent more time cooking meals. By 1900 the typical housewife worked six hours a day on just two tasks: meal preparation and cleaning. This was in addition to the time they spent on other household tasks.

The Lost Crafts

Although workers complained regularly about wages and hours, they were equally disturbed by several other results of industrialization. The late-nineteenth-century industries differed from the preindustrial workshop in four important areas: size, discipline, mechanization, and displacement of skill. The informality of the preindustrial workshop, with only a handful of employees, was an inevitable casualty. Huge plants demanded an organized, disciplined work force. Work became formalized and structured, and workers were carefully regulated to ensure maximum productivity.

Mechanization of work led to both the large factories and the incredible boom in productivity. It also caused an erosion of certain skilled trades. Imaginative inventors designed machines that performed tasks previously done by skilled artisans. Where once a single tailor took a piece of cloth, cut it, fashioned it, sewed it, and made it into a pair of pants, by 1859 a Cincinnati clothing factory had divided the process into 17 different semiskilled jobs. The replacement of highly skilled workers by semiskilled laborers was a characteristic of the factory system.

By the end of the century it appeared to many observers that all work was being mechanized and moving toward the factory mode. Even farmers followed the mechanization march. By the early 1880s one Dakota Territory wheat farm stretched over 30,000 acres, used 20 reapers and 30 steam-powered threshers, and employed 1,000 field hands.

Worker Discontent

In the long run, industrialization brought much to many. Between 1860 and 1920 the volume of manufactured goods increased almost 14-fold. Consumer goods, which once only the rich could afford, came into the purchasing range of the middle class. Newspapers and magazines advertised, and department stores displayed, a wide variety of factory products.

From a worker's perspective, however, industrialization was often an inhumane process. Factory labor tended to be monotonous, and machines made work more dangerous. Industrial accidents were alarmingly common, and careless or tired workers sacrificed their fingers, hands, arms, and sometimes even lives. Frequent speedups increased the chances of injury.

To make matters even worse, owners often assumed an uncaring attitude toward their laborers. Concerned with production quotas and cost efficiency, owners seemed insensitive to workers' needs; and in fact, many *were* insensitive. As one factory manager proclaimed, "I regard my people as I regard my machinery. So long as they can do my work for what I choose to pay them, I keep them, getting out of them all I can."

Workers did not passively accept industrialization and the changes caused by that enormous process. At almost every step they resisted change, and they had formidable weapons at their disposal. On one level, resistance entailed a simple, individual decision not to change completely. Factory managers demanded a steady, dependable work force, but they were plagued by chronic absenteeism. Immigrant workers refused to labor on religious holidays, and in some towns factories had to shut down on the day the circus arrived. Across America, heavy drinking on Sunday led to "blue Mondays," a term used to describe absenteeism.

Another form of individual protest was simply quitting. Most industrial workers changed jobs at least every three years, and in many industries the annual turnover rate was over 100 percent. Some quit because they were bored, "forced to work too hard," or because they were struck by spring wanderlust and simply wanted to move. Others quit because of severe discipline, unsafe working conditions, or low wages. Compulsive quitting was a clear indication that perhaps 20 percent of the work force never came to terms with industrialization.

Workers were similarly quick to take collective action. The late nineteenth century witnessed the most sustained and violent industrial conflict in the nation's history. Strikes were as common as political corruption during the period. Between 1881 and 1890 the Bureau of Labor Statistics estimated that 9,668 strikes and lockouts had occurred. Although most of the conflicts were relatively peaceful, some were so violent that citizens across the nation feared that America was moving toward another revolution.

Early Labor Violence

An examination of several conflicts indicates clearly the relative power of industrialists and workers. An early violent conflict occurred in the anthracite coal region of eastern Pennsylvania. The late 1860s and early 1870s were troubled times for this socially and ethnically divided area. Mine owners competed ruthlessly against each other, and they all distrusted the miners and their union, the Workingmen's Benevolent Association (WBA). Added to economic and class tensions, the area was torn by ethnic conflicts. American-born and Protestant Scots-Irishmen owned most of the mines, and Welshmen and Englishmen served as mine superintendents. Increasingly, however, the miners were Irish-Catholic immigrants. Old World prejudices thus mingled with New World economics.

Matters became worse during the depression of the mid-1870s, when the mine owners came together and agreed to cut wages and increase workloads. The Irish responded much as they had done in the old country. While the WBA battled the owners at the negotiation table, the Ancient Order of Hibernians, a secret fraternal society of Irish immigrants, and its inner circle, the Molly Maguires, waged a violent guerrilla war. They disrupted the operation of several mines and attacked a handful of mining officials.

The mine owners managed to infiltrate the Molly Maguires with a secret agent, Irish-born James McParlan, who agreed to inform on his fellow Irishmen for the Pinkerton agency. While McParlan was gathering information, the WBA went on strike. Disorder and violence followed. The public blamed the WBA for the violence, and the strike was broken. Shortly thereafter, McParlan's testimony was used to destroy both the Mollies and the WBA. Altogether, 20 Mollies were convicted and executed.

In eastern Pennsylvania and elsewhere, the greatest weapon against strikers was the community's fear of violence. If industrialists could convince the public that unions promoted violence, then they could characterize their own union-busting tactics as a sincere defense of law and order.

The same depression that convulsed the Pennsylvania coal fields shook the rest of the country as well. To keep from going under, many businessmen cut rates and attempted to recoup their losses by reducing labor costs. This was true especially in the highly competitive railroad business. Repeatedly, workers suffered wage cuts, and usually unskilled wages were slashed more than the skilled.

During mid-July 1877 the Baltimore and Ohio Railroad (B&O) announced its third consecutive 10 percent wage cut. Angry, frustrated, and led by the new Trainmen's Union, railroad workers along the line went on strike. When trouble followed, B&O workers seized an important junction at Martinsburg, West Virginia. The state militia and local sheriffs sympathized with the workers and could not end the strike. As a result, President Rutherford B. Hayes sent in federal troops to protect an army of strikebreakers.

From Martinsburg the strike spread. Railroad workers walked off their jobs, and trains sat unused and deserted. The strike paralyzed transportation in the Midwest and much of the industrial Northeast. In Baltimore the state militia shot into a mob and killed ten persons; in Pittsburgh rioters burned 2,000 freight cars, looted stores, and torched railroad buildings; in Buffalo, Chicago, and Indianapolis workers and police engaged in bloody battles.

When local police and state militiamen failed to quell the problems, President Hayes ordered more federal troops to do the job. Eventually, superior force restored peace and the trains started rolling again, but not before more than a hundred strikers were killed.

Like most spontaneous strikes, the Great Strike of 1877 failed. But the anger it revealed frightened America. Although some authorities labeled the disturbances as the work of communist agitators, more thoughtful observers realized it was caused by legitimate grievances. For owners and workers alike, the strike was a lesson. Owners learned that workers were not merely passive partners in the industrial process. Labor learned that when pressed, the federal government was not neutral—it would side with capital.

Employers Gain Power

Between 1877 and 1886 industrialists grew in organizational and economic power. In the steel, oil, coal, railroad, and meat industries ruthless competition and consolidation produced industrial giants. Workers could not match the power of Rockefeller, Carnegie, and Swift, who controlled their industries and were the victors in the competitive industrial wars.

The power of industrialists can be seen in the famous Haymarket Square riot of 1886. In 1885 skilled molders won a 15 percent pay increase after a strike at McCormick Harvester Machine Company in Chicago. Reacting angrily to the union's activities, McCormick introduced pneumatic molders that could be run by unskilled workers. Again in 1886, the skilled workers went on strike, but this time the result was different. The combined forces of McCormick and local police ensured the safety of an army of strikebreakers and the plant's output continued until the strike was broken.

Tempers, however, remained high, and violence resulted. In May, after the strike ended, police and workers clashed once again, and a handful of laborers were killed and wounded. Disturbed by the violent force used by police in defense of industrialists' positions, August Spies, a Chicago anarchist and labor agitator, called for a protest meeting in Haymarket Square. The meeting took place on May 4 before a generally unenthusiastic crowd of about 3,000 labor supporters. But as the peaceful meeting was breaking up, local police unexpectedly charged the crowd. Then somebody—to this day no one knows who—threw a bomb into the melee, killing police and protesters alike. The police opened fire, shooting protesters and even, accidentally, each other.

Industrialists, city officials, ministers, and the local press convinced the public that the bombing was a prelude to anarchistic revolution. Despite a lack of evidence, police arrested eight local radicals, including Spies, and charged them with conspiracy. The eight were tried and convicted, and seven were sentenced to be hanged. One man committed suicide in his cell and three were eventually pardoned, but Spies and three others were

The famous Haymarket Square riot of 1886 began as a peaceful protest meeting but ended in violence. The arrest of eight local radicals without real evidence sent a message to workers that the police and public opinion sided with the industrialists.

executed. For radicals, labor agitators, and unionists, the message was clear: police and public opinion were on the side of the industrialists.

The excessive violence of the Molly Maguires, the great strike of 1877, and the Haymarket Square riot was not necessarily typical of disputes between labor and management. Although labor violence continued unabated in the 1890s, late-nineteenth-century labor disputes were often settled peacefully. In most cases, however, management won the conflicts. Only in small towns, where prolabor and anti-industrial sentiment knew no class lines, did labor battle management on anything approaching even terms.

Unorganized and Organized Labor

Historians have used the term "robber barons" to characterize late-nineteenth-century industrialists. Whether "robber" is accurate or not is debatable, but "baron" is a fitting description. They controlled their industries as medieval barons ruled their fiefs. Their word was usually final, and such a modern concept as democracy found an unsympathetic environment inside factory walls.

Unfortunately, during the last third of the nineteenth century, labor was unable to form organizations powerful enough to deal with capital on equal terms. Before 1900 most unions were weak, and their goals were often out of touch with the changing American economy. In addition, the labor force itself was divided along ethnic, racial, gender, and craft lines. It was during this period, then, that labor attempted to overcome its own divisions and fumbled its way toward a clearer vision of what were its own best interests.

Before the 1870s most American unions were locally rooted, craft-based organizations. They were geared to the small Jacksonian workshop, not to the large modern factory. The first union to attempt to organize all workers was the short-lived National Labor Union (NLU). Founded in Baltimore in 1866, the NLU was a consciously national organization. In addition to shorter hours and higher wages, its ambitious program included women's and blacks' rights, monetary reform, and worker-owned industries. Rich in ideas and solutions, the NLU was poor in organization and finances. The NLU, whose reach exceeded its grasp, died during the depression of the mid-1870s.

The vision of the NLU was carried on by the Noble and Holy Order of the Knights of Labor. Begun in 1869 as a secret fraternal order as well as a union, the Knights remained small and unimportant until 1878 when they went public. Led by Terence V. Powderly, in 1881 the Knights opened their membership to all wage earners. The Knights excluded only bankers, lawyers, liquor dealers, speculators, and stockbrokers, whom they viewed as money manipulators and exploiters.

Complete worker solidarity was the Knights' goal. They welcomed and spoke for all laborers—women and men, black and white, immigrant and native, unskilled and skilled. Like the NLU, the Knights rejected industrial capitalism and favored cooperatively owned industries. Although critics labeled the Knights "wild-eyed, utopian visionaries," they are best understood in the context of exploited workers searching for a less exploitive alternative to industrial capitalism. If their rhetoric was extreme, their suffering was real.

An able leader, Powderly called for reforms of the currency system, the abolition of child labor, regulation of trusts and monopolies, an end to alien contract labor networks, and government ownership of public utilities. He favored peaceful arbitration of labor disputes, opposed strikes, and also opposed the formation of narrow trade unions, instead advocating that skilled workers should assist the unskilled. Harmony and fellowship ultimately dominated his vision of America's future. Consensus, not conflict, was his goal.

The Knights' rhetoric found sympathetic listeners among American workers. During the early 1880s membership rolls grew. Then came 1884, the beginning of what labor historians have called "the great upheaval." Strikes erupted in the coal fields of Pennsylvania and Ohio and the railroad yards of Missouri and Illinois. The labor conflicts continued into 1885 and 1886. Labor won some, but by no means all, of the strikes. Although their role was small, the Knights had a part in several important labor victories. By mid-1886 perhaps 750,000 workers had joined the Knights.

From that high point, however, the decline was rapid. From the start, the Knights could not weld together their diverse rank and file. Administrative and organizational problems surfaced, and Powderly's relatively conservative leadership was opposed by more radical members, who fully accepted strikes and conflict. In 1886 the Haymarket Square bombing branded all unions as un-American and violent in the public mind. By 1893, when Powderly was driven from office, the Knights' membership had declined precipitously. Weakened and divided, they failed to survive the depression of the mid-1890s.

Unlike the Knights and the NLU, the American Federation of Labor (AFL) did not aspire to remake society. Its leaders accepted industrial capitalism and rejected partisan politics and the dreams of radical visionaries. Instead the AFL concentrated on practical, reachable goals: higher wages, shorter workdays, and improved working conditions. Most important, it only recruited skilled laborers, recognizing that easily replaceable unskilled workers were in a poor position to negotiate with employers.

Formed in 1886 by the coming together of skilled trade unions, the AFL was ably led by Samuel Gompers, a Jewish immigrant who had been the president of a New York cigar makers' union. As the head of the AFL for almost 40 years, Gompers used his considerable "moral power" and organizational ability to fight for achievable goals. American laborers were divided over religious, racial, ethnic, gender, and political issues, but they all desired higher wages, more leisure time, and greater liberty. Gompers battled for those unifying issues, focusing on the real world, not the best of all possible worlds. For this reason, he opposed "theorizers" and "intellectuals" in the labor movement. Once effectively organized, he maintained, labor could deal with capital on equal terms.

Gompers's approach toward working with capital and organizing labor proved successful in the long run. Before 1900, however, the AFL was not more successful than the Knights or the NLU. In fact, workers benefited little from unions before the turn of the century. All together fewer than 5 percent of American workers joined trade unions, and the major areas of industrial growth were the least unionized. Nevertheless,

As head of the American Federation of Labor (AFL), Samuel Gompers worked for higher wages, shorter hours, industrial safety, and the right of skilled workers to organize.

the experimentation during the late nineteenth century taught workers valuable lessons. To combat the power of capital, labor needed equal power. During the twentieth century labor would finally gain that power.

Conclusion

In 1986 the Statue of Liberty was given a good cleaning. Its copper was shined as much as copper turned green can be shined, and its structure was refortified. America celebrated, and television newscasters recited once again Emma Lazarus's poem on the base of the statue. Few asked the question, "What are we celebrating?"

What the United States celebrated was nothing less than the emergence of modern America. In 1876 when France shipped the Statue of Liberty to the United States, the country, despite a recent civil war, was remarkably uniform. Most Americans traced their ancestry to Great Britain

Chronology of Key Events

1866	National Labor Union founded in Baltimore
1871	Knights of Labor founded
1877	Great railroad strike; 20 Molly Maguires convicted and executed for terrorism
1882	Chinese Exclusion Act suspends Chinese immigration for ten years
1886	Statue of Liberty unveiled; Haymarket Square riot in Chicago; American Federation of Labor founded
1887	Dawes Severalty Act
1890	U. S. soldiers kill more than 300 Sioux at Battle of Wounded Knee
1892	Homestead strike
1894	Pullman strike
1896	President Cleveland vetoes literacy requirement for adult immigrants
1915	Leo Frank lynched
1921	Emergency Quota Act restricts immigration
1924	National Origins Act lowers imigration quotas; Snyder Act grants citizenship to all U. S.-born Indians

and northern Europe, worshiped in a Protestant church, and lived on farms or in small villages. If they were divided, it was along political and economic lines, not along ethnic and religious ones. The United States was not a world leader. Its navy was small, its diplomats uninfluential, and its industry still largely underdeveloped.

By 1900 America had changed radically. Unprecedented immigration had transformed the country into the most diverse nation in the world as a host of immigrants crowded into American cities. For some it was an exciting, hopeful time; for others a painful, disillusioning one. Old America gave way to a New America with startling speed. In fact, most Americans in 1900 had not yet adjusted to the massive changes. What role would the new immigrants play in American life? What rights did workers have in the large industries? These and other questions would be answered in the next century.

Suggestions for Further Reading

For in-depth examinations of American immigration see John Bodnar, *The Transplanted* (1985); Roger Daniels, *Coming to America* (1990); Alan M. Kraut, *The Huddled Masses* (1982); Philip Taylor, *The Distant Magnet* (1971).

Experiences of specific ethnic groups are analyzed in John Duff, *The Irish in the United States* (1971); Yuji Ichioka, *The Issei: The World of the First Generation Japanese Americans* (1988); Helen Znaniecka Lopata, *Polish Americans* (1976); Joseph Lopreato, *Italian Americans* (1970); Kerby A. Miller, *Emigrants and Exiles: Ireland and the Irish Exodus to North America* (1985); Charles C. Moskos, Jr., *Greek Americans,* 2d ed. (1989); Moses Rischin, *The Promised City: New York's Jews, 1870–1914* (1962).

To gain additional insight into the lives of women immigrants see Cecyle S. Neidle, *America's Immigrant Women* (1975); Sydney Weinberg, *The World of Our Mothers: Lives of Jewish Immigrant Women* (1988). For nativist reaction to the immigrant exodus see David H. Bennett, *The Party of Fear* (1988); Robert Carlson, *The Quest for Conformity* (1975).

Issues facing industrial workers are examined in Melvyn Dubofsky, *Industrialism and the American Worker,* 2d ed. (1985); Herbert Gutman, *Work, Culture, and Society in Industrializing America* (1976); Alice Kessler-Harris, *Out to Work: A History of Wage-Earning Women in the United States* (1982); S. J. Kleinberg, *The Shadow of the Mills* (1989).

Chapter *19*

The Rise of an Urban Society and City People

New Cities and New Problems
Transforming the Walking City
City Technology
The Segregated City
The Problems of Growth
From Private City to Public City

City Culture
Nightlife
From the Genteel Tradition to Realism and Naturalism
Describing the Urban Jungle
Painting Urban Reality
The Sounds of the City

Entertaining the Multitudes
Of Fields and Cities
Bloody Knuckles
The Excluded Americans
From Central Park to Coney Island
The Magic of the Flickering Image
The Agony of Painless Escape

Andrew Borden had, as the old Scottish saying goes, short arms and long pockets. He was cheap, not because he had to be frugal but because he hated to spend money. He had dedicated his entire life to making and saving money, and tales of his unethical and parsimonious business behavior were legendary in his hometown of Fall River, Massachusetts. Andrew, however, was not interested in rumors or the opinions of other people; he was concerned with his own rising fortunes. By 1892 he had amassed over half a million dollars, and he controlled the Fall River Union Savings Bank as well as serving as the director of several companies.

Andrew was rich, but he did not live like a wealthy man. Instead of living alongside the other prosperous Fall River citizens in the elite neighborhood known as The Hill, Andrew resided in an area near the business district called the flats. He liked to save time as well as money, and from the flats he could conveniently walk to work. For his daughters, Lizzie and Emma, whose eyes and dreams focused on The Hill, life in the flats was an intolerable embarrassment. Their house was grim, lacking both comfort and privacy. The only washing facilities were a cold-water faucet in the kitchen and a laundry room water tap in the cellar, where the only toilet in the house was located. To make matters worse, the house was not connected to the Fall River gas main. Andrew preferred to use kerosene to light his house because it was less expensive. To save even more money, he and his family frequently sat in the dark.

The Borden home was far from happy. Lizzie and Emma, ages 32 and 42 in 1892, strongly disliked their stepmother Abby and resented Andrew's penny-pinching ways. Lizzie especially felt alienated from the world around her. Although Fall River was the largest cotton-manufacturing town in America, it offered few opportunities for the unmarried daughter of a prosperous man. Society expected a woman of Lizzie's social position to marry, and while she waited for a proper suitor, her only respectable social outlets were church and community service. She kept herself busy by teaching Sunday School classes and participating in the Woman's Christian Temperance Union and other organizations, but she was not happy.

In August 1892 strange things started to happen in the Borden home. They began after Lizzie and Emma learned that Andrew had secretly changed his will. Abby became violently ill. In time so did the Borden maid Bridget Sullivan and Andrew himself. Shortly thereafter Lizzie went shopping for prussic acid, a deadly poison she said she needed to clean her sealskin cape. When a Fall River druggist refused her request, she left the store in an agitated state. Later in the day she told a friend that she feared an unknown enemy of her father's was after him.

On August 4, 1892, Bridget awoke early and ill, but she still managed to prepare a large breakfast. After a hearty meal, Andrew left for work.

Bridget also left to do some work outside. This left Abby and Lizzie in the house alone. Then somebody did something very specific and very grisly. As Abby was bent over making the bed in the guest room, someone moved into the room unobserved and killed her with an ax.

Andrew came home for lunch earlier than usual. He asked Lizzie where Abby was, and she said she did not know. Unconcerned, Andrew, who was not feeling well, lay down on the parlor sofa for a nap. He never awoke. Like Abby, he was slaughtered by someone with an ax. Lizzie "discovered" his body, still lying on the sofa.

Experts have examined and reexamined the crime, and most have reached the same conclusion: Lizzie killed her father and stepmother. In fact, Lizzie was tried for the gruesome murders. Despite a preponderance of evidence, however, an all-male jury found her not guilty. They arrived at their verdict without debate or disagreement. A woman of Lizzie's social position, they affirmed, simply could not have committed such a terrible crime.

Even before the trial began, newspaper and magazine writers had judged Lizzie innocent for the same reasons. As one historian has noted, "Americans were certain that well-brought up daughters could not commit murder with a hatchet on sunny summer mornings." Criminal women, they believed, originated in the lower classes and even looked evil. They did not look like round-faced Lizzie Borden.

Jurors and editorialists alike judged Lizzie according to their preconceived notions of Victorian womanhood. They believed that such a woman was gentle, docile, and physically frail, short on analytical ability but long on nurturing instincts. Too uncoordinated and weak to accurately swing an ax and too gentle and unintelligent to coldly plan a double murder, women of Lizzie's background simply had to be innocent because of their basic virtue.

Preconceived notions of Victorian femininity saved Lizzie Borden from being convicted of murdering her father and stepmother.

While Lizzie was being tried and found innocent, Victorian notions were being challenged. In the larger cities of America a new culture was taking form, one based on freedoms, not restraints. Immigrants could become millionaires, and women could vote and hold office. Rigid Victorian concepts crumbled under the weight of new ideas; but the new freedoms came with a high price. In both the cities and the culture that flourished within them, a new order had to be constructed out of the chaos of freedom.

New Cities and New Problems

Transforming the Walking City

In an age before reliable mass transportation, when only the rich could afford a carriage, the majority of city dwellers had to walk to and from work. This simple fact dictated the type of cities that emerged in America. They were compact and crowded, their sizes normally limited to about two miles radius from center city or the distance a person could walk in half an hour. Even America's largest cities—New York, Philadelphia, and Boston—conformed to these standards.

Inside these cities, houses, businesses, and factories sat side by side. Tightly packed near the waterfront were shops, banks, warehouses, and business offices, and not far away were the residences of the people who owned or worked in those enterprises. There was little residential segregation. If the rich occupied the finest houses in the center city, the poor lived in the alleys and dirty streets close by. Rich and poor, native-born and immigrant, black and white—they all walked along the same streets and worked in the same area.

Booming industrialization during the last third of the century shattered this arrangement. As industrialists built their new plants in or near existing cities, urban growth accelerated at an alarming rate. Like twin children, factories and cities grew and matured together, each helping the other to reach its physical potentials. In 1860, before America's industrial surge, 20 percent of the population lived in cities. By 1900 almost 40 percent of the population lived in cities or towns, and that figure climbed to more than 50 percent in 1920. At the same time, the numbers of large cities (those with a population of over 100,000) increased at an even faster rate. In 1860 America had only nine large cities. The numbers rose to 38 in 1900 and 68 in 1920.

Immigrant as well as native sources fueled the urban explosion. Although most of the late-nineteenth-century immigrants came from rural communities, they settled in America's industrial heartland. Added to these were the native-born migrants who moved from poor rural areas to the cities. As in Europe and Asia, rural opportunities in the United States were dwindling at the same time that the rural population was growing. Thus ten farm sons moved to the cities for each son who became a farm owner.

Black migration from the rural South to the urban North further expanded the labor pool in the industrial cities. Slow at first, it increased each decade, as blacks left the land of their bondage determined to forge a better life for themselves and their families in the northern cities. Between 1897 and 1920 almost one million blacks left the South, and of those, 85 percent settled in the urban North.

City Technology

Even the largest of the walking cities was unprepared to meet the demands the newcomers placed on it. Cities were already crowded, and construction technology was not yet sufficiently advanced to accommodate the recent arrivals. But in time, engineers and scientists discovered ways to expand cities. During the half century after 1870 horizontal and vertical growth changed the skyline and living conditions of urban America.

Better transportation facilities, constructed and owned by entrepreneurs, solved the basic limitation of the walking city. As early as the 1830s, the horse-drawn omnibus, which carried 12 to 20 passengers along a fixed route, permitted a handful of wealthier urbanites to escape life in the crowded center city. Faster than walking, it was too expensive for unskilled laborers. Similarly the commuter railroads, which also dated back to the 1830s and 1840s, served only the wealthier classes.

The horse railway expanded the city for the middle-class urbanites, white-collar workers, and skilled workers. For 5 cents, these horse-drawn omnibuses carried passengers over steel rails at a speed of 6 to 8 miles per hour. By the 1880s over 300 American cities and towns had constructed horsecar lines, and they significantly expanded the size of cities. Now a person could live 5 miles from his or her place of work and still travel there in less than an hour. The age of walking was almost over.

The cable car, introduced during the 1870s, proved a blessing for urban dwellers in hillier cities like San Francisco and Pittsburgh. Utilizing steam power, cable cars were faster and cleaner than horse-drawn transportation. Even relatively flat cities such as Kansas City and Chicago installed cable cars. Pulled by a moving underground cable, these cars, engineers believed, would be the public transportation of the future—but the system's problems were considerable. Expensive to install and quick to break down, the cable car soon became outmoded, a victim of the electric trolley, which was cheaper to run and more dependable.

Employing the electrical current in overhead wires, trolleys could operate in stop-and-go traffic and travel at average speeds of 10 to 12 miles

This watercolor of New York City's Bowery at night by W. Louis Sonntag, Jr.,
shows how steam, steel, and electricity played a major part in transforming cities.

per hour. By 1902, 97 percent of urban transit mileage had been electrified. Trolleys connected not only city with suburb, but also city with city.
By 1920 a person could travel from Boston to New York entirely by trolleys known as interurbans.

Trolleys were not without their problems, either. The overhead wires
gave cities a weblike appearance, and in the winter the electric wires
snapped from the cold and created serious dangers. In addition, they sometimes frightened horses and thus worsened traffic problems. Altogether, by
the 1890s, the mixture of horsecars, cable cars, and trolleys jostling each
other and pedestrians on city streets created immense traffic jams.

Clogged streets inspired engineers to search for other transportation
solutions. Looking above and below ground, they designed elevated railway lines and subways, such as the Chicago "el" (elevated railway) and the
New York City subway. Electricity powered both, and each helped to ease
transportation for the masses.

While mass transportation allowed cities to spread miles beyond their
cores, steel and glass permitted cities to reach for the sky. At midcentury,
few buildings were higher than five stories. Church spires still dominated

the urban skyline. Buildings, like cities themselves, were personal; they did not dwarf the individual. That, however, soon changed.

In 1885 New York architect William LeBaron Jenney, using light masonry over an iron and steel skeleton, built the Home Insurance Building in Chicago. Although only ten stories high, it was the first true skyscraper in history. Steel, light masonry, and eventually glass revolutionized building construction, and the use of electric elevators made skyscrapers functional.

Louis Henri Sullivan demonstrated the architectural possibilities of the skyscraper. Working in Chicago, Sullivan became the leading exponent of skyscraper technology. Turning his back on classical models, he preached the doctrine that "form follows function," and designed many of the most beautiful and practical skyscrapers in America, including the Wainwright Building in St. Louis and the Transportation Building in Chicago. By the turn of the century, skyscrapers had changed the profile of American cities as surely as industrialism had altered the American landscape.

The Segregated City

The outward and upward growth of cities brought an end to the more personal walking city. Mass transportation freed the upper and middle classes to move to the "streetcar suburbs." They commuted to work and no longer mixed on a daily basis with their economic inferiors.

The working class moved into areas and even houses deserted by wealthier families. Brownstone homes that had served the upper classes were divided into small apartments that satisfied the new demand for inexpensive housing. Since architects had not designed the houses to be used as multiunit apartments, numerous problems resulted. Heatless, sunless, and poorly ventilated rooms became increasingly common.

Ethnic groups and races, like economic classes, tended to stake out neighborhoods in the new, larger cities. In addition, real estate brokers and landlords restricted blacks and immigrants to particular areas. For the first time black ghettos emerged in the major northern cities. In Chicago, New York, Boston, and Philadelphia, English became a foreign language in ethnic neighborhoods. These neighborhoods reproduced in their finer details Old World communities. Familiar faces, foods, churches, and speech patterns comforted lonely immigrants.

Since members of the ethnic working class were too poor for even moderately priced mass transit, they tended to settle close to their places of work. In New York City Jews and Italians lived within walking distance of the Lower East Side garment factories. In Chicago Poles and Lithuanians who worked in the meat-packing industry lived near the stockyards.

Just as new residential trends separated rich and poor, the central business district underwent important changes. Prices for central city real estate shot up at an incredible rate, which only businesses and industries could afford. The central cities were turned over to high-income businesses, banks, warehouses, railroad terminals, and the recently developed department stores. It became an area where money was made, not where people lived.

The Problems of Growth

By the 1890s British observers despaired over what had become of the once small American cities. The uncontrolled growth, they suggested, had created ugliness on an almost unprecedented scale. Although English author Rudyard Kipling had seen the suffering and overcrowded conditions of Bombay and Cairo, he was appalled by Chicago: "This place is the first American city I have encountered . . . Having seen it, I urgently desire never to see it again."

Kipling's opinion was not that of an anti-American foreigner. Numerous American observers echoed this view. American cities were unprepared for the incredible growth they experienced during the late nineteenth century. Housing, clean water, competent police, and adequate public services were all in short supply. Finally, health standards were low everywhere, and scientists had barely begun to study the problems and diseases created by crowded urban conditions.

High crime rates plagued rich and poor. Pickpockets, robbers, con artists, and violent gangs roamed the streets and alleyways of American cities. Urban officials had established police forces in the 1830s and 1840s. In the 1850s police were outfitted with uniforms and badges and allowed to carry clubs and revolvers, but they still could not control or seriously curtail urban crime. Police corruption was common. Officers took bribes from saloon keepers and streetwalkers to overlook illegal activities, and owed their loyalty to the political boss who hired them. Not until the end of the century would there be successful attempts to bring professionalism and civil service reform to police departments.

Housing presented an even more pressing problem. The immigrants disembarking at the ports of entry and the farmers arriving at the train depots had to have some place to live. The situation created opportunities as well as problems. The building industry was one of the great urban boom industries, and its leaders largely determined the shape and profile of the modern city. Like the other businesspeople, they worked in an essentially unregulated economic world, bent on maximizing their profits and equipped with a lofty disregard of public opinion.

In urban housing, money talked. The rich built opulent mansions on New York's Fifth Avenue along Central Park. The "homes" of the leaders of New York's—and often the nation's—society, business, commerce, and industry shouldered each other for their place in the sun. High ceilings, European furnishings, and spacious rooms were commonplace, and even the new apartments of the upper classes were designed and constructed by gifted architects and artisans.

Tenements, built to minimal codes but overcrowded and undermaintained, greeted urban newcomers without money. They were designed to cram the largest number of people into the smallest amount of space. Like skyscrapers, tenements made use of vertical space by piling family upon family into small, poorly lighted, badly ventilated apartments. By 1900 portions of the Jewish Tenth Ward in New York's Lower East Side had reached population density levels of 500,000 persons to one square mile and as many as one person per square foot of land in the most crowded areas.

Dumbbell tenements were the most notorious examples of exploitative urban housing. Each building had an indentation in the middle—thus giving it a dumbbell shape—that allowed for better ventilation. Although they conformed to the Tenement Reform Law of 1879, which required all rooms to have access to light and air, they made maximum use of standard 25- by 100-feet urban lots. The problems inherent in dumbbell tenements were obvious from the first, but the design was not outlawed in New York until 1901.

Street conditions, unlike housing, were more democratic in that they plagued rich and poor alike. Well into the 1870s, pigs rooted for food amid trash and thousands of pounds of horse manure. Spring rains turned thoroughfares into fetid quagmires, and winter freezes left them with hard deep ruts. Waste not dumped onto the streets often found its way into the rivers that flowed through the major cities or the harbors that bordered them. By the turn of the century, 13 million gallons of sewage were emptied each day into the Delaware River, the major source for Philadelphia's drinking water. In Baltimore, according to Satirist H. L. Mencken, the bay smelled like a "billion polecats." Pittsburgh's rivers were blackened by the industrial waste poured into them.

Overcrowded housing, polluted streets and rivers, uncollected garbage—these problems and others contributed to the notoriously unhealthy urban environment. Unfortunately, advances in medicine and public health lagged behind technological and industrial progress. Diseases ranging from yellow fever and smallpox to diphtheria and typhoid claimed victims by the thousands. In 1878 a yellow fever epidemic, known as the American Plague, killed more than 9,000 people. Physician Walter Reed's discovery in 1900 that the disease was carried by the *Aedes aegypti* mosquito led to a cure for the dreaded scourge.

Smallpox proved a more persistent problem. Although not as deadly as yellow fever, it struck more people and left millions of faces scarred by pockmarks. Like diphtheria and scarlet fever, smallpox flourished in the overcrowded and garbage-strewn cities.

Tenement life on the Lower East Side of New York was overcrowded, filthy, and dangerous.

Death, suffering, and massive inconvenience prodded city officials to move toward a more systematic approach to their problems. It was a slow transition, involving the replacement of political appointees with trained experts. Yet during the late nineteenth century remarkable progress was made, particularly after the discovery of the germ theory in the 1880s, which linked contagious diseases to environmental conditions.

Health officials and urban engineers vigorously attacked the sewage and water problems. Without good sewers and clean drinking water, urban civilization was almost a contradiction of terms. To improve conditions, cities replaced cesspools and backyard privies with modern sewer systems. Most large cities turned to filtration and chlorination to assure pure water supplies.

From Private City to Public City

In housing, pure water, and clean streets, the battle lines in most cities were drawn between individual profits and public need. Individual entre-

For the wealthy, city life could be quite luxurious, as the rooms of Alexander
T. Stewart's Fifth Avenue mansion show.

preneurs shaped the modern American city with horsecar and trolley
lines, skyscrapers, apartments, and tenements. Motivated by profit like
their industrial counterparts, they worked, planned, and invested, putting
their pocketbooks before their civic responsibilities. The result was that
they provided good housing and services for only those city dwellers who
could pay.

Historians have termed this type of city the "private city." Allowing
the profit motive to determine urban growth created numerous problems.
It led to such waste and inefficiency as competing trolley lines and such
inconveniences as poorly cleaned streets. Most important, it stood contrary to planned urban growth. Urban entrepreneurs were generally unconcerned about the city as a whole, regarding parks as uneconomic use
of real estate and battling against the idea of zoning. In the end, they contributed to the ugliness and problems of Pittsburgh, New York, Chicago,
and other American cities.

By the turn of the century, urban engineers and other experts began
calling for planned urban growth and more concern for city services. Advocates of the "public city," they wanted efficient, clean, healthy cities

where rich and poor alike could enjoy a decent standard of life. College educated, these professionals brought knowledge and administrative expertise to government service. After 1900 they would increasingly dominate the quest for better services and public responsibility, but in many cities their voices were heard too late. The scars of the private city remained on the urban landscape.

City Culture

Nightlife

At 3:00 P.M. on September 4, 1882, Thomas Edison's chief electrician threw the switch on the inventor's Pearl Street station in New York City. Four hundred electric lights went on. Wall Street buildings were for the first time illuminated by the clearest of all artificial lighting. Just as trolleys spelled the end for the horse car, electric lights eventually replaced gaslights, candles, kerosene, and oil lamps.

Electricity soon bathed America's leading cities in light. In the rural regions life revolved around the sun. Farmers awoke with the sun, labored during the daylight hours, and went to sleep soon after the sun disappeared over the horizon. Although one's labor changed depending on the season, the order of one's day was changeless. In cities and industries, however, night became more than just a time to rest. Labor and leisure claimed their share of the night.

This new nightlife fired the imaginations of urbanites. If nighttime labor proved a plague for the working class, nighttime leisure animated the lives of the wealthy. For New York's "fast set" the real fun began after the theaters closed. They moved down Broadway, stopping for a late-night dinner at one of the exclusive restaurants where eating became a refined pleasure and not just a physical necessity. The variety of dishes available at city eateries was but another example of the yawning gap between the values of an older rural America and those of the emerging urban society. The American diet expanded along with the nation's cities.

The middle and upper classes not only consumed different types of food, they consumed more of everything. Like the new diet, this shift in consumption patterns signaled a break with the past. The traditional Victorian ethos emphasized production and values—thrift, self-control, delayed gratification, and hard work—that encouraged production. But with industrial success came a general fear of overproduction, and increasingly advertisers and economic advisers attempted to transform Americans from "savers" to "spenders." In various ways, they told people to give in to their desire for luxury.

In large American cities not only restaurants but also department stores and hotels fostered this new attitude. John Wanamaker in Philadelphia, Marshall Field in Chicago, and Rowland H. Macy in New York opened department stores that catered to and pampered the middle and upper classes by offering an unequaled range of products and quality service. The architecture and plush interiors of the department stores inspired extravagant spending. Grand hotels, like the Waldorf Astoria in New York, trafficked in the same luxury. Inside the giant hotels and department stores the austerity doctrines of the early nineteenth century were easily forgotten.

It is difficult to imagine the impression electric lights, department stores, and grand hotels made on the people who lived in or visited American cities. They underscored a style of life clearly different from what existed in rural America. City life presented a strange new world that inspired American writers, painters, and musicians with feelings of excitement and revulsion. This ambivalent reaction formed the basis of a new urban culture which combined the energies and experiences of all city people—black and white, male and female, immigrant and native-born.

From the Genteel Tradition to Realism and Naturalism

Frank Norris was born in Chicago, grew up in San Francisco, and lived for a time in Paris. He restlessly moved about the world looking for action. As a newspaper reporter he traveled to Cuba to cover the Spanish-American War, and to South Africa to chronicle the Boer War. In his journalism and in his novels he fed his readers bloody slices of the real world. Shortly before he died at 32 of appendicitis in 1902, he boasted, "I never truckled. I never took off the hat to fashion and held it out for pennies. I told them the truth. They liked it or they didn't like it. What had that to do with me?"

How literature had changed during the previous generation! At the end of the Civil War the American literary tradition had little to do with harsh truth. Conforming to a "genteel tradition," great writers endeavored to reinforce morality, not portray reality. Real life was too sordid, corrupt, and mean; it was far too coarse, violent, and vulgar. Literature, these arbiters decided, should transcend the real and anchor to the ideal. Sex, violence, and passion were taboo.

Out of rural America came the first challenge to the genteel tradition. Such local colorists as Bret Harte, who set his stories in the rough mining camps of the West, emphasized regional differences and used regional dialects to capture the flavor of rural America. In their own way, the local colorists were as confined by their approaches to writing as the defenders of the genteel tradition. Although their characters used real American speech, they were hardly realistically presented. Humor and innocence were the hallmarks of local colorists.

Only Mark Twain, whose real name was Samuel Langhorne Clemens, transcended the genre. Like a local colorist, he used regional dialects, humor, and sentimentality in all his novels, but he also explored the darker impulses of human nature. *The Adventures of Huckleberry Finn* (1884), his classic work, exposes the greed, violence, and corruption in American society. Nowhere is Twain more insightful than when he deals with American racism. In one scene, Huck invents a story about a riverboat explosion. A woman asks if anyone was injured. "No'm," Huck responds. "Killed a nigger." Relieved, she replies, "Well, it's lucky; because sometimes people do get hurt."

Although Twain never outgrew his obsession with life on the Mississippi River, the impact of industrialism and city life on the American character fascinated most of the other great writers of his generation. They wanted to show American life in all its harsh and sordid reality. Realism, the name of their movement, soon replaced the genteel sentimentality of the previous generation. Defined as "the truthful treatment of material" by its leader William Dean Howells, realism centered on average individuals dealing with concrete ethical choices in realistic circumstances.

As realism matured in the largely unregulated and highly competitive cities, it turned into naturalism. A more pessimistic movement, naturalism portrayed the individual as a helpless victim, battered defenseless by natural forces beyond a person's control. Influenced by the writings of Charles Darwin, Karl Marx, and eventually Sigmund Freud, naturalists described a world in which biological, social, and psychological forces determined a person's fate. They were particularly interested in how the uncaring forces of industrialization and urbanization determined the course of individual lives. Even when they wrote about the problems of rural America, the power of factory and city worked in the shadows.

Describing the Urban Jungle

The premier naturalistic writer was Theodore Dreiser. Unlike most earlier American novelists, he was not the product of Protestant, Anglo-Saxon, middle-class respectability. His German-Catholic immigrant father's life was the flip side of the American success story. After a promising beginning, he and his family slid deeper and deeper into poverty and despair. Throughout his life, Dreiser remained sympathetic to those who had suffered.

Unlike better-educated writers, Dreiser had no genteel tradition to shed or rebel against. His first novel, *Sister Carrie* (1900), unflinchingly describes the effect of modern urban society on the lives of one woman and one man. Carrie travels to Chicago from the countryside in search of happiness, which she equates with material possessions, but she discovers only poverty, exploitation, and hardship. Like the course of Dreiser's own family, the likeable, friendly Carrie sinks ever deeper into physical and moral despair. The novel shocked most readers, and as a result Dreiser's genius was generally unappreciated during his lifetime.

Like Dreiser, Stephen Crane was also interested in the effects poverty and urban life had on individual character. His first novel, *Maggie: A Girl of the Streets* (1893), traces the life of a girl raised in a New York City slum. In rapid order, she loses her innocence, her virginity, and her life. It was not a story of a character being rewarded or punished; issues of personal good or evil were irrelevant. A victim of her environment, poverty determined Maggie's fate.

Taken together, naturalistic writers challenged the traditional idea that individuals had the power to control their own destinies. Rugged individualism, that cherished frontier ideal, seemed poor protection against the forces of urban poverty and industrial exploitation. Although neither *Maggie* nor *Sister Carrie* was a blueprint for reform, both suggested a pressing need for change. The same private city that offered opportunity for the wealthy held little promise for the poor.

Painting Urban Reality

American artists shared with American writers and social critics a general aesthetic and philosophical dislike of the city. As Americans moved west, artists like Albert Bierstadt focused on the dramatic landscape. Even the great, late-nineteenth-century realists—Winslow Homer, Thomas Eakins, and John LaFarge—harbored a suspicion, if not an outright fear, of the city.

By the end of the century, however, the varied urban landscape began to intrigue artists. Steel bridges, colorful immigrant costumes, smoke-filled, congested streets, clashing boxers, washed clothes hanging between tenements, pigeons soaring over flat apartment roofs—each demonstrated the everyday beauty of the city. The energy, conflict, and power of the city seemed to explode with artistic possibilities.

Appropriately enough, the center of this new movement was New York City. The leader of the school—often described as "ashcan" because of its urban orientation—was Robert Henri, an artistic and political radical. Skyscrapers thrilled him, and he saw beauty in the most squalid slum. He was joined by such other artists who shared his love of city life and political radicalism as John Sloan, George Luks, Maurice Prendergast,

Everett Shinn, W. J. Glackens, and Ernest Lawson. Their paintings were generally in the impressionistic style, but they were more concerned with content than technique. Like Theodore Dreiser, who admired the ashcan school, Henri and his followers used their talent to depict problems in the growing cities such as overcrowded tenement conditions and urban traffic.

Maturing along with the ashcan painters was a second school of artists that also gained inspiration from the urban landscape. Labeled modernists, they championed the pure freedom of nonrepresentational abstract painting. Their intellectual leader was Alfred Stieglitz, who used his studio at 291 Fifth Avenue in New York to exhibit the modernist paintings of Georgia O'Keeffe, Marsden Hartley, John Marin, Max Weber, and Arthur Dove. Like the ashcanners, the modernists chose the city—rife with conflict and power—as the prevalent theme for abstract art.

In 1913 the ashcanners and the modernists participated in the most important art exhibition in American history. Held at the Sixty-ninth Regiment Armory in New York, the show also included works by Cézanne, Van Gogh, Picasso, and other leaders of the European Postimpressionists. The Armory Show drew some sharp criticism; Marcel Duchamp's cubist *Nude Descending a Staircase* was called "an explosion in a shingle factory." Other critics and collectors maintained that the exhibition marked a new age for American art. Its more important result was to fuse European and American art movements. It further signaled the ascendancy of the modernists, who dominated the next generation of American art.

The Sounds of the City

Modern American music began in the nation's large cities, and from the very first was the language of the oppressed. Before the late nineteenth century critics regarded American music as decidedly inferior to European music. America had produced no great classical composers in the European tradition, and what music it did create was largely the sounds of work and worship. Uninfluenced by European traditions, American blacks adapted the rhythms and melodies of Africa to meet American conditions. African music centered on rhythmical complexity and used notes that did not conform to the standard scale. Repetition, call and response, and strong beat became the hallmarks of black American music.

The two traditions, African and European, existed independently in the United States until the 1890s, when they were suddenly thrown together in New Orleans. As in most southern cities, Jim Crow laws passed during the 1890s legally and forcefully separated the races in New Orleans. For the history of American music this process had unexpected results. Before the 1890s wealthy mulatto Creoles had lived in the affluent downtown section of New Orleans and followed European musical traditions. Segregation, however, forced them uptown, where poorer blacks who followed African musical traditions lived. Although Creoles and poor blacks did not mix socially, they did forge new musical styles.

The result was jazz, a musical form based on improvisation within a structured band format, which used both African and European traditions. Storyville, the New Orleans red-light district, provided employment for the jazz musicians, who could earn far more than even skilled laborers. Ragtime and the blues also flourished in Storyville. Ragtime, a syncopated piano style, needed only one performer and was therefore popular as café and bordello entertainment. Scott Joplin, a Texas-born black who had formal musical training, wrote several scores of popular rags, and his "Maple Leaf Rag" (1899) probably sold a million copies in sheet music form. Blues musicians, mostly from the Mississippi Delta region, performed in cheap saloons and expressed the pain of life in a hostile world.

During World War I, government officials closed Storyville, charging it was a health hazard. The talented black musicians headed north—to St. Louis, Chicago, Memphis, Kansas City, and New York. They continued

Jazz combined European and African-American music styles into a new musical form. Here King Oliver's Creole Jazz Band poses for a rare picture.

to play jazz and the form continued to evolve. White musicians, trained in the European tradition, soon put their imprint on the American musical form. Although larger jazz bands dominated music during the next generation, they were an outgrowth of the New Orleans sound.

Jazz was the result of the mixture of European and African traditions, and could only have happened in the fertile atmosphere of the cities, where old and new, black and white, immigrant and native-born combined to create new literary, artistic, and musical forms.

Entertaining the Multitudes

City sports, like city music, were loud and raucous. Before the urbanization of the late nineteenth century, the sports and games that Americans played tended to be informal and participant oriented. Rules varied from region to region, and few people even considered the standardization of rules desirable. By 1900 this cozy informality had changed dramatically. Entertainment became a major industry, and specialized performers competed for the right to entertain the multitudes.

The emergence of commercialized entertainment was the result of changes in both American technology and values. Transportation improvements allowed professional entertainers and sports teams to move across America more easily and cheaply, and technological advances in communications allowed the results of games and entertainment news to be spread quickly throughout the country. Added to this was the decline in the Victorian notion that associated popular entertainment with immorality, swearing, and drinking.

In the second half of the nineteenth century a new outlook challenged Victorian values. Immigrants brought with them to America a culture that was at odds with Victorian notions of work and play. In addition, immigrants tended to marry later than native-born Americans; even at midcentury 40 percent of men between the ages of 25 and 35 were unmarried. These men formed a "bachelor subculture" that centered around saloons, gambling halls, race tracks, boxing rings, billiard rooms, and cockpits. Toward the end of the century as the Victorian economic and social order began to crumble, upper-class and then middle-class Americans became interested in the activities of the bachelor subculture. The result was a new attitude toward sport and leisure.

Of Fields and Cities

"Baseball," wrote Mark Twain, "is the very symbol, the outward and visible expression of the drive and push and struggle of the raging, tearing, booming nineteenth century." It captured the bustle and hustle of city life. More than any other sport of the period, baseball was an urban game. All of the early professional teams were located in cities, and most of the paid players were products of the cities.

Ironically, the symbols of the game also recalled America's rural past. Unlike most modern sports, no clock governed the pace of a baseball game. In crowded, dirty cities, baseball was played on open, grassy fields with such bucolic names as Sportsman Park, Ebbets Field, and the Polo Grounds. The field even had fences and bullpens, and the game was played during the planting and harvesting seasons of spring, summer, and fall.

If the symbols and mythology of baseball were rural, the game itself was very urban. Team managers, like their industrialist counterparts, preached the values of hard work, punctuality, thrift, sobriety, and self-control to their players. Baseball, they emphasized, was like modern life, ruthlessly competitive and demanding sacrifice for the "good of the team." Like modern corporate society, modern sports reinforced the ideal of teamwork.

During the last third of the nineteenth century, as men like Rockefeller and Carnegie struggled to bring order to their industrial empires,

Baseball was the leading sport of the late nineteenth century. It brought a sense of America's rural past into the country's urban present.

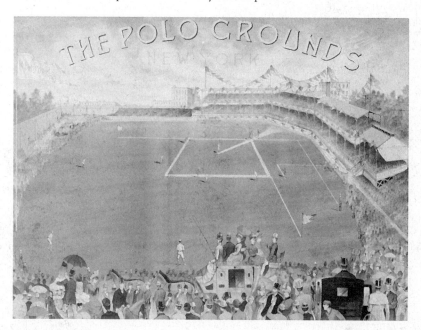

modern baseball took form. Rules were standardized, and owners attempted to make the sport suitable for the urban middle class. They banned the spitball, arranged games to fit the urban professionals' schedules, fined players for using profanity, and encouraged women to attend the games.

Most important, they formed competitive professional leagues centered in the industrial cities of America. In 1869 Harry Wright took his all-professional Cincinnati Red Stockings on a barnstorming tour, traveling on the recently completed Transcontinental Railroad. During the year the team traveled 11,877 miles by rail, stage, and boat, and entertained more than 200,000 spectators.

The Cincinnati club impressed Americans with its professionalism, and demonstrated to entrepreneurs that there was money to be made in sports. In 1876 William A. Hulbert and several associates formed the National League. In business terms, the league was a loosely organized cartel designed to eliminate competition among franchises for players. Poorly paid and restricted in their ability to negotiate for higher salaries, the players revolted in 1890 and formed their own league. The Players' League was an experiment in workers' control of an industry that players felt was dominated by owners who were only concerned with profits. Lofty in ideals, the Players' League was badly managed and lasted only one year.

With the failure of the Players' League, the National League increased its control over professional baseball. It either crushed rival leagues or absorbed them. In 1903, for example, after a short business war the National League entered into a partnership with the American League. The only losers were the players, whose salaries decreased with the absence of competition. Nevertheless, the popularity of the sport soared. By 1909, when William Howard Taft established the practice of the president opening each season by throwing out the first ball, baseball had become the national pastime.

Bloody Knuckles

Only boxing rivaled baseball in popularity during the late nineteenth century. Like baseball, boxing began the period as a largely unstructured sport, but by 1900 entrepreneurs had reorganized the activity into a profitable business. Although boxing remained illegal in most parts of America, it produced some of the first national sports heroes.

Bare-knuckle boxing, the forerunner of modern boxing, was a brutal, bloody sport. It involved two men fighting bare-fisted until one could not continue. A round lasted until one of the men knocked or threw down his opponent. At that point both men rested for 30 seconds and then started to fight again. Fights could and often did last over 100 rounds and as long as seven or eight hours. After such a fight it took months for the men to recover.

Boxers, unlike baseball players, often emerged from poor immigrant families. Irish-Americans dominated the sport during the late nineteenth century, and they used boxing as a means of social mobility. John L. Sullivan, who won the bare-knuckle world heavyweight title in 1882, became the greatest known American athlete during the nineteenth century. Born in Boston of Irish immigrant parents, Sullivan was a loud boastful man who loved to fight. Politicians, actors, writers, and merchants avidly followed his exploits, but Sullivan never lost touch with his immigrant, working-class origins.

During the 1880s the sport gained greater respectability and, like baseball, underwent a series of reforms. The traditional challenge system for arranging fights was replaced by modern promotional techniques. Fighters started wearing gloves and adopted the Marquis of Queensberry Rules, which standardized a round at three minutes, allowed a one-minute rest period between rounds, and outlawed all wrestling throws and holds. The new rules also replaced the fight to the finish with a fight to a decision over a specified number of rounds. Although the new rules did not reduce the violence of the sport, they did provide for more orderly bouts.

The Excluded Americans

Although promoters talked about the democratic nature of sports, this was far from the case. To be sure, a number of Irish and German men—often immigrants or sons of immigrants—prospered in professional sports. Far more Americans were excluded from the world of sports.

In large cities the lines between social classes tended to blur, much to the discomfort of the wealthy who struggled to separate themselves from the masses. The rich moved to the suburbs and employed other methods of residential segregation to isolate themselves. Another tactic to protect their exclusive status was to allow their children to marry only within their narrow group of acquaintances.

One way to exclude the masses was to engage in sports that only the very rich could play. Yachting and polo demanded nearly unlimited free time, expensive equipment, and a retinue of hired helpers. The New York Yacht Club was founded in 1884, and by the 1890s every major eastern seaboard city had its exclusive yacht club. Each summer the richest yacht owners sailed their splendid vessels to Newport, Rhode Island, the most exclusive of the summer colonies.

Athletic clubs devoted to track and field, golf, and tennis were similarly exclusive, and catered to more than the members' athletic concerns. Each club had an elaborate social calendar filled with dress balls and formal dinners. When they did schedule sporting events, participation and the privilege of watching were normally on an invitation-only basis.

To prevent the various social classes from mixing too freely in athletics, wealthy patrons advocated the code of amateurism, which separated the professionals—who often came from the poorer classes—from the more prosperous athletes who participated in a sport simply for the love of the game. The revival of the Olympic Games in 1896 strengthened the amateur code. Thus when it was discovered that Jim Thorpe, an Oklahoma Indian who had attended the Carlisle Indian School and who won the decathlon and the pentathlon in the 1912 Stockholm Games, had briefly played baseball for a minor league professional team, the International Olympic Committee stripped him of his medals.

Although amateurism was a subtle attack on the working class, sports leaders moved more forcefully against blacks. During the 1870s and 1880s blacks and whites competed in sports against each other on a fairly regular basis. A number of blacks even rose to become world champions. With the advent of the Jim Crow laws, however, most sports became segregated. In 1892 John L. Sullivan issued his famous challenge to fight all contenders: "In this challenge I include all fighters—first come, first served—who are white. I will not fight a Negro. I never have and I never shall." By the 1890s major league baseball also excluded blacks, and it would remain so until Jackie Robinson broke the "color barrier" in 1946.

Cultural expectations and stereotypes also limited the development of women athletes. Compared to men, they were considered weak and uncoordinated. Although women might ride a bicycle or gently swing a croquet mallet, men ridiculed women who were interested in serious competitive athletics. The cult of domesticity, which idealized women as nurturers and maintained that women's proper sphere was the home, also militated against female participation in competitive sports.

Even during the 1890s, when women became more interested in sports and exercise, women's athletics developed along different lines than men's. Male and female physical educators considered women to be uncompetitive and decided that women's sports should serve a utilitarian function. Sports, they emphasized, should promote a woman's physical and mental qualities and thus make her more attractive to men. They also believed that sports and exercise would sublimate female sexual drives. As one physical educator noted, "There is a time in the life of a girl when it is better for her and for the community to be something of a boy rather than too much of a girl." Not until 1924 were women allowed to compete in Olympic track and field events, and even then on a limited basis.

From Central Park to Coney Island

Like sports, parks changed to satisfy new urban demands. Mid-nineteenth-century park designers felt uneasy about the urban environment.

In parks they saw an antidote for the tensions and anxieties caused by living in cities. Frederick Law Olmsted, the most famous park architect, believed cities destroyed community ties and fostered ruthless competition. He designed Central Park to serve as a rural retreat in the midst of New York. Surrounded by rolling hills and quiet lakes, city dwellers would be moved toward greater sociability.

Olmsted's vision of a quiet, orderly park was shared by other leaders of Victorian culture. They believed that culture and leisure activities should serve society by smoothing the rough edges of the urban masses. Instead of supporting baseball and boxing, they built parks, libraries, and museums. In 1870, for example, both the Metropolitan Museum of Art in New York and the Museum of Fine Arts in Boston were opened. Visitors to these repositories of culture were expected to behave in an orderly, quiet, respectful manner.

The quiet world offered by Central Park and the new museums, however, was too tame for many urbanites. They wanted entertainment and excitement, desires that entrepreneurs were quick to satisfy. During the 1890s a series of popular amusement parks opened in Coney Island. Unlike Central Park, which was constructed as a rural retreat, the Coney Island parks glorified the sense of adventure and excitement of the cities. They offered exotic, dreamland landscapes; wonderful, novel machines; and a free, loose social environment. At Coney Island men could remove their coats and ties, and both sexes could enjoy a rare personal freedom.

Coney Island also encouraged new values. If, as Olmsted believed, Central Park reinforced self-control, sobriety, and delayed gratification, Coney Island stressed the emerging consumer-oriented values of extravagance, gaiety, abandon, revelry, and instant gratification. It attracted working-class Americans who longed for at least a taste of the "good life."

The Magic of the Flickering Image

Coney Island showed workers that machines could liberate as well as enslave. It offered an escape from an oppressive urban landscape to an exotic one. The motion picture industry, however, offered a less expensive, more convenient escape. During the early twentieth century it developed into a major popular culture form, one that reflected the hopes and ambitions, fears and anxieties of an urban people.

The first "movies," as the new form was soon called, presented brief vaudeville turns or glimpses of everyday life. Still the movies attracted considerable interest, and filmmakers began to experiment with such new techniques as editing and intercutting separate "shots" to form a dramatic narrative. In 1903 the release of Edwin S. Porter's *The Great Train Robbery*, the first "western" and the first film to exploit the violence of armed robbery, fully demonstrated the commercial possibilities of the invention. Although *The Great Train Robbery* ran only 12 minutes, it mesmerized audiences.

During the early twentieth century movies developed a strong following in ethnic, working-class neighborhoods. Local entrepreneurs converted stores and saloons into nickelodeons and introduced immigrants to a silent world of promise. Movies provided inexpensive and short escapes from the grimmer realities of urban life. In addition, since the movies were silent, they required no knowledge of English to be enjoyed.

Ministers, politicians, and other guardians of traditional Victorian morality criticized the new form of entertainment for encouraging idleness, careless spending, and sexual temptation at the expense of work. Soon local boards of censorship formed to protect innocent boys and girls, and perhaps not so innocent men and women, from being corrupted by movies.

In the cities censorship movements ultimately failed. Furthermore, attempts by white, native-born American entrepreneurs to control the new industry similarly failed. Ironically, while films were beginning to attract middle-class audiences, control of the industry shifted to immigrant entrepreneurs, most of whom were Jewish and had come to America from eastern Europe. They proved better able than native-born businessmen to develop the possibilities of the medium. They emerged from a culture that valued laughter, cooperation, and entertainment. Committed to giving the people what they wanted, they were less constrained by the traditional Victorian code of morality.

To better entertain the public, film moguls started producing feature-length films and moved the industry from the East Coast to sunny Hollywood, where they could shoot outdoors and, not incidentally, escape union difficulties. While such "stars" as Charlie Chaplin, Douglas Fairbanks, and Mary Pickford captured the hearts of America, producers such as Adolph Zukor, William Fox, Louis B. Mayer, and Harry Warner forged a multimillion-dollar industry.

The Agony of Painless Escape

Coney Island and movie theaters provided one form of escape, and the criticism of both was fairly uniform. At the same time as popular culture was exploring the theme of mechanized instant gratification, however, Americans were seeking escape in other, more ominous forms, such as narcotics.

Like the whirring machines at Coney Island and the flickering images on the silent, silver screen, the mindless escape of narcotics attracted millions of Americans. During the late nineteenth and early twentieth centuries, as the nation underwent the trauma of industrialization and urbanization, Americans took drugs in unprecedented amounts. Apologists blamed this development on the Civil War. They claimed that soldiers became addicted to morphine after using the drug as a painkiller. Yet France, Germany, Great Britain, Russia, and Italy also fought wars in the second half of the nineteenth century, and their drug addiction rates were far below those of the United States.

Part of the problem was that before 1915 there were few restrictions on the importation and use of opium, its derivatives, and cocaine. Physicians prescribed opiates for a wide range of ailments, and patent medicine manufacturers used morphine, laudanum, cocaine, or heroin in their concoctions. Coca-Cola used cocaine as one of its secret ingredients, and the Parke Davis Company produced coca-leaf cigarettes, cheroots, and a Coca Cordial.

Cocaine in particular was regarded as a wonder drug. By the late 1890s, however, its harmful effects had become obvious. Eventually, angry citizens and the federal and state governments launched the first great American crusade against cocaine. It culminated with the Harrison Anti-Narcotic Act in 1914, which controlled the distribution of opiates and cocaine; but drug addiction remained a problem in American cities.

Robert Louis Stevenson's *Dr. Jekyll and Mr. Hyde,* which he wrote under the influence of cocaine, described the dangers of challenging society's standards and altering one's personality, but in America's cities a new culture had taken shape. It opposed Victorian restraints, glorified the freedoms of urban life, and at the same time worried about the implications of a liberated life-style. Social, as well as economic, freedom came with a price. By the 1890s many Americans believed some new regulations were needed to check the social and economic freedom unleashed in urban America.

Conclusion

On January 17, 1906, Marshall Field, the dry-goods merchant and founder of the large Chicago department store that bears his name, died. "The first as well as the richest citizen" in Chicago, noted the *New York Sun,* Field left his children over $140 million. Americans questioned how one man could accumulate such a fortune. "No man could earn a million dollars honestly," said politician William Jennings Bryan. Another critic suggested that Field's fortune was made at the expense of his more than 10,000 employees, 95 percent of whom earned $12 dollars a week or less.

Most Americans, however, focused on what Field offered shoppers more than what he paid his employees. Department stores brought order to shopping and emphasized standardization of products. Serving urban markets and satisfying urban desires, they enabled customers to buy a

*C*hronology of Key Events

1869	Cincinnati Red Stockings begin barnstorming tour of America
1870	Metropolitan Museum of Art in New York and Museum of Fine Arts in Boston open
1873	Cable car introduced
1878	Yellow fever epidemic
1879	New York City adopts Tenement Reform Law
1882	Electric lighting comes into widespread use for the first time in New York City
1884	Mark Twain's *The Adventures of Huckleberry Finn* published
1885	William LeBaron Jenney erects the Home Insurance Building in Chicago
1888	Electric-power trolley introduced
1892	Stephen Crane publishes his first novel, *Maggie: A Girl of the Streets*
1899	Scott Joplin composes "Maple Leaf Rag"
1900	Theodore Dreiser publishes *Sister Carrie*
1903	Edwin S. Porter's *The Great Train Robbery* released
1912	Jim Thorpe wins the decathlon and pentathlon at Olympic Games in Stockholm
1913	Armory Show in New York City includes works from artists of ashcan and modernist schools
1914	Harrison Anti-Narcotic Act controls distribution of opiates and cocaine

wide range of products hitherto unavailable under one roof. Inside one of the great department stores, consumers isolated themselves from the garbage in the streets, the filth in the air, and the sounds of traffic and commerce that dominated the outside world. They chose not to think about the workers who made the goods they purchased.

Both the orderly world of the department store and the chaotic one of the streets were the products of urban entrepreneurs who fashioned the modern cities. In pursuit of profits they were capable of producing dazzling monuments to commerce and terrible tributes to greed. By 1900 their days of absolute dominance were numbered. Although they would remain a vital part of American capitalism, in the future they would be rivaled by governmental planners—people who wanted to extend the smooth, efficient order of the department store to the outside streets.

The emergence of the great cities changed American life. They dominated not only the nation's economy but the American imagination. In the cities the clash of ideas and beliefs, of peoples and traditions created an exciting, new heterogeneous culture. The result was evident at places such as Coney Island and the Armory Show, it was visible in many of the movies, and it was audible at a New Orleans jazz café. As the nineteenth century drew to a close, a new culture was clearly emerging. It would add a new element to the new century.

Suggestions for Further Reading

Valuable overviews of the urbanization of America include Sean D. Cashman, *America in the Gilded Age* (1984); Howard P. Chudacoff, *The Evolution of American Urban Society* (1975); Raymond A. Mohl, *The New City* (1985); John Stilgoe, *Borderland: Origins of the American Suburb* (1988).

Aspects of urban culture and society are examined in Gunther Barth, *City People* (1980); Burton J. Bledstein, *The Culture of Professionalism* (1976); Lawrence W. Levine, *Highbrow/Lowbrow: the Emergence of Cultural Hierarchy in America* (1988); Martin V. Melosi, *Garbage in the Cities* (1982); Lewis O. Saum, *The Popular Mood of America* (1990).

The role of professional sports is analyzed in Melvin L. Adelman, *A Sporting Time* (1986); Warren Goldstein, *Playing for Keeps: A History of Early Baseball* (1989); Allen Guttmann, *A Whole New Ball Game: An Interpretation of American Sports* (1988); Donald J. Mrozek, *Sport and American Mentality* (1983); Randy Roberts, *Papa Jack: Jack Johnson and the Era of White Hopes* (1983), and *Jack Dempsey: The Manassa Mauler* (1979).

On the development of the arts consult Robert Crunden, *American Salons* (1992); Neil Leonard, *Jazz and the White Americans* (1962); Russell Lynes, *The Lively Audience* (1985); Richard J. Powell, *The Blues Aesthetic* (1989).

Chapter *20*

End of the Century Crisis

Equilibrium and Inertia: The National Political Scene
Divided Power: Republicans and Democrats
The Bases of Party Loyalty
The Business of Politics: Party Organization
Women and Politics

Style over Substance: Government in the Gilded Age
Hayes and the "Money Question"
Garfield, Arthur, and the Patronage Issue
Cleveland, the Railroads, and Tariffs
Harrison and Big Business
Minority Rights and Social Issues

The Farmers Revolt
Grievances: Real and Imagined
The Farmers Organize
The Agrarian Agenda
Emergence of the Populist Party

Depression and Turbulence in the 1890s
The Panic of 1893
Expressions of Worker Discontent
Deteriorating Race Relations
The Tide Is Turned: The Election of 1896

On July 9, 1896, thirty-six-year-old William Jennings Bryan rose to speak to the delegates at the Democratic National Convention in Chicago. A congressman from Nebraska, Bryan had become the champion of the "free silver" movement. In the 1890s many American farmers favored expanding the amount of money in circulation by coining more silver dollars. Such an inflationary policy, they believed, would raise crop prices and alleviate their heavy debt burdens. Many rural residents felt the national government had not been responsive to their needs—that both political parties had been captured by industrialists, railroad owners, and bankers. In 1896 silver was a symbol for popular grievances. Among other things, silver represented rural values, the common people, and a growing discontent with northeastern political domination.

By the time of the 1896 Democratic convention the Republicans had nominated William McKinley and adopted a platform calling for the gold standard—or currency backed entirely by gold supplies in the federal treasury. The Democrats were divided between the "silverites" and the "Gold Democrats," monetary conservatives who supported President Grover Cleveland. Control of the party by the Northeast was being challenged by southern and western delegates when Bryan finally rose to speak.

Called "the Great Commoner," Bryan voiced the frustrations of farmers with the failure of traditional politicians to meet their needs. A compelling orator, he enthralled the crowd from the beginning, but his closing words created pandemonium. "We will answer the demand for a gold standard," he roared, "by saying to them: 'You shall not press down upon the brow of labor this crown of thorns, you shall not crucify mankind upon a cross of gold.'" As Bryan spoke his fingers first traced the course of imaginary trickles of blood from his temples. He closed with his arms outstretched as if he were nailed to a cross.

Bryan's "Cross of Gold" speech won him the Democratic nomination and clinched the victory of the party's silverites. President Cleveland's supporters, however, refused to support him, and nearly half the Democratic newspapers opposed his candidacy. As a result, Bryan was only able to raise the meager sum of $500,000.

Taking his campaign directly to the people, Bryan relied on his oratorical genius and electrifying charisma. He crisscrossed the country, railing against big business and corporate financiers and appealing to the sectional and class animosities of his listeners. He made his own travel arrangements, bought his own tickets, carried his own bags, altogether logging more than 18,000 miles and giving 600 speeches before election day.

In the 1896 election, Republicans sought to convince voters that Bryan (at right and below in the campaign poster) was a radical who threatened American values and institutions, while McKinley would guarantee stability, order, and integrity.

With a Republican campaign fund of more than $3.5 million, McKinley wisely refused to follow Bryan's course. Between June and November, McKinley conducted a "front porch" campaign, leaving his home in Canton, Ohio, for only three days. Huge crowds were brought in by railroad to McKinley's lawn for special events organized by the candidate's staff. McKinley stressed national unity rather than division in a calm and dispassionate style that contrasted sharply with the frenzied oratory of his opponent.

On election day Bryan and his wife rose at 6:30 A.M. and voted at a local fire station in Omaha, Nebraska. He then gave seven speeches in his hometown before collapsing, exhausted, in bed that evening. McKinley walked to his polling place and stood in line to vote. He then returned home to wait for the returns—his lawn and porch in worse shape than he was. All over the nation people waited to find out which man and party would preside over the dawning of the twentieth century.

The election came in a decade of turbulence that saw an increasingly militant labor movement, rising racial tensions, and agrarian unrest—all of which intensified after a major depression began in 1893. The social fabric seemed to be unraveling rapidly, which is why the election of 1896 was considered so important. For the first time since the 1870s voters were given a clear choice between two very different candidates and platforms.

Following Reconstruction, national politics were colorful but not very significant. No important policy differences separated the two major parties; the campaigns revolved around personalities, gimmicks, emotional slogans, and local issues. As elections were trivialized, they also became a major source of entertainment, and voters turned out in record numbers. This triumph of style over substance in politics, as well as culture, caused the era to be labeled the "Gilded Age." By 1890 both the Democratic and Republican parties were out of touch with the sentiments of large blocks of voters. The losers in the great national drive toward economic modernization were unable to unite around a viable progam. The issues they raised, however, appeared regularly on political agendas in the twentieth century.

Equilibrium and Inertia: The National Political Scene

In the late nineteenth century patronage, or the granting of political favors and offices, had become more important than issues to the two major parties. Close elections caused the parties to be careful not to alienate potential supporters. Most people also believed in limited government. Political parties were therefore organized more to win offices than to govern.

The result was a failure by government to deal effectively with the enormous changes wrought by industrialization and urbanization.

Divided Power: Republicans and Democrats

After Reconstruction both the Democratic and Republican parties emerged with sizable and stable constituencies. For the 20 years between 1876 and 1896 they shared a rare equality of political power. Elections were so close that until 1896 no president won office with a majority of the popular vote. Two (Hayes and Harrison) even entered the presidency without a plurality. Most of the time Congress itself was split, with Democrats generally taking the House and the Republicans the Senate. Very few seats shifted parties in any given election.

The party division of Congress inevitably weakened the presidents of the era. None was elected to consecutive terms; none was noteworthy in his accomplishments. To be fair, all were competent men, most with considerable public service. One reason they were so forgettable was the era's concept of the presidency. Presidents were only supposed to implement laws passed by Congress—occasionally vetoing ill-advised legislation. None considered it his duty to propose legislation. Congress was also hampered by outdated, complex rules and lax party discipline. Thus there was little possibility of formulating and enacting any coherent legislative program.

The lack of legislative action did not seem to be a serious problem at the start of the Gilded Age, since most people rejected the idea of an activist government. Widely accepted doctrines of laissez-faire and Social Darwinism limited what people expected of government. Both parties basically accepted a narrow vision of federal responsibility. When vetoing a small appropriation for drought relief in Texas, Democrat Cleveland asserted that "though the people support the Government, the Government should not support the people."

Such antigovernment sentiment tended to increase the power of the judicial branch. Many saw the courts as a bastion against governmental interference in the economy, and the courts certainly fulfilled that role. On the basis of the Fourteenth Amendment, judges were especially active in striking down state laws to regulate business. The courts narrowly interpreted the Constitution on federal authority—ruling that the power to tax did not extend to personal incomes and that the power to regulate interstate commerce applied only to trade, not manufacturing. Congress also indirectly gave judges more power by enacting vague laws that relied upon the courts for both definition and enforcement.

The Bases of Party Loyalty

One consequence of the equal power shared by the Democrats and Republicans was the reluctance of either party to chance losing voters by taking clear positions on the issues. Perhaps this reluctance was also based on the memories of the divisive 1860 election and its devastating impact on party and national unity. In addition, few Americans criticized industrialization and modernization during the early stages, and there was widespread agreement on many issues.

Until 1896 the parties shared numerous similarities. Both were led by wealthy men but still tried to appeal to wage earners and farmers as well as merchants and manufacturers. Most members of both parties believed in protective tariffs and "sound currency." Both rejected economic radicalism and positive programs to aid workers. Presidents of both parties sent federal troops to break up strikes. Business leaders had so little to fear from either party that they contributed generously to both.

Ironically, for all their similarities the parties evoked fierce loyalty from a heterogeneous mix of people, which was one reason party platforms were so innocuous. Because of its antislavery past, the Republican party retained the support of activist reformers, idealists, and African Americans. Yet most Republicans came from established, "old stock" families. The more wealth a man had, the more likely he was to vote Republican. The Democrats were even more mixed. The party's constituency, comprised of such disparate elements as Southern whites, immigrants, Catholics, and Jews, sometimes seemed united mainly by opposition to the Republicans.

For historical and cultural reasons, party loyalty was frequently determined by three factors: region, religion, and ethnic origin. The regional factor was most evident in the support white Southerners gave to the Democratic party. To vote for the party of abolition and Reconstruction was considered treason and a threat to white supremacy. On the other hand, the Republicans could count on heavy support from New Englanders, who saw the Democrats as members of the party of traitorous rebellion against the Union. The Republicans frequently "waved the bloody shirt," reminding Northerners of the Democrats' role in causing the Civil War.

For various reasons immigrants had long gravitated toward the Democratic party. Many were members of the poorest classes, which traditionally voted Democratic. Most of the "new immigrants" of the Gilded Age settled in cities controlled by Democratic political machines that won their loyalty by meeting the immigrants' needs. As immigration swelled, increasing Democratic strength, Republicans became more and more restrictionist. In fact, immigration policy was one of the very few substantive issues on which the parties took clearly different stands.

Religious affiliations also helped determine party loyalty, partly because of the positions on immigration. Many of the late-nineteenth-century immigrants were Catholics and Jews who were suspicious of the Protestant-dominated Republican party. There were also fundamental differences in the religious orientation of most Republicans and Democrats. Republicans frequently sought to legislate morality, supporting prohibition of alcohol and enforcement of Sunday blue laws, which barred various activities on the sabbath—including baseball. By contrast, many Democrats did not believe that personal morality could or should be a matter of state concern. Thus, the Republicans became known as the "party of morality," the Democrats the "party of personal liberty." Democrats not only rejected government interference in their personal life; in the nineteenth century they were also more suspicious of government action of any sort.

Because of their mixed constituencies, the differences and divisions *within* parties were often as great as those between them. Democrats could count on the South for all of that region's electoral votes, but conservative southern Democrats frequently broke party ranks when voting on legislation favorable to farmers, on financial and economic issues, as well as on immigration restriction.

The Republicans were even more deeply divided into factions. One group, led by Roscoe Conkling of New York, was labeled the "Stalwarts." Followers of James G. Blaine of Maine were called "Half-breeds." The only significant item of dispute between the two was who would receive the numerous jobs appointed by the president. Since the distribution of patronage was a prime function of both parties of the era, the rivalry was a bitter one.

There was one faction of the Republican party that did have some ideological basis. Composed of reformers whose primary concern was honest and effective government, they had bolted the party in 1872 because of the corruption of the Grant regime, and they bolted again in 1884. Party regulars ridiculed them, calling them "Mugwumps," asserting that they had their "mugs" on one side of the fence and their "wumps" on the other.

The divisions within the Democratic and Republican parties reflected the fact that the politicians of the day were less concerned with issues and ideology than with winning office and distributing patronage. Rather than confront the problems facing the nation, they put their energies into electioneering and party management.

The Business of Politics: Party Organization

The Gilded Age saw the largest voter turnouts in the nation's history, a phenomenon that had more to do with the ability of sophisticated party organizations to get out the vote than with compelling political issues. In the elections from 1860 to 1900 an average of 78 percent of eligible voters cast ballots. Outside of the South (where African Americans were increasingly prevented from voting and where the Democratic nomination determined the general election), the turnout sometimes reached 90 percent.

There was one main difference in Republican and Democratic party organization. Republicans generally depended on strong state organizations, and Democrats tended to rely on urban political machines to win and control votes. Since city governmental structures did not keep pace with the huge population increases, the political machines provided many of the social services for which government would later be held responsible. In return, the politicians were paid in votes from the people, bribes from legal and illegal businesses, and graft from contractors. The system worked so well that the Democrats usually carried the big cities.

Dominated by skilled professionals, Gilded Age politics was a rough and frequently corrupt business. In 1888 when Benjamin Harrison won the presidency, a Republican party boss noted that Harrison "would never know how close a number of men were impelled to approach the gates of a penitentiary to make him president." Electoral corruption was not limited to one party. In the same year a Mississippi Democrat admitted that "we have been stuffing ballot boxes, committing perjury, and . . . carrying the elections by fraud and violence."

Gilded Age politics was undoubtedly the prime form of mass entertainment. The drama of emotional tent meetings rivaled circuses. The pageantry of parades also provided excitement. Almost everyone got caught up in the elections, displaying such paraphernalia as buttons, handkerchiefs, hats, banners, and posters emblazoned with their party's symbol or slogan.

Many politicians surely must have enjoyed their status as "media stars" and folk heroes. For some, whose ethnic or class backgrounds closed conventional doors of opportunity, politics provided a vehicle of upward social mobility, similar to professional entertainment, athletics, or trade union leadership. Yet politics as a vocation offered other rewards. Elected and appointed officials not only received salaries but also openly accepted gifts from lobbyists and free passes from railroads, and sometimes used their governmental status to promote their private interests. One quip claimed that the United States had the best Congress money could buy.

Women and Politics

Politics during the Gilded Age remained a pastime enjoyed almost exclusively by males. In 1874 the Supreme Court ruled that citizenship did not automatically confer the vote and that suffrage could be denied specific groups, such as criminals, the insane, and women. Under the leadership of Elizabeth Cady Stanton and Susan B. Anthony, the National Woman Suffrage Association (NWSA) in 1878 succeeded in getting a constitutional amendment introduced into the Senate that stated that "the right to vote shall not be denied or abridged by the United States or by any state on account of sex." It continued to be submitted for the next 18 years but was usually killed in committee and only rarely reached the floor of the Senate.

At the state level, the American Woman Suffrage Association (AWSA) enjoyed somewhat more success. By 1890, 19 states allowed women to vote on school issues, and three states extended women the franchise on tax and bond issues; yet only the territory of Wyoming had granted women full political equality.

In 1890 the groups merged to form the National American Woman Suffrage Association (NAWSA). As male resistance mounted, the movement seemed to lose steam. No other state acted to grant full suffrage rights to women until 1910. Many men agreed with a Texas senator that "equal suffrage is a repudiation of manhood."

Style over Substance: Government in the Gilded Age

Politics provided great entertainment, but governmental inertia in Washington left many Americans dissatisfied. As discontent rose, many problems were first tackled by city, county, and state governments before becoming a part of the national agenda. Such issues as the currency and tariffs, however, could only be solved at the national level. Others, such as demands for honest government, were undertaken at all levels. On the whole, the states responded more vigorously than the national government to the problems created by economic changes—only to have the Supreme Court sometimes tie their hands. People began to look to Washington for solutions. The presidents and Congress responded timidly. National elections still focused mainly on trivial issues. When backed to the wall, Congress would enact laws to quiet popular cries for action, but such laws were limited in scope and often unenforceable. Style triumphed over substance, and most problems remained unsolved.

Hayes and the "Money Question"

Rutherford B. Hayes is probably best remembered for removing the remaining federal troops from the South in 1877, thus marking the end of Reconstruction. Hayes was honest, competent, and did much to establish the Republican party as the "party of morality" after the corruption of the Grant regime.

When Hayes came into office, the country was still in the throes of an economic depression that began with the Panic of 1873. As a result of hard times, a complex and heated political debate arose over federal monetary policy. At its root was a long period of deflation following the Civil War. Prices fell because the production of goods was growing faster than the supply of money. Farmers were particularly hard hit. Wheat, corn, and cotton prices declined more than other prices in the late nineteenth century. Farmers had also borrowed heavily to expand production, and they were caught in a debt squeeze with their mortgage payments remaining high while the prices they received for their goods fell.

Farmers and debtors of all occupations saw inflation as the cure to their problems. They advocated increasing the amount of "greenbacks"— paper money not backed by gold or silver—which had first been issued during the Civil War. Advocates of that solution organized the Greenback party in 1874. A conservative Congress, however, steadfastly supported a "hard money" policy, and one year later passed the Specie Resumption Act, gradually withdrawing the greenbacks then in circulation.

Some inflationists then turned their attention to silver. Since the 1790s the nation had been on a bimetallic standard. The value of a dollar was based on both gold and silver, and for years dollars were coined at a 16 to 1 mint ratio. In other words, a dollar contained 16 times as much silver as gold. By the 1870s this ratio did not reflect the market prices of the metals. Silver prices were so high that producers sold it on the open market rather than take it to the mint to be coined. Unable to buy silver at that ratio, Congress had passed the Coinage Act of 1873 that halted the minting of silver dollars.

Soon thereafter, the discovery of large deposits of silver drove prices down. Then it was in the interest of both silver miners and inflationists to return to the coining of silver at 16 to 1. Together they formed a large lobby that wrested minor concessions from Congress. The Bland-Allison Act of 1878 required the government to buy between $2 and $4 million worth of silver each month. However, the act proved ineffective; it neither raised silver prices nor inflated the currency significantly. Like much of the legislation of the Gilded Age, the Bland-Allison Act was a cosmetic answer to popular demands.

Garfield, Arthur, and the Patronage Issue

In the 1880 election neither of the two major parties focused on substantial issues but instead relied on slogans and gimmicks to win votes. The battle for the Republican nomination was between the Half-Breed and Stalwart factions since Hayes refused to run for a second term. On the thirty-sixth ballot the party picked James A. Garfield, a Civil War veteran but relatively unknown Ohio congressman. Chester A. Arthur, a Conkling henchman, became the vice-presidential nominee.

The Democrats nominated an even more obscure figure, General Winfield Scott Hancock, a hero of the Battle of Gettysburg. He was described as "a good man weighing 250 pounds." Despite the blandness of both candidates, the 1880 election was one of the closest of the century in popular vote. Garfield received a mere 39,000 vote plurality out of almost ten million ballots cast.

Once the election was over, the currency question was overshadowed by the issue of patronage because of returning prosperity and a tragic event. Only four months after Garfield's inauguration he was shot by a deranged office seeker named Charles Guiteau. His successor, Chester A. Arthur, was considered by many to be a party hack, but Arthur surprised them by becoming a champion of governmental reform.

During the 1870s the Mugwumps and other reformers had become increasingly concerned with the "spoils system" of patronage. Since the early 1800s government jobs had been considered the "spoils" of political victory to be awarded to party workers regardless of their qualifications. The problem had worsened as the federal government grew, and after the Civil War presidents spent much of their time appointing party loyalists to some 100,000 federal jobs.

Revulsion at Garfield's assassination finally prompted Congress to take action. With the support of President Arthur, Congress enacted the Pendleton Act in 1883. It outlawed political contributions by appointed officeholders and established competitive examinations for federal positions to be given by the Civil Service Commission. The act was rather timid—only applying to about ten percent of government employees. Moreover, since it was to apply only to future appointees, the act served to protect incumbents. The political system was becoming modernized, but some questioned whether it was being improved.

Cleveland, the Railroads, and Tariffs

Arthur's actions won him more favor from the public than from his party, and in 1884 the Republicans bypassed him and nominated James G. Blaine. Handsome and charismatic, Blaine was nonetheless a tainted political commodity. While in Congress he had become very rich without any visible means of outside income. Copies of letters were circulated that seemed to indicate Blaine was up for sale to the railroads. This revelation was more than the Mugwumps could stomach, and they refused to support him.

Realizing the potential advantage of a Mugwump defection, the Democrats selected Grover Cleveland, a reform governor of New York. Although he was neither physically attractive nor charismatic, he was honest. Because Cleveland and Blaine did not disagree on the major issues, their campaign revolved around personalities and became one of the most scurrilous in the nation's history.

Blaine's tainted past was obvious fodder for the Democrats' campaign. Unable to find a shred of evidence to challenge Cleveland's honesty, Republicans publicized a more personal scandal. As a bachelor, Cleveland had supported an illegitimate child since 1874, even though his paternity was questionable. Thus Republicans countered Democratic chants with "Ma! Ma! Where's my pa? Going to the White House? Ha! Ha! Ha!" In the end Cleveland won, in part because Republican efforts to portray the Democrats as the party of Roman Catholicism backfired, enabling the Democrats to rally Catholic voters to win key states.

The major legislation of Cleveland's first presidency came as the result of public pressure and actions of the courts. The power and discriminatory rates of the railroads scared and angered many Americans, and actions to regulate the railroads had started at the state level. By 1880, 14 states had established railroad commissions. The most active advocate of regulation was the Patrons of Husbandry, a farmers' group organized into local chapters called "granges." The Grangers and their allies, especially in the Midwest, got stronger legislation enacted that set maximum rates and charges within their states.

The railroad companies naturally attacked the so-called Granger laws through the courts. At first the railroads lost. In the 1877 *Munn* v. *Illinois* decision, the Supreme Court ruled that when "private property is affected with a public interest it . . . must submit to be controlled by the public for the common good." Nevertheless, it was difficult for states to regulate railroads chartered by other states and doing business across state lines. Then in a resounding defeat for the Grangers, the Supreme Court ruled in 1886 in *Wabash* v. *Illinois* that only Congress had the right to regulate interstate commerce.

Pressure began to build for federal action, and Congress responded with the 1887 Interstate Commerce Act. It prohibited pools, rebates, and rate discriminations; provided that all charges by the railroads should be "reasonable and just"; and established the Interstate Commerce Commission (ICC).

The commission was significant as the first federal regulatory agency, but its power was woefully limited. It could investigate charges against the railroads and issue "cease and desist" orders, which could only be enforced by the courts. Conservative courts soon nullified 90 percent of the commission's orders, and between 1887 and 1905 the Supreme Court ruled against the ICC in 15 of 16 cases.

The Interstate Commerce Act temporarily satisfied the "popular clamor" for reform without alienating railroad owners. It therefore did

Public anger over railroad power finally pushed Congress to pass the Interstate Commerce Act in 1887.

not become a partisan issue for either party. However, during Cleveland's term, a major issue on which Democrats and Republicans actually differed emerged: the tariff. Both parties supported these taxes on imports in order to raise revenue and to protect American products from being undersold by foreign competitors. The question was merely how high these tariffs should be. Supporters of protectionism were those who sold on the domestic markets; opponents depended on foreign markets. Both groups included some farmers and manufacturers from every region.

Like most Democrats, Cleveland had long been less enthusiastic about high tariffs. While in office he found that existing tariff rates were producing treasury surpluses that tempted congressmen to propose programs and appropriations that he considered a dangerous expansion of federal activities. Thus he became an advocate of tariff reduction, and made the tariff a focus of his reelection bid in 1888.

Harrison and Big Business

In 1888 the Democrats renominated Cleveland and wrote tariff reduction into their platform. The Republicans chose Benjamin Harrison and cheerfully picked up the gauntlet—denouncing Cleveland's "free trade" as unpatriotic. They also promised generous pensions to veterans. Voters at last were given a choice on a real issue. When Cleveland lost, Republicans erroneously interpreted his narrow defeat as a mandate for protectionism. Congress then enacted the McKinley Tariff, which raised the average duties to the highest level yet. A wave of public resentment followed. No longer able to afford foreign-made goods, many Americans saw the act as evidence of the tremendous power wielded by manufacturing interests in the nation's capital.

Growing hostility toward big business was also seen in the popular demand for legislative action against monopolistic trusts. Again action started on the state level; 15 southern and western states had passed antitrust legislation by the mid-1880s. Companies responded by incorporating in more sympathetic states. The laws were both ineffective and likely to be overturned by federal courts, but they did reflect popular outrage. Congress responded by enacting the Sherman Antitrust Act in 1890. On the surface it seemed to doom the trusts, prohibiting any "contract, combination in the form of trust or otherwise, or conspiracy in restraint of trade or commerce." But, as with the Interstate Commerce Act, appearances were deceiving.

The Supreme Court emasculated the law in *United States* v. *E. C. Knight Co.* (1895), ruling that it applied to commerce but not manufacturing. Thus the E. C. Knight Co., a sugar trust controlling 98 percent of the industry, was not in violation. Until 1901 the antitrust law was virtually unenforced; the Justice Department instituted only 14 suits and failed to get convictions in most of them. Indeed, the only effective use made of the act in its first decade was as a tool to break up labor strikes by court injunctions.

The currency issue continued to serve as a lightning rod for public protest against the new economic order. Following the Bland-Allison Act of 1878, the money supply continued to grow too slowly for the expanding economy, leading to increased pressure to coin more silver. In 1890 Congress responded with the Sherman Silver Purchase Act. It required the government to buy 4.5 million ounces of silver each month at the unrealistic ratio of 16 to 1. Paper money to pay for the purchases was redeemable in gold or silver, keeping the inflationary impact minimal. The act was a compromise that satisfied no one; consequently, the silver issue would grow more heated in the 1890s.

During Harrison's presidency Congress was more active than previously—passing the McKinley Tariff, the Sherman Antitrust Act, the Sherman Silver Purchase Act, and the first billion-dollar budget. At the same time the Republican party was becoming alienated from its abolitionist past and more closely tied to big business.

Minority Rights and Social Issues

To African Americans the Republicans remained the party of black rights, but following the election of 1876 the party did less and less to earn that label. By 1890, however, conditions finally moved some Republicans to action. Dismayed by increasing southern assaults on the black vote, Senator Henry Cabot Lodge and others drafted a federal elections bill which sought to protect voter registration and guarantee fair congressional elections by establishing mechanisms to investigate charges of voting fraud and to deal with disputed elections.

Outraged white Southerners and Northern Democrats joined to defeat the measure. Although in 1890 Republicans controlled both houses of Congress, they finally bartered away the Lodge Election Bill to gain support for the McKinley Tariff. Protection of manufacturers was more important to them than the protection of African Americans.

Other measures of the era affected minorities—but usually in a negative way. Southern white Democrats enacted discriminatory legislation against blacks at the local and state level. A movement for immigration restriction, usually initiated by Republicans, led to the Chinese Exclusion Act of 1882 and other legislation banning certain categories of immigrants and giving the federal government control of overseas immigration. In 1887 the Dawes Act attacked the tribal roots of American Indian culture by trying to make Native Americans homesteading farmers, and resulted unintentionally in making them dependent wards of the state.

Although most social issues received short shrift at the federal level, at the local and state level some—especially education and prohibition—received passionate attention. Alarmed by the seeming increase in alcohol consumption, Republicans moved beyond the educative temperance movement to attempt to make drinking alcohol a crime. They also sought to increase compulsory school attendance, but their efforts were often linked to moves to undermine parochial schools and schools that taught immigrants in their native tongues. In most areas these Republican actions backfired, losing more voters than they gained.

By 1890 very little effective legislation had been adopted to deal with the problems arising from a pluralistic society experiencing rapid social and economic change. This pattern resulted partly from a political equilibrium that bred inertia, as well as from traditional, widely held views regarding the limited nature of government. Nevertheless, public demands for change were growing. No group challenged the status quo more than the nation's farmers.

The Farmers Revolt

Cries for change naturally came from the losers in the new economic order. The declining prosperity of American farmers led many to the conclusion that the cards had been stacked against them. By the 1890s, many desperate farmers agreed with Populist leader Mary E. Lease that it was time "to raise less corn and more hell." Their success was limited, but they led the first American mass movement to reject Social Darwinism and laissez-faire principles. They also promoted the "radical" idea that "it is the duty of government to protect the weak, because the strong are able to protect themselves." Some even questioned basic tenets of industrial capitalism.

Grievances: Real and Imagined

The basic cause of the farmers' problems was the decline of agricultural prices—primarily because of overproduction. Farmers had a hard time believing, however, that they could produce too much, especially since there were still poorly clad and fed Americans.

Overproduction was an abstract, invisible enemy; many farmers sought more tangible, personal villains—the railroads, bankers, and monopolists. Farmers believed they were being robbed by high freight and credit costs, an unfair burden of taxation, middlemen who exploited their marketing problems, and an inadequate currency.

Although there was no conspiracy by the "monopolists" to fleece the farmers, their grievances did contain a germ of truth. Freight rates were higher for farmers in the West because of the long distances to markets and the scattered and seasonal nature of grain shipments. Although western farmers generally paid the same interest rates as easterners, they were more dependent on mortgages to finance their operations than the corporations. Southern farmers also paid dearly through higher credit prices for goods obtained by crop liens. Their large debts increased farmers' marketing problems. All the crops in a region were usually harvested at the same time, and farmers had to sell them immediately to pay off loans. Middlemen took advantage of the glutted markets, buying the crops at low prices and selling them after the prices rose.

Governmental policy also seemed to hurt more than help. Property taxes hit farmers hard because they had lots of land but little income. The tariffs generally hurt most farmers by both raising the prices they paid for

By the late 1880s many farmers were already suffering from severe economic dislocation. This 1889 cartoon shows a poor, hungry farmer gazing at a banquet for tariff-gorged industrialists while Congressman McKinley pours whiskey.

goods and making it harder for them to sell their crops on the international market. The deflationary policy of the federal government especially hurt the farmers because of their great indebtedness. Every economic downturn brought a wave of farm foreclosures and frustration. Thousands of dreams died slowly, as one Kansas farmer's letter reveals.

> At the age of 52 years, after a long life of toil, economy and self-denial, I find myself and family virtually paupers. With hundreds of cattle, hundreds of hogs, scores of good horses, and a farm that rewarded the toil of our hands with 16,000 bushels of golden corn, we are poorer by many dollars than we were years ago. What once seemed a neat little fortune and a house of refuge for our declining years . . . has been rendered valueless.

The Farmers Organize

In the age of economic consolidation farmers realized early the need to unite and cooperate. They were never able, however, to do so as effectively as the industrialists and railroad magnates, due to their greater geographic separation as well as a frontier-bred individualism. The first national farm organization was the Patrons of Husbandry, founded in 1867. Organized into local granges that sponsored lectures, dances, and picnics, the group met a deep hunger for social interaction, and the membership grew to more than one million by 1874.

The Grangers soon moved beyond their social functions to address the economic grievances of the farmers. In addition to their efforts to regulate the railroads, the Grangers established buying cooperatives, which were formed to purchase in bulk directly from manufacturers, thus eliminating retail markups. In some places granges established cooperative banks, grain elevators, cotton gins, insurance companies, processing plants, and even plants to manufacture farm implements. However, most of the cooperatives were short on capital and skilled management, and in the late 1870s the granges began to decline.

Economic grievances remained, however, and the farmers' organizational response shifted to the Farmers' Alliance movement. Although never very effective, a northwestern Allliance was formed in 1880. In the South the Alliance movement was more radical and more successful. By 1890 the southern Alliance was a national organization with about 1.5 million members, with an additional 1 million members in the Colored Alliance, its African-American affiliate.

Like the Grangers, Alliance members sought to establish cooperatives, mostly without long-term success. They also conducted wider social and educational programs and boasted about 1,000 newspapers. Self-help, however, proved inadequate. In 1890 they turned to political action to redress farmers' grievances, either by seeking to capture their state Democratic organizations or by establishing independent third parties.

The Agrarian Agenda

The demands of the farmers mixed rhetoric, radicalism, and realism. Their words expressed an anger that had flared white-hot after years of smouldering resentment. Rejecting certain aspects of capitalism, they spoke in a language that divided the nation into "haves" and "have-nots." They saw a division between the toiling masses who produced wealth and the parasitic capitalists who expropriated it. In response they proclaimed that "wealth belongs to him who creates it."

Scorned by critics, the movement did have its unsavory aspects. A few agrarians espoused simplistic and often anti–Semitic conspiracy theories. Other flamboyant demagogues such as "Pitchfork Ben" Tillman of South Carolina exploited rural anger for their personal political ambitions. Thus, with a mixture of contempt and fear, critics called the rural reformers "crackpot radicals" and "hayseed socialists."

By Gilded Age standards, agrarian demands were indeed radical, even though most have since been adopted. Many farmers called for government ownership and operation of the railroads and telegraph and telephone lines. As landowners they rejected socialism, but some did believe that transportation and communication facilities were "natural monopolies" that could only be run efficiently under centralized management and were too important to the public welfare to be in the hands of private monopolies.

The remainder of the agrarian political agenda reflected a rather realistic and moderate response to the farmers' problems. To ease their credit crisis farmers advocated an inflated, more flexible currency and the subtreasury plan. Considered by the Alliance members to be the keystone of their program, subtreasuries (federal warehouses) were to be constructed as places where farmers could store their crops until prices rose to relieve them of the pressure to sell immediately. To finance government programs farmers also called for a graduated income tax.

Believing that many of their problems could be relieved by a more responsive government, farmers called for greater popular participation in the political process. They advocated the direct election of senators, which would allow the people to elect senators instead of having state legislatures select them. They also called for initiative and referendum procedures, which would enable voters to propose legislation through petitions and enact laws by popular vote, thereby bypassing the state legislatures that seemed unwilling to act on their grievances.

Although the farmers failed to address the fundamental problem of overproduction, adoption of the agrarian demands could have relieved somewhat the agricultural distress fueling their anger. Thus the farmers became increasingly involved in political organization.

Emergence of the Populist Party

In 1890 Alliance members entered politics in the West and the South with remarkable success. Under independent party banners, western Alliance members elected a governor in Kansas, gained control of four state legislatures, and sent U.S. senators from Kansas and Nebraska. Working through the existing Democratic state parties, southern Alliance members elected four governors, 44 congressmen, and several senators.

Western Alliance farmers interpreted this success as a mandate to establish a national third party. Although at first Southerners were apprehensive, the Alliances joined hands in St. Louis to create the People's or Populist party. In July 1892 the Populist party's national convention in Omaha drafted a platform and gave its presidential nomination to James B. Weaver of Iowa, formerly a Union general and Greenback presidential candidate.

The Populist platform included all the agrarian demands: the subtreasury plan; an income tax; free coinage of silver to inflate the currency; government ownership of railroads, telephone, and telegraph; and the political reforms intended to restore government to "the hands of the people."

Most Populists were small-scale farmers in the South and West whose farms were minimally mechanized. Many relied on a single cash crop, had unsatisfactory access to credit, and lived in social isolation some distance from towns and railroads. The majority owned some land, but sizable numbers of sharecroppers and tenant farmers joined the party. Prosperous, large-scale, diversified farmers found little appeal in the party's platforms or activities.

The Populists realized the need to broaden the base of their constituency. Therefore, the Omaha platform included planks to appeal to urban workers. They advocated an eight-hour day, urged immigration restriction, opposed strikebreaking, and favored "fair and liberal" pensions to veterans. In the South some Populist leaders, such as Tom Watson of Georgia, sought to woo black voters. He told audiences of black and white farmers: "You are made to hate each other because upon that hatred is rested the keystone of the arch of financial despotism which enslaves you both."

The Populists conducted colorful campaigns, which one Nebraska Democrat called a blend of "the French Revolution and a western religious revival." Their anger fostered a revolutionary spirit that appealed to large numbers of farmers. In 1892 Weaver won more than one million popular votes—the first third-party candidate to do so—and 22 electoral votes. Although the Populists failed to carry a single southern state, it was a remarkable showing for a new party, revealing the extent of popular discontent. The next year brought the panic of 1893, which produced more discontent and gave the Populists great hopes for the election of 1896.

Depression and Turbulence in the 1890s

While the Populists made their bid for office in the election of 1892, the two major parties featured a rerun of the election of 1888. Once again Cleveland and Harrison faced each other over the issue of the tariff. The unpopular McKinley Tariff helped create a different outcome, and Cleveland entered the White House, the only president to serve two nonconsecutive terms.

The Panic of 1893

No sooner had Cleveland been inaugurated than the nation plunged into the worst depression it had yet experienced. A downturn in the European economy had caused overseas buyers to reduce their purchases of American goods, while at the same time foreign investors began to withdraw from American markets. These factors led to a serious shortage of currency, which in turn led to rapidly falling prices. There had also been serious overexpansion of the economy, especially in railroad construction. The collapse of several important railroads sent shock waves through the American economy. Confidence faltered, the stock market crashed, and banks failed.

The panic ushered in a depression in which unemployment reached 20 percent of the work force. Farm prices plummeted, and farm foreclosures reached new highs. Sharp wage cuts and massive layoffs took place in virtually every industry. Still opposed to direct federal aid, President Cleveland's only response was repeal of the Sherman Silver Purchase Act and the sale of lucrative federal bonds to a banking syndicate, headed by J. P. Morgan, aimed at protecting the nation's gold reserves.

The Democrats did pass the Wilson-Gorman Tariff in 1894, which reduced rates by 10 percent. Disappointed with the moderate cuts, reformers were appeased by a provision placing a 2 percent tax on incomes (ruled unconstitutional a year later). In the face of massive suffering, many people wanted the government to do more.

Expressions of Worker Discontent

Even before the Panic of 1893 violence in labor-management relations was on the rise. In 1892, for example, Andrew Carnegie and the Amalgamated Association of Iron and Steel Workers clashed at Carnegie's Homestead plant near Pittsburgh. In an effort to crush the union, Carnegie slashed wages, and, expecting a confrontation, he fortified his steel mills, hired strikebreakers, and employed the Pinkerton Agency to protect them.

On July 5 strikers and Pinkerton agents clashed in a battle that left ten men killed and another 70 wounded. Carnegie's manager and partner Henry Frick appealed for help to the governor of Pennsylvania, who dispatched 8,000 militiamen to Homestead to reopen the plant. In late July an anarchist named Alexander Berkman, who had no connections with the steel union, tried to assassinate Frick but only wounded him. The local and national press linked unionism with radicalism, as public support for the steel workers quickly subsided. The powerful forces of capital, government, and press had combined to defeat the strike and destroy the union.

During the depression employers frequently cut wages to preserve profits. In 1894 the workers in the Pullman plant at Chicago found their wages reduced several times while their rent for company-owned housing remained the same. When management refused to negotiate with the union, members of the American Railway Union (ARU) refused to handle any cars made in the Pullman plant. The boycott totally disrupted railroad traffic in the Midwest. When the liberal governor of Illinois, John P. Altgeld, refused to interfere, railroad executives turned to U.S. Attorney General Richard Olney, a former railroad corporation lawyer. Olney and Cleveland responded quickly, using the excuse of protecting the mails to send 2,000 troops to the Chicago area. When ARU president Eugene V. Debs defied a court injunction ordering union leaders to discontinue the strike, he was imprisoned. Federal troops managed to crush the strike, but only after bitter fighting and extensive damage to railroad property.

Such repressive force drove some workers to the political left. Prior to 1894, the Socialist Labor party had been able to muster only a small following. After the Pullman strike Eugene V. Debs emerged from prison a socialist and made socialism more respectable. Born in Indiana in 1855, Debs delivered with a Hoosier twang a version of socialism based upon distinctly American values. The movement thus acquired a fiery and effective orator. Under Debs's leadership the larger and stronger Socialist party of America began to form and directly challenge unrestrained capitalism.

The mass suffering during the depression also provoked some to urge the federal government to provide work for the unemployed. One such person was Jacob S. Coxey, an Ohio businessman who advocated putting men to work on the roads. To demand action and dramatize the plight of the unemployed, he staged a march on Washington that gained nationwide attention. Federal authorities, however, took a dim view of such expressions of popular protest. When some of the marchers straggled into the capital on May 1, 1894, they were forcibly dispersed; their leader was arrested for walking on the grass. Once again the national government seemed out of touch with a large segment of the electorate and insensitive to its grievances.

Deteriorating Race Relations

The turbulent 1890s was also one of the worst decades of racial violence in the nation's history. The Republican party and all three branches of government deserted African Americans, and Populists failed to unite blacks and whites on the basis of class interests. Lynching increasingly became a tool for controlling both black votes and actions. Under the pretext of "maintaining law and order" vigilante mobs hanged, mutilated, and burned African Americans in increasing numbers. During the decade of the 1890s an average of two to three black southerners were lynched each week.

Attempts to limit black voting began in 1890 when Mississippi established poll taxes, literacy tests, and residency requirements. The Supreme Court displayed its disregard for black rights by upholding the so-called Mississippi Plan. Other states soon adopted similar measures. Later, to woo lower-class white voters, "grandfather" clauses were added—providing exemptions to the sons and grandsons of those who had voted prior to the Reconstruction Acts, a requirement that blacks, of course, could not meet.

Once whites stripped away black political power, discriminatory social legislation soon followed. Although segregation had long existed in a haphazard, informal way, it now became a legalized system of repression. Constitutional obstacles to this new means of racial control, such as the Fourteenth Amendment, were removed by the Supreme Court, which ruled in its 1896 *Plessy* v. *Ferguson* decision that public accommodations for blacks could be "separate but equal." With segregation legalized, southern states passed "Jim Crow" laws to require the separation of the races. Some states even passed laws prohibiting interracial checker playing and requiring textbooks used in black schools to be stored separately from those used in white schools.

The Tide Is Turned: The Election of 1896

As a new century approached, the United States seemed to be a nation torn by racial, class and regional antagonisms. The turbulence prompted one of the major parties to respond in 1896 to the popular clamor for reform, and in so doing brought the political equilibrium that had characterized the Gilded Age to an end.

The Populists had hoped to ride silver to power because of the growing popularity of the issue, but the Democrats stole their thunder by choosing William Jennings Bryan, an advocate of free silver. To nominate someone else would split the silver votes and ensure a victory for McKinley. Yet to nominate Bryan meant the loss of their identity and momentum.

Many Populists argued fervently against a union with the Democrats, who focused almost exclusively on silver at the expense of the rest of the Populist demands. In the end the Populists bit the bullet and nominated Bryan for president but chose Tom Watson for vice president rather than the Democratic choice, Arthur Sewall.

McKinley carried the popular vote 7.1 million to 6.5 million and the electoral college votes 271 to 176. The defeat of Bryan and the silver forces marked the beginning of an era of Republican dominance. Millions of disaffected Democrats joined the ranks of the Republicans, who won the presidency in seven of the nine contests between 1896 and 1928, and controlled both houses of Congress 17 of the next 20 sessions.

The Populists suffered the most from the election results: their party disappeared. Their attempt to unite farmers and laborers, blacks and whites, had failed. Like the Socialists and other radicals, the Populists were never able to recruit organized labor to forge a broadly based working-class movement because labor leaders argued that farmers' goals were not compatible with labor's interests. In the South, race proved to be more important than class, and many disillusioned white Populists such as Tom Watson became antiblack activists following their defeat.

*C*hronology of Key Events

1867	The Grangers, first national farmers' organization, founded
1873	Coinage Act declares that gold alone will back paper money
1875	Specie Resumption Act
1877	Southern Farmers' Alliance founded; *Munn* v. *Illinois* upholds constitutionality of state regulation of railroads
1878	Bland–Allison Act
1881	President James A. Garfield assassinated; Chester Arthur becomes twenty-first president
1883	Pendleton Act authorizes competitive examination for civil service positions
1886	*Wabash* case reverses *Munn* v. *Illinois* decision
1887	Congress establishes the Interstate Commerce Commission
1890	Founding of the National American Woman Suffrage Association; Congress passes Sherman Antitrust Act; Sherman Silver Purchase Act allows U. S. to issue paper money based on silver; Mississippi Plan to restrict black voting through poll taxes, literacy tests, and residency requirements
1892	Populist party formed; Homestead strike
1893	Panic of 1893; severe economic depression
1894	Pullman strike; Coxey's Army marches on Washington to protest unemployment
1895	*United States* v. *E. C. Knight Co.* weakens Sherman Antitrust Act
1896	*Plessy* v. *Ferguson;* William McKinley elected twenty-fifth president

Americans had come to a turning point in 1896 and chose the conservative path. The Republican administration quickly raised duties with the Dingley Tariff of 1897, and three years later officially put the nation on the gold standard by requiring all money to be redeemable in gold. Ironically, new discoveries of gold and more efficient extracting methods brought the inflation that farmers had sought from silver. Prosperity began to return, which undermined the agrarian movement as rising prices eased farmers' economic distress.

Conclusion

After Reconstruction, national politics entertained the masses rather than solved the emerging problems of industrialization. The two major parties differed little in their laissez-faire support of business and seemed more concerned with the spoils of office than with the suffering of farmers, workers, and minorities. Finally, a challenge to unrestrained capitalism arose from the losers in the race toward economic modernization. Led by disgruntled farmers, the Populists sought to unite large segments of the American population on the basis of class interest. As a result, the election of 1896 provided a real choice for American voters.

The conservative victory brought about the death of Populism, but many of the problems the farmers addressed in the 1890s continued into the twentieth century. Time vindicated their demands. A large number of their rejected solutions were adopted in the first two decades of the new century; most of their remaining agenda was enacted in modified form during the New Deal of the 1930s.

Suggestions for Further Reading

For general overviews of America during the Gilded Age see Sean Dennis Cashman, *America in the Gilded Age* (1984); John A. Garraty, *The New Commonwealth* (1968); Alan Trachtenberg, *The Incorporation of America* (1982).

Books that focus on political developments during the late nineteenth century include John M. Dobson, *Politics in the Gilded Age* (1972); Michael E. McGerr, *The Decline of Popular Politics* (1986); H. Wayne Morgan, *From Hayes to McKinley* (1969); Leonard D. White, *The Republican Era* (1958); R. Hal Williams, *Years of Decision* (1978).

For studies of women's issues consult Eleanor Flexner, *Century of Struggle*, rev. ed. (1975); Margaret Forster, *Significant Sisters* (1984); Aileen Kraditor, *The Ideas of the Woman's Suffrage Movement* (1965).

The currency debate is the focus of Walter T. K. Nugent, *Money and American Society* (1968); Allen Weinstein, *Prelude to Populism* (1970). For more on the spoils system and corruption in government see Ari Hoogenboom, *Outlawing the Spoils* (1961); Gerald McFarland, *Mugwumps, Morals and Politics* (1975); John C. Sproat, *The Best Men* (1968).

The Populist movement is analyzed in Lawrence Goodwyn, *Democratic Promise: The Populist Moment in America* (1976). Other valuable studies of the agrarian revolt include Steven Hahn, *The Roots of Southern Populism* (1983); Robert McMath, Jr., *Populist Vanguard* (1975); Norman Pollack, *The Populist Response to Industrial America* (1962).

Race relations during the Gilded Age are covered in Howard N. Rabinowitz, *Race Relations in the Urban South* (1978); C. Vann Woodward, *The Strange Career of Jim Crow,* rev. ed. (1974).

Chapter *21*

Imperial America, 1870–1900

Congressional Control and the Reduction of American Power
Foreign Service
Reduction of the Military
Seward's Dreams

The Spirit of American Greatness
American Exceptionalism
Sense of Duty
Search for Markets
The New Navy
Shaping Public Opinion

The Emergence of Aggression in American Foreign Policy
Confronting the Germans in Samoa
Teaching Chile a Lesson
The Hawaiian Pear
Facing Down the British

The War for Empire
The Cuban Revolution
The Yellow Press
The Spanish-American War
Freeing Cuba
The Imperial Debate
The War to Crush Filipino Independence
Keeping the Doors Open

Dreams of expansion came easily to Americans during the 1800s. For most of the century they expanded westward, moving into Texas and Kansas, pushing across the Great Plains, and occupying California and the Pacific Northwest. But they did not restrict their dreams to the millions of acres between Mexico and Canada. They cast covetous eyes toward Central America and the islands of the Caribbean and the Pacific. Plans to annex Nicaragua, Cuba, Santo Domingo, the Virgin Islands, Hawaii, and Samoa fired politicians' imaginations. Before the Civil War the debate over slavery blocked these larger expansionist efforts. Once the Union was preserved, however, expansionists returned to their plans with revived energy and enthusiasm.

President Ulysses S. Grant had a pet expansionist project of his own. He eyed the Dominican Republic, the eastern two-thirds of the Caribbean island of Santo Domingo. Annexation, he maintained, would benefit America in a number of ways. The island was rich in mineral resources, possessed an important natural harbor, and its inhabitants were eager to buy American products. Most important for Grant, who was ever mindful of America's race problem, the Dominicans were black. The island could serve as a haven for black Americans, a retreat from Ku Klux Klan harassment.

With so much to gain, Grant put his full political weight behind annexation. His conduct was less than presidential. First, he sent his personal secretary and close friend Orville Babcock to Santo Domingo on a "fact-finding" mission. Unimpressed by the islanders, Babcock found them "indolent and ignorant." Nonetheless, he concluded that the Dominican Republic was a commercial and strategic prize worthy of annexation. Moreover, Buenaventura Baez, the unscrupulous president of the republic, was anxious to sell his country so he could afford to move to Paris or Madrid because, as Babcock noted, the Dominican Republic was "a dull country." The promise of American dollars had convinced Baez that his country should belong to the United States.

Unrest at home added fuel to Baez's willingness to sell. His government was threatened both by neighboring Haiti and a strong force of Dominican rebels. So difficult was Baez's position that Babcock had to order a United States Navy ship to protect the Baez government during the annexation negotiations, which were completed in the late fall of 1869.

The treaty of annexation, however, would have to be ratified by the Senate, a body more difficult to satisfy than Baez's government. Deciding to forego presidential protocol, Grant made a personal visit to the home of Charles Sumner, the chairman of the Senate Foreign Relations Committee. After listening to the president's arguments in favor of annexation,

Sumner promised his "most careful and candid consideration." Grant departed for his short walk back to the White House believing he had won Sumner's full support.

After consideration and considerable investigation, Sumner decided that the entire annexation scheme was distasteful. He was disturbed by Babcock's and Baez's unethical financial dealings and was enraged that the United States Navy had been used to keep the Dominican president in power. Not a person to mince words, Sumner accused Grant of being "a colossus of ignorance." By a vote of five to two, the Foreign Relations Committee voiced its disapproval of the treaty of annexation.

Grant was furious, and refused to concede defeat. He hinted that if the United States did not take the Dominican Republic, one of the European powers would, and he reported the results of a rigged plebiscite in which the Dominicans supposedly supported annexation by the suspiciously lopsided vote of 15,169 to 11. Grant's efforts to gain support failed, however, and on June 30, 1870, the Senate rejected the treaty.

The failed attempt to annex the Dominican Republic is important for the themes it underscored. It demonstrated both the desire for expansion by the president and his advisers and the power of Congress in foreign affairs. During the remainder of the century the scenario would be repeated again and again, often with different results. Gradually, presidents wrested more control over foreign affairs from Congress, which for its part came to accept a more expansionist foreign policy. As presidents and Congress found common ground, America expanded outward into the Caribbean and the Pacific. The expansion took different forms. Sometimes the United States annexed countries outright. Other times America remained content to exercise less forceful control over nominally independent countries. The results were the same. The United States ultimately acquired an overseas empire and expanded its influence over the Western Hemisphere.

Congressional Control and the Reduction of American Power

Foreign Service

In 1869 when Grant took office, congressmen and other Americans held the State Department and the diplomatic service in low esteem. Once regarded as a stepping-stone to the presidency, politicians increasingly viewed the post of secretary of state as a reward for outstanding party men or the refuge for defeated presidential aspirants. Even the diplomats themselves did not escape criticism. Some politicians considered the foreign service "a nursery of snobs" and viewed diplomats as an expensive, nearly useless luxury. A few reformers even advocated the abolition of the foreign service, arguing that international lawyers could be hired to handle really serious international crises.

The irreverent treatment of the State Department reflected the national mood. Concerns over the currency, civil service reform, Reconstruction, the tariff, the Indian problem, and railroad building dwarfed interest in foreign affairs. During the 1870s and 1880s, when a powerful Congress largely dictated foreign policy, the spirit of Washington's Farewell Address, which advised America to steer clear of foreign entanglements, and the Monroe Doctrine, which elevated isolationism to a national obsession, guided the country. Separated from a powerful Europe by the Atlantic, Congress saw no reason to spend time or money on the State Department or foreign affairs.

Using its control over the budget as a sword, Congress trimmed the State Department to the bone. In 1869 Congress allowed the State Department a paltry 31 clerks; by 1881 presidential efforts had succeeded in raising that number to a still inadequate 50.

Reduction of the Military

The sword that trimmed the State Department was also used on America's army and navy once the Civil War had ended. In 1865 the United States had the largest and perhaps the most powerful navy in the world. To be sure, it was a ragtag navy, but it numbered 971 vessels, ranging from the powerful *Monitor*-class ironclads to modest yachts. Within nine months of Appomattox, the fleet was reduced to 29. While the world's best navies converted to steel and steam, American naval leaders remained tied to wood and sails.

As Congress watched unconcerned, the navy declined intellectually as well as physically. The men appointed as the secretaries of the navy were mostly political appointees who knew little and cared less about ships. There were far too many officers, and with promotions based strictly upon length of service, any officer who lived long enough could become an admiral. Thus the system almost guaranteed poor leadership.

The power and effectiveness of the army were similarly reduced. Demobilization after the Civil War occurred quickly and haphazardly. In May 1865 the army contained 1,034,064 volunteers; by November 1866 only 11,043 remained in uniform. Eventually even the number of regular troops was reduced until, by the end of Reconstruction, the army was a skeleton of its former self. In 1876 the maximum strength stood at 27,442 troops.

Certainly in 1876 the United States did not need an active foreign service and a powerful army and navy to secure its borders. No countries threatened America. Geography defended the United States, and the European balance of power discouraged foolish European designs on any part of the Western Hemisphere. At the same time, the relative weakness of its foreign service, army, and navy discouraged the United States from attempting to extend its influence beyond its own borders. All in all, most congressmen were entirely happy with the situation.

Seward's Dreams

Not everyone in government agreed with congressional leadership in foreign affairs. William Henry Seward was among those who called for a more forceful, expansionist policy. While serving as secretary of state under Lincoln and Johnson, Seward advocated vigorous expansionism and dreamed of an American empire that would dominate the Pacific and Caribbean basins. He negotiated with Denmark to purchase the Danish West Indies (Virgin Islands), with Russia to buy Alaska, and with Santo Domingo for the Dominican harbor of Samana Bay. In addition, his plan for an American empire encompassed Haiti, Cuba, Iceland, Greenland, Honduras's Tigre Island, and Hawaii.

Congress, which did not share Seward's vision, balked. During Seward's term, America did acquire the Midway Islands in the middle of the Pacific Ocean, but few Americans even noticed. The purchase of Alaska in 1867 drew more comments, most of which were negative. Some senators claimed that $7.2 million was too much money for a frozen wasteland that only Eskimos and seals could love. But in the end the Senate, influenced by a few well-placed bribes, reluctantly ratified the treaty.

Articulate and aggressive anti-imperialists blocked the remainder of Seward's dreams during the late 1860s and the 1870s, when congressional power was at a high tide. Seward and President Andrew Johnson were no match for Congress, which consistently found other issues more pressing than foreign affairs. Some congressmen pushed for money to enact a fair Reconstruction policy. Others freely gave money to railroad construction companies and Union veterans to bolster their own reelection chances. But they drew America's purse strings tight when confronted with most expansionist schemes.

The Spirit of American Greatness

Although Congress was reluctant to endorse expansionist schemes, during the last third of the nineteenth century many citizens had become convinced that the United States had to adopt a more aggressive and forceful

During the turn of the century, the United States increasingly tried to influence world affairs. Here, Uncle Sam assumes a forceful attitude.

foreign policy. Their reasons varied. Some believed expansion would be good for American business. Others felt the United States had a duty to spread its way of life to less fortunate countries. Still others maintained that economic and strategic security required that the country acquire overseas bases. Behind all these arguments, however, rested a common assumption: the United States was a great country, and it should start acting the part.

American Exceptionalism

The idea of American exceptionalism—that the nation houses God's chosen people—has deep roots in the country's history. Puritan concepts of "a city upon a hill" mixed easily with talk of the greatness of republicanism and democracy and the manifest destiny of America. The teachings of

Social Darwinists added "scientific proof" to the concept of American exceptionalism. With such Darwinian phrases as "natural selection" and "survival of the fittest," American intellectuals praised the course of American history.

There was, however, a dark side to American exceptionalism, and this too many Americans were quick to endorse: if white Anglo-Saxon Americans were biologically superior, then other races and other nations had to be inferior. During the late nineteenth century such Social Darwinists as Herbert Spencer in England and John Fiske in the United States helped to make racism intellectually acceptable. Catering to white audiences, Social Darwinists advanced one pseudoscientific theory after another to "prove" the superiority of Anglo-Saxons.

From the idea of superiority to the acceptance of domination was a short step. If Americans were God's chosen people, why shouldn't they dominate and uplift less fortunate countries and peoples? This was the question posed by advocates of a more aggressive American foreign policy.

Sense of Duty

Religious leaders noted the duty that American exceptionalism implied. Talk of the "white man's burden" was rife during the period. Protestant missionaries carried their faith and beliefs to the far corners of the world. In addition to preaching salvation and saving souls, they also extolled the virtues of American civilization, which included everything from democracy and rule by law to sanitation, material progress, sewing machines, and cotton underwear. Defining good and bad, progress and savagery by American standards, they attempted to alter native customs and beliefs to conform to a single American model.

Popular writer and religious leader Reverend Josiah Strong voiced what other missionaries and true believers acted upon when he wrote: "The Anglo-Saxon is the representative of two great ideas . . . civil liberty [and] a pure *spiritual* Christianity." These two ideas, he added, are destined to elevate all humankind, and "the Anglo-Saxon . . . is divinely commissioned to be . . . his brother's keeper."

Search for Markets

Strong's message was not lost on the business leaders of America. They fully agreed that missionaries should preach the benefits of American material progress as well as the glories of the Protestant faith. Looking south toward Latin America and west toward Asia, American businesspeople and farmers

Many foreign missionaries sought to unite the people of the world by extolling the virtues of Western civilization.

saw vast virgin markets for their industrial and agricultural surpluses as well as endless sources of raw materials. Sensing that American markets, filled with low-paid workers, offered few new opportunities, they entertained fabulous visions of hungry Latin Americans and shoeless Chinese.

Although the United States had become the leading industrial and agricultural country in the world, domestic consumption did not keep pace with galloping production. In addition, throughout the period the government pursued tight-money policies, and the real income of laborers made only modest gains. The result was a boom and bust economy that witnessed spectacular growth as well as severe depressions.

In part, the United States was a victim of its own spectacular success. Increased production without increased consumption led only to glutted markets and falling prices. Increasingly, farmers and industrialists looked toward foreign markets. Too often, export trade spelled the difference between prosperity and bankruptcy. Although American businesspeople and bankers had yet to develop overseas marketing networks and foreign branch banks to market their goods and finance sales, they clearly saw the need for such additions. The future of America, many economic leaders believed, would be determined by the ability of the government to find and secure overseas markets.

During the depression years the lure of foreign trade proved particularly strong. Depressions meant farm foreclosures and industrial unemployment, problems that led to social unrest. The Grange and Populist movements, the two largest agrarian revolts, and such labor confrontations as the violent railroad strikes of 1877, the Haymarket riot of 1886, and the Pullman strike of 1894 occurred during lean economic times. For many Americans the issue was simple: the United States must acquire foreign markets or face economic hardship and revolution at home.

The State Department was in full agreement. Both William Henry Seward and his successor as secretary of state during the Grant administration, Hamilton Fish, believed firmly that the United States needed new markets. Seward especially coveted the lucrative markets of Asia, and he wanted the United States to acquire islands in the Pacific as stepping-stones toward that prize. Furthermore, American economic control, he believed, should be extended to include Canada and Latin America. Although both Seward and Fish had to contend with a cautious, isolationist Congress, several important strides toward the Asian markets were made during their terms in office.

During the late 1870s and 1880s economic hard times quickened the search for new markets. The United States successfully negotiated bilateral reciprocity treaties with many Latin American countries. These treaties lowered tariffs and thus stimulated trade between the United States and Latin America.

By the mid-1880s efforts in favor of expansion combined with economic and social problems at home convinced Congress to reevaluate its isolationist policies. The time had come to look at our oceans not as defensive barriers but as paths toward new markets and increased prosperity. A final problem, however, remained. America's navy and merchant marine seemed woefully unfit for the challenge.

The New Navy

If the United States hoped to compete for world markets, it had to upgrade its navy. During the 1880s advocates of a new navy moved Congress to action, and by 1890 great gains had been made. But serious problems remained. While England and Germany were building large, heavily armored battleships, the ships built by the United States were lightly armored, fast cruisers, inadequate for any major naval engagement. In 1890 Congress appropriated money for the construction of three first-class battleships and a heavy cruiser. It was the beginning of a new, offensive navy for the United States.

Talk of empire, navy, trade, and national greatness came together in 1890 in the publication of a monumentally important book, *The Influence of Sea Power upon History,* by Captain Alfred Thayer Mahan. According to Mahan, naval power was the key to national greatness. He attempted to demonstrate that countries rise to world dominance by expanding their foreign commerce and protecting that commerce with a strong navy. Without a powerful navy, Mahan emphasized, a nation could never enjoy full prosperity and security; in short, no nation could ever hope to be a world power.

Shaping Public Opinion

Mahan's writings were applauded by American politicians and businesspeople who felt it was time for the United States to assume the rights and responsibilities of world power status. These men of wealth, education, and influence like Henry Cabot Lodge, Theodore Roosevelt, Albert J. Beveridge, and John Hay were powerful politicians and administrators. They believed that the United States was destined to be the greatest of world powers. Increasingly after 1890, these and other men of like mind dominated and shaped America's foreign policy.

The expansionists often shared common experiences and beliefs. Most were prosperous Republicans from old-line American families, and most had traveled abroad widely. Anglo-Saxon by heritage, they tended to be ardent Anglophiles, full of praise for Great Britain's imperial efforts. They believed that the United States should join "Mother England" in administering to the "uncivilized" corners of the globe.

Lodge and other expansionists called for a bold foreign policy. They advocated the construction of a canal through Central America to allow American ships to move between the Atlantic and Pacific oceans more rapidly. To protect the canal, the United States would have to exert control over Cuba and the other strategically located Caribbean islands. The United States, they believed, also needed coaling stations and naval bases across the Pacific. Secure bases in Hawaii, Guam, Wake Island, and the Philippines would allow the United States to exploit the seemingly limitless China market. Finally, a powerful navy would have to protect the entire American empire.

The Emergence of Aggression in American Foreign Policy

Expansionists talked loudly about peace, but their rhetoric was couched in aggressive language. "To be prepared for war is the most effectual means to promote peace," said Theodore Roosevelt. The more they talked about peace, the closer war seemed. It is not surprising that the United States launched a more belligerent foreign policy at the same time it was building and launching more powerful ships. The two developments originated from the same source: a ready acceptance of force as the final arbiter of international disputes. This acceptance of force almost led to several wars in the late nineteenth century and culminated in the Spanish-American War in 1898. The Spanish-American War was not an aberrant event. Rather, it was the result of a more aggressive American foreign policy, one aimed at acquiring both world respect and an empire.

Confronting the Germans in Samoa

Changing American attitudes toward foreign policy were first seen in Samoa, a group of 14 volcanic islands lying 4,000 miles from San Francisco along the trade route to Australia. Throughout the nineteenth century American whalers stopped in Samoa, the harbors of which had often provided refuge for ships caught in Pacific storms. If the natives were quarrelsome among themselves, they were exceptionally friendly with Americans.

The U.S. government's interest was decidedly more mercenary. In 1878 the Senate ratified a treaty granting the United States rights to a naval station at the harbor of Pago Pago. Unfortunately for American interests, England and especially Germany were also determined to influence events on the islands.

Like the United States, Germany was just beginning to think in terms of empire. German Chancellor Otto von Bismarck decided that Samoa should belong to Germany. England sided with the "iron chancellor." President Cleveland firmly disagreed. Germany and the United States were set on a collision course.

When a conference between the three countries held in Washington in 1887 failed to solve the problem, war seemed inevitable. Neither Germany nor the United States had much money invested in the islands, but both felt their national pride was at stake. "We must show sharp teeth," remarked Bismarck. Nature, however, had the most powerful weapon. On the morning of March 16, 1889, a typhoon swept across Samoa, destroying the American and German warships anchored in Apia harbor.

The violent winds seemed to calm the ruffled emotions of the United States and Germany. That same year, Germany, the United States, and England met for a conference in Berlin, and without consulting the Samoans, they decided to partition the islands. Everyone seemed satisfied—except the Samoans who were deprived of their independence and saddled with an unpopular king. The plan lasted until 1899, when Germany and the United States ended the facade of Samoan independence and officially made colonies of the islands. The United States gained Tutuila, with the harbor of Pago Pago, and several smaller islands. Many expansionists believed that America's aggressive stand against Germany had paid handsome dividends.

Teaching Chile a Lesson

American expansionists had something to show for their confrontation with Germany over Samoa. Pago Pago was, after all, an ideal coaling station for ships running between San Francisco and Australia. American troubles with Chile, however, are more difficult to understand, since trade and strategic policy played small roles. More than anything else, touchy pride and jingoism pushed the United States toward war with Chile.

Had people not died, the background to the confrontation would have been amusing. In 1891 a revolutionary faction, which the United States had opposed, gained control of the Chilean government and initiated a foreign policy that was unfriendly toward America. Shortly thereafter, on October 16, 1891, an American cruiser, the *Baltimore,* anchored off the coast of Chile, sent about 100 members of its crew ashore on leave at Valparaiso. Many of the sailors did what sailors normally do on leave: they retired to a local saloon and drank. As the men left the saloon, a riot broke out. An angry, anti-American mob attacked the sailors, killing two and injuring 16. To make matters worse, the Chilean police, who had done nothing to halt the fighting, carried the surviving Americans off to jail.

It was an unfortunate affair, and the United States loudly protested, demanding a formal apology and "prompt and full reparation." The Chilean government refused. Incensed, President Benjamin Harrison threatened to break off diplomatic relations—a serious step toward war—unless the United States received an immediate apology. The American public supported Harrison's tough stand. Finally the Chilean government backed down. It apologized for the attack on the sailors and paid an indemnity of $75,000. The threat of force had again carried the day. Advocates of the new navy, a jingoistic press, and aggressively nationalistic Americans cheered.

The Hawaiian Pear

Throughout the late nineteenth century Hawaii figured prominently in American foreign policy planning. Earlier in the century, the islands had been a favorite place for many American missionaries, who went to Hawaii to spread Christianity and ended up settling and raising their families in the tropical paradise. More important still was the location of the islands. Not only were they ideally situated along the trade routes to Asia, but they offered a perfect site for protecting the Pacific sea lanes to the American

West Coast and the potential locations of an isthmus canal. In Hawaii, religious, economic, and strategic concerns met in complete harmony

By the mid-1880s expansionists who dreamed of Hawaii found willing allies in Congress. In 1884 a treaty between Hawaii and the United States set aside Pearl Harbor for the exclusive use of the American navy. After some debate the Senate ratified the treaty in 1887, and Hawaii officially became part of American strategic planning. By that time the islands were already tied economically to the United States. An 1875 treaty had allowed Hawaiians to sell their sugar in the United States duty-free, giving them a two cents per pound advantage over other foreign producers. The legislation encouraged American speculators to invest in Hawaiian sugar and to import Chinese and Japanese laborers to the islands to work on the large plantations. The investments returned incredibly high dividends, and for a time business boomed.

Problems arose suddenly in 1890. The McKinley Tariff Act removed all tariffs on foreign sugar and protected domestic sugar producers by awarding American sugar a bounty of two cents per pound. Hawaiian sugar prices plummeted, costing island producers about $12 million. U.S.-Hawaiian relations worsened when Queen Liliuokalani acceded to the throne in 1891. Adopting a strong anti-American policy, she wanted to purge American influences in Hawaii and disenfranchise all white men except those married to native women.

The white population in Hawaii reacted quickly. On January 17, 1893, white islanders overthrew her government. Supported by the American minister in Honolulu and aided by American sailors and marines, the revolution was fast, almost bloodless, and successful. The U.S. minister proclaimed Hawaii an American protectorate and wired his superiors in Washington that "the Hawaiian pear is now fully ripe, and this is the golden hour for the United States to pluck it."

The revolutionaries in Hawaii favored prompt American annexation of the islands. In Washington the Harrison administration, which was due to leave office on March 4, agreed. It negotiated a treaty of annexation with "indecent haste" and sent it to the Senate for ratification.

Before the Senate could ratify the treaty, Cleveland took office. An anti–imperialist, Cleveland had grave misgivings about the revolution, America's reaction, and the treaty. Five days after his inauguration, he recalled the treaty from the Senate and sent a special agent to Hawaii to investigate the entire affair. Upon learning that the majority of native Hawaiians opposed annexation, Cleveland killed the treaty.

This did not end the controversy. A white American minority continued to govern Hawaii. To correct the situation, Cleveland sent another representative to Hawaii to convince the new government to step down and allow Queen Liliuokalani to return to the throne, but Sanford B. Dole, president of a large Hawaiian pineapple corporation, refused. "Queen Lil" did not help matters by refusing to promise full amnesty for the revolutionaries if she were returned to power, vowing instead to behead those involved in the affair. In the end, Cleveland washed his hands of the entire matter, and the revolutionaries proclaimed an independent Hawaiian republic on July 4, 1894. Four years later, during the Spanish-American War, the United States finally annexed Hawaii.

Facing Down the British

Potentially the most serious conflict the United States faced during the 1890s originated in a border dispute between Venezuela and British Guiana. For almost 50 years this dispute remained peacefully unsettled, but the discovery of gold in the jungle region in the 1880s increased the importance of the issue. It was a rich deposit, and both Britain and Venezuela wanted it for their own. In response to Venezuelan requests for help, several times the United States offered to arbitrate the matter, and each time Britain refused the offer.

By June 1895 Cleveland and his new secretary of state, Richard Olney, had decided that Britain's actions were in violation of the spirit, if not the letter, of the Monroe Doctrine. In a strongly worded message to Great Britain, Olney affirmed U.S. sovereignty in the Western Hemisphere, and demanded that Britain submit the dispute to arbitration, hinting that the United States might intervene militarily if its wishes were not honored.

Britain waited four months to reply to Olney's note, and then answered, in effect, that the dispute did not involve either the United States or the Monroe Doctrine. Olney and the president were furious. In a special message to Congress, Cleveland asked for funds to establish a commission to determine the actual Venezuelan boundary, and he insisted that he would use force if necessary to maintain that boundary against any aggressors. Both houses of Congress unanimously approved Cleveland's request. The excitement of war was in the air.

America's bellicose reaction surprised British officials. England certainly did not want war, particularly at that time when it was becoming involved in a conflict in South Africa. It allowed a commission to arbitrate the dispute. In the end, the tribunal gave Britain most of the land it claimed.

America, however, felt it was the real winner. Cleveland had faced the British lion and won. The Monroe Doctrine and American prestige soared to new heights. More important for the future, Cleveland's actions, coupled with his handling of the Hawaiian revolution, significantly increased the power of the president over foreign affairs. Relations between the United States and Britain would quickly improve, and relations between America and Venezuela would rapidly deteriorate, but future presidents would not soon relinquish their control over foreign policy.

The War for Empire

During the Venezuela crisis and throughout the 1890s many Americans seemed openly to invite and look forward to the prospect of war. Viewed as a whole, it was a decade of strident nationalism and aggressive posturing. It was also a troubled and violent decade. Racked by the depression of 1893, frustrated by the problems created by monopolies and overproduction, and plagued by internal strife, Americans turned on each other, often with violent results. Strikes in Pullman, Illinois, and Homestead, Pennsylvania, saw laborers battle federal and state authorities. Populist protest dramatized the widening gulf between city and country, rich and poor. Anarchists and socialists talked about the need for violent solutions to complex problems.

Popular culture in America reflected this aggressive mood. Americans looked to arenas of conflict for their heroes. They glorified boxers like the great John L. Sullivan, and they cheered as violence increased on the Ivy League football fields. They admired body-builders like Bernard Macfadden, who declared, "Weakness Is a Crime." And in the parlors of the wealthy, Teddy Roosevelt stressed, "Cowardice in a race, as in an individual, is the unpardonable sin." Between Sullivan and Roosevelt, and the Americans that admired both men, was a bond forged by the love of violence and power.

This attitude led to the glorification of war and jingoistic nationalism. In public schools throughout the country administrators instituted daily flag salutes and made the recitation of the new pledge of allegiance mandatory. Even the popular music of the day, such as John Philip Sousa's "Stars and Stripes Forever" (1897), had a particularly martial quality and captured the aggressive, patriotic, and boisterous mood of the country.

As the disputes with Germany, Chile, and Great Britain demonstrated, neither the American people nor its leaders feared war. The horrors of the Civil War were dying with the generation that had known them. A younger generation of men, filled with romantic and idealized conceptions of battle and heroism, now openly sought a war of its own. In Washington some politicians even began to view war as a way to unite the country, to quell the protests of angry farmers and laborers.

The Cuban Revolution

In 1895 an independence revolt broke out in Cuba. Indirectly the United States had contributed to the turmoil that gripped the island; one year earlier Congress had passed the Wilson-Gorman Tariff, which raised the duty on foreign sugar, thus crippling the island's most important industry and causing great economic hardship. From the start, Americans expressed far more than casual interest in the rebellion. American businesses had invested over $50 million in Cuba, and the annual trade between the two countries totaled almost $100 million. Overall, however, economics played a relatively unimportant role in forming America's attitude toward the revolution.

Humanitarianism was a far more important factor. Americans cheered the underdog. In Cuba's valiant fight they saw a reenactment of their own war for independence. And the resourceful Cubans made sure that Americans stayed well supplied with stories of Spanish atrocities and Cuban heroism. The Cuban junta (central revolutionary committee) established bases in New York City and Tampa, Florida, and daily provided American newspapers with stories aimed at sympathetic American hearts.

Not all the stories were false. The Cuban—and Spanish—suffering was real enough. Unable to defeat the Spanish army in the field, Cuban revolutionaries resorted to guerrilla tactics. They burned sugarcane fields and blew up mills. They destroyed railroad tracks and bridges. They vowed to win their independence or destroy Cuba in the process. Supported by the populace, the guerrillas succeeded in turning Cuba into an economic and military nightmare for Spanish officials.

In 1896 Spain sent Governor-General Valeriano Weyler y Nicolau to Cuba to crush the rebellion. A man of ruthless clarity, he understood the nature of guerrilla warfare. Guerrillas could not be defeated by conventional engagements; their weapons were patience and endurance and popular support. Weyler knew this, and he decided to fight the guerrillas on their own terms.

His first plan was to rob the guerrillas of their base of support, the rural villages and the sympathetic peasants. He divided the island into military districts and relocated Cubans into guarded camps. He forced more than a half million Cubans from their homes and crowded them into shabbily constructed and unsanitary camps. The food was bad, the water worse. Disease spread with frightful speed and horrifying results. Perhaps 200,000 Cubans died in the camps as Weyler earned the sobriquet "the Butcher."

The Yellow Press

In the United States reports of the suffering Cuban masses filled the front pages of newspapers. In New York City William Randolph Hearst's *New*

York Journal and Joseph Pulitzer's *New York World* used the junta's lurid stories as ammunition in a newspaper war for increased circulation. Reporters freely engaged in "yellow journalism," exaggerating conditions and sensationalizing stories that were in truth depressingly sad and inhumane. Such coverage not only biased American opinion against Spain; it also sold newspapers. When Hearst bought the *Journal* in 1895 it had a daily circulation of 77,000 copies; by the summer of 1898 sales had increased to more than 1.5 million daily.

"Yellow journalism" persuaded many Americans to call for U.S. intervention in the Cuban Revolution. Grover Cleveland, however, was not easily moved by newspaper reports. His administration wanted to protect American interests in Cuba, but was dead set against any sort of military intervention in the conflict, and tried instead to convince Spain to grant "home rule." Unprepared to move beyond vague warnings, Cleveland passed the Cuban problems in 1897 to his successor William McKinley. Like Cleveland, McKinley deplored war. Before he would even consider military intervention, McKinley was determined to exhaust every peaceful alternative.

As many influential Americans called for U.S. intervention, McKinley worked diplomatically to end the fighting. Rather than inflame public opinion, he attempted to remove the issue from public debate. In his inaugural address, for example, he did not even mention Cuba. For a time it appeared that his efforts would succeed. In October 1897 a new government in Spain moved toward granting more autonomy to Cuba. It removed Weyler and promised to end his hated reconcentration program.

Spain moved with glacial slowness, only halfheartedly committed to reform. In Cuba the bloodshed continued, and pressure on McKinley to take stronger action mounted. In May 1897 he dispatched a trusted adviser, William J. Calhoun, to Cuba to provide him with an independent report of conditions on the island. The report confirmed the grim picture presented in American newspapers. "The country was wrapped in the stillness of death and the silence of desolation," Calhoun observed.

In early February 1898, William Randolph Hearst acquired with the help of the Cuban junta a private letter from Enrique Dupuy de Lôme, the Spanish minister in the United States, to a Spanish friend in Cuba. Reprinted on the front page of the *Journal,* the letter contained de Lôme's unguarded and undiplomatic opinion of McKinley. De Lôme called McKinley "weak and a bidder for the admiration of the crowd." Even worse, De Lôme suggested that Spain's new peace policy was mere sham and propaganda.

The letter hit the American public like a bombshell. Although de Lôme resigned, America was in no mood to forget and forgive. Less than one week later a second event rocked America. On the still evening of February 15 an explosion ripped apart the *Maine,* a U.S. battleship anchored in Havana harbor. The ship quickly sank, killing over 250 officers and men. An investigation in 1898 ruled that an external explosion had sunk the *Maine.* Although a recent study blamed the sinking on an internal explosion, in truth, no one knows the definitive answer. At the time, however, Americans were not in an impartial or philosophical mood. Through the streets of American cities went the cry, "'Remember the *Maine!* To Hell with Spain!'"

War was in the air, and it is doubtful if McKinley or any other president could have long preserved peace. Congress was ready for war, and on March 8 approved McKinley's request for $50 million in defense appropriations without a single dissenting vote. Although McKinley continued to work for a diplomatic solution to the crisis, his efforts lacked his earlier energy and optimism. By early April diplomacy had reached its end.

The sinking of the *Maine* was one of the major events leading to the Spanish-American War. It is still uncertain who or what caused the explosion that sank the ship.

On April 11 an exhausted McKinley sent a virtual war message to Congress, asking for authority to use force to end the Cuban war. On April 19 Congress officially acted. It proclaimed Cuba's independence, called for Spain's evacuation, and authorized McKinley to use the army and navy to achieve those ends. In the Teller Amendment, Congress added that the United States had no intention of annexing Cuba for itself. For some Americans it was a great and noble decision. For the men and boys who would have to fight the battles, the war would soon seem considerably less noble.

The Spanish-American War

No simple explanation can account for the Spanish-American War. Economics and imperial ambitions certainly played a part, but no more so than did humanitarianism and selfless concern for the suffering of others. President McKinley tried to find a peaceful solution, but he failed. Some historians and many of his contemporaries have viewed McKinley as a weak, hollow president, a messenger boy for America's financial community. Such was not the case. McKinley did have a vision—a peaceful vision—of America's role in world affairs. But the unpredictability of events and the mood of the nation were more powerful than the president.

In theory the United States had prepared for war with Spain. In 1897 the Navy Department had drawn up contingency plans for a war against Spain for the liberation of Cuba. It had envisioned a war centered mainly in the Caribbean, but the navy had plans to attack the Philippine Islands, which belonged to Spain, and even the coast of Spain, if necessary. In the Caribbean the navy planned to blockade Cuba and assist an army invasion of the island.

In reality, however, the military was not ready for war. The process of mobilizing troops was chaotic and the training given volunteers was inadequate. In addition, the army faced severe supply shortages. Volunteers suffered the most. They were herded into camps, often without such basic equipment as tents and mess kits. Long before they ever faced enemy guns or even saw Cuba, they battled thick wool uniforms, bad food, and deadly sanitary conditions. Far more volunteers died in stateside camps than were killed by Spanish bullets.

For black troops, regulars and volunteers, racism exacerbated already difficult conditions. Since most of the large camps were located in the South—in places such as Tampa, New Orleans, Mobile, and Chickamauga Park, Tennessee—they also had to battle Jim Crow laws and other forms of racial hostility. Once in the camps, they were given the lowest military assignments.

While mobilization was taking place, the navy moved into action. During the tense weeks before the United States went to war against Spain, Theodore Roosevelt, then acting secretary of the navy, wired his friend Commodore George Dewey, leader of America's Asiatic Squadron, to prepare for offensive operations in the Philippine Islands in the event that war against Spain was declared.

Dewey had been anxiously waiting for just that order. At the break of light on the morning of May 1, 1898, Dewey's ships destroyed Spain's Asiatic fleet in Manila Bay. It was a stunning victory. Only one American died, and he of heat prostration.

Not every victory came so easily. Closer to home, the main Spanish forces in Cuba were in control of the strategically important Santiago Bay. To defeat the Spanish it would take the combined efforts of the army and the navy. With this in mind, McKinley ordered 17,000 American troops under the command of Major General William R. Shafter from Tampa to Santiago. Delays, confused orders, and other problems slowed the process, foreshadowing future difficulties. Finally, toward the end of June, American troops landed at the ports of Daiquiri and Siboney.

From there they moved toward Santiago, but the road was little more than a rutted, dirt trail. Slowly the army moved forward, more concerned with broken wagons mired in the mud and tropical diseases than Spanish soldiers.

On July 1 American soldiers learned firsthand the horrors of battle. Blocking the American advance, Spanish troops had dug in along the San Juan Heights and the hamlet of El Caney. From the first, American plans broke down in the face of stiff Spanish opposition. U.S. troops struggled up Kettle and San Juan hills, moving very slowly and suffering alarming casualties. Although outnumbered more than ten to one, Spanish soldiers made U.S. troops pay for every foot they advanced. After America finally secured the enemy positions, correspondent Richard H. Davis wrote, "Another such victory as that of July 1 and our troops must retreat."

Shafter had neither the disposition nor the ability to lead an energetic campaign. Fortunately for him, Spain's forces in Cuba were even less ready to fight. In Santiago, Spanish soldiers faced shortages of food, water, and ammunition. On July 3 the Spanish squadron tried to break an American blockade and force its way out of Santiago Bay. The act was a suicidal move. American guns destroyed the Spanish fleet and killed some 500 Spanish sailors. Only one American died in the decisive engagement.

Little fighting remained. On July 17 the leading Spanish general in Cuba surrendered to Shafter. Timid in war, Shafter was petty in victory. He refused to permit any naval officers to sign the capitulation document, nor would he allow any Cubans to participate in the surrender negotiations and ceremonies. The Cubans who had fought so long and bravely for their independence were denied the glory of their success.

Before the full Spanish surrender, the United States extended its influence in the Caribbean. In late July, General Nelson A. Miles invaded Puerto Rico, Spain's other Caribbean colony. Without any serious resistance U.S. forces took the island. Finally, on August 12, Spain surrendered, granting Cuban independence and ceding Puerto Rico and Guam to the United States. Both countries agreed to settle the fate of the Philippines at a postwar peace conference to be held in Paris.

For America, it had been a short, successful war. Spanish bullets killed only 379 Americans, the smallest number in any of America's declared wars. Disease and other problems cost over 5,000 more lives. If the army's mobilization had been chaotic, its troops had performed heroically under fire. And the navy, which took most of the credit for winning the war, demonstrated the wisdom of its planners. Finally, the war served to bring the North and South closer together as the two sections fought alongside each other rather than against each other. All in all, many Americans agreed with U.S. Ambassador to England John Hay that it had been a "splendid little war."

There was nothing little about the consequences of the war. With the Spanish-American War the United States became an imperial power. The war increased America's appetite for overseas territories. The McKinley administration used the war to annex Hawaii and part of Samoa. In addition, at the Paris Peace Conference the United States wrested the Philippines, Puerto Rico, and Guam from Spain. Although the United States paid Spain $20 million for the Philippines, there was no question that Spain had to negotiate under duress. These new imperial possessions gave the United States strategic bases in the Caribbean and along the trade routes to Asia.

Freeing Cuba

Many Americans favored the annexation of Cuba. In the land grab that ended the war, the idealism of the Teller Amendment and the war's beginning was all but forgotten. When the war ended, U.S. troops stayed in Cuba, and the country was ruled by an American-run military government, which was to remain until "complete tranquility" and a "stable government" existed on the island. Under General Leonard Wood, the military government helped Cuba recover from its terrible conflict with Spain. Wood restored the Cuban economy and promoted reforms in the legal system, education, sanitation, and health care.

In 1903 the United States finally recognized Cuban independence—but under certain conditions. According to the Platt Amendment of 1901, Cuba could exercise self-government, but it could sign no treaties that might limit its independence. Should Cuban independence ever be threatened, the Platt Amendment authorized the United States to intervene in the island's internal and external affairs. The amendment was also written into the 1901 Cuban constitution. In short, for Cuba, independence had the look and feel of an American protectorate.

The Imperial Debate

Compared to the Philippines, Cuba was a minor problem. McKinley's decision to annex the Philippines pleased some Americans and angered many more. Businessmen who dreamed of the rich China markets applauded McKinley's decision. Naval strategists similarly believed it was a wise move. They argued that if the United States failed to take the Philippines, then one of the other major powers—Germany, Japan, or England—probably would. Finally, Protestant missionaries favored annexation to facilitate their evangelical efforts among the Filipinos, undeterred by the knowledge that the Filipinos already favored Roman Catholicism.

Opposed to the annexation of the Philippines was a heterogeneous group of Americans that included such notables as agrarian leader William Jennings Bryan, steel magnate Andrew Carnegie, labor organizer Samuel Gompers, and writer Mark Twain. Their reasons for being anti–imperialists were as varied as their occupations and backgrounds. Some were high-minded idealists who believed that the Filipinos had the right to govern themselves. Others had more selfish reasons for opposing annexation. Samuel Gompers, for example, feared that annexation would lead to an influx of Filipino workers into the United States and hurt the American labor movement. Still others opposed annexation on racial grounds. The annexation of "dependencies inhabited by ignorant and inferior races," noted the *Nation* editor E. L. Godkin, could only lead to trouble.

During early 1899 the imperial debate raged. Even Andrew Carnegie's offer to write a personal check for $20 million to buy the independence of the Philippines failed to end the debate. Ultimately, imperialists and anti–imperialists had different visions for America, and no bridge could span the gulf between these two groups.

The issue was settled on February 6, 1899, when the Senate voted on the Treaty of Paris. Strained tempers were evident in the tense atmosphere. For a time it appeared that the imperialists would not be able to muster the two-thirds majority needed to ratify the treaty. Anti–imperialist William Jennings Bryan ironically saved the imperialist cause. Not wanting to prolong the war by rejecting the treaty, he urged fellow Democrats to vote for ratification. In the close vote of 57 to 27 the Senate ratified the treaty. Undoubtedly Bryan hoped to use the issue of Philippine independence to capture the presidency in 1900, but such was not the case. With ratification of the treaty, the issue lost its sense of urgency and Americans grew tired of the debate.

The War to Crush Filipino Independence

Filipino independence, however, was not an abstract debate in the Philippines. Led by Emilio Aguinaldo, Filipinos had fought bravely against the Spanish both before and after Dewey arrived in Manila. They had no intention of allowing one colonial master to replace another. When it was clear that the United States did not have Filipino interests at heart, Aguinaldo and his followers resumed their fight for independence.

Between 1899 and 1902 American troops and Filipino revolutionaries fought an ugly and destructive colonial war. American soldiers faced a difficult task. Some did not know what they were fighting for, whose interests they were defending, or what rights they were protecting. Others regarded the Filipinos as subhuman. Black American troops fighting to destroy Filipino freedom faced an even greater and more painful

American Empire, 1900

dilemma. Many black soldiers readily identified with Filipino aspirations. Although the majority of black troops professionally followed the orders of their white officers, an unusually large number deserted.

For black and white soldiers alike, however, the actual fighting was bloody and frustrating. Aguinaldo's men were efficient guerrilla warriors. They fought only when victory was certain, usually ambushing small patrols. They burned bridges, destroyed railroads, sniped, and sabotaged. They filled pits with sharpened stakes and tortured prisoners. Some American captives had their ears cut off, and many Filipinos who supported the United States were hacked to death with bolos or buried alive. Aguinaldo's hope was that eventually the game would not be worth the prize and that the American president would call his troops home.

McKinley was not about to do any such thing, and American troops proved just as vicious as the Filipino insurgents. The "water cure," used to obtain information, entailed forcing a prisoner to drink gallons of water and then emptying his stomach quickly with a kick or a punch. In one especially violent campaign U.S. troops were ordered to kill all males ten years old or older who were capable of bearing arms against the United States. Using tactics reminiscent of General Weyler's in Cuba, U.S. troops herded more than 300,000 civilians into concentration centers, where many died of disease and starvation.

Aguinaldo hoped that anti–imperialist Bryan would defeat McKinley for the presidency in 1900, but the November election dashed his hopes. Five months later American troops captured the Filipino leader. That same year McKinley sent a commission under the leadership of William Howard Taft, a federal judge, to the Philippines to improve the country's transportation, education, and public health systems. Aguinaldo's capture and the efforts of the Taft Commission doomed the Philippine independence movement. Approximately 4,200 Americans and over 20,000 Filipino soldiers had died in the struggle. Perhaps another 200,000 Filipino civilians died of famine, disease, and war-related incidents.

Keeping the Doors Open

The war against the Filipinos led to congressional investigations and shocked many Americans. Political and business leaders, however, continued to believe that the Philippines had been worth the fight because the islands were of strategic importance both as a military base and a stepping-stone toward the Asian markets. Yet policymakers understood the popular mood; they knew that the American public would be hostile to any U.S. military venture into China *just* to support trade.

To prevent other countries from carving up China, in 1899 Secretary of State John Hay issued an "open door" note. Hay believed that imperial competition in China was dangerous and economically inefficient. It stimulated costly anticolonial resistance and rebellion and gave no incentive to European countries to improve their economic efficiency. Hay's "open door" note was an attempt to prevent further European partitioning of the Manchu empire and to protect the principle of open trade in China. Under the terms of the Open Door policy, all countries active in China would respect each other's trading rights by imposing no discriminating duties and closing no ports within their spheres of influence. Although most European countries expressed little interest in Hay's Open Door policy—which, after all, benefited the United States the most—in 1900 Hay announced that the European powers had accepted his proposal.

The Chinese themselves had other plans. In the late spring of 1900 a group of Chinese nationalists, known as the Boxers, besieged the Legation Quarter in Peking, calling for the expulsion or death of all westerners in China. By late summer, 1900, a western expeditionary force had crushed the Boxer Rebellion.

These additional troops in China threatened Hay's Open Door policy. On July 3, 1900, during the tensest moment of the Boxer Rebellion, he issued a second "open door" note, calling on all western powers to preserve Chinese independence and uphold "the principle of equal and impartial trade with all parts of the Chinese Empire." Once again, few European countries paid attention to Hay's Open Door policy. Mutual distrust and the fear of provoking a general European war—more than any American plan—prevented the major European powers from dismembering China. Out of Hay's Open Door policy came the idea, held mostly in America, that the United States was China's protector. It was another example of the increasingly active role the United States had taken in world affairs.

Conclusion

Thirty-two years separated the inauguration of Ulysses S. Grant and the assassination of William McKinley, but during that generation America and the presidency changed radically. Part of the change can be attributed to growth—industry boomed, the population swelled, agricultural production increased. The growth was also psychological. During those years many Americans achieved a new sense of confidence. After 250 years of looking westward across America's seemingly limitless acres of land, they

Chronology of Key Events

1867	Russia sells Alaska to the United States
1870	Annexation of the Dominican Republic rejected by U.S. Senate
1889	Britain, Germany, and the United States agree to share control of Samoa
1890	Captain Alfred Thayer Mahan's *The Influence of Sea Power upon History* published
1893	Queen Liliuokalani of Hawaii deposed
1895	Venezuela border dispute; Cuban revolt against Spain begins
1898	*Maine* explodes in Havana harbor; Spanish-American War begins; Hawaii is annexed
1899	Filipino rebellion begins; Open Door note issued to prevent further partitioning
1900	Boxer Rebellion; Second Open Door note issued
1901	Platt Amendment
1902	Philippine revolt ends

began to look toward the oceans and consider the possibilities of a new form of expansion. They also began to follow the imperial examples of England, France, Italy, and Germany. Talk of world power, world outlook, and world responsibilities colored their rhetoric.

This outward thrust was accompanied and enhanced by the growth of presidential power. Grant worked hard for the annexation of the Dominican Republic, but Congress blocked his efforts. By the turn of the century, however, Congress clearly expected the president to lead the nation in the area of foreign affairs. Although the presidents pursued different policies, they agreed that the United States should have a greater influence in world affairs. None questioned the fundamental fact that the United States was and should be a world power.

Many questions, nevertheless, remained unanswered. What were the rights of a world power? What were its responsibilities? What were its duties? The limits and possibilities of American power had yet to be defined and explored. The next three presidents—Roosevelt, Taft, and Wilson—would help to define how the United States would use its new found power.

Suggestions for Further Reading

Overviews of American imperialism include Charles S. Campbell, Jr., *Transformation of American Foreign Relations* (1976); David F. Healy, *U.S. Expansionism: Imperialist Urge in the 1890s* (1970), and *Drive to Hegemony: The United States in the Caribbean* (1988); Walter LaFeber, *The New Empire* (1963); Thomas G. Paterson and Stephen C. Rabe, *Imperial Surge: The United States Abroad* (1992).

For studies focusing on the Spanish-American War see Philip Foner, *The Spanish-American-Cuban War and the Birth of American Imperialism,* 2 vols. (1972); Frank Freidel, *The Splendid Little War* (1958); Stuart C. Miller, *"Benevolent Assimilation": The American Conquest of the Philippines* (1982); David F. Trask, *The War with Spain in 1898* (1981).

For information on the anti-imperialists consult Robert L. Beisner, *Twelve Against Empire* (1968). Concerning the home front during the war see Gerald F. Linderman, *The Mirror of War: American Society and the Spanish-American War* (1974). Issues confronting black Americans during the age of imperialism are examined in Willard B. Gatewood, Jr., *Black Americans and the White Man's Burden* (1975).

Chapter 22

The Progressive Struggle

The Progressive Impulse
America in 1901
Voices for Change

Progressives in Action
The Drive to Organize
Urban Beginnings
Reform Reaches the State Level

Progressivism Moves to the National Level
Roosevelt and New Attitudes Toward Government Power
Taft and Quiet Progressivism
Wilson and Moral Progressivism

Progressivism in the International Arena
Big Stick Diplomacy
Dollar Diplomacy
Missionary Diplomacy

Progressive Accomplishments, Progressive Failures
The Impact of Legislation
Winners and Losers

Times had changed by 1902 when George F. Baer declared "anthracite mining is business and not a religious, sentimental or academic proposition." Those tough-minded words might have won public approval at an earlier time, but many believed that Baer, spokesperson for mine owners in Pennsylvania, was merely being pig-headed in his response to a request by John Mitchell of the United Mine Workers (UMW) for arbitration of a labor dispute. There was an unusual amount of support for the coal miners' position. Exposés had increased popular awareness of miserable working conditions, and the union's demands seemed reasonable: a nine-hour day, recognition of the union, a 10 to 20 percent increase in wages, and a fair weighing of the coal mined. Mitchell repeatedly stated the miners' willingness to accept arbitration, both before and after 50,000 miners walked out of the pits in May 1902.

Skillfully led, the coal miners stood firm month after month. By September, the nation's coal reserves were running short and prices were rising. With winter approaching, newspaper after newspaper expressed disgust with the mine owners, and some tentatively suggested government ownership of the mines.

On October 3 President Theodore Roosevelt presided over a conference in the White House attended by Mitchell, Baer, Attorney General Philander C. Knox, and other labor leaders and mine operators. Baer was still not in a mood to be cooperative. Refusing to speak directly to Mitchell, Baer urged Roosevelt to prosecute UMW leaders under the Sherman Antitrust Act and to use federal troops to break the strike, just as Cleveland had done in the 1894 Pullman strike. While Mitchell "behaved like a gentleman" according to Roosevelt, Baer remained obstinate.

When the mine owners returned to Pennsylvania, they took actions that indicated they might use force to break the strike. Roosevelt's response was to begin preparations to send 10,000 federal troops to take over and operate the mines. A compromise was soon reached, under which the miners returned to work and Roosevelt appointed a commission to arbitrate the dispute.

Decidedly pro-business, the commission's findings were essentially conservative: a 10 percent wage increase, reduction of working hours to eight hours a day for a handful of miners and to nine for most, no recognition for the union, and continuation of the traditional manner of weighing coal. The commission also suggested a 10 percent increase in the price of coal.

Nevertheless, for the first time, a president did not give knee-jerk support to business. The federal government became not merely a champion of the status quo, but also an arbiter of change. This retreat from laissez-faire principles was motivated by the demands of the middle class and

President Roosevelt, surrounded here by coal miners after their 1902 strike, set a precedent by threatening the use of force against management rather than labor.

workers. By 1902 many middle-class citizens had rejected the heavy-handed tactics of management, and sought instead a more orderly, stable, and just society through government intervention. Workers began flexing their political muscles at the ballot box, and Americans of all classes were learning the limits of individualism and joining together in organizations to accomplish their goals. National leaders such as Roosevelt began to recognize the need for change in order to preserve stable government and the capitalist system. For a variety of motives, a plethora of legislation was enacted—sometimes with unintended results.

The Progressive Impulse

Americans exalted progress as a basic characteristic of their nation's distinctiveness. Technology was reshaping the human environment in dramatic ways. In the late 1890s, as people seemed to stop and look around at their new world, much filled them with pride. Some of what they saw seemed outmoded or disruptive, but these problems appeared eminently solvable. Modern minds were explaining and harnessing natural forces. Could they not also understand and control human behavior? Could they not eliminate conflict and bring harmony to competing interests through some simple adjustments in the system? Americans increasingly answered "yes" and called themselves "progressives."

America in 1901

The twentieth century opened with a rerun of the 1896 election between William Jennings Bryan and William McKinley. Although the outcome was the same, much was different. By 1900 the crises of the 1890s had largely passed. Prosperity had returned and was shared by many. The nation also reveled in its newfound international power following the Spanish-American War. The social fabric seemed to be on the mend, but memories of the depression of the 1890s still haunted Americans, and society's blemishes appeared more and more intolerable.

Unequal distribution of wealth and income persisted. Four-fifths of Americans lived on a subsistence level, while a handful lived in incredible opulence. In 1900 Andrew Carnegie's income was $23 million; the average working man earned $500. The wealth of a few was increased by the exploitation of women and children. One out of five women worked, earning wages as low as $6 a week, while the sacrifice of the country's young to the god of economic growth was alarming.

Factory working conditions were horrifying, and for many Americans housing conditions were as bad or worse. One investigator described a Chicago neighborhood, remarking on the "filthy and rotten tenements . . . dilapidated outhouses, the broken sewer pipes, the piles of garbage fairly alive with diseased odors." At the same time the Vanderbilts summered in a "cottage" of 70 rooms.

The middle class experienced neither extreme. Its members did have their economic grievances, however. Prosperity increased the cost of living by 35 percent in less than a decade, while many middle-class incomes remained the same. Many blamed the monopolies and watched with alarm as trusts, proving to be immune to the Sherman Act, proliferated rapidly, thereby decreasing competition and opportunity. People came to believe that they had to find political solutions to wrestle government from the hands of a few and return it to the "people" in order to solve the nation's problems. The great democratic experiment seemed to have run afoul of wealthy industrialists, corrupt state and federal legislators, and urban political machines.

Most of these problems were not new; neither were the proposed solutions. Progressivism was rooted in the Gilded Age, but while reform had been a sideshow earlier, it now became a national preoccupation. Progressivism was more broadly based and enjoyed greater appeal than any previous reform movement. One reason it did so was the diversity and pervasiveness of the voices calling for change.

Voices for Change

By 1900 Americans had done nothing less than reinterpret their understanding of their world. Under the old, classical interpretation, the universe was governed by absolute, natural laws. There was divine logic to all and truth was universal—the same at all times. According to this vision, public policy should not attempt to change the course of those laws through human-made ones. Such logic justified the concentration of wealth as well as the lack of governmental regulation of business and assistance to the poor and weak.

Social Darwinism, laissez-faire economics, and the Gospel of Wealth never enjoyed total acceptance. Throughout the Gilded Age, challenges and alternative visions had chipped away at their bases of support. In 1879 Henry George wrote *Progress and Poverty* which addressed the unequal distribution of wealth. His solution was a "single tax" on land to control speculative profits. In *Looking Backward* (1888) Edward Bellamy provided a glimpse of a utopian society based upon a state-controlled economy propelled by cooperation rather than competition. These writings profoundly influenced the Populists, the Socialists, and many who called themselves progressive.

In literary circles, realist writers dethroned romanticism, describing the world as it was, not as it should be. The naturalists portrayed the powerlessness of the individual against the uncaring forces of urbanization and industrialization. Artists of the "ashcan" school painted urban scenes teeming with problems as well as life. Thus art and literature became mirrors of social concerns.

A revolution was also taking place in the academic world. One of the most important changes was the democratization of higher education. From 1870 to 1910 the number of colleges and universities nearly doubled. Higher education became less elitist, white, religious, and male, as female and black enrollment increased. Professors at these institutions became increasingly middle-class, and therefore had less interest in supporting the status quo.

Another academic change was the revolt against formalism. Intellectuals had once sought to explain the world by formulating abstract, universal theories. The new scholars, especially in the emerging social sciences, began by collecting concrete data which did not support the so-called natural laws propounded by their predecessors.

Whereas theories had prescribed limits to human action, facts now became weapons for change. A new breed of economists conducted field research to gather data, and their findings challenged traditional laissez-faire doctrines. To continue policies based on competition seemed absurd in an economy dominated by monopolies. A group of sociologists calling themselves "Reform Darwinists" rejected Spencer's Social Darwinism as another tool of exploitation. They accepted evolutionary principles and the influence of environment, but denied that people were merely pawns manipulated by natural forces. Human intelligence was an active factor that could control and change the environment, especially when people worked together. The goal of many social scientists was a more orderly society, based on rational planning and social engineering to do away with strife and unregulated growth.

Legal scholars also joined the assault on formalism. During the Gilded Age courts had read laissez-faire principles into their interpretation of the Constitution. Decisions striking down regulatory and reform legislation invoked such abstract principles as the sanctity of property rights and contracts. Challenging laissez-faire jurisprudence, Supreme Court Justice Oliver Wendell Holmes, Jr. rejected the idea that laws had ever been the logical result of pure, universal principles, arguing instead that laws had been and should be based on "the felt necessities of the time." Lawyer Louis D. Brandeis successfully argued these ideas in 1908. That year the Supreme Court upheld a ten-hour law for women working in Oregon laundries in *Muller v. Oregon*, primarily because of social research documenting the damage done to women's health by long working hours.

As Americans began to reject absolute truths and universal principles, the remaining question was how to determine right from wrong and good from bad. The answer came from philosopher William James with his doctrine of pragmatism. Ideas, he argued, were to be judged by their results. An idea that produced a socially desirable end was right and good. Philosophical thought was useless unless it focused on solving problems. Pragmatism was a distinctly American philosophy and found many adherents. One of them, John Dewey, applied its principles to education. Arguing against rote memorization of a static body of facts, he advocated that education should be based on experience and directed toward creativity and personal growth.

The literary and intellectual currents of the era helped to set the stage for reform, but the impact of organized religion on progressivism was even more profound. Embracing what became known as the Social Gospel movement, theology schools added courses in Christian sociology to teach "the application of our common Christianity to . . . social conditions." The Social Gospelers used the tools of scientific inquiry to root out and solve human problems in order to usher in the "Kingdom of God on Earth." Many settlement-house workers, such as Jane Addams, sought to use their Christian faith to solve social problems.

A final spark that ignited public interest in reform was popular journalism. The expansion of education and the growth of cities provided a mass audience for low-priced magazines such as *Collier's* and *McClure's*. Their editors quickly discovered people's fascination with evil and launched a series of exposés by investigative reporters. Labeled "muckrakers" by Teddy Roosevelt, they brought to light corruption in almost every facet of society.

Whether published serially in magazines or published as books, the exposés of the muckrakers shocked the public with their indictments of child labor, unscrupulous industrialists, or corrupt politicians. Ida Tarbell called Standard Oil "one of the most gigantic and dangerous conspiracies ever attempted." Lincoln Steffens denounced urban politics in *The Shame of the Cities,* and the socialist Upton Sinclair described the horrifying conditions in the meat-packing industry in *The Jungle.*

Progressives in Action

Voices of change echoed a genuine transformation of popular sentiment. Americans of all classes began calling themselves "progressives" and sought to reform whichever social evil captured their attention. Most believed problems could be legislated away, and that human progress would come through cooperation rather than competition. Thus they organized themselves into diverse groups that shared their own particular vision of a better world.

So varied were the aims of people calling themselves progressive that to think of progressivism as a movement is a mistake. There was little unity except in the idea that people could improve society. Most progressives, however, were middle-class moderates who abhorred radical solutions. Motivated by a fear and hatred of class conflict, such progressives sought to save the capitalists from their own excesses and thereby salvage the system. Their goal was an orderly and harmonious society.

The Drive to Organize

Organizing was a major activity at the turn of the century. Such professional groups as the American Medical Association (AMA) began to emerge in modern form. These groups reflected the rise of a new professionalism that helped to create a body of "experts" to be tapped by progressives wanting to impose order and efficiency on social institutions.

The organizations themselves also acted to effect change. The AMA's major goal was to improve professional standards. The government assisted by enacting laws that required licenses to practice medicine. Minimum standards for medical education were adopted, closing the doors of dozens of marginal medical schools, several of which trained minority doctors. The result of the new professionalism in most fields was to limit the number of practitioners. This helped weed out incompetents, but it also increased the incomes of the remaining practitioners and often reduced minority participation. In other words, order, stability, and improved standards often came at the cost of decreased opportunity.

To a large extent, middle-class women led in the organization of reform. Technology and domestic help lessened the burdens of running a home for these women, but a stigma remained on paid employment. Women's clubs provided an outlet for the energies and abilities of many competent and educated women. Local organizations flourished and reform groups founded and led mainly by women sprang up. The majority of activist, middle-class women became involved in movements closely linked to their assigned social roles as guardians of morality and nurturers of the family. One movement dominated by women's groups that enjoyed a strong resurgence in the late nineteenth century was prohibition.

By 1898 the Woman's Christian Temperance Union had 10,000 local branches. It was assisted by the Anti-Saloon League and such church organizations as the Temperance Society of the Methodist Episcopal church. Some of the prohibitionists were Protestant fundamentalists who considered the consumption of alcohol a sin; others saw it as the root cause of many social problems. While the AMA reported the physically devastating effects of alcoholism, urban reformers saw the consequences of alcohol abuse in domestic violence, accidents, and pauperism.

Many middle-class women came to believe that aid to the poor was an inadequate response to society's ills. By attacking the causes of poverty, they sought to improve wages and working conditions, especially for women, and to protect children from exploitation. The National Consumers League lobbied for protective legislation for women and children as well as better working and living conditions for all. Like most progressives, child labor reformers gathered data and photographs to document horrors for legislators at the local, state, and finally federal level.

Some reformers were not content to be merely advocates for the poor and the weak; they wanted to become directly involved with such people in an effort to educate them and organize them to help themselves. Here again middle-class women played a key role. Foremost among such activities was the settlement house movement. Following the lead of Jane Addams of Hull House in Chicago, many young college-educated women moved into slum neighborhoods to live and work with those they sought to help.

More than unselfishness motivated such women, some of whom wanted more freedom than marriage and part-time volunteer work seemed to offer. One appeal of settlement work was that men did not control it. The result was a growing social feminism that cut across class lines.

At first, such activity seemed to draw attention away from the suffrage movement. Women's roles in progressive reforms, however, convinced many people that women not only deserved the right to vote but also that their political participation would be socially beneficial. Arguments based on women's "special role," however, cut both ways. Some male writers charged that voting was so "unnatural" for women that pregnant women would miscarry and nursing mothers' milk would cease to flow.

Convinced that only national action could be effective, the National American Woman Suffrage Association, led by Carrie Chapman Catt after 1915, began a broad-based campaign for a federal amendment to the Constitution. More militant women who followed Alice Paul, founder of the National Woman's party in 1914, preferred the tactics of British suffragists who had picketed, gone on hunger strikes, and actively confronted both politicians and police.

Another group in the social justice movement worked to protect the rights of African Americans. White Southerners had continued to devise

Women employed a variety of tactics in their fight for the vote. Here Dr. Anne Shaw and Carrie Chapman Catt lead 20,000 marchers down Fifth Avenue in New York City.

forms of racial control to replace slavery, using legal segregation, disfranchisement, and violence. From the beginning, blacks resisted white efforts to suppress them. In city after city, African Americans utilized almost every tool and tactic that would prove successful in the 1960s—marching, lobbying, petitioning, challenging court decisions, and boycotting. Under the leadership of Booker T. Washington, they also tried conciliation. But nothing stemmed the rising tide of racism.

As conditions grew worse, educated African Americans became increasingly disenchanted with Booker T. Washington's conciliatory approach, his suppression of dissent by his fellow blacks, his influence with white politicians and philanthropists, and his control of much of the black press. The so-called anti–Bookerite radicals found their spokesperson in W. E. B. Du Bois. Unlike Washington, who had been born into slavery and educated at an industrial school, Du Bois was born to free parents in Massachusetts and became the first African American to receive a doctorate from Harvard.

Du Bois expressed the frustrations and dreams of his fellow blacks and criticized Washington's leadership in *The Souls of Black Folk* (1903). Du Bois took exception to Washington's refusal to recognize the importance of the vote, his emphasis on industrial education at the expense of higher education, his reluctance to criticize as well as praise white actions, and his willingness to give up previously won rights. Rejecting Washington's gradualist approach, Du Bois believed the key to black advancement was in cultivating what he called the "Talented Tenth." To him, more of the limited education funds should go to train the ablest ten percent of African Americans for leadership through liberal arts and professional schooling.

Relations between Washington and Du Bois deteriorated steadily. By 1905 their differences were so great that Du Bois joined William Monroe Trotter in forming the Niagara Movement, an organization devoted to two main objectives: opposition to Washington's leadership of the black community and the demand for "full manhood rights." Although only about 50 educated African Americans—mainly northerners—joined, it played an important role in convincing northern white progressives that an alternative to Washington was desirable. When a white mob in Springfield, Illinois, went on a rampage against African Americans, concerned whites joined with Du Bois to found the National Association for the Advancement of Colored People (NAACP) in 1909. At first the group was led and dominated by whites; Du Bois was the only African American to hold a responsible position. The organization became more black over time, but the focus of its activities remained essentially the same: education and propaganda, court challenges to discrimination, and lobbying for such legislation as a federal antilynching law.

Immigration policy became another source of organizational activity. The American Protective Association (1887) sought to control and limit the access of immigrants by lobbying for literacy tests and quotas. Some progressive Americans, however, welcomed the nation's new pluralism, and formed the North American League for Immigrants to "protect the newcomers from unscrupulous bankers, steamship captains and fellow countrymen."

Even if most were middle-class citizens, progressives obviously came from all classes, and within classes there was a diversity of responses to the modernization of society and the economy. Many businesspeople organized to fight regulatory and labor legislation in such groups as the National Association of Manufacturers. Others joined moderate reformist groups such as the Chamber of Commerce. Even more liberal was the National Civic Federation, which sought to bring together employers and employees to discuss industrial problems.

The drive to organize pervaded American society, creating such diverse groups as the Boy Scouts of America (1910), the Rotary Club (1915), the National Collegiate Athletic Association (1906), and the National Birth Control League (1915). As Americans came to believe in cooperative efforts to achieve goals, they also began to look to government for answers—starting at the local level and moving up to Washington.

Urban Beginnings

Progressivism was largely a response to modernization. It first confronted the most visible problems, most of which were found in the cities. Incredibly rapid increases in urban populations outpaced the ability of "small-town" governments to meet the challenges. Political machines provided needed services but came under attack in the 1890s as inefficient and corrupt.

Reformers demanded that governments be run "not by partisans, either Republican nor Democratic, but by men who are skilled in business management and social service." In their struggle for efficient, nonpartisan government, urban reformers fought for the secret ballot and voter registration. In an effort to do away entirely with "boss rule," many municipalities hired city managers or appointed commissioners to conduct city business.

Middle-class progressives sometimes found their will thwarted by lower-class voters. Breaking up urban machines often destroyed the informal welfare networks that met the needs of the poor. In 1901 the Tammany Hall machine recaptured New York with the campaign slogan "To hell with reform." Poor immigrants did not accept that their ignorance and "foreign ways" were at the root of urban problems.

In a number of cities voters elected mayors who sympathized with working-class objectives. Tom L. Johnson, elected mayor of Cleveland in 1901, expanded social services and brought about the public ownership of the waterworks, gas and electric utilities, and public transportation, thereby reducing their costs to the poor. After his election in 1899, Mayor Samuel "Golden Rule" Jones of Toledo, Ohio, reformed the police department and worked to provide free kindergartens, playgrounds, golf courses, and concerts. Advocating public ownership of utilities, many Socialists also showed growing strength at the local level. In 1910 Milwaukee elected a Socialist mayor, and by 1912 about 1,000 held offices in 33 states and 160 cities and towns.

Urban progressivism was obviously not a coherent, unified movement. Different groups succeeded at different times in different cities. Social services were cut to lower business taxes in some cities and expanded in others. In most cities the progressives attacked unhealthy living conditions with varying degrees of success. By the turn of the century, however, more and more people began to look to the states to solve problems.

Reform Reaches the State Level

Because cities had little power and the federal government seemed too remote, the states became major battlegrounds for reform. Leadership of state progressivism was as diverse and complex as urban progressivism, and drew its support from equally diverse constituencies.

State progressives pursued four major goals: establishing "direct democracy," protecting the public by regulating the economy, increasing state services, and social control. By World War I many states had adopted political procedures designed to give the people a more direct say in running the government, such as initiative, referendum, and recall. An initiative allowed voters to propose legislative changes, usually by petition; a referendum gave the public a mechanism for voting directly on controversial legislation; recall provided a way to remove elected officials. Many states also established direct primaries, the secret ballot, voter registration, and corrupt practices legislation. The drive for direct democracy culminated in the Seventeenth Amendment to the Constitution (1913), which substituted the popular election of senators for their election by state legislatures.

The victories of women suffragists at the state level also expanded democracy. Washington became the fifth state to give women the vote in 1910. California acted the next year, and four other western states followed suit by 1916. That year Jeannette Rankin was elected to Congress from Montana. These victories encouraged the efforts to obtain a constitutional amendment allowing women to vote.

Clearly, progressive actions to protect the public and regulate the economy took many forms. In the West, especially, the emphasis was on regulating railroads and utilities, and legislatures created commissions to regulate the rates charged by both.

In the industrialized states workmen's compensation became a major goal. Then in 1911 a major tragedy chilled the hearts of Americans when a fire broke out at the Triangle Shirtwaist Company in New York City. Because the doors were locked and many fire escape ladders were either broken or missing, 147 workers, mostly women and girls, lost their lives in the blaze. The relatives of many victims sued the company, and some received large settlements. After the Triangle fire, the idea of mandatory insurance grew in popularity with the support of many factory owners, who did not want the expense of lawsuits filed by workers. Between 1910 and 1916, 32 states enacted workmen's compensation laws.

The work of the National Child Labor Committee and other organizations moved states to legislate protection for women and children. Progressives gathered evidence of the harm done by long working hours and unsafe, unhealthy conditions, and demanded state action. By 1916, 32 states had laws regulating the hours women and children could work. Eleven had specified minimum wages for women, and every state regulated child labor in some manner. Other protective legislation included building and sanitary codes.

A number of states also expanded social services. Because of lobbying by settlement house workers, by 1914 some 20 states had provided mother's pensions to widows or abandoned wives with dependent children. Funding for education also increased, with the expansion of compulsory education to the high school level. Support often came from businesses, which saw public education as a means of preparing individuals for life in an industrial society. As a result, very few public schools were modeled on John Dewey's progressive educational doctrines, and instead promoted discipline and punctuality.

In the South progressivism was for whites only. Increased school funding was common, but the bulk went to educating white children, the *Plessy* v. *Ferguson* formula of "separate but equal" facilities notwithstanding. In 1919 southern states spent an average of $12.16 per white student and $3.29 per black student. More interested in social control than in social justice, southern whites trumpeted segregation as a reform, and often had the tacit approval of many northern progressives.

Other forms of social control, such as prohibition, also enjoyed considerable success at the state level. Prohibitionists won many victories in the states, especially in the South, where Protestant fundamentalism and the race question figured prominently in the debate. One southern prohibitionist argued that "whiskey must be taken out of the Negro's hands," and that it was the duty "of the stronger race to forego its own personal liberty for the protection of the weaker race." By 1916 nineteen states had adopted prohibition.

The legacy of progressivism in the states was mixed, as were the motives of state reformers. Regardless of their goals, most eventually turned to the federal government for help. They had little choice. As one reformer stated: "When I was in the city council . . . fighting for a shorter work day, [my opponents] told me to go to the legislature; now [my fellow legislators] tell me to go to Congress for a national law. When I get there and demand it, they will tell me to go to hell."

Progressivism Moves to the National Level

When McKinley was reelected in 1900, few expected a national reform leader; but for a quirk of fate they would have been right. On September 6, 1901, anarchist Leon Czolgosz shot McKinley, and eight days later Vice President Theodore Roosevelt became president. Many remembered that during the Pullman strike Roosevelt had suggested shooting the strikers. Most therefore did not expect the action he took in the 1902 coal strike. Nor did they think Roosevelt would help usher in an era of reform that would span almost two decades, resulting in a massive amount of legislation and four constitutional amendments by 1920.

Roosevelt and New Attitudes Toward Government Power

Roosevelt became the most forceful president since Lincoln, but few men have looked or sounded less presidential. He was short, nearsighted, beaver-toothed, and talked in a high-pitched voice. A frail, asthmatic child, he seemed intent on proving his manliness. Thus his life became a robust adventure of sports, hunting, and camping. His exuberance, vitality, and wit captivated most Americans. To understand him, an observer declared, one had to remember "the president is really only six years old." He was not a simple man, however. His hobbies included writing history books, and he displayed a keen intellect that he had honed as a student at Harvard.

Born into an aristocratic Dutch family in New York, Roosevelt rejected a leisurely life for the rough and tumble world of politics. His privileged background made him an unlikely candidate for a reformer, yet he ended up making reform both fun and respectable. He saw himself as a conservative, but felt that in in order to preserve what was vital, one had to reform.

Roosevelt shared two progressive sentiments. One was that government should be efficiently run by able, competent people. The other was that industrialization had created the need for expanded governmental action. Roosevelt reorganized and revitalized the executive branch, modernized the army command structure and the consular service, and pursued the federal regulation of the economy that has characterized twentieth-century America.

Although he was later remembered more for his "trust-busting" and "Square Deal," Roosevelt considered conservation his greatest domestic accomplishment. In 1902 he backed the Newlands Reclamation Act, which set aside the proceeds from public land sales for irrigation and reclamation projects. He also used presidential power to add almost 150 million acres to national forests and to preserve valuable coal and water sites for national development. With his chief forester, Gifford Pinchot, he sponsored a National Conservation Congress in 1908.

Some businesspeople already disliked Roosevelt for his conservation policies. He further alienated the business community by his handling of the coal strike, and again when the Justice Department filed a suit against the Northern Securities Company under the Sherman Antitrust Act. Northern Securities was a wise choice for action. It was a highly unpopular combination of northwestern railroad systems controlled by such heavyweights as James J. Hill and J. P. Morgan. In 1904 the Supreme Court ordered the company's dissolution. That same year, in a case against the major meat packers, the Court also reversed the *E. C. Knight* ruling of 1895 that exempted manufacturing from federal antitrust law.

The rulings pleased Roosevelt, who rejected the Court's earlier narrow, strict interpretations of the Constitution. Roosevelt's trust-busting was an answer to progressive prayers, since antimonopoly was a strong component of progressivism. Yet Roosevelt was not a true convert to trust-busting. He attacked trusts that abused their power and left alone trusts that acted responsibly. He preferred to negotiate differences, and to do so he established in 1904 a Bureau of Corporations within the recently formed Department of Commerce and Labor.

Campaigning on the promise to provide a "Square Deal" for all Americans, Roosevelt easily defeated the Democratic candidate Alton B. Parker in the 1904 presidential election. Now elected in his own right, he launched into expanding the regulatory power of the federal government. His top priority over the objection of conservative Republican senators was to control the railroads by expanding the power of the Interstate Commerce Commission (ICC). Although the Elkins Act, passed in 1903, had already eliminated rebates, Roosevelt wanted to give the ICC the power to set shipping rates. Through shrewd political maneuvering he got this with the Hepburn Act of 1906.

The publication of Upton Sinclair's *The Jungle* in that same year caused a consumer uproar for regulation of the food and drug industries. An investigation of the meat-packing industry ordered by Roosevelt proved the truth of Sinclair's charges of filth and contamination. As a result, Congress passed the Pure Food and Drug Act and the Meat Inspection Act on the same day in 1906. By 1908 Roosevelt had left his indelible mark on the nation and decided not to run for reelection. He cast his support to William Howard Taft, who easily defeated William Jennings Bryan, the Democratic nominee and loser for the third time. Roosevelt then retired and went off to hunt lions in Africa.

Taft and Quiet Progressivism

William Howard Taft brought to the presidency a distinguished record of public service. An Ohio lawyer, he had served as a federal judge, the first civil governor of the Philippines, and secretary of war. Weighing more than 350 pounds, Taft was far from charismatic and indeed quite shy. He was incapable of rallying public support for any cause, and reformers were especially skeptical about him.

Taft was essentially more conservative than Roosevelt, especially in his view of limited rather than expansive governmental power. On the other hand, Taft was far more the trust-buster than Roosevelt, initiating 43 antitrust indictments during his one term in office. He also supported the eight-hour day and favored legislation to improve mine safety. He urged passage of the Mann-Elkins Act of 1910, which increased the rate-setting power of the ICC and extended its jurisdiction to telephone and telegraph companies.

Nevertheless, Taft was not forceful enough to preside effectively over the growing divisions within the Republican party. The conservatives, led by the powerful Senator Nelson W. Aldrich, were determined to draw the line against further reform, while progressive Republicans such as Robert La Follette and George Norris were growing rebellious. Conflict came on several fronts. The first was the tariff. In his campaign Taft had promised a lower tariff, but in the end he accepted the much compromised Payne-Aldrich Tariff, which actually raised some key duties. It disappointed reformers immensely. Taft had suffered a defeat, but foolishly did not admit it; instead he called the tariff the "best" ever passed.

Caught in the middle of several conflicts, Taft eventually alienated the progressive wing of his party as well as Teddy Roosevelt. He first supported and then abandoned party insurgents who challenged the power of conservative Speaker of the House "Uncle Joe" Cannon. Later, when chief forester Gifford Pinchot protested a sale of public lands by Secretary of the Interior Richard A. Ballinger, Taft fired him, an action that infuriated both conservationists and Roosevelt.

By 1912 progressive Republicans were ready to bolt the party if Taft were renominated, and Roosevelt declared his intention to run. The fight for the nomination became bitter, but, as president, Taft was able to control the party convention. The defeated Roosevelt walked out with his supporters and formed a third party, known as the Progressive or Bull Moose party.

The Progressive Party's platform endorsed such wide-ranging reforms as abolition of child labor; federal old-age, accident, and unemployment insurance programs; an eight-hour day; and women's suffrage. At Roosevelt's request, however, a plank supporting black equality was deleted.

With the Republicans divided, Democratic chances of recapturing the White House increased. A hard fight for the Democratic nomination ensued, which New Jersey's progressive governor, Woodrow Wilson, won on the forty-sixth ballot. The Socialist party nominated Eugene V. Debs, making it a four-way race.

As soon became apparent, the real battle was between Wilson and Roosevelt. The campaign produced an unusually high level of debate over the proper role of government in a modern, industrialized society. Labeling his program the "New Freedom," Wilson aimed to restore competition by trust-busting. Roosevelt, on the other hand, believed that big business was not necessarily bad, but needed to be regulated. His answer was the "New Nationalism"—the expansion of federal power to control rather than dismantle the trusts. Big government would offset the power of big business. The rhetoric of the two candidates differed sharply, but in their presidencies each practiced a little of both the "New Freedom" and "New Nationalism."

The split in the Republican party enabled the Democrats to capture not only the White House but also the Senate. Democrats also consolidated their control of the House, so Wilson entered the presidency with his party solidly in power, even though he did not receive a majority of the popular vote. He got 6.3 million votes, Roosevelt 4.1 million, Taft 3.5 million, and Debs nearly 1 million. In the electoral college, however, Wilson won an impressive 435 votes to Roosevelt's 88 and a mere 8 for Taft.

Table 22.1

Election of 1912

Candidate	Party	Popular Vote	Electoral Vote
Woodrow Wilson	Democratic	6,296,547	435
Theodore Roosevelt	Progressive (Bull Moose)	4,118,571	88
William H. Taft	Republican	3,486,720	8
	Minor Parties	1,135,697	—

Wilson and Moral Progressivism

The son and grandson of Presbyterian ministers, Woodrow Wilson grew up in the South and practiced law in Atlanta before receiving his doctorate from Johns Hopkins University. His book *Congressional Government* was published in 1895, and he became president of Princeton University in 1902 before being elected governor of New Jersey. His religion was an important factor in his personality, and he exuded a self-righteousness which was not endearing. Although much less charismatic, Wilson did resemble Roosevelt in his view of the role of the president. Roosevelt had called the presidency a "bully pulpit," and Wilson agreed that the president should be the "political leader of the nation."

Wilson's activism coincided with growing demands for further reform. Investigations and amendments launched earlier came to fruition during his presidency. The result was an outpouring of legislation. In 1913, his first year in office, Congress passed the Underwood Tariff, which significantly lowered duties for the first time since the Civil War. To recoup lost revenues, a graduated income tax was added to the act, and was ratified as the Sixteenth Amendment.

Congress passed banking reform the same year. Following the panic of 1907, Congress launched investigations into its causes. Everyone, including bankers, had come to believe the nation's banking system needed to be stabilized by governmental action. As a result, the Federal Reserve Act of 1913 was a compromise. It established the Federal Reserve System of 12 regional banks owned by bankers but under the control of a presidentially appointed Federal Reserve Board.

In 1914 Congress also took actions to deal with monopolies and to regulate business. In September it established the Federal Trade Commission to replace the Bureau of Corporations. The five-person body was charged with investigating alleged violations of antitrust law and could issue "cease and desist" orders against corporations found guilty of unfair trade practices. The next month the Clayton Antitrust Act sought to close some of the loopholes of the Sherman Act and prohibited a number of business practices such as price discrimination. One provision declared that labor unions were not to be considered illegal combinations in restraint of trade—a move designed to undermine the use of court injunctions against strikers.

At that point Wilson believed he had accomplished his agenda. A firm opponent of paternalistic government, he did not support further labor legislation or farm-credit plans. As the election of 1916 approached, however, progressives reminded him of the importance of the farm and labor vote. Legislation to win those votes soon followed. Farmers were

A distinguished professor, Woodrow Wilson brought both competence and a grim moral determination to the presidency.

given the Federal Farm Loan Act, which provided low-interest credit, and federal funding for agricultural specialists in each county. Labor got the Keating-Owen Child Labor Act, which barred goods made by children under 16 from interstate commerce; the Adamson Act, which established an eight-hour day for railroad workers; and the Workman's Compensation Act, which provided protection to federal employees. Progressives were also pleased by Wilson's appointment of Louis Brandeis to the Supreme Court. All of these actions helped to ensure victory over the Republican nominee Charles Evans Hughes in 1916.

Progressivism in the International Arena

Progressive victories on the home front, further bolstered by the nation's economic growth and victory in the Spanish-American War, expanded Americans' confidence in their ability to solve problems on the international level. Just as people differed over what alterations, if any, were required in domestic policies, various visions of a new American foreign policy also emerged. For some, progressivism simply redefined and reinvigorated the old ideas of America's manifest destiny. Other progressives believed that democratic principles required that all people, even foreigners, be free to determine their own destinies. Order and justice were two progressive goals that sometimes conflicted, both in the domestic and the international arenas.

Big Stick Diplomacy

Theodore Roosevelt's foreign policy reflected the same kind of vigor he displayed in everything else. Asserting that Congress was "not well fitted for the shaping of foreign policy," he expanded presidential power in the conduct of diplomacy. Order having been restored in Cuba and the Philippines by 1903, Roosevelt launched the United States into the role of policeman. His doctrine was to "speak softly and carry a big stick," but he really only lived up to the second half of the slogan.

Possession of the Philippines brought with it concern over turbulent Asian politics. Most alarming was the emergence of Japan after its unexpected victories in the Russo-Japanese War (1904–1905). Often playing the role of arbiter at home, Roosevelt now shifted his arena and mediated an end to the war at a conference held in Portsmouth, New Hampshire, in August 1905. Japan remained a formidable rival, however. In order to intimidate the Japanese, Roosevelt's "big stick" was displayed by conspicuous stops in the Pacific during a 1907–1909 tour of America's "Great White Fleet."

Within the Western Hemisphere Roosevelt was even less reluctant to threaten or use force. In 1906 he responded to Cuban demonstrations against the Platt Amendment by sending in marines, who stayed until 1909. "I am doing my best," he declared, "to persuade the Cubans that if only they will be good, they will be happy." The marines could be very persuasive.

Progress and strategic considerations also demanded that a canal in Central America link the Atlantic and Pacific oceans. Roosevelt was determined to make it happen. There were two possible routes: one through Nicaragua and one across the Panamanian isthmus, which belonged to Colombia. A start had been made in Panama by a French company, which ran out of funds and was reorganized as the New Panama Canal Company. The new company's major asset was its concession from Colombia that extended to 1904.

Deciding that the Panama route was preferable, the Roosevelt administration negotiated the Hay-Herrán Treaty, which provided the United States with rights to a six-mile-wide zone across the isthmus in return for a $10 million payment to Colombia and an annual rental fee of $250,000.

As in the United States, ratification required the consent of the Colombian senate, which in August 1903 rejected the treaty unanimously.

Roosevelt was furious. "The blackmailers of Bogotá," he roared, should not be allowed "permanently to bar one of the future highways of civilization." He considered taking the canal zone by force, but a different solution presented itself when Philippe Bunau-Varilla, the chief engineer of the French canal company, incited a Panamanian revolt. Roosevelt promptly dispatched the USS *Nashville* to prevent Colombian troops from even getting to the so-called revolution. Three days after its start, Roosevelt recognized the independence of the Republic of Panama. Secretary of State John Hay and Bunau-Varilla then quickly drafted the Hay-Bunau-Varilla Treaty with essentially the same terms as the Hay-Herrán Treaty—only now the payment went to the rebels, not Colombia.

At first Roosevelt denied any part in the revolution, but he eventually admitted, "I took the Canal Zone and let Congress debate; and while the debate goes on the Canal does also." In 1914, the canal, a monument to both progress and Yankee imperialism, was completed.

At the same time, Latin American countries sometimes fell behind in debt payments to such European powers as Britain and Germany. As a result those two nations blockaded Venezuela in 1902–1903. A year later,

American Interventions in the Caribbean

Early in the twentieth century, the United States policed the Western Hemisphere and often took action when it judged Latin American countries were not managing.

Roosevelt announced that the United States would assume the responsibility of seeing that the nations of the Caribbean behaved themselves and paid their debts in order to thwart European intervention and assure American dominance in the region. Known as the Roosevelt Corollary to the Monroe Doctrine, this policy justified U.S. intervention in such places as the Dominican Republic, Nicaragua, and Haiti. Roosevelt's "big stick" diplomacy established America as the "policeman of the Western Hemisphere"—a role that would last long into the twentieth century.

Dollar Diplomacy

By nature less aggressive than his predecessor, William Howard Taft believed in the need for order and stability as well as the limited capacity of armed force for solving problems. He also realized that the United States had a new source of power—its economic clout. From 1898 to 1909 American overseas investments had risen from about $800 million to more than $2.5 billion.

Called "dollar diplomacy," Taft's approach was to use dollars instead of bullets to ensure stability and order. He wanted American capital to replace European capital in Latin America in order to increase U.S. influence there. When British bondholders wanted to collect their debts from Honduras in 1909, Taft asked American financiers to assume the debt. In 1910 he convinced New York bankers to take over the assets of the National Bank of Haiti. When needed, however, Taft also wielded a big stick. He refused to recognize a revolution in Nicaragua until the leaders agreed to accept American credits to pay off British debts, and he sent in marines to punctuate his point.

Missionary Diplomacy

As in domestic policies, Woodrow Wilson's foreign policy differed more in style than substance from his predecessors. Wilson's moralism did not stop at national boundaries. Indeed his sermonistic foreign policy has sometimes been called "missionary diplomacy." His gospel was American-style democracy. "When properly directed," he declared, "there is no people not fitted for self-government."

The rhetoric was different from his predecessors', but the results were the same. Renouncing both big stick and dollar diplomacy, Wilson continued to maintain stability and order in the Caribbean by similar measures. He sent marines to the Dominican Republic and Haiti, and kept them in Nicaragua. His interventionism ran into more trouble in Mexico, where the overthrow of longtime dictator Porfirio Diaz in 1911 began a cycle of revolution. Just before Wilson entered office, General Victoriano Huerta seized power through assassination. To the surprise of many, the moralistic Wilson refused to extend diplomatic recognition to Huerta's government, which he called a "government of butchers."

American business interests were dismayed by Wilson's stand. They controlled 75 percent of Mexico's mines, 60 percent of its oil, and 70 percent of its rubber. Determined to unseat Huerta, Wilson persevered. His tactics escalated from diplomatic pressure to landing troops at Veracruz, a move that infuriated Mexicans more than Huerta's despotism. Even after Huerta was overthrown, civil war continued between the government forces of Venustiano Carranza and rebels led by Pancho Villa.

In an attempt to draw the United States into the fracas, Villa launched a raid into New Mexico in March 1916. The tactic worked, and Wilson sent an expedition to capture Villa. Led by General John Pershing, American troops failed to find him. Soon they were 300 miles deep into Mexican territory and, as a result, on the brink of war with Carranza's government. In January 1917, however, America was being drawn into World War I, and Wilson decided to withdraw the troops. In the end he got basically the kind of government he wanted for Mexico, but Mexicans continued to believe that their government was their business and deeply resented the American intervention.

American involvement in World War I diverted attention not only from the crisis with Mexico. Domestic reform took a backseat to "making the world safe for democracy." Yet progressivism did not entirely die. Indeed, prohibitionists, women suffragists, and immigration restrictionists won their greatest victories in the wake of war.

Progressive Accomplishments, Progressive Failures

Measured by direct results, most progressive reforms proved disappointing. In some cases unintended consequences actually worked against the intended goals of laws. Nevertheless, progressives established important precedents that opened doors to later, more effective reform.

The Impact of Legislation

Attempts to promote direct democracy were among the least effective. Direct election of senators did not seem to alter the kinds of people elected. Initiative, referendum, and recall were rarely used, since the expense and organization needed for petition drives were beyond the reach of any but well-financed pressure groups. An unintended result of democratization was to increase the power of urban machines, as the move toward popular voting increased the political power of the most populous cities and the machines that controlled them. Nevertheless, in some states, such as Wisconsin, government did become more responsive to public needs, and urban machines often adopted reform measures to maintain power.

Other kinds of urban reforms had varying results. City government did indeed become more efficiently and economically run. The competency and honesty of officials generally increased. Occasional consequences, however, were cuts in social services in less affluent neighborhoods.

Attempts to regulate the railroads on either the state or national level rarely produced dramatic benefits for the general public. The chief advocates and beneficiaries of railroad regulation were frequently large shipping interests that did not share lower costs with consumers. With the Hepburn Act, Roosevelt did accomplish his primary goal of giving the ICC the power to set rates, but the act was more significant as a precedent for expanded governmental power than as an immediate solution to problems, since the courts ruled in favor of the railroads in most rate disputes.

Antimonopoly actions also did not always produce the intended results. For example, the breakups of Standard Oil and the American Tobacco Company did not increase competition or lower prices. The Clayton Antitrust Act was considered too vague for effective enforcement. Perhaps the only legislation to fulfill the promise of the New Freedom was the Underwood Tariff, and it was reversed by tariff legislation in the 1920s.

The Federal Trade Commission (FTC) did not become an aggressive watchdog either. Wilson's appointments were fairly pro-business, and the appointments of the 1920s were even more so. In the end, the FTC proved most beneficial to big business by protecting firms from unexpected suits and by outlawing many "unfair trade practices," many of which had promoted competition at the expense of stability. On the other hand, the FTC was also an important precedent.

Proclaimed victories for labor frequently turned out to be more symbolic than real. In the arbitration of the 1902 coal strike, for example, the United Mine Workers did not win recognition. Yet the symbolism was important. The precedent that the government would not automatically support the demands of management was later built upon during the New Deal of the 1930s.

Some labor legislation brought benefits but also produced unintended results. Child labor laws in combination with compulsory education legislation decreased the number of children from ages 10 to 15 who worked for wages, while the number of students enrolled in secondary education increased. Both were desirable results, but in the short run at least the poor received a mixed blessing. The incomes of a family's children were often crucial to its welfare, and no alternatives were provided. Much the same can be said about limits imposed on women's working hours.

Laws establishing minimum wages for women helped somewhat to offset earning losses resulting from child labor legislation. In any event, laws such as the Child Labor Act were declared unconstitutional in the 1920s.

Workmen's compensation laws were an improvement over existing procedures but were not an unqualified victory of labor over management. Indeed, businesspeople eventually welcomed the relief from the growing number of suits instituted by lawyers on a contingency fee basis, which made it possible for poor workers to take legal action. For the industrialists, a predictable premium replaced the uncertainty of court actions, decreasing the risks and increasing stability in the cost of doing business.

The establishment of the Federal Reserve System also favored order and stability. Everyone benefited from the maintenance of cash reserves for emergencies, a more flexible currency, and national check-clearing facilities. The banking system became more resistant to panics but, as 1929 would prove, not immune to them. Wall Street was not a big loser; three of the five seats on the Federal Reserve Board went to important bankers. The new system was a significant improvement, but far from a radical change.

From the consumer's point of view, the Pure Food and Drug Act and the Meat Inspection Act were great victories. After the rise of mass production and mass marketing, only federal action could provide adequate protection from adulteration of the nation's foodstuffs. Unintended beneficiaries, however, were the large drug and meat-packing companies that could more easily afford the increased expenses of meeting required production standards. Thus the effect was anticompetitive. Like much progressive legislation, the final act did provide protection for consumers, but in a way agreeable to big business.

Other progressive legislation left mixed legacies. Roosevelt's conservation measures prevented the squandering of natural resources, but also aided the larger lumber companies. Prohibition proved to be a boon to organized crime and also fostered widespread disrespect for the law. With a maximum rate of six percent, the income tax did little to redistribute huge fortunes but did establish an important revenue raising precedent. Another significant precedent was set by the Adamson Act, through which the federal government first dabbled in wage and hour legislation. Many other progressive reforms were illusory or short-lived. In the 1920s lax enforcement and hostile court decisions reversed many of them. Nevertheless, laissez-faire had suffered an irreversible blow. That was a major accomplishment and perhaps as much as many progressives wanted.

Winners and Losers

Before the era ended, people from almost every class and occupation had sought to take advantage of the climate of change to promote their interests. Obviously not all were equally successful; some gained far more than others, and some lost more than they gained. Clearly, large corporations were among the biggest winners. Other winners included members of the growing body of middle-class technocrats. At all levels of government the search for orderly, efficient management created new job opportunities for engineers, health professionals, trained managers, and other experts. Reforms that diminished the influence of political parties also increased the power of special interest groups working for particular social and economic goals. Consumers of all classes shared benefits from government regulation.

In general, most of the winners were white, urban, Protestant, and middle-class. Working-class ethnics won a few victories in some cities and states. African Americans came closest to being unqualified losers. For them, the only lasting advances came from such organizations as the NAACP, which survived to become an important force later in the century. Other victories were mainly token; the defeats, however, were concrete.

Of the three presidents, Roosevelt was the most sympathetic to blacks. In 1901 he invited Booker T. Washington to dine at the White House, consulted with him on some southern appointments, and named a few African Americans to federal positions. His actions hardly reflected an acceptance of black equality, however.

Theodore Roosevelt gave the appearance of supporting African Americans when he invited Booker T. Washington to the White House, but like many white leaders, he did not promote equality between blacks and whites.

When Taft became president, he approved of southern disfranchisement and appointed white-supremacist Republicans to federal jobs. As a result, some African Americans, including W. E. B. Du Bois, supported Wilson in 1912. They made a mistake. The influence of Wilson's southern upbringing and advisers became apparent when he allowed his cabinet to segregate federal employees and to demote black officeholders, especially those "who boss white girls." Jim Crow moved to Washington, and Wilson's defense of these actions indicated the blindness and paternalism of many white progressives on ths subject of race.

Conclusion

At the start of the new century, Americans confronted the problems that had accompanied the forces of modernization and industrialization. They were determined to do something to achieve more social justice and stability. Numerous solutions were proposed and victories won. In the end, however, Americans rejected radicalism and ignored major problems.

Once again the nation resolutely refused to come to terms with its ethnic and cultural diversity. Rather than protect minorities, most actions infringed on their personal liberties and sought to control rather than accommodate their differences. Women won some victories, but the majority of Americans did not accept the radical feminists' vision of true equality. Socialists' dreams of a peaceful, democratic redistribution of the country's wealth fell on deaf ears. In the end, there was no significant change in the distribution of either wealth or power. Nonetheless, the vigor and diversity of progressive actions brought to light many problems and provided later generations with a body of experience in dealing with them.

Suggestions for Further Reading

Valuable overviews of progressivism include John W. Chambers, *The Tyranny of Change* (1980); Robert M. Crunden, *Ministers of Reform* (1982); Richard Hofstadter, *The Age of Reform* (1955); Gabriel Kolko, *The Triumph of Conservatism* (1963); Arthur S. Link and Richard L. McCormick, *Progressivism* (1983); Robert Wiebe, *The Search for Order* (1967).

For specific aspects of the Progressive agenda, consult Jerold S. Auerbach, *Unequal Justice* (1976); Harold U. Faulkner, *The Quest for Social Justice* (1931); Thomas Haskell, *The Emergence of Professional Social Science* (1977); David W. Marcell, *Progress and Pragmatism* (1974).

Chronology of Key Events

1879	Henry George's *Progress and Poverty* published
1888	Edward Bellamy's *Looking Backward* published
1889	Jane Addams founds Hull House
1901	President William McKinley assassinated; Theodore Roosevelt becomes twenty-sixth president
1902	Three states adopt initiative and recall; United Mine Workers' strike
1903	W. E. B. Du Bois's *The Souls of Black Folk* published; Elkins Act bars railroad rebates
1904	Northern Securities broken up; Lincoln Steffins's *Shame of the Cities* published; United States obtains right to build the Panama Canal; announcement of Roosevelt Corollary to the Monroe Doctrine, asserting the right of the United States to exercise international police power in the Caribbean
1905	Treaty of Portsmouth ends Russo-Japanese War
1906	Upton Sinclair's *The Jungle* published; Meat Inspection Act enforces standards; Pure Food and Drug Act; Hepburn Act
1908	First city manager hired; *Muller* v. *Oregon*
1909	National Association for the Advancement of Colored People (NAACP) founded; Mann-Elkins Act
1912–1917	Twelve states adopt minimum wage laws for women; 30 states adopt industrial accident insurance
1912	Progressive party created; Woodrow Wilson elected the twenty-eighth president
1913	Sixteenth Amendment; Underwood-Simmons Tariff; Seventeenth Amendment; Federal Reserve System created
1914	Federal Trade Commission established; Clayton Antitrust Act; U.S. Navy captures Veracruz
1915	U.S. marines dispatched to Haiti
1916	U.S. troops enter Mexico to search for Pancho Villa; U.S. marines sent to Dominican Republic; Adamson Act; Federal Workmen's Compensation Act; Keating-Owen Act
1919	Eighteenth Amendment prohibits liquor
1920	Nineteenth Amendment grants women voting rights

Social and intellectual currents are examined in David W. Noble, *The Progressive Mind,* rev. ed. (1981); Frank Tariello, *The Reconstruction of American Political Ideology* (1982); John L. Thomas, *Alternative America* (1983); Morton White, *Social Thought in America: The Revolt Against Formalism* (1975).

Studies of women's and children's issues include Nancy S. Dye, *As Equals and Sisters* (1980); Ellen Condliffe Lagemann, *A Generation of Women: Education in the Lives of Progressive Reformers* (1979); Ruth Rosen, *The Lost Sisterhood: Prostitution in America, 1900–1918* (1982).

The United States role in the international arena is the focus of P. Edward Haley, *Revolution and Intervention* (1970); Walter LaFeber, *The Panama Canal,* rev. ed. (1989); Lester Langley, *The United States and the Carribean* (1980); Dana G. Munro, *Intervention and Dollar Diplomacy in the Caribbean* (1964); Whitney Perkins, *Constraints of Empire: The United States and Caribbean Interventions* (1981); Robert E. Quirk, *An Affair of Honor: Woodrow Wilson and the Occupation of Veracruz* (1962).

Chapter *23*

The United States and World War I

The Road to War
American Neutrality
Allied Violations of Neutrality
Submarine Warfare
Preparedness Campaign
The End of Neutrality

American Industry Goes to War
Voluntarism
Peace with Labor
Financing the War

The American Public Goes to War
Selling the War
Political Repression
Wartime Reform
Blacks and the Great Migration

The War Front
Raising an Army
The Defeat of Germany

Social Unrest After the War
Labor Unrest and the Red Scare

The Treaty of Versailles
The Fourteen Points
Discord Among the Victors
The Struggle for Ratification
The Election of 1920

Disillusioned writers of the 1920s honored Randolph Bourne as "the intellectual hero of World War I," yet his appearance was anything but heroic. An unusually messy forceps delivery crushed one side of Bourne's skull at birth, leaving him with a misshapen ear, a partially paralyzed face, and a mouth permanently askew in a horrible grimace. Then, when he was four, an attack of spinal tuberculosis twisted his frame and left him a hunchback dwarf.

Bourne's brain, however, was razor sharp. A brilliant student, Bourne attended Columbia University, graduating on the eve of World War I. Determined to become a writer, he settled in New York's Greenwich Village, where self-styled literary radicals had declared war on the smugness and the optimism of American culture. While his interests ranged wide and far, he made his reputation as a critic of America's entrance into World War I.

Bourne loathed President Woodrow Wilson, but he directed his choicest barbs at fellow intellectuals who supported Wilson's policies. In effect, he accused them of not doing their job as thinkers. Instead of questioning Wilson's policies, they had betrayed their duty by "opening the sluices and flooding the public with the sewage of the war spirit."

Bourne refused to endow the war with lofty purposes. Hardly a knee-jerk pacifist, he knew that some wars were unavoidable, perhaps even necessary. In his judgment, however, World War I was not a struggle to make the world safe for democracy; it was nothing more than "frenzied mutual suicide." To those who argued that this war could somehow be converted into an instrument of progress and democracy, Bourne replied that World War I would unleash "all the evils that are organically bound up with it." America's allies would reject Wilson's call for a "peace without victory," and instead would try to win the war and "then grab what they can."

On the home front, warned Bourne, there would be the suppression of civil liberties and the growth of big government. "War is the health of the State," he declared in one of his most famous lines. "It automatically sets in motion throughout society those irresistible forces for uniformity, for passionate cooperation with the Government in coercing into obedience the minority groups and individuals which lack the larger herd sense."

Like many of his contemporaries, Bourne feared the state. During wartime the state's power grew exponentially, making it "the inexorable arbiter and determinant of men's businesses and attitudes and opinions." Most alarming of all, the war would kill reform by diverting public attention from the unfinished work of progressivism. It would "leave the country spiritually impoverished because of the draining away of sentiment into the channels of war."

A few days after the Armistice was signed in 1918, Bourne died, a victim of the influenza epidemic that killed 500,000 Americans that winter. Although he had no visible impact on Wilson's administration, Bourne raised important questions about the relationship between the individual and the state during wartime, and many of his fears proved prophetic. In the end, the United States had little choice but to enter the conflict on the side of the Allies. The war itself was a terrible human tragedy, and did not make "the world safe for democracy" or serve as the "war to end all wars" as President Wilson promised. Rather, World War I sowed the seeds of World War II.

The Road to War

On June 28, 1914, terrorists assassinated Archduke Franz Ferdinand, the heir to the Austro-Hungarian throne. A complicated system of alliances pitting the Triple Entente of France, Russia, and Great Britain against the Central Alliance of Germany, Austria-Hungary, Italy, and Turkey triggered a chain reaction that started World War I. In the Far East, Japan, England's ally since 1902, also declared war on Germany. A year after the war began, Italy switched sides and joined the fight against Germany.

World War I caught most people by surprise. Lulled by a century of peace that began with the defeat of Napoleon in 1815, many observers had come to regard armed conflict as a thing of the past. Convinced that the major powers had advanced too far morally and materially to fight, these optimists believed that nation states would settle disputes through diplomacy. World War I shattered these beliefs, demonstrating that death and destruction had not yet been banished from human affairs.

Both sides expected a swift victory; both sides miscalculated. After the Allies halted Germany's massive offensive through France and Belgium at the Marne River in September 1914, the Great War bogged down into trench warfare and a ghastly stalemate ensued, in which the two armies burrowed into the ground and fought pitched battles over narrow strips of blood-soaked earth.

Airplanes, tanks, hand grenades, and poison gases distinguished the Great War from earlier conflicts, but the machine gun did most of the killing. The grim cycle repeated itself countless times: Officers cried "Attack!"; men rose in waves; and the opposing forces opened fire with machine guns, spewing out death at the rate of eight bullets per second. In minutes, thousands of men lay wounded or dead, savage evidence of how efficiently military technology and insane tactics could slaughter a generation of young men. When the war ended, Germany had lost 1,800,000 men; Russia, 1,700,000; France, 1,385,000; Austria-Hungary, 1,200,000; and Great Britain, 947,000.

American Neutrality

Like the combatants, Americans did not see the war coming, and most felt relieved when President Woodrow Wilson issued an official declaration of neutrality on August 4. Mindful of the wisdom embodied in Washington's Farewell Address, steeped in a long tradition of isolation from Europe's wars, and shielded from the hostilities by the Atlantic Ocean, they hoped to avoid the conflict.

Two weeks after the official declaration of neutrality, Wilson asked his countrymen to remain impartial "in thought as well as in action." Yet the president himself could not meet this standard. Privately, his sympathies lay with the Allies, especially Great Britain, whose culture and government he had long admired. Moreover, with the notable exception of William Jennings Bryan, his secretary of state, Wilson's advisors all favored Great Britain, and pushed the president to side with the Allies. Yet Wilson saw the war's causes as complicated and obscure; simple prudence dictated that the United States must avoid taking sides.

Internal divisions underscored the wisdom of neutrality. Wilson knew his countrymen felt deeply divided over the war. Ties of language and culture prompted many Americans to side with the Allies, and, as the war progressed, the British adeptly exploited these bonds with anti-German propoaganda. Yet the Central Powers had their sympathizers, too, since more than ten million Americans were of German, Austrian, or Italian descent. Furthermore, millions of Irish-Americans sided with the Central Powers because they hated the English.

Domestic politics reinforced Wilson's determination to remain neutral. In 1914 the United States stood at the end of two decades of bitter social and political debate. Labor unrest, corporate growth, trust-busting, and the arrival of 12 million new immigrants since the turn of the century had opened deep fissures in American society. As Wilson struggled to correct these problems through legislation, he feared his domestic program would be endangered if neutrality failed.

Allied Violations of Neutrality

Because German armies held the edge in the land war, Great Britain had no choice but to press her naval superiority. During the early part of the war British efforts to control the seas posed repeated threats to Anglo-American relations. Immediately after war erupted, the British navy attempted to blockade Europe. In February 1915 British ships mined the North Sea and started seizing American vessels bound for neutral countries, often without offering compensation. The British captured not ony war matériel, but also noncontraband items, including food and cotton, bound for neutral nations such as Holland for reshipment to Germany. In 1916 Britain blacklisted some 87 American companies accused of trading with Germany and censored the mail coming from Europe to the United States.

These actions, coupled with England's ruthless suppression of the Irish Rebellion in 1916, infuriated Wilson. In retaliation, the State Department bombarded England with a flurry of protests. Although the British interpreted his ardent defense of neutral rights as petty, legalistic quibbling, they realized they could not push Wilson too far, since they needed American trade to survive.

Wilson could have ended the controversy over neutral rights by clamping an embargo on trade with the belligerents, but he refused to take this action because wartime trade was stimulating the American economy. The United States had been in a recession when Wilson entered office in 1913, and the war had quadrupled its exports to the Allied nations.

The huge volume of trade quickly exhausted the Allies' cash reserves, forcing them to ask the United States for credit. After hesitating several months, Wilson agreed in October 1915 to permit loans to belligerents, a decision that favored Great Britain and France far more than Germany. The United States became a creditor nation for the first time, giving Americans a strong economic interest in an Allied victory.

Submarine Warfare

Given Britain's overwhelming naval superiority, Germany decided to rely on a new weapon, the submarine, and on February 4, 1915 Germany proclaimed a "war zone" around the British Isles. Henceforth all enemy merchant ships that entered the zone would be torpedoed without warning, and neutral ships would not be guaranteed safe passage.

A new development in naval technology, the submarine posed serious challenges to international law. The law required ships that attacked other vessels on the high seas to warn their intended victims, allow time for passengers to reach lifeboats, and then rescue survivors after the sinking. By its very nature, the submarine could not abide by these regulations. A silent assassin whose effectiveness depended on the element of surprise, it had to strike from below the surface, in violation of international law.

Wilson's approach to foreign affairs was both legalistic and moralistic. He expected nation-states to behave like gentlemen; and, above all, that meant living up to the letter of international law and respecting the rights of every nation. To Wilson, German submarines were committing criminal acts. In contrast to British violations of American neutrality, which merely resulted in property losses, submarine warfare threatened to kill innocent civilians. In unusually blunt language, he warned Berlin that it would be held "strictly accountable" for American lives lost to submarine attacks. While international law did not guarantee the safety of neutrals who traveled on belligerents' ships, Wilson acted as though it did.

On March 28, 1915, a German submarine torpedoed the *Falaba,* a British liner, killing 104 passengers, including one American. Wilson was furious, but Secretary of State Bryan reminded the president of numerous British violations of American neutrality in her attempt to blockade Germany. "Why be shocked at the drowning of a few people," asked Bryan, "if there is no objection to the starving of a nation?"

On May 1 the German Embassy took out ads in New York newspapers warning Americans not to travel on Allied ships. Undeterred, 197 Americans sailed for the British Isles on board the British *Lusitania.* On May 7, 1915, a German submarine torpedoed the *Lusitania* off the coast of Ireland. She sank in 18 minutes, killing 1,198 persons, 128 of them Americans. The public was shocked and outraged. The *New York Nation* called the sinking "wholesale murder on the high seas," and a small minority of Americans demanded war. It did not matter that the *Lusitania* (like the *Falaba*) was transporting munitions in her hull and had secret orders to ram submarines on sight.

In a sharply worded dispatch, Wilson ordered Germany to apologize for the sinking, compensate the victims, and pledge to stop attacking merchant ships. When Berlin equivocated, Wilson sent a second *Lusitania* note repeating his demands. This time the Germans met him halfway, expressing regret over the·*Lusitania* and agreeing to pay an indemnity. However, the Imperial Government refused to stop sinking merchant ships without warning, explaining that Germany's survival depended on full use of the submarine. Convinced that Wilson's policies would lead to war, Bryan resigned from the cabinet to protest what he saw as a dangerous tilt toward Great Britain.

On March 24, 1916, a submarine attacked the *Sussex,* an unarmed French passenger ship, killing more than 80 people in the attack and severely wounding seven Americans. Wilson threatened to sever diplomatic relations unless Germany promised to stop sinking all merchant and passenger ships without warning. Anxious to keep the United States neutral, Berlin agreed. The so-called *Sussex* pledge reduced tensions between the United States and Germany for the remainder of 1916, but the fragile peace depended solely on German restraint.

Preparedness Campaign

As the submarine threatened to draw the United States into the fighting, the American people and their leaders debated whether or not to make ready for war. Initially, Wilson's policy toward preparedness reflected cautious hostility.

Many Americans saw the issue differently. Wilson increasingly found himself assailed by prominent and highly vocal critics who insisted that the best way to preserve peace was to prepare for war. The pugnacious Theodore Roosevelt called the president "the popular pacifist hero," while Tin Pan Alley produced songs with titles such as "I Did Not Raise My Boy to Be a Coward."

Yet Wilson felt pressured by groups opposed to war. Socialists such as Eugene V. Debs dismissed the war as a struggle for assets among capitalist nations. Radicals such as anarchist Emma Goldman and "Big Bill" Haywood, head of the Industrial Workers of the World, shared this view. Liberal reformers feared that war would destroy the spirit of progressivism. Pacifists such as social worker Jane Addams opposed the war on moral grounds. Most troubling of all, Wilson had to worry about opposition from within his own party. Speaking for the peace Democrats, former Secretary of State Bryan warned that a preparedness campaign would transform the United States into "a vast armory with skull and crossbones above the door."

In the end, Wilson threw his support behind a moderate preparedness program. Throughout January and February 1916 he stumped the country pleading for a military force powerful enough to protect the nation's honor. In June Congress increased the army from 90,000 to 175,000 men, and a few months later appropriated more than $500 million for new ships. Though of small importance militarily, both acts drew fire from those who predicted that armaments would lead to war.

Despite his own support for military preparedness, Wilson decided to make peace the key issue in his bid for reelection in 1916. The Republicans chose Charles Evans Hughes, a former governor of New York and a Supreme Court justice who had earned a solid reputation as a liberal. Wilson charged that Hughes's election would plunge the United States into Europe's madness. "He kept us out of war" became the Democrats' rallying cry.

The race was extremely close. On election eve the *New York Times* and the *New York World* both awarded victory to Hughes, who went to bed believing he had won. However, Wilson won in the electoral college by a vote of 277 to 254, with a popular vote margin of 9.1 million to Hughes's 8.5 million.

The End of Neutrality

Interpreting his reelection as a vote for peace, Wilson attempted to mediate an end to the war. In January 1916 Wilson urged both sides to embrace his call for "peace without victory," but neither welcomed his overtures. Randolph Bourne was right. Above all else, the belligerents wanted victory.

Any hope for a negotiated settlement ended when Germany announced that after February 1, 1917, all vessels caught in the war zone, neutral or belligerent, armed or unarmed, would be sunk without warning. Driven to desperation by the British blockade and unable to break the impasse on land, Germany had decided to risk everything on a furious U-boat campaign designed to starve Britain into submission.

Members of his cabinet pressed Wilson to declare war, but he broke diplomatic relations instead, viewing war as the defeat of reason. For weeks he seemed indecisive and confused, unable to accept the fact that "strict accountability" demanded war once the Germans started sinking American ships.

The Zimmermann telegram snapped Wilson out of his daze. In January, British cryptographers intercepted a secret message from Arthur Zimmermann, the German foreign minister, to the German ambassador to Mexico, proposing an alliance between Germany and Mexico in the event Germany went to war with the United States. Germany promised to help Mexico recover the territory it had lost in the 1840s, roughly the present-day states of Texas, New Mexico, California, and Arizona. The British revealed the scheme to Wilson, hoping to draw the United States into the war.

The Zimmermann telegram convinced Wilson and millions of Americans that Germany would stop at nothing to satisfy her ambitions and that those ambitions posed a serious danger to America's rights and security. On March 12 Wilson issued an executive order arming merchant ships and instructing them to shoot submarines on sight.

At this critical juncture, with the United States and Germany virtually at war, the Russian Revolution erupted. Suddenly, the Czar's government was swept away, and in its place stood the provisional government of a Russian Republic, complete with a representative parliament. With the only autocratic regime among the Allies transformed overnight into a fledgling democracy, the war now truly seemed to pit the forces of democracy against the forces of despotism.

Pale and solemn, Wilson delivered his war message to Congress on April 2. The United States "had no quarrel with the German people," he insisted, but their "military masters" had to be defeated in order to make the world "safe for democracy." The next day the Senate approved the war resolution, 82 to 6; the House followed on April 6, 373 to 50. The president signed the declaration on April 7, 1917, and America was at war.

For more than two years Wilson had worked frantically to keep the United States at peace: Why did he now lead the nation to war? Cultural ties and economic motivations did not decide the issue. Wilson drew the sword, although reluctantly, because he concluded that German submarines had violated international law and made a mockery of America's long-standing commitment to freedom of the seas. His strong defense of neutral rights left him no choice but to declare war once Germany resumed its attacks on American ships.

One additional factor weighed heavily on Wilson—his desire to help shape the peace. By entering the war, the United States would be guaranteed a place at the peace table. "I hate this war," an anguished Wilson confided to an aide, "and the only thing I care about on earth is the peace I am going to make at the end of it."

Most Americans supported Wilson's call to arms. John Dewey, the famed educator, spoke for progressives when he described war as an ugly reality that had to be converted into an instrument for benefiting mankind. Randolph Bourne disagreed. "If the war is too strong for you to prevent," he asked pointedly, "how is it going to be weak enough for you to control and mould to your liberal purposes?"

American Industry Goes to War

The United States entered the Great War unprepared. The problems went far beyond the puny size of the military forces. Americans themselves had no idea of what the war would ask of them as a society. Decisions had to be made about mobilization, but the public had not formed a consensus on the proper role of government in society, especially during wartime. As a result, Wilson hesitated to mobilize by decree. Instead, he tried to create a system of economic incentives that would encourage Americans to support the war in a spirit of voluntary cooperation.

Voluntarism

It took nearly a year to organize an effective war administration. Wilson established a war cabinet with six key boards, each with broad powers to promote voluntarism. The War Industries Board (WIB), organized early in 1918 under the leadership of Bernard M. Baruch, a Wall Street financier, assumed the task of managing the economy by fixing prices, setting priorities, and reducing waste. To increase production, the WIB appealed to the profit motive, setting prices artificially high, permitting profits to triple during the war.

The Fuel Administration, the War Trade Board, the Shipping Board, and the U.S. Railroad Administration adopted similar policies. The Fuel Administration increased production by two-fifths and conserved supplies through voluntary "lightless nights" and "gasless Sundays." By offering large profits to railroads and high wages to workers, the Railroad Administration established an efficient rail system under national control.

Agricultural production came under the jurisdiction of the Food Administration, headed by Herbert Hoover, a self-made millionaire who had served with distinction as director of relief operations in Belgium. Appealing to the spirit of patriotism, he preached "the gospel of the clean plate." Americans "Hooverized" with wheatless Mondays and Wednesdays, meatless Tuesdays, and porkless Thursdays and Saturdays.

No foe of profits, Hoover set farm prices at high levels to encourage production, stabilized the grain market by guaranteeing farmers a minimum price, and purchased raw sugar and then sold it to refineries at a fixed rate. The policies worked. Overall, real farm incomes rose 30 percent during the war, food production increased by one-quarter, domestic food consumption fell, and America's food shipments to the Allies tripled.

Peace with Labor

The government also made concessions to labor. Gradually, Wilson recognized labor's right to organize and to engage in collective bargaining, and he sanctioned other key demands, including the eight-hour workday. To settle labor disputes, Wilson created the National War Labor Board (WLB). Though it lacked legal authority, the WLB had the president's backing and a commitment from industry and labor to accept its decisions.

While Wilson embraced moderate unions like the AFL, his administration opposed the militant Industrial Workers of the World (IWW or the "Wobblies"), which demanded higher wages and better working conditions, and went out on strike to win them. Because the Wobblies frequently employed the rhetoric of class warfare to dramatize their demands, their strikes frightened many Americans who feared social revolution. Businessmen played upon these fears to demand suppression of the radical unions. The Wobblies were "traitors," they sneered, and the IWW stood for "I Won't Work."

The AFL shrewdly separated itself from the militant workers, pledging not to strike for the duration of the war. The AFL supported the war and joined the administration's attack on socialist critics. In return, the AFL won a voice in home-front labor policy. Union men occupied seats in wartime agencies, where they pushed for the eight-hour day and staved off pressure from employers bent on preserving the open shop. Real income of manufacturing workers and coal miners rose, hours were reduced, and AFL membership jumped from 2.7 million in 1916 to 4 million in 1919.

Financing the War

By 1920 the war had cost $33.5 billion—33 times the federal government's revenues in 1916. Conservatives favored a regressive tax policy: consump-

Wilson's administration opposed militant labor unions like the Industrial Workers of the World (IWW), shown here striking against Oliver Steel in Pennsylvania. Such strikes did little to help the war effort at home. Samuel Gompers, who wanted to separate members of the American Federation of Labor (AFL) from more militant workers, pledged not to strike until the war was over.

tion taxes, borrowing, and, if necessary, a slight increase in income taxes. Reformers and radicals demanded a progressive tax policy: inheritance and excess profits taxes coupled with higher income taxes. Wilson walked the middle ground, but the heaviest burdens fell on the wealthy through taxes on large incomes, corporate profits, and estates. By 1919 the tax burden in the highest income brackets had risen to 77 percent.

World War I brought an important change in the sources of federal tax revenues. Before the war nearly three-quarters of federal revenues had come from excise and customs taxes. After the war, America's tax structure shifted from taxing consumption to taxing wealth, proof that progressives had won an important victory in the struggle to make upper-income groups pay a large share of the cost of government. On the tax issue Randolph Bourne was wrong.

The American Public Goes to War

Although Wilson preferred to rely on voluntary efforts rather than mandated government interference, federal powers were greatly expanded during World War I. Wilson's decision to substitute voluntarism for statutory controls on industry placed the burden of supporting the war on the profit motive and the public's sense of patriotism. This policy avoided the clash between Wilson and industry that would have resulted from strict government control over the economy, but it did so at a huge cost to civil liberties.

Selling the War

Throughout the war the government directed its coercion at people rather than industries, largely through the Committee on Public Information (CPI). Ably led by George W. Creel, the CPI became America's first propaganda agency. Creel immediately drafted a voluntary censorship agreement with newspapers to keep sensitive military information out of print. The CPI hired hundreds of musicians, writers, and artists to stage a patriotic campaign, sponsored 75,000 speakers to deliver war pep talks in vaudeville and movie theaters across the country, and got movie stars to sell war bonds.

Indeed, the CPI found a powerful ally in Hollywood. Quick to perceive the link between patriotism and profits, studio moguls cranked out scores of crude propaganda films with titles such as *The Prussian Cur, The*

Claws of the Hun, and *To Hell with the Kaiser,* which reduced World War I to a conflict between good and evil, heroes and villains.

Popular culture reflected the CPI's influence. Suddenly, dissent meant treason, Germans devolved into Huns, and German-Americans all spied for the fatherland. It did not matter that the vast majority of German-Americans supported the United States; the CPI consistently attacked their loyalty. At its best the CPI may have sold war bonds, discouraged

Hollywood and Tin Pan Alley did their parts to encourage patriotism by putting out scores of war films and a large number of music pieces like the one shown here.

war stoppages, and convinced the public to support the war; at its worst the CPI fostered a witch-hunt.

In the name of patriotism, musicians no longer played Bach and Beethoven, schools stopped teaching the German language, and Americans renamed sauerkraut "liberty cabbage." Cincinnati, with its large German-American population, even removed pretzels from the free lunch counters in saloons. More alarming, vigilante groups attacked anyone suspected of being unpatriotic. Many German-Americans became the victims of mob violence. Workers who refused to buy war bonds often suffered harsh retribution, and attacks on labor protesters were nothing short of brutal. The legal system backed the suppression. Juries routinely released defendants accused of violence against individuals or groups critical of the war.

Political Repression

The government fueled the hysteria. In June 1917 Congress passed the Espionage Act, which gave postal officials the authority to ban newspapers and magazines from the mails and threatened individuals convicted of obstructing the draft with $10,000 fines and 20 years in jail. Congress passed the Sedition Act in 1918, which made it a federal offense to use "disloyal, profane, scurrilous, or abusive language" about the Constitution, the government, the American uniform, or the flag. The government prosecuted over 2,100 people under these acts. Randolph Bourne's prediction that civil rights would fall victim to the power of the state rang true.

Political dissenters bore the brunt of the repression. Eugene V. Debs, who urged socialists to resist militarism, went to prison for nearly three years. In September 1917 the Justice Department staged massive raids on IWW officers, arresting 169 of its veteran leaders. Many observers thought the judicial system would protect dissenters, but the courts handed down stiff prison sentences to the Wobblies.

World War I did not cause repression; it merely intensified old fears, offering intolerant citizens a chance to lash out at those who had changed America. Immigrants, radical labor organizers, socialists, anarchists, Communists, and critics of any kind became victims of intolerance.

Wartime Reform

The war hysteria bred a curious alliance between superpatriots and old style reformers. Prohibitionists had little difficulty turning World War I to their advantage. In 1917 Congress prohibited the use of grain for the production of alcoholic beverages, insisting that foodstuffs must be used to feed America's soldiers and Allies. Prohibitionists joined the anti-German craze, warning that German-Americans controlled the nation's breweries. Congress passed the Eighteenth Amendment in 1917. The Volstead Act, which banned the manufacture, transportation, and sale of alcoholic beverages, took effect in 1920.

Like prohibition, women's suffrage benefited from the emergency atmosphere of World War I. Most women's organizations supported the war effort. As blue-collar female workers started pouring into defense industries, middle-class women showed their support by volunteering to help the sick and the wounded. Thousands of women joined the Red Cross and the American Women's Hospital Service, serving overseas as nurses, physicians, clerks, and ambulance drivers. Thousands more enlisted after the army established the Army Corps of Nurses in 1918.

Suffragists demanded the vote in return for their support of the war. Wilson had long opposed women's suffrage, but political reality ultimately forced his hand. Most western states had granted women the vote before he entered the White House. Alice Paul, head of the National Woman's Party, pressed the issue by organizing around-the-clock picketing in front of the White House. Determined to prevent women's suffrage from becoming a political issue in the congressional elections of 1918, Wilson told the Senate that the vote for women "is vital to the winning of the war." In 1919 Congress passed the Nineteenth Amendment, granting women the right to vote. Ratification followed in the summer of 1920.

Apart from voting rights, World War I brought few permanent changes for women. Women had hoped the war would open new jobs for them. Instead, employment opportunities proved meager and brief. Labor unions opposed hiring women and tolerated their presence solely as a wartime necessity, arguing that industrial jobs belonged to men and should be returned to them as soon as the war ended. As a result, the number of women who remained in the work force in 1920 dropped below the 1910 figures.

Blacks and the Great Migration

Like women, blacks wanted to use the war to improve their status. While the government had given blacks little reason to shed their blood, most black newspapers backed the war. W. E. B. Du Bois urged blacks to "close ranks" with whites, hoping that blacks, by demonstrating patriotism and bravery, could win public respect and earn better treatment after the war.

At first military leaders even denied blacks the right to fight for their country. The marines accepted no blacks; the navy used them only as mess boys; and the army planned to make them laborers and stevedores.

When the National Association for the Advancement of Colored People (NAACP) and other black organizations protested, however, the army agreed to compromise. Following the Civil War example, the army created black regiments commanded almost exclusively by white officers. Black regiments committed to battle fought bravely, but only one-fifth of the black troops ever saw combat. Instead, most were assigned to move supplies.

Back home the record was equally mixed. In the decades following the Civil War a steady trickle of blacks had left the South to search for jobs in northern cities. During World War I the trickle became a flood. When labor agents appeared in 1916 promising jobs in the North, blacks responded eagerly. By November 1918 the "Great Migration" had brought half a million southern blacks to the "Land of Hope." Many found jobs in northern factories and packinghouses. Still, regardless of the industry, discrimination forced blacks to the bottom of the ladder, where they took over the menial, backbreaking jobs that had been vacated by the most recent wave of immigrants.

The 369th Infantry Regiment returned from the war in February 1919. They were awarded the *Croix de Guerre* (war cross) for bravery in the Meuse-Argonne.

The Great Migration angered southern whites. The price of cotton tripled during the war; southern planters, fearing the loss of their labor force, resorted to intimidation and mob violence to stop the exodus. Northern whites opposed the Great Migration, too. Manufacturers welcomed cheap black labor (especially as strikebreakers), but most northerners felt threatened by the newcomers. Increasingly, they turned to segregation, discrimination, and violence; and blacks, hoping for a better life in the North, fought back. Race riots erupted in 26 cities in 1917, with the most serious violence occurring in East St. Louis, where at least 39 blacks died in the fighting.

Clearly, World War I meant different things to different groups: for the administration, a test of the limits of voluntarism; for businessmen and technocrats, a chance to pull the levers of government; for nativists and superpatriots, an excuse to lash out at "undesirable" elements; for radicals and dissenters, repression and hardship; for manufacturers and farmers, high profits; for reformers, victories on women's suffrage and prohibition; for trade unions, the right to organize for better pay; and for blacks, a chance to escape from southern poverty.

The War Front

The United States entered World War I without a large army or the ships to transport one to Europe. With the Allies ready to collapse due to huge casualties, low morale, and a dwindling supply of food, Wilson ordered the navy to act immediately. Six destroyers reached Ireland on May 4; 35 ships had arrived by July; and 343 ships patrolled the seas surrounding England by the war's end.

To cut down losses of merchant ships, which in April alone totaled 881,027 tons, the Americans proposed a convoy system—using warships to escort merchant ships to Great Britain. By December the convoy system had cut losses in half.

Raising an Army

Wilson's choice to lead the American Expeditionary Force (AEF) was Major General John J. "Black Jack" Pershing. Despite urgent requests from Allied commanders, Pershing refused to send raw recruits to the front, and he rejected demands that American units be integrated into British and French regiments. Instead, Pershing insisted on keeping American troops as independent units under his command. To bolster Allied morale, the War Department hurriedly dispatched the First Division to France, where it marched through Paris on July 4, 1917, to the cheers of thousands.

A bitter debate erupted over how to raise the troops. Despite heavy pressure from Theodore Roosevelt and others who favored a volunteer army, Wilson insisted on conscription. Congress passed the Selective Service Act on May 18, 1917.

To assign soldiers to the right military tasks, the army launched an ambitious program of psychological testing. Though the tests supposedly measured native intelligence, in reality they favored men with the most schooling, and thus reinforced the class structure of American society. Native-born whites achieved the highest scores, while blacks and recent immigrants consistently scored lower.

Apart from selecting officers, the army made little use of the test data. Ordinary soldiers were not assigned tasks on the basis of test scores. All the testing really accomplished was to sell the public on the idea of mental testing and lay the groundwork for a thriving peacetime industry. After the war, numerous businesses adopted mental tests to screen personnel, and many colleges began requiring them for admission. Few legacies of the war had a more lasting or widespread impact on American society.

The Defeat of Germany

As the American army trained, the situation in Europe deteriorated. Mutiny within the French army was spreading; the eastern front dissolved in March when the Bolsheviks, who had seized power in Russia in November, accepted Germany's peace terms; and German and Austrian forces had all but routed the Italian armies. In fact, by late 1917 the war had come down to a race between American mobilization and Germany's war machine.

On March 21, 1918, the Germans launched a massive offensive on the western front in the Valley of the Somme in France. For a time, it looked as though the Germans would succeed. Badly bloodied, the Allied forces lost ground. But with German troops barely 50 miles from Paris, Marshal Ferdinand Foch, the leader of the French army, assumed command of the Allied forces. Foch's troops, aided by 85,000 American soldiers, launched a furious counteroffensive, hitting the Germans hard in a series of bloody assaults. By the end of October the German army had been pushed back to the Belgian border.

During the final months of fighting, American troops hit Europe like a tidal wave. In June 279,000 American soldiers crossed the Atlantic; in July more than 300,000; in August, 286,000. All told, 1.5 million American troops arrived in Europe during the last six months of the war.

Fresh and battle ready, Pershing's forces made the crucial difference in the war. Buoyed by the fresh manpower, the Allies pressed their advantage. Their furious offensive in the summer of 1918 broke the opposition, and within a few months the Central Powers faced certain defeat. The Austro-Hungarian Empire asked for peace; Turkey and Bulgaria stopped fighting; and Germany requested an armistice. In a direct slap at the kaiser, Wilson announced he would negotiate only with a democratic regime in Germany. When the military leaders and the kaiser wavered, a brief revolution forced the kaiser to abdicate, and a civilian regime assumed control of the government.

Germany's new government immediately accepted the armistice and agreed to negotiate a treaty. At 11:00 A.M., November 11, 1918, the guns stopped. Throughout the Western world, crowds filled the streets to celebrate peace.

Social Unrest After the War

Peace did not restore stability to the United States. Race relations deteriorated, as tensions rose in the North because of competition between whites and blacks for jobs and housing. In the South whites felt threatened by the return of 400,000 black veterans, many of whom had been trained in the use of firearms, even if many had not seen actual combat. Moreover, many black veterans had served in France where they were treated as equals, and southern whites feared they would demand the same treatment at home. Determined to keep blacks repressed, southern whites instituted a reign of terror. About 70 lynchings occurred in the first year of peace.

As the heat of summer brought tensions to a boil, race riots broke out in 25 cities. The worst violence erupted on a Chicago beach where 17-year-old Eugene Williams strayed into waters claimed by whites. A rock-throwing mob kept him from reaching shore, and Williams drowned. Fighting broke out when police refused to arrest his killers. Thirteen days of street violence followed, leaving 38 dead, 578 injured, and 1,000 families homeless. Racial injustice remained a defining feature of American life throughout the Progressive Era, despite American efforts abroad to make the world "safe for democracy."

Labor Unrest and the Red Scare

Labor was another trouble spot. Most workers demonstrated their patriotism by not striking during the war, but the Armistice ended their truce with management. High inflation, job competition from returning veterans, and government policies all contributed to labor's discontent. Of the three, inflation hit workers the hardest. Food prices more than doubled between 1915 and 1920; clothing costs more than tripled. Wilson had made peace with trade unions only as a wartime necessity. After the fighting stopped, he removed controls on industry, and business leaders closed ranks to roll back concessions to workers.

The first strike came four days after the Armistice; many more occurred in the months that followed. Strikers ranged from clothing and textile workers to actors, miners, and telephone operators. In the steel industry 365,000 workers went on strike; even the Boston police force walked out. By the end of 1919 more than four million workers (20 percent of the work force) had staged over 3,600 strikes nationwide.

The strikes frightened middle- and upper-class Americans, who feared the country might be swept by revolution. The government made matters worse by blaming the strikes on Communists. In 1919 Russian Bolsheviks called for socialists and workers in Europe and the United States to seize their governments and join the worldwide revolution. When Communist revolts erupted in eastern Europe, Americans braced themselves for trouble at home.

A bomb scare brought public fears to a head. On the eve of May 1 (May Day), 1919, authorities discovered 20 bombs in the mail of prominent capitalists, including John D. Rockefeller and J. P. Morgan, Jr., as well as government officials like Justice Oliver Wendell Holmes. A month later bombs exploded in eight American cities. Anarchists were probably responsible, but the public blamed the Communists.

Fear sparked by the labor unrest, Communism, and the bombings plunged the United States into the "Red Scare." Every threat to national security, real or imagined, fed the public's anxiety. Vigilantism flourished as juries across the country acquitted individuals accused of violent acts against Communists. Federal authorities, breaking up the IWW, arrested 1,000 Wobblies and slapped the union's leaders with stiff prison sentences. The nation had lost confidence in its ability to survive without police-state tactics. Civil liberties became the first victim of the hysteria, for the Bill of Rights was all but suspended. Again, Randolph Bourne's warnings hit the mark.

Attorney General A. Mitchell Palmer led the attack on radicalism. Determined to become president in 1920, Palmer hoped to ride a wave of public hysteria against radicalism into the White House. To root out sedition, he created a General Intelligence Division (the precursor of the Federal Bureau of Investigation) in the Justice Department under the direction of J. Edgar Hoover. Hoover collected the names of thousands of known or suspected Communists and made plans for a coordinated government attack on their headquarters.

Within the course of three months, raids ordered by Palmer in 45 cities netted more than 4,000 arrests of alleged Communists, many of whom were jailed without bond, beaten, and denied food and water for days. Local authorities freed most of them in a few weeks, except for 600 aliens, who were deported. While Palmer insisted he was ridding the country of the "moral perverts," to cooler heads his tactics gave off the unmistakable odor of a police state. Suddenly on the defensive, Palmer tried to rally public support by predicting a second wave of terrorist attacks on May Day, 1920. Federal troops went on alert, and police braced themselves in cities across the country, but May Day came and went without incident. Palmer's bid for the White House fizzled, and the Red Scare faded into memory.

The Treaty of Versailles

Long before the war's military outcome became clear, the Allies started planning for peace, signing secret treaties plotting harsh peace terms for Germany. Their plans made a mockery of Wilson's call for "peace without victory." Wilson, however, felt a punitive treaty would sow the seeds of future wars. He repeatedly elaborated his ideas on the interdependence of democracy, free trade, and liberty, and on January 8, 1918, he unveiled the Fourteen Points, his personal peace formula.

The Fourteen Points

Among other things, Wilson called for "open covenants openly arrived at," freedom of the seas, free trade, arms reduction, and self-determination. Other points demanded partial or full independence for minorities and a recognition of the rise of nationalist sentiments. The fourteenth point, which Wilson considered the heart of his plan, called for a League of Nations, an international organization to promote world peace.

Economically, the Fourteen Points projected Wilson's vision of liberal capitalism onto a world stage. His call for freedom of the seas and free trade was designed to protect free market capitalism from monopolistic restrictions and open huge markets to booming American industries. Self-determination would offer independence to Europe's minorities and thereby delight millions of recent immigrants back in the United States, most of whom were drifting into the Democratic party. The League of

Nations would enable the world to police aggression and relieve the United States of that responsibility.

Wilson's personal prestige peaked with the Armistice. During the war Democrats and Republicans had closed ranks behind his leadership. Europeans saw Wilson as the moral leader of the Western democracies, and his authority rested not only on words but on might. Economically, the United States was now the most powerful nation on earth.

Yet Wilson proved to be his own worst enemy in marshaling support for his peace plans. His first mistake was in asking voters to support Democratic candidates at the polls in 1918. His request offended Republicans who had faithfully supported the administration throughout the war. When voters gave Republicans a narrow majority (primarily reflecting local issues), Wilson looked as if he had lost a national referendum on his leadership.

The American Peace Commission's composition further alienated Congress. Wilson elected to take personal responsibility for negotiating the peace, a role no previous president had assumed. In addition, he named only one Republican to the five-man commission; the other three men were loyal Democrats. The failure to include a prominent Republican senator, such as Henry Cabot Lodge, the newly elected chairman of the powerful Senate Committee on Foreign Relations, was a serious tactical error. The treaty had to be approved by two-thirds of the Senate, and Republicans picked up five new Senate seats in the congressional elections of 1918, giving them a two-vote majority.

Discord Among the Victors

The delegates, who arrived in Europe early in January 1919, confronted three basic issues: territory, reparations, and future security. On each of these issues, Wilson and the Allies disagreed. Early in the war the Allies decided to divide Germany's territorial possessions among themselves, but the Fourteen Points called for self-determination. Devastated by the war, the Allies (especially France) wanted to saddle Germany with huge reparations to pay for the war. The Fourteen Points rejected punishment, arguing it would only lead to future wars. On the issue of security, France wanted Germany dismembered while the other Allies favored treaties and alliances.

Only five nations played an important role in the proceedings (the Allies refused to allow Russia's Communist government a place at the peace table). Prime Minister David Lloyd George of Great Britain proved to be Wilson's staunchest ally, yet he also defended Britain's colonial ambitions and insisted on reparations. Premier Georges Clemenceau of

France was determined to break up the German empire and bleed the German people dry in order to rebuild France. Premier Vittorio Orlando of Italy was bent on pressing Italy's territorial ambitions in the Tyrol and on the Adriatic. When Wilson refused to sanction Italy's sovereignty over the largely Yugoslav population near Fiume, Orlando stormed out of the peace conference in disgust. The final important negotiator was Count Nobuaki Makino, the spokesman for Japan, who demanded control over German interests in the Far East.

To achieve any treaty at all, Wilson had to compromise. In the end he tried to scale down the Allied demands and pinned his hopes on the League of Nations. Under the territorial compromise, the Allies gained control of Germany's colonies as "mandates" under the League of Nation's supervision. Japan acquired Germany's Pacific islands under mandate and assumed Germany's economic interest in China's Shantung peninsula. In eastern Europe the delegates created the nation-states of Poland, Yugoslavia, Czechoslovakia, Estonia, Latvia, Lithuania, and Finland. Eu-

At the Versailles peace conference Wilson met with Prime Minister David Lloyd George, Premier Vittorio Orlando, and Premier Georges Clemenceau.

rope's political map for the first time roughly resembled its linguistic and cultural map.

Over the misgivings of most delegates, Wilson insisted on making the League of Nations an integral part of the final treaty. France remained dubious that any international organization could protect French borders and demanded a buffer zone. To satisfy Clemenceau, the delegates gave France a buffer zone to protect it from future German aggression. After Wilson and Lloyd George both signed security treaties guaranteeing these arrangements, France grudgingly agreed to join the League of Nations.

Despite promises of a just peace, the treaty imposed a harsh settlement on Germany, burdening the country with a $34 billion reparations bill, far more than Germany could pay. In addition, Germany lost territories that contained German people. Moreover, the war guilt clause in the reparations bill required Germany to accept the blame for World War I and dismantle its war machine. Germany felt betrayed. Clearly, this was not a peace based upon the Fourteen Points. Rather, it brought to life Bourne's prediction of victors who "grab what they can."

Wilson derived no joy from the Treaty of Versailles. He accepted the treaty's territorial and punitive provisions in order to ensure the adoption of the League of Nations, which he hoped would secure world peace and eventually redress the treaty's inequities. The League consisted of a general assembly, and an executive council composed of the United States, Great Britain, France, Italy, Japan, and four other states to be elected by the assembly. But the heart of the League was clearly Article 10, which pledged all members "to respect and uphold the territorial integrity and independence of all members of the League." It embodied Wilson's dream of an international organization that would keep the peace by giving all nations (large and small) equality and protection.

The Struggle for Ratification

Wilson knew the treaty faced stiff opposition back home. In February 1919, 39 Senate Republicans had signed a petition warning that they would not approve the League in its present form. To court domestic support, Wilson persuaded the delegates in Europe to acknowledge the Monroe Doctrine, omit domestic issues from the League's purview, and permit member states to withdraw after two years' notice. Though he worked to include provisions the Senate wanted, Wilson refused to separate the League from the treaty.

Senate opposition broke into three groups. The first, 14 "irreconcilables," were staunch isolationists who opposed the League of Nations in any form. Though their attack was broad-based, they concentrated their fire on Article 10, which called for the mutual protection of the territorial integrity of all member states. Critics charged that this article gave the League the authority to commit American troops to foreign military actions. Henry Cabot Lodge of Massachusetts spoke for the "strong reservationists." Lodge and his followers were basically in favor of the treaty and could have been won over if Wilson agreed to their modifications. Like the irreconcilables, they were also opposed to Article 10, insisting that only Congress had the right to commit American troops. The third group of opponents could have been won over by relatively minor alterations. They approached international affairs as cautious nationalists, favoring an independent foreign policy as the best tool for protecting American interests. With their backing and the support of Senate Democrats, the treaty would have passed easily.

As Wilson sailed back to the United States, polls suggested that most Americans favored the League in some form. All he had to do was compromise and the treaty would pass. Dismissing his opponents as "blind and little provincial people," he declared that the "Senate must take its medicine."

Fearing Senate debate had eroded popular support for the treaty, Wilson decided to take his case directly to the people. Although in poor health, he launched a nationwide tour in September 1919, covering 8,000 miles in 33 days and delivering 32 major addresses. He started in the Midwest where opposition to the treaty was strongest, gradually moving west where he met cheering crowds. Totally exhausted, Wilson collapsed on September 25 in Pueblo, Colorado. Four days after returning to Washington, he suffered a severe stroke that paralyzed the left side of his body.

Unable to work, the president did not meet his cabinet for more than six months. Since the law made no provision for removing an incapacitated president, Wilson's second wife, Edith, assisted by a few close aides, ran the government, operating under a cloak of silence about the president's condition.

As the Senate vote on the treaty drew near, Wilson, whose stroke may have impaired his judgment, remained intransigent. He ordered all Democrats to vote against the treaty if it contained any changes. On November 19 the Senate defeated the revised version of the treaty, 55 to 39; a few minutes later the Senate defeated the treaty without changes, 39 to 53.

The Senate's failure to reach a compromise must be blamed on Wilson. When the treaty's supporters tried again in March, many of the Democrats disobeyed the president and voted for a revised version. But 23 Democrats followed Wilson's orders, and the treaty fell seven votes short of adoption. It would be wrong to interpret the treaty's defeat as an endorsement of isolationism. In essence, the Senate rejected both isolationism and Wilsonian internationalism in favor of preserving a nationalistic foreign policy that would allow the United States to act independently.

The refusal of the Senate to ratify the Treaty of Versailles and join the League of Nations is satirized in this cartoon.

The Election of 1920

When the Democratic convention met in San Francisco, the delegates ignored Wilson's pathetic anglings for a third term and nominated Governor James M. Cox of Ohio. The Republicans nominated Senator Warren G. Harding of Ohio. A stalwart party regular on domestic issues, Harding had voted for the Treaty of Versailles with the Lodge reservations.

While Cox barnstormed the country, campaigning unequivocally for the League of Nations and the Treaty of Versailles, Harding waffled on the issue. Tired of foreign crusades, voters clearly wanted a change, giving Harding 61 percent of the popular vote. In the electoral college Harding trounced Cox 404 to 127.

Harding interpreted his victory as a mandate to reject the League. America never joined the League of Nations, opening the way for those who later blamed the United States for the rise of fascism in Italy and Nazism in Germany. Critics went so far as to claim that America's failure to join the League caused World War II. If the United States had only joined, they insisted, the League would have been able to deter German and Japanese aggression by presenting a united front. The war's main legacy, then, was not peace without victory, but bitterness and suspicion.

*C*hronology of Key Events

1914	World War I begins
1915	U.S. marines dispatched to Haiti; Germans sink *Lusitania,* British passenger ship
1916	*Sussex* pledge temporarily reduces tensions between U.S. and Germany
1917	Zimmermann telegram urges Mexico and Japan to join Central Powers; United States enters the war in Europe; Espionage Act passed; Russian Revolution begins; War Industries Board created to coordinate industrial production; Selective Service Act
1918	Wilson outlines plan for peace in his Fourteen Points; National War Labor Board created to arbitrate labor-management disputes; Sedition Act passed; Germany surrenders
1919	Treaty of Versailles ends World War I
1920	Red Scare; Senate rejects Treaty of Versailles; Nineteenth Amendment adopted; Warren Harding is elected twenty-ninth president

Conclusion

World War I made Randolph Bourne a prophet. The changes in American life between 1914 and 1919 bore out his fear that war obliterates idealism and brings out the dark side of the human spirit. World War I accelerated social and economic changes, expanded the power of the federal government, and unleashed extraordinary fears that led to attacks on labor unions, blacks, immigrants, and radicals. Similar confusion gripped America's foreign policy. The United States emerged from the Great War as the premier economic power on earth, with global interests requiring protection. Those responsibilities terrified a country that had been lulled into a sense of security by three centuries of geographic isolation. Tired and disillusioned, Americans attempted to flee their responsibilities rather than make global political commitments commensurate with their new economic interests.

The result was an upsurge in isolationist sentiment in the United States during the 1920s and 1930s that made it very difficult for America's leaders to respond strongly to the rise of despotic governments in Europe and the Far East. The Great War did not make the world "safe for democracy." It left humankind a legacy of bitterness, hatred, and suspicion, creating rich soil for the seeds of future conflicts.

In 1920, however, most Americans felt too numb to give much thought to the future. When President Harding promised a return to "normalcy," he struck a responsive chord. Millions of Americans thought he meant resurrecting rural villages and a small farm economy, restoring Anglo-Protestant culture, and forgetting about the rest of the world. The 1920s proved they were in for a surprise.

Suggestions for Further Reading

For excellent overviews of analyses of America and World War I, consult Ross Gregory, *The Origins of American Intervention in the First World War* (1971); Ellis W. Hawley, *The Great War and the Search for a Modern Order* (1979); Gordon Levin, Jr., *Woodrow Wilson and World Politics* (1968); Bernadotte Schmitt and Harold C. Vedeler, *The World in the Crucible* (1984).

Women during and after the war are examined in Maurine Weiner Greenwald, *Women, War, and Work* (1980); Christine A. Lunardini, *From Equal Suffrage to Equal Rights: Alice Paul and the National Woman's Party* (1986).

Other sociopolitical issues are examined in James R. Grossman, *Land of Hope: Chicago, Black Southerners, and the Great Migration* (1989); David M. Kennedy, *Over Here: The First World War and American Society* (1980);

Frederick C. Luebke, *Bonds of Loyalty: German-Americans and World War I* (1974); Carole Marks, *Farewell—We're Good and Gone: The Great Black Migration* (1989).

The contentious debates surrounding the Treaty of Versailles are discussed in Herbert F. Margulies, *The Mild Reservationists and the League of Nations Controversy in the Senate* (1989); Arno J. Mayer, *Politics and Diplomacy in Peacemaking: Containment and Counterrevolution at Versailles* (1967); Ralph A. Stone, *The Irreconcilables* (1970); William C. Widenor, *Henry Cabot Lodge and the Search for an American Foreign Policy* (1980).

The most in-depth biography of Woodrow Wilson remains Arthur S. Link, *Wilson*, (5 vols. (1947–1965). For a study of Randolph Bourne, see James R. Vitelli, *Randolph Bourne* (1981). Bourne's essays can be found in Randolph S. Bourne, *War and the Intellectuals: Collected Essays* (1915–1919) (1964).

Chapter *24*

Modern Times, the 1920s

The Clash of Values
The Growth of Cities
Black Protests
The Harlem Renaissance
The New Woman and the Sex Debate

The Revolt of the Traditionalists
Prohibition
The Scopes Trial
Xenophobia and Restricting Immigration
The Ku Klux Klan

The Rise of Urban Culture
The Consumer Culture
The Lost Generation
The Communication Revolution
The Rise of Suburbs
Leisure Time

The Republican Restoration
Handsome Harding
Silent Cal
The Twilight of Progressivism
The Election of 1928

The Great Crash

In 1898 the Physicians Club of Chicago held a symposium on "sexual hygiene" to give its members some practical tips on marriage counseling. To those married women who wanted information on birth control, Chicago physicians offered this advice: "Get a divorce and vacate the position for some other woman, who is able and willing to fulfill all a wife's duties as well as to enjoy her privileges."

Most Americans shared this view. They did not believe sex should be separated from procreation. To the male custodians of morality, birth control challenged patriarchy. It would lead to sexual promiscuity and an epidemic of venereal diseases, they charged, and weaken the family by raising the divorce rate. Many women condemned birth control just as soundly. Taught from childhood to embrace the cult of domesticity, they accepted childbearing as their "biological duty" and rejected birth control as immoral and radical.

Yet by 1950 most Americans regarded birth control as a public virtue rather than a private vice. The person most responsible for this amazing transformation was Margaret Sanger, a tireless crusader who possessed an iron will and the soul of a firebrand. Sanger's mother, Margaret Higgins, bore 11 children, all ten-pounders or more; Michael Higgins, her father worked as a stonecutter. Her mother died of pulmonary tuberculosis at 43; her father lived to 84. For the rest of her life, Sanger blamed her mother's suffering on the absence of effective family planning.

An unhappy marriage also pushed Sanger toward reform work. While still in nursing school, she married William Sanger, an architect and would-be artist. After bearing three children in rapid succession, Sanger overcame her own struggle with tuberculosis, finished school, and began a nursing career. Feeling trapped by married life and determined to achieve her own identity, Margaret plunged into New York's labor movement. As her marriage to William slowly dissolved, she devoted herself to the working poor.

Convinced that large families placed a terrible economic burden on poor people, Sanger came to regard family planning as the most important issue of her day because birth control would make abortion, as well as unwanted babies, unnecessary. When male labor leaders refused to add contraception to their reform agenda, Sanger left the labor movement, resolving to make birth control her life's work.

From 1914 to 1937 Sanger campaigned to make birth control morally acceptable. She built a network of clinics where women could get accurate information about contraception and obtain inexpensive, reliable birth control devices. After World War II she helped organize the international planned parenthood movement and played a key role in the development of "the pill." Through her birth control work, Margaret Sanger probably had a greater influence on the world than any other American woman of her day.

Margaret Sanger, a nurse who had watched many women suffer from
unwanted births and die from illegal abortions, was one of the founders of the
modern American birth control movement. After spending a year studying
medical literature and learning about contraceptives, Sanger began publishing
the journal *The Woman Rebel.*

Sanger played a key role in the transition to modern times. Her career
illustrates how the reform spirit of the Progressive Era survived the conservative climate of the 1920s to touch the lives of future generations. No
legacy of progressivism was more far-reaching than the birth control
movement, which reformed sexual mores, redefined women's role in society, and redistributed power within the family. But the birth control
movement represented just one symptom of a society in flux, one in
which urban growth, ethnic diversity, and economic development set the
stage for controversy.

The Clash of Values

In the wake of the Great War's carnage and failed promises, many Americans disagreed on a host of issues. Wets battled drys, atheists ridiculed
fundamentalists, nativists denounced the "new immigrants," whites
lashed out against blacks. Rural folks debated the dubious morals of city
dwellers, while farmers glowered at industrialists. Yet none of these disputes was new. Each was a continuing, if sharpening, controversy that had
been building for decades. At bottom these conflicts were the unavoidable

growing pains of a nation struggling to come to grips with cultural pluralism and changing values.

The Growth of Cities

Cities underwent dramatic and visible changes. By 1920, more Americans dwelled in cities than in the country for the first time in the nation's history. Most urbanites lived in small towns and cities, but a surprising number resided in large cities of 50,000 or more. During the 1920s nearly 15 million Americans moved to cities.

Urban growth drove up land values and reshaped the skyline of America's cities, especially in central business districts, where office space more than doubled during the 1920s. Skyrocketing land prices forced architects to build "up" instead of "out," launching the first great era of skyscrapers.

America's cities attracted large numbers of new immigrants from southern and eastern Europe. These immigrants poured into the industrial cities of the Northeast and Midwest, filling them with new sights, sounds, and smells that many old-stock Americans found offensive. World War I briefly stopped the flow of immigrants, but between 1919 and 1926, more than 3.2 million immigrants poured into the United States.

Blacks contributed to the new urban growth. In 1910 three out of every four black Americans lived on farms, and nine out of ten lived in the South. World War I changed that profile. Hoping to escape the tenant farming, sharecropping, and peonage of the South, 1.5 million blacks moved to cities in the 1920s. Some went to southern cities, but most settled in major northern metropolises such as New York, Philadelphia, Cleveland, and Chicago.

Black migration intensified housing shortages, making competition for limited housing a source of friction between blacks and whites. In city after city, whites closed ranks against blacks, blocking access to white neighborhoods. Cities passed municipal residential segregation ordinances; white realtors refused to show blacks houses in white areas; and white property owners formed "neighborhood improvement associations," largely in order to keep blacks out. After the Supreme Court declared municipal residential segregation ordinances unconstitutional in 1917, whites resorted to the restrictive convenant, a formal deed restriction binding white property owners in a given neighborhood not to sell to blacks. Whites who broke these agreements could be sued by "damaged" neighbors. Not until 1948 did the Supreme Court strike down restrictive covenants. Zoning laws offered a more subtle means of segregating blacks. Originally designed to keep businessmen and industries out of residential neighborhoods, zoning restrictions had become the tool of choice for segregating people on the basis of wealth by the 1930s.

Racial animosity, restrictive covenants, and zoning restrictions confined blacks to certain neighborhoods. Between World War I and World

War II scores of American cities developed cities within cities. These "black metropolises" resembled ethnic ghettos of the late nineteenth and early twentieth centuries, with one major difference: racial prejudice made it all but impossible for their residents to escape to the suburbs.

Black Protests

In the 1920s several black organizations stepped up their protests against discrimination, which heightened the fears of many old-stock Americans. Closely identified with Booker T. Washington's conciliatory approach to race relations, the National Urban League, organized in 1911 by social workers, white philanthropists, and conservative blacks, concentrated on finding jobs for urban African Americans. Despite the nation's postwar prosperity, blacks made scant progress on the job front during the 1920s.

Leaving economic issues to the Urban League, the National Association for the Advancement of Colored People (NAACP), formed in 1909, concentrated on civil rights and legal action. The NAACP won important Supreme Court decisions against the grandfather clause (1915) and restrictive covenants (1917). The NAACP also fought school segregation in northern cities during the 1920s, and lobbied hard, though unsuccessfully, for a federal antilynching bill. Though progress on these fronts did not come until after World War II, the NAACP became the nation's leading civil rights organization.

Black radicals dismissed the Urban League and the NAACP as too conservative. A. Philip Randolph, the editor of the Socialist monthly, the *Messenger,* called for a "New Negro" who would meet violence with violence to end discrimination and achieve racial equality. Randolph also urged blacks to seek admission into trade unions. Though Randolph addressed the black masses, he appealed to the college-educated, black elite. Most blacks neither read nor understood his theories.

Marcus Garvey spoke for the black masses. A flamboyant and charismatic figure from Jamaica, Garvey rejected integration and preached racial pride and black separatism, exhorting his followers to glorify their African heritage. In 1914 Garvey organized the Universal Negro Improvement Association (UNIA) to promote black migration to Africa. Under the slogan, "Africa for the Africans, at home and abroad," the UNIA's Black Star Steamship Line sold stock to thousands of members, promising to help blacks migrate to Africa. Garvey also advocated economic self-sufficiency for those who remained in the United States. To enable his followers to buy only from black-owned businesses, the UNIA opened a chain of laundries, groceries, restaurants, a hotel, a doll factory (whose products all had black bodies), and a printing plant.

The UNIA collapsed in the mid-1920s after the Black Star Line went bankrupt. Garvey was charged with mail fraud, jailed, and finally deported, but this "Black Moses" left behind a rich legacy. At a time when magazines and newspapers overflowed with advertisements for hair straighteners and skin-lightening cosmetics, Garvey's message of racial pride struck a responsive chord in many black Americans.

The Harlem Renaissance

The movement for black pride found its cultural expression in the Harlem Renaissance. Located in New York's upper Manhattan, Harlem attracted black intellectuals who migrated from small towns or rural areas where they had felt stifled and oppressed.

By the 1920s the Harlem Renaissance was in full bloom. Langston Hughes probed the past in his elegant poem, "The Negro Speaks of Rivers." In *Cane,* Jean Toomer, perhaps the most gifted prose writer of the renaissance, explored the lives of blacks who toiled in Georgia's sawmills in the 1880s. Yet for all its artistic promise, the Harlem Renaissance had little influence on the black masses, most of whom never knew it existed. Moreover, the Harlem Renaissance often reflected the cultural stereotypes of white liberals, who underwrote the renaissance by providing scholarships, prizes, and grants to aspiring young black artists. Leaders of the Harlem Renaissance shied away from controversial social issues and all but ignored jazz, one of the most important black contributions to American popular culture.

The New Woman and the Sex Debate

"If all girls at the Yale prom were laid end to end, I wouldn't be surprised," sighed Dorothy Parker, the official wit of New York's smart set. Parker's quip captured the public's perception that America's morals had taken a nosedive. Practically every newspaper featured articles on prostitution, venereal disease, sex education, birth control, and the rising divorce rate.

City life nurtured new sexual attitudes. With its crowded anonymity, urban culture eroded sexual inhibitions by relaxing community restraints on individual behavior. Cities also promoted secular, consumer values, and city people seemed to tolerate, if not welcome, many forms of diversity.

If cities spawned a new environment for sexual values, the new psychology of Sigmund Freud provided the ideas. A Vienna physician, Freud revolutionized academic and popular thinking about human behavior by arguing that unconscious sexual anxieties cause much of human behavior. Freud also explained how sexual desires and fears develop in infancy and stay with people throughout their lives. During the 1920s physicians, academics, advice columnists, women's magazines, and preachers debated Freud's theories.

The image of the "flapper"—the liberated woman who bobbed her hair, painted her lips, raised her hemline, and danced the Charleston—personified the public's anxiety about the decline of traditional morality. In the 1950s Alfred C. Kinsey, a researcher at Indiana University, found that women born after 1900 were twice as likely to have had premarital sex as their mothers, with the most pronounced changes occurring in the generation reaching maturity in the early 1920s.

Sexual permissiveness had eroded Victorian values, but the "new woman" posed less of a challenge to traditional morality than her critics

The image of the "flapper," who bobbed her hair, bared her knees, and smoked and drank in public, alarmed a public still clinging to Victorian codes of morality.

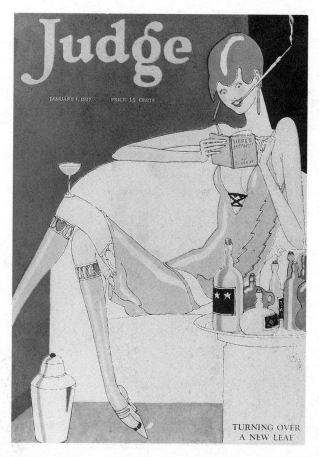

feared. Far from being promiscuous, her sexual experience before marriage was generally limited to one or two partners, one of whom she married. In practice, this narrowed the gap between men and women and moved society toward a single standard of morality. Instead of turning to prostitutes, men made love with their sweethearts, who in many instances became their wives.

Moreover, the sexual revolution did not redefine gender roles for women. The "new woman" embraced the traditional duties of wife and mother. In fact, the most striking theme of women's history in the 1920s was its continuity with the past. Nowhere was the absence of change more evident than in politics. Most feminists had viewed suffrage as the key to ending discrimination against women. After the Nineteenth Amendment passed, reformers talked about female voters uniting to clean up politics, improve society, and end discrimination in the marketplace.

None of these dreams came true during the 1920s. Women failed to organize into a bloc vote, and generally did not vote differently than men. Even more galling to feminists, substantial numbers of women during the 1920s failed to vote at all.

Nor did women win new opportunities in the marketplace. Although the American work force included eight million women in 1920, more than half were black or foreign-born. Domestic service remained the largest occupation, followed by secretaries, typists, and clerks—all low-paying jobs. The American Federation of Labor (AFL) remained openly hostile to women because it did not want females competing for male jobs. Female professionals, too, made little progress. They consistently received less pay than their male counterparts. Moreover, they were concentrated in traditionally "female" occupations—teaching and nursing.

Most Americans regarded working women as an anomaly. Young women could work during the interlude between leaving home and marriage, but they were expected to make homemaking their career after marriage. While economic necessity forced many poor women to continue working after marriage, most middle-class women of the 1920s abandoned any hope of combining careers with marriage.

Americans had not resolved the basic conflict between equal rights for women and the sexual division of labor that continued to confine women to the domestic sphere. Feminists had secured the vote, not true equality.

The Revolt of the Traditionalists

Teeming cities, crowded ghettos, unfamiliar immigrants, black migration, civil rights protests, and new sexual mores all proved deeply threatening to traditional white Protestants. During the 1920s old-stock Americans vented their fears and frustrations by attacking alcohol, smoking, evolution, immigrants, and radicals.

Prohibition

Like the sex debate, prohibition exposed deep fissures in American society. The issue turned on the class, ethnic, and religious makeup of individual communities, not merely on whether the community was rural or urban.

At first prohibition's apparent success muted its critics. Distilleries and breweries shut down, saloons locked their doors, arrests for drunkenness declined, and alcohol-related deaths all but disappeared. Compliance, however, had less to do with piety and public support than the law of supply and demand: since illegal liquor remained in short supply, its price rose beyond the average worker's means.

Private enterprise filled the void. Smugglers supplied wealthy imbibers, but the less affluent had to rely on small-time operators who produced for local consumption. Much of this booze ran the gamut from swill to poison. According to one story, a potential buyer who sent a liquor sample to a laboratory for analysis was shocked when the chemist replied: "Your horse has diabetes." For others the problem of "killer batches" was no laughing matter. Hundreds, perhaps thousands, died from drinking these illegal concoctions.

Neither federal nor state authorities had enough funds to enforce prohibition. Lax enforcement, coupled with huge profits, enticed organized crime to enter bootlegging. Long a fixture of urban life, with gambling and prostitution as its base, organized crime had operated on a small, local scale. Liquor, however, demanded production plants, distribution networks, and sales forces. Bootlegging turned into a gold mine for organized crime. By the late 1920s liquor sales generated revenue in excess of $2 billion annually. Chicago's Al Capone had a gross income of $60 million in 1927. A ruthless figure accused of ordering numerous gangland killings, he preferred to think of himself as a businessman.

From the outset, cynics insisted prohibition could not be enforced. They were right. Particularly in large cities, people openly defied the law. On more than one occasion journalists saw President Warren G. Harding's bootlegger deliver cases of liquor to the White House in broad daylight.

In 1923 New York became the first state to repeal its enforcement law, and by 1930 six more states had followed suit. Others remained firmly committed to prohibition. After a presidential commission reported prohibition could not be enforced, Congress finally repealed it in 1933, making liquor control a state and local matter.

The campaign to outlaw cigarette smoking was closely allied to the prohibition movement. Opposition to tobacco was not new. During the nineteenth century the antitobacco campaign remained an appendage of the temperance movement. After the introduction of machine-made cigarettes in the 1880s, however, opponents concentrated their fire specifically on the "little white slavers."

As early as the Civil War, a few cities had banned smoking in restaurants, theaters, public buildings, trolleys, and railway cars. After antismokers organized the National Anti-Cigarette League in 1903, scores of prominent leaders joined the crusade. By 1923, 14 states outlawed the sale of cigarettes, prompting calls for a constitutional amendment for national prohibition. By the end of the decade. however, every state had repealed its law against cigarette sales. A national consensus had not formed against tobacco, and the tobacco industry opposed every effort to restrict the sale of cigarettes, spending millions of dollars on advertisements. Thus smokers had no difficulty defending their right to smoke—at least for the present.

The Scopes Trial

Many custodians of small-town morality also fretted over the teaching of evolution in public schools, and they got their day in court in the celebrated "Monkey Trial." In 1925 the Tennessee legislature passed a bill that prohibited the teaching of evolution in public schools. Immediately afterwards, a 24-year-old science teacher, John Scopes, from Dayton, Tennessee, provoked a test case by declaring publicly he taught biology from an evolutionary standpoint.

Scopes was brought to trial in the summer of 1925. William Jennings Bryan, rural America's defender of the faith, agreed to join the team of prosecutors, and Clarence Darrow, the celebrated trial lawyer and self-proclaimed agnostic, volunteered his services to defend Scopes.

The trial opened on July 10, 1925. As Holy Rollers from the surrounding regions held revivals and religious zealots exhorted people to read their Bibles, huge crowds poured into Dayton to watch Bryan and Darrow do combat. Near the end of testimony the defense surprised everyone by asking Bryan to take the stand as an expert witness on the Bible. His simple, direct answers to Darrow's sarcastic questions revealed an unshakable faith in the literal truth of the Bible. Bryan insisted "it is better to trust in the Rock of Ages than to know the ages of rocks."

The outcome was never in doubt. Scopes admitted he had broken the law. He was convicted and fined $100. (Tennessee's supreme court later rescinded the fine on a technicality.) What gave the trial its drama was the clash between Bryan and Darrow and the opposite images of America they represented. Bryan, who died five days after the trial ended, left the courtroom believing he had carried the day. His opponents, however, thought he had been humiliated and proclaimed the Scopes trial a victory for academic freedom. In the end, the Scopes trial merely illustrated how little tolerance secular and fundamentalist groups had for each other.

Xenophobia and Restricting Immigration

Cultural fears unleashed a new wave of nativism in the 1920s. Organized labor, bent upon protecting high wages, resented competition from cheap labor; staunch nativists and superpatriots warned that foreign influences would corrupt the American character; and assorted businessmen denounced immigrants as dangerous radicals.

To protect the United States these groups demanded drastic changes in the nation's immigration policy. Congress passed the National Origins Act of 1924, establishing an annual immigration quota of two percent of each national group counted in the 1890 census, and barring Asians entirely. Since southern and eastern Europeans did not begin arriving in large numbers until the turn of the century, the law gave western and northern Europeans a big edge over the "new immigrants."

Hostility to immigrants also surfaced in the Sacco and Vanzetti case. On April 15, 1920, two unidentified gunmen robbed a payroll messenger from a shoe factory in South Braintree, Massachusetts, killing a paymaster and a guard. Two Italian immigrants, Nicola Sacco and Bartolomeo Vanzetti, both avowed anarchists, were arrested and charged with the crime. Although the state failed to prove its case, prosecutors succeeded in parading the radical political views of both men before the jury. On July 14, 1921, Sacco and Vanzetti were convicted and sentenced to death.

The trial brought a storm of protest from Italian-Americans, liberals, and civil rights advocates. Despite lengthy appeals, the conviction was upheld, and Sacco and Vanzetti, asserting their innocence to the end, went to the electric chair on August 23, 1927.

The Ku Klux Klan

Fear of political radicals and ethnic minorities found its most strident voice during the 1920s in the rebirth of the Ku Klux Klan. The secret organization, led by Colonel William Joseph Simmons, stood for "100 percent pure Americanism" and limited its membership to white, native-born Protestants. Membership remained small until Simmons hired two advertising specialists, Edward Young Clarke and Elizabeth Tyler, to market the Klan nationwide. Klan policy was set at the local level, varying from community to community to accommodate local prejudices, be they directed at blacks, Catholics, Jews, Mexicans, Orientals, foreigners, or "Reds."

Many people felt that Sacco and Vanzetti, Italian-born admitted anarchists, were persecuted for their immigrant status and radical views rather than for any real crime. Their trial, shown here in a painting by Ben Shahn, became an important symbol in the fight for civil liberties and brought about violent protest in America and abroad. Ben Shahn, *Bartholomeo Vanzetti and Nicola Sacco* (1931–32). Tempera on paper over composition board, 10 × 14; dp. Gift of Mrs. John D. Rockefeller, Jr./The Museum of Modern Art, New York.

Clarke and Tyler hired an army of organizers to canvas the country selling memberships in the Klan. (Membership cost $10; the sheet was $4 extra.) Working on commission and molding their pitch to match their clientele, they enjoyed astounding success. By 1921 the Klan had become a national organization with over 90,000 paying members; by 1925 it claimed a membership of five million. The Klan was strongest (and most violent) in the South, but it had a large following in the Southeast, the Far West, and the Midwest. Its natural habitat was not the countryside, but middling towns and small cities. Most members were not "poor white trash," but members of the lower middle class from old-stock, respectable families.

In the mid-1920s the Klan was a political force to reckon with. It influenced the election of several governors and state legislatures. In addition the Klan sought to intimidate individuals, using night ridings, cross

The Ku Klux Klan exploited postwar confusion and fear of anything "un-American." Although the Klan had flourished in small, rural towns across the South, during the 1920s it spread to working-class and middle-class neighborhoods of large cities, where people felt threatened by the influx of African-American and immigrant workers.

burnings, tar and featherings, public beatings, and lynchings as forms of coercion. The Klan did not limit its wrath to ethnic and religious offenders, but also lashed out against wife beaters, drunkards, bootleggers, gamblers—anyone who violated time-honored standards of morality.

In the end poor leadership and the absence of a political program destroyed the Klan. Once they attained office, Klan-supported officials offered no constructive legislation. Even more damaging, several Klan leaders became involved in sex scandals, and several more were indicted for corruption. By 1930 the white sheets and cross burnings vanished from public view, only to return again a few decades later when the civil rights movement challenged white supremacy.

The Rise of Urban Culture

Despite all the upheavals, a new force for social cohesion was drawing Americans together during the 1920s. The United States was rapidly evolving a consumer culture that blunted regional differences and imposed similar tastes and life-styles. Centered in the cities and propelled by revolutions in transportation, advertising, communications, and entertainment, a new consumer society emerged during the 1920s, enshrining materialism and self-indulgence as the dominant cultural motifs of prosperity's decade.

The Consumer Culture

In 1900 only 8,000 motor vehicles were registered in the United States and the automobile was little more than a rich man's toy; by 1920 Americans owned more than nine million automobiles. By 1925 Henry Ford had lowered the price of his sturdy Model T to less than $300, about three-months' pay for the average urban worker, and by 1930 automobile registrations had risen to 26,531,999. No previous form of transportation (except walking) had been so widely available. The great American love affair with the automobile had begun.

Enthusiasts claimed the automobile promoted family togetherness through evening rides, picnics, and weekend excursions. Critics decried squabbles between parents and teenagers over use of the automobile, and an apparent decline in church attendance resulting from Sunday outings. Worst of all, charged critics, automobiles gave young people freedom and privacy, "portable bedrooms" that couples could take anywhere. Critics also blamed the automobile for undermining the public's devotion to thrift. In the past, people had paid cash for consumer goods or done without. With auto manufacturers and banks encouraging the public to buy the car of their dreams on credit, this thrift ethic slowly eroded.

The increasing availability of electricity offered the key to another vast new market, appliances. As more and more of America's households received electricity, refrigerators, washing machines, vacuum cleaners, and toasters quickly took hold. Appliances eased the sheer physical drudgery of housework, but they did not shorten the average housewife's work week. Women had to do more because standards of cleanliness kept rising. Sheets had to be changed weekly; the house had to be vacuumed daily. In short, social pressure expanded household chores to keep pace with the new technology. Far from liberating women, appliances imposed new standards and pressures.

The Lost Generation

While most Americans embraced the consumer culture, others found it thoroughly disgusting. Disillusioned by the collapse of Wilsonian idealism, the hypocrisy of prohibition, and the upsurge of nativism, writers of this so-called Lost Generation felt alienated. To these cultural critics, America had become a nation of conspicuous consumption, awash in materialism and devoid of spiritual vitality.

No author captured these themes better than Sinclair Lewis, who in 1930 became the first American to win the Nobel Prize for literature. In *Main Street* (1920) he satirized small-town American life, with its narrow-minded complacency, while in *Babbitt* (1922) Lewis attacked the spiritual conformity that drove Americans to follow the crowd.

H. L. Mencken mounted a scathing attack on his countrymen. As editor of *Mercury* magazine, he wrote hundreds of essays mocking practically every aspect of American life. Calling the South a "gargantuan paradise of the fourth rate," and the middle class the "booboisie," Mencken directed his choicest barbs at reformers, whom he blamed for the bloodshed of World War I and the gangsters of the 1920s. "If I am convinced of anything," he snarled, "it is that Doing Good is in bad taste."

F. Scott Fitzgerald and Ernest Hemingway made the same points more obliquely. In novels such as *The Great Gatsby* (1925) and *Tender Is the Night* (1929) Fitzgerald exposed the decadence and materialism of American culture. Hemingway lionized toughness and "manly virtues" as a counterpoint to the softness of American life. In *The Sun Also Rises* (1926) and *A Farewell to Arms* (1929) he emphasized meaningless death and the importance of facing stoically the absurdities of the universe.

The Communication Revolution

In 1897 the United States had less than one telephone for every hundred residents; by 1930 the number stood at one in six. The telephone hastened the transition from the written to the electronically transmitted word, brought the home in closer contact with the outside world, and reduced household visiting among neighbors as friends picked up the phone instead of dropping in.

Radio had an even greater impact. It drew the nation together by bringing news, entertainment, and advertisements to more than ten million households by 1929. Radio not only offered something for everyone—news adventure shows, sports and "soaps"—but also helped create mass culture by blunting regional differences. Moreover, no other media had the power to create heroes and villains so quickly. When Charles Lindbergh became the first person to fly nonstop across the Atlantic from New York to Paris in 1927, the radio brought this incredible feat into American homes and made him a celebrity overnight.

In contrast, radio also brought the nation decidedly unheroic images. "Amos and Andy," one of the most popular shows of the depression, spread vicious racial stereotypes into homes whose white occupants knew little about black people. Other minorities fared no better. The Italian gangster, the bloodthirsty Indian, the Mexican with the singsong voice, the tightfisted Jew, and the Irish thug became stock characters in radio programming.

The Rise of Suburbs

Americans who bought the same products and listened to the same programs also shared new housing arrangements. New forms of transportation made the suburbs possible.

For much of the nation's history, cities could not grow larger because workers had to live within walking distance of their jobs. After the Civil War trolleys and streetcars permitted workers to move beyond the walking radius surrounding factories. In the twentieth century the automobile opened up vast new regions for housing, giving workers numerous options about where to live. Though suburbs had once been the exclusive domain of the well-to-do, the automobile enabled working-class families to move there, too.

Yet optimists who hoped to escape the city's congestion by moving to the suburbs got fooled. The sharp rise in road construction following the Federal Highway Act of 1916 produced complicated lateral traffic flows within cities and traffic congestion became worse. City planners counterattacked with traffic circles, synchronized stoplights, divided dual highways, and grade separation of highways from city streets, but nothing could free motorists from rush hour and holiday traffic jams.

Leisure Time

Thanks to the unprecedented prosperity of the 1920s, Americans had more money for leisure activities than ever before. Among the most popular were parlor games—mahjong sets, crossword puzzles, and the like. Contract bridge became the most durable of the new pastimes, followed closely by photography. Americans hit golf balls, played tennis, and bowled. Dance crazes like the fox trot, the Charleston, and the jitterbug swept the country.

While Lewis, Mencken, Fitzgerald, and Hemingway found a wide audience, millions of Americans preferred the new popular literature, largely because it resolved rather than explored cultural tensions. Edgar Rice Burroughs' *Tarzan of the Apes* became a runaway best-seller. For readers who felt concerned about urbanization and industrialization, the adventures of a lone white man in "dark Africa" revived the spirit of the frontier and individualism. Zane Grey's novels, such as *Riders of the Purple Sage,* enjoyed even greater popularity, using the tried but true formula of romance, action, and a moralistic struggle between good and evil, all put in a western setting. Between 1918 and 1934 Grey wrote 24 books and became the best-known writer of popular fiction in the country.

Other readers wanted to be titillated, as evidenced by the boom in "confession magazines." Urban values, liberated women, and Hollywood films had all relaxed Victorian standards. Confession magazines rushed to fill the vacuum, purveying stories of romantic success and failure, divorce, fantasy, and adultery. Writers survived the censors' cuts by placing moral tags at the end of their stories, advising readers to avoid similar mistakes in their own lives.

Spectator sports attracted vast audiences in the 1920s. The country yearned for heroes in an increasingly impersonal, organized society, and sports provided them. Prizefighters like Jack Dempsey became national idols. Team sports flourished, but Americans focused on individual superstars, people whose talents or personalities made them appear larger than life. Harold "Red" Grange, the "Galloping Ghost" halfback for the University of Illinois, raised professional football to new heights when he signed a contract with the Chicago Bears in 1926.

Baseball drew even bigger crowds than football. George Herman ("Babe") Ruth ruled as the sport's undisputed superstar. Up until the 1920s Ty Cobb's defensive brand of baseball, with its emphasis on base hits and stolen bases, dominated the sport. Ruth transformed baseball into the game of the home-run hitter. As a New York Yankee, Ruth set four home run records, hitting 60 in his best year, and led the team to four World Series. Between 1915 and 1930, the total number of home runs in major league baseball increased from 384 a year to 1,565. Baseball became the game of the big hitter, and none was bigger, literally or figuratively, than Babe Ruth.

Despite the mania for athletics, Americans shelled out ten times more money on movies than on spectator sports. By 1929, 90 million Americans—three fourths of the population—went to the movies every week to see Hollywood spectacles such as Cecil B. DeMille's *Ten Commandments* with its "cast of thousands" and dazzling special effects. Comedies, such as slapstick masterpieces starring Charlie Chaplin and Buster Keaton enjoyed great popularity as well. Like radio and sports, movies helped create a new popular culture, with common speech, dress, behavior, and heroes. And like radio, Hollywood did its share to reinforce racial stereotypes by denigrating minority groups. Mexicans appeared as sleepy-eyed peasants, while the only parts for blacks went to actors like Stepin Fetchit, who got rich playing superstitious, blithering idiots. The wooden box and the silver screen both molded and mirrored mass culture.

The Republican Restoration

The Republican party dominated American politics in the 1920s. When Republican leaders promised to restore prosperity, most Americans embraced the conservative rhetoric, hoping to find in politics the stability they found lacking in their culture. Talk about trust-busting and regulating big business gave way in New Era politics to calls for a partnership between government and industry, one that would promote the interests of American corporations at home and abroad.

Handsome Harding

By and large the presidents of the New Era were mediocre figures. Senator Warren G. Harding of Ohio, who led off the decade, suited the times perfectly. Handsome enough to be a movie star, he not only looked great, but promised voters what they wanted: a return to "normalcy." He appeared to be a moderate, responsible leader who would avoid extremes and guide the country into a decade of prosperity.

Harding, a fun-loving man who liked to play poker, drink whiskey, and shoot the breeze with old pals, left government to his cabinet members and the Supreme Court. Political conservatives all, they equated the people's interests with those of big business, championing American business interests abroad, denouncing government regulation, and slashing taxes on the rich.

Business leaders had contributed $8 million to the GOP's campaign chest in 1920; in return they expected the federal government to roll back the gains organized labor had made during World War I. They were not disappointed. Under the leadership of Chief Justice William Howard Taft, the Court took a narrow view of federal power, assigning the responsibility for protecting individual citizens to the states. During the 1920s the Court outlawed picketing, overturned national child labor laws, and abolished minimum wage laws for women.

The decade's most capable figure was Herbert Hoover, secretary of commerce under both Harding and his successor, Calvin Coolidge. A successful engineer, Hoover abhorred destructive competition and waste in the economy, which he proposed to eliminate through "associationism." Hoover called for voluntary trade associations to foster cooperation in industry and agriculture through commissions, trade practice controls, and ethical standards. By 1929 more than 2,000 trade associations were busily at work implementing Hoover's vision of a stable and prosperous economy. No other Harding appointment matched Hoover's talent and vision.

In fact, several of Harding's appointees proved to be disasters. Harding found it hard to say "no" to old friends and cronies, members of the so-called Ohio Gang, when they asked for government jobs. In the end this motley assortment of political hacks and hangers-on plunged his administration into disgrace, as major scandals involving bribes and kickbacks erupted in the Justice Department and in the Veterans Bureau. Shortly after these disclosures, Harding died of a cerebral embolism on August 2, 1923. Immediately after his death, more misdeeds came to light. In the infamous Teapot Dome oil scandal, Interior secretary Albert B. Fall was convicted of accepting $360,000 in bribes in exchange for leasing drilling rights on federal naval oil reserves, the first cabinet member in American history convicted for crimes in office. Attorney General Harry Daugherty, accused of accepting payoffs for selling German chemical patents controlled by the Alien Property Office, was forced to resign in disgrace.

Silent Cal

The election of 1924 symbolized, in a variety of ways, the tensions and concerns of the 1920s. Despite the Harding scandals, President Calvin Coolidge remained extremely popular, largely because of the nation's prosperity. Deeply divided over such issues as immigration, prohibition, and the Ku Klux Klan, the Democrats nominated a compromise candidate, John W. Davis, a Wall Street attorney.

A coalition of labor leaders, social workers, and former progressives bolted both major parties and formed the Progressive party, which nominated Wisconsin Senator Robert La Follette for president. Their platform called for government ownership of natural resources, abolition of child labor, elimination of monopolies, and increased taxes on the rich. In the end, no issue could match the GOP's prosperity crusade. Coolidge won the election by a comfortable margin.

Coolidge was a stern-faced, tight-lipped New Englander. Born in Plymouth Notch, Vermont, where five generations of Coolidges had worked the same family farm, he epitomized the rural values threatened by immigration, urbanization, and industrialization. As governor of Massachusetts, Coolidge had crushed a police strike in Boston in 1919 by calling out the National Guard, prompting the Republicans to give him the number two slot on their ticket in 1920.

Coolidge had no desire to be a strong president in the tradition of a Teddy Roosevelt or a Woodrow Wilson. A firm believer in the wisdom of inactivity, Coolidge slept ten hours a night, napped every afternoon, and seldom worked more than four hours a day. A staunch conservative,

Coolidge was positively consumed by his reverence for the corporate elite. "The man who builds a factory builds a temple," said Coolidge. "The man who works there, worships there." Government, he believed, should do everything in its power to promote business interests. While Coolidge set the tone for his administration, he left it to his cabinet members, the courts, and Congress to devise strategies for consummating the marriage between business and government.

The Twilight of Progressivism

The government's tilt toward business signaled a retreat from progressivism. With the Democrats in disarray and Teddy Roosevelt's wing of the GOP all but dead, conservative Republicans were riding high. Still, the reform impulse did not disappear entirely during the 1920s. A small band of beleaguered reformers, led by Robert La Follette of Wisconsin and George Norris of Nebraska, kept progressivism alive in Congress, where they worked for farm relief, child labor laws, and regulation of wages and working hours for women.

In keeping with their historic pattern, progressives had better luck at the state and local level than at the federal level, where they ran into stiff opposition from Congress or from Coolidge himself. Social workers and women's groups spearheaded campaigns which sponsored a broad range of welfare legislation. By 1930, 43 states had passed laws providing assistance to women with dependent children, and 34 states had adopted workers' compensation laws. Under the leadership of Governor Alfred Smith, New York granted women a 40-hour work week and instituted the nation's first public housing program.

Welfare opponents counterattacked, arguing labor reforms would increase production costs and leave states that passed welfare legislation at a competitive disadvantage with states without such laws. Asked to choose between social welfare programs and jobs, Congress, along with most states, opted for jobs.

The Election of 1928

After Coolidge announced his retirement from politics in 1928, the Republicans nominated Herbert Hoover, while the Democrats turned to Alfred E. Smith. Since both parties adopted nearly identical platforms, the election turned on personalities and images. Few elections have pitted opponents who better defined the two faces of America—one rural, the other urban.

A native of Iowa, Hoover depicted himself as a simple farmboy who, through hard work and pluck, had grown up to become wealthy and famous. Orphaned as a boy and cared for by a variety of relatives, Hoover worked his way through Stanford University, earning a degree in mining engineering. Brilliant and hard-working, he was a millionaire 12 years after landing his first engineering job. As a self-made man, Hoover presented a portrait of a safe, reassuring world.

Yet Hoover was also a spokesman for the future. He thought the federal government had a responsibility to coordinate the competing interests of a modern economy. He accepted the reality of industrialization, technology, governmental activism, and global markets, and in contrast to Harding and Coolidge, believed the president should lead the nation. According to Hoover, technology and expertise would make economic prosperity a permanent feature of American life.

The son of immigrants, Smith was an Irish Catholic from Hell's Kitchen in New York City who had started public life with nothing and had climbed the political ladder as a faithful son of the New York Democratic machine. Smith also represented the future, not so much in terms of science, technology, and organization, but in terms of cultural pluralism and urbanization. America's future lay with her cities, and the cities contained large groups of ethnic Americans struggling for acceptance and their share of the good life.

Aided by prosperity, Hoover coasted to an easy victory. Smith was hurt by his failure to bridge the North-South, urban-rural split in the Democratic party; by anti-Catholic sentiment; and by his opposition to prohibition. The Democrats were so divided that six states from Dixie abandoned the Solid South and defected to Hoover. Yet even in defeat, Smith's campaign revealed the most significant political change of the 1920s—the growing power of urban and ethnic voters and the shrinking influence of the rural element within the Democratic party.

Herbert Hoover's election marked the climax of New Era politics. As president he advocated total cooperation between government and business. Optimistic businesspeople, bankers, and stockbrokers applauded Hoover's promises, predicting a future of prosperity and progress. Ironically, the stock market crashed before their cheers had stopped echoing.

The Great Crash

Economic historians have been hard pressed to explain why "prosperity's decade" ended in financial disaster. Employment was high, prices were stable, and production was soaring. Manufacturing output nearly doubled between 1921 and 1929, and the real wages of industrial workers rose by about 17 percent. Not everyone prospered, to be sure. Strapped with long-term debts, high taxes, and a sharp drop in crop prices, farmers lost ground throughout the decade. Most blacks and Hispanics lived in poverty, large numbers of poor whites haunted southern Appalachia, and virtually every large American city had its ghetto. Still, more people were comfortable, well-to-do, or rich during the 1920s than ever before in American history.

Rampant speculation, in real estate and the stock market, was a by-product of the nation's newfound prosperity. Many speculators sought to make their fortunes in the Florida land boom of the mid1920s, until two devastating hurricanes brought land prices back down to earth. The Great Bull Market offered even more Americans the chance to vent their passion for speculation. Beginning in 1924 the price of securities began to rise steadily, until 1928 when the rate of increase switched from measured steps to vaulting leaps. In March of 1928 alone, the value of stocks shot up more than ten percent, with the price of individual stocks rising as much as 20 percent in a single day.

Credit provided the yeast for the Great Bull Market. Buying on margin—using a broker's loan to finance a large portion of the transaction—allowed the purchaser to buy securities at a fraction of their face value. Speculators could get all the benefits of ownership without paying the full purchase price. Investment borrowing transmuted itself into an orgy of speculation. Contrary to popular belief, the masses did not join in the fun. Most speculators were wealthy people or members of the upper middle class. Most working-class Americans did not own stocks, let alone play the market.

The Federal Reserve Board found itself in a real dilemma. If it raised interest rates to stifle speculation, it risked slowing down the economy and creating unemployment. If it lowered interest rates to stimulate the economy, it risked making securities speculation worse. Confused and uncertain, the Federal Reserve Board pursued contradictory policies. Between 1927 and 1929 the board raised and lowered interest rates several times in a futile attempt to slow Wall Street down without harming the economy. In the end, private greed and government impotence combined to create a catastrophe.

Financial analysts for the *New York Times* warned investors that the huge gap between stock prices and the rate of economic growth was bound to end in disaster. The bubble burst in September and October of 1929 when the market finally crashed. By November the value of the average stock had dropped 50 percent. The market continued its downward spiral for the next several years.

But the Great Crash did not cause the Great Depression. Whole segments of the American economy, including agriculture, banking, manufacturing, and foreign trade, were shaky long before the stock market collapsed. Farm prices had been depressed ever since the end of World War I,

York Times.

THE WEATHER
Cloudy and continued cold today; tomorrow fair and warmer.

FRIDAY, OCTOBER 25, 1929.

TWO CENTS

WORST STOCK CRASH STEMMED BY BANKS; 12,894,650-SHARE DAY SWAMPS MARKET; LEADERS CONFER, FIND CONDITIONS SOUND

FINANCIERS EASE TENSION

Five Wall Street Bankers Hold Two Meetings at Morgan Office.

CALL BREAK 'TECHNICAL'

Lamont Lays It to 'Air Holes' —Says Low Prices Do Not Depict Situation Fairly.

FINDS MARGINS BEING MET

Sees Market 'Susceptible of Betterment'—Mitchell, Potter, Wiggin, Prosser at Talks.

Wall Street Optimistic After Stormy Day; Clerical Work May Force Holiday Tomorrow

Confidence in the soundness of the stock market structure, notwithstanding the upheaval of the last few days, was voiced last night by bankers and other financial leaders. Sentiment as expressed by the heads of some of the largest banking institutions and by industrial executives as well was distinctly cheerful and the feeling was general that the worst had been seen. Wall Street ended the day in an optimistic frame of mind.

The opinion of brokers was unanimous that the selling had got out of hand not because of any inherent weakness in the market but because the public had become alarmed over the steady liquidation of the last few weeks. Over their private wires these brokers counseled their customers against further thoughtless selling at sacrifice prices.

Charles E. Mitchell, chairman of the National City Bank, declared that fundamentals remained unimpaired after the decline of the last few days. "I am still of the opinion," he added, "that this reaction has badly overrun itself."

Lewis J. Pierson, chairman of the board of the Irving Trust Company, issued last night the following statement:

"Severe disturbances in the stock market are nothing new in American experience. The pendulum always swings widely and it would seem as though the long-expected break should bring about an equilibrium.

"The position of the Federal Reserve Bank is unusually strong and the borrowings of member banks are moderate.

"Considering the record-breaking earnings in many industries, we may well remember that whenever fundamental values are lost sight of by the unthinking majority it is time for courage on the part of those investors who have a real sense of basic worth."

Because the clerical facilities of brokerage houses are overtaxed as a result of the recent phenomenally heavy trading, an agitation was started yesterday in favor of a suspension of trading on the New York Stock Exchange tomorrow.

It is thought possible that the governing committee will take action today, without waiting for a petition from the membership. In many brokerage houses the posting of books has fallen far behind and some relief will have to be afforded, according to brokers, unless the market quiets down shortly.

LOSSES RECOVERED IN PART

Upward Trend Starts With 200,000-Share Order for Steel.

TICKERS LAG FOUR HOURS

Thousands of Accounts Wiped Out, With Traders in Dark as to Events on Exchange.

SALES ON CURB 6,337,415

Prices on Markets in Other Cities Also Slump and Rally —Wheat Values Hard Hit.

The most disastrous decline in the biggest and broadest stock market of history rocked the financial district yesterday. In the very midst of the collapse five of the country's most influential bankers hurried to the office of J. P. Morgan & Co., and after a brief conference gave out word that they believe the foundations of the market to be sound, that the market break has been caused by technical rather than fundamental considerations, and that many sound stocks were selling too low.

Suddenly the market turned about, on buying orders thrown into the pivotal points, and before the final quotations were tapped out, four hours and eight minutes after the 3 o'clock bell, most stocks had regained a measurable part of their losses.

BIG DROP IN WHEAT; PIT IN A TURMOIL

Break of 12 Cents a Bushel to New Season Low and 8-Cent Rally Mark Wild Trading.

STOCKS TUMBLE IN CHICAGO

Selling Swamps Exchange in 1,200,000-Share Day—Part of Big Losses Recovered.

TREASURY OFFICIALS BLAME SPECULATION

Drastic Market Decline Found Not Due to Any Basic Business Weakness.

STILL PLAN TAX REDUCTION

Reserve Board Meets Twice a Day and Keeps in Constant Touch With Markets Here.

This newspaper headline from October 25, 1929, tried to reassure the public that the economy was fundamentally sound, but the downward spiral continued through 1932, when prices were 80 percent below their 1929 highs.

when European agriculture revived. Caught with declining incomes, farmers tried to recover their losses and make their debt payments by increasing production. The collective result of millions of farmers raising output was larger surpluses and lower prices, a vicious cycle that persisted throughout the decade. Moreover, the decline in farm income reverberated throughout the economy: Rural consumers stopped buying farm implements, tractors, automobiles, furniture, and appliances.

Millions of farmers defaulted on their debts, placing tremendous pressure on the banking system. Between 1920 and 1929 more than 5,000 of the country's 30,000 banks failed. Afraid to put their money in banks, large numbers of people began hoarding cash, which by 1930 removed more than $1 billion from circulation. Following the stock market crash in 1929 and the continued downward spiral through 1933, the banking system saw more of its assets destroyed. Between 1929 and 1933, when the entire banking system collapsed, another 5,000 banks went under.

Because of the banking crisis, thousands of small businesspeople failed because they could not secure working capital loans. Thousands more went bankrupt because they had lost their working capital in the stock market. Instead of plowing some of their profits during the 1920s back into their businesses and expanding capacity, many gambled on the securities markets instead. When the crash came, these small businesses shut their doors.

Labor formed another weak link in the chain. Like farmers, workers did not have enough purchasing power to sustain the economy. While business leaders promoted the consumer culture through advertising, they refused to give workers the wage increases needed to buy products. Drops in consumer spending led inevitably to reductions in production and worker layoffs. Unemployed workers then spent less and the cycle repeated itself.

Installment buying also weakened the economy. In the 1920s consumers went on a spending binge, encouraged by "buy now and pay later" advertising. Demand for automobiles and furniture, high in the early 1920s, ultimately reached a saturation point. By 1927 both industries found themselves with excess capacity and had to lay off workers.

Finally, Republican tariff policies damaged the economy by depressing foreign trade. Anxious to protect American industries from foreign competitors after World War I, Congress passed the Fordney-McCumber Tariff of 1922 and the Hawley-Smoot Tariff of 1930, raising tariff rates to unprecedented levels. Along with serious weaknesses in the European economies, American tariffs stifled international trade, making it difficult for European nations to pay off their debts.

All these factors sapped the economy, leaving it ripe for disaster. Yet the depression did not strike instantly; it infected the country gradually, like a slow-growing cancer. Measured in human terms, the Great Depression was the worst economic catastrophe in American history. It hit urban and rural areas, blue- and white-collar families alike. In the nation's cities, unemployed men took to the streets to sell apples or shine shoes. Thousands of others, many of whom deserted their wives and children, hopped freight trains and wandered from town to town looking for jobs or handouts.

Unlike most of Western Europe, the United States had no federal system of unemployment insurance. The relief burden fell on state and municipal governments working in cooperation with private charities, such as the Red Cross and the Community Chest. Created to handle temporary emergencies, these groups lacked the resources to alleviate the massive suffering created by the Great Depression. Poor southerners, whose states had virtually no relief funds, were particularly hard hit.

Urban centers in the North fared little better. Most city charters did not permit public funds to be spent on work relief. Adding insult to injury, several states disqualified relief clients from voting, while other cities forced them to surrender their automobile license plates. "Prosperity's decade" had ended in economic disaster.

Conclusion

Janus, the two-faced god of antiquity, offers an intriguing symbol for America in the 1920s. The nation's image was divided, with one profile looking optimistically to the future and the other staring longingly at the

*C*hronology of Key Events

1914	Marcus Garvey organizes the Universal Negro Improvement Association (UNIA)
1915	Ku Klux Klan revived
1917–1925	Approximately 600,000 black Americans migrate to northern industrial cities in the Great Black Migration
1920	Palmer raids arrest suspected Communists Sacco and Vanzetti tried on charges of murder and executed in 1927; Sinclair Lewis's *Main Street* published
1921	Warren Harding becomes twenty-ninth president
1922	Fordney-McCumber Tariff raises duties on imports
1923	President Harding dies; Calvin Coolidge becomes thirtieth president
1924	Teapot Dome oil-leasing scandal uncovered
1925	Scopes trial attacks teaching theory of evolution in public schools; F. Scott Fitzgerald's *The Great Gatsby* published
1929	Herbert Hoover becomes thirty-first president; stock market crashes
1930	Hawley-Smoot Tariff raises import duties

past. Caught between the disillusionment of World War I and the economic malaise of the Great Depression, the 1920s witnessed a gigantic struggle between an old and a new America.

No longer a nation of farms and villages, the United States had become a nation of factories and cities. The Protestant culture of rural America was being undermined by the secular values of urban society. Country against city, native against immigrant, worker against farmer, Protestant against Catholic and Jew, fundamentalist against liberal, conservative against progressive, wet against dry—all these confrontations reflected different images of the same battle: a colossal identity crisis that saw the United States struggling to come to terms with secular values and cultural pluralism. But what World War I started, the Great Depression interrupted. The intense cultural upheavals of the 1920s gave way to the equally intense economic debates of the 1930s as cultural politics took a backseat to the politics of survival.

Suggestions for Further Reading

Overviews of the 1920s include Frederick Lewis Allen, *Only Yesterday* (1931); William E. Leuchtenburg, *The Perils of Prosperity, 1914–32* (1958); Geoffrey Perrett, *America in the Twenties: A History* (1982).

Women's changing roles and the issues confronting women in the 1920s are examined in Dorothy Brown, *Setting a Course* (1987); William H. Chafe, *The American Woman* (1972); John D'Emilio and Estelle B. Freedman, *Intimate Matters* (1988); J. Stanley Lemons, *The Woman Citizen* (1973); Winifred D. Wandersee, *Women's Work and Family Values* (1981). On Margaret Sanger and the birth control movement see James Reed, *From Private Vice to Public Virtue* (1978).

On the Harlem Renaissance see Houston A. Baker, Jr., *Modernism and the Harlem Renaissance* (1987); Nathan Huggins, *Harlem Renaissance* (1971); Ira Katznelson, *Black Men, White Cities* (1973); David L. Lewis, *When Harlem Was in Vogue* (1981).

On the traditionalists and their opposition to modernization see David Chalmers, *Hooded Americans: The First Century of the Ku Klux Klan* (1965); Norman Furniss, *The Fundamentalist Controversy* (1954); Ray Ginger, *Six Days or Forever?* (1958); John Higham, *Strangers in the Land* (1955); Kenneth T. Jackson, *The Ku Klux Klan in the City* (1967); Don S. Kirshner, *City and Country* (1970).

Intellectual and cultural developments of the 1920s are examined in Loren Baritz, ed., *The Culture of the Twenties* (1970); Robert Crunden, *From Self to Society* (1972); Paula Fass, *The Damned and the Beautiful* (1977); Frederick Hoffman, *The Twenties: American Writing in the Postwar Decade*, rev. ed. (1962);

Roderick Nash, *The Nervous Generation* (1970); Robert Sklar, *Movie-Made America* (1975).

Good analyses of the stock market crash and the Great Depression include John Kenneth Galbraith, *The Great Crash, 1929* (1955); Jim Potter, *The American Economy Between the World Wars,* rev. ed. (1985); James Prothro, *The Dollar Decade: Business Ideas in the 1920s* (1954); Albert U. Romasco, *The Poverty of Abundance* (1965); Robert Sobel, *The Great Bull Market* (1968); George Soule, *Prosperity Decade* (1947).

Chapter 25

The Age of Roosevelt

Herbert Hoover and the Great Depression
Conservative Responses
Government Loans
Families in the Depression

Franklin Roosevelt and the First New Deal
The Election of 1932
The First 100 Days
The National Recovery Administration
Farm Policy
Job Programs
Protest from the Left

The Second New Deal
Roosevelt Moves Toward the Left
The Election of 1936

The New Deal and Minorities
Mexican Americans
Native Americans
Women

The New Deal in Decline

To fans of authentic folk music, Woodrow Wilson "Woody" Guthrie was a "Shakespeare in overalls," the finest American frontier balladeer of the twentieth century. His nasal, high-pitched singing voice was definitely an acquired taste, but Guthrie's lyrics were at once simple and penetrating. He sang of vagabonds who wandered in search of work, of union men who saw their comrades on the picket lines knocked to the ground by company goons, and of farmers who watched with horror as their land dried up and turned into a dust bowl. In short, he put to music the hardships and struggles of working-class Americans trapped in the Great Depression.

Guthrie drew his material from his life. Born in 1912, Woody grew up in Oklahoma and the Texas Panhandle in a family star-crossed by disasters. When he was still a boy his older sister died from setting herself on fire; his father, once a prosperous land speculator, sank into alcoholism; and his mother slipped slowly into madness and had to be committed to the state mental hospital.

In the face of these tragedies the Guthrie household simply dissolved, leaving Woody pretty much on his own. He passed the time by learning to play the guitar and harmonica. Eventually, he dropped out of school and became a drifter, driven by an internal restlessness that kept him on the road for the rest of his life.

Guthrie spent the Great Depression riding the rails, playing his music and visiting "his" people, along the boxcars, hobo jungles, and migrant camps from Oklahoma to California. He saw families sleeping on the ground and children with distended bellies who cried from hunger while guards hired to protect the orchards prevented them from eating fruit that lay rotting on the ground. Over time a quiet anger began to eat at him and he blamed the nation's "polli-Tish-uns" for not doing more to relieve the people's suffering. By 1940 Guthrie had recorded several albums of Dust Bowl ballads and union protest songs. His home-grown radicalism made him an instant hit with socialist and communist intellectuals and entertainment figures who saw his music as a powerful weapon in the class struggle. They saw Guthrie as an authentic folk hero, the very embodiment of the proletarian artist.

In truth, Guthrie held more radical political views than most Americans. Nevertheless, he aptly fulfilled his role as the "voice of the people" by putting to music the most important themes to emerge in American life during the 1930s—the common man's defiant pride, his will to survive in the face of adversity, and the extraordinary love Americans felt for their country.

In "God Blessed America" (which later generations of Americans would recognize by its first line, "This land is your land, this land is my land"), Guthrie sang of "endless skyways," "golden valleys," "diamond

Woody Guthrie often inscribed the phrase, "This machine surrounds hate and destroys it" on his guitars.

deserts," and "wheat fields waving," evoking the country's grandeur with a poet's sense of beauty. What gave the song its power, however, was the idea that America belonged to the people; every verse closed with the refrain, "God blessed America for me."

Even in the depths of the Great Depression, Guthrie found much of enduring value in America. In ballad after ballad, he celebrated the fortitude and dignity of the American people. They provided the glue that held things together while President Franklin D. Roosevelt experimented with policies and programs designed to promote relief, recovery, and reform.

Herbert Hoover and the Great Depression

When the Great Depression struck, most political and economic leaders regarded recessions as inevitable—a natural part of the business cycle. The prevailing economic theory held that government intervention was both unnecessary and unwise. Previous financial panics had failed to elicit much response from government; and many economists in 1929 continued to extol the virtues of inaction, arguing that the economy would recover by itself. President Hoover disagreed. Though Hoover saw the Great Crash as a temporary slump in a fundamentally healthy economy, he believed the president should try to facilitate economic recovery.

Conservative Responses

First, Hoover resorted to old-fashioned "jawboning." Shortly after the stock market crashed, he summoned business and labor leaders to the White House. Industrial leaders promised to maintain prices and wages, and labor spokesmen pledged not to strike or demand higher wages. While Hoover remained hopeful voluntary measures would suffice, business struggled to survive, forcing employers to lay off workers.

Next, the president tried cheerleading. The contrast between Hoover's speeches and conditions in the country was jarring. In 1930, according to Hoover, the economy was fundamentally sound, and recovery was just around the corner. His rosy pronouncements prompted critics to accuse Hoover of being insensitive to the unemployed and the dispossessed. Cynics called the shantytown slums on the edges of cities "Hoovervilles." Newspapers became "Hoover blankets" and empty pockets turned inside out, "Hoover flags."

Neither cruel nor insensitive, Hoover was tormented by poor people's suffering. Yet he could not bring himself to sanction large-scale federal public works programs because he honestly believed recovery depended on the private sector, because he wanted to maintain a balanced budget, and because he feared federal relief programs would undermine individual character by making the recipient dependent on the state.

Government Loans

When jawboning and cheerleading failed to revive the economy, Hoover reluctantly adopted other measures. In 1932 Congress created the Reconstruction Finance Corporation (RFC) and authorized it to loan $2 billion to banks, savings and loan associations, railroads, and life insurance companies. Blaming the depression on tight credit, Hoover believed federal loans would enable businesses to increase production and hire workers. The same principle applied to the Federal Home Loan Bank System (FHLBS), created by Congress in July 1932 to lend up to $500 million to savings and loan associations to revive the construction industry.

Yet by early 1933 Hoover's agencies had failed to make a dent in the Great Depression. The real problem was not tight credit but the soft demand for goods, a problem that flowed both from the chronic low wages paid to the bulk of American workers and the massive layoffs following the Great Crash. It was a vicious cycle. Unemployed workers could not buy goods, so businesspeople cut back production and laid off additional workers. Businesspeople did not ask banks for working capital loans, which the RFS and FHLBS were created to provide, because they had no interest in increasing production.

In the meantime, thousands of banks across the country went bankrupt, the unemployment rate climbed to 25 percent, and life got worse for millions of people.

Down to the bitter end, Hoover refused to admit people were starving in America, even though his opponents placed the responsibility squarely at the White House door.

Families in the Depression

The Great Depression did not affect everyone equally. Many rich people, insulated by their wealth, maintained opulent life-styles, and perhaps as many as 40 percent of Americans made it through these years without experiencing real hardships. Still, the majority of Americans saw the Great Depression as a wolf at the door. "Mass unemployment," as one journalist observed, "is both a statistic and an empty feeling in the stomach." Hunger pains were intense in 1933, the year Franklin D. Roosevelt took office, when one-quarter of the nation's families had no breadwinner.

For all but the most fortunate, the Great Depression reduced family income. In 1929 the average American family earned $2,300; by 1933 the figure had declined to $1,500, a 35 percent drop. Most of the loss resulted

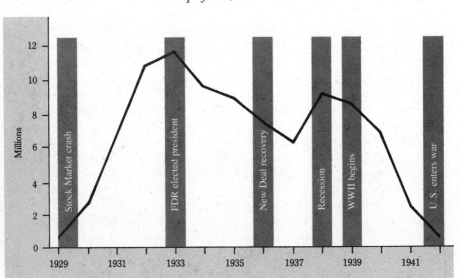

Unemployment, 1929–1942

from unemployment, but it also reflected reduced wages for those who kept their jobs. By 1933 nine out of ten companies had cut wages (some by as much as 50 percent), and more than half of all employers had converted their work force from full- to part-time jobs, averaging roughly 60 percent of the normal work week.

The depression had a powerful impact on families. It forced couples to delay marriage, lowered the divorce rate (many couples could not afford to maintain separate households or pay legal fees to obtain divorces), and drove the birthrate below the replacement level for the first time in American history. Many unemployed fathers saw their status lowered by the Great Depression. With no wages to punctuate their authority, they lost power as primary decision makers. Large numbers of men lost self-respect, became immobilized, and stopped looking for work, while others turned to alcohol, became self-destructive or abusive to their families, or simply walked out the door, never to return.

In contrast to men, many women saw their status rise during the depression. To supplement the family income, married women entered the work force in large numbers. Although most women worked in menial occupations, the fact that they were employed and bringing home paychecks elevated their position within the family and gave them a say in family decisions.

Despite the hardships it inflicted, the Great Depression drew some families closer together. As one observer noted, "Many a family has lost its automobile and found its soul." Families had to devise strategies for getting through hard times because their survival depended on it. They pooled their incomes, moved in with relatives in order to cut expenses, bought day-old bread, ate in soup kitchens, and did without. Many families drew comfort from their religion, sustained by the hope things would turn out well in the end, while others placed their faith in themselves, in their own dogged determination to survive that so impressed observers like Woody Guthrie. But many Americans no longer believed the problems could be solved by people acting alone or through voluntary associations. Increasingly, they looked to the federal government for help.

Franklin Roosevelt and the First New Deal

Franklin D. Roosevelt won the Democratic nomination in June 1932. At first glance he did not look like a man who could relate to other peoples' suffering, for Roosevelt had spent his entire life in the lap of luxury. A fifth cousin of Teddy Roosevelt, he was born in 1882 to a wealthy New York family. Roosevelt enjoyed a privileged youth. He attended Groton, an exclusive private school, Harvard, and Columbia Law School. After three years in the New York state senate, Roosevelt was tapped by President Wilson to serve as assistant secretary of the navy in 1913. His status as the rising star of the Democratic party was confirmed when James Cox chose Roosevelt as his running mate in the presidential election of 1920.

The Election of 1932

Handsome and outgoing, Roosevelt seemed to have a bright political future. Then disaster struck. In 1921 he was stricken with polio. The disease left him paralyzed from the waist down and confined to a wheelchair for the rest of his life. Instead of retiring, however, Roosevelt labored diligently to return to public life. "If you had spent two years in bed trying to wiggle your toe," he later declared, "after that anything would seem easy."

Buoyed by an exuberant optimism and devoted political allies, Roosevelt won the governorship of New York in 1928, one of the few Democrats to survive the Republican landslide. Surrounding himself with able advisors, Roosevelt labored to convert New York into a laboratory for reform, involving conservation, old age pensions, public works projects, and unemployment insurance.

In his acceptance speech before the Democratic convention in Chicago, Roosevelt promised "a New Deal for the American people." Although his speech contained few concrete proposals, Roosevelt radiated confidence, giving many desperate voters hope. He even managed during the campaign to turn his lack of a blueprint into an asset, offering instead a policy of experimentation. "It is common sense to take a method and try it," he declared, "if it fails, admit it frankly and try another."

The Republicans stuck with Hoover. Dejected and embittered, he projected despair and failure. What little chance he had for reelection was dashed by his callous treatment of the "Bonus Army." A bedraggled collection of unemployed veterans and their families, the Bonus Army marched on Washington in the spring of 1932 to ask Congress for immediate payment of their war service bonuses, which did not come due until 1945. More than 15,000 strong, they erected a shantytown, camped out in vacant lots, and occupied empty government buildings. Though the House gave them what they wanted, the Senate killed the bill after Hoover lobbied against it.

Most of the veterans then left Washington, D.C., but a few thousand stayed behind because they had no place to go. At Hoover's request, Congress appropriated $100,000 to help pay their expenses home. When police tried to evict some of the marchers in late July, a riot broke out in which two policemen and two marchers died. Hoover then ordered General Douglas MacArthur to use federal troops to remove them from government buildings. Exceeding his orders, MacArthur used tanks and tear gas to drive the veterans from the city. Newsmen captured the melee in vivid photographs which papers carried the next day.

Although Hoover was appalled by what happened he publicly accepted the responsibility and endorsed MacArthur's charge that the bonus marchers included dangerous radicals who wanted to overthrow the government. Most Americans felt outraged by the government's harsh treatment of the Bonus Army, and Hoover encountered resentment everywhere he campaigned.

Upon learning of the Bonus Army incident, Franklin D. Roosevelt remarked: "Well, this will elect me." Roosevelt was correct; he buried Hoover in November, winning 22,809,638 votes to Hoover's 15,758,901, and 472 to 59 electoral votes. In addition, the Democrats won commanding majorities in both houses of Congress.

Roosevelt appealed to a wide range of voters, wooing southerners back into the Democrat fold, as well as new groups of voters, including young people, women, and ethnic Americans. Urban Catholics, Jews, and members of the Eastern Orthodox Church voted overwhelmingly for Roosevelt, the first of many elections to come in which the Democratic party's fortunes would be strongly affected by these groups.

The First 100 Days

The New Deal was a jumble of hastily improvised legislation and executive orders. Most of the legislation was economic and came in three spurts: one in 1933, during the first "100 days" of Roosevelt's administration, the second in 1935, and the last in 1938. From beginning to end, the New Deal represented an intensely personal enterprise unified only by Roosevelt's personality. In place of a well-defined political philosophy, he pursued a vague commitment to moderate reform, leavened with keen political instincts and a desire to help people.

Roosevelt's greatest asset was his ability to persuade, and no president has ever encountered a Congress so eager to follow. Promising decisive action, he called Congress into special session and demanded "broad executive power to wage a war against the emergency, as great as the power that would be given me if we were in fact invaded by a foreign foe." Across the nation people held their breaths waiting to see what the new president would do.

Roosevelt attacked the banking crisis first. In the months before he took office America's banking system had all but disintegrated. Hundreds of banks had collapsed, wiping out the life savings of nearly ten million people. On March 5 Roosevelt declared a national bank holiday, stopping all banking transactions. A few days later he sent Congress the Emergency Banking Relief Bill, which it immediately approved. The new law permitted solvent banks to reopen under government supervision, and allowed the RFC to buy the stock of troubled banks and keep them open until they could be reorganized. The law gave the president broad powers over the Federal Reserve System.

To generate support for his programs, Roosevelt appealed directly to the people. On March 12 he conducted the first of many radio "fireside chats." Using the radio the way later presidents exploited television, he explained what he had done in plain, simple terms and told the public to have "confidence and courage." When the banks reopened the following day, people demonstrated their faith by making more deposits than withdrawals. One of Roosevelt's key advisors did not exaggerate when he later boasted, "Capitalism was saved in eight days."

Three months later Congress passed the Glass-Steagall Banking Act of 1933. To protect depositors from risky projects, the law separated investment banking from commercial banking. It also established the Federal Deposit Insurance Corporation (FDIC), which guaranteed all deposits up to $2,500, to restore the public's confidence in banks.

Banking reform was just the beginning. During the "100 days," Congress rammed through 15 major bills, more legislation than any preceding session had passed in history. Most of the early bills were conservative and deflationary, reflecting Roosevelt's desire to pursue moderate reform within a balanced budget.

Within days after taking office, President Franklin Delano Roosevelt moved to restore the public's confidence in the banking system.

Table 25.1

Depression Shopping List: 1932–1934

Automobiles		Furniture	
Pontiac Coupe	$585.00	Dining room set, 8-piece	$ 46.50
Chrysler Sedan	995.00	Lounge chair	19.95
Dodge	595.00	Double bed and mattress	14.75
Studebaker	840.00	Mahogany coffee table	10.75
Packard	2150.00	Chippendale sofa	135.00
Chevrolet 1/2-ton pickup truck	650.00	Louis XV walnut dining table	124.00
		Wing chair	39.00
Clothing		Grand piano	395.00
Women's			
Mink coat	$585.00	**Toys**	
Leopard coat	92.00	Doll carriage	$ 4.98
Cloth coat	6.98	Sled	1.45
Wool dress	1.95	Tricycle	3.98
Wool suit	3.98	Bicycle	10.98
Wool sweater	1.69	Fielder's glove and ball	1.25
Silk stockings	.69		
Leather shoes	1.79	**Food**	
		Sirloin steak/lb	$ .29
Men's		Rib roast/lb	.22
Overcoat	$ 11.00	Bacon/lb	.22
Wool suit	10.50	Ham/lb	.31
Trousers	2.00	Chicken/lb	.22
Shirt	.47	Pork Chops/lb	.20
Pullover sweater	1.97	Salmon (16 oz can)	.19
Silk necktie	.55	Milk (quart)	.10
Stetson hat	5.00	Butter/lb	.28
Shoes	3.85	Eggs (dozen)	.29
		Bread (20 oz loaf)	.05
Household Items		Coffee/lb	.26
Silverplate flatware, 26 pieces	$ 4.98	Sugar/lb	.05
Double-bed sheets	.67	Rice/lb	.06
Bath towel	.24	Potatoes/lb	.02
Wool blanket	1.00	Tomatoes (16 oz can)	.09
Wool rug (9' × 12')	5.85	Oranges/dozen	.27
		Cornflakes (8 oz box)	.08
Appliances			
Electric iron	$ 2.00	**Air Travel**	
Electric coffee percolator	1.39	New York to Chicago,	
Electric mixer	9.95	round trip	$ 86.31
Vacuum cleaner	18.75	Chicago to Los Angeles,	
Electric washing machine	47.95	round trip	207.00
Gas stove	23.95		
Electric sewing machine	24.95		

The later bills of the "100 days" marked a change in direction. Distancing himself from Hoover's tight-money policies, Roosevelt provided relief to debtors and exporters by devaluing the dollar, abandoning the gold standard, and ordering the Federal Reserve System to ease credit. This shift reflected the declining clout within his administration of conservatives, and the growing influence of a group of economists and college professors who came to be known as the "brain trust." The "brain trust" supplied Roosevelt with economic ideas and oratorical ammunition. These advisors saw "bigness" as the natural product of a mature industrial economy. Instead of busting trusts, they believed government should accept consolidation and enforce regulations designed to promote open and fair competition. Acting on their advice, Roosevelt launched two major reforms, one directed at industry, the other at agriculture.

The National Recovery Administration

Roosevelt called the National Recovery Administration (NRA), established by the National Industrial Recovery Act (NIRA), "the most important and far-reaching legislation ever passed by the American Congress." The NRA, which sought to define a working relationship between government and industry, had much in common with Teddy Roosevelt's philosophy of "New Nationalism." The NRA proposed to resolve the major causes of economic instability (ruinous competition, overproduction, labor-management confrontations, and price fluctuations) through economic planning. Under the NRA, boards of industrial leaders, labor representatives, and government officials would draft codes of competition to limit production, assign quotas among individual producers, and impose strict price guidelines.

Participation in the NRA was purely voluntary, but businesses that joined were exempted from antitrust prosecution. In practice, this meant that the codes offered businesspeople the chance to fix prices. To attract labor's support, Section 7A of the NIRA guaranteed maximum hours, minimum wages, and collective bargaining. In short, the NRA proposed to restore economic health by letting industry regulate itself and by conferring the government's blessing on labor unions.

Led by General Hugh Johnson, the new agency got off to a promising start. By midsummer 1933, over 500 industries had signed codes covering 22 million workers. By the end of the summer the nation's ten largest industries had been won over, as well as hundreds of smaller businesses. All across the land businesses displayed the "Blue Eagle," the insignia of the NRA, in their windows.

The NRA's success was short-lived. Johnson proved to be an overzealous leader who alienated many businesspeople. Instead of creating a smooth-running corporate state, Johnson presided over a chorus of endless squabbling. The NRA boards, which were dominated by representatives of big business, drafted codes that favored their interests over those of small competitors. Moreover, even though they controlled the new agency from the outset, many leaders of big business resented the NRA for interfering in the private sector.

For labor the NRA was a mixed blessing. On the positive side, the codes abolished child labor and established the precedent of federal regulation of minimum wages and maximum hours. In addition, the NIRA boosted the labor movement by drawing large numbers of unskilled workers into unions. On the negative side, however, the NRA codes set wages in most industries well below what labor demanded, and large occupational groups, such as farm workers, fell outside the codes' coverage.

The NIRA also tried "pump priming," to promote industrial recovery, a favorite scheme of the "brain trusters." They advocated large public construction projects to stimulate the economy. The Public Works Administration (PWA), led by the overly cautious Harold Ickes, sponsored a variety of building projects, such as schools, hospitals, bridges and courthouses. The PWA eventually pumped $3 billion into the economy, but Ickes's prudence and fear of waste prevented the funds from being spent fast enough to have any measurable impact.

Other New Deal agencies followed the same pattern as the PWA. While the New Deal was remarkably scandal free, the government often worked at cross-purposes with itself, permitting concern for potential corruption to hamper prompt and decisive action.

Farm Policy

The Great Depression all but destroyed America's farmers. Between 1929 and 1933 farmers saw their income fall 60 percent, leaving them with crops they could not sell and mortgages they could not pay. To make matters worse, their current woes followed a decade of hard times in the 1920s. Small wonder farmers looked back wistfully to the brief period of prosperity they had enjoyed on the eve of World War I.

The New Deal attacked farm problems through a variety of programs. As late as 1935 more than six million of America's 6.8 million farms had no electricity. Unlike their sisters in the city, farm women had no washing machines, refrigerators, or vacuum cleaners. Nor did private utility companies intend to change things. Private companies insisted that it would be cost prohibitive to provide electrical service to rural areas.

Roosevelt disagreed. He wanted to break the private monopoly of electric power in rural areas, envisioning a future in which electric power would serve broader goals, including flood control, soil conservation, reforestation, diversification of industry, and a general improvement in the quality of life for rural Americans. Settling on the 40,000 square-mile valley of the Tennessee River as his test site, Roosevelt decided to put the government into the electric business.

Two months after he took office Congress passed a bill creating the Tennessee Valley Authority (TVA). The bill authorized the TVA to build 21 dams to generate electricity for tens of thousands of farm families. In 1935 Roosevelt signed an executive order creating the Rural Electrification Administration (REA) to bring electricity generated by government dams to America's hinterland. Between 1935 and 1942 the lights came on for 35 percent of America's farm families.

Nor was electricity the only benefit the New Deal bestowed on farmers. The Soil Conservation Service helped farmers battle erosion; the Farm Credit Administration provided some relief from farm foreclosures; and the Commodity Credit Corporation permitted farmers to use stored products as collateral for loans. Roosevelt's most ambitious farm program, however, was the Agriculture Adjustment Act (AAA).

Like the NRA, the AAA, led by Secretary of Agriculture Henry Wallace, sought a partnership between the government and major producers. Together the new allies would raise prices by reducing the supply of farm goods. Under the AAA, the large producers, acting through farm cooperatives, would agree upon a "domestic allotment" plan that would assign acreage quotas to each producer. Participation would be voluntary. Farmers who cut production to comply with the quotas would be paid for land left fallow.

Unfortunately for its backers, the AAA got off to a horrible start. Because the 1933 crops had already been planted by the time Congress established the AAA, the administration ordered farmers to plow their crops under, paying them over $100 million for mowing down ten million acres of cotton. The government also purchased and slaughtered several million pigs, salvaging only one million pounds for the needy. The public neither understood nor forgave the agency for destroying food while jobless people went hungry.

Overall, the AAA's record was mixed. Farm income doubled between 1933 and 1936, but large farmers reaped most of the profits. The AAA did little to help sharecroppers and tenant farmers, the groups hardest hit by the agricultural crisis. The problem of overproduction was never solved as technology and mechanization dramatically increased crop yields. As a result, between 1932 and 1935, three million Americans abandoned farming and moved to the city.

Job Programs

To provide short-term assistance for the unemployed, Roosevelt reluctantly turned to welfare programs. In March 1933 Congress created the

Civilian Conservation Corps (CCC) to offer young people jobs in national parks. By midsummer, the government had hired 300,000 young men between the ages of 18 and 25 who planted saplings, built fire towers, stocked depleted streams, and restored historic battlefields. By 1942, 2.5 million men had served in Roosevelt's "Tree Army."

No New Deal program enjoyed greater popularity. The CCC offered young men fresh air, exercise, healthy food, and educational programs. In addition to room and board, they received a modest wage, most of which went home to their families. Still, the CCC's economic impact was small. It excluded women, imposed rigid quotas on blacks, and offered employment to only a small number of the young people who needed work.

Much more ambitious was the Civil Works Administration (CWA), established in November 1933. Under the energetic leadership of Harry Hopkins, the CWA put 2.6 million men to work in its first month, and within two months it employed four million men building 250,000 miles of road, 40,000 schools, 150,000 privies, and 3,700 playgrounds.

In March 1934, however, Roosevelt scrapped the CWA because he (like Hoover) did not wish to create a permanent dependent class. Roosevelt badly underestimated the crisis. As government funding slowed

For $30 a month, workers in the Civilian Conservation Corps (CCC) planted trees and dug drainage ditches. Such federal work relief programs helped many retain their self-respect.

down and economic indicators leveled off, the depression deepened in 1934, triggering a series of violent strikes, which culminated on Labor Day, 1934, when garment workers launched the single largest strike in the nation's history. All across the land, critics attacked Roosevelt for not doing enough to combat the depression, charges that did not go unheeded in the White House.

Following the congressional elections of 1934, in which the Democrats won 13 new House seats and 9 new Senate seats, Roosevelt abandoned his hopes for a balanced budget, deciding that bolder action was required. He had lost faith in government planning and the proposed alliance with business, which left only one other road to recovery—government spending. Encouraged by the CCC's success, he decided to create more federal jobs for the unemployed.

In January 1935 Congress created the Works Progress Administration (WPA), Roosevelt's program to employ 3.5 million workers at a "security wage"—twice the level of welfare payments but well below union scales. To head the new agency, Roosevelt again turned to Harry Hopkins. Since the WPA's purpose was to employ men quickly, Hopkins opted for labor-intensive tasks, creating jobs that were often makeshift and inefficient. Jeering critics said the WPA stood for "We Piddle Along," but the agency built many worthwhile projects. In its first five years alone the WPA constructed or improved 2,500 hospitals, 5,900 schools, 1,000 airport fields,

---

Table 25.2

Legislation Enacted During the Hundred Days, March 9–June 16, 1933	
March 9	Emergency Banking Relief Act
March 20	Economy Act
March 22	Beer-Wine Revenue Act
March 31	Unemployment Relief Act
March 31	Civilian Conservation Corps Act
May 12	Agricultural Adjustment Act
May 12	Federal Emergency Relief Act
May 18	Tennessee Valley Authority Act
May 27	Securities Act of 1933
June 5	Gold Repeal Joint Resolution
June 13	Home Owners' Refinancing Act
June 16	Farm Credit Act
June 16	Banking Act of 1933
June 16	Emergency Railroad Transportation Act
June 16	National Industrial Recovery Act

and nearly 13,000 playgrounds. By 1941 it had provided jobs to 40 percent of the nation's unemployed, pumping $11 billion into the economy.

The WPA also sponsored several cultural programs. While folksingers like Woody Guthrie honored the nation in ballads, other artists were hired to catalog it, photograph it, paint it, record it, and write about it. In photojournalism, for example, the Farm Security Agency (FSA) employed scores of photographers to create a pictorial record of America and its people. Under the auspices of the WPA, the Federal Writers Project sponsored an impressive set of state guides and dispatched an army of folklorists into the backcountry in search of tall tales. Oral historians collected slave narratives, and musicologists compiled an amazing collection of folk music. Other WPA programs included the Theatre Project, which produced a live running commentary on everyday affairs, and the Art Project, which decorated the nation's libraries and post offices with murals of muscular workmen, bountiful wheat fields, and massive machinery.

Valuable in their own right, the WPA's cultural programs had the added benefit of providing work for thousands of writers, artists, actors, and other creative people. In addition, these programs established the precedent of federal support to the arts and the humanities, laying the groundwork for future federal programs to promote the life of the mind in America.

Protest from the Left

The WPA marked the zenith of Roosevelt's influence over Congress. Following its passage, Congress dallied for several months over the remainder of his program. Opposition came from both the right and the left, as the New Deal's failure to end the depression by 1935 led to growing frustration. Three figures stepped forward to challenge Roosevelt: Huey Long, a Louisiana senator; Father Charles Coughlin, a Catholic priest from Detroit; and Francis Townsend, a retired California physician.

Of the three, Huey Long attracted the widest following. Ambitious, endowed with supernatural energy, and totally devoid of scruples, Long was a fiery, spellbinding orator in the tradition of southern populism. As governor and then senator, he ruled Louisiana with an iron hand. Yet the people of Louisiana loved him because he attacked the big oil companies, increased state spending on public works, and improved public schools. Although he backed Roosevelt in 1932, Long quickly abandoned the president and opposed the New Deal as too conservative.

Early in 1934 Long announced his "Share Our Wealth" program. Vowing to make "Every Man a King," he promised to soak the rich by imposing a stiff tax on inheritances over $5 million and by levying a 100 percent tax on annual incomes over $1 million. The confiscated funds, in turn, would be distributed to the people, guaranteeing every American family an annual income of no less than $2,000, in Long's words more than enough to buy "a radio, a car, and a home." By February 1935 Long's followers had organized over 27,000 "Share Our Wealth" clubs. Roosevelt had to take him seriously, for a Democratic poll revealed Long could attract three to four million voters to an independent presidential ticket.

Like Long, Father Charles Coughlin was an early supporter who turned sour on the New Deal. Speaking on the radio to an estimated 30 million Americans from his Catholic parish in a Detroit suburb, Coughlin blamed the depression on greedy bankers and challenged Roosevelt to solve the crisis by nationalizing banks and inflating the currency. When Roosevelt refused to heed his advice, Coughlin broke with Roosevelt and formed the National Union for Social Justice.

Roosevelt's least strident opponent was Dr. Francis Townsend, a California public health officer who found himself unemployed at the age of 67, with only $100 in savings. Seeing many people in similar or worse straits, Townsend embraced old age relief as the key to ending the depression. In January 1934 Townsend announced his plan, demanding a $200 monthly pension for every citizen over the age of 60. In return, recipients had to retire and spend their entire pension every month within the United States. Younger Americans would inherit the jobs vacated by senior citizens, and the economy would be stimulated by the increased purchasing power of the elderly. Although critics lambasted the Townsend plan as ludicrous, several million Americans found his plan refreshingly simple.

The Second New Deal

Roosevelt could not afford to ignore his critics. In a close election Long, Coughlin, and Townsend commanded more than enough votes to tip the scales in favor of a Republican candidate. Thus, Roosevelt slowly abandoned his dream of building a coalition that would unite all Americans behind the New Deal. To remain in office, Roosevelt had to shift policies.

Roosevelt Moves Toward the Left

Alarmed by his critics, Roosevelt called for the further expansion of federal authority. Opposition from the Supreme Court also prodded Roosevelt in this direction. On May 26, 1935, the Court struck down the NRA in *Schechter* v. *United States*—the famous "sick chicken" case, in which the Court held unanimously that the federal government did not have the power to regulate the sale of poultry in Brooklyn. The ruling, a stinging rebuke to the president and his New Deal, infuriated Roosevelt. In June he refused to dismiss Congress until they passed his new legislative agenda. The result was the "Second Hundred Days."

The National Labor Relations Act (Wagner Act) came first. Senator Robert F. Wagner of New York, the bill's sponsor, seized the opportunity to replace Section 7A of the NIRA with what he called "labor's Magna Carta." Up to this point Roosevelt had resisted any drastic change in labor policy, but once the Wagner Act's passage seemed assured he gave it his belated blessing. The bill represented the government's most important concession to labor to date. It guaranteed labor's right to organize by creating the National Labor Relations Board (NLRB), which had the power to conduct labor elections, determine bargaining units, and restrain business from "unfair labor practices."

The Wagner Act inspired an unprecedented burst of labor organizing and increased union membership in many industries, giving labor the bargaining power to push its demands. In late 1936 Walter Reuther and the United Automobile Workers (UAW) launched "sit down" strikes in which workers occupied factories but refused to work. The automobile companies responded with violence, but the union prevailed. In February 1937 General Motors recognized the union, and UAW membership increased from 30,000 to more than 400,000 in less than a year. Under the effective leadership of John L. Lewis, the newly formed Congress of Industrial Organizations (CIO) enjoyed remarkable success in organizing the steel, automotive, and textile industries, and quickly became a powerful force in the labor struggle. The Wagner Act had put the full weight of the federal government behind labor's right to bargain collectively.

Social Security

A goal of reformers since the Progressive Era, the 1935 Social Security Act aimed to alleviate the plight of America's visible poor—dependent children, the elderly, and the handicapped. A major political victory for Roosevelt, the Social Security Act was a triumph of social legislation. It offered workers 65 or older monthly stipends based on previous earnings, and it gave the indigent elderly small relief payments, financed by the federal government and the states. In addition, it provided assistance to blind and handicapped Americans, and to dependent children who did not have a wage-earning parent. The act also established the nation's first federally sponsored system of unemployment insurance. Mandatory payroll deductions levied equally on employees and employers financed both the retirement system and the unemployment insurance.

While conservatives argued that the Social Security Act placed the United States on the road to socialism, the legislation was also profoundly disappointing to reformers, who demanded "cradle to grave" protection as the birthright of every American. The new system authorized pitifully small payments; its retirement system left huge groups of workers uncovered, such as migrant workers, civil servants, domestic servants, merchant seamen, day laborers; its budget came from a regressive tax scheme that placed a disproportionate tax burden on the poor; and it failed to provide health insurance.

Despite these criticisms, the Social Security Act introduced a new era in American history. It committed the government to a social welfare role by providing for elderly, disabled, dependent, and unemployed Americans. By doing so, the act greatly expanded the public's sense of entitlement, and the support people expected government to give to all citizens.

The remaining "must legislation" of the Second Hundred Days included utilities regulation, banking reform, and a new tax proposal. Yet none of these measures represented a drastic change in American politics or society. On the whole, the Second New Deal merely sought to make capitalism more humane. The majority of Americans did not want dramatic changes, and Roosevelt never contemplated, much less achieved, a social revolution. He made no attacks on private property; the well-to-do retained their privileges; wealth was not redistributed; and the poor remained poor.

To hear many wealthy conservatives tell it, however, Roosevelt was a wild-eyed radical who threatened the very foundation of capitalism. William Randolph Hearst ordered his newspapers to substitute the words "Raw Deal" for "New Deal." Firmly committed to a balanced budget, conservatives viewed heavy government spending as sacrilege, and they were appalled by the growth of the bureaucracy in Washington, D.C. By 1940 the number of federal employees in the nation's capital had risen to 139,770, nearly double what it had been in 1932. Conservatives feared government's growth would increase federal power at the expense of states' rights and individual liberties, and they believed Roosevelt would raise rich people's taxes to finance his relief programs. Viewing Roosevelt as a traitor to his class, many wealthy Americans saw the election of 1936 as their chance to save the country.

The Election of 1936

To carry its banner in 1936, the GOP picked Alfred M. Landon of Kansas, the only Republican governor who survived the 1934 elections. Landon was far more liberal than many of his backers. He had opposed the KKK, backed business regulation, and supported many New Deal programs. A poor public speaker, Landon offered few alternatives to Roosevelt's programs.

To win in 1936 the GOP needed help from a third party, but this assistance never arrived. Huey Long's organization fell apart following his assassination in 1935; Francis Townsend's campaign, already weakened by passage of the Social Security Act in 1935, collapsed in the spring of 1936 under charges of corruption; and by 1936 Father Coughlin had been reduced to an abusive name-caller who had been publicly rebuked by the Catholic church.

Roosevelt enjoyed the race, lashing out at "economic royalists" who opposed the New Deal. The Democrats were aided by positive economic indicators: In 1936 industrial output more than doubled its 1933 figures, and the national income rose half again as much. Roosevelt carried every state but Maine and Vermont. Democrats won an equally lopsided victory in the congressional races: 331 to 89 in the House and 76 to 16 in the Senate.

The Democratic victory rested on a broad base of support. Roosevelt's backers included poor people, organized labor, urban ethnics, the Democratic South, blacks, and many intellectuals. A formidable alliance of diverse groups, Roosevelt's New Deal coalition would shape the contours of American politics for decades to come.

The New Deal and Minorities

Until the New Deal, blacks had shown their traditional loyalty to the party of Lincoln by voting overwhelmingly Republican. By the end of Roosevelt's first administration, however, one of the most dramatic voter shifts in American history had occurred. In 1936, 75 percent of black voters supported the Democrats. Blacks turned to Roosevelt in part because his spending programs gave them a measure of relief from the depression and in part because the GOP had done little to repay their earlier support.

Still, Roosevelt's record on civil rights was modest at best. Instead of using New Deal programs to promote civil rights, the administration consistently bowed to discrimination. In order to pass major New Deal legislation, Roosevelt needed the support of southern Democrats. Time and time again, he backed away from equal rights to avoid antagonizing southern whites, although his wife, Eleanor, did take a public stand in support of civil rights.

Most New Deal programs discriminated against blacks. The NRA, for example, not only offered whites the first crack at jobs but authorized separate and lower pay scales for blacks. The Federal Housing Authority

(FHA) refused to guarantee mortgages for blacks who tried to buy in white neighborhoods, and the CCC maintained segregated camps. Furthermore, the Social Security Act excluded those job categories blacks traditionally filled.

The story in agriculture was particularly grim. Since 40 percent of all black workers made their living as sharecroppers and tenant farmers, the AAA acreage reduction hit blacks hard. White landlords could make more money by leaving land untilled than by putting land into production. As a result, the AAA's policies forced more than 100,000 blacks off the land in 1933 and 1934.

Even more galling to black leaders, the president failed to support an antilynching bill and a bill to abolish the poll tax. Roosevelt feared that conservative southern Democrats, who had seniority in Congress and controlled many committee chairmanships, would block his bills if he tried to fight them on the race question.

Yet the New Deal did record a few gains in civil rights. Roosevelt named Mary McLeod Bethune, a black educator, to the advisory committee of the National Youth Administration (NYA), and thanks to her efforts, blacks received a fair share of NYA funds. The WPA was color-blind, and blacks in northern cities benefited from its work relief programs. Harold Ickes, a strong supporter of civil rights who had several blacks on his staff, poured federal funds into black schools and hospitals in the South. Most blacks appointed to New Deal posts, however, served in token positions as advisors on black affairs. At best they achieved a new visibility in government.

Mexican Americans

Like blacks, most Mexican Americans reaped few benefits from the New Deal. Affected in much the same way as sharecroppers and tenant farmers, many Mexican-American migrant workers lost their jobs due to AAA acreage reductions or competition in the fields from unemployed whites.

Mexican Americans faced serious opposition from organized labor, which resented competition from Mexican workers as unemployment rose. Bowing to union pressure, federal, state and local authorities deported more than 400,000 people of Mexican descent during the 1930s to prevent them from applying for relief. Since this group included many who had been born in the United States, the deportations constituted a gross violation of civil liberties.

Still, the New Deal offered Mexican Americans a little help. The Farm Security Administration established camps for migrant farm workers in California, and the CCC and WPA hired unemployed Mexican

Americans on relief jobs. Many, however, did not qualify for relief assistance because as migrant workers they did not meet residency requirements. Furthermore, agricultural workers were not eligible for benefits under workers' compensation, Social Security, and the National Labor Relations Act.

Native Americans

The so-called "Indian New Deal" was the only bright spot in the administration's treatment of minorities. In 1933 Roosevelt appointed John Collier as commissioner of Indian affairs. At Collier's request, Congress created the Indian Emergency Conservation Program (IECP), a CCC-type project for the reservations which employed more than 85,000 Indians. Collier also made certain that the PWA, WPA, CCC, and NYA hired Native Americans.

Collier had long been an opponent of the 50-year-old government allotment program, in which tribal lands had been broken up and distributed to individual Native Americans and whites. In 1934 Congress passed the Indian Reorganization Act, which terminated the allotment program of the Dawes Severalty Act of 1887; provided funds for tribes to purchase new land; offered government recognition of tribal constitutions; and repealed prohibitions on Native American languages and customs. That same year, federal grants were provided to local school districts, hospitals, and social welfare agencies to assist Native Americans.

Women

Women achieved measured progress under the New Deal. Frances Perkins, the secretary of labor and the first woman cabinet member in American history, brought many women into government; Molly Dewson, the director of the Women's Division of the Democratic Committee, helped place women throughout the administration. By 1939 women held one-third of all positions in the independent agencies and almost one-fifth of the jobs in the executive departments.

Eleanor Roosevelt deserves much of the credit for the progress made by minorities. The first president's wife to stake out an independent public position, she provided the social conscience of the New Deal. The First Lady worked tirelessly to persuade her husband and the heads of government agencies to hire well-qualified women and blacks. More courageous than her husband and less restricted politically, she did not hesitate to take a public stand on civil rights.

The New Deal in Decline

As Roosevelt's first term drew to a close, the Supreme Court turned on the New Deal. In 1935 the Court ruled the NRA unconstitutional, and in 1936 it struck down the AAA. These decisions convinced Roosevelt the Supreme Court was at odds with the other two branches of government, and was threatening the success of his New Deal. In an effort to make his opponents on the Supreme Court resign so he could replace them with justices more sympathetic to his policies, Roosevelt announced a plan to add one new member to the Supreme Court for every judge who had reached the age of 70 without retiring (six justices were over 70). To offer a carrot with the stick, Roosevelt also outlined a generous new pension program for retiring federal judges.

The court-packing scheme was a political disaster. Conservatives and liberals alike denounced Roosevelt for attacking the separation of powers, and critics accused him of trying to become a dictator. Fortunately, the Court itself ended the crisis by shifting ground. In two separate cases the Court upheld the Wagner Act and approved a Washington state minimum wage law, furnishing proof that it had softened its opposition to the New Deal.

Yet Roosevelt remained too obsessed with the battle to realize he had won the war. He lobbied for the court-packing bill for several months, squandering his strength on a struggle that had long since become a political embarrassment. In the end, the only part of the president's plan to gain congressional approval was the pension program. Once it passed, Justice Willis Van Devanter, the most obstinate New Deal opponent on the Court, resigned. By 1941 Roosevelt had named five justices to the Supreme Court. Few legacies of the president's leadership proved more important, for the new "Roosevelt Court" significantly expanded the government's role in the economy and in civil liberties.

Roosevelt's second blunder involved fiscal policy. Secretary of the Treasury Henry Morganthau urged Roosevelt to cut federal spending in an effort to balance the federal budget and restore business confidence. Reassured by good economic news in 1936, Roosevelt slashed government spending the following year. The budget cuts knocked the economy into a tailspin. By early 1938 economic indicators dipped nearly as low as they had been in 1932, forcing Roosevelt to reverse himself and ask Congress to resume welfare spending.

By the end of 1938 the reform spirit was gone. A conservative alliance of southern Democrats and northern Republicans in Congress blocked all efforts to expand the New Deal. Yet if Roosevelt could not pass any new measures, neither could his opponents dismantle his programs. The New Deal ended in stalemate, but with several reforms ensconced as permanent features of American politics.

Conclusion

From a purely economic perspective, the New Deal barely made a dent in the Great Depression. Roosevelt's programs suffered from poor planning and moved with considerable caution. By 1939 national productivity had barely reached 1929 levels, and ten million men and women remained unemployed. Roosevelt simply could not bring himself to support huge federal budgets. As a result, government expenditures stayed below $10 billion a year, not nearly enough to fuel economic recovery. World War II, not the New Deal, snapped America out of the depression, for then and only then did unemployment disappear.

Yet whatever its shortcomings, the New Deal blunted the worst effects of the Great Depression. Through economic reforms and public works projects Roosevelt managed to preserve the public's faith in capitalism and in democratic government at a time when both seemed on the verge of collapse. Roosevelt accomplished this, in large measure, by reaching out to groups that Washington had largely neglected in the past. The Social Security program, while it ignored many, made the government responsible for old age pensions and welfare payments to citizens who could not support themselves. The NIRA and the Wagner Act encouraged the growth of unions; minimum wage laws benefited many workers; and child labor was finally abolished in industry (though it remained in agriculture). While the New Deal stopped far short of providing equal treatment under the law for minorities, it offered them a measure of relief from the depression.

The New Deal encouraged Americans to look to the White House for strong executive leadership. Roosevelt responded to the situation with decisive action. Increasingly, the public expected the other branches of government to support presidential initiatives. Roosevelt's administrative style, creating special agencies to handle specific problems and placing people in charge who answered directly to him, further enhanced presidential power. On a purely partisan level, the New Deal enabled Roosevelt to forge a Democratic coalition of diverse groups—labor, blacks, urban ethnics, intellectuals, and southern whites—that helped shape American politics for the next several decades.

Above all, the New Deal made the federal government responsible for safeguarding the nation's economic health. Prior to the 1930s, if people

Chronology of Key Events

1928   Herbert Hoover elected thirty-first president

1929   Stock market crashes

1930   Hawley-Smoot Tariff raises import duties

1932   Reconstruction Finance Corporation created to lend money to banks, railroads, and insurance companies; Federal Home Loan Bank System created to lend money to savings and loan associations; Bonus Army dispersed by federal troops in Washington, DC; Franklin Roosevelt elected thirty-second president

1933   Emergency Banking Relief Act addresses banking crisis; Civilian Conservation Corps created to employ young men in reforestation, road construction, and flood control projects; Federal Emergency Relief Act provides federal funds for state and local relief efforts; Civil Works Administration created to provide federal jobs for unemployed; Agricultural Adjustment Act sets up system of farm price supports and production limits; National Industrial Recovery Act (NIRA) created to revive business through a series of fair-competition codes; Tennessee Valley Authority constructs dams and hydroelectric plants in Tennessee River valley; Twenty-first Amendment repeals prohibition; Glass-Steagall Act creates Federal Deposit Insurance Corporation to insure savings accounts against bank failures; Farm Credit Administration and Home Owners' Loan Corporation provide low-interest loans to farmers and home owners

1934   Huey Long's "Share Our Wealth" program announced; Indian Reorganization Act repeals prohibitions on Native American customs

1935   Schechter v. United States; Emergency Relief Appropriation Act; National Labor Relations Act; Social Security Act creates federal system of old-age pensions

1937   Roosevelt proposes "court-packing" scheme

1938   Fair Labor Standards Act bans child labor, sets minimum wages and maximum hours were asked how the government affected them, they probably thought in terms of state or even local government. The New Deal, however, made the federal government such a daily presence in people's lives that they now expected Washington to involve itself in everything from farm subsidies to the sale of stocks and securities.

Suggestions for Further Reading

Good overviews of America during the Great Depression include Sean Dennis Cashman, *America in the Twenties and Thirties* (1989); William E. Leuchtenburg, *Franklin D. Roosevelt and the New Deal* (1963); Robert S. McElvaine, *The Great Depression: America* (1984).

Studies of the Hoover administration include William J. Barber, *From New Era to New Deal* (1985); Martin L. Fausold, *The Presidency of Herbert Hoover* (1985).

Good biographies of Franklin D. Roosevelt include James M. Burns, *Roosevelt: The Lion and the Fox* (1956); Frank Freidel, *Franklin D. Roosevelt,* 4 vols., (1952–1976); Arthur Schlesinger, Jr., *The Age of Roosevelt,* 3 vols. (1957–1960).

For specific New Deal policies, useful studies include Barbara Blumberg *The New Deal and the Unemployed* (1979); Bernard Bellush, *The Failure of the NRA* (1975); Ellis Hawley, *The New Deal and the Problem of Monopoly* (1966);

For opposition to Roosevelt's New Deal, consult Alan Brinkley, *Voices of Protest: Huey Long, Father Coughlin, and the Great Depression* (1982); T. Harry Williams, *Huey Long* (1969). Women's issues are examined in Susan Ware, *Beyond Suffrage: Women in the New Deal* (1981). Issues confronting minorities during the 1930s are dealt with in Abraham Hoffman, *Unwanted Mexican Americans in the Great Depression* (1974); James H. Jones, *Bad Blood: The Tuskegee Syphilis Experiment,* rev. ed. (1992); Lawrence C. Kelly, *The Assault on Assimilation* (1983); Kenneth Philp, *John Collier's Crusade for Indian Reform* (1977); Nancy J. Weiss, *Farewell to the Party of Lincoln: Black Politics in the Age of FDR* (1983); Raymond Wolters, *Negroes and the Great Depression* (1970).

Chapter **26**

The End of Isolation: America Faces the World, 1920–1945

Diplomacy Between the Wars
The Isolationist Mirage
The Good Neighbor Policy

The Coming of World War II
Conflict in the Pacific
The Rome-Berlin Axis
Conflict in Europe
An "Arsenal of Democracy"
Pearl Harbor

America at War
Economic Mobilization
Controlling Inflation
Election of 1944
Molding Public Opinion

Social Changes During the War
Women
Minorities
Fear of Enemy Aliens

The War in Europe
The Grand Alliance
Stemming the Tide
Liberating Europe
The Yalta Conference

The War in the Pacific
Island-Hopping
Truman and the Dawn of the Atomic Age

Allied armies won the decisive battles of World War II, but the Allied victory rested squarely on America's economic might. The gross national product rose from $91 billion in 1939 to $166 billion in 1945, and industrial production soared by an astonishing 96 percent. By 1943 America's productivity outstripped all its enemies combined; by 1944 it was twice as great.

No one symbolized this economic miracle better than Henry J. Kaiser. Before the war his Six Companies consortium built Boulder Dam and sank the piers for the Golden Gate Bridge. When World War II erupted, Kaiser immediately used his experience with government contracts and officials to become one of the leading industrial architects of the Allied victory.

Kaiser built ships—tankers, small aircraft carriers, troop ships, and Liberty ships, the basic cargo carrier of the war. He would not tolerate delays in production schedules. By 1945 his shipyards won more than $3 billion in government contracts and turned out a ship a day. With enemy submarines sinking everything in sight, Kaiser stressed speed and large-scale production, not efficiency, cost, or quality.

Kaiser's shipyards formed a microcosm of American society. Teeming with migrants from farms and small towns, they employed 125,000 men

One of the biggest producers of war goods was Henry Kaiser. Almost one quarter of America's entire wartime output of merchant shipping came from his shipyards.

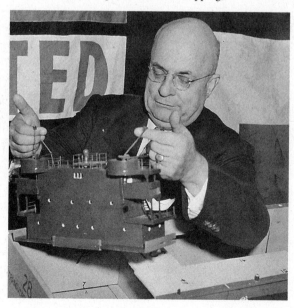

and women who faced problems ranging from overcrowded housing to nonexistent child care. Kaiser devised ingenious ways to attract workers. He paid good wages, built a modern hospital or clinic near every shipyard, enrolled workers and their families in an excellent health plan, and experimented with round-the-clock nurseries and child-care centers.

After the war Kaiser praised himself as the embodiment of rugged individualism, but in truth his success derived from "welfare capitalism." Government loans financed his shipyards, and cost-plus government contracts guaranteed his profits. Yet his concern for workers and their families tempered capitalism with compassion, creating a model of corporate management that survived long after the last of his ships went into mothballs.

Diplomacy Between the Wars

World War I's horrible casualties, disappointments over the Treaty of Versailles, the United States' failure to join the League of Nations, and the Red Scare left the public suspicious of foreign crusades. During the 1920s and much of the 1930s, the United States concentrated on improving its status in the Western Hemisphere and on avoiding European entanglements.

The Isolationist Mirage

Throughout the 1920s Republican leaders debated and ultimately refused to join the League of Nations or the World Court. Such commitments, they feared, might involve the United States too deeply in global politics. Yet Washington remained keenly interested in preserving international stability and tried to promote world peace through diplomatic means.

In December 1921 Secretary of State Charles Evans Hughes convened a disarmament conference in Washington, D.C., which produced the Five-Power Naval Treaty the following year. The treaty established a ten-year moratorium on the construction of battleships and set tonnage for battleships at a ratio of 525,000 tons for the United States and Great Britain, 300,000 tons for Japan, and 175,000 tons for France and Italy. In 1922 the United States also signed the Nine-Power Treaty, an agreement to preserve the "Open Door" in China, and the Four-Party Treaty, which committed the United States, Great Britain, France, and Japan to consult before going to war in Asia. None of these treaties, however, contained any provision for enforcement.

Several years later the United States and France launched an international crusade to banish war from world affairs. In 1928 the French foreign minister, Aristide Briand, and Secretary of State Frank B. Kellogg negotiated the Kellogg-Briand Pact, which renounced war as an instrument for resolving international disputes and symbolized the post-World War I era's disillusionment with naked power. If attacked, however, the signatories, 62 in all, could defend themselves by force. While it raised hopes for peace and earned Kellogg the Nobel Peace Prize, the Kellogg-Briand Pact had no chance of preventing future bloodshed, since it, too, lacked an enforcement mechanism.

The Good Neighbor Policy

During the 1920s Republican administrations inched away from gunboat diplomacy and tried to develop better relations with Latin America. Progress was uneven and Washington's policies occasionally reverted to heavy-handed interventions, but the thrust of Republican diplomacy during the 1920s—more trade and less military involvement—clearly anticipated the shift toward improved relations with Latin America, which the Democrats dubbed the "Good Neighbor Policy" in the 1930s.

In 1924, for example, the United States pulled the marines out of the Dominican Republic, and the following year American troops left Nicaragua, only to be sent back a few months later when a revolution broke out. President Herbert Hoover continued the diplomacy of reconciliation. He announced plans to withdraw marines from Nicaragua and Haiti, and he resisted pressure from Congress to establish a customs receivership in El Salvador when the government there defaulted on its bonds. In 1930 Hoover repudiated the Roosevelt Corollary to the Monroe Doctrine, which for 25 years had justified U.S. intervention in Latin America.

In his first inaugural address President Franklin D. Roosevelt dedicated the United States "to the policy of the good neighbor." Secretary of State Cordell Hull stunned Latin America in December 1933 by declaring, "no state has the right to intervene in the international or external affairs of another." The marines left Nicaragua in 1933 and Haiti in 1934. The United States also nullified the Platt Amendment, thereby surrendering the right to intervene in the affairs of Cuba, and gave Panama its political independence. Furthermore, when Mexico expropriated foreign oil properties in 1938, Roosevelt rejected calls to send in troops and let the action stand. The Good Neighbor Policy did not solve all the problems with Latin America, but it promoted better relations just when the United States needed hemispheric solidarity to meet the threat of global war.

The Coming of World War II

Conflict in the Pacific

The first major threat to international stability following World War I came in the Far East. Chronically short of raw materials, Japan was desperate to establish hegemony in Asia. In September 1931 the Japanese invaded Manchuria. President Hoover, a peaceful man, rejected military intervention. He also refused to impose economic sanctions against Japan, fearing such reprisals might hurt American exports or, worse yet, lead to war. Instead, Secretary of State Henry Stimson revived the Wilsonian policy of refusing to recognize governments based on force.

Expecting bolder measures, Japan ignored the Stimson Doctrine and concluded that the United States would not use military might to oppose its designs on the Far East. In 1937 Japan invaded China. In response, the League of Nations sponsored a conference at Brussels in November 1937. As the delegates debated whether or not to impose economic sanctions against Japan, the United States announced it would not support sanctions. The conference adjourned after passing a report mildly criticizing Japanese aggression.

Any doubts regarding the U.S. desire to avoid war vanished when a Japanese plane bombed the *Panay*, a U.S. gunboat stationed on the Yangtze Rivern in December 1937, killing three Americans. While the attack angered the public, few calls for war rang out similar to those following the sinking of the *Maine* or the *Lusitania*. Secretary Hull sent sharply worded protests to Tokyo, but the United States quickly accepted Japan's "profound apology," which included indemnities for the injured and relatives of the dead, promises against future attacks, and punishment of the pilots responsible for the bloodshed. In short, by the end of 1937, as one historian has noted, "America's Far Eastern Policy had retreated to inaction."

The Rome-Berlin Axis

The modern world had never known a leader like Adolf Hitler. Charismatic and a spellbinding orator, Hitler possessed a unique ability to articulate a nation's darkest fears and hatreds and then turn them to his own twisted purposes. Hitler found a receptive audience among many Germans, who were prepared to embrace any leader offering to restore the national honor which had been surrendered in the Treaty of Versailles in 1919. At that time, Germany had been forced to sign a "war guilt" clause, accepting full responsibility for the war. In addition, in 1921 the Allies presented Germany with a reparations bill of $34 billion to cover war damages. Unable to make the interest payments, let alone the principal, Germany staggered beneath the burden until its economy dissolved into severe unemployment and hyperinflation.

Confronted by Germany's imminent economic collapse, the United States offered a measure of relief. In 1924 Charles Dawes, a prominent American banker, worked out a proposal (the Dawes Plan) that reduced the reparations bill and provided Germany with an American loan. With prodding from the United States, Great Britain and France agreed to cut reparations to $2 billion in 1929, but even that proved too much when the Great Depression struck. Germany entered the 1930s with its economy in shambles.

Hitler came to power in 1933, vowing to reclaim Germany's position as a world leader. True to his word, he immediately pulled Germany out of the League of Nations. In 1935 he rearmed Germany and started a peacetime draft, clear violations of the Treaty of Versailles. Recognizing Germany's right to rearm, Great Britain and France did not oppose Hitler's actions.

Next Hitler concentrated on forging alliances with nations that shared Germany's taste for expansion and aggression. Germany and Japan signed the Anti-Comintern Pact (forerunner of a full-scale military alliance) in 1936. Shortly thereafter Hitler formed the Rome-Berlin Axis with Italy's fascist dictator, Benito Mussolini, who had recently attacked Ethiopia. Also in 1936, German troops reoccupied the Rhineland, the German-speaking region between the Rhine River and France. Once again, France and Great Britain did not oppose Hitler's bold advance, for they believed (or wanted to believe) the Rhineland would satisfy his ambitions.

But the Rhineland only whetted Hitler's appetite. Intent on reuniting all German-speaking peoples of Europe under the "Third Reich," Hitler annexed Austria in 1938. Once again, the British and the French acquiesced. Later that year he seized the Sudetenland, the German-speaking region of western Czechoslovakia.

This time France and Great Britain felt compelled to act. In September 1938 French and British leaders met with Hitler in Munich, Germany, to demand whether he had further designs on Europe. Fearing they could not count on each other to use force, they eagerly accepted Hitler's promises not to seek additional territory.

By 1938, then, Hitler had kept his promise to avenge the humiliations Germans had suffered at Versailles. Germany's frontiers were larger than they had been in 1914, Germany was rearmed, and German national pride had been restored. In addition, Germany had acquired powerful allies in Japan and in Italy. All this had transpired virtually unopposed by the victors of World War I. The League of Nations had failed to

Benito Mussolini and Adolf Hitler share their diplomatic triumph over France and England in Munich in 1938.

act and its member states had offered only feeble protests. Their caution reflected the mood of a war-weary world. Everyone hoped the Germans, Italians, and Japanese would be satisfied with their acquisitions and stop expanding. In retrospect, such hopes were clearly wrong, but at the time they did not appear unfounded. Western leaders assumed they were dealing with reasonable men; they had no way of knowing appeasement would only fuel the Axis dictators' appetites for expansion.

The United States responded to Europe's turmoil with caution. Preoccupied with the Great Depression, President Roosevelt had little time or energy to deal with foreign affairs. Yet America's timidity also reflected the strength of isolationist sentiment. Congress, not the president, played the dominant role in foreign affairs for much of the 1930s, and Congress was determined to keep the United States out of another European conflict.

Roosevelt's first diplomatic initiative involved the Soviet Union. Hoping to expand foreign trade and to use the Soviet Union to balance Japan in the Far East, he formally recognized the Soviet Union in 1933, provoking the wrath of isolationists and anti-Communists alike.

Meanwhile, isolationist forces were gaining strength. In 1934 Gerald P. Nye, a Republican senator from North Dakota, blamed international bankers and weapons manufacturers for involving the United States in World War I. While Nye's charges were never substantiated, they fed the public's fears that the United States had been suckered into the conflict by "merchants of death" who put profits above the national interest.

Privately, Roosevelt opposed the retreat into isolation. In his view, the United States had to play an important role in world affairs because it had become a major power. But Roosevelt's freedom to act was severely limited by isolationists in Congress. Between 1935 and 1937 Congress passed three separate neutrality laws that clamped an embargo on arms sales to belligerents, forbade American ships from entering war zones and prohibited them from being armed, and barred Americans from traveling on belligerents' ships. Clearly, Congress was determined to avoid what it regarded as the mistakes that had plunged the United States into World War I.

The neutrality laws troubled Roosevelt. Convinced that these laws posed a serious threat to presidential power, Roosevelt delivered a speech in October 1937 in which he spoke of the need to "quarantine the aggressors." But he immediately retreated into silence when it became clear that the public did not support vigorous action. This was where matters stood when Hitler decided to take advantage of the world's indecisiveness.

Conflict in Europe

On August 24, 1939, Germany and the Soviet Union signed the Nazi-Comintern Pact, a nonaggression treaty. In exchange for a sphere of influence over parts of Eastern Europe, Stalin approved Germany's designs on western Poland and Lithuania. His eastern flank protected, Hitler invaded Poland on September 1, 1939. Two days later, France and Great Britain honored their treaty obligations to defend Poland and declared war on Germany. World War II had formally begun.

Poland was no match for Germany. Though its people fought bravely, it fell in a few weeks. Land fighting in Europe then stopped for several months. The next "blitzkrieg" by Nazi forces came in April 1940, when German tanks swept through Denmark and Norway, then into the Netherlands, which fell in five days.

In May Nazi forces moved against France, which many observers expected to to be a more formidable opponent. But French leaders capitulated six weeks later; only the heroic boatlift at Dunkirk saved 300,000 British and French troops from capture.

Like Wilson before him, Roosevelt responded to Europe's war by declaring America's neutrality. Unlike the idealistic Wilson, however, he did not ask his countrymen to be "neutral in thought as well as in action." After France fell, Roosevelt feared a German victory would threaten America's future security, and he resolved to save England at all costs—including war.

Before he could rescue Britain, however, Roosevelt first had to regain control of American foreign policy. Soon after Germany invaded Poland, he pushed an act through Congress which modified earlier legislation by permitting belligerents to purchase war materials, provided they paid cash and carried the goods away in their own ships. This act was pro-British because England controlled the Atlantic. Acting on his own authority, Roosevelt then rushed thousands of planes and guns to Britain. In September 1940 he persuaded Congress to pass the first peacetime draft in American history and signed an executive agreement with Great Britain transferring 50 destroyers in exchange for 99-year leases on eight British bases in the Western Hemisphere. Most Americans, gravely concerned with events in Europe, supported the destroyers-for-bases deal.

Fearing Roosevelt was duplicating Wilson's mistakes, isolationists of both parties opposed the tilt toward Britain. Their most powerful argument was that Europe's war did not threaten "fortress America." Germany had no designs on the Western Hemisphere, they insisted. Therefore, the United States should sit this war out.

An "Arsenal of Democracy"

The war dominated the election of 1940. Running for an unprecedented third term, Roosevelt handily defeated Republican challenger Wendell Willkie 27 million votes to 22 million votes, and 449 electoral votes to 82. As New York City Mayor Fiorello La Guardia put it, Americans preferred "Roosevelt with his known faults to Willkie with his unknown virtues."

After the election, Churchill informed Roosevelt that England had run out of money and no longer could purchase war supplies. Consequently, the president replaced "cash and carry" with a "lend-lease" bill, which Congress passed after a bitter debate and Roosevelt signed in March 1941. With "this legislation," he declared, "our country has determined to do its full part in creating an adequate arsenal of democracy."

To cement the Anglo-American bond, Roosevelt met with Churchill in August 1941 on board the USS *Augusta* off the coast of Newfoundland. There they negotiated the Atlantic Charter, which pledged mutual support for democracy, freedom of the seas, arms reductions, and a just peace. In everything but name the United States and Great Britain were now allies.

While the public strongly supported aid for Great Britain, many Americans balked at helping the Russians, who had been invaded by Hitler in June 1941. Roosevelt, however, immediately offered lend-lease aid to the Soviet Union, and in November 1941 the United States allocated $1 billion in lend-lease to the Soviets. By 1945 America's allies had received $50 billion, four times the amount loaned to the allies in World War I.

In April 1941 the United States went beyond financial assistance by constructing bases in Greenland and escorting convoys as far as Iceland to protect them from German submarines. The American navy started tracking German submarines and signaling their locations to British destroyers. After a German submarine attacked an American destroyer in September, Roosevelt ordered the navy to "shoot on sight" any German ships in the waters around Iceland. Yet the president stopped short of asking Congress for a formal declaration of war; for a few more months the United States maintained the fiction of neutrality.

Pearl Harbor

Thanks to the public's preoccupation with Europe, Roosevelt had a relatively free hand in the Far East, where Japan was on the march to acquire an empire that would encompass large parts of China and the western Pacific. Yet Japan's dream of expansion clashed with the two main pillars of America's Far Eastern policy—preserving the "Open Door" for trade and protecting China's territorial integrity.

After Japan invaded China in 1937, relations between Washington and Tokyo deteriorated rapidly. The United States pressured Japan to withdraw, but Tokyo refused. In July 1939 Secretary of State Cordell Hull, aware that American exports fueled Japan's war machine, threatened to impose economic sanctions. Roosevelt, however, held back, fearing Japan would attack the Dutch East Indies to secure the oil it needed.

Events quickly forced Roosevelt's hand. In 1940 Japan occupied northern Indochina, an obvious step toward the Dutch East Indies. Late in September Roosevelt placed an embargo on scrap iron and steel, hoping economic sanctions would strengthen moderates in Japan who wished to avoid conflict with the United States.

When these actions failed to deter Japanese aggression, Roosevelt in July 1941 froze Japanese assets in the United States and cut off steel, oil, and aviation fuel exports to Japan. Hurt by these sanctions, Japan negotiated with the United States throughout 1941. Instead of compromising, however, the United States asked Japan to withdraw immediately from Indochina and China, concessions that would have ended Japan's dream of economic and military hegemony in Asia.

In a last-ditch effort to avoid war, Japan promised not to march further south, not to attack the Soviet Union, and not to declare war against the United States if Germany and America went to war. In return, Japan asked the United States to abandon the Chinese. Roosevelt refused. In

October 1941 the Japanese government fell and General Hideki Tojo, the leader of the militants, seized power. The new regime offered to compromise if Washington would soften its demands, but Secretary of State Hull refused to negotiate. War was imminent.

Most military experts expected Japan to attack the Dutch East Indies to secure oil and rubber. Before striking there, however, Japan moved to neutralize American power in the western Pacific. At 8:00 A.M. on Sunday morning, December 7, 1941, Japanese planes hit the U.S. naval base at Pearl Harbor, Hawaii, executing the most daring surprise attack in military history. In less than two hours Japan reduced the base to flames, sank two battleships, and heavily damaged six others. The remainder of the fleet was either damaged or destroyed. The United States lost more than 2,400 dead, while Japan sustained minimal losses.

Yet Japan had won a costly victory. Its planes failed to destroy America's aircraft carriers, and, more important, the attack united the American

In a little less than two hours, the surprise attack at Pearl Harbor had killed more than 2,400 American sailors and damaged or sunk eight battleships, including the USS *Arizona* pictured here.

public as nothing else could have. Opposition to Roosevelt simply evaporated. On December 8 Congress declared war on Japan with but one dissenting vote. Germany declared war on the United States on December 11.

America at War

Practically everyone agreed what had to be done: jump-start the economy, raise an army, and win the war. Yet the economic challenges facing the United States were truly mind-boggling. New plants had to be built and existing ones expanded; raw materials had to be procured and distributed where needed; labor had to be kept on the job; production had to be raised; and all this had to be accomplished without producing soaring inflation.

Economic Mobilization

Like Wilson before him, Roosevelt wished to make the transition to a wartime economy without government controls; he, too, would fail. Like Wilson, Roosevelt increased the size and power of the federal bureaucracy to meet the demands of the war effort. In January 1942 the president created the War Production Board (WPB) to "exercise general responsibility" over the economy.

Business leaders responded coolly to the call for economic conversion. With profits already booming because of the war in Europe, many industrialists did not wish to jeopardize their position in the domestic market by converting factories to military production. Others worried about getting stuck with inflated capacity after the war ended.

To gain their support, Washington offered even greater returns. The armed services suspended competitive bidding, offered cost-plus contracts, guaranteed low-cost loans for retooling, and paid huge subsidies for plant construction and equipment. Lured by huge profits, the automotive industry enthusiastically made the switch to military production. In 1940 6,000 planes rolled off Detroit's assembly lines; production jumped to 47,000 in 1942; and by the end of the war it exceeded 100,000, more than doubling Roosevelt's original goal.

Most military contracts went to big businesses because large-scale production simplified buying. At Roosevelt's insistence the Justice Department stopped prosecuting antitrust violators, a policy which accelerated business consolidations. Overall, industrial profits doubled, but small industries, lacking the capital to convert to war production, got crowded away from the federal trough.

Government-supported research became a major new industry during World War II. To counter Germany's scientific and technological superiority, especially in tanks and artillery, Roosevelt created the Office of Scientific Research and Development (OSRD) in 1942. Its most ambitious undertaking was the Manhattan Project, the code name for the atomic bomb, which cost more than $2 billion and employed 500,000 workers. Federal funds also supported the development of radar, flame throwers, antiaircraft artillery, and rockets. Thanks in large part to penicillin and new blood plasma techniques, the death rate of wounded soldiers who reached medical installations was half that of World War I. Moreover, antimalarial drugs and insecticides dramatically reduced the incidence of mosquito-carried diseases among troops in the Mediterranean and in the Pacific.

No less than industry, American agriculture performed impressively during World War II. To encourage production, Roosevelt allowed farmers to make large profits by setting crop prices. Good weather, mechanization, and a dramatic increase in the use of fertilizers did the rest. Cash income for farmers jumped from $2.3 billion in 1940 to $9.5 billion in 1945.

The distribution of profits in agriculture followed the same pattern as in industry: most went to large-scale operators who could afford expensive machinery and fertilizers. Many small farmers, saddled with huge debts from the depression, abandoned their farms for jobs in defense plants or the armed services. Over five million farm residents left rural areas during the war.

Overall, the war brought unprecedented prosperity to Americans. Workers never had it so good. The total income of families increased dramatically as large numbers of women joined the work force, creating millions of two-income families. In fact, World War II brought Americans more money than they could spend, for the production of consumer goods could not keep pace with the new buying power. Everything from toasters to diapers was in short supply.

Controlling Inflation

The shortages led to inflation. Prices rose 18 percent between 1941. Fearing inflation would destroy the economy, Congress created the Office of Price Administration (OPA) in January 1942, which quickly instituted price controls as well as rationing programs on such items as food, gasoline, and clothing. Relying on voluntarism and patriotism, the OPA extolled the virtues of self-sacrifice, telling people to "Use it up, wear it out, make it do, or do without."

In addition to rationing, Washington attacked inflation by reducing the public's purchasing power. The government encouraged the sale of war bonds, which not only helped finance the war but also absorbed more than 7 percent of the real personal income of Americans. Tax reforms were also used to combat inflation. To cool off consumer purchasing power, Congress passed the Revenue Act of 1942, which raised corporate taxes, increased the excess profits tax, and levied a 5 percent withholding tax on anyone who earned more than $642 a year. Tax reforms forced citizens to pay more than 40 percent of the war's total cost as the war progressed, and laid the foundation for postwar tax policies. Wage controls offered another tool for controlling inflation. The War Labor Board (WLB), established in 1942, had the power to set wages, hours, and working conditions. Thanks to overtime, however, the weekly paychecks of some workers rose 70 percent.

Working together, these programs brought inflation under control. Still, the administration's methods pleased no one. Everyone groused about taxes; manufacturers and farmers denounced price controls; and labor officials condemned wage freezes.

Yet American workers clearly reaped a bonanza from World War II, which created 17 million new civilian jobs. After Pearl Harbor, labor soared to an absolute premium, drawing into the work force previously unemployed and underemployed groups such as women, teenagers, blacks, senior citizens, and the handicapped. The war also gave labor unions a lift. Under the benevolent hand of government protection, unions rebounded from their sharp decline of the 1920s and early 1930s.

Despite these gains, labor unrest increased throughout the war. increased throughout the war. After Pearl Harbor, union officials pledged not to strike until the war ended, but inflation and wage restrictions quickly eroded their goodwill. Work stoppages rose, though most ended quickly and did not harm the war effort. Although most Americans condemned strikes as unpatriotic, Roosevelt remained a model of restraint with labor leaders. After all, labor formed a vital element of the New Deal coalition.

In contrast to Roosevelt, Congress took a hostile stand toward labor. Over the president's veto, it passed the Smith-Connally Act, which banned strikes in war industries, authorized the president to seize plants useful to the war effort, and limited political activity by unions. The Smith-Connally Act reflected a resurgence of conservatism, both in Congress and in the country at large. Though the Democrats continued to maintain a thin majority in both houses of Congress throughout the war, a coalition of Republicans and conservative Democrats after 1942 could defeat any measure.

Election of 1944

With reform in retreat, the Republicans expected to win the election of 1944. Thomas E. Dewey, the dapper, 42-year-old governor of New York, won his party's nomination on the first ballot. While Dewey accepted the New Deal as part of American life, he opposed its expansion. No distance separated the two major candidates on foreign affairs.

Despite his declining health, Roosevelt easily captured his party's nomination for a fourth term. To counter the resurgence of conservatism, he selected Senator Harry S Truman, a moderate from Missouri, as vice president. The campaign revitalized Roosevelt. He unveiled plans for a "GI Bill of Rights," promising liberal unemployment benefits, educational support, medical care, and housing loans for veterans, which Congress approved overwhelmingly in 1944. The president easily won reelection. Unwilling to switch leaders while at war, the public stuck with Roosevelt to see the crisis through.

Molding Public Opinion

Having witnessed the mistakes of World War I, Roosevelt did not want government propaganda to arouse hatreds or fuel false hopes. Shortly before Pearl Harbor, he created the Office of Facts and Figures, which soon became embroiled in bureaucratic struggles with government agencies, the armed services, and the Office of Strategic Services. By 1944 the government had all but abandoned its efforts to shape public opinion about the war.

Private enterprise filled the void. Movies, comic strips, newspapers, books, and advertisements reduced the war to a struggle between good and evil as the Allies engaged in mortal combat with Japan and Germany. The Japanese bore the brunt of the propaganda, especially during the first two years of fighting. Caricatured with thick glasses and huge buck teeth, public portraits of the Japanese grew more ugly and vicious as deeply ingrained racism fed the stereotypes, reviving old fears of the "yellow peril."

Germans, by contrast, elicited more complex attitudes in Americans, largely because racism did not inflame passions. At first, Americans blamed Hitler for the war. As eyewitness accounts of German atrocities began to filter back from the front, however, the public's views shifted. Gradually, Americans came to blame not just the Nazis, but all Germans for the war.

Motion pictures emerged as the most important instrument of propaganda during World War II, but Hollywood made little effort to confront the war's complexities. Instead, the industry churned out a series of simple morality plays, aimed at inspiring the public's patriotism. Movies such as *Back to Bataan* and *Guadalcanal Diary* showed a few Americans outfighting Japanese hordes. Hollywood produced 982 movies during the war, enough for three new movies each week at the neighborhood theater.

Social Changes During the War

World War II produced important changes in American life, some subtle, others profound. Above all, it set families in motion, pulling them off farms, out of small towns, and packing them into large urban areas. Urbanization had virtually stopped during the depression, but the war saw the number of city dwellers leap from 46 to 53 percent of the population.

Women

The war had a dramatic impact on women. Easily the most visible change involved the sudden appearance of large numbers of women in uniform. The military organized women into auxiliary units with special uniforms, their own officers, and, amazingly, equal pay. By 1945 more than 250,000 women had joined the Women's Army Corps (WAC), the Army Nurses Corps, the Women Accepted for Voluntary Emergency Service (WAVES), the Navy Nurses Corps, the marines, and the Coast Guard. Most women who joined the armed services either filled traditional women's roles, such as nursing, or replaced men in noncombat jobs.

Women also substituted for men on the home front. For the first time in American history the majority of married women worked outside the home. The war challenged the conventional image of female behavior, as "Rosie the Riveter" became the popular symbol of women who abandoned traditional female occupations to work in defense industries.

Women paid a price for their economic independence. Outside employment did not free wives from domestic duties. They had not one job now, but two, and the only way they could fill both was to sacrifice relaxation, recreation, and sleep. Outside employment also raised the problem of child care. A few industries, such as Kaiser Steel, offered day-care facilities, but most women had to make their own arrangements.

Many women, however, elected to cling to the familiar by embracing the traditional roles of housewives and mothers. From 1941 to 1945 the marriage rate rose, as did the birthrate, rebounding sharply from the all-time low during the depression. Overall, the "baby boom" did not signal a return to large families; rather, the birthrate rose because women married at younger ages and had their families earlier in life.

Hasty marriages between young partners often proved brittle. Wartime separations forced newlyweds to develop new roles and become self-reliant. Although the divorce rate rose, Americans had not soured on marriage. The divorce rate had been climbing steadily (except during the depression years) since 1900. Most Americans who divorced during the 1940s promptly remarried; they had rejected their mates, not marriage.

Minorities

World War II accelerated long-developing social trends for blacks. More than one million migrated to the North during the war (twice the number who did so in World War I), and more than two million found work in defense industries. Yet blacks continued to be the last hired and the first fired, and other forms of discrimination remained blatant, especially in housing and in employment.

Black leaders fought discrimination vigorously. In the spring of 1941 black labor leaders, backed by the NAACP, threatened to stage a march on Washington to protest discrimination in defense industries. Embarrassed and concerned, Roosevelt issued an executive order prohibiting discrimination in defense industries and creating the Fair Employment Practices Commission (FEPC). But the FEPC's tiny staff lacked the power and resources to enforce its decisions. During the war the FEPC did not even process most complaints, and contractors ignored 35 of the 45 compliance orders it issued.

Blacks fared no better in the public sector. Most blacks in the federal bureaucracy worked as janitors, and the armed services treated blacks as second-class citizens. The marines excluded blacks; the navy used them as servants; and the army created separate black regiments commanded mostly by white officers. The Red Cross even segregated blood plasma.

Not surprisingly, racial tensions deepened during the war. Many blacks joined the armed services hoping to find social mobility. Instead, they encountered segregation and discrimination. They resented white officials who denounced Nazi racism but remained silent about discrimination against blacks. On the home front, as urban areas swelled with defense workers, housing and transportation shortages exacerbated racial tensions. In 1943 a riot broke out in Detroit in a federally sponsored housing project. White soldiers from a nearby base joined the fighting, and other federal troops had to be brought in to disperse the mobs. The violence left 35 blacks and 9 whites dead.

Similar conflicts erupted across the nation, exposing in each instance the same jarring contradiction: white Americans espoused equality abroad but practiced discrimination at home. Many blacks responded to the rising tensions by joining such civil rights organizations as the NAACP, which intensified its legal campaign against discrimination. Some blacks, however, considered the NAACP too slow and too conciliatory. Rejecting legal action, the Congress of Racial Equality (CORE), founded in 1942, organized a series of "sit-ins." While black activists won few gains during World War II, they forged new demands and tactics that shaped the civil rights movement after the war.

World War II affected Mexican Americans no less than blacks. Almost 400,000 Mexican Americans served in the armed forces. As soldiers, they expanded their contacts with Anglo society, visiting new parts of the country and meeting for the first time large groups of people who held few prejudices against them. For Mexican Americans in the civilian sector, jobs in industry provided an escape hatch from the desperate poverty of migratory farm labor.

The need for farm workers rose dramatically after Pearl Harbor, prompting several hundred thousand Mexican workers to immigrate to the Southwest. Commercial farmers welcomed them, but labor unions resented the competition, leading to animosity and discrimination against Mexicans and Mexican Americans alike.

In Los Angeles, Anglo society both feared and resented newly formed Mexican-American youth gangs, whose members celebrated their ethnicity by wearing flamboyant "zoot suits." In June 1943 riots broke out between Anglo sailors on shore leave and Mexican-American youths. The local press blamed Mexican-American gangs, and the riots did not end until military police ordered sailors back to their ships.

Despite the outbursts of violence and discrimination, World War II benefited the poor of all races. Thanks to full employment and progressive taxation, people at the bottom saw income redistributed in their favor. Still, the gains made by poor people came from the state of the economy (the need for soldiers and workers), not from federal policies or the efforts of organized labor.

Fear of Enemy Aliens

On December 8, 1941, Roosevelt issued an executive order regarding enemy aliens. It suspended naturalization proceedings for Italians, Germans, and Japanese immigrants, required them to register, restricted their mobility, and prohibited them from owning items that might be used for sabotage, such as cameras and shortwave radios. In practice, however, the government did not accord enemy aliens the same treatment: Italian and German aliens received lenient treatment, while Japanese aliens suffered gross injustices.

Jewish refugees complicated the German question. Reflecting a nasty strain of anti-Semitism, Congress in 1939 refused to raise immigration quotas to admit 20,000 Jewish children fleeing Nazi oppression. Instead of relaxing quotas, American officials worked in vain to persuade Latin American countries and Great Britain to admit Jewish refugees.

While Hitler's death camps killed millions, American officials who knew the ghastly truth publicly downplayed press reports of genocide. Air reconnaissance missions had taken scores of photographs of the death camp at Auschwitz, and military intelligence officers had learned the locations of several other concentration camps. Not until January 1944 did Roosevelt create the War Refugee Board, which set up refugee camps in Italy, North Africa, and the United States. But America's response offered too little, too late. During the 18 months of the War Refugee Board's existence, Hitler killed far more Jews than the War Refugee Board saved.

Like Jews, Japanese Americans got a bitter taste of discrimination during World War II. They comprised a tiny portion of the population in 1941, totaling no more than 260,000 people, most of whom lived in Hawaii and on the West Coast. After Pearl Harbor, military authorities moved against Japanese Americans. In Hawaii, where the local economy depended on their labor, the military did not force Japanese Americans to relocate. On the West Coast, however, authorities ordered the Japanese to leave, drawing no distinction between aliens and citizens. Forced to sell their property for pennies on the dollar, most Japanese Americans suffered severe financial losses. Relocation proved next to impossible, as no other states would take them.

When voluntary measures failed, Roosevelt created the War Relocation Authority. It resettled 100,000 Japanese Americans in ten relocation camps, resembling minimum security prisons, in seven western states. In these camps American citizens who had committed no crimes were locked behind barbed wire, crowded into ramshackle barracks, and forced to endure bad food, inadequate medical care, and poorly equipped schools. Nearly 18,000 Japanese-American men won release from those camps to fight for the United States Army. In one of the most painful scenes in American history, Japanese-American parents, still locked inside concentration camps, received posthumous Purple Hearts for their sons.

Japanese Americans protested their treatment, claiming numerous civil rights violations. Finally, in December 1944, the Supreme Court ruled that the War Relocation Authority had no right to incarcerate law-abiding citizens. Two weeks later the federal government began closing down the camps, ending one of the most shameful chapters in American history.

Japanese Americans of all ages, tagged like pieces of luggage, awaited their relocation to one of ten detention camps in seven western states. This family was from Hayward, California.

The War in Europe

The Grand Alliance

Following Pearl Harbor, the Axis Powers of Germany, Japan, and Italy faced the Grand Alliance, composed of the United States, Great Britain, the Soviet Union and, later, the French government-in-exile. Yet from the beginning the Grand Alliance was an uneasy coalition, born of necessity and filled with tension. Apart from the need to defeat the enemy, the Allies found it difficult to agree on anything.

Winston Churchill, Great Britain's prime minister, approached international affairs in spheres-of-influence, balance-of-power terms. He wanted to block Soviet expansion, and was determined that Britain play a major role in postwar Europe. Furthermore, he wanted Britain to emerge from the war with its colonial empire intact.

France's goals reflected the vision of one man—General Charles de Gaulle, who after the fall of France in 1940 had established in London a French government-in-exile. Above all, de Gaulle wanted to restore France

World War II, European Theater

to greatness. By nature aloof and suspicious, like Churchill he fought to retain his country's empire, and as the war progressed American officials came to regard de Gaulle as a political extremist. In policy disputes he often sided with Britain to oppose American and Soviet demands.

Joseph Stalin spoke for the Soviet Union. Iron-willed and deeply paranoid, Stalin rose to power by crushing all rivals during the turbulent years following the Bolshevik revolution. A formidable negotiator, he pressed for a postwar settlement that would guarantee the Soviet Union's future security and open new lands for communism. To protect the Soviet Union from future attacks, Stalin insisted upon Germany's total destruction. As additional insurance, he demanded parts of Poland and Finland and all of the Baltic states. Eastern Europe would then form a buffer against future aggression from the West, provide colonies for rebuilding the Soviet economy, and add new territory to the communist world map.

Roosevelt had his own ideas about how the world should look after the war. In broad terms, he opposed colonialism and the spread of communism; and he supported open markets, democratic elections to counter spheres of influence, and a new League of Nations to promote world peace. Among these objectives, anticolonialism and support for free markets were his top priorities, and both goals reflected Roosevelt's remarkable ability to join political principle with economic advantage.

No less than his counterparts, Roosevelt's personality shaped his policies. Because he disliked the rough and tumble of hard bargaining, he tried to avoid clashes with other leaders by postponing difficult decisions and by relying too heavily on his personal charm. In addition, Roosevelt's pragmatic approach to problem solving made him seek compromises whenever possible, which meant that he often sacrificed principles in order to preserve Allied cooperation.

From the outset, then, dissent riddled the Grand Alliance. In pursuit of its own national interest, each ally had a separate agenda, its own set of demands, and its own vision of the how the world map should look when the war ended. Given these conflicts, the Allies could look forward not to harmony but to clashes over military strategy throughout the war, bitter debates over peace terms at the war's end, and decades of international strife in the postwar era.

Stemming the Tide

For six months after Pearl Harbor, Japan looked unbeatable. Japanese forces captured Guam, Wake Island, the Philippines, Hong Kong, and Malaya and slashed deep into Burma. General Douglas MacArthur was driven from the Philippines in March 1942. In a matter of months Japanese troops had conquered a vast expanse extending from the Gilbert Islands through the Solomons and from New Guinea to Burma, leaving India and Australia vulnerable to attack.

Nor did the Allied cause look any brighter in Europe. During the first ten months of 1942, German submarines sank over 500 American merchant ships. With its lend-lease supplies threatened, Great Britain stood in danger of collapsing before the United States could mobilize. On the Russian front, German troops pressed toward Stalingrad, and in North Africa, where German Field Marshal Erwin Rommel, the famous "Desert Fox," was sweeping toward the Suez Canal, the situation seemed equally bleak. In short, World War II opened badly for the Allies. Axis victories in the Pacific, Europe, and Africa served notice that the war would be long and costly.

Roosevelt decided to assign Germany top priority for two reasons: first, he doubted Hitler could be defeated if Britain fell; and, second, Roosevelt wanted to placate Stalin, whose troops were bearing the brunt of the German war machine. As the Germans drove deep into Soviet territory in 1942, Stalin demanded a second front in France to force Germany to divide her armies, thereby relieving some of the pressure on the Soviet Union.

By the autumn of 1942 the tide was beginning to turn on the eastern front. In September the Red Army won a key victory at Stalingrad, then launched a furious counterattack, beginning the long drive to push the Germans back across the Ukraine. Despite Soviet victories and Stalin's repeated pleas for a second front, the Allies, at Churchill's insistence, decided to attack the Germans in North Africa instead of France. Stalin saw this as a betrayal and his suspicions deepened.

Allied victories in Africa seemed to confirm Churchill's wisdom. British Field Marshal Sir Bernard Montgomery drove the Germans back to Tunis in October, and in November 1942 General Dwight David Eisenhower led a force of 400,000 Allied soldiers in a full-scale invasion of North Africa. Complete victory came on May 12, 1943, when the remnants of the Axis armies surrendered. Germany and Italy had suffered a major defeat and Allied shipping could now cross the Mediterranean in safety.

Cheered by the North African victory, Churchill and Roosevelt met in Casablanca, French Morocco, in January 1943. Stalin did not attend, explaining he could not leave the Soviet Union at this critical juncture of the war. Churchill pushed hard for an attack on Sicily and then Italy. The United States initially opposed the plan, arguing it would delay the invasion of France, but Churchill prevailed. Vowing publicly to make peace with the Axis powers only on the basis of unconditional surrender, the two leaders also renewed their pledge to open a second front, although they kept Stalin in the dark about the decision for several months.

Sicily fell in August 1943 after a campaign of slightly more than a month. In Italy, however, victory did not come cheaply for the Allies. The terrain was mountainous, and the Germans offered fierce resistance. Stalin deeply resented the commitment of Allied troops there, which further postponed the long-promised second front. Moreover, since Soviet troops had not fought in the Italian campaign, Roosevelt and Churchill refused to permit Stalin to participate in organizing an occupation government there. The next time Stalin wanted a voice in a region he made certain to have his armies on site.

Liberating Europe

In November 1943 Roosevelt, Churchill, and Stalin held their first face-to-face meeting in Teheran, the capital of Iran. Buoyed by military success, Stalin sounded conciliatory as the three leaders discussed a second front. The leaders set May 1944 as the target date for Operation Overlord, the code name for the invasion of France. To increase the odds for success, Stalin promised to coordinate Russia's spring offensive with the invasion.

Once the leaders turned to postwar issues, however, the conference dissolved into bitter controversy. Stalin demanded Soviet control over Eastern Europe and insisted Germany be divided into several weak states. Opposing both demands, Churchill proposed democratic governments for Eastern Europe, especially in Poland, for which England had gone to war, and argued that the balance of power in postwar Europe required a united Germany. Roosevelt, on the other hand, knew Stalin had the inside track in Eastern Europe. Convinced he could handle "Uncle Joe," Roosevelt decided to leave territorial questions to a postwar international organization dominated by the victors. Apart from reaching agreement on the second front, the Teheran Conference merely aired the leaders' conflicting demands.

In preparation for the invasion, the Allies instituted saturation bombing, dropping more than two and a half million tons of bombs on German territory, killing 305,000 civilians. While these air raids were supposed to wipe out the German war machine and break the people's will to resist, missions such as the firebombing of Dresden, which killed 100,000 people, made many Germans believe Hitler's ravings about the evil Allies and stiffened their will to fight.

As the bombers pounded Germany, the Allies prepared for the invasion of France, massing more than three million soldiers in England under the command of General Dwight D. Eisenhower. D-Day came on June 6, 1944. After two weeks of desperate fighting on the beaches of Normandy, the Allies began to push inland. A month later Allied troops were sweeping across Europe in a race for Berlin. They liberated Paris in August, and by mid-September Allied forces had crossed the German border. True to his word, Stalin synchronized his spring offensive with the invasion. Soviet troops engaged the Germans in furious combat all across Eastern Europe, tying up men and materials that otherwise could have been hurled against the Allies.

On December 16, 1944, German troops launched a massive western counteroffensive. In the Battle of the Bulge German armored divisions slashed 60 miles to the Franco-Belgian border before being defeated by General George Patton's Third Army. Meanwhile, the eastern front had turned into a rout. By January 1945 Soviet troops had captured Warsaw, and by February they were within 45 miles of Berlin.

The Yalta Conference

With victory in Europe at hand, Roosevelt, Churchill, and Stalin met in February 1945 at Yalta, on the Black Sea, to settle the shape of the postwar world. They concurred on the partition of Germany, but there the agreement stopped. Stalin demanded $20 billion in reparations payments from Germany, half of which would go to Russia. Churchill opposed him, rejecting any plan that would leave Germany financially prostrate after the war.

Eastern Europe was the most divisive issue at Yalta. Stalin had long insisted on Soviet control over the Baltic states, as well as portions of Finland, Poland, and Romania as the price of Russian participation in an anti-German alliance. Moreover, in October 1944, Stalin and Churchill had met secretly in Moscow, where they agreed to divide Eastern Europe into British and Russian spheres of influence for the duration of the war. Consistent with these earlier demands, Stalin laid claim to eastern Poland at the Yalta Conference, reminding Churchill and Roosevelt that since he had not opposed their political decisions in Italy, he would not tolerate any interference in Eastern Europe. Under pressure from Roosevelt and Churchill, however, Stalin grudgingly agreed to hold free elections in

Stalin, Roosevelt, and Churchill met at Yalta in February 1945 to discuss the state of the postwar world.

Poland itself, and promised that any new government formed there would include democratic elements. Yet as one of Roosevelt's chief military advisors warned the president, Stalin tacked so many amendments onto the Polish agreement that the Soviets "could stretch it all the way from Yalta to Washington without technically breaking it."

The remaining issues at Yalta proved less troublesome. Stalin promised to enter the war against Japan within three months after Germany surrendered, and he renewed his pledge to join the United Nations. Roosevelt considered both concessions important victories because he wanted Soviet help in defeating Japan and because he remained hopeful that the United Nations could negotiate peaceful solutions to the disputes between the United States and the Soviet Union after the war.

Critics have denounced Roosevelt for his role at Yalta, insisting Stalin would have surrendered Eastern Europe had the president held firm. Yet this argument seriously discounts Stalin's obsession with protecting his homeland from future attacks. The Soviet Union had paid a staggeringly high price for victory in World War II. When the war finally ended, the country had suffered approximately 18 million military and civilian deaths. More Soviets died at Stalingrad than the United States lost in all theaters of the war combined. Stalin's determination to maintain Soviet control of Eastern Europe was also bolstered by the fact that the Red Army occupied Eastern Europe in the spring of 1945. Stalin was not about to lose at the conference table what he had won on the battlefield.

Allied victories came rapidly after the Battle of the Bulge. On March 4, American troops reached the Rhine River, and in April they joined forces with the Soviet army 60 miles south of Berlin. After Roosevelt's death on April 12, however, Stalin immediately tested the new president, Harry S Truman. Stalin ordered the execution of democratic leaders in Eastern Europe and replaced them with Communist governments. Truman deplored Stalin's disregard for the Yalta agreements, but like Roosevelt he refused to fight the Soviets to save Eastern Europe. Instead, he followed General Eisenhower's advice about finishing off Germany. On April 22 Soviet troops reached Berlin and occupied the city after house-to-house fighting. On April 30 Hitler committed suicide, and Germany surrendered one week later. On May 8, 1945, the Allies celebrated V-E (Victory in Europe) Day.

The War in the Pacific

Though Europe received top priority, American forces managed to halt Japanese advances in the Pacific by late summer 1942. In May a Japanese troop convoy was intercepted and destroyed by the U.S. Navy at Coral

Sea, preventing a Japanese attack on Australia. In early June, at Midway Island in the Central Pacific, the Japanese launched an aircraft carrier offensive to cut American communications and isolate Hawaii to the east. In a three-day naval battle the Japanese lost three destroyers, a heavy cruiser, and four carriers. The Battle of Midway broke the back of Japan's navy.

Island-Hopping

On August 7, 1942, American forces attacked Guadalcanal in the Solomon Islands, and after six months of hard fighting drove the Japanese troops into the sea, securing the Allied supply line to Australia. The victory also protected the Allies' eastern flank, enabling General Douglas MacArthur, commander of southwest Pacific forces, to seize the northern coast of nearby New Guinea in September 1943. Instead of assaulting Japanese strong points on the island, MacArthur leapfrogged up the coast. By capturing isolated positions, MacArthur cut Japanese supply lines and forced Japanese troops to abandon their fortifications. By July 1944 MacArthur's forces controlled all of New Guinea.

Meanwhile, Admiral Chester Nimitz's naval and marine forces in the Central Pacific were "island-hopping" toward Japan, capturing important positions, building airstrips, and then moving on to the next island. After securing the Gilbert Islands and the Marshall Islands, Nimitz attacked

World War II, Pacific Theater

Saipan, Tinian, and Guam, from which the Americans could strike the main Japanese islands with B-29 bombers. Determined to protect their homeland against air raids, Japanese commanders resolved to fight to the last man. In the battle for Saipan, 30,000 of the island's 32,000 Japanese defenders died, and 6,000 of the island's 12,000 Japanese civilians committed suicide rather than surrender. Tinian and Guam fell to the Americans in early August, and B-29s began regular bombing raids over Japan in November 1944.

On October 21, 1944, General MacArthur invaded the Philippines. That same month the navy won a stunning victory at the Battle of Leyte Gulf, where the Japanese lost virtually their entire remaining battle fleet. American submarines now controlled Pacific shipping lanes, sealing the Japanese Islands off from military and food supplies. In January, Allied forces invaded Luzon, the main island of the Philippines, and Allied troops claimed victory five months later.

While MacArthur was reclaiming the Philippines, the American island-hopping strategy was entering its final phase. By early March the island of Iwo Jima fell to U. S. marines. Its capture enabled fighter planes to link up with B-29s heading out of Saipan, providing escorts for their raids on Japan. On April 1, 1945, American troops attacked Okinawa, 350 miles southwest of Japan. Japanese resistance was fierce. Kamikaze attacks (suicide flights by Japanese pilots) rose dramatically. Okinawa fell in June, after 70,000 Japanese soldiers had died defending it. In the meantime, B-29s firebombed Japan, killing more than 330,000 civilians and cutting deeply into its war production.

Confronted with certain defeat, many moderate leaders in Japan wanted to avoid an invasion, but strong factions within the military vowed to keep fighting. In an effort to save Japan, the emperor switched his support to the peace party in February 1945. He then sent out peace feelers to Stalin, who in turn conveyed them to Truman at the Potsdam Conference in July 1945.

Truman and the Dawn of the Atomic Age

Few presidents have been asked to conduct diplomacy with less preparation than Harry S Truman. He had risen to power as a loyal machine politician in Kansas City. As vice president and former senator from Missouri he knew next to nothing about foreign affairs, especially since Roosevelt had kept him largely in the dark. Yet Truman brought certain assets to the challenge. A man who possessed the courage of his convictions, he fully intended to be a strong president and to make decisions resolutely.

Truman's first test came at Potsdam, a suburb of Berlin, where the Allied leaders convened in July 1945 for their last wartime meeting. Though new to the job, Truman had been in office long enough to believe Roosevelt had been too soft on Stalin, whom he viewed as a liar and a bully. Deadlocked on Eastern Europe, Truman and Stalin turned their attention to Japan. The Potsdam Declaration of July 26 demanded immediate "unconditional surrender," warning that any other action would lead to "prompt and utter destruction."

During the Potsdam negotiations Truman learned that American scientists had successfully tested the first atomic bomb. However, many scientists who had worked on the Manhattan Project, as well as several key political figures, pleaded with Truman not to use the bomb because they foresaw its implications for a postwar arms race with the Soviet Union. Others, arguing from a moral position, wanted the United States to warn the Japanese about the bomb's terrifying power, giving them a chance to surrender.

Truman rejected these alternatives and decided to drop the bomb. Military considerations played a large role in his decision. According to the best intelligence reports, an invasion of the Japanese Islands might cost one million Allied casualties, with the Japanese suffering several times that figure. Ironically, the bomb had the potential to save countless lives on both sides by ending the war immediately. Yet Truman's decision also reflected his growing frustration with the Soviet Union. He wanted to

This photo of the remains of the Nagasaki Medical College shows the almost total destruction by the atomic blast. The buildings that remained standing were made of reinforced concrete.

demonstrate the bomb's awesome power to impress Stalin so that the Soviets would be easier to deal with after the war.

Following Japan's rejection of the Potsdam Declaration, Truman gave the final order. On August 6 three B-29s flew over Hiroshima and the lead bomber, the *Enola Gay*, dropped an atomic bomb that destroyed 4.4 square miles and killed 100,000 people instantly. Two days later the Soviets entered the war against Japan, making good on Stalin's promise at Yalta. Because Japan failed to surrender immediately, Truman ordered a second atomic strike. On August 9 Nagasaki was obliterated, killing another 35,000 Japanese instantly. The following day Japan asked for peace.

V-J Day (Victory in Japan) came on September 2, 1945, when Japanese officials surrendered unconditionally to General MacArthur aboard the battleship *Missouri* in Tokyo Bay. Truman refused to permit the Soviets to attend the ceremony or to play any role in creating an occupation government for Japan.

World War II was over. The fascist governments had been destroyed, their military machines crushed, their economies shattered, their major cities reduced to rubble, and their people ravaged by disease and starvation. Yet the war left the Allies hardly less devastated, except for the United States, which emerged from the fighting stronger than ever. Much of the world had to be reordered and rebuilt, but the conflicts between the United States and the Soviet Union that festered throughout the war raised grave doubts about the prospects for future cooperation.

Conclusion

World War II cost America one million casualties, and over 300,000 deaths. In both domestic and foreign affairs, its consequences were far-reaching. It had an immediate and spectacular impact on the economy by ending the Great Depression. Fueled by government contracts, the economy expanded dramatically, soaring to full employment and astounding the world with its productivity. The war accelerated corporate mergers and the trend toward large-scale agriculture. Labor unions also grew during the war as the government adopted pro-union policies, continuing the New Deal's sympathetic treatment of organized labor.

Presidential power expanded enormously during World War II, anticipating the rise of what postwar critics termed the "imperial presidency." The Democrats reaped a political windfall from the war. Roosevelt rode the wartime emergency to unprecedented third and fourth terms. Despite these victories, however, the reform spirit waned, a victim, it seemed, of the country's unmistakable swing to the right in politics.

Chronology of Key Events

1921	Washington Naval Conference places limits on construction of large warships
1922	Mussolini seizes power in Italy
1924	Dawes Plan to help Germany pay reparations
1928	Kellogg-Briand Pact renounces war "as an instrument of national policy"
1931	Japan invades Manchuria
1932	Stimson Doctrine declares that U.S. would not recognize Japanese territorial gains in China.
1933	Adolf Hitler appointed chancellor of Germany; Roosevelt announces Good Neighbor Policy, withdraws marines from Haiti, and nullifies Platt Amendment
1935–37	Neutrality Acts bar arm sales, loans to belligerents, and shipments of nonmilitary goods
1936	German troops reoccupy the Rhineland
1937	Japan invades China
1938	Germany annexes Austria; Munich Pact hands over a third of Czechoslovakia to Germany
1939	Soviet Union and Germany sign a nonaggression pact; World War II begins
1940	Destroyers for bases deal; United States institutes military draft; Roosevelt elected to third term
1941	Lend-Lease Act lets U.S. lend war material to Britain; Germany invades USSR; Japan attacks Pearl Harbor
1942	Office of Price Administration created to control prices and ration scarce goods; Japanese-Americans interned; Philippine Islands surrender; U.S. naval victory at Battle of Midway
1943	British and U.S. forces defeat Axis forces in North Africa; U.S. marines secure control of Guadalcanal in the Solomon Islands; Allies invade Italy; Soviets halt German advance into Soviet Union
1943–1944	U.S. forces seize Guam and New Guinea
1944	D-Day—Allied amphibious invasion of northern France; U.S. forces begin an invasion of Philippine Islands, launch aerial attacks on Japan; Allies victorious in Battle of the Bulge; both sides suffer heavy casualties
1945	Roosevelt, Churchill, and Stalin meet at Yalta to discuss Soviet entry into war against Japan, postwar division of Europe, and plans for United Nations; Roosevelt dies; Harry S Truman becomes thirty-third president; Germany surrenders; Potsdam conference plans postwar settlement in Europe and final attack on Japan; United States drops atomic bombs on Hiroshima and Nagasaki; Japan surrenders

The war's social effects varied from group to group. For most people, it had a disruptive influence—separating families, overcrowding housing, and creating a shortage of consumer goods. The war also accelerated the movement from the countryside to the cities; and it challenged gender and racial roles, opening new opportunities for women and minority groups. Yet sexual and racial barriers remained, highlighting reforms left unfinished at home even as American troops fought totalitarian forces abroad.

In foreign policy, the many disagreements between the Allies regarding military strategy and peace terms foreshadowed major conflicts which dominated the postwar era. Gone forever was the notion of fortress America, isolated and removed from world affairs. In its place stood a strong internationalist state, determined to exercise power on a global scale. Second only to the victory the Allies won for freedom, the war's most important legacy was the end of isolation and the rise of America's commitment to international security.

Suggestions for Further Reading

Excellent analyses of World War II include Martha Hoyle, *A World in Flames* (1970); Donald Watt, *How War Came* (1989); Gordon Wright, *The Ordeal of Total War* (1968).

The American reaction to the outbreak of war in Europe is examined in Selig Adler, *The Uncertain Giant* (1969); Wayne S. Cole, *Roosevelt and the Isolationists* (1983); Robert Divine, *The Reluctant Belligerent,* 2d ed. (1979). The attack on Pearl Harbor is the focus of Herbert Feis, *The Road to Pearl Harbor* (1950); Gordon W. Prange, *At Dawn We Slept* (1981). For Roosevelt's handling of the war, see Eric Larrabee, *Commander in Chief: Franklin Delano Roosevelt, His Lieutenants, and Their War* (1987).

Social and cultural aspects of the American home front are the focus of John Morton Blum, *V Was for Victory* (1976); Richard Lingeman, *Don't You Know There's a War On?* (1970); Richard Polenberg, *The War and Society* (1972). For information on the issues facing women and minorities, consult Karen Anderson, *Wartime Women* (1981); A. Russell Buchanan, *Black Americans in World War II* (1977); Sherna B. Gluck, *Rosie the Riveter Revisited* (1987); Susan M. Hartmann, *The Home Front and Beyond: American Women in the 1940s* (1982); Peter H. Irons, *Justice at War: The Story of the Japanese American Internment Cases* (1983); Mauricio Mazón, *The Zoot-Suit Riots* (1984).

Studies of American diplomacy include Diane Shaver Clemens, *Yalta* (1970); Gaddis Smith, *American Diplomacy During the Second World War* (1965). The decision to drop the atomic bomb is discussed in Gar Alperovitz, *Atomic Diplomacy,* rev. ed. (1985); Herbert Feis, *The Atomic Bomb and the End of World War II* (1966); Dan Kurzman, *Day of the Bomb.*

Chapter *27*

Waging Peace and War

Containing the Russian Bear
Origins of the Cold War
A World Divided
Tough Talk
The Truman Doctrine
The Marshall Plan: "Saving Western Europe"

The Containment Policy
Berlin Test
Troubling Times
The Korean War

The Cold War at Home
Adjusting to Peace
Confronting the Demands of Labor
Failure of the Fair Deal
Searching for the Enemy Within
The Rise and Fall of Joseph McCarthy

The Paranoid Style
HUAC Goes to Hollywood
"What's Wrong with Our Kids Today?"

I t was Sunday, August 27, 1948. Whittaker Chambers appeared calm as he answered questions on "Meet the Press," a weekly radio news show. He knew he was on enemy ground and that questions were the ammunition of the war. The question he had been waiting for soon came. Edward T. Folliard, a reporter for the *Washington Post,* asked, "Are you willing to say now that Alger Hiss is or ever was a Communist?" Chambers paused a second before answering, for the answer could open him up to a slander or libel suit. Then came his terse, important reply: "Alger Hiss was a Communist and may be now."

The road to "Meet the Press" began for Chambers with an unhappy childhood that left him rebellious and feeling unwanted. Forced to withdraw from Columbia University for writing a mildly sacrilegious play, Chambers then flirted with radical political philosophies, moved through a succession of love affairs, and kicked about Europe. In 1926 his brother Richard committed suicide. Grief-stricken and needing a new direction and purpose in his life, Chambers committed himself fully to the Communist party.

During the late 1920s and early 1930s, as the United States sank deeper and deeper into the Great Depression, other Americans joined Chambers in the Communist party. Feeling betrayed by capitalism, they looked toward the Soviet Union, which appeared less affected by the depression than the West, for political and economic inspiration. Still more Americans joined the party because only the Soviets seemed to be standing up against the Fascist threat posed by Hitler and Mussolini.

Chambers met Alger Hiss in 1934, when they both belonged to the same Communist "cell" in Washington, D.C. In appearance and personality they were complete opposites. Chambers was overweight and sloppy, and his face had a sleepy, slightly disinterested cast. Hiss, then a legal assistant for a Senate committee investigating the munitions industry, was handsome, thin, and aristocratic looking. Popular with influential superiors and coworkers, Hiss seemed marked for success. It was during that time, Chambers later testified, that Hiss began to give him secret government documents.

Like many of his American comrades, Chambers abandoned the ideology of communism during the late 1930s. By 1938 news of Stalin's purges, which would eventually lead to the death of millions of Soviets, had reached the West. Such gross disregard for humanity shook many American Communists. In addition, in 1939 Stalin signed a nonaggression pact with Hitler's Germany. Once seen as the bulwark against Nazi expansion, the Soviet Union now joined Germany in dividing Poland. Although the United States and the Soviet Union later became allies, Communist ideology ceased to attract many American followers.

Chambers not only quit the Communist party, he turned against it with a vengeance. As an editor for *Time* magazine, he openly criticized Communist tactics and warned about the evils of the Soviet Union. Finally, in 1948 he went before the House Un-American Activities Committee (HUAC) and told his life story, carefully naming all his former Communist party friends and associates, among them the brilliant New Dealer Alger Hiss. Now a well-known and well-respected career diplomat, Hiss had gone to the Yalta Conference with President Roosevelt, helped to organize the United Nations, and served as the president of the Carnegie Endowment for International Peace.

Hiss denied Chambers's allegations. He too appeared before HUAC. Well-dressed and relaxed, he testified, "I am not and never have been a member of the Communist Party. . . . I have never followed the Communist Party line, directly or indirectly." As he answered questions, he smiled and confidently stood on his record of public service. Unlike his nervous, rumpled accuser, Hiss was the picture of placid truthfulness. His testimony satisfied most of the committee members, but not all.

After hearing both Chambers and Hiss, Richard Nixon, a junior congressman from California, still was not sure Hiss was as innocent as he seemed. Nixon, whose struggling background contrasted sharply with Hiss's career, insisted that Hiss and Chambers be brought together before HUAC. At that meeting, Chambers demonstrated his encyclopedic knowledge about Hiss, his family, and his life. He discussed the furniture in Hiss's house and Hiss's hobbies. He showed beyond any doubt that he had been close to Hiss. For once, Hiss's confident equanimity vanished. He challenged Chambers to make his accusations in public, where he would not be protected against a libel suit.

Chambers accepted the challenge, and on "Meet the Press" he repeated his charges. In response, Hiss sued Chambers for defamation. During the involved trials that followed, Chambers proved his case. He even produced a series of classified, microfilmed documents he had stored in a hollowed-out pumpkin on his Maryland farm that incriminated Hiss. Hiss was indicted for perjury by a federal grand jury. The first trial ended in a hung jury, but in January 1950 he was found guilty of perjury and sentenced to five years in prison.

The Hiss-Chambers affair was one of the major episodes of the late 1940s. It was a time of momentous changes. The United States took an active and aggressive stand in world affairs and accepted the responsibilities of world leadership. Across the globe it clashed with the Soviet Union over a series of symbolic and real issues. Labeled the Cold War, these ideological battles affected American domestic and foreign policy. Americans attacked the Communist threat inside as well as outside the United States. In an atmosphere charged with fear, anxiety, paranoia, and hatred, the United States waged peace and war with equal emotional intensity.

Alger Hiss (left), accused of being a Communist spy by Whittaker Chambers (right), was convicted of perjury. This episode helped heighten American fear of communism at home.

Containing the Russian Bear

During World War II, when the United States and the Soviet Union were allies, Joseph Stalin was known as Uncle Joe. The media portrayed him as a stern but fair leader and pictured communism as strikingly like capitalism. Even Hollywood cooperated in this image-making process, producing films in which Stalin appeared as a gentle, pipe-smoking, sad-eyed friend of America.

In reality Stalin was a determined, ruthless leader who had over the years systematically eliminated his actual and suspected political rivals. Between 1933 and 1938 he violently eliminated over 850,000 members of the Communist party, and perhaps one million more died in labor camps. He was apparently suspicious of almost everyone. If his attitude was extreme, it was not totally irrational. Twice in his lifetime Russia had been invaded from the West. Twice Germans had pushed into his country, killing millions upon millions of Russians. For Stalin, the West stood unalterably opposed to communism and could not be trusted.

Stalin, however, was not the only suspicious world leader. The newest Western leader, President Harry Truman, was wary of Stalin, but assumed he could deal with him. Advisers told Truman that Stalin was a tough, no-nonsense leader, characteristics that the tough, no-nonsense Truman could appreciate. But their totally different backgrounds and philosophies separated the two leaders from the start, and the directions in which they led their countries drove them farther apart. The United States and the Soviet Union emerged from World War II as the two most powerful countries in the world, even though the Soviet Union had suffered tremendous industrial, agricultural, and human losses during the war. Both countries were inexperienced as world leaders, but both knew exactly what they wanted, and what they wanted guaranteed future conflicts. The Cold War was the result.

Origins of the Cold War

World War II had ended successfully for the Allies, but too many issues had been left unresolved at Yalta and Potsdam. Anxious to avoid straining their uneasy wartime alliance, the Soviet Union, Great Britain, and the United States decided to set aside thorny issues until after the war. One of the thorniest was the fate of Eastern Europe and Germany. The debate centered on the fate of Poland, which Stalin was determined to maintain as a buffer zone against future invasions. Although Truman conceded that the Soviets had the right to expect any Polish government to be friendly toward the Soviet Union, he insisted that the Soviets allow free and democratic elections in Poland.

In America Poland's fate was no abstract diplomatic issue. Millions of Americans of Eastern European origins pressed Truman to take a tough stand. Truman complied. He told Soviet Foreign Minister V. M. Molotov that the United States would not tolerate Poland being made into a Soviet puppet state. His speech was salted with profanity. Molotov remarked, "I have never been talked to like that in my life."

Truman's tough language, however, did not impress Stalin. He was not now about to give away Poland or any other territory the Red Army occupied simply because of Truman's colorful phrases. As he had bluntly stated at Yalta, "For the Russian people, the question of Poland is not only a question of honor but also a question of security . . . of life and death for the Soviet Union."

Confronted by an inflexible opponent, Truman played his trump card. He threatened to cut off economic aid to the Soviet Union. Devastated by World War II, the Soviet Union needed the aid, but Stalin would not back down and accepted the loss of American money. In the end, Truman was powerless. Americans would certainly not accept a war with the Soviet Union to liberate Poland, and in 1945 the Soviet Union was not about to leave Poland voluntarily. Relations between the United States and the Soviet Union were strained to the breaking point.

A World Divided

The most contentious issue in Soviet-American relations was the degree of control over other nations. America's control was based on its strong economy as much as its military muscle. Even as the country demobilized, American leaders were confident that they could use foreign aid to exert influence on the future development of the world. They were also confident that what was good for America would indeed be good for the world. The Soviet Union's control in all of Eastern Europe depended on the physical presence of the Red Army. Stalin freely granted America and England their spheres of influence, but he wanted the West to recognize his own.

Truman refused. A believer in free trade, national self-determination, and the virtues of democracy, he opposed Stalin's use of military force as a diplomatic weapon. Approaching issues from different perspectives, the Soviet Union and the United States arrived at different conclusions. The fate of Germany illustrates the basic conflict between the two powers. The Soviets wanted to punish Germany by stripping the country of its industry and imposing harsh reparation payments. Only a prostrate Germany, unarmed and unthreatening, would satisfy Stalin. As Truman lost confidence in the Soviet Union, he came to believe in the need for a strong Germany to act as a block against Soviet expansion. The result of these conflicting approaches was a divided Germany. Occupied by the Red Army, East Germany became a Soviet satellite state. West Germany fell under the American, British, and French spheres of influence and soon became part of the postwar democratic alliance.

Control over atomic weapons also divided the two powers. The United States developed and used the first atomic bomb—demonstrating to the world that it possessed not only the scientific knowledge to construct the bomb but also the will to use it—but realized that future world safety depended on some plan to control the awesome potential of the weapon. Publicly Truman seemed favorable to international control of the world's fissionable materials. Yet privately he used the threat of the bomb in his negotiations with the Soviet Union. Stalin reacted with suspicion and bitterness to this contradictory policy, distrusting any atomic control plan that originated in the United States. Rather than make Stalin more manageable, America's atomic diplomacy stiffened his resolve, heightened his suspicions, and made him cling even more firmly to Eastern Europe as a buffer. The result was an atomic arms race, not international cooperation.

In February 1946 Stalin warned all Soviet citizens not to expect a lasting peace with the capitalistic West. Economic sacrifices and perhaps more warfare lay ahead. The next month, in Fulton, Missouri, Winston Churchill announced that "from Stettin in the Baltic to Trieste in the

Adriatic, an iron curtain has descended across the continent." Fortunately, Churchill emphasized, "God has willed" the atomic bomb to America. Dramatic words and ominous warnings, threats and counterthreats—the Cold War had clearly begun.

Tough Talk

Although real issues divided the United States and the Soviet Union, the emotionally charged rhetoric and the emergence of Cold War myths hardened the battle lines. Truman lacked the skill and the language of a diplomat, and followed the advice of those who encouraged him to take a hard line toward the Soviet Union. Remembering how the British and the French had given in to Hitler at the Munich Conference of 1938, American foreign policymakers were determined not to allow history to repeat itself. Equating Stalin's goals with Hitler's, however, was a grave mistake. Stalin was concerned more with security than expansion; he wanted to protect his country from a future attack, not initiate World War III.

The Truman Doctrine

America's rise as a world power was paralleled by Britain's decline. England, like much of the rest of Europe, suffered terribly during World War II. The war shattered its economy, and burned-out buildings and miles of fresh graveyards gave silent testimony to the country's physical and human losses. By early 1947 Britain could no longer stand as the leader of the Western democracies. On Friday, February 21, 1947, England passed the torch to America, when the British ambassador announced that his nation could no longer economically support Greece and Turkey in their fight against Communist rebels. If these two vital countries, which stood between the Soviet Union and the Mediterranean and the Middle East, were to be kept as Western allies, the United States had to aid their cause.

Truman was prepared to assume the burden, but there were doubts whether the country was. Republicans had regained control of Congress in the November 1946 elections, and they were not anxious to shoulder expensive new foreign programs. In addition, rapid demobilization after World War II had drastically reduced the size and effectiveness of American military forces. Truman's advisers and congressional leaders recommended that he speak directly to the American people. But as Republican Senator Arthur Vandenberg warned, to win public support the president would have to "scare the hell out of the American people."

On March 12, 1947, Truman appeared before a joint session of Congress and described the Greek and Turkish situations as battles between the forces of light and the legions of darkness. Congress sounded its approval as Truman came to his climactic sentence: "I believe that it must be the policy of the United States to support free peoples who are resisting attempted subjugation by armed minorities or outside pressures." Labeled the Truman Doctrine, the statement set the course U.S. foreign policy would follow during the next generation.

Specifically, Truman called for economic and financial aid to "save" Greece and Turkey. Congress responded by appropriating $400 million. In the future, the United States would send billions of dollars in economic and military aid to countries fighting communism, even though the leaders of some of those nations were themselves dictators. In Truman's morality play, however, "anti-Communists" and "free peoples" became synonymous.

Although Truman succeeded in getting aid for Greece and Turkey and in arousing the American public, a few foreign policy experts believed that his scare tactics did more harm than good. George Kennan deplored the sweeping language of the Truman Doctrine, which placed U.S. aid to Greece "in the framework of a universal policy rather than in that of a specific decision addressed to a specific set of circumstances."

The Marshall Plan: "Saving Western Europe"

The millions of dollars sent to Greece and Turkey stabilized the pro-American governments of the two countries. But at the same time the United States was losing support in Western Europe, a far more vital region. Although the war had ended in the spring of 1945, Europe's problems continued. It lacked the money to rebuild its war-torn economies and scarred cities. To make matters worse, the winters of 1946 and 1947 were brutally cold. The winter hardships fueled the Communist party, which made marked gains. American leaders assumed that economic distress would continue to breed political extremism.

At the Harvard University commencement on June 5, 1947, Secretary of State George C. Marshall announced a plan to bolster the recovery of Europe. Marshall suggested that America could not afford to send a Band-Aid to cover the deep European wounds; a complete cure in the form of massive economic aid was in order. Although the cost might seem high, without America's help "economic, social, and political deterioration of a very grave character" would result. And from a more selfish point of view, the United States needed a strong democratic Europe to provide rich markets for American goods and to act as a check against Soviet westward expansion.

In early 1948 Congress appropriated $17 billion to be spent over the next four years for the Marshall Plan. The program put food in the mouths of hungry children, coal in empty furnaces, and money in near-empty banks. More important, it rebuilt the economic infrastructure of Western Europe and restored economic prosperity to the region. In the process it created stable markets for American goods. Americans were proud of the Marshall Plan, and Europeans were grateful for the help. All told, the Marshall Plan greatly restored America's prestige abroad, fueled Europe's recovery, and served America's Cold War strategy by diminishing the threat of Communist expansion.

The Containment Policy

Money, even billions of dollars, could not substitute for a concrete foreign policy to guide U.S. actions: an explicit policy that mixed the international idealism of the Truman Doctrine and the economic realism of the Marshall Plan with the will to meet the real or perceived Soviet threat. The policy was not long in coming; its author was George Kennan, the government's foremost authority on Russian history. Kennan had spent his adult life in the U.S. foreign service where he carefully studied the Soviet scene. During World War II he was stationed in Moscow and was able to observe Soviet political behavior. Although he believed Russians were a "great and appealing people," he distrusted the Soviet government. In a 1947 *Foreign Affairs* article, published anonymously, Kennan expressed his views of the Soviet Union. He believed that Soviet communism was driven by two engines: the need for a repressive dictatorship at home and the belief that there could never be any sense of true accord with the capitalist West. But, Kennan argued, Stalin and the leaders in the Kremlin were more interested in security than expansion, and would only expand when allowed by American weakness. In short, the Soviet Union could be *contained* within its present borders by a politically, economically, and militarily active United States.

Although Kennan later argued that he was talking about the political containment of communism, in 1947 his article was viewed as a military blueprint. Once implemented, the policy of containment involved confronting the spread of communism across the globe. As Americans soon learned, the policy came with a heavy price tag. It meant supporting our allies around the world with billions of dollars in military and economic aid, and it meant thousands of Americans dying in foreign lands. Since containment was a defensive policy, it involved a permanent Cold War without any hope of ultimate victory. Unlike World War I and World War II, the Cold War emphasized the doctrine of limited wars fought for limited goals. It was a policy bound to breed frustration and anxiety—certain to influence domestic as well as foreign policy.

Berlin Test

During the late 1940s containment seemed to fit American needs. American-Soviet tensions centered particularly on the future of Germany. The United States maintained that the economic revival of Western Europe depended on a prosperous Germany. The Soviets believed that a reindustrialized Germany was a dangerous Germany. An early test of the two different viewpoints came in Berlin, a divided city located in the heart of East Germany, deep within the Soviet zone. In June 1948, Stalin decided to stop all road and rail traffic between West Germany and Berlin. It was a crisis tailor-made for the containment policy.

Stalin could close highways and railways, but he could not effectively close the skyways. For almost one year the United States and Britain kept West Berlin alive and democratic by a massive airlift. Food, coal, clothing, and all other essentials were flown daily into West Berlin. It was an heroic feat, a triumph of technology. Western pilots logged 277,264 flights into West Berlin; they hauled in 2,343,315 tons of food, fuel, medicine, and clothing. Finally, on May 12, 1949, Stalin lifted his blockade of West Berlin. In the West, containment had passed an important test.

Troubling Times

Truman scored a series of triumphs during 1947 and 1948. The Truman Doctrine, the Marshall Plan, and the Berlin Airlift strengthened his popularity at home and U.S. prestige abroad. In the election of 1948 Truman won a remarkable upset victory over Republican challenger Thomas E. Dewey. Then in 1949 eleven western democracies joined the United States in signing the North Atlantic Treaty Organization (NATO), a mutual defense pact. But difficult times for Truman, containment, and the United States lay ahead. In late August 1949 American scientists detected traces of radioactive material in the Soviet atmosphere. The cause was as clear as a mushroom-shaped cloud. The Soviets had the bomb—a full decade before American intelligence had predicted.

Between 1945 and 1949 the threat of the bomb had given teeth to American foreign policy. It was the country's check to the Red Army, and U. S. policymakers seldom allowed Soviet leaders to forget it. Now that the Soviet Union had entered the atomic age, Truman responded by asking his scientists to accelerate the development of a hydrogen bomb; Congress responded by voting appropriations for Truman's latest defense requests.

On the heels of the Soviet bomb came more unwelcome news—the establishment of the Communist government in China after a bitter civil war between Mao Zedung's (Mao Tse-tung) Communists and Jiang Jieshi's (Chiang Kai-shek) Nationalists. Although the United States had provided Jiang with more than $3 billion in aid between 1945 and 1949, it was unable to prop up a government that was structurally unsound, inefficient, and corrupt. In May 1949, Jiang fled to Taiwan, and on September 21 Mao proclaimed Red China's sovereignty.

The Truman administration tried to put the best face possible on the turn of events. Secretary of State Dean Acheson issued a thousand-page White Paper explaining how Mao had won the civil war. It detailed the rampant corruption in the Nationalist government and Jiang's many mistakes. For the American public, however, that explanation was not good enough. Republicans and supporters of Jiang in America blamed Truman for "losing" China. Led by Henry Luce, the influential publisher of *Time* and *Life* who was the China-born son of American missionaries, an informal group known as the China Lobby blasted the Truman administration. They claimed "phony liberals" had "sold China into atheistic slavery." Millions of Americans took their loud cries seriously.

Facing intense political pressure at home, Truman refused to recognize the Communist People's Republic of China. Instead he insisted that Jiang's Nationalist government on Taiwan was the legitimate regime. It was an unrealistic policy, but one that future presidents found politically difficult to reverse. The United States and the People's Republic of China did not establish formal diplomatic relations until 1979.

The Korean War

The rhetoric of the Truman administration tended to simplify complex issues, intensify the Cold War rivalry, and tie foreign policy to domestic politics. Failure abroad could have calamitous consequences for politicians at home. After "China fell," Truman was more than ever determined to contain communism.

The mood of the Truman administration is clearly evident in National Security Council Paper Number 68 (NSC-68), one of the most important documents of the Cold War. Completed in April 1950, it expressed the view that communism was a monolithic world movement directed from the Kremlin. NSC-68 extended the Truman Doctrine and called for the Unied States to protect the world against the spread of communism. The cost would be great—NSC-68 estimated it at 20 percent of the gross national product or more than a 300 percent increase in military appropriations—but planners warned that without the commitment the United States faced the prospect of a world moving toward communism. Two months later, in June 1950, America went to war in Korea.

Korea, like Germany, was a divided country. When the Japanese surrendered its forces in Korea after World War II, Soviet troops accepted the surrender north of the 38th parallel, American troops south of that line.

With the deepening of the Cold War, the temporary division line became permanent. North of the 38th parallel, the Soviet-backed communist government forged a modern, disciplined army during the late 1940s. South Korea, which received strong aid and support from the United States, opposed any reconciliation with Communist North Korea.

In an unfortunate speech before the National Press Club on January 12, 1950, Secretary of State Dean Acheson stated that South Korea lay outside America's primary "defense perimeter." In late June North Korea attacked, sending 90,000 men across the 38th parallel into South Korea. A weak, disorderly South Korean army quickly retreated.

Truman assumed that North Korea was acting on orders from Moscow, although there is little evidence to support this contention. Since both Koreas were technically wards of the United Nations, the Truman administration decided to take the matter to the Security Council. With the Soviet Union absent, the Security Council by a 9 to 0 vote condemned the North Korean assault and demanded an immediate cease-fire. Encouraged by the United Nations' prompt action and without consulting Congress, Truman pledged American support to South Korea

Truman termed the conflict a "UN police action" and, in fact, a number of UN member nations sent troops, but for all practical purposes it was a war that initially matched the United States and South Korea against North Korea. When bombing the Communist supply line failed to slow the North Korean advance, Truman took the fateful step of ordering American troops to Korea. They soon joined their South Korean allies in a headlong retreat. For six weeks the allies fell steadily back until they stabilized a perimeter in southeast Korea around the port city of Pusan.

North Korean troops besieged the city for two months. Determined to reverse the stalemate, U.N. commander General Douglas MacArthur, a bold, even arrogant man, decided to split his forces and launch a surprise attack against the North Koreans' rear. On the morning of September 15, 1950, American marines began an amphibious attack on Inchon, a port city just below the 38th parallel. It was a bold, risky, but successful maneuver.

Faced with an enemy to their front and their rear, North Korean troops retreated above the 38th parallel. Truman had achieved his objective: to restore the 38th parallel as the border between the two Koreas. But MacArthur wanted more—he wanted victory on the battlefield. And he said so, loudly and publicly.

After receiving MacArthur's reassurances that Red China would not intervene, Truman decided to allow U.S. forces to "liberate" North Korea. This time boldness failed. North Korea was a difficult country to invade. The American army had no reliable maps, and mountainous terrain rendered traditional military tactics impossible. In addition, as MacArthur's forces moved recklessly north toward Manchuria, Chinese officials sent

Korean War

informal warnings to the United States that unless the advance stopped, their country would enter the fray. MacArthur ignored Chinese warnings and kept moving. In late November Communist China struck, pouring more than 300,000 troops across the border and sending American forces reeling back across the 38th parallel.

Despite this stunning setback, McArthur continued to talk about absolute victory. If a nation was going to fight a war, he sermonized, it should fight to win. In Washington, however, the Truman administration was shifting back to the pre-Inchon policy of containment. When MacArthur publicly criticized the administration's newest approach, an angry Truman replaced him, a move that raised a firestorm of protest and contributed to the president's low public approval ratings.

The Korean War dragged on. Formal peace negotiations began on July 10, 1951, but they proved to be a long, difficult process. While diplomats talked, American soldiers fought and died. Altogether, 34,000 Americans were killed and 103,000 wounded during the Korean War. Finally, on July 26, 1953, the war ended as it began, with North Koreans above the 38th parallel and South Koreans below it. The war represented a victory for Truman's containment policy, but for millions of Americans it somehow tasted like defeat.

The Cold War at Home

As Truman waged the Cold War abroad, Cold War issues gradually came to dominate the American domestic scene. During the ensuing Red Scare, the fear of communism disrupted American life, and the freedoms that Americans took for granted came under attack. At home as well as abroad, Americans battled real and imagined Communist enemies.

Adjusting to Peace

Truman and his advisers approached the end of World War II with their eyes on the past. Memories of the Great Depression and the painful social and economic adjustment after World War I clouded their thinking. They knew that massive wartime spending, not the New Deal, had ended the decade of depression, and they worried that peace might bring more economic suffering. Peace with prosperity was their goal.

The solution to the problem of converting back to a peacetime economy, Truman believed, lay in the continuation, at least for a time, of wartime government economic controls. During the war the Office of Price Administration (OPA) had controlled prices and held inflation in check. To ensure prosperity, Truman asked Congress to continue price controls. He also advocated such economic measures as a 65-cents-an-hour minimum wage, nationalization of the housing industry, and stronger fair employment practices legislation.

Congress responded halfheartedly. It did pass the Employment Act of 1946 which, although less than Truman requested, provided the institutional framework for more government control over the economy. The act also created the Council of Economic Advisers, and in the decades after 1946 the council exerted a powerful influence over economic policy.

On the other hand, Republicans and southern Democrats balked at a return to more "New Dealism." Consequently, Congress destroyed the OPA by relaxing its controls, a policy that created immediate inflation, and refused to pass Truman's economic package. The American economy, however, was basically sound, and wartime employment and wartime saving had created a people whose money was burning holes in their pockets. Given the demand for consumer goods and the short supply, inflation was inevitable. But, as industries converted to peacetime production, consumer supplies rose to meet the new demands.

Confronting the Demands of Labor

During the war labor unions had taken "no strike" pledges, and through their efforts America became the "arsenal of democracy." Workers labored long and hard, agreeing to speedups and higher production quotas. As the war came to an end, however, workers demanded rewards for their wartime efforts and their loss of overtime pay. During 1946 more than 4.5 million laborers went on strike.

Truman was in no mood to coddle labor. When two national railway brotherhoods threatened to disrupt the transportation system, Truman proposed to draft the workers. Confronted by hostile public opinion and an unsympathetic president, the brotherhoods went back to work.

Labor was angry. As winter approached, United Mine Workers leader John L. Lewis took his men out on strike. The prospect of a cold winter created anxiety, and Truman reacted angrily. He threatened to take over the mines and lashed out publicly at the defiant Lewis. Finally, Truman appealed directly to the miners, asking them to go back to work for the good of the nation. It worked. Lewis called off the strike.

The congressional elections of 1946, which brought the conservative, Republican-controlled Eightieth Congress, added to labor's problems. Led by Robert Taft, Congress pushed through the Taft-Hartley Act in 1947 over Truman's veto, which outlawed the closed shop (a business or industry in which all the employees are required to join a union), gave presidents power to delay strikes by declaring a "cooling-off" period, and curtailed the political and economic power of organized labor. The act signified the conservative mood of the country.

It was a bad period for all industrial workers, but for female workers it was especially hard. During the war they had filled a wide range of industrial jobs, but returning soldiers quickly displaced them. What was worse, when new jobs opened employers hired and trained younger males rather than rehire the experienced females. Thus, while male workers complained about the antilabor mood of the country, many unemployed women laborers lamented the antifemale prejudices among employers.

Failure of the Fair Deal

Political experts expected America to vote Republican in the 1948 presidential elections. Truman's policies had angered liberals, labor, southerners, and most of Congress. Moreover, Democrats had occupied the White House since 1933. Republicans reasoned that it was time for a change. They nominated Thomas E. Dewey of New York, the GOP candidate in 1944. The Democrats stayed with Truman, even though large numbers of southerners and liberals deserted the party to follow third-party movements. Southerners, angered by Truman's support of civil rights, formed the States' Rights Democratic party—better known as the Dixiecrats—and nominated Governor J. Strom Thurmond of South Carolina for president. Liberals formed the Progressive party, which nominated FDR's former vice president Henry A. Wallace.

An underdog from the start, Truman rolled up his sleeves and took his cause to the people. Campaigning across the country by train, at each stop Truman blasted the "do-nothing" Eightieth Congress. "If you send another Republican Congressman to Washington, you're a bigger bunch of suckers than I think you are," he lectured. "Give 'em hell, Harry!" was the popular refrain. By contrast, Dewey's cold personality failed to move American voters.

By election day Truman had closed the gap. The old Roosevelt coalition—midwestern farmers, urban ethnics, organized labor, blacks, and southerners—remained sufficiently strong to send Truman back to the White House. Neither the Dixiecrats nor the Progressives hurt Truman in any substantial way. Most Democrats chose to remain in the center of the party with Truman rather than drift toward the radical fringes. The election was a testimony to the legacy of FDR as well as Truman's scrappiness, and to the often overlooked fact that Democrats outnumbered Republicans in the nation.

"Keep America Human With Truman," read one of his campaign posters. In 1949 the president announced a plan to do just that. Known as the Fair Deal, the legislative package included an expansion of Social Security, federal aid to education, a higher minimum wage, federal funding for public housing projects, a national plan for medical insurance, civil rights legislation for minorities, and other measures to foster social and economic justice.

Congress extended Social Security and raised the minimum wage to 75 cents an hour, but otherwise failed to enact Truman's plan. The more original proposals of the Fair Deal—civil rights legislation, a national health insurance program, an imaginative farm program, and federal aid to education—were rejected by a Congress that opposed anything defined as "creeping socialism."

Truman, as well as Congress, contributed to the ultimate failure of the Fair Deal to achieve its objectives. To be sure, Republicans and southerners joined forces in opposition to civil rights and government spending programs. But on domestic issues Truman demonstrated an almost total inability to work with Congress. In addition, by 1949 foreign policy dominated the president's attention and claimed an increasing share of the federal budget.

Searching for the Enemy Within

While Congress tampered with Truman's Fair Deal, Cold War winds were chilling the country's political landscape. The tough diplomatic rhetoric of Truman, Acheson, and other policymakers encouraged Americans to view the rivalry between the Soviet Union and the United States in simplistic terms. America became the "defender of free people," the Soviet Union the "atheistic enslaver of millions." Every time a world event did not go America's way, it was seen as a Soviet victory. The suspicion thus took shape that "enemies within" America were secretly aiding the Soviet cause and sabotaging U.S. foreign policy.

Were spies working against American interest to further the Soviet cause? Unquestionably, yes. In 1945 a Communist spy ring working in Canada and the United States was uncovered. The evidence led to the arrest of two British physicists who had worked on the Manhattan Project. The investigation led to a group of American radicals—among them Julius and Ethel Rosenberg—who had passed atomic secrets to the Soviets during the war. Whether this information helped the Soviet Union develop an atomic bomb remains largely conjecture.

The espionage issue soon became an instrument of partisan politics. Republicans accused Democrats of being "soft" on communism—in fact, of harboring spies in the State Department and other government agencies. California congressman Richard M. Nixon announced that Democrats were responsible for "the unimpeded growth of the communist conspiracy in the United States." As proof, Republicans pointed to the "fall" of China, the atomic bomb in the Soviet Union, and Alger Hiss in the State Department.

Truman reacted to such criticism as early as 1947 by issuing Executive Order 9835 establishing the Federal Employee Loyalty Program, which authorized the FBI to investigate all government employees. Although the search disclosed no espionage or treason, thousands of employees were forced to resign or were fired because their personal lives or past associations did not meet government inspection. Homosexuality, alcoholism, unpaid debts, contributions to left-wing causes, support of civil rights—all became grounds for dismissal.

Ethel and Julius Rosenberg paid the supreme price. They were Communists, and at least one—Julius—may have been a spy, but the death penalty was not mandatory for their crime. Judge Irving R. Kaufman, nevertheless, made an example of them, and ordered the couple's execution for treason. On June 19, 1953, the Rosenbergs, parents of two young sons, died in the electric chair.

The Rise and Fall of Joseph McCarthy

More than any other person, Wisconsin Senator Joseph McCarthy capitalized on the anticommunism issue. Although he did not start the crusade or even join it until 1950, the entire movement bears the name "McCarthyism." His career, which caused so much suffering for so many, illuminated the price the country had to pay for temporarily placing anticommunism above the Constitution.

First elected to the Senate in 1946, McCarthy spent four years in relative obscurity, all the while demonstrating his incompetency and angering his colleagues. Then on February 9, 1950, he gave a speech in Wheeling, West Virginia. Warning his audience about the threat of communism to America, he boldly announced, "While I cannot take the time to name all of the men in the State Department who have been named as members of the Communist Party and members of a spy ring, I have in my hand a list of 205 . . . a list of names that were known to the Secretary of State and who nevertheless are still working and shaping the policy of the State Department." McCarthy had no real list; he had no names. But within days he became a national sensation.

McCarthy dealt in simple solutions to complex problems. He told Americans that the United States could control the outcome of world affairs if it would get the Communists out of the State Department. It was those "State Department perverts," those "striped-pants diplomats" who "gave away" Poland, "lost" China, and allowed the Soviet Union to develop the bomb. It was the "bright young men who are born with silver spoons in their mouths" who were "selling the Nation out." His arguments found receptive ears among Catholics who had relatives in Eastern Europe, political outsiders who resented the power of the "Ivy League Eastern Establishment," and pragmatic Republicans who wanted to return to the White House in 1952. And with the outbreak of the Korean War in the early summer of 1950, Joseph McCarthy's support grew.

McCarthy's origins were humble; he worked his way through high school and a Catholic university. He was in all ways the opposite of Secretary of State Dean Acheson, whose Ivy League degrees, waxed mustache, and aristocratic accent were a red flag to McCarthy. Throughout the early 1950s McCarthy bitterly attacked "Red Dean" and the State Department. But in the end, McCarthy ferreted out no Communists, espionage agents, or traitors.

McCarthy's basic tactic was never defend. Caught in a lie, he told another; when one case dissolved, he created another. He attacked Truman and Eisenhower, Acheson and Marshall, the State Department and the U.S. Army. No authority or institution frightened him. In 1954 his campaign against the army became so bitter that the Senate arranged special hearings. Televised between April 22 and June 17, the Army-McCarthy hearings attracted a high audience rating. But for once McCarthy's attention-getting methods backfired badly. It was the first time that most Americans saw McCarthy in action—the bullying of witnesses, the cruel use of innuendo, the tasteless humor.

After the hearings, McCarthy's downfall was as rapid as his rise. When the polls showed that his popularity had swung sharply downward, his enemies mounted an offensive. On December 2, 1954, the Senate voted to censure McCarthy for his unsenatorial behavior. Newspapers stopped printing his outlandish charges. He sank back into relative obscurity, and died on May 2, 1957.

The end of the Korean War and McCarthy's downfall signaled the end of the Red Scare. The Cold War remained, but most Americans soon realized that there was no significant domestic Communist threat. They

Senator Joseph McCarthy's downfall came about as a result of his unsubstantiated charges of Communist infiltration in the U.S. Army.

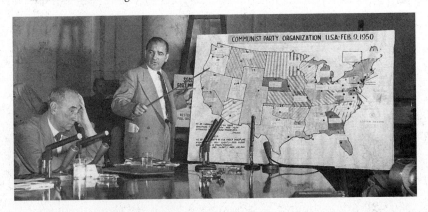

learned that an occasional spy was part of the price that free societies pay for their personal freedom, and that "McCarthyism" can be the result of a curtailment of that freedom.

The Paranoid Style

The Cold War mentality left its imprint on politics and culture during the late 1940s and early 1950s, giving rise to a national mood that has been termed the "paranoid style." The nature of the fight against communism contributed to the paranoid style. Politicians warned Americans that communism was silently and secretly destroying the country from within. Although directed from Moscow, its aim was subversion through the slow destruction of a country's moral fiber. No one knew which institution it would next attack, or when. It might be the State Department or the YMCA; it might be the presidency, the army, the movie industry, or the Cub Scouts. Politicians counseled vigilance. They told Americans to watch for the unexpected, to suspect everyone and everything. As a result, between 1945 and 1955 a broad spectrum of institutions, organizations, and individuals came under suspicion. Whether it was the Mafia or the fluoridation of drinking water, Americans sought the answers to complex problems in the workings of conspiracies.

HUAC Goes to Hollywood

The House of Representatives established the Un-American Activities Committee (HUAC) in the late 1930s to combat subversive right-wing and left-wing movements. From the first it tended to see subversive Communists everywhere at work in American society. HUAC even announced that the Boy Scouts were Communist-infiltrated. During the late 1940s and the early 1950s HUAC picked up the tempo of its investigations, which it conducted in well-publicized sessions. Twice during this period HUAC traveled to Hollywood to investigate Communist infiltration in the film industry.

HUAC first went to Hollywood in 1947. A group of radical screenwriters and producers were called upon to testify. Asked if they were Communists, the "Hollywood Ten" refused to answer questions about their political views, believing that the First Amendment protected them. In the politically charged late 1940s, however, their rights were not protected. Those who refused to divulge their political affiliations were tried for contempt of Congress, sent to prison, and blacklisted.

HUAC went back to Hollywood in 1951. This time it called hundreds of witnesses from both the political right and the political left. Conservatives told HUAC that Hollywood was littered with "Commies." Walt Disney even recounted attempts to have Mickey Mouse follow the party line. Of the radicals, some talked but most remained silent. To cooperate with HUAC entailed "naming names"—that is, informing on one's friends and political acquaintances. Again, those who refused to name names found themselves unemployed and unemployable.

The HUAC hearings and blacklisting convinced Hollywood producers to make strongly anticommunist films. Between 1947 and 1954 they released more than 50 such films. Most were second-rate movies, starring third-rate actors. The films assured Americans that Communists were thoroughly bad people—they didn't have children, they exhaled cigarette smoke too slowly, they murdered their "friends," and they went berserk when arrested. If the films were bad civics lessons, they did have an impact. They seemed to confirm HUAC's position that Communists were everywhere, that subversives lurked in every shadow. They reaffirmed the paranoid style and helped to justify McCarthy's harangues and Truman's Cold War rhetoric.

"What's Wrong with Our Kids Today?"

At the same time that it turned out films about Communists, Hollywood produced movies that contributed to the fear that something was terribly wrong with the youth of America. Films such as *The Wild One* (1954), *Blackboard Jungle* (1955), and *Rebel Without a Cause* (1955) portrayed adolescents as budding criminals, emerging homosexuals, potential Fascists, and pathological misfits—everything but perfectly normal kids.

FBI reports and congressional investigations reinforced the theme of adolescent moral decline. J. Edgar Hoover, head of the FBI, linked the rise in juvenile delinquency to the decline in the influence of family, home, church, and local community institutions. Frederic Wertham, a psychiatrist who studied the problem extensively, agreed, emphasizing particularly the pernicious influence of comic books. He believed that crime and horror comic books fostered racism, fascism, sexism, and even homosexuality in their readers. Far from being an unheard voice, Wertham's attack generated congressional investigations of and local attacks against the comic book industry. In response, the comic book industry passed several self-regulatory codes designed to restrict the violent and sexual content of comic books.

For a number of critics, sports were an antidote to the ills of wayward youths. "Organized sport is one of our best weapons against juvenile

Movies like *Rebel Without a Cause,*
starring James Dean, depicted the
futility and hopelessness of American
youth in the 1950s.

delinquency," remarked J. Edgar Hoover. Youths who competed for
championship trophies felt no inclination to steal cars. Nor would they
turn to communism. As Senator Herman Welker of Idaho bluntly put it,
"I never saw a ballplayer who was a Communist."

Given these widespread beliefs, the sports scandals of the early 1950s
shocked the nation and raised fresh questions about the morality of
American adolescents. In February 1951 New York authorities disclosed
that players for the City College of New York (CCNY) basketball team
had accepted money to fix games. By the time the investigations ended,
seven other colleges were implicated in the scandal, which involved forging transcripts and paying players as well as fixing games. In August, a
cheating scandal at the U.S. Military Academy at West Point resulted in
he dismissal of 90 cadets, half of them football players.

The West Point scandal struck especially at the nation's heart, for half
a world away in Korea American soldiers were battling to contain communism. What of their moral fiber? They too had read comics, watched
films written by left-wing screenwriters, and been exposed to other "subversive" influences. Did they have the "right stuff"? These questions
swirled around the Korean prisoner of war (POW) controversy. Early reports suggested the American POWs in Korea were different from, and inferior to, those of World War II. Journalists portrayed them as undisci-
plined, morally weak, susceptible to "brainwashing," uncommitted to

traditional American values, and prone to collaborate with their communist guards.

What was wrong? Who was corrupting the youth of America? The Republican *Chicago Tribune* blamed the decline on the New Deal. The Communist *Daily Worker* said it was the fault of Wall Street, bankers, and greedy politicians. The paranoid style, after all, had no party affiliation. Other Americans, without being too specific, simply felt that there was some ominous force working within the United States against Americans.

Sociologists and historians have demonstrated that Korean POWs behaved in much the same way as POWs from earlier wars. During the late 1940s and 1950s juvenile delinquency was not on an upswing, nor were alien, subversive forces undermining American morality. But the rhetoric of the Cold War and McCarthyism created a political atmosphere that proved fertile for the paranoid style.

Conclusion

By 1953 and 1954 there were indications of a thaw in the Cold War. First came the death of Joseph Stalin in 1953. Shortly thereafter Georgi Malenkov told the Supreme Soviet, the highest legislative body of the Soviet Union: "At the present time there is no disputed or unresolved question that cannot be settled peacefully by mutual agreement. . . . This applies to our relations with all states, including the United States of America." That summer the Korean War ended in a stalemate that allowed both the United States and the Communist forces to save face. In America, 1954 saw the fall of McCarthy. Certainly these events did not end the paranoid style in either the United States or the Soviet Union, but they did ease the tension.

In addition, by 1954 both the United States and the Soviet Union had become more comfortable in their positions as world powers and had begun to realize that neither side could readily win the Cold War. Between 1945 and 1954 each had carved out spheres of influence. The Soviet Union and its sometime-ally China dominated most of Eastern Europe and the Asian mainland. America and its allies controlled Western Europe, North and South America, most of the Pacific, and to a lesser extent Africa, the Middle East, and Southeast Asia. Throughout much of the Third World, however, emerging nationalistic movements challenged both U.S. and Soviet influences.

In the United States the containment policy was seldom even debated. The Truman Doctrine governed foreign policy decisions, but economic and political questions lingered. How much would containment cost?

Chronology of Key Events

1938 House Un-American Activities Committee (HUAC) created to investigate Communist subversion

1945 United Nations is founded

1947 Truman Doctrine declared; Truman establishes Federal Employee Loyalty Oath Program; Marshall Plan provides economic aid for European recovery; Taft-Hartley Act bans closed shop; HUAC investigates Communist infiltration of the film industry

1948 West Germany founded; Soviet Union imposes Berlin blockade; ex-Communist Whittaker Chambers charges former State Department official Alger Hiss

1949 NATO founded; Berlin blockade ends; Mao Zedong's Communist forces win China's civil war; Soviet Union successfully tests atomic bomb

1950 Senator Joseph McCarthy claims to have names of State Department employees who are Communists; Korean War begins; UN forces invade North Korea; Chinese troops enter North Korea

1951 Ethel and Julius Rosenberg are sentenced to death for atomic espionage

1953 Joseph Stalin dies; Dwight D. Eisenhower inaugurated thirty-fourth president; cease-fire in Korean War

1954 Army-McCarthy hearings

Where would the money come from? Which Americans would pay the most? Would it mean the end of liberal reform? During the next decade American leaders would wrestle with these and other crucial questions.

Suggestions for Further Reading

Valuable studies of American foreign policy during the Cold War include Stephen E. Ambrose, *Rise to Globalism,* 5th ed. (1988); John L. Gaddis, *The United States and the Cold War* (1992); Walter LaFeber, *America, Russia, and the Cold War,* 5th ed. (1985); Thomas G. Paterson and Robert J. McMahon, *The Origins of the Cold War,* 3d ed. (1991).

Specific studies of Cold War foreign policy crises include Bruce Cumings, *The Origins of the Korean War,* 2 vols. (1981–1990); Michael Hogan, *The Marshall Plan* (1987); Howard Jones, *A New Kind of War* (1989); Akira Iriye, *The Cold War in Asia* (1974); Avi Shlaim, *The United States and the Berlin Blockade* (1983).

For American social, cultural, and political developments during this period see James Aronson, *The Press and the Cold War* (1970); William Leuchtenburg, *A Troubled Feast,* rev. ed. (1983); Larry Ceplair and Steven Englund, *The Inquisition in Hollywood* (1980); Nora Sayre, *Running Time: Films of the Cold War* (1982); Stephen J. Whitfield, *The Culture of the Cold War* (1991).

Examinations of McCarthy and McCarthyism include David M. Oshinsky, *A Conspiracy So Immense* (1983); Thomas C. Reeves, *The Life and Times of Joe McCarthy* (1982); Athan Theoharis, *Seeds of Repression: Harry S Truman and the Origins of McCarthyism* (1971). The Hiss-Chambers case is examined in Allen Weinstein, *Perjury* (1978), and in Hiss's own memoir, *Recollections of a Life* (1988).

Chapter 28

Ike's America

Quiet Changes
I Like Ike
A Country of Wheels
Ike, Dulles, and the World
A New Face in Moscow
1956: The Dangerous Year
Sputnik and Sputtering Rockets
Third-World Challenges
Not with a Bang, But a Whimper

We Shall Overcome
Taking Jim Crow to Court
A Failure of Leadership
The Word from Montgomery

The Sounds of Change
Father Knows Best
The Other Side of the Coin
The Meaning of Elvis
A Different Beat

Mose Wright stood and surveyed the courtroom. Most of the faces he saw were white. The two accused men were white. The 12 jurors were white. The armed guards were white. Slowly, Wright, a 64-year-old black sharecropper, extended his right arm. "Thar he," Wright answered, pointing at J. W. Milam. He then pointed at Roy Bryant, the second defendant. In essence, Wright was accusing the two whites of murdering Emmett Till, his 14-year-old nephew—accusing them in a segregated courtroom in Sumner, Mississippi. As Wright later recalled: "It was the first time in my life I had the courage to accuse a white man of a crime, let alone something as terrible as killing a boy. I wasn't exactly brave and I wasn't scared. I just wanted to see justice done."

It was 1955, but the march of racial justice in the South had been painfully slow. In 1954 the Supreme Court of the United States in the landmark *Brown* v. *Board of Education of Topeka* decision had ruled that segregated schooling was "inherently unequal." News of the *Brown* decision drew angry comments and reactions from all corners of the Jim Crow South. Throughout Dixie, Klansmen burned crosses while other white leaders organized Citizens' Councils. These self-proclaimed protectors of white America vowed "to make it difficult, if not impossible, for any Negro who advocates desegregation to find and hold a job, get credit, or renew a mortgage."

Into this racially charged atmosphere came Emmett Till in August 1955. Taking a summer vacation from his home on the South Side of Chicago, he went to visit relatives living near Money, Mississippi. Emmett had known segregation in Chicago, but nothing like what he found in Money. Although his mother told him what to expect and how to act, Emmett had a mind and a mouth of his own. He told his cousins that he was friends with plenty of white people in Chicago; he even had a picture of a white girl, *his* white girl, he said. "Hey," challenged a listener, "there's a [white] girl in that store there. I bet you won't go in there and talk to her."

Emmett accepted the challenge. He entered Bryant's Grocery and Meat Market and browsed about. As he left, he said, "Bye, Baby" to Carolyn Bryant and gave a "wolf call" whistle. Outside an old black man told Emmett to scat before the woman got a pistol and blew "his brains out." Emmett beat a hasty retreat.

After midnight the following Saturday, Roy Bryant and his half-brother, J. W. Milam, drove to Mose Wright's unpainted cabin. They demanded the "boy who done the talkin'." Mose tried to explain that Emmett was from "up nawth," and was unfamiliar with southern ways.

The logic of the argument was lost on the two white men, who drove away with Emmett. What happened next is uncertain. According to Milam and Bryant's account, they had only meant to scare the northern youth. But Emmett did not beg for mercy. Therefore they *had* to kill him.

Mose Wright and his three boys, seated in the "colored" section of the courtroom, attended the trial of Bryant and Milam, accused of killing Emmett Till in Mississippi.

"What else could we do? " Milam asked. "He was hopeless. I'm no bully; I never hurt a nigger in my life. I like niggers in their place. I know how to work 'em. But I just decided it was time a few people got put on notice."

Three days later Emmett's badly beaten body was found in the Tallahatchie River. A gouged-out eye, crushed forehead, and bullet in his skull gave evidence to the beating he took. Around his neck, attached by barbed wire, was a 75-pound cotton gin fan. At the request of his mother, the local sheriff sent the decomposing body to Chicago for burial.

Mamie Bradley, Emmett's grieving mother insisted on an open casket funeral. Thousands of black Chicagoans attended, and the black press closely followed the episode. *Jet* magazine even published a picture of the mutilated corpse. In the black community the Till murder case became a cause célèbre.

In Money, white southerners rallied to Bryant and Milam's side. Supporters raised a $10,000 defense fund, and southern editorials labeled the entire affair a "Communist plot" to destroy southern society. Few people expected that Bryant and Milam would be judged guilty because few expected any blacks would testify against white men in Mississippi.

Mose Wright proved them wrong. He dramatically testified against the defendents, as did several other relatives of Emmett Till. But in his closing statement, John C. Whitten, one of the defense attorneys, told the all-white, all-male jury: "I'm sure that every last Anglo-Saxon one of you has the courage to free these men in the face of that [outside] pressure."

The jury returned a "not guilty" verdict in one hour and seven minutes. But if there was no fairness on that day in 1955, there were clear signs of change. A black man had demanded justice in white-controlled Mississippi. Soon other voices would join Mose Wright's. Their peaceful but insistent cries would be heard across America. They would force the United States to come to terms with its own ideology. After a heroic struggle against fascism and during a cold war against communism, Americans no longer could ignore racial injustice and inequality at home.

Slow, painful, poignant, occasionally uplifting—the march toward justice moved forward. It was part of other significant social and economic changes taking place in America. Against the backdrop of Dwight D. Eisenhower's calm assurances, a new country was taking shape.

Quiet Changes

Most white Americans during the late 1940s and the early 1950s were unconcerned about the struggles of their black compatriots. Other concerns seemed more urgent. In November 1952 the Korean War was dragging into its third year, and the chances for a satisfactory peace were fading. Joseph McCarthy was still warning Americans about the Communist infiltration of the U.S. government. At the polls Americans were ready to vote for change.

I Like Ike

The Democrats had occupied the White House for the previous 20 years. In 1952 they nominated Governor Adlai Stevenson of Illinois. A political moderate, the witty, sophisticated Stevenson was burdened by Truman's unpopularity.

Stevenson's Republican opponent was Dwight David Eisenhower. An aging war hero, Eisenhower promised to end the war in Korea and battle communism and corruption at home. His message and grandfatherly image appealed to many voters. "I like Ike" campaign buttons and posters captured the public sentiment. Eisenhower won a landslide victory, even carying several southern states and winning big in urban areas, traditional Democratic strongholds.

Few people had advanced so far while making so few enemies. An accomplished athlete and a good student, Ike earned an appointment to West Point, where he graduated in 1915. As an army officer, Eisenhower demonstrated rare organizational abilities and a capacity for complex detail work. With the outbreak of World War II, he was promoted with star-tling rapidity. General George C. Marshall passed over 366 more senior officers to promote Eisenhower to major general and appoint him com-mander of the European Theater of Operations. It was Ike who planned and oversaw America's invasions of North Africa, Sicily, and Italy, and who led the combined British-American D-Day invasion of France. By the end of the war, Ike was a four-star general and an international hero.

As president, Eisenhower practiced a brand of leadership that was strikingly different from Roosevelt and Truman. Preferring a behind-the-scenes approach to his executive duties, Eisenhower in public seemed friendly, outgoing, quick to please, but only slightly interested in being president. His "hidden hand" leadership relied upon a chain-of-command system that allowed him to delegate authority while keeping the major de-cisions of his administration in his own hands. Ike was in charge, but he left the detail work and the political battling to his subordinates.

Ike called himself a conservative, "but an extremely liberal conserva-tive," one who was concerned with fiscal prudence but not at the expense of human beings. Throughout his eight years in office Eisenhower fo-cused closely on two major priorities: U.S.–Soviet relations and a bal-anced budget. These issues, not civil or other important social concerns, occupied most of his attention. Ike termed his approach "modern Repub-licanism." In practice this approach led his administration to cut spend-ing but not to attempt any rollback of New Deal social legislation.

During Ike's two terms the country made steady and at times spectac-ular economic progress. In 1955 the minimum wage was raised from 75 cents to $1 per hour, and during the 1950s the average family income rose 15 percent. Work was plentiful, and unemployment was extremely low. Stable prices, full employment, and steady growth were the economic hallmarks of the 1950s. Although the population increased by 28 million people, the country was on the whole better housed and fed than ever be-fore. Especially for white Americans, "modern Republicanism" seemed a viable alternative to New Dealism.

A Country of Wheels

If Eisenhower labored to curtail the role of the federal government in some areas, he expanded it in others. As an expert on military logistics, Ike frequently expressed concern about the sad state of the American highway system. During World War II he had been impressed by Hitler's system of *Autobahnen,* which allowed the German dictator to deploy troops to different parts of Germany with incredible speed. From his first days in office Eisenhower worked for legislation to improve America's highway network.

A loose collection of pressure groups, including the automobile, trucking, bus, oil, rubber, asphalt, and construction industries, pushed for a new federally subsidized interstate highway system. Not only would such a project provide millions of new jobs, it would contribute to a safer America by making it easier to evacuate major cities in the event of a nuclear attack.

As a result of presidential and lobby pressure, in 1956 Congress passed the National System of Interstate and Defense Highways Act, the most significant piece of domestic legislation enacted under Eisenhower. As planned, the system would cover more than 40,000 miles, cost $26 billion, and take 13 years to construct. Although it took longer to complete and cost far more than Congress projected, it did create thousands of jobs and provided the United States with the world's most extensive superhighway system.

More than any other piece of legislation, the Highways Act also changed America, altering its culture and landscape. It accelerated the decline of the inner city and the flight to the suburbs. As downtown businesses, hotels, and theaters closed, suburban shopping malls with multiscreen cinemas and roadside motels began to dot the American highway landscape. Drive-in theaters, gasoline service stations, mobile homes, and multicar garages signified the birth of a new extended society, one without a clear center or focus.

America's commitment to highways and cars created numerous problems. Mass transportation suffered most conspicuously. Streetcars and commuter railroads languished, as did the country's major interstate railroads. In the years since the end of World War II, 75 percent of government expenditures for transportation have gone for highways as opposed to one percent for urban mass transit. As a result, those without the use of automobiles—the old, the very young, the poor, the handicapped—became victims of America's automobile obsession.

Ike, Dulles, and the World

For Eisenhower, "modern Republicanism" was more than simply a domestic economic credo. It also implied an internationalist foreign policy. As with domestic policy, in foreign policy Ike preferred to operate behind the scenes. But he did make all major foreign policy decisions.

The point man for Ike's foreign policy was Secretary of State John Foster Dulles. Rigid and moralistic, Dulles took himself, his Presbyterian religion, and the world seriously. One Washington correspondent described him as "a card-carrying Christian," and he frequently delivered lectures on the evils of "atheistic, materialistic Communism." Although Eisenhower and Dulles had strikingly different public styles, they shared a common vision of the world. Both were internationalists and cold warriors who believed that the Soviet Union was the enemy and that the United States was and should be the protector of the free world. Peace was their objective, but never a peace won by appeasement. To keep honorable peace, both were willing to consider the use of nuclear weapons and go to the brink of war.

Occasionally Dulles's impassioned anti-Communist rhetoric obscured the actual policies pursued by the Eisenhower administration. In public, Dulles rejected the containment doctrine as a "negative, futile and immoral policy" and advocated the "liberation" of Eastern Europe, using nuclear weapons if necessary to achieve America's objectives.

In reality, Eisenhower's objectives were far more limited and his approach toward foreign policy much more cautious. Ike supported containment, but he viewed Truman's approach as unorganized and far too expensive. Ike believed that the United States could not support every country that claimed to be fighting communism. If America continued Truman's policies, the costs would soon become higher than Americans would be willing to pay. A change, Ike maintained, was needed.

Eisenhower termed his adjustments of the containment doctrine the "New Look." In order to save money, he decided to emphasize nuclear weapons over conventional weapons, a "more bang for the buck" approach that drew angry criticism. Congressional hawks claimed that Eisenhower was "putting too many eggs in the nuclear basket," and liberals suggested that the program would inevitably lead to nuclear destruction.

Whatever the criticisms, the New Look did save money. While air and missile forces were expanded, the army's budget was greatly reduced. The results of Eisenhower's approach were dramatic. Between 1953 and 1956 the defense budget was cut by $14.6 billion, and troop levels were reduced by almost one-third.

The New Look took an unconventional approach to conventional warfare. Ike had learned from Truman's mistakes in Korea. America could not send weapons and men to all corners of the world to contain communism. Instead, the New Look emphasized the threat of massive retaliation to keep order, and reinforced America's position with a series of foreign alliances that encouraged indigenous troops and peoples to resist Communist expansion. Finally, Eisenhower used the Central Intelligence Agency as a covert foreign policy arm. Through assassinations and political coups engineered by the CIA, Eisenhower was able to prevent—or at least forestall—the emergence of anti-America regimes.

A New Face in Moscow

The world changed dramatically a few months after Eisenhower took office. In March 1953, Joseph Stalin died. Always fearful of rivals, Stalin did not groom a successor. The result was a power struggle within the Kremlin, from which Nikita Khrushchev emerged as the winner.

Short, rotund, and bald, Khrushchev, unlike Stalin, enjoyed meeting people, making speeches, and traveling abroad. If occasionally he lost his temper and uttered belligerent remarks (he once even took off his shoe and pounded it on a table at the United Nations), Khrushchev did try to lessen the tensions between the Soviet Union and the United States.

Ike shared Khrushchev's dream for peaceful coexistence between the two nations and used Stalin's death as an opportunity to extend an olive branch. The Soviet Union peacefully responded. During 1955 the nations resolved several thorny issues: The Soviets repatriated German prisoners of war held since World War II, established relations with Greece and Israel, gave up claims to Turkish territory, and withdrew from their occupation zone in Austria.

In July 1955 the two leaders met in Geneva, Switzerland, for a summit conference. During the meeting Eisenhower suggested that the United States and the Soviet Union allow aerial surveillance and photography of each other's nations to lessen the chance of a possible surprise attack. Although Khrushchev rejected this "open skies" proposal, the two leaders seemed to be working toward the same peaceful ends. "A new spirit of conciliation and cooperation" had been achieved, Ike announced. Unfortunately, "the Spirit of Geneva" would not survive the confrontations ahead.

1956: The Dangerous Year

While working toward peaceful coexistence, both Eisenhower and Khrushchev had to satisfy critics at home. In Washington, Dulles continued to call for the "liberation" of Eastern Europe and hinted that the United States would rally behind any Soviet-dominated country that rebelled. In reality, Eisenhower was not about to risk war with the Soviet Union over Eastern Europe.

At the same time, Khrushchev often promised more than he would or could deliver. On February 24, 1956, for example, Khrushchev delivered a four-hour speech before the Twentieth Party Congress, in which he condemned the former dictator's domestic crimes and foreign policy mistakes, endorsed "peaceful coexistence" with the West, and indicated that he was willing to allow greater freedom behind the "iron curtain." Although the speech was supposed to be secret, the CIA obtained copies and distributed them throughout Eastern Europe.

Poland took Khrushchev at his word and moved in a more liberal, anti-Stalinist direction. Since it did not attempt to withdraw from the Soviet bloc, Khrushchev allowed Poland to move along its more liberal course. What Poland had won, Hungary wanted—and more. In October 1956, an uprising in Budapest brought a more liberal government to power which the Soviets recognized. However, when the new government announced that it planned to pull out of the Warsaw Pact (the Soviet-dominated defense community that was created in response to NATO), Khrushchev sent Soviet tanks and soldiers into Budapest to crush what he now termed a "counterrevolution." Killing hundreds of demonstrators, the Soviets brutally restored their control over Hungary. All the while the Eisenhower administration watched, demonstrating that the notion of "liberation" was mere rhetoric, not policy.

At the time of the Soviet move into Budapest, Eisenhower was more concerned with problems in Egypt, whose nationalistic leader, President Gamal Abdel Nasser, was struggling to remain neutral in the Cold War. When Nasser recognized the People's Republic of China and pursued amicable relations with the Soviet Union, the Eisenhower administration withdrew a proposed loan to help build the Aswan Dam on the Nile. Nasser struck back by nationalizing the Suez Canal, the waterway linking the oil-rich Gulf of Suez and the Mediterranean. Half of Western Europe's oil came through the Suez Canal, which many considered essential to the security of Western Europe. British and French leaders were outraged, loudly claiming that the seizure threatened their Middle Eastern oil supplies. Eisenhower counseled caution, but Britain, France, and Israel resorted to "drastic actions." On October 29, 1956 Israel invaded Egypt, and Britain and France used the hostilities as a pretext to seize the Suez Canal.

Furious, Eisenhower refused to support the invasion. He interrupted his reelection campaign to return to Washington. Ike told Dulles to inform the Israelis that "we're going to apply sanctions, we're going to the United Nations, we're going to do everything that there is so we can stop this thing." Cut off from American support and faced with angry Soviet threats, Britain, France, and Israel halted their operations.

Sputnik *and Sputtering Rockets*

In foreign affairs, Eisenhower's second term was less successful than his first. Age and health may have contributed to this turn of events. During his first four years in office, Ike suffered a heart attack and a bout with ileitis, which entailed a serious operation. During his second term, he was more apt to take vacations and play golf and bridge with his close friends.

John Foster Dulles's health was also declining. During the Suez crisis doctors discovered that he had cancer. Acute physical pain punctuated his last years as secretary of state, and he died in 1959.

More than ill health plagued Ike's foreign policy. Soviet technological advances created a mood of edginess in American foreign policy and military circles. In 1957 the Soviet Union successfully launched *Sputnik,* the first artificial satellite to orbit the earth. Less than one month later, the Soviet Union launched its second *Sputnik,* this one built on a larger and grander scale, carrying a small dog which was wired with devices to gauge the effects of zero gravity on bodily functions. If the first *Sputnik* demonstrated that the Soviets had gained the high ground, the second indicated that they intended to go higher and to place men in space.

Before the year was out, the United States tried to respond with a satellite of its own. Code-named *Vanguard,* the satellite was placed on the top of a three-stage navy rocket that was launched on December 6. The rocket blew up only seconds after lift-off. It was the first of a series of highly publicized American rocket launches that ended with the sputtering sound of failure.

Sputnik forced Americans to question themselves and their own values. Had the country become soft and overly consumer-oriented? While Soviet students were studying calculus, physics, and chemistry, had American students spent too much time in shop, home economics, and driver education classes? More important, did *Sputnik* give the Soviet Union a military edge over the United States? If a Soviet rocket could put a thousand-pound ball in orbit, could the same rocket armed with a nuclear warhead hit a target in the United States? Such questions disturbed ordinary Americans and U.S. policymakers alike.

In truth, Americans overrated the importance of *Sputnik.* Launching a satellite was one thing; delivering a warhead to a specific target was quite another matter. That entailed sophisticated guidance systems, which the Soviet Union had not developed. Nonetheless American policymakers responded with more money for "defense-related" research and funneled more dollars into American higher education. In an attempt to improve science and mathematics skills, Congress passed the National Defense Education Act (1958) to help finance the undergraduate and graduate educations of promising students. Congress also organized the National Aeronautics and Space Administration (NASA) and allotted the agency huge sums of money in order to get ahead in the "space race."

Third-World Challenges

If *Sputnik* was largely an illusionary challenge, nationalist movements in the Third World created more serious problems. Eisenhower's response to

U.S. efforts to compete with the Soviet Union's space advances suffered a major setback when the *Vanguard* exploded two seconds after takeoff on December 6, 1957.

such movements varied from case to case. On the one hand, he opposed Britain and France's efforts to use aggression to whip Egypt into line. On the other hand, Ike employed covert CIA operations to achieve his foreign policy goals. In 1953 the CIA planned and executed a coup d'état that replaced a popularly elected government in Iran with a pro-American regime headed by Shah Mohammad Reza Pahlavi. The reason for the coup was that the elected government had taken over Iranian oil resources that the British had been exploiting. One year later the CIA masterminded the overthrow of a leftist government in Guatemala and replaced it with an unpopular but strongly pro-American government.

To keep order in what he believed were areas vital to American interests, Eisenhower would even resort to armed intervention. In 1958 Lebanese Moslems, backed by Egypt and Syria, threatened a revolt against the Beirut government dominated by the Christian minority. President Camille Chamoun appealed to Eisenhower for support. Concerned with Middle Eastern oil, Ike ordered marines from America's Sixth Fleet into Lebanon. Once order was restored and Lebanese politicians had agreed on a successor to Chamoun, Ike withdrew the troops.

In 1959 revolutionary Fidel Castro overthrew Fulgencio Batista, a right-wing dictator who had encouraged American investments in Cuba at the expense of the Cuban people. Castro quickly set about to change the situation. He confiscated land and properties in Cuba owned by Americans, executed former Batista officials, built hospitals and schools, ended racial segregation, improved workers' wages, and moved leftward. Before long, Castro had begun to jail writers and critics, hold public executions, postpone elections, and condemn the United States.

Instead of waiting for Cuba's anti-American feelings to subside, Eisenhower decided to move against Castro. He gave the CIA permission to plan an attack on Cuba by a group of anti-Castro exiles, a plan that would culminate with the disastrous Bay of Pigs invasion (see Chapter 29). As one of his last acts as president, in 1961 Eisenhower severed diplomatic relations with Cuba. Such actions only increased Castro's anti-American resolve and further drove him into the arms of the Soviet Union.

Ultimately, the Truman and Eisenhower brands of containment were unsuccessful in dealing with nationalistic independence movements. Such movements dominated the postwar world. Between 1944 and 1974, for example, 78 countries won their independence. These included more than one billion people, or close to one-third of the world's population. As the CIA activities in Guatemala, Iran, and Cuba indicated, short-term benefits came with long-term costs. Increasingly, the United States became identified with unpopular, undemocratic, and intolerant right-wing regimes. Such actions tarnished America's image in the Third World.

Not with a Bang, But a Whimper

Going into his last year in office, Eisenhower hoped to improve on the foreign policy record of his second term. Since his last meeting with Khrushchev in Geneva, the Cold War had intensified. In particular, the Soviets were once again threatening to cut off Western access to West

Berlin, an action Eisenhower feared might lead to a nuclear war. To solve the problem—or at least to neutralize it—Khrushchev visited the United States and agreed to a formal summit meeting set for May 1960 in Paris.

The two world leaders never again had serious talks. Just before the meeting the Soviets shot down an American U-2 spy plane over their territory. During the previous few years, U-2 missions had kept Eisenhower abreast of Soviet military developments and convinced him that *Sputnik* posed no military threat to the United States. Nevertheless, the existence of such planes was a military secret, and U-2 pilots had strict orders to self-destruct their planes rather than be forced down in enemy territory.

Assuming that the pilot had followed orders, Eisenhower responded to the Soviet charges of spying by publicly announcing that the Soviets had shot down a weather plane that had blown off course. Unfortunately for Ike, the pilot, Francis Gary Powers, had not followed orders, and the Soviets had him and the wreckage of his plane. Trying to save the summit, Khrushchev offered Eisenhower a way to save face. The Soviet leader indicated that he was sure that Eisenhower had not known about the flights. Eisenhower, however, accepted full personal responsibility and refused to apologize for actions he deemed were in defense of America. Rather than appear soft himself, Khrushchev refused to engage in the Paris summit.

Eisenhower's presidency ended on this note of failure. A chance to improve Soviet-American relations had been lost. But the end of his presidency should not obscure his positive accomplishments. He had concluded one war, kept America out of several others, limited military spending, and presided over seven and a half years of relative peace. Like George Washington, when Eisenhower left office he issued warnings to America about possible future problems. In particular, he noted, the "military-industrial complex"—an alliance between government and business—could threaten the nation's democratic processes.

We Shall Overcome

When Dwight Eisenhower took office in early 1953, racism—often institutionalized, sometimes less formal—was the order of the day. Below the Mason-Dixon line it reached its most virulent form in the Jim Crow laws that governed the everyday existence of southern blacks, and subjected them to daily bouts of degradation and soul-destroying humiliation. Whites framed these laws to separate the races and to demonstrate white superiority and black inferiority. Jim Crow dictated that whites and blacks eat in separate restaurants, drink from separate water fountains, sleep in separate hotels, and learn in separate schools. Jim Crow etiquette dictated that blacks give way on sidewalks to whites, speak respectfully to whites of all ages (whites addressed blacks of all ages by their first names), and give up their seats to whites when buses were full. Although the underpinning of the Jim Crow laws was the "separate but equal" doctrine enunciated in *Plessy* v. *Ferguson* (1896), both blacks and whites realized that subjugation, not equality, was the object of the laws.

North of Dixie the situation was not much better. To be sure, rigid Jim Crow laws did not exist, but blacks were informally excluded from the better schools, neighborhoods, and jobs. Whites argued that the development of ghettos was a natural process, not some sort of racist agreement between white realtors. Such, however, was not the case. William Levitt, the most famous post-World War II builder of suburban housing, attempted to keep blacks out of his developments by drafting neighborhood covenants that denied occupancy to blacks. Even after the courts struck down such restrictions, Levitt instructed his realtors not to sell to blacks. Indeed, *Shelley* v. *Kraemer* (1948), the case that stated that state courts could not uphold housing restrictions, only declared such restrictions legally unenforceable; it did not outlaw such practices per se.

When Ike left office in 1961, segregation remained largely unchanged. During his years in office, however, African Americans did make significant strides in their quest for civil rights. In particular, during the decade after 1954 blacks won a series of legal victories that in theory if not always in practice buried Jim Crow. These were years of joy and years of sadness, when the best as well as the worst aspects of the American character were clearly visible.

Taking Jim Crow to Court

World War II underscored the yawning gap between the promise and reality of life in America. Fighting against Nazi racist theories helped to draw attention to real racial problems at home. After the war, conditions improved, but at a snail's pace. With an eye on black Democratic northern voters, Truman established the President's Committee on Civil Rights, which issued a report that most white politicians ignored. While Truman called for "fair employment throughout the federal establishment" and ordered the racial desegregation of the armed services, southern politicians railed against these moderate reforms.

By the late 1940s African Americans realized that they would have to lead the fight against racial injustice themselves. In the early years of the battle the NAACP spearheaded the struggle. But the organization faced a number of problems, both within and outside the black community. For example, many blacks believed the NAACP was racist and elitist, since the organization was staffed by educated middle-class blacks who seemed out of touch with the majority of their race.

Mindful of white hostility, the NAACP moved cautiously. Instead of attacking segregation head-on and demanding full equality, the organization chose to chip away at the legal edges of Jim Crow. The separate but equal doctrine was particularly vulnerable, as NAACP lawyers demonstrated the impossibility, even the absurdity, of applying the yardstick to graduate education and law schools. The Supreme Court agreed. If, the court implied, separate but equal educational systems were to be continued, then states had to pay more than lip service to equality.

In grade school and high school education, just as in higher education, the South translated separate but equal to read "separate and highly unequal." In South Carolina's Clarendon County, for example, the county spent $179 per year on each white student and $43 per year on each black student. Intellectual and financial considerations were not the only factors that precluded equality. Psychologists argued that segregation instilled feelings of inferiority among black children, causing grave psychological damage.

In 1952 the NAACP consolidated a series of cases under the name of the first case—*Brown* v. *Board of Education of Topeka*—which challenged the very existence of the separate but equal doctrine. After months of deliberation, Chief Justice Earl Warren read the Supreme Court's unanimous decision on May 17, 1954: "Separate educational facilities are inherently unequal."

The *Chicago Defender* labeled the *Brown* decision "a second emancipation proclamation," and the *Washington Post* called it "a new birth of freedom." But such court decisions have to be enforced. As Charles Houston, an NAACP lawyer, remarked, "Nobody needs to explain to a Negro the difference between the law in the books and the law in action."

A Failure of Leadership

A year after the *Brown* decision the Supreme Court ruled that schools should desegregate "with all deliberate speed." This second decision placed the burden of desegregation in the hands of local, state, and national leaders. If the process was to be accomplished with the minimum amount of conflict, those leaders would have to be firm in their resolve to see justice done. Such, however, would not be the case.

On the national level, Eisenhower moved uncomfortably and cautiously on the issue of civil rights and desegregation. Having spent most of his life in a segregated army, Ike did not see racism as a great moral issue, and he was unresponsive to the black demand for equality. He believed that the *Brown* decision had been a mistake. When questioned about the case, he claimed, "I don't believe you can change the hearts of men with laws or decisions."

The brand of Ike's leadership and his ambitions for the Republican party further weakened his response. His behind-the-scenes approach led him to avoid speaking out clearly and forcefully on the subject. Moral outrage was not his style. In addition, he was popular in the South and harbored hopes of bringing that section of the country into the Republican party. Finally, his commitment to integration was lukewarm at best, and he placed controlling military spending above desegregating the South.

If Eisenhower had acted decisively in support of the *Brown* v. *Board of Education* decision—if he had placed the full weight of his office behind desegregation—there is some evidence that the South would have complied peacefully with the verdict. By not acting forcefully, however, Eisenhower strengthened the position of southern opponents of desegregation.

The Little Rock crisis demonstrated the failure of national and state leadership. In 1957 in Little Rock, Arkansas, school officials were ordered to desegregate their classrooms. As they prepared to do so, Governor Orval Faubus, locked in a reelection fight, intervened. He announced that any integration attempt would disrupt public order and sent in the National Guard to prevent black children from entering Central High. While Eisenhower quietly tried to maneuver behind the scenes, a crisis brewed. On the morning of September 23, 1957, when black children attempted to attend school, they were inhospitably greeted by an angry mob.

Television turned the ugly episode into a national drama. Millions of Americans witnessed violent racism for the first time. Television gave a face to racism, a concept that for many white Americans was still an abstraction. For the first but not last time, television aided the cause of civil rights by conveying the human suffering caused by racism.

To restore order, Eisenhower federalized the Arkansas National Guard and sent 1,000 paratroopers from the 101st Airborne Division to Little Rock. Although their presence desegregated Central High in 1957, the following year Faubus closed Little Rock's public schools. Taken together, Faubus's shortsighted political moves and Eisenhower's refusal to take action until public order had been disrupted created a crisis that more decisive leadership might have avoided.

The Word from Montgomery

The failure of white leaders convinced African Americans that court orders would not magically produce equal rights. Many blacks realized this

Paratroopers escorted black students to and from school in Little Rock, Arkansas, after violence erupted when the schools were instructed to desegregate.

even before the Little Rock crisis. On a cold afternoon in 1955 in Montgomery, Alabama, Rosa Parks, a well-respected black seamstress who was active in the NAACP, took a significant stride toward equality. She boarded a bus and sat in the first row of the "colored" section. The white section of the bus quickly filled, and, according to Jim Crow rules, blacks were expected to give up their seats rather than force whites to stand. Mrs. Parks, however, stayed seated. The bus stopped, the driver summoned the police, and Rosa Parks was arrested.

Black Montgomery rallied to Mrs. Parks's side. Like her, they were tired of riding in the back of the bus, tired of giving up their seats to whites, tired of having their lives restricted by Jim Crow. Local black leaders decided to organize a boycott of Montgomery's white-owned and white-operated bus system. They hoped that economic pressure would force changes that court decisions could not. For the next 381 days, more than 90 percent of Montgomery's black citizens participated in a heroic and successful demonstration against racial segregation.

To lead the boycott, Montgomery blacks turned to the new minister of the Dexter Avenue Baptist Church, a young man named Martin Luther King, Jr. Reared in Atlanta, the son of a respected minister, King had a doctorate in theology from Boston University. King believed in the power of nonviolent, direct action, and he possessed a gift for oratory that stirred people's souls. In King, the civil rights movement had found a genuine spokesperson, one who preached a doctrine of change guided by Christian love, not racial hatred. "In our protest," he observed, "there will be no cross burnings. No white person will be taken from his home by a hooded Negro mob and brutally murdered. There will be no threats and no intimidation."

The success of the Montgomery boycott inspired nonviolent black protests elsewhere in the South. Increasingly, young African Americans took the lead. Within a few months of the successful conclusion of the Montgomery boycott, demonstrations erupted in 54 cities in nine states. The protesters were arrested, jailed, beaten, and even knocked off their feet by high-pressure fire hoses, but still they challenged the traditional order.

The protests were widely reported in the country's newspapers and televised nightly on the news shows. They confronted Americans everywhere with the stark reality of segregation. As the violence continued, pressure mounted on white national politicians to take decisive action. By the early 1960s the time had come for freedom to become a reality.

The Sounds of Change

Beginning in the 1970s, American advertisers started to market a new commodity—the fifties. They marketed it as a Golden Decade, an age of innocence, tranquility, and static charm, a carefree time before the assassination of John F. Kennedy, the Vietnam War, and Watergate. According to the popular myth, kids in the 1950s thought "dope" referred to a dull-witted person, parents married for life, and major family problems revolved around whether or not "sis" had a date for the prom. In truth, however, that carefully packaged Golden Decade hardly existed. Instead, the decade was alive with dynamic, creative tensions.

Father Knows Best

The stock television situation comedy of the 1950s centered on a white family with a happily married husband and wife and two or three well-adjusted children. Most often, the family lived in a white, two-story suburban home, from which the father ventured daily to his white-collar job. The wife did not work outside the house—the husband made a comfortable living and, in any case, mothers were supposed to stay home and tend the children. "Father Knows Best," which ran from 1954 to 1962, was the classic example of this genre.

Television programs of the 1950s often centered around a happy, well-adjusted suburban family with two or three children.

The picture these sitcoms presented was generally correct. Starting after World War II, Americans moved steadily toward the suburbs, which during the 1950s grew six times faster than cities. Several factors contributed to this migration. The high price of urban real estate had driven industries out of the cities, and as always in American history, the population followed the jobs. In addition, developers built abundant, inexpensive homes, which newly married couples, aided by VA and FHA loans, purchased.

The television image of predominantly white suburban families was an accurate reflection of American demographic patterns. A far greater percentage of whites than blacks moved to the suburbs. Housing and job restrictions worked to keep blacks in the central cities while allowing whites to inhabit the suburban areas.

Even the sitcom image of the suburban housewife preoccupied with her husband and her family was correct. American women in the 1950s married younger, had children sooner, and raised larger families than they had in the previous two decades. The best-sellers list indicated America's concern with children and its glorification of motherhood. Between 1946 and 1976 the pocket edition of Dr. Benjamin Spock's *Baby and Child Care* sold over 23 million copies. The best-seller *Modern Woman: The Lost Sex* went so far as to say that an independent woman was "a contradiction in terms." The ideal woman, writers observed, was content being a wife and a mother or, in a word, a homemaker.

The Other Side of the Coin

"Father Knows Best" and other television shows portrayed an ideal world where serious problems seldom intruded and where life lacked complexity. In fact, the move to suburbia and the changes in family life forced Americans to reevaluate many of their beliefs.

Some observers claimed that life in suburbia fostered mindless conformity. Social critic Lewis Mumford described suburbs as "a multitude of uniform, unidentifiable houses, lined up inflexibly, at uniform distances, on uniform roads, in a treeless communal wasteland, inhabited by people of the same class, the same income, the same age group."

Some writers feared the United States had become a country of unthinking consumers driven by advertisers to desire only the latest gadget. Americans bought automobiles, houses, and electrical appliances as never before. While this enormous buying spree fueled the tremendous economic growth between 1945 and 1970, was it beneficial to the individuals who spent more and more of their time in their cars and watching their televisions? Cultural observers despaired.

Some women also expressed frustration about their roles as wives and mothers. Although many women worked, cultural stereotyping prevented most of them from rising to the higher paying, more prestigious positions. In addition, Betty Friedan, a leader in the women's rights movement, noted that those women who did place a career above marriage or family were regarded as abnormal.

Numerous films, novels, and articles explored the problems of suburban life. The film *Invasion of the Body Snatchers* (1956) was an outstanding example of the fear that suburbia had created a nation of conformists. In the movie, the inhabitants of the town Santa Mira are turned into emotionless shells by giant pods from outer space. Utterly lacking individuality, the pod people, as one explains, had been "reborn into an untroubled world, where everyone's the same." In that world, "there is no need for love or emotion." For such cultural critics as David Riesman, author of *The Lonely Crowd* (1955), America's acceptance of conformity threatened to make podism a form of reality.

The critics, however, overreacted to the "suburban threat." If the houses looked the same, the people were individuals. In the suburbs, white working-class families could afford for the first time to purchase homes and live middle-class lives. This was a real accomplishment. The problems that critics observed in the suburbs—the tendency toward conformity, cultural homogeneity, materialism, and anxiety over gender roles—were urban problems as well.

The Meaning of Elvis

The harshest critics of "suburban values" were American youths. Their criticism took different forms. Some of it was thoughtful and formalized, the result of the best efforts of young intellectuals. At other times it took a more visceral form, a protest that came from the gut rather than the mind. Of the second type of protest, none was more widely embraced by youths—or roundly attacked by adults—than rock and roll.

Rock and roll was the product of a heterogeneous American culture. It combined black rhythm and blues with white country music. It was made possible by the post–World War II demographic changes. The movement of southern blacks and whites to the cities of the upper South and North threw together different musical traditions and forged an entirely new sound.

Confronting conventional morality, rock and roll was openly vulgar. Its lyrics and heavy beat challenged the accepted standards of "good taste" in music. The very term—"rock 'n' roll"—had long been used in blues songs to describe lovemaking, and early black rock-and-roll singers, such as Little Richard and Bo Diddley, glorified physical relationships.

From its emergence in the early 1950s, rock and roll generated angry criticism. In the South white church groups attacked it as part of a plot to corrupt the morals of southern youths and foster integration. Between 1954 and 1958 there were numerous crusades to ban rock and roll from the airwaves.

Much of the criticism of rock and roll focused on Elvis Presley, who more than any other artist most successfully fused country music with rhythm and blues. Presley exuded sexuality. When he appeared on the Ed Sullivan Show, network executives instructed cameramen to avoid shots of Elvis's suggestive physical movements. Presley upset segregationists by performing the music of black artists. The head of Sun Records, Sam Phillips, had once claimed, "If I could find a white man who had the

Negro sound and the Negro feel, I could make a million dollars." Presley was that white man.

In the end, however, the protests implicit in Elvis Presley and rock and roll were largely co-opted by middle-class American culture. Record producers, most of whom were white, smoothed the jagged edges of rock and roll. Sexually explicit black recordings were rewritten and rerecorded—a process known as "covering"—by white performers and then sold to white youths. By 1959 rock and roll had become an accepted part of mainstream American popular culture.

A Different Beat

Rock-and-roll artists never rejected the idea of success in America. If they challenged conventional sexual mores and tried to create a unique sound, they accepted the rewards of success in a capitalistic society. Not all youth protests, however, were so easily absorbed into middle-class culture. The Beat movement, for example, questioned the values at the heart of that culture.

The Beat Generation extolled the very things that conventional Americans abhorred, and they rejected what the others prized. Beats scorned

Elvis Presley, one of the great pioneers of rock-and-roll music, was the target of much controversy throughout his life.

materialism, traditional family life, religion, sexuality, and politics. Instead, they valued spontaneity and intuition, searching for truth through Eastern mysticism and drugs. Allen Ginsberg, the leading poet of the Beat Generation, preached a life based on experimentation and developed an authentic poetic voice. In 1955 he wrote "Howl," the prototypical Beat poem. Written under the influence of drugs, "Howl" is a literary kaleidoscope, a breathless succession of stark images and passionate beliefs.

Ginsberg and Jack Kerouac, the leading Beat novelist, outraged adults but discovered followers on college campuses and in cities across America. They tapped an underground dissatisfaction with the prevailing blandness of conventional culture. In this their appeal was similar to that of rock and roll. Both were scattering seeds that would bear fruit during the next decade.

*C*hronology of Key Events

1944	GI Bill of Rights grants veterans aid for education, loans for homes and businesses
1948	President Truman bans segregation in armed forces
1953	Dwight D. Eisenhower becomes thirty-fourth president; Stalin dies; Nikita Khrushchev emerges as leader of Soviet Union; CIA helps bring Shah Mohammad Reza Pahlavi to power in Iran
1954	CIA masterminds overthrow of leftist government of Guatemala; *Brown* v. *Board of Education of Topeka* holds that "separate educational facilities are inherently unequal"
1955	Emmett Till murder; Montgomery, Alabama, bus boycott; Eisenhower and Khrushchev hold summit in Geneva, Switzerland
1956	Hungarian uprising crushed; Suez crisis
1957	Troops sent to Little Rock, Arkansas; *Sputnik* launched
1958	U.S. marines intervene in Lebanon; Congress passes the National Defense Education Act to provide federal aid to schools and colleges
1959	Cuban Revolution
1960	U-2 spy plane is shot down over the Soviet Union

Conclusion

Ike's America was both more and less than what it seemed. In foreign and domestic affairs Eisenhower appeared to allow his subordinates to run the country, when in reality he made the important decisions. Whether it was national highways or the Middle East, Eisenhower's vision of order helped shape American policy. He was more influential than most Americans during the 1950s realized.

If Eisenhower was more active than he appeared, then the country was more dynamic than it seemed on the surface. Although critics railed against the conformity of suburban America, everywhere there were signs of change. During the 1950s African Americans quickened the pace of their struggle for equality and youths experimented with alternatives to traditional behavior. And increasingly these two rebellions merged to form a distinct subculture. During the 1960s the war in Vietnam would give a political edge to that subculture.

Suggestions for Further Reading

Good overviews of social, cultural, and political developments in postwar America can be found in William H. Chafe, *The Unfinished Journey*, 2d ed. (1991); William Leuchtenburg, *A Troubled Feast*, rev. ed. (1983); Richard Polenberg, *One Nation Divisible* (1980); Emily and Norman Rosenberg, *In Our Times*, 4th ed. (1991); Howard Zinn, *Postwar America* (1973).

Important studies of the Eisenhower presidency include Stephen E. Ambrose, *Eisenhower*, 2 vols. (1983–1984); Fred I. Greenstein, *The Hidden-Hand Presidency* (1982). Foreign policy during the Eisenhower years is dealt with in Robert A. Divine, *Eisenhower and the Cold War* (1981); Townsend Hoopes, *The Devil and John Foster Dulles* (1973); Richard Immerman, *The CIA in Guatemala* (1982); Richard Melanson and David Mayers, eds., *Reevaluating Eisenhower* (1987); Richard Welch, Jr., *Response to Revolution: The United States and the Cuban Revolution* (1985).

The postwar civil rights movement is examined in William Berman, *The Politics of Civil Rights in the Truman Administration* (1970); Richard Dalfiume, *Desegregation of the U.S. Armed Forces* (1969); David Garrow, *Bearing the Cross* (1986); David L. Lewis, *King*, 2d ed. (1978); Richard Kluger, *Simple Justice* (1976); Manning Marable, *Race, Reform, and Rebellion* (1991); Stephen B. Oates, *Let the Trumpet Sound: The Life of Martin Luther King, Jr.* (1982); Harvard Sitkoff, *The Struggle for Black Equality* (1981).

For studies of specific social and cultural trends, see Erik Barnauw *Tube of Plenty*, 2d ed. (1990); Carl Belz, *The Story of Rock*, 2d ed. (1972); Bruce Cook,

The Beat Generation (1971); David Marc, *Demographic Vistas: Television in American Culture* (1984); Douglas Miller and Marion Nowak, *The Fifties* (1977); David Riesman, *The Lonely Crowd* (1950); Lynn Spigel, *Make Room for TV* (1992).

The suburbanization of America is examined in Scott Donaldson, *The Suburban Myth* (1969); James Flink, *The Car Culture* (1975); John Kenneth Galbraith, *The Affluent Society,* 4th ed. (1984); Herbert Gans, *The Levittowners* (1967); Kenneth Jackson, *The Crabgrass Frontier* (1985).

Chapter **29**

Vietnam and the
Crisis of Authority

The Illusion of Greatness
Television's President
The "Macho" Presidency
Something Short of Camelot
Cuba Libre Revisited

Vietnam: America's Longest War
A Small Corner of a Bigger Picture
Kennedy's Testing Ground
Texas Tough in the Gulf of Tonkin
Lyndon's War
To Tet and Beyond
The Politics of a Divided Nation

The Tortuous Path Toward Peace
Vietnamization
A "Decent Interval"
The Legacy of the War

Ho Chi Minh was a tiny, frail, splinter of a man. He was gentle, and in public always deferential. Even after he had come to sole power in North Vietnam, he steadfastly avoided all the trappings of authority, favoring the simple shorts and sandals worn by the Vietnamese peasants. He was sure of who he was, certain of his place in Vietnamese history, and he had no desire to impress others with his position. To his followers, he was "Uncle Ho," who treated all Vietnamese citizens like the children he never had. But in the pursuit of Vietnamese independence and the realization of a Communist nation, Ho could be cold-blooded and ruthless.

Born around 1890 in a village in a central province of Vietnam, Ho left Vietnam in 1912 and began a generation-long world odyssey. Signing aboard a French freighter, he moved from one port to the next, including Boston, New York City, and San Francisco. He was amazed not only by America's skyscrapers but also by the fact that immigrants in the United States enjoyed the same legal rights as American citizens. He was also struck by the impatience of the American people, their expectations of immediate results. (Later, during the Vietnam War, Ho would say to his military leaders, "Don't worry, Americans are an impatient people. When things begin to go wrong, they'll leave.")

After three years of almost constant travel, Ho settled in London, where he lived in squalid quarters and learned that poverty existed even in the wealthiest, most powerful countries. Then it was on to Paris, where he came in contact with the French Left. There he studied, and his nationalist ambitions became tinged with revolutionary teachings. He was still in Paris when World War I ended and the world leaders came to Versailles

Ho Chi Minh was influenced by French socialism and Soviet communism in his goal to liberate Vietnam from the French.

for the Peace Conference. Inspired by Woodrow Wilson's call for national self-determination, Ho wanted to meet Wilson to plead for his country's independence from France. Wilson ignored his request. Ho moved on— farther east and further Left.

He traveled to Moscow, where Lenin had denounced capitalist imperialism. In the Soviet Union Ho embraced communism. In the ideology he saw a road to his ultimate goal, the liberation of Vietnam. By the early 1920s he was actively organizing Vietnamese exiles into a revolutionary force. He lived a life of secrecy, moving from place to place, changing his name, renouncing anything even remotely resembling a personal life.

In 1941 Ho returned to his homeland. The time was right, he believed, to free Vietnam from colonial domination. During the early part of World War II the Japanese had won control of the country from the French; now Ho and his followers would force out the Japanese. Ho allied himself with the United States. Working alongside American Office of Strategic Services (OSS) agents, Ho impressed them with his bravery, intelligence, and unflagging devotion to his cause. On September 2, 1945, borrowing passages from the American Declaration of Independence, Ho declared Vietnamese independence.

The French reasserted their control over Vietnam after the war, but Ho's struggle continued. Although he did not expect to live to see Vietnam free of French domination, he believed that the struggle of others would eventually secure independence. Ho's patience was only one of many qualities that the West found difficult to understand.

A deep intellectual chasm divided Vietnam and the West. The West viewed history as a straight line in which progress was the governing principle. Emphasizing technological advancements and material improvements, westerners glorified change and prized individualism. The Vietnamese were products of different beliefs. Notions of competition, individualism, and technological change were anathema to tradition-bound Vietnamese. For a thousand years they had survived using the same rice-cultivating methods. To survive, the Vietnamese organized life around villages and practiced cooperative existence. Rich people were considered selfish because they gained wealth at the expense of others.

Like wealth, individualism threatened the corporate nature of village life, which was based on social harmony, not individual rights. Nor did the Vietnamese believe in intellectual freedom, which fostered debate and discord, rather than community stability. Americans considered Soviet communism evil in part because it discouraged the exchange of free ideas; Ho Chi Minh was drawn to the doctrine because it provided a set of answers not subject to question.

Motivated by the Cold War, during the period between 1954 and 1973, U.S. officials became convinced that they had to "save" Vietnam from Ho Chi Minh and his Communist brand of nationalism. Given Vietnamese leadership, traditions, and desire for independence, the American intervention in Vietnam was almost certain to fail.

The Illusion of Greatness

Television's President

John Fitzgerald Kennedy was made for television. His tall, thin body gave him the strong vertical line that cameras love, and his tanned looks appealed to women without intimidating men. His public persona, too, was tailor-made for television—wit, irony, and understatement, all delivered with a studied nonchalance.

In the 1960 presidential race Kennedy challenged his Republican opponent Richard M. Nixon to a series of television debates. At the time, Kennedy faced an uphill battle. Kennedy was considered by many to be too young, too handsome, and too wealthy to make an effective president. His undistinguished political record stood in stark contrast to Nixon's work in Congress and eight years as Eisenhower's vice president. In addition, Kennedy was Catholic, and Americans had never elected a Catholic president. Behind in the polls, Kennedy needed a dramatic boost. Against the advice of his campaign manager, Nixon accepted Kennedy's challenge.

The first debate was held in Chicago on September 26, 1960, only a little more than a month before the election. Nixon arrived looking ill and weak. Still recuperating from an infected kneecap, he appeared pale and haggard. Makeup experts offered to hide his heavy beard and soften his jowls, but Nixon accepted only a thin coat of pancake makeup. Kennedy looked very much better, needing neither makeup nor special lighting. He did, however, change suits from gray to dark blue, a color he thought would look better under the bright television lights.

Kennedy spoke first. Although he was nervous, he exuded confidence. Disregarding prearranged ground rules, Kennedy shifted what was supposed to be a debate on domestic issues to one on foreign policy. Nixon fought back. He perspired, scored debating points, produced memorized facts, and struggled to win. But while they heard a knowledgeable candidate, viewers saw an uncertain man, one whose clothes did not fit and whose face looked pasty and white. Kennedy was the clear winner. Only later did Nixon realize that the telecast had been a production, not a debate.

The polls registered the results. Most of the people who were undecided before watching the debate voted for Kennedy. That proved to be the margin of victory. Only one tenth of one percent separated the two candidates. Perhaps the most important result of the election, however, was not Kennedy's victory but the demonstration of the power of television. It came into its own in 1960.

The "Macho" Presidency

John F. Kennedy was the first American president born in the twentieth century, the torchbearer for "a new generation." Competition and an aggressively masculine view of the world ran through his life. He was the son of a multimillionaire who demanded excellence of all his sons and who believed that as Boston Irish Catholics they had to try harder and be tougher than their Protestant neighbors. This was particularly difficult for John Kennedy, who suffered throughout his life from a series of illnesses and chronic physical problems.

During the Kennedy-Nixon debates, John F. Kennedy demonstrated that for television politics, style was as important as substance.

But Kennedy never used—and his father never accepted—pain as an excuse for inactivity. At Harvard University he played football and other sports; during vacations at the family home in Hyannis Port he rough-housed with his brothers and sisters. Throughout his life, Kennedy maintained this physical view of life.

Kennedy's macho ethos extended to his attitude toward women, whom he viewed first and foremost as sexual objects. During his Washington years as a U.S. senator, he moved from one affair to the next, a habit that continued after he was married and elected president. When he wanted companionship and conversation he turned to his male friends.

Kennedy brought this masculine attitude to his presidency. He surrounded himself with advisers who shared his energetic approach to work and play. He seemed charged with a sense of urgency and often expressed the belief that America was entering a period of crisis. Without crisis, Kennedy believed, no person could achieve greatness, and he desired greatness.

Something Short of Camelot

From the very first, journalists associated the Kennedy administration with Camelot. According to the popular legend, King Arthur established in the realm of Camelot a period of unparalleled peace and prosperity. Although Kennedy himself encouraged the Camelot comparisons, the record of his administration fell short of the ideal.

Several factors worked to limit the success of Kennedy's domestic programs. To begin with, Kennedy lacked both political support in Congress and a firm commitment to push for liberal reforms. Ideologically, he was a centrist Democrat. In addition, although his party held a solid majority in the House, 101 of 261 Democratic representatives came from southern and border states, and they normally voted with conservative Republicans. Added to this problem was Kennedy's distaste for legislative infighting and his poor working relations with many senators. He limited his domestic agenda, which he named the "New Frontier," to such traditional Democratic proposals as a higher minimum wage, increased Social Security benefits, and modest housing and educational programs. In the final analysis, Kennedy was so concerned with the "crises abroad" that he risked little of his political capital on unpopular domestic reforms.

There were small successes. Congress raised the minimum wage, expanded Social Security, and appropriated a few billion dollars for public housing and aid to economically depressed areas. However, these gains were offset by the setbacks, which Kennedy accepted perhaps too stoically. Congress defeated the president's plan for federal aid to education, a health insurance plan for the aged, and programs to help migrant workers, unemployed youths, and urban commuters.

African Americans were especially disappointed with Kennedy's performance. For blacks, the early 1960s were difficult, violent years that tested their resolve. White segregationists confronted blacks' nonviolent desegregation efforts with unprovoked ferocity. In city after city violence erupted.

Through his first two years in office Kennedy remained largely silent on the issue of civil rights. Although his brother, Attorney General Robert Kennedy, aided protesters when federal laws were violated, JFK and the FBI staked out a conservative position. As one historian noted, "Civil rights workers were assaulted and shot at—systematically, often openly, frequently by law enforcement officials themselves. And through it all, in virtually every case, federal authorities did nothing."

In 1963 Kennedy changed his position. In part this about-face was the result of Robert Kennedy's prodding. In part it was the result of television, which daily showed shocking examples of brutality in the South and accelerated the demand for change. In late May 1963, Kennedy eloquently announced his new position.

Perhaps Kennedy was convinced that the time had come for "the nation to fulfill its promise." Perhaps, as his supporters claim, Kennedy was beginning to fulfill his own promise. His death in November 1963 left questions unanswered, potential unrealized. Judged by his accomplishments, however, Kennedy's Camelot, like King Arthur's, existed largely in the realm of myth. Although he could inspire people to follow, too often on domestic issues he chose not to lead.

Cuba Libre *Revisited*

Foreign affairs consumed Kennedy's interest. Kennedy generally continued the essentially Cold War policies of Truman and Eisenhower. He accepted the strategy of containment and the notion that the Soviet Union would take advantage of any sign of weakness by the United States. Unlike domestic politics, international conflicts were more clear-cut, and the divisions between "us" and "them" more certain.

Kennedy's handling of Cuban relations revealed his bellicose tendencies. Like Eisenhower, Kennedy was dismayed by the success of Fidel Castro. Just as Americans during the 1890s had cried "*Cuba Libre*," on taking office Kennedy began to search for a way to "free" Cuba, this time from Castro's communism rather than Spain's colonialism. His desire to strike a blow against communism led him to embrace a CIA plot to overthrow Castro.

Hatched during the Eisenhower administration, the CIA plan entailed the assassination of Castro and the training and transporting of a force of Cuban exiles to Cuba, where they would launch a counterrevolution. It was a plan that even the joint chiefs of staff believed would probably fail. Making matters worse, the plan was a poorly kept secret, known even to Cuban authorities.

The invasion on April 17, 1961, at the Bay of Pigs was an unmitigated disaster. The Cuban people did not rise up to join the invaders, who were trapped on the beaches. Nor would Kennedy authorize U.S. air support for the anti-Castro forces. As a result, all but 300 of the 1,500 invaders were killed or captured. If anything, the Bay of Pigs fiasco strengthened Castro's position in Cuba.

In the fall of 1962 a more serious Cuban crisis arose when the Soviet Union began to install intermediate-range ballistic missiles (IRBMs) on the island. Instead of trying to work through proper diplomatic avenues—a process that would have taken time and might have hurt the Democrats in the upcoming election—Kennedy announced the alarming news on television. After showing the public the American cities that the missiles could destroy, Kennedy said he would not permit Soviet ships transporting the weapons to enter Cuban waters.

Behind the scenes, Kennedy and Soviet Premier Nikita Khrushchev searched for a way to defuse the crisis. In the end, the world leaders achieved a solution. Khrushchev agreed to remove the missiles under United Nations inspection in return for an American pledge not to invade Cuba. The two "superpowers" had stood at the brink, gazed into the abyss, and stepped back.

The Kennedy administration interpreted the result as a victory. "We're eyeball to eyeball and I think the other fellow just blinked," Secretary of State Dean Rusk observed during the episode. And, indeed, the Soviet Union could hardly disagree. The missile crisis provided the ammunition to force Khrushchev out of power.

Friends of Kennedy claimed that he reached maturity during the crisis and that it motivated him to move toward détente—an easing of tensions—with the Soviet Union. In several 1963 speeches he called for "not merely peace in our time but peace for all time" and a "world safe for diversity." And he did support a treaty banning all atmospheric testing of nuclear weapons.

On November 22, 1963, Lee Harvey Oswald assassinated Kennedy in Dallas, Texas. (Later investigations, however, questioned whether Oswald acted alone.) The tragedy moved the nation. Once again, television gave the event a mythical quality. Americans mourned together, eyes fixed on their television sets; and immediately commentators began to evaluate Kennedy's presidency in terms of not what was but what might have been.

Vietnam: America's Longest War

How did the war start? And when? Even in the 1960s most Americans, including some foreign policy experts, were not exactly sure of the answers to such basic questions. Lyndon B. Johnson said he was continuing Kennedy's policy, who had continued Eisenhower's, who had continued Truman's, who had acted as he believed Roosevelt would have acted. The answers stretch back into time.

A Small Corner of a Bigger Picture

For almost 2,000 years Vietnam had battled China for its own independence. The French came next. During the seventeenth, eighteenth, and nineteenth centuries French traders and missionaries established their control over Vietnam. The Japanese took over the country during World War II.

In 1945 the Vietnamese declared their independence, but the same year the French returned, bent on the resubjugation of the country. The struggle continued, with the Communist Vietminh under Ho Chi Minh controlling the north of the country and the French the south. Between 1945 and 1954 both sides suffered terrible losses in the bitter guerrilla warfare.

The United States faced a difficult decision. During World War II Franklin Roosevelt had favored Vietnamese independence and aided Ho's fight against the Japanese. Roosevelt recognized that the age of colonialism was doomed, but he also believed that a strong postwar Western Europe was essential to American security, and he did not want to alienate Britain or France by pressing too hard for an end to empires.

Harry Truman inherited FDR's problems. Even more than his former boss, he advocated a strong Western Europe, even if that strength had to be based on the continuation of empires. In the game of Cold War politics Vietnam became a pawn. Truman wanted French support against the Soviet Union; in return, he willingly agreed to aid France's ambitions in Vietnam.

The success of Mao Zedong's Communist revolution in China strengthened America's support of the French in Vietnam. Obsessed with the idea of an international Communist conspiracy, Truman and his advisers contended that Stalin, Mao, and Ho were united by the single ambition of world domination. They overlooked the historical rivalries that pulled Russia, China, and Vietnam apart.

By the late 1940s the United States had assumed a large part of the cost of France's effort to regain its control over Vietnam. The price escalated during the early 1950s. By 1952 the United States was shouldering roughly one-third of the cost of the war, and between 1950 and 1954 America contributed $2.6 billion to France's war effort. But it was not enough. France was unable to defeat Ho's Vietminh forces.

In 1954 the war reached a crisis stage. In an effort to lure the Vietminh into a major engagement, the ranking French commander moved more than 13,000 soldiers to Dien Bien Phu, a remote outpost in a river valley in northwest Vietnam. The Vietminh surrounded the fort and moved artillery pieces to the hills above the French airstrip. From there they mounted a siege of Dien Bien Phu. As the months passed, French troop strength and prestige suffered punishing blows. Finally, on May 7, 1954, the French surrendered.

At the peace talks in Geneva the countries involved agreed to temporarily divide Vietnam at the 17th parallel into two countries and hold elections in the summer of 1956 to reunify Vietnam. Eisenhower supported the independent government established in South Vietnam under the leadership of Ngo Dinh Diem, a staunch anti-Communist. As a popular leader, however, he had no appeal. A Roman Catholic in an overwhelmingly Buddhist nation, Diem successfully alienated almost everyone who came into contact with him. Even United States intelligence sources rated his chances of establishing order in South Vietnam as "poor."

Diem, nevertheless, was America's man. Vietnam had become a test case, an opportunity for the United States to battle communism in Asia with dollars instead of U. S. troops. When the time came to hold the unification election, Diem, with American backing, refused. Instead, he held "free" elections in South Vietnam, where he received an improbable 98.2 percent of the popular vote. In Saigon, where there were only 405,000 registered voters, Diem received 605,000 votes.

By the end of 1957 Vietminh guerrillas in South Vietnam—often called the Vietcong—were in open revolt. Two years later North and South Vietnam resumed hostilities. The United States increased its aid, most of which went toward improving the South Vietnamese military or into the pockets of corrupt officials. The United States spent little money on improving the quality of life of the peasants. Nor did the United States object strongly to Diem's dictatorial methods.

By the end of Eisenhower's second term the United States had become fully committed to Diem and South Vietnam. To be sure, problems in Vietnam were not America's major concern. In fact, most Americans were unaware of their country's involvement there. More than anything, Vietnam was a small corner of a bigger picture. U.S. policy there was determined by larger Cold War concerns. America's presence in Vietnam, however, would soon be expanded.

Kennedy's Testing Ground

On taking office, John Kennedy reaffirmed his country's commitment to Diem and South Vietnam. The president announced his intention to be even more aggressive than Truman or Eisenhower. In Vietnam, Kennedy saw an opportunity to "prove" his nation's resolve and strength. In the end, South Vietnam as a country was less important to Kennedy than the challenge it presented.

Kennedy believed that the United States needed a fresh military approach. Eisenhower's "massive retaliation" was too rigid. It was of no use in a guerrilla war like Vietnam. Kennedy labeled his approach "flexible response," which entailed the development of conventional and counterinsurgency (antiguerrilla) forces as well as nuclear weapons. Vietnam rapidly became the laboratory for counterinsurgency activities, a place for Special Forces (Green Berets) units to develop their own tactics.

To "win" in Vietnam, Kennedy realized that he would have to strengthen America's presence there. In November of 1961 he decided to deploy American troops to South Vietnam. By the end of 1961, 3,205 American "advisers" were in Vietnam. Kennedy increased this force to 11,300 in 1962 and 16,300 in 1963.

As U.S. involvement deepened, Diem's control over South Vietnam declined. He alienated peasants by refusing to enact meaningful land reforms and Buddhists by passing laws to restrict their activities. Responding to Diem's pro-Catholic policies, Buddhists conducted hunger strikes and nonviolent protests, and one Buddhist monk, in full view of American reporters and cameras, burned himself to death on a busy, downtown Saigon intersection.

More fiery suicides followed. Protests mounted. Outside of Saigon, Diem exerted little influence. The Kennedy administration soon reached the conclusion that Diem had to go. Behind the scenes, Kennedy encouraged Vietnamese generals to overthrow Diem. On November 1, 1963, Vietnamese army officers arrested and murdered Diem and his brother. Although Kennedy did not approve of the assassination, the United States quickly aided the new government.

Three weeks later Kennedy was assassinated in Dallas. Several friends of the slain president have suggested that he had begun to reevaluate his Vietnam policy and that after the 1964 election he would have started the process of American disengagement. But whatever his future plans, Kennedy had increased U.S. involvement in Vietnam.

Unfortunately for Kennedy's successor, the prospects for South Vietnam's survival were less than they had been in 1961. By 1963 South Vietnam had lost the fertile Mekong Delta to the Vietcong and with it most of the country's rural population. From the peasants' perspective, the

Saigon government stood for heavy taxes, no services, and military destruction; and increasingly they identified the United States with Saigon. Such was the situation Lyndon B. Johnson inherited.

Texas Tough in the Gulf of Tonkin

Lyndon Baines Johnson was a complex man—shrewd, arrogant, intelligent, sensitive, vulgar, and occasionally cruel. He loved power, and he knew where it was, how to get it, and how to use it. Everything about Johnson seemed to emphasize or enhance his power. He was physically large, and seemed even bigger than he was. He used both his size and the famous "Johnson treatment"—a backslapping, hugging sort of camaraderie—as tools of persuasion.

A legislative genius, Johnson had little experience in foreign affairs. Reared in the poverty of the Texas hill country, educated at a state teachers' college, and concerned politically with domestic issues, before becoming president LBJ had expressed little interest in foreign affairs. "Foreigners are not like the folks I am used to," he often said, and whether it was a joke or not he meant it.

Yet to say Johnson had little experience in foreign affairs is not to suggest that he did not have strong opinions on the subject. Like most politicians of the period, Johnson was an unquestioning Cold Warrior. In addition, along with accepting the domino theory (the idea that if Vietnam fell, other nations would also fall to communism) and a monolithic view of communism, Johnson cherished a traditionally southern notion of honor and masculinity. It was his duty, he maintained, to honor commitments made by earlier presidents. Leaving Vietnam, Johnson believed, would be a dishonorable act, dangerous for the nation's future. To show weakness and back down was worse than cowardly—it was unmanly. Furthermore, Johnson believed that any retreat from Vietnam would destroy him politically. He had not forgotten that Truman had been blamed by the Republicans for the collapse of China. He was determined not to "lose" Vietnam.

Before winning in Vietnam, however, Johnson had to win in the United States. The presidential election in 1964 was his top priority. He was pitted against Barry Goldwater, the powerful Arizona senator from the Republican Right. "Extremism in the defense of liberty is no vice," Goldwater said, and if elected he promised to defend South Vietnam at any cost. He also preached against the welfare state, Social Security, the Nuclear Test Ban Treaty of 1963, and any rapprochement with the Soviet Union or China. Democrats suggested that Goldwater might start a nuclear war, a view that Goldwater did little to discourage, even going so far as to coin the uncomfortably comforting phrase "conventional nuclear weapon."

Johnson's campaign strategy was to appear as the thoughtful, strong moderate. He would not lose Vietnam, he told voters, but neither would he use nuclear weapons or send American troops "to do what Asian boys ought to be doing themselves." Johnson promised that, if elected, he would create a "Great Society" at home and honor American commitments abroad. Voters rewarded him with a landslide victory in the November election.

Behind the scenes, however, the Johnson administration was maneuvering to obtain a free hand for conducting a more aggressive war in Vietnam. He did not want a formal declaration of war, which might frighten voters. Rather he desired a quietly passed resolution giving him the authority to deploy American forces. Such a resolution would allow him to act without the consent of Congress. Johnson and his advisers were planning to escalate American involvement in the Vietnam War, but they hoped it would go unnoticed.

Johnson used two reported North Vietnamese attacks on the American destroyer *Maddox* as a pretext for going before Congress to ask for the resolution. Actually, he was less than truthful about the circumstances of the attack. The first incident occurred in the Gulf of Tonkin in early August 1964 when the North Vietnamese suspected the *Maddox* of aiding a South Vietnamese commando raid into North Vietnam. The American ship and supporting navy jets opened fire, sinking one of the North Vietnamese ships and crippling two others; the *Maddox* was not hit and suffered only superficial machine gun damage. The second of the Gulf of Tonkin incidents probably never occurred. Assaulted by high waves, thunderstorms, and freak atmospheric conditions, the *Maddox's* sonar equipment apparently malfunctioned, registering 22 invisible enemy torpedoes. Soon after the incident the commander of the *Maddox* reached the conclusion that no attack had ever taken place.

Johnson realized the dubious nature of the second attack. Nevertheless, he went on national television and announced, "Aggression by terror against the peaceful villages of South Vietnam has now been joined by open aggression on the high seas against the United States of America." A few days later Johnson pressed Congress for a resolution authorizing him to "take all necessary measures" to prevent aggression, and protect American security. Almost without debate, the Senate passed the Tonkin Gulf resolution on August 7 with only two dissenting votes, and the House of Representatives endorsed it unanimously. In the years that followed Johnson used his new powers to escalate the war.

Lyndon's War

Lyndon Johnson liked to personalize things. Once a military aide tried to direct him to the correct helicopter, saying "Mr. President, that's not your

Vietnam Conflict, 1964–1975

helicopter." "Son, they're all my helicopters," Johnson replied. So it was with the Vietnam War. He did not start the war, but once reelected he quickly made it "his war," exercising complete control.

When he became president it was still a relatively obscure conflict for most Americans. By the end of 1964 there were 23,300 military personnel in Vietnam, most of whom were volunteers. Only a few people strongly opposed America's involvement. All this would change dramatically during the next four years.

With the election behind him, Johnson in early 1965 started to reevaluate the position of the United States. In Saigon crisis followed crisis as one unpopular government gave way to the next. Something had to be done, and Johnson's advisers suggested two courses. The military and most of LBJ's foreign policy experts called for a more aggressive military presence in Vietnam, including bombing raids into North Vietnam and more ground troops. Other advisers, notably Under Secretary of State George Ball, believed that a land war in Indochina was not in America's best strategic interests and that bombing North Vietnam would only stiffen the Communists' resolve.

Johnson chose the first course, claiming it would be dishonorable not to come to South Vietnam's aid. In February 1965 Vietcong troops attacked the American base in Pleiku, killing several soldiers. Johnson used the assault as a pretext to commence air raids into the North. Codenamed Rolling Thunder, the operation was designed to use American technological superiority to defeat North Vietnam. At first, Johnson limited U.S. air strikes to enemy radar and bridges, but as the war dragged on, he ordered pilots to hit military targets in metropolitan areas. Between 1965 and 1973 American pilots flew more than 526,000 sorties and dropped 6,162,000 tons of bombs on enemy targets, almost three times more than were dropped in World War II.

However, the bombs did not lead to victory. Ironically, as Ball had predicted, the bombing missions actually strengthened the Communist government in North Vietnam. As a U.S. intelligence report noted, the bombing had enabled Ho's regime "to increase its control of the populace and perhaps even to break through the political apathy and indifference which have characterized the outlook of the average North Vietnamese in recent years." The massive use of air power also undermined U.S. counterinsurgency efforts. By using bombing raids against the enemy in both the North and South, U.S. forces inevitably killed large numbers of civilians, the very people they were there to help.

A larger air war also led to more ground troops; between 1965 and 1968 the escalation of American forces was dramatic. Needless to say, escalation of American troops and deaths went hand in hand. The year-end totals for the United States between 1965 and 1968 were:

1965: 184,300 troops; 636 killed.
1966: 385,300 troops; 6,644 killed.
1967: 485,600 troops; 16,021 killed.
1968: 536,000 troops; 30,610 killed.

But still there was no victory.

To Tet and Beyond

Throughout the escalation Johnson was less than candid with the American people. He argued that there had been no real change in American policy and that victory was in sight. Anyone who said otherwise, he roundly criticized. Increasingly he demanded unquestioning loyalty from his close advisers. Such demands led to an administration "party line." As the war ground on, the "party line" bore less and less similarity to reality.

In late 1967 General William Westmoreland, commander of U.S. forces in Vietnam, returned to America briefly to assure the public that he could now see the "light at the end of the tunnel," and that the enemy was "increasingly resorting to desperation tactics." At the time, the American press focused most of its attention on the battle of Khe Sanh, and Westmoreland assured everyone that victory there was certain.

Then with a suddenness that caught all America by surprise, North Vietnam struck into the very heart of South Vietnam. On the morning of January 30, 1968, North Vietnam launched the Tet offensive. A Vietcong suicide squad broke into the U.S. embassy in Saigon, and Vietnamese Communists attacked cities, towns, and hamlets in South Vietnam.

For a few weeks the fighting was ferocious and bloody. In order to re-take Hue, an ancient city close to the border between North and South Vietnam, U.S. troops had to destroy part of the city. Before they evacuated, North Vietnamese and Vietcong soldiers killed several thousand political leaders, teachers, and other civilians, many of whom were buried alive in one mass grave. In another village, where victory came at a high price, the liberating American general reported, "We had to destroy the town to save it."

Technically, the Tet offensive was a military defeat for North Vietnam, but it was also a profound psychological victory. Johnson, his advisers, and his generals had been proclaiming that the enemy was on the run and almost defeated. Tet demonstrated that the contrary was true. The Tet offensive, more than any other single event, turned the media against the war and exposed the widening "credibility gap" between official pronouncements and public beliefs.

After Tet, Americans stopped thinking about victory and turned toward thoughts of how best to get out of Vietnam. In the polls Johnson's popularity plummeted, and in the New Hampshire primary Democratic peace candidate Eugene McCarthy received surprisingly solid support. On the night of March 31, 1968, LBJ went on television and made two important announcements. First, he said that the United States would limit its bombing of North Vietnam and would enter into peace talks any time and at any place. And second, Johnson surprised the nation by announcing his decision not to seek another term as president.

A major turning point had been reached. The gradual escalation of the war was over. The period of de-escalation had started. Even in official government circles, peace had replaced victory as America's objective in Vietnam.

The Politics of a Divided Nation

As Johnson himself realized, his policies had deeply divided the nation. Instead of fully committing the United States by calling up the reserves and National Guard and by pushing for higher taxes to pay for the war, Johnson had gambled that a slow, steady escalation would be enough to force North Vietnam to accept a negotiated peace. During the buildup, LBJ told the American people that he was not drastically changing policy and that victory was in sight. After Tet, many Americans refused to believe such assurances.

Dissatisfaction with Johnson's policy surfaced first among the young, the very people who were being asked to fight and die for the cause. In the early years of "Lyndon's war," many soldiers sincerely believed that they were fighting—and dying—to preserve freedom and nourish democracy in Southeast Asia. As the war lengthened, however, an ever-growing number of soldiers expressed disillusionment. Some turned to drugs to relieve the constant stress and fear that the war engendered. A 1969 Pentagon study estimated that nearly two of every three American soldiers in Vietnam were using marijuana and that one of every three or four had tried heroin.

Other soldiers reacted by viewing all Vietnamese as the enemy. In part the nature of the war against the Vietcong caused this attitude. In a village of "civilians" any man, woman, or child *might* be the enemy. Tension and anxiety were ever present.

Empty government phrases, however, also contributed to the problem. How could soldiers win the "hearts and minds" of villagers one day and rain napalm on them the next? Reacting to the surface idealism of U.S. policy, one experienced soldier commented, "All that is just a *load* man. We're here to kill gooks, period." The My Lai massacre, which saw American soldiers kill more than 100 (the official figure was 122 but it was probably many more) South Vietnamese civilians, was the sad extension of this attitude.

As the war lengthened, the morale of American soldiers plummeted. Desertion and absent-without-leave (AWOL) rates skyrocketed. Even worse, "fragging"—the term soldiers used to describe the assassination of overzealous officers and noncommissioned officers (NCOs) by their own troops—increased at an alarming rate. The army claimed that at least 1,011 officers and NCOs were killed or wounded by their own troops during the Vietnam War.

At home, thousands of university students, most of whom had draft exemptions, also reacted to the war and Johnson's policies. They were the earliest and most vocal critics of the Vietnam War. If they lacked a coherent ideology, they were strong in numbers and energy. Not all students demonstrated against the war; most protesters were from upper middle-class families and could afford the intellectual luxury of being political idealists. Led by such leftist groups as Students for a Democratic Society (SDS), they called for a more just society in which political life was governed by morality, not greed. During the early 1960s they focused on the civil rights movement, participating in freedom rides and voter registration drives. By the mid-1960s, however, they were increasingly shifting their attention to America's "unjust and immoral" war in Southeast Asia; and with the shift their numbers swelled. By 1968 the SDS boasted more than 100,000 members. By then, too, older voices had joined the student chorus of condemnation.

It was the older voices, energized by the idealism of youth, that led to Johnson's decision not to seek reelection in 1968. For many, it seemed as if the future of American politics belonged to the proponents of peace and morality. Students initially flocked to presidential candidate Eugene McCarthy's peace cause. After Johnson pulled his hat out of the ring, Robert Kennedy announced his candidacy. Although RFK had started in political life as an aggressive cold warrior, by 1968 he had radically reevaluated these beliefs. An eloquent spokesman for the cause of humanity and peace, Kennedy exhibited the passion and commitment that McCarthy lacked.

By the conclusion of the primaries Kennedy had become the Democratic front-runner. But the hopes of American liberals for a candidate who spoke their language and addressed their concerns abruptly ended when, moments after giving a speech at a party celebrating his victory in the California primary, Kennedy was shot in the head by a Palestinian fanatic, Sirhan B. Sirhan.

The Democratic party went to the Chicago convention without a candidate. There party leaders battled among themselves—young and old; radical, liberal, and conservative. In the streets, outside the convention hall, police beat protesters in full view of television cameras. An official commission later termed it a "police riot." Inside the convention hall the fighting was largely verbal, but it was just as intense and bitter. In the end, the Democratic party chose Hubert Humphrey, Johnson's liberal vice president. Instead of change, the Democratic party chose a representative of the "old politics."

In a more tranquil convention in Miami the Republican party endorsed Richard M. Nixon, who promised when elected to end the Vietnam War honorably, move against forced busing of black children to white schools, and restore "law and order." Nixon claimed to speak for the great majority of Americans who obeyed the nation's laws, paid their taxes, regularly attended church, and loved their country.

In a similar vein, Alabama's governor George Wallace, running in 1968 on the American Independent ticket, spoke for millions of working-class white Americans, young and old alike, who opposed forced integration of schools and neighborhoods, radical college students, and what they believed was the country's drift toward the Left. Although Humphrey finished the campaign strong, Nixon's and Wallace's appeal to traditional values had an undeniable attraction. And on election day Nixon received 43.4 percent of the popular vote, Humphrey 42.7 percent, and Wallace 13.5 percent. Given the combined votes for Nixon and Wallace—57 percent—it was clear that the country was moving Right rather than Left.

The Tortuous Path Toward Peace

During the presidential campaign of 1968 Richard Nixon sported a new public image, which the press often referred to as the "new Nixon"—experienced, statesmanlike, mature, and well adjusted. But in many respects the new Nixon was not very different from the old. He still considered himself something of an outsider, a battler against an entrenched political establishment. Reared on the West Coast in humble circumstances, he had to overcome considerable obstacles in his rise to power. In the process certain character traits emerged. He was a hard worker—careful, studious with a tendency toward perfectionism. He was also a loner—shy, introverted, humorless, uncomfortable in social situations.

As a restless outsider, Nixon harbored a heightened suspicion of political insiders. On taking office he therefore surrounded himself with close advisers who held noncabinet titles. Cabinet appointees, and particularly his secretary of state, William Rogers, had almost no voice in key decisions. Personal aides H. R. Haldeman and John Ehrlichman advised Nixon on domestic political issues. Vice President Spiro Agnew assumed the role of the administration's hatchet man, attacking liberals with the ferocity of a professional wrestler verbally abusing an archrival. For foreign affairs, Nixon relied on his national security adviser, Henry Kissinger. Vain, articulate, and intellectual, Kissinger shared Nixon's desire to alter the very nature of the country's foreign relations and to make history. Both men were attracted by the diplomacy of secrecy and intrigue.

Vietnamization

During his campaign Nixon had promised "peace with honor" in Vietnam. One thing was certain: Nixon knew that he could not continue Johnson's policy. Whatever else he did, Nixon realized that to ensure some semblance of domestic tranquillity he would have to begin to remove American troops from Vietnam. In May 1969, the president announced that henceforth South Vietnamese soldiers would carry more of the combat burden. Certainly the United States would continue to aid materially any anticommunist struggle, but the aid would not include the wholesale use of American troops.

Nixon's Vietnamization policy was based on the questionable premise that the South Vietnamese government of Nguyen Van Thieu was stable and prepared to assume greater responsibility for fighting the war, Nixon announced that he planned gradually to de-escalate American military involvement. Increasingly U.S. aid would be limited to war matériel, military advice, and air support. He coupled Vietnamization with a more strenuous effort to move along the peace talks.

Actually, the idea of Vietnamization was hardly new. Advisers for Eisenhower, Kennedy, and Johnson had suggested one variation or another of the plan as the solution to the war. The major problem was that the South Vietnamese could not successfully fight the war on their own. But faced with angry criticism at home, Nixon had no choice but to implement the policy.

At the same time as he extended the olive branch, he expanded the nature of the conflict. Hoping to slow down the flow of North Vietnamese supplies and soldiers into South Vietnam, Nixon ordered American B-52 pilots to bomb the Ho Chi Minh Trail both in Vietnam and Cambodia. He kept this violation of Cambodian neutrality secret from the American public. It was a bold move, but the bombs only reduced the flow of men and supplies by approximately 10 percent.

When both increased bombings of North Vietnam and Kissinger's peace talks with North Vietnamese officials failed to end the war, Nixon decided to send American ground forces into Cambodia to destroy Communist supply bases. On April 30, 1970, he went on television to announce a joint American and South Vietnamese "incursion" into Cambodia's border regions to be limited to 60 days.

Militarily the "incursion" fell far short of success. Although American forces captured large stockpiles of weapons and supplies, the operation did not end the war. But the "incursion" had dangerously enlarged the battlefield.

More important, the invasion of Cambodia reignited the fires of the peace movement at home, as colleges and universities shut down in protest. At Kent State University in Ohio a volley of gunshots fired by National Guardsmen broke up a peaceful demonstration, killing 4 students and wounding 11 others. Less than two weeks later, policemen shot two more innocent students at Jackson State University in Mississippi. Instead of victory or even peace, Nixon's efforts had further divided America.

In the spring of 1970, Ohio National Guardsmen fired into a group of protesting students at Kent State University, killing four.

As an effective policy for ending the war, Vietnamization was a fail-ure. To be sure, the policy allowed Nixon to bring home American com-bat troops. When Nixon took office, 540,000 American troops were in Vietnam; four years later only 70,000 remained. But American reductions were not accompanied by a marked improvement in the South Viet-namese army. If anything, South Vietnam became more dependent on the United States during the years of Vietnamization.

A "Decent Interval"

By 1972 Nixon simply wanted to end the war with as little embarrass-ment as possible. Without an active U.S. military presence, Vietnam's demise was a foregone conclusion. Negotiations presented the only way out. Nixon and Kissinger hoped to arrange for a peace that would permit the United States and South Vietnam to save face and allow a "decent in-terval" of time to ensue between the American departure and the collapse of the government in Saigon. In pursuit of this goal, Nixon changed the character of American foreign policy.

The Soviet Union and the People's Republic of China aided and ad-vised North Vietnam. Yet the two large Communist nations were hardly allies themselves. In fact, the Sino-Soviet split demonstrated to American

U.S. troop levels in Vietnam

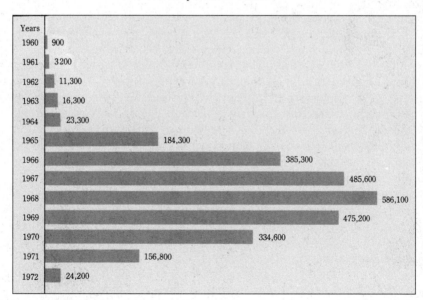

leaders the fallacy of the old Cold War theme of a monolithic Communist movement. Nixon and Kissinger were astute enough to use the Sino-Soviet rift to improve U.S. relations with both countries. Improved relations, they believed, would move the United States several steps closer to an "honorable" peace in Vietnam. Unfortunately, Nixon and Kissinger greatly overestimated the influence of the Soviet Union and China on North Vietnam.

From his first days in office Nixon had his eyes on the People's Republic of China, a nation that the United States had refused to recognize. Nixon's Cold War record—his opposition to any concession to the Communists—was well known. But he understood that his very record would protect him from public cries of being soft on communism.

In the summer of 1971 Kissinger made a very secret trip to China, which paved the way for Nixon's own very public trip to China in February 1972. American television cameras recorded Nixon's every move as he toured the Great Wall, the Imperial Palace, and the other sites of historic China. Nixon thoroughly enjoyed the event, going so far as quoting Chairman Mao at an official toast and learning to eat with chopsticks. Although full diplomatic relations would not be established until 1979, Nixon's trip to China was the single most important event in the history of the relations between the United States and the People's Republic of China. It bridged, as Chinese foreign minister Chou En-lai remarked, "the vastest ocean in the world, twenty-five years of no communication."

Concerned about the growing rapprochement between China and America, the Soviet Union sought to move closer to the United States. Once again, Nixon and Kissinger were pleased to oblige. In late May 1972, after many months of preparatory talks, Nixon traveled to Moscow to sign the Strategic Arms Limitation Treaty (SALT I) with Soviet leader Leonid Brezhnev. Although the treaty froze intercontinental ballistic missile (ICBM) deployment, it did not alter the buildup of the more dangerous multiple independent reentry vehicles (MIRVs). As so often was the case during the Cold War, SALT I provided more a warm breeze than the real heat wave necessary for a complete thaw of the Cold War. Both the United States and the Soviet Union hoped that SALT I would lead to other, more comprehensive, arms reductions treaties.

In other areas the United States and the Soviet Union made more substantial progress. American businesspeople forged inroads into the Soviet market place, and some farmers also reaped significant rewards when disastrous harvests at home led the Soviet Union to purchase several billion dollars worth of American wheat, corn, and soybeans.

Thus, although Nixon had not been able to end the Vietnam War, his 1972 triumphs in the Soviet Union and China gave him more influence with North Vietnam's major allies and dazzled voters at home. In 1972 Nixon easily defeated Democratic candidate George McGovern, capturing 61 percent of the popular vote and 521 of the 538 votes of the electoral college. Nixon's success with blue-collar workers, conservative Roman Catholics, and southerners signified the end of the New Deal coalition.

Once reelected, Nixon again focused on Vietnam. A month before the election, Kissinger had announced, "Peace is at hand," but no sooner was Nixon safely reelected than the peace talks broke down once again. Nixon's response was more and heavier bombing of North Vietnam. Starting on December 18, 1972 and continuing for the next ten days, the Christmas bombings—code-named Operation Linebacker II—attacked military targets in Hanoi and Haiphong and killed more than 1,500 civilians. When the bombings concluded, the warring nations resumed peace talks.

In a week North Vietnam and the United States hammered out a peace strikingly similar to the October proposal. On January 27, 1973, America ended its active participation in the Vietnam War. The peace treaty provided for the release of all prisoners of war and U.S.'s military withdrawal from Vietnam. It also established a monitored cease-fire between North and South Vietnam and set up procedures aimed at solving the differences between the two countries. Nixon quickly claimed that he had won an honorable peace. The war had claimed the lives of 58,000 American, 107,000 South Vietnamese, more than 500,000 North Vietnamese soldiers and, of course, the lives of many thousands of Vietnamese civilians.

But the war was not yet over. All the peace provided for was a "decent interval" between America's withdrawal and North Vietnam's complete victory. Almost as soon as the ink on the treaty was dry, North Vietnam and the Vietcong were once again engaged in a war with the government in South Vietnam. Finally, in the spring of 1975 South Vietnamese forces collapsed. On April 30 South Vietnam formally announced its unconditional surrender. Vietnam was finally unified. Free elections in 1956 might have accomplished the same results.

The Legacy of the War

At home, the controversy engendered by the war raged on long after the American withdrawal. Much of the controversy centered on the returning veterans. Reports of drug use and "fragging" shocked many Americans who had come no closer to the war than their television sets. And veterans—most of whom had served their country faithfully and to the best of their abilities—were angered by the cold, hostile reception they received when they returned to the United States.

During the 1970s and 1980s the returning Vietnam War veteran loomed large in American popular culture. He was first portrayed as a dangerous killer, a deranged time bomb that could explode at any time and in any place. He was Travis Bickle in *Taxi Driver* (1976), a veteran wound so tight that he seemed perpetually on the verge of snapping, or he was Colonel Kurtz in *Apocalypse Now* (1979), who adjusted to a mad war by going mad himself. Not until the late 1970s did popular culture begin to treat the Vietnam War veteran as a victim of the war or even as a hero, rather than a madman produced by the war.

The transformation of the veteran that took place in the late 1970s and 1980s indicated a fundamental shift in America's attitude toward the war. Millions of Americans began once again to see the war in terms of a noble crusade that could have been won. As John Rambo said in *Rambo: First Blood II,* "Do we get to win this time?" His former commander replied: "This time it's up to you." This message fit well with the political message of Ronald Reagan's America.

Conclusion

The Vietnam War confused and divided the nation. Tim O'Brien captured something of this confusion in his acclaimed novel *Going after Cacciato* (1978). After fighting in the war, his protagonist "didn't know who was right, or what was right; he didn't know if it was a war of self-determination or self-destruction, outright aggression or national liberation; he didn't know which speeches to believe, which books, which politicians; he didn't know if nations would topple like dominos or stand separate like trees; he didn't know who started the war, or why, or when, or with what motives; he didn't know if it mattered."

Vietnam destroyed Lyndon Johnson's presidency, and it helped to undermine Nixon's. Both men had injured their cause by using conscious deception in dealing with the American people. It was a war that left scars—on the people who fought in it and on the people who opposed and supported it; on Americans and on Vietnamese; and on America's position in the world.

The most constructive outcome of the war was the lessons it taught. Congress learned that it had to take a more active role in foreign affairs. The War Powers Act (1973), which requires the president to account for his actions within 48 hours of committing troops in a foreign conflict,

Chronology of Key Events

1954 Dien Bien Phu falls to Vietnamese nationalists; Geneva conference divides Vietnam

1961 John F. Kennedy inaugurated thirty-fifth president; Alliance for Progress pledges aid to Latin America; Cuban exiles stage abortive invasion of Cuba at Bay of Pigs; Berlin Wall erected

1962 Cuban missile crisis; American advisers in South Vietnam increased to approximately 16,000

1963 Limited test ban treaty; President Diem murdered; President Kennedy assassinated; Lyndon Johnson becomes thirty-sixth president

1964 Gulf of Tonkin Resolution gives president authority to retaliate against North Vietnamese aggression

1965 Operation Rolling Thunder; first American ground combat troops sent to South Vietnam

1968 Tet offensive: bombing of North Vietnam suspended; Johnson decides not to run for reelection; Robert F. Kennedy assassinated; Richard M. Nixon elected thirty-seventh president

1969 Nixon Doctrine announced

1970 Invasion of Cambodia; antiwar protests at Kent State University and Jackson State University; Congress repeals Gulf of Tonkin Resolution

1972 Nixon travels to China; Strategic Arms Limitation Treaty freezes intercontinental ballistic missile deployment

1973 United States ends active participation in the Vietnam War

1975 Fall of Saigon

demonstrated that the Gulf of Tonkin Resolution had taught Congress a painful lesson. Ho Chi Minh's nationalism taught policymakers that communism was not a monolithic movement and that not all small nations are dominos. Perhaps politicians, policymakers, and citizens alike even learned that national policy should be based on the realities of specific situations and not the kind of stereotypes generated by the Cold War.

Suggestions for Further Reading

For information on Kennedy and his presidency see David Burner, *John F. Kennedy and a New Generation* (1988); Henry Fairlie, *The Kennedy Promise* (1973); Bruce Miroff, *Pragmatic Illusions: The Presidential Politics of JFK* (1976); Herbert S. Parmet, *JFK: The Presidency of John F. Kennedy* (1983); Thomas C. Reeves, *A Question of Character* (1991).

The Kennedy administration's Cuban crises are examined in James G. Blight and David A. Welch, *On the Brink* (1989); Herbert S. Dinerstein, *The Making of a Missile Crisis* (1976); Louise FitzSimons, *The Kennedy Doctrine* (1972); Trumbull Higgins, *The Perfect Failure* (1987); Richard Walton, *Cold War and Counterrevolution* (1972); Peter Wyden, *Bay of Pigs* (1979).

Studies of American involvement in Vietnam include Larry Berman, *Planning a Tragedy* (1989); Larry E. Cable, *Unholy Grail: The War in Vietnam* (1991); Philip Caputo, *A Rumor of War* (1977); Frances FitzGerald, *Fire in the Lake* (1972); David Halberstam, *The Making of a Quagmire*, rev. ed. (1988); George C. Herring, *America's Longest War*, 2nd ed. (1986); Stanley Karnow, *Vietnam, A History* (1983); David Levy, *The Debate over Vietnam* (1991); James S. Olson and Randy Roberts, *Where the Domino Fell* (1991); Marilyn Young, *The Vietnam Wars: 1945–1990* (1991).

A thorough study of Lyndon Johnson's early career is Robert Dallek, *Lone Star Rising* (1991). For a more critical analysis, see Robert Caro, *Means of Ascent* (1990). For Johnson's presidential years, see Doris Kearns, *Lyndon Johnson and the American Dream* (1976). Studies of Richard Nixon and his administration include Stephen E. Ambrose, *Nixon, the Education of a Politician;* William Shawcross, *Sideshow: Kissinger, Nixon, and the Destruction of Cambodia*, rev. ed. (1987). See also Richard Nixon's autobiography, *RN*, 2 vols. (1978).

Chapter *30*

The Struggle for a Just Society

The Struggle for Racial Justice
Freedom Now
To the Heart of Dixie
"Bombingham"
Kennedy Finally Acts
Black Nationalism and Black Power
The Civil Rights Movement Moves North
The Great Society
White Backlash
The Struggle Continues

The Youth Revolt
The New Left
The Making of a Counterculture

Liberation Movements
Women's Liberation
Radical Feminism
Sex Discrimination
Impact of the Women's Liberation Movement
Mexican-American Liberation
The Native American Power Movement

He has been called the nation's nag. He has denounced soft drinks for containing excessive amounts of sugar; and warned Americans about the health hazards of red dyes used as food colorings and of nitrates as preservatives in hot dogs. He has even denounced high heels: "It is part of the whole tyranny of fashion, where women will inflict pain on themselves . . . for what, to please men." His name is Ralph Nader and since the mid-1960s he has been the nation's leading consumer advocate.

An extraordinarily frugal and committed crusader on behalf of the nation's consumers, Nader credits his parents with instilling the sense of justice and civic duty that has inspired his career. Born in 1934, Nader received his bachelor's degree from Princeton and earned a law degree at Harvard, where he found his initial cause: automobile safety. After learning that auto accidents were the fourth leading cause of death (behind

Ralph Nader is the best-known advocate of consumer protection laws in the United States. His group of attorneys, nicknamed "Nader's Raiders," have investigated such wide-ranging problems as automobile safety, the rights of the handicapped, tax reform, the environment, and public health. Here, Nader looks on during a demonstration showing the operation of an automobile air bag safety restraint.

heart disease, cancer, and strokes), he launched a study of auto injury cases. His research convinced him that the law placed too much emphasis on driver mistakes and not enough on the unsafe design of cars.

In 1963 Nader decided to devote his life to consumer protection. Two years later he published a best-seller, *Unsafe at Any Speed*, which charged that automakers stressed styling, comfort, speed, power, and a desire to cut costs at the expense of safety. General Motors Corporation was so unhappy with the book it hired a detective to investigate Nader's politics, religion, and sex life. GM was forced to apologize for this invasion of privacy and eventually paid Nader a $425,000 settlement. Nader used the money to establish more than two dozen public interest groups. The people who work for these groups are known as "Nader's Raiders."

During the 1960s and 1970s Nader was the driving force behind the passage of more than two dozen landmark consumer protection laws, including the National Traffic and Motor Vehicle Safety Act (which set up a federal agency to establish auto-safety standards and order recalls of cars that failed to meet them), the Occupational Safety and Health Act (which established another agency to set standards for on-the-job safety), the Consumer Products Safety Act, and the Freedom of Information Act (which allows citizens to request and see government records). His efforts have been instrumental in obtaining job protection for employees who expose corrupt or abusive business practices, federal financing of presidential elections, and the creation of the Environmental Protection Agency. Few Americans have ever compiled such a long and impressive list of legislative accomplishment.

But Nader's ultimate goal was not simply to protect consumers from shoddy or dangerous products. It was to reinvigorate the nation's ideal of democracy by encouraging active grass-roots citizen participation in politics. The best answer to society's problems, he believed, was for ordinary citizens to campaign for safer consumer products, better schools, a cleaner environment, and safer workplaces.

During the late 1970s and 1980s, Nader's influence seemed to wane. In 1978, Congress defeated his proposal for a Consumer Protection Agency. Critics dismissed him as a "scold." In a decade of deregulation, his call for greater regulations seemed out of step with the times.

As the 1980s ended and the 1990s began, however, it was clear that Nader remained a major force in American politics. He played a central role in passing a California initiative that rolled back the cost of auto insurance. He led a bitter fight against a proposed 51 percent congressional pay raise. And his long campaign for auto safety achieved an important breakthrough when the major automobile manufacturers agreed to install air bags in most of their cars.

Ralph Nader illustrates in vivid terms the difference that one person's life can make. His life also epitomizes the idealism and activism of the 1960s—a decade when hundreds of thousands of Americans gave new life to the nation's democratic ideals. African Americans used sit-ins, freedom rides, and protest marches to fight segregation, poverty, and unemployment. Feminists demanded equal employment opportunities and an end to sexual discrimination. Mexican Americans protested discrimination in voting, education, and employment. Native Americans demanded that the government recognize their land claims and the right of tribes to govern themselves.

Although these and other grass-roots activists seemed to fade from public view during the 1980s, they—like Ralph Nader—never abandoned their causes and today remain a significant force in American life. Indeed, the success of their efforts has led to a conservative grass-roots reaction, one in which equally committed Americans have denounced busing, affirmative action, quotas, and abortion.

The Struggle for Racial Justice

For African Americans in 1960 the statistics were grim. Their average life span in 1960 was seven years less than that of white Americans. Their children had only half the chance of completing high school, only a third the chance of completing college, and a third the chance of entering a profession when they grew up. On average, black Americans earned half as much as white Americans and were twice as likely to be unemployed.

Despite a string of court victories during the late 1950s, many blacks were still second-class citizens, due to lax enforcement of civil rights laws. Six years after the landmark *Brown* v. *Board of Education* decision, only one percent of black schoolchildren in the 11 states of the old Confederacy attended public school with white classmates. Less than a quarter of the South's voting-age black population could vote, and in certain southern counties blacks could not serve on grand juries and trial juries, or frequent all-white beaches, restaurants, and hotels.

In the North, too, African Americans suffered humiliation, insult, embarrassment, and discrimination. Many neighborhoods, businesses, and unions almost totally excluded blacks. Unemployment soared as laborsaving technology eliminated many semiskilled and unskilled jobs that historically provided many blacks with work. Black families experienced severe strain; the proportion of black families headed by women jumped from 8 percent in 1950 to 21 percent in 1960.

During the 1960s, however, a growing hunger for full equality arose among African Americans. The Rev. Dr. Martin Luther King, Jr., gave voice to the new mood when he said: "We can't wait any longer. Now is the time."

Freedom Now

"Now is the time." These words became the credo and rallying cry for a generation. On Monday, February 1, 1960, four black freshmen at North Carolina Agricultural and Technical College walked into the F.W. Woolworth store in Greensboro, North Carolina, and sat down at the lunch counter. Each asked for a cup of coffee. A waitress told them that she would only serve them if they stood.

Instead of walking away, the four college freshmen stayed in their seats until the lunch counter closed, giving birth to the "sit-in." The next morning, the four college students reappeared at Woolworth's, accompanied by 25 fellow students. By the end of the week protesters filled Woolworth's and other lunch counters in town. Although the student protesters subscribed to King's doctrine of nonviolence, their opponents did not—assaulting the students both verbally and physically. When the police were called, they often arrested black protesters, not the whites who tormented them.

By the end of February lunch counter sit-ins had spread through 30 cities in seven southern states. This form of protest was also used against segregated libraries and other facilities. In April, 142 student sit-in leaders from 11 states met in Raleigh, North Carolina, and voted to set up a new group to coordinate the sit-ins, the Student Nonviolent Coordinating Committee (SNCC). The Rev. Dr. Martin Luther King, Jr., told the students that their willingness to go to jail would "be the thing to awaken the dozing conscience of many of our white brothers."

In the summer of 1960 sit-ins gave way to "wade-ins" at segregated public beaches. In Atlanta, Charlotte, Greensboro, and Nashville, black students lined up at white-only box offices of segregated movie theaters. By the end of 1960, 70,000 people had taken part in sit-ins in over 100 cities in 20 states. Police arrested and jailed more than 3,600 protesters. Nevertheless, the new tactic worked. By August 1 lunch counters in 15 states had been integrated. By the end of the year protesters had succeeded in integrating eating establishments in 108 cities.

The Greensboro sit-in initiated a new, activist phase in black America's struggle for equal rights. Fed up with the slow, legalistic approach that characterized the civil rights movement in the past, southern black college students began to attack the Jim Crow laws directly. In the upper South, federal court orders and student sit-ins successfully desegregated lunch counters, theaters, hotels, public parks, churches, libraries, and beaches. But in three states—Alabama, Mississippi, and South Carolina—segregation remained intact. In those states young civil rights activists launched new assaults against segregation.

To the Heart of Dixie

In early May 1961, 13 men and women, black and white, set out from Washington, D.C., on two buses. They called themselves "freedom riders," and they wanted to demonstrate that despite a federal ban on segregated travel on interstate buses, segregation prevailed throughout much of the South. The freedom riders' trip was sponsored by the Congress of Racial Equality (CORE), a civil rights group dedicated to breaking down racial barriers through nonviolent protest.

In Virginia and North Carolina the freedom riders met little trouble. But in Winnsboro, South Carolina, police arrested two black freedom riders, and outside Anniston, Alabama, a white hurled a bomb through one of the bus's windows, setting the vehicle on fire. Waiting white thugs beat the freedom riders as they tried to escape the smoke and flames. Eight other whites boarded the second bus and assaulted the freedom riders before police restrained the attackers.

In Birmingham and Montgomery, Alabama, another mob of whites attacked the freedom riders with clubs, blackjacks, and pipes. Local law enforcement agencies were slow in aiding the protesters. Explained Montgomery's police commissioner: "We have no intention of standing police guard for a bunch of troublemakers coming into our city."

President Kennedy was appalled by the violence. He hastily deputized 400 federal marshals and Treasury agents and flew them to Alabama to protect the freedom riders' rights. The president publicly called for a "cooling-off period," but conflict continued. When the freedom riders arrived in Jackson, Mississippi, 27 were arrested for entering a "white-only" washroom and were sentenced to 60 days on the state prison farm.

The threat of racial violence in the South led the Kennedy administration to pressure the Interstate Commerce Commission to desegregate air, bus, and train terminals. In more than 300 southern terminals signs saying "white" and "colored" were taken down from waiting room entrances and lavatory doors.

Civil rights activists next aimed to open state universities to black students. Many southern states opened their universities to black students without incident. Other states were stiff-backed in their opposition to integration. A major breakthrough occurred in September 1962, when a federal court ordered the state of Mississippi to admit James Meredith to the University of Mississippi in Oxford. Governor Ross Barnett vowed that he would go to jail rather than permit Meredith to register for classes. Barnett flew into Oxford, named himself special registrar of the university, and ordered the arrest of federal officials who tried to enforce the court order.

James Meredith refused to back down. He arrived at the Ole Miss campus in the company of police officers, federal marshals, and lawyers. Angry white students waited, chanting, "Two, four, six, eight—we don't want to integrate."

Four times James Meredith tried unsuccessfully to register at Ole Miss. He finally succeeded on the fifth attempt, escorted by several hundred federal marshals. The ensuing riot left two people dead and 375 injured, including 166 marshals. Ultimately, President Kennedy sent 16,000 troops to put down the violence.

"Bombingham"

By the end of 1961, protests against segregation, job discrimination, and police brutality had erupted from Georgia to Mississippi and Tennessee to Alabama. Staunch segregationists responded by vowing to defend the Jim Crow laws. The symbol of unyielding resistance to integration was Alabama governor George C. Wallace. Elected on an extreme segregationist platform, Wallace declared at his inauguration in January 1963: "I draw the line in the dust and toss the gauntlet before the feet of tyranny, and I say segregation now, segregation tomorrow, segregation forever."

It was in Birmingham, Alabama, that civil rights activists faced the most determined resistance. A sprawling steel town of 340,000 people, Birmingham had a long history of racial acrimony. In open defiance of Supreme Court rulings Birmingham had closed its public playgrounds, swimming pools, and golf courses rather than integrate them. Calling Birmingham "the most thoroughly segregated city in the United States," Martin Luther King announced in early 1963 that he would lead demonstrations in the city until demands for fair hiring practices, desegregation, and amnesty for previously arrested civil rights demonstrators were met.

Day after day, well-dressed men, women, and children marched against segregation—only to be jailed for demonstrating without a permit. On April 12 King himself was arrested—and while in jail wrote his now-famous "Letter from Birmingham City Jail," a scathing response to a group of white clergymen who had publicly criticized King for staging the demonstrations.

For two weeks all was quiet, but in early May demonstrations resumed with renewed vigor. On May 2 and again on May 3 more than a thousand of Birmingham's black youths marched for equal rights. In response, the local police chief, Eugene "Bull" Connor, unleashed police dogs and sprayed the marchers with high-pressure fire hoses. Watching the willful brutality on television, millions of Americans, white and black, were shocked by the face of segregation.

Tension mounted as police arrested 2,543 blacks and whites between May 2 and May 7, 1963. Under intense pressure, the Birmingham Chamber of Commerce reached an agreement on May 9 with black leaders to desegregate public facilities, hire blacks as clerks and salespersons, and release demonstrators without bail in return for an end to the protests.

King's goal was nonviolent social change—but the short-term result of protest was violence and confrontation. On May 11 white extremists firebombed an integrated motel. That same night a bomb destroyed the

Police used dogs, high-pressure water hoses, clubs, and electric cattle prods to break up the nonviolent civil rights demonstration in Birmingham, Alabama, in May 1963. Scenes such as this one, broadcast on television to millions of viewers, aroused public indignation and sympathy for the civil rights movement.

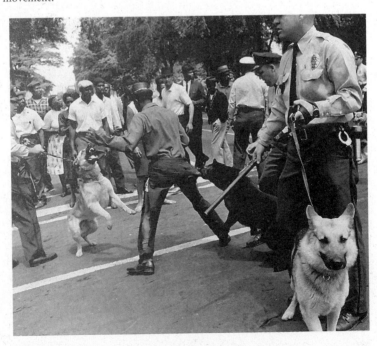

home of King's brother. Shooting incidents and racial confrontations quickly spread across the South. In June a gunman killed Medgar Evers, the NAACP field representative in Mississippi. In September an explosion destroyed Birmingham's Sixteenth Street Baptist Church, killing four black girls and injuring 14 others. All told, ten people died during racial protests in 1963, 35 black homes and churches were firebombed, and 20,000 people were arrested during civil rights protests.

Kennedy Finally Acts

The eruption of violence forced the Kennedy administration to introduce legislation to guarantee black civil rights. Twice before, in 1957 and 1960, the federal government had adopted weak civil rights acts designed to provide federal protection for African American voting rights. Now Kennedy responded to the racial violence by proposing a new stronger civil rights bill that required the desegregation of public facilities, outlawed discrimination in employment and voting, and allowed the attorney general to initiate school desegregation suits.

Kennedy's record on civil rights inspired little confidence. He had voted against the 1957 Civil Rights Act, and in the 1960 campaign many African American leaders backed Richard Nixon, even though Kennedy worked hard to court the black vote by promising new civil rights legislation and declaring that as president he would end housing discrimination. A few weeks before the 1960 election, Kennedy broadened his black support by helping to secure the release of Martin Luther King from an Atlanta jail, where he had been imprisoned for leading an antisegregation demonstration.

Once in office, however, Kennedy moved slowly on civil rights issues, both because he feared alienating white southern Democrats and because he had no deep commitment to the cause. Although Kennedy's administration filed 28 suits to protect black voting rights (compared to ten suits filed during the Eisenhower years), it was not until November 1963 that Kennedy took steps to fulfill his campaign promise to end housing discrimination.

The violence that erupted in Birmingham and elsewhere in 1961 and 1962 alarmed many veteran civil rights leaders. Eager to rededicate the movement to the principle of nonviolence, African American leaders decided that a massive march for civil rights and jobs might provide the necessary pressure to prompt Kennedy and Congress to act.

On August 28, 1963, over 200,000 people gathered around the Washington Monument and marched to the Lincoln Memorial. Ten speakers addressed the crowd, but the event's highlight was an address by Martin Luther King. After he finished his prepared text King launched into his legendary closing words. "I have a dream," he declared, "that one day on the red hills of Georgia the sons of former slaves and the sons of former slaveowners will be able to sit down together at the table of brotherhood. . . . I have a dream that one day even the state of Mississippi, a state sweltering with people's injustices, sweltering with the heat of oppression, will be transformed into an oasis of freedom and justice." As the audience roared its approval, King continued: "I have a dream that one day this nation will rise up and live out the true meaning of its creed: 'We hold these truths to be self-evident; that all men are created equal.'"

For seven months, debate raged in the halls of Congress. In a futile effort to delay the Civil Rights Bill's passage, opponents proposed over 500 amendments and staged a protracted filibuster in the Senate. On July 2, 1964—a little over a year after President Kennedy had sent it to Congress—the Civil Rights Act was enacted into law, skillfully pushed through Congress by President Lyndon Johnson. The act prohibited discrimination in voting, employment, and public facilities such as hotels and restaurants, and it established the Equal Employment Opportunity Commission to prevent discrimination in employment on the basis of race, religion, or gender.

Although most white southerners accepted the new federal law without resistance, many violent incidents occurred as angry whites vented their rage. Even so, the Civil Rights Act was a success. In the first weeks under the 1964 civil rights law segregated restaurants and hotels across the South opened their doors to black patrons. Over the next ten years the Justice Department would bring hundreds of suits against school districts, hotels, restaurants, taverns, gas stations, and truck stops charged with racial discrimination.

The 1964 Civil Rights Act prohibited discrimination in employment and public accommodations. But many African Americans were denied an equally fundamental constitutional right, the right to vote. The most effective barriers to black voting were state laws requiring prospective voters to read and interpret sections of the state constitution. In Alabama, voters had to provide written answers to a 20-page test on the Constitution and state and local government.

In an effort to bring the issue of voting rights to national attention, Martin Luther King in early 1965 launched a voter registration drive in Selma, Alabama. Even though blacks slightly outnumbered whites in the city of 25,000, Selma's voting rolls were 99 percent white and one percent black. For seven weeks King led hundreds of black residents to the county courthouse to register to vote. Nearly 2,000 black demonstrators, including King, were jailed by County Sheriff James Clark for contempt of court and parading without a permit. After a federal court ordered Clark not to interfere with orderly registration, the sheriff forced black applicants to stand in line for up to five hours before being permitted to take a "literacy" test. Not a single black voter was added to the registration rolls.

When a young black man was killed during a riot in nearby Marion, King responded by calling for a march from Selma to the state capital of Montgomery, 50 miles away. On March 7, 1965, black voting-rights demonstrators began their march, but were attacked by 200 mounted state police as they crossed a bridge spanning the Alabama River. The march resumed on March 21 with federal protection. The marchers chanted: "Segregation's got to fall . . . you never can jail us all." On March 25 a crowd of 25,000 gathered at the state capitol to celebrate the march's completion.

Two measures adopted in 1965 helped safeguard the voting rights of black Americans. On January 23 the states completed ratification of the Twenty-fourth Amendment to the Constitution barring a poll tax in federal elections. At the time, five southern states still had a poll tax. On August 6 President Johnson signed the Voting Rights Act, which prohibited literacy tests and sent federal examiners to seven southern states to register black voters. Within a year, 450,000 southern blacks registered to vote.

Black Nationalism and Black Power

At the same time that such civil rights leaders as Dr. Martin Luther King fought for racial integration, other black leaders emphasized separatism and identification with Africa. One of the most important expressions of the separatist impulse during the 1960s was the rise of the Black Muslims, which attracted 100,000 members. Founded in 1931, the Nation of Islam drew its appeal from among the growing numbers of urban blacks living in poverty.

The Black Muslims, led by Elijah Muhammad, elevated racial separatism into a religious doctrine and declared that whites were doomed to destruction unless they acceded to the Muslim separatist demands. The Black Muslims did more than vent anger and frustration. The organization was also a vehicle of black uplift and self-help. The Black Muslims called upon black Americans to "wake up, clean up, and stand up" in order to achieve true freedom and independence. To root out any behavior that conformed to racist stereotypes, the Muslims forbade eating pork and cornbread, drinking alcohol, and smoking cigarettes. Muslims also emphasized the creation of black businesses.

The most controversial exponent of black nationalism was Malcolm X. The son of a Baptist minister who had been an organizer for Marcus Garvey's United Negro Improvement Association, he was born Malcolm

Little in Omaha, Nebraska, and grew up in Lansing, Michigan. A reformed drug addict and criminal, Malcolm X learned about the Black Muslims in prison. After his release in 1952, he adopted the name Malcolm X to replace "the white slave-master name which had been imposed upon my paternal forebears by some blue-eyed devil."

He quickly became one of the Black Muslims' most eloquent speakers. His main message was that discrimination led many black Americans to despise themselves. Self-hatred, he argued, caused black Americans to lose their identity, straighten their hair, and become involved in crime, drug addiction, and alcoholism. Condemned by some whites as a demagogue for such statements as "If ballots won't work, bullets will," Malcolm X gained widespread public notoriety by attacking Martin Luther King as a "chump" and an Uncle Tom, by advocating self-defense against white violence, and by emphasizing black political power.

In March 1964 Malcolm X withdrew from Elijah Muhammad's organization and set up his own Organization of Afro-Americans. Less than a year later, his life ended in bloodshed. On February 21, 1965, in front of

Malcolm X, frustrated with moderate civil rights advocates, spoke sharply against racism and called for African-American self-defense against white violence. In 1964, he founded the Organization of Afro-American Unity.

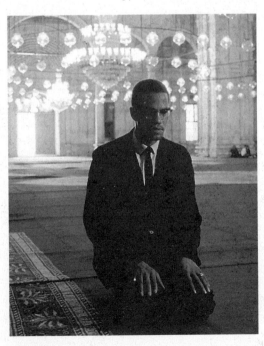

400 followers, he was shot and killed, apparently by followers of Black Muslim leader Elijah Muhammad.

Inspired by Malcolm X's example, young black activists embraced the new spirit of radicalism and increasingly challenged the traditional leadership of the civil rights movement and its philosophy of nonviolence. The single greatest contributor to the growth of militancy was the continued violence perpetrated by white racists. One of the most publicized incidents took place in the summer of 1964, when three civil rights workers—two whites, Andrew Goodman and Michael Schwerner, and one black, James Chaney—disappeared near Philadelphia, Mississippi. Six weeks after they were reported missing, the bodies of the men were found buried under a dam; all three had been beaten, then shot. David Dennis, a black civil rights leader, spoke at James Chaney's funeral. He angrily declared: "I'm sick and tired of going to the funerals of black men who have been murdered by white men. . . . I've got vengeance in my heart."

In 1966 two key civil rights organizations—SNCC and CORE (the Congress of Racial Equality)–embraced black nationalism. In May, Stokely Carmichael was elected chairman of SNCC and proceeded to transform the group from an interracial organization committed to nonviolence and integration into an all-black organization committed to "black power." "Integration is irrelevant," declared Carmichael. "Political and economic power is what the black people have to have." Although Carmichael initially denied that "black power" implied racial separatism, he eventually called on blacks to form their own separate political organizations. In July 1966 CORE also endorsed black power and repudiated nonviolence.

Of all the groups advocating racial separatism and black power, the one that received the widest publicity was the Black Panther party. Formed in October 1966 in Oakland, California, the Black Panthers were an armed revolutionary socialist organization advocating self-determination for black ghettoes. The Black Panthers gained public notoriety by entering the gallery of the California State Assembly brandishing guns and by following police to prevent brutality toward blacks.

Separatism and black nationalism attracted no more than a small minority of African Americans, and public opinion polls indicated that the overwhelming majority of blacks considered Martin Luther King their favored spokesperson. The older civil rights organizations such as the NAACP rejected black power, viewing it as an abandonment of the goals of nonviolence and integration.

Yet despite their relatively small following, black power advocates exerted a powerful and positive influence upon the civil rights movement. In addition to giving birth to a host of community self-help organizations, supporters of black power spurred the formation of black studies programs in universities and encouraged black Americans to take pride in their racial background. A growing number of African Americans began to wear "Afro" hairstyles and take African or Islamic surnames. Singer James Brown captured the new spirit: "Say it loud—I'm black and I'm proud."

In an effort to maintain support among more militant blacks, civil rights leaders began to address the problems of the poor blacks who lived in the cities. By the mid-1960s Martin Luther King had begun to move toward the political Left. King denounced the Vietnam War as "an enemy of the poor," and urged a radical redistribution of wealth and political power in the United States to provide medical care, jobs, and education for all of the nation's people.

The Civil Rights Movement Moves North

On August 11, 1965, five days after President Lyndon Johnson signed the Voting Rights Act, the arrest of a 21-year-old for drunk driving ignited a

A major achievement of the black power movement was to increase educational opportunities for minorities in universities across the country.

riot in Watts, a predominantly black section of Los Angeles. The violence lasted five days and resulted in 34 deaths, 3,900 arrests, and the destruction of over 744 buildings in a 20-square-mile area. Rioters smashed windows, hurled bricks and bottles from rooftops, and looters stripped store shelves.

Over the next four summers the nation's inner cities experienced a wave of violence and rioting. The last major wave occurred following the assassination of Martin Luther King in Memphis, Tennessee, on April 4, 1968. Violence erupted in 168 cities, leaving 46 dead, 3,500 injured, and $40 million worth of damage. In Washington, D.C., fires burned within three blocks of the White House.

In 1968 President Johnson appointed a commission to examine the causes of the race riots of the preceding three summers. The commission attributed racial violence to "white racism" and its heritage of discrimination and exclusion. Joblessness, poverty, a lack of political power, decaying and dilapidated housing, police brutality, and poor schools bred a sense of frustration and rage that had exploded into violence. The commission warned that unless major steps were taken, the United States would inevitably become "two societies, one black, one white—separate and unequal."

Until 1964 most white northerners regarded race as a peculiarly southern problem that could be solved by extending political and civil rights to southern blacks. Beginning in early 1964, however, thousands of blacks throughout the North staged sit-ins, boycotts, and demonstrations to protest school segregation as well as job, housing, and employment discrimination. Americans learned that discrimination and racial prejudice were nationwide problems.

In the North African Americans suffered from de facto discrimination in housing, schooling, and employment—discrimination that lacked the overt sanction of law. The most obvious example of de facto segregation related to schooling. An overwhelming majority of northern black children attended predominantly black inner-city schools while most white children attended schools with an overwhelming majority of whites. In 1968—fourteen years after the *Brown* v. *Board of Education* decision—federal courts began to order busing as a way to deal with de facto segregation brought about by housing patterns. In April 1971 in the case of *Swann* v. *Charlotte-Mecklenburg Board of Education* the Supreme Court upheld "bus transportation as a tool of school desegregation."

The Great Society

Lyndon B. Johnson had a vision for America. Believing that problems of housing, income, employment, and health were ultimately a federal responsibility, Johnson used the weight of the presidency and his formidable political skills to enact the most impressive array of reform legislation since the days of Franklin Roosevelt, a figure Johnson greatly admired. He envisioned a society without poverty or discrimination, in which all Americans enjoyed equal educational and job opportunities. He called this vision the "Great Society."

A major feature of Johnson's Great society program was the "War on Poverty." The federal government raised the minimum wage and enacted programs to train poorer Americans for new and better jobs, including the 1964 Manpower Development and Training Act and the Economic Opportunity Act, which established such programs as the Job Corps and the Neighborhood Youth Corps. To assure adequate housing, Congress in 1966 adopted the Model Cities Act to attack urban blight, set up a cabinet-level Department of Housing and Urban Development, and began a program of rent supplements.

To promote education, Congress passed the Higher Education Act in 1965 providing student loans and scholarships, the Elementary and Secondary Schools Act of 1965 to pay for textbooks, and the Educational Opportunity Act of 1968 to help the poor finance college educations. To address the nation's health needs, the Child Health Improvement and Protection Act of 1968 provided for prenatal and postnatal care, the Medicaid Act of 1968 paid for the medical expenses of the poor, and Medicare, established in 1965, extended medical insurance to older Americans under the Social Security system.

Johnson also prodded Congress to pass a broad spectrum of civil rights laws, ranging from the Civil Rights Act of 1964 and the Voting Rights Act of 1965 to the 1968 Fair Housing Act barring discrimination in the sale or rental of housing. In 1965 LBJ issued an executive order requiring government contracts to ensure that job applicants and employees were not discriminated against. It required all contractors to prepare an "affirmative action plan" to achieve these goals.

Johnson broke many other color barriers. In 1966 he named the first black cabinet member and appointed the first black woman to the federal bench. In 1967 he appointed Thurgood Marshall to become the first black American to serve on the Supreme Court. The first southerner to reside in the White House in half a century, Johnson showed a stronger commitment to improving the position of black Americans than any previous president.

When President Johnson announced his Great Society program in 1964, he promised substantial reductions in the number of Americans living in poverty. When he left office, he could legitimately argue that he had delivered on his promise. In 1960, 40 million Americans, 20 percent of the population, were classified as poor. By 1969, their number had fallen to 24 million, 12 percent of the population. Johnson also pledged to qualify the poor for new and better jobs, to extend health insurance to the poor and elderly to cover hospital and doctor costs, and to provide better housing for low-income families. Here too Johnson could say he had delivered. Infant mortality among the poor, for example, fell by one-third in the decade after 1965 as a result of expanded federal medical and nutritional programs.

Although critics argued that Johnson took a shotgun approach to reform and pushed poorly thought-out bills through Congress, supporters responded that at least Johnson tried to move toward a more compassionate society. During the 1960s median black family income rose by 53 percent, while black employment in professional, technical, and clerical occupations doubled. The proportion of blacks below the poverty line fell from 55 percent in 1960 to 27 percent in 1968. The black unemployment rate fell 34 percent. The country had taken major strides toward extending equality of opportunity to African Americans. In addition, the number of whites below the poverty line dropped dramatically, and such poverty-plagued regions as Appalachia made significant economic strides.

White Backlash

Ghetto rioting, the rise of black militancy, and resentment over Great Society social legislation combined to produce a backlash among many whites. Commitment to bringing black Americans into full equality declined. In the wake of the riots, many whites fled the nation's cities. The Census Bureau estimated that 900,000 whites moved each year from central cities to the suburbs between 1965 and 1970.

The 1968 Republican candidate Richard Nixon promised to eliminate "wasteful" federal antipoverty programs and to name conservatives to the Supreme Court. As presidnet, Nixon moved quickly to keep his commitments. In an effort to curb Great Society social programs, Nixon did away with the Model Cities program and the Office of Economic Opportunity. The administration urged Congress not to extend the Voting Rights Act of 1965 and to end a fair housing enforcement program.

Nixon also made a series of Supreme Court appointments that brought to an end the liberal activist era of the court. During the 1960s the Supreme Court greatly increased the ability of criminal defendants to defend themselves. In *Mapp* v. *Ohio* (1961) the high court ruled that evidence secured by the police through unreasonable searches must be excluded from trials. In *Gideon* v. *Wainwright* (1963) it declared that indigent defendants have a right to a court-appointed attorney. In *Escobedo* v. *Illinois* (1964) it ruled that suspects being interrogated by police have a right to legal counsel.

As president, Nixon promised to alter the balance between the rights of criminal defendants and society's rights. He selected Warren Burger, a moderate conservative, to replace Earl Warren as chief justice of the Supreme Court and then nominated two conservative white southerners for a second court vacancy, only to have both nominees rejected (one for financial improprieties, the other for alleged insensitivities to civil rights). He eventually named four justices to the high court: Burger, Harry Blackmun, Lewis Powell, and William Rehnquist.

Under Chief Justice Burger and his successor William Rehnquist, the Supreme Court defined the remedies that can be used to clarify past discrimination. In 1974 the court limited the use of school busing for purposes of racial desegregation. In 1978 in the landmark *Bakke* case, the court held that educational institutions could take race into account when screening applicants, but could not use rigid racial quotas. The following year, however, the court ruled that employers could legally establish voluntary programs, including the use of quotas, to aid minorities and women in employment.

The Struggle Continues

Over the past quarter century African Americans have made impressive social and economic gains, yet full equality remains an elusive dream. State-sanctioned segregation was eliminated, and many barriers to equal opportunity were shattered. In political representation, educational attainment, and representation in white-collar and professional occupations, black Americans have made striking gains. Between 1960 and 1988 the number of black political officeholders rose from just 300 to nearly 6,600. Black mayors have governed many of the nation's largest cities, including Chicago, Detroit, Los Angeles, Philadelphia, and Washington, D.C.

Nevertheless, millions of African Americans still do not share fully in the promise of American life, and separation of the races in housing and schooling remains widespread. According to census figures, blacks still suffer twice the unemployment rate of whites and earn only about half as much. The poverty rate among black families is three times that of whites, the same ratio as in the 1950s. Forty percent of black children are raised in fatherless homes and almost half of all black children are born into families earning less than the poverty level.

Although the United States has eliminated many obstacles to black progress, reformers maintain that much remains to be done before the country attains the equality Martin Luther King and Lyndon Johnson envisioned.

The Youth Revolt

During the 1960s one age group of Americans loomed larger than any other: youth. As a result of the depressed birthrates during the 1930s and the postwar baby boom, there was a sudden explosion in the number of teenagers and young adults. Unlike their parents, whose values had been shaped by the depression and World War II, young people of the 1960s grew up during a period of prosperity. This sense of economic security allowed them to seek personal fulfillment and to dismiss the older generation's success-oriented lives. Their skepticism of corporate and bureaucratic authority, their strong emotional identification with the underprivileged, and their intense desire for stimulation and instant gratification shaped the nation's politics, dress, music, and film.

At no earlier time in American history had the gulf between the generations seemed so wide. Blue jeans, long hair, psychedelic drugs, casual sex, hippie communes, campus demonstrations, and rock and roll all became symbols of the distance separating youth from the world of conventional adulthood.

The New Left

Late in the spring of 1962 five dozen college students gathered at a lakeside camp near Port Huron, Michigan, to discuss politics. For four days and nights the members of an obscure student group known as Students for a Democratic Society (SDS) talked passionately about such topics as civil rights, foreign policy, and the quality of American life. The gathering ended with the participants agreeing on a political platform. This manifesto, one of the pivotal political documents of the 1960s, became known as the Port Huron Statement. Its chief author was Tom Hayden, who had spent much of 1961 in the South, working with SNCC in the civil rights movement. Hayden would become a key figure in the student movement.

The goal set forward in the Port Huron Statement was the creation of a radically democratic political movement in the United States that rejected hierarchy and bureaucracy. In its most important paragraphs the document called for "participatory democracy"—direct individual involvement in the decisions that affected their lives. This notion would become the battle cry of the student movement of the 1960s—a movement that came to be known as the New Left.

During the 1960s thousands of young college students became politically active. The first issue to spark student radicalism was the modern university, which many students criticized for being too bureaucratic and impersonal. Students questioned university requirements, restrictions on student political activities, and dormitory rules. Restrictions on students handing out political pamphlets on university property led to the first campus demonstrations that broke out at the University of California at Berkeley, led by Mario Savio and the Berkeley Free Speech Movement. The protests soon spread to other campuses.

Involvement in the civil rights movement in the South initiated many students into radical politics. In the early 1960s many white students from northern universities began to participate in voter registration drives, freedom schools, sit-ins, and freedom rides to help desegregate the South.

Student radicalism also drew inspiration from a literature of social criticism that flourished in the 1950s. During that decade, many of the most popular films, novels, and writings aimed at young people criticized conventional middle-class life. Popular films, like *Rebel Without a Cause* (1955), and popular novels, like J. D. Salinger's *Catcher in the Rye* (1951), celebrated sensitive, directionless, alienated youths unable to conform to the conventional adult values of suburban and corporate America. Sophisticated works of social criticism, by such maverick sociologists, psychologists, and economists as Herbert Marcuse, Norman O. Brown, Paul Goodman, Michael Harrington, and C. Wright Mills, documented the growing concentration of power in the hands of social elites, the persistence of poverty in a land of plenty, and the stresses and injustices in America's social order.

Above all, student radicalism owed its support to student opposition to the Vietnam War. SDS held its first antiwar march in 1965, which attracted at least 15,000 protestors to Washington, and commanded wide press attention. Over the next three years opposition to the war brought thousands of new members to SDS. In addition to its antiwar activities, members of SDS also tried to organize a democratic "interracial movement of the poor" in northern city neighborhoods.

Many members of SDS quickly grew frustrated by the slow pace of social change and began to embrace violence as a tool to transform society. After 1968, SDS rapidly tore itself apart as an effective political force, and its final convention in 1969 degenerated into a shouting match between radicals and moderates. That same year the Weathermen, a surviving faction of SDS, attempted to launch a guerrilla war in the streets of Chicago—an incident known as the "Days of Rage." Finally, in 1970 three members of the Weathermen blew themselves up in a Greenwich Village brownstone trying to make a bomb out of a stick of dynamite and an alarm clock.

Throughout the 1960s the SDS and other radical student organizations claimed to speak for the nation's youth, and in thousands of editorials and magazine articles journalists accepted this claim. In reality, SDS represented only a small minority of college students, who themselves composed a minority of the country's youth. Far more young Americans voted for George Wallace in 1968 than joined SDS, and most college students during the decade spent more time studying and enjoying the college experience than protesting. Nevertheless, radical students did help to draw the nation's attention to the problem of racism in American society and the moral issues involved in the Vietnam War. In that sense, their impact far exceeded their numbers.

The Making of a Counterculture

The New Left had a series of heroes, ranging from Marx, Lenin, and Ho, to Mao, Fidel, and other revolutionaries. It also had its own uniforms, rituals, and music. Faded blue work shirts and jeans, wire-rimmed glasses, and work shoes were *de rigueur;* so was the political protest folk music of Greenwich Village—of Phil Ochs, Bob Dylan, and Joan Baez.

But the New Left was only one part of youth protest during the 1960s. While the New Left labored to change the world and remake American society, other youths attempted to alter themselves and reorder consciousness. Variously labeled the counterculture, hippies, or flower children, they had their own heroes, music, dress, and approach to life.

In theory, supporters of the counterculture rejected individualism, competition, and capitalism, and challenged prevailing middle-class standards of behavior. Adopting rather unsystematic ideas from oriental religions, they sought to become one with the universe. Rejection of monogamy and the traditional nuclear family gave way to the tribal or communal ideal, where members renounced individualism and private property and shared food, work, and sex. In such a community, love was a general abstract ideal rather than a focused emotion.

The quest for oneness with the universe led many youths to experiment with hallucinogenic drugs. LSD had a particularly powerful allure. Under its influence, poets, musicians, politicians, and thousands of other Americans claimed to have tapped into an all-powerful spiritual force. Timothy Leary, the Harvard professor who became the leading prophet of LSD, asserted that the drug would unlock the mysteries of the universe.

Although LSD was outlawed in 1966, the drug continued to spread. Perhaps some takers discovered profound truths, but by the late 1960s drugs had done more harm than good. The history of the Haight-Ashbury section of San Francisco illustrated the problems caused by drugs. In 1967 Haight was the center of the "counterculture," the home of the "flower children." In the "city of love" hippies ingested LSD, smoked pot, listened to "acid rock," and proclaimed the dawning of a new age. Yet the area was suffering from severe problems. High levels of racial violence, venereal disease, rape, drug overdoses, and poverty ensured more bad trips than good.

Even music, which along with drugs and sex formed the counterculture trinity, failed to alter human behavior. In 1969 journalists hailed the Woodstock Music Festival as a symbol of love. But a few months later a group of Hell's Angels violently interrupted the Altamont Raceway music festival. As Mick Jagger sang "Sympathy for the Devil" an Angel stabbed a black man to death.

Like the New Left, the counterculture fell victim to its own excesses. Sex, drugs, and rock and roll did not solve the problems facing the United States. And by the early 1970s the counterculture had lost its force.

Liberation Movements

The struggle of African Americans for racial justice inspired a host of other groups to seek full equality. Women, Mexican Americans, Native Americans, and many other deprived groups protested against discrimination and organized to promote social change.

Women's Liberation

One of the most popular daytime television shows of the 1950s was "Queen for a Day." Five times a week, three women, each with a hard luck story, recited their tales of woe—diseases, difficult children, poverty—and the studio audience, with the aid of an applause meter, decided which woman was the most miserable. She became "Queen for a Day." Gifts for the winner included cosmetics, a makeover, and kitchen appliances—everything a woman needed to be a prettier and better housewife.

One woman in the television audience was Betty Friedan. A 1942 honors graduate of Smith College and former psychology Ph.D. candidate at the University of California at Berkeley, Friedan had quit graduate school, married, moved to the New York suburbs, and bore three children. American culture told her that husband, house, children, and electric appliances were true happiness. But Friedan was not happy. And she was not alone.

In 1957 Friedan sent out questionnaires to fellow members of her college graduating class. The replies amazed her. Again and again, she found women suffering from "a sense of dissatisfaction." Over the next five years Friedan interviewed hundreds of other women, and she repeatedly found an unexplainable sense of melancholy and incompleteness. Friedan was not the only observer to detect a widespread sense of discontent among American women. Doctors identified a new female malady, the housewife's syndrome, characterized by a mixture of frustration and exhaustion. When *Redbook* magazine asked for examples of this problem, in an article entitled "Why Young Mothers Feel Trapped," it received 24,000 replies.

Why, Friedan asked, were American women so discontented? In 1963 she published her answer in a book entitled *The Feminine Mystique*. Friedan analyzed and criticized the role of educators, psychologists, sociologists, and the mass media in conditioning women to believe that they could only find fulfillment as housewives and mothers. By requiring women to subordinate their own individual aspirations to the welfare of their husbands and children, the "feminine mystique" prevented women from achieving self-fulfillment and inevitably left women unhappy.

One of the most influential books ever written by an American, *The Feminine Mystique* helped launch a new movement for women's liberation. The book touched a nerve, but the origins of the movement lay much deeper—in the traditional role of females in American society.

During the 1950s many American women reacted against the poverty of the depression and the upheavals of World War II by placing renewed emphasis on family life. Young women married earlier than had their mothers, and had more children and bore them faster—producing a population growth rate approaching that of India. Growing numbers of women decided to forsake higher education or a full-time career and achieve emotional fulfillment as wives and mothers.

Politicians, educators, psychologists, and the mass media all echoed the view that women would find their highest fulfillment managing a house and caring for children. Women's magazines pictured housewives as happy with their tasks and depicted career women as neurotic, unhappy, and dissatisfied.

Already, however, a series of important social changes was underway that would contribute to a rebirth of feminism. A dramatic upsurge took place during the 1950s in women's employment and education, as more and more married women entered the labor force; the number of women receiving college degrees also rose. Meanwhile, beginning in 1957 the birthrate began to drop as women elected to have fewer children. A growing discrepancy had begun to appear between the popular image of happy women as full-time housewives and mothers and the actual realities of many women's lives.

Women in 1960 played a limited role in American government. Although women comprised about half of the nation's voters, there were no female Supreme Court justices, federal appeals court justices, governors, cabinet officers, or ambassadors. Only two of 100 U.S. senators and 15 of 435 representatives were women.

Economically, women workers were concentrated in low-paying service and factory jobs. The overwhelming majority worked as secretaries, waitresses, beauticians, teachers, nurses, and librarians. Lower pay for women doing the same work as men was commonplace. One out of every three companies had separate pay scales for male and female workers. Altogether, the earnings of women working full-time averaged only about 60 percent of those of men.

In many parts of the country the law discriminated against women. In three states—Alabama, Mississippi, and South Carolina—women could not sit on juries. Many states restricted married women's right to make contracts, sell property, engage in business, control their own earnings, and make wills. In practically every state men had a legal right to have intercourse with their wives and to administer an unspecified amount of physical punishment.

Women were often portrayed in the mass media in unrealistic ways. Magazines like *Reader's Digest* and television shows like "I Love Lucy" often stereotyped women as stupid or foolish, jealous of other women, irresponsible about money, and overanxious to marry.

In December 1961 President Kennedy placed the issue of women's rights on the national political agenda by establishing a President's Commission on the Status of Women. Chaired by Eleanor Roosevelt, the commission issued its report in 1963, the year that Betty Friedan published *The Feminine Mystique*. The report's recommendations included a call for an end to all legal restrictions on married women's right to own property, to enter into business, and to make contracts; equal opportunity in employment; and greater availability of child-care services. The most important reform to grow out of the commission's investigations was the 1963 Equal Pay Act, which required equal pay for men and women who performed the same jobs under equal conditions. The Equal Pay Act was the first federal law to prohibit discrimination on the basis of gender.

The next year Congress developed a new weapon in the fight against sex discrimination. Title VII of the 1964 Civil Rights Act prohibited discrimination in hiring or promotion based on race, color, religion, national origin, or gender by private employers and unions. The act made it illegal for employers to discriminate against women in hiring and promotion unless the employer could show that gender was a "bona fide occupational qualification" (for example, hiring a man as an attendant for a men's restroom). To investigate complaints of employment discrimination, the act set up the Equal Employment Opportunity Commission (EEOC).

At first, the EEOC focused its enforcement efforts on racial discrimination and largely ignored sex discrimination. To pressure the EEOC to enforce the law prohibiting such discrimination, Betty Friedan and 300 other women formed the National Organization for Women (NOW) in 1966. With Friedan as president, NOW filed suit against the EEOC "to force it to comply with its own government rules." It also sued the country's 1,300 largest corporations for sex discrimination and lobbied President Johnson to issue an executive order that would include women within federal affirmative action requirements.

At its second national conference in November 1967 NOW drew up an eight-point bill of rights for women. It called for adoption of an Equal Rights Amendment (ERA) to the Constitution, prohibiting sex discrimination; equal educational, job training, and housing opportunities for women; and repeal of laws limiting access to contraceptive devices and abortion.

Two proposals produced fierce dissension within the new organization. One source of disagreement was the Equal Rights Amendment, which stated: "Equality of rights under the law shall not be denied or abridged by the United States or by any state on account of sex." It had originally been proposed in 1923 and was submitted to Congress at almost every session for the next 40 years. The other issue that generated controversy was the call for reform of laws that made abortion a criminal offense.

Despite internal disagreements, NOW's membership grew rapidly, reaching 40,000 by 1974 and 175,000 by 1988. The group broadened its attention to include such issues as the plight of poor and nonwhite women, domestic violence, rape, sexual harrassment, the role of women in sport, and the rights of lesbians. At the same time, the organization claimed a number of achievements. Two victories were particularly important. In 1967 NOW persuaded President Johnson to issue Executive Order 11375, which prohibited government contractors from discriminating on the basis of gender and required them to take "affirmative action" to ensure that women were properly represented in their work force. The next year the EEOC ruled that separate want ads for men and women were a violation of Title VII of the 1964 Civil Rights Act.

Radical Feminism

Alongside NOW, other more radical feminist groups emerged during the 1960s. In cities across the country, independent women's groups sprouted up, establishing the first feminist bookstores, battered women's shelters, rape crisis centers, and abortion counseling centers. Women within these organizations resented their status as "second class citizens" in a male-dominated culture. In 1968 radical women's groups staged a protest of the Miss America pageant, concluding their rally by crowning a sheep Miss America.

In 1971 Gloria Steinem and others published *Ms.,* the first national feminist magazine. The first 300,000 copies were sold out in eight days. Meanwhile, radical new ideas began to fill the air, and a host of new words and phrases entered the language, such as "consciousness raising," "bra burning," "sexism," and "male chauvinist pig."

In the years following the publication of *The Feminine Mystique* feminists developed a large body of literature analyzing the economic, psychological, and social roots of female subordination. It was not until 1970, however, that the more radical feminist writings reached the broader reading public with the publication of Shulamith Firestone's *The Dialectic of Sex,* Germaine Greer's *The Female Eunuch,* and Kate Millett's *Sexual Politics.* These books argued that gender distinctions structure virtually every aspect of individual lives, not only in such areas as law and employment, but also in personal relationships, language, literature, religion, and an individual's internalized self-perceptions. Even more controversially, these works attributed female oppression to men and an ideology of male supremacy. "Women have very little idea how much men hate them," declared Greer. As examples of misogyny, these authors cited pornography, grotesque portrayals of women in literature, sexual harrassment, wife abuse, and rape.

Sex Discrimination

Despite its conservative image, the Supreme Court under chief justices Warren Burger and William Rehnquist were active in the area of sex discrimination and women's rights. The Burger Court issued its first important discrimination decision in 1971. In its landmark decision, *Griggs* v. *Duke Power Company,* the Court established the principle that regardless of an employer's intentions, any employment practice is illegal if it has a "disparate" impact on women or minorities and "if it cannot be shown to be related to job performance."

The court's most controversial decision involving women's rights was delivered in 1973 in the case of *Roe* v. *Wade.* The court struck down a nineteenth-century Texas law prohibiting abortion and all similar laws in other states. In its ruling, the court declared that the decision to have an abortion is a private matter of concern only to a woman and her physician, and that only in the last three months of pregnancy could the government limit the right to abortion.

Many Americans—including many Roman Catholic lay and clerical organizations—bitterly opposed the Supreme Court's *Roe* v. *Wade* decision and banded together to form the "right to life" movement. The major legislative success of the right-to-life movement was adoption by Congress of the so-called Hyde Amendment, which permitted states to refuse to fund abortions for indigent women.

In March 1972 Congress passed an Equal Rights Amendment (ERA) to the United States Constitution, prohibiting gender discrimination. Before the year was over, 22 state legislatures ratified the ERA, only 16 short of the 38 states required before the amendment would be added to the Constitution. Over the next five years, only 13 more states ratified the amendment—and five states rescinded their ratification. In 1978 Congress gave proponents of the amendment 39 more months to obtain ratification, but no other state gave its approval.

The ERA was defeated in part by organized labor, which feared that the amendment would eliminate state "protective legislation" that established minimum wages and maximum hours for women workers. Increasingly, however, resistance to the amendment came from conservative activists such as Phyllis Schlafly, a Radcliffe-educated mother of six. Schlafly argued that the ERA was unnecessary because women were already protected by the Equal Pay Act of 1963 and the Civil Rights Act of

Women have been involved in protest movements throughout the years. Here women march in support of the Equal Rights Amendment. Failure to achieve ratification by the required three-fourths of states sent the amendment to its final defeat in 1982.

1964, which barred sex discrimination, and that the amendment would outlaw separate public rest rooms and deny wives the right to financial support. She also raised the "women in combat" issue by suggesting that the passage of the ERA would mean that women would have to fight alongside men in wartime.

Impact of the Women's Liberation Movement

Since 1960 women have made impressive social gains. Advances in employment have been particularly noteworthy. During the 1970s the number of working women climbed 42 percent and much of the increase was in what traditionally was considered "men's" work and professional work—lawyers, professors, doctors, managers, and administrators.

Striking gains have been made in undergraduate and graduate education. Today, for the first time in American history, women constitute a majority of the nation's college students and nearly as many women as men receive master's degrees. In addition, the number of women students receiving degrees from professional schools—including dentistry, law, and medicine—has shot upward, from just 1,425 in 1966 to over 20,000 by the early 1990s. Women comprise nearly a third of the students attending law school and medical school.

Women have also made substantial political gains. In 1988 more than two dozen women served in Congress, and 80 served as mayors of large cities. In 1981 Sandra Day O'Connor became the first woman to sit on the Supreme Court, and in 1984 a major political party nominated a woman, Geraldine Ferraro, as its vice presidential candidate.

In spite of all that has been achieved, however, problems remain. Most women today continue to work in a relatively small number of traditional "women's" jobs, and a full-time female worker earns only 68 cents for every $1 paid to men. Even more troubling is the fact that large numbers of women live in poverty. Today, nearly half of all marriages end in divorce and many others end in legal separation and desertion—and the economic plight of these women is often grave. Although female-headed familes constitute only 15 percent of the U.S. population, they account for over 50 percent of the poor population.

Mexican-American Liberation

On election day, 1963, hundreds of Mexican Americans in Crystal City, Texas, did something that many had never done before: vote. Although Mexican Americans outnumbered Anglos two to one, Anglos controlled all five seats on the Crystal City council. For three years, organizers struggled to register Mexican-American voters. When the election was over, Mexican Americans had won control of the city council. "We have done the impossible," declared Albert Fuentes, who led the voter registration campaign. "If we can do it in Crystal City, we can do it all over Texas."

As the 1960s began, Mexican Americans shared problems of poverty and discrimination with other minority groups. The median income of a Mexican-American family was just 62 percent of the median income of the general population. Unemployment was twice that of non-Hispanic whites, and four-fifths of employed Mexican Americans were concentrated in semiskilled and unskilled jobs, a third in agriculture.

Educational attainment lagged behind other groups (Mexican Americans averaged less than nine years of schooling as recently as 1970), and Mexican-American pupils were concentrated in predominantly Mexican-American schools, less well staffed and supplied than non-Mexican-American schools, with few Hispanic or Spanish-speaking teachers. Gerrymandered election districts and restrictive voting legislation resulted in the political underrepresentation of Mexican Americans. They were underrepresented or excluded from juries by requirements that jurors be able to speak and understand English.

During the 1960s a new Mexican-American militancy arose. In 1962 César Chávez began to organize California farm workers, and three years later, in Delano, California, he led his first strike. At the same time that Chávez launched his struggle for higher wages and union recognition, Reies Lopez Tijerina fought to restore the legal rights of heirs to Spanish and Mexican land grants that had been guaranteed under the treaty ending the Mexican War.

In Denver, Rodolfo "Corky" Gonzales formed the Crusade for Justice in 1965 to protest school discrimination; provide legal, medical, and financial services and jobs for Chicanos; and foster the Mexican-American cultural heritage. La Raza Unida political parties arose in a number of small towns with large Mexican-American populations. On college campuses across the Southwest, Mexican Americans formed political organizations.

In 1968 Congress responded to the demand among Mexican Americans for equal educational opportunity by enacting legislation encouraging school districts to adopt bilingual education programs to instruct non-English speakers in both English and their native language. In a more recent action, Congress moved in 1986 to legalize the status of many immigrants, including many Mexicans, who entered the United States illegally. The Immigration Reform and Control Act of 1986 provided permanent legal residency to undocumented workers who had lived in the United States since before 1982 and prohibits employment of illegal aliens.

Since 1960 Mexican Americans have made important political gains. During the 1960s four Mexican Americans were elected to Congress. In

1974 two Chicanos were elected governors, becoming the first Mexican-American governors since early in this century. In 1981 Henry Cisneros of San Antonio became the first Mexican-American mayor of a large city.

Today, the 10.5 million Mexican Americans, the nation's second largest minority group, continue to struggle to expand their political influence, improve their economic position, and preserve their distinctive culture.

The Native American Power Movement

In November 1969, 200 Native Americans seized the abandoned federal penitentiary on Alcatraz Island in San Francisco Bay. For 19 months Indian activists occupied the island in order to draw attention to conditions on the nation's Indian reservations. Alcatraz, the Native Americans said, symbolized conditions on reservations: "It has no running water; it has inadequate sanitation facilities; there is no industry, and so unemployment is very great; there are no health care facilities; the soil is rocky and unproductive."

On Thanksgiving Day, 1970, 350 years after the Pilgrims' arrival, Wampanoag Indians, who had taken part at the first Thanksgiving, held a National Day of Mourning at Plymouth, Massachusetts. A tribal representative declared, "We forfeited our country. Our lands have fallen into the hands of the aggressor. We have allowed the white man to keep us on our knees." Meanwhile, another group of Native Americans established a settlement at Mount Rushmore, to demonstrate Indian claims to the Black Hills.

During the late 1960s and early 1970s a new spirit of political militancy arose among Native Americans, just as it had among black Americans and women. No other group, however, faced problems more severe than Native Americans. Throughout the 1960s Indians were the nation's poorest minority group, worse off than any other group according to virtually every socioeconomic measure. In 1970 the Native American unemployment rate was 10 times the national average, and 40 percent of the Indian population lived below the poverty line. In that year, Native-American life expectancy was just 44 years, a third less than that of the average American. Half a million Indian families lived in unsanitary, dilapidated dwellings that lacked indoor plumbing.

During World War II Native Americans began to revolt against such conditions. In 1944 they formed the National Congress of American Indians (NCAI), the first modern intertribal association. Among the group's primary concerns were protection of Indian land rights and improved educational opportunities. When Congress voted in 1953 to allow states to assert legal jurisdiction over Indian reservations without tribal consent and the federal government sought to transfer federal Indian responsibilities for a dozen tribes to the states (a policy known as "termination") and to relocate Indians into urban areas, the NCAI rallied opposition to these measures.

By the 1960s a new spirit of Indian nationalism had arisen. In 1961 a militant new Indian organization appeared, the National Indian Youth Council, which began to use the phrase "Red Power" and sponsored demonstrations and protest marches. Native Americans in the San Francisco Bay area in 1964 established the Indian Historical Society to present history from the Indian point of view, while the Native American Rights Fund brought legal suits against states that had taken Indian land and abolished Indian hunting, fishing, and water rights in violation of federal treaties. Many tribes also took legal action to prevent strip-mining or spraying of pesticides on their lands.

The best known of the Native-American groups was AIM, the American Indian Movement, formed by a group of Chippewas in 1966 to protest alleged police brutality. In the fall of 1972 AIM seized the offices of the Bureau of Indian Affairs in Washington, D.C., and occupied them for a week to dramatize Indian grievances. In the spring of 1973, 200 heavily armed Indians took over the town of Wounded Knee, South Dakota, site of an 1890 massacre of 300 Sioux by the U.S. army cavalry, and occupied the town for 71 days.

Indians are no longer a vanishing group of Americans. The 1980 census recorded an Indian population of 1.38 million in the United States, 72 percent over the figure reported in 1970 and four times the number recorded in 1950. About half live on reservations. The largest Native-American populations are located in Alaska, Arizona, California, New Mexico, and Oklahoma.

Although Native Americans continue to face severe problems of employment, income, and education, they have demonstrated that they will not abandon their Indian identity and culture or be treated as dependent wards of the federal government.

Conclusion

In the early 1960s black college students and religious groups, impatient with the slow pace of change, staged protests to challenge legal segregation in the South. Their efforts led the federal government to pass the Civil Rights Act of 1964, prohibiting discrimination in public facilities and employment, and the Twenty-fourth Amendment to the Constitution and the Voting Rights Act in 1965, guaranteeing black voting rights.

Despite significant legal gains, and the far-reaching effort of Lyndon Johnson's Great Society program, many African Americans felt a growing sense of frustration and anger. The violence perpetrated by white racists and

Chronology of Key Events

1960 First sit-ins held to protest segregation; Student Nonviolent Coordinating Committee (SNCC) founded

1961 Congress of Racial Equality (CORE) stages freedom rides; *Mapp* v. *Ohio* rules that evidence obtained by unreasonable search must be excluded

1962 James Meredith enrolls at University of Mississippi; SDS issues Port Huron Statement; César Chávez organizes California farm workers

1963 Martin Luther King, Jr., leads Birmingham, Alabama, demonstrations; racial violence sweeps the South; Betty Friedan's *The Feminine Mystique* published; Equal Pay Act requires equal pay for equal work; *Gideon* v. *Wainright;* Civil rights march on Washington, D.C.; John F. Kennedy assassinated; Lyndon Johnson becomes thirty-sixth president

1964 War on Poverty announced; Manpower Development and Training Act and Economic Opportunity Act establish the Job Corps and Neighborhood Youth Corps; *Escobedo* v. *Illinois;* Civil Rights Act prohibits discrimination in employment; Twenty-fourth Amendment prohibits poll taxes in federal elections

1965 Malcolm X assassinated; Martin Luther King, Jr., leads demonstrations in Selma, Alabama; Voting Rights Act prohibits literacy tests; Watts riot; Medicare extended to older Americans; Ralph Nader publishes *Unsafe at Any Speed*

1966 SNCC and CORE embrace black nationalism; Black Panther party organized; National Organization for Women formed; Model Cities Act passed to attack urban blight

1967 Riots in 127 cities

1968 Medicaid expanded to cover the poor; Martin Luther King, Jr. assassinated; riots in 168 cities

1971 *Swann* v. *Charlotte-Mecklenburg Board of Education* upholds busing as tool to achieve racial integration

1973 *Roe* v. *Wade* legalizes abortion

1986 Immigration Reform and Control Act provides permanent legal residency to undocumented workers who have lived in United States since 1982

a growing white backlash against civil rights led black nationalists to downplay the goal of integration and instead emphasize black power and black pride. Frustration was particularly evident in urban ghettoes, where the black poor faced problems that were not addressed by civil rights legislation.

The example of the civil rights movement inspired other groups to press for equal opportunity. The women's movement fought for passage of antidiscrimination laws, equal educational and employment opportunities, and a transformation of traditional views about women's place in society. Mexican Americans battled for bilingual education programs in schools, unionization of farm workers, improved job opportunities, and increased political power. Native Americans pressed for control over Indian lands and resources, the preservation of Indian cultures, and tribal self-government.

Suggestions for Further Reading

For insight into America during the 1960s consult Taylor Branch, *Parting the Waters* (1988); William H. Chafe, *Unfinished Journey,* 2d ed. (1991); Richard N. Goodwin, *Remembering America* (1988); Allen Matusow, *The Unraveling of America* (1984); William O'Neill, *Coming Apart* (1971).

The literature on the civil rights movement is voluminous. Besides those mentioned in the bibliography in Chapter 28, valuable analyses include Michel Belknap, *Federal Law and Southern Order* (1987); Derrick Bell, *And We Are Not Saved* (1987); David R. Goldfield, *Black, White, and Southern* (1990); Vincent Harding, *There is a River* (1981); Richard Kluger, *Simple Justice* (1975); Steven Lawson, *Running for Freedom* (1991); Nicholas Lemann, *The Promised Land* (1991); Doug McAdam, *Freedom Summer* (1988); Harvard Sitkoff, *The Struggle for Black Equality* (1981); Juan Williams, *Eyes on the Prize* (1987).

Useful books on feminism include Mary Frances Berry, *Why ERA Failed* (1986); William H. Chafe, *Women and Equality* (1977); Sara Evans, *Personal Politics* (1979); Leila Rupp and Verta Taylor, *Survival in the Doldrums* (1987).

The Mexican American struggle for equal rights is discussed in Rodolfo Acuña, *Occupied America,* 3d ed. (1988); Albert Camarillo, *Hispanics in a Changing Society* (1979); Mario T. García, *Mexican Americans* (1989); and Juan Gómez-Quiñones, *Chicano Politics* (1990). Books on Native Americans include Peter Iverson, *The Navajo Nation* (1981); Roger Nichols, *The American Indian: Past and Present,* 3d ed. (1985).

The youth movement and the rise of the New Left are examined in Paul Buhle, *History and the New Left* (1990); Morris Dickstein, *Gates of Eden* (1977); Todd Gitlin, *The Sixties* (1987); Maurice Isserman, . . . *If I Had a Hammer* (1987); W. J. Rorabaugh, *Berkeley at War* (1989); Theodore Roszak, *The Making of a Counter Culture* (1969); Kirkpatrick Sale, *SDS* (1973); Irwin Unger, *The Movement.*

Chapter 31

America in Our Time

Crisis of Political Leadership
Restraining the Imperial Presidency
New Style Presidents

Wrenching Economic Transformations
The Age of Inflation
Oil Embargo
Foreign Competition
Whipping Stagflation

A New American Role in the World
Détente
Foreign Policy Triumphs
No Islands of Stability

The Reagan Revolution
The Gipper
Reaganomics
The Celebration of Wealth
The Reagan Doctrine
A Remarkable Ideological Turnaround
The Reagan Revolution in Perspective

The Bush Presidency
A Kinder, Gentler Nation
Economic Policy
Foreign Policy
Collapse of Communism
The Persian Gulf War
Enter Bill Clinton

Shortly after 1 A.M. on the morning of June 17, 1972, a security guard at the Washington, D.C., Watergate office complex spotted a strip of masking tape covering the lock of a basement door. He removed it. A short while later, he found the door taped open again. He called the police, who found two more taped locks and a jammed door leading into the offices of the Democratic National Committee. Inside they discovered five men carrying cameras and electronic eavesdropping equipment.

At first, the Watergate break-in seemed like a minor incident. The identities of the burglars, however, suggested something more serious. One, James McCord, was chief security coordinator of the Committee for the Reelection of the President (CREEP). Others had links to the CIA.

Over the course of the next year, it became clear that the break-in was one of a series of secret operations coordinated by the White House. Financed by illegal campaign contributions, these operations posed a threat to America's constitutional system of government and eventually forced Richard Nixon to resign the presidency.

The Watergate break-in had its roots in Richard Nixon's obsession with secrecy and political intelligence. To stop "leaks" of information to the press, in 1971 the Nixon White House assembled a team of "plumbers," consisting of former CIA operatives. This private police force, paid for in part by illegal campaign contributions, engaged in a wide range of criminal acts, including phone tapping and burglary, against those on its "enemies list."

In 1972 when President Nixon was running for reelection, CREEP authorized another series of illegal activities. It hired Donald Segretti to stage "dirty tricks" against potential Democratic nominees, which included mailing letters that falsely accused one candidate of homosexuality and fathering an illegitimate child. It considered a plan to use call girls to blackmail Democrats at their national convention and to kidnap anti-Nixon radical leaders. The committee also authorized $250,000 for intelligence-gathering operations. Four times the committee sent burglars to break into Democratic headquarters.

Precisely what the campaign committee hoped to learn from these intelligence-gathering activities remains a mystery. It seems likely that it was seeking information about the Democratic party's campaign strategies and any information the Democrats had about illegal campaign contributions to the Republican party.

On June 23—six days after the botched break-in—President Nixon ordered aides to block an FBI investigation of White House involvement in the break-in on grounds that an investigation would endanger national security. He also counseled his aides to lie under oath, if necessary.

The Watergate break-in did not hurt Nixon's reelection campaign. Between the activities of the burglars and the president were layers of deception that had to be carefully peeled away. *Washington Post* reporters Bob Woodward and Carl Bernstein, sensing that the break-in was only part of a larger scandal, slowly pieced together part of the story. Facing long jail terms, some of the burglars began to tell the truth, and the truth illuminated a path leading to the White House.

If Nixon had few political friends, he had legions of enemies. Over the years he had offended or attacked many Democrats—and a number of prominent Republicans. His detractors latched onto the Watergate issue with the tenacity of bulldogs.

The Senate appointed a special committee to investigate the Watergate scandal. Most of Nixon's top aides continued the cover-up. John Dean, the president's counsel, did not. Throughout the episode he had kept careful notes, and in a quiet precise voice he told the Senate Watergate Committee that the president was deeply involved in the cover-up. The matter was still not solved. All the committee had was Dean's word against the other White House aides.

On July 16, 1973, a former White House employee dropped a bombshell by testifying that Nixon had recorded all Oval Office conversations. Whatever Nixon and his aides had said about Watergate in the Oval Office, therefore, was faithfully recorded on tape.

Nixon tried to keep the tapes from the committee by invoking executive privilege, insisting that a president had a right to keep confidential any White House communication, whether or not it involved sensitive diplomatic or national security matters. When Archibald Cox, a special prosecutor investigating the Watergate affair, persisted in demanding the tapes, Nixon ordered his attorney general, Elliot Richardson, to fire him; Richardson refused and resigned; Richardson's assistant, William Ruckelshaus, also resigned. Ruckelshaus's assistant, Robert Bork, finally fired Cox, but Congress forced Nixon to name a new special prosecutor, Leon Jaworski.

In the midst of the Watergate investigations another scandal broke. Federal prosecutors accused Vice President Spiro Agnew of extorting payoffs from building contractors while he was Maryland's governor and Baltimore County executive. In a plea bargain, Agnew pleaded no contest to a relatively minor charge—that he had falsified his income tax in 1967—in exchange for a $10,000 fine. Agnew was succeeded as vice president by Gerald Ford, whom Nixon appointed.

The Watergate scandal gradually came to encompass not just the cover-up but a wide range of presidential wrongdoings, including political favors to powerful business groups in exchange for campaign contributions; misuse of public funds; deceiving Congress and the public about the secret bombing of Cambodia; authorization of illegal domestic political surveillance and espionage against dissidents, political opponents, and journalists; and attempts to use FBI investigations and income tax audits by the IRS to harass political enemies.

On July 24, 1974, the House Judiciary Committee recommended that the House of Representatives impeach Nixon for obstruction of justice, abuse of power, and refusal to relinquish the tapes. On August 5 Nixon obeyed a Supreme Court order to release the tapes, which confirmed Dean's detailed testimony. Nixon had indeed been involved in a cover-up. On August 9 he became the first American president to resign from office. The following day Gerald Ford became the new president. "Our long national nightmare," he said, "is over."

Crisis of Political Leadership

The Vietnam War and the Watergate scandal had a profound effect on the presidency. The office suffered a dramatic decline in public respect, and Congress became increasingly unwilling to defer to presidential leadership. Congress enacted a series of reforms that would make future abuses

On August 9, 1974, Richard Nixon resigned the presidency after the release of secret tapes revealed that he had been involved in a cover-up of the Watergate affair.

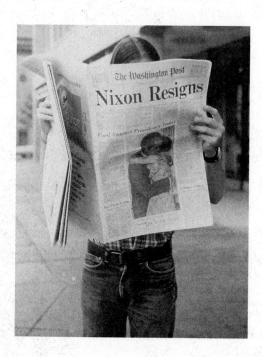

of presidential authority less likely. In the process Congress recaptured constitutional powers that had been ceded to an increasingly dominant executive branch.

Restraining the Imperial Presidency

Over the course of the twentieth century the presidency gradually supplanted Congress as the center of federal power. Presidential authority increased, presidential staffs grew in size, and the executive branch gradually acquired a dominant relationship over Congress.

Beginning with Theodore Roosevelt, the president, and not Congress, established the nation's legislative agenda. Increasingly, Congress ceded its budget-making authority to the president. Presidents even found a way to make agreements with foreign nations without congressional approval. After World War II presidents substituted executive agreements for treaties requiring approval of the Senate. Even more important, presidents gained the power to take military action, despite the fact that Congress is the sole branch of government empowered by the Constitution to declare war.

No president went further than Richard Nixon in concentrating powers in the presidency. He refused to spend funds that Congress had appropriated; he claimed executive privilege against disclosure of information on administration decisions; he refused to allow key decision makers to be questioned before congressional committees; he reorganized the executive branch and broadened the authority of new cabinet positions without congressional approval; and during the Vietnam War, he ordered harbors mined and bombing raids launched without consulting Congress.

Watergate brought a halt to the "imperial presidency" and the growth of presidential power. Over the president's veto, Congress enacted the War Powers Act (1973), which required future presidents to obtain authorization from Congress to engage U.S. forces in foreign combat for more than 90 days. Under the law, a president who orders troops into action abroad must report the reason for this action to Congress within 48 hours.

In the wake of the Watergate scandal Congress passed a series of laws designed to reform the political process. Disclosures during the Watergate investigations of money-laundering led Congress to provide public financing of presidential elections, public disclosure of sources of funding, limits on private campaign contributions and spending, and enforcement of campaign finance laws by an independent Federal Election Commission. To make it easier for the Justice Department to investigate crimes in the executive branch, Congress now requires the attorney general to appoint a special prosecutor to investigate accusations of illegal activities. To reassert its budget-making authority, Congress created a Congressional Budget Office and specifically forbade a president to impound funds without its approval. To open government to public scrutiny, Congress opened more committee deliberations and enacted the Freedom of Information Act, which allows the public and press to request the declassification of government documents.

Some of the post-Watergate reforms have not been as effective as reformers anticipated. The War Powers Act has never been invoked. Campaign financing reform has not curbed the ability of special interests to curry favor with politicians or the capacity of the very rich to outspend opponents.

On the other hand, Congress has had somewhat more success in reining in the FBI and the CIA. During the 1970s congressional investigators discovered that these organizations had, in defiance of federal law, broken into the homes, tapped the phones, and opened the mail of American citizens; illegally infiltrated antiwar groups and black radical organizations; and accumulated dossiers on dissidents; which had been used by presidents for political purposes. Investigators also found that the CIA had been involved in assassination plots against foreign leaders, among them Fidel Castro, and had tested the effects of radiation, electric shock, and drugs (such as LSD) on unsuspecting citizens. In the wake of these investigations, the government severely limited CIA operations in the United States and laid down strict guidelines for FBI activities. To tighten congressional control over the CIA, Congress established a joint committee to supervise its operations.

New Style Presidents

In contrast to Nixon's abuses of presidential power, the next two presidents, Gerald Ford and Jimmy Carter, cultivated reputations as honest, forthright leaders. Both were men of decency and integrity, but neither established reputations as strong, dynamic leaders. Although many Americans admired their honesty and sincerity, neither Ford nor Carter succeeded in winning the confidence of the American people. Moreover, neither administration had a clear sense of direction. Both Ford and Carter seemed to waffle on major issues of public policy. As a result, both came to be regarded as unsure, vacillating presidents.

A 13-term congressman from Grand Rapids, Michigan, Gerald Ford dismissed the possibility of pardoning Richard Nixon for his Watergate misdeeds, then changed his mind. In the realm of economic policy, he began by urging tax increases, but later called for a large tax cut. His energy policy was crippled by the same indecision. At first, he tried to raise prices by imposing import fees on imported oil and ending domestic price controls; then he abandoned that position in the face of severe political pressure.

Carter, too, suffered from the charge that he modified his stances in the face of political pressure. A two-term Democratic governor from Georgia who defeated Ford in the 1976 presidential election, Carter came to office determined to cut military spending, calling for the abolition of nuclear weapons and the withdrawal of American troops from South Korea. By the end of his term, however, Carter spoke of the need for sustained growth in defense spending, upgrading nuclear forces in Europe, and developing a new strategic bomber.

Both men were described as "passionless presidents" who failed to project a clear vision of where they wanted to lead the country. But in their defense, both faced serious problems, ranging from dealing with rising oil prices to confronting third-world terrorists.

Wrenching Economic Transformations

At one time, the car makers in Detroit produced automobiles that mirrored America's strength and power. They were big, heavy, powerful cars, with such expensive options as power windows, power brakes, and power steering. So what if they were not energy-efficient (most got 10 to 13 miles per gallon)? Gas was cheap; just 37 cents a gallon in 1973. The public kept buying big cars, Detroit kept producing them, and the automobile industry reaped big profits.

By the late 1970s the rising costs of Middle Eastern oil forced the American automotive industry to rethink its strategy. Emerging Arab nationalism and the solidarity of the Organization of Petroleum Exporting Countries (OPEC) drove the price of a gallon of gas toward the dollar mark. American drivers started purchasing smaller, better-engineered, fuel-efficient cars from Japan and Europe. By 1982 Japanese cars had captured 30 percent of the U.S. market.

Since 1973, the American economy has undergone a series of wrenching economic transformations. Economic growth slowed; productivity flagged; inflation rose; and major industries faltered in the face of foreign competition. Despite a massive influx of women into the work force, family wages stagnated. A quarter century of rapid post-World War II economic growth had come to an end.

The Age of Inflation

In 1967 the average price of a three-bedroom house was $17,000. A brand new Cadillac convertible went for $6,700 and a new Volkswagen

$1,497; a Hershey chocolate bar sold for a nickel; a pound of sirloin for 89 cents. Two decades later the prices of these products had quadrupled.

The upsurge in inflation started when Lyndon Johnson decided to fight the Vietnam War without raising taxes enough to pay for it. By 1968 the war was costing the United States $3 billion dollars a month, and the federal budget skyrocketed to $179 billion. With hundreds of thousands of Americans in the military service and even more working in defense-related industries, unemployment fell, wages rose, and government deficits increased. Inflation was further fueled by a series of crop failures and sharp rises in commodities, especially oil.

High inflation had many negative effects on the American economy. It wiped out many families' savings. It provoked labor turmoil, as workers went on strike for higher wages. It encouraged speculation in tangible assets—like art, precious metals, and real estate—rather than productive investment in new factories and technology. Above all, certain organized interest groups were able to keep up with inflation, while other less powerful groups, such as welfare recipients, saw the value of their benefits decline significantly.

Inflation reduced the purchasing power of most Americans. For over a decade, real family wages remained flat. By the end of the 1970s they had climbed just $36 over 1973 levels. Yet inflation raised the prices of virtually all goods and services. Health care and housing, in particular, experienced price rises far above the inflation rate. The consequences were a sharp increase in the number of Americans unable to afford health insurance, and a dramatic increase in the cost of housing, which resulted in an increase in homelessness.

Oil Embargo

Political unrest in the oil-rich Middle East contributed significantly to America's economic troubles. After suffering a humiliating defeat at the hands of Israel in the 1973 "Yom Kippur" war, Arab leaders unsheathed a new political weapon—oil. In order to pressure Israel out of territory conquered in the 1967 and 1973 wars, Arab nations cut oil production 25 percent and embargoed all oil exports to the United States. Leading the way was OPEC, which had been founded by Iran, Saudi Arabia, and Venezuela in 1960 to fight a reduction in prices by oil companies.

Because Arab nations controlled 60 percent of the oil reserves in the non-Communist world, they had the western nations over a barrel. Production cutbacks produced an immediate global shortage. The United States imported a third of its oil from Arab nations; Western Europe imported 72 percent from the Middle East; Japan, 82 percent. Gas prices rose, long lines formed at gas pumps, some factories shortened the work-week, and some shopping centers restricted business hours.

The oil crisis brought to an end an era of cheap energy. Americans had to learn to live with smaller cars and less heating and air conditioning. But the crisis did have a positive side effect. It increased public consciousness about the environment and stimulated awareness of the importance of conservation. For millions of Americans the lessons were painful to learn.

Foreign Competition

In 1947 the United States was truly the world's factory. Half of all the world's manufacturing took place in the United States. Americans made 57 percent of the world's steel and 80 percent of the world's cars. It was inevitable that other countries would eventually challenge the dominance that American manufacturers had enjoyed in the aftermath of World War II. During the early 1960s foreign manufacturers produced 6 percent of the cars purchased by Americans. That figure climbed to 20 percent in the late 1970s.

The foreign penetration extended far beyond the market for compact cars. Foreign countries began to dominate the highly profitable, techno-logically advanced fields such as consumer electronics, luxury automo-biles, and machine tools. Americans discovered that technologies their country had pioneered—such as semiconductors, color televisions, and videocassette recorders—were now produced almost exclusively by for-eign manufacturers. The decline in the American share of the market meant fewer jobs in the American automobile, steel, rubber, and electron-ics industries. In addition, American and even Japanese companies shifted low-skill production work to such places as South Korea, Taiwan, Hong Kong, Singapore, and Indonesia, where goods could be produced more cheaply because of lower wage scales.

Few economic developments aroused as much public concern during the 1970s as the loss of American jobs in basic industry. According to one estimate, 30 million jobs disappeared. Displaced workers saw their sav-ings depleted, mortgages foreclosed, and health and pension benefits lost. Even when they found new jobs, they typically had to settle for wages substantially below what they had earned before. Plant shutdowns and closings had profound effects on entire communities, which lost their tax bases at the time when they needed to fund health and welfare services.

Whipping Stagflation

During the 1960s the primary goal of economic policy was to encourage growth and keep unemployment low. But by the early 1970s the economy started to suffer from *stagflation*—high unemployment and inflation coupled with stagnant economic growth. This presented economic policymakers with a new and perplexing dilemma, since unemployment and inflation usually do not coexist.

The problem with stagflation was the pain of its options. To attack inflation by reducing consumer purchasing power only made unemployment worse. The other choice was no better. Stimulating purchasing power and creating jobs also drove prices higher. Not surprisingly, economic policy during the 1970s was a nightmare of confusion and contradiction.

By 1971 pressures produced by the Vietnam War and federal social spending, coupled with the increase in foreign competition, pushed the inflation rate to 5 percent and unemployment to 6 percent. President Richard Nixon responded by increasing federal budget deficits and devaluing the dollar in an attempt to stimulate the economy and to make American goods more competitive overseas. Nixon also imposed a 90-day wage and price freeze, followed by a mandatory set of wage-price guidelines, and then by voluntary controls. Inflation stayed at about 4 percent during the freeze, but once controls were lifted, inflation resumed its upward climb.

In 1974 during the first oil embargo, inflation hit 12 percent. Gerald Ford, the new president, initially attacked the problem in a traditional Republican fashion, tightening the money supply by raising interest rates and limiting government spending. In the end, his economic program proved to be no more than a series of ineffectual wage and price guidelines monitored by the federal government. In the subsequent recession unemployment reached 9 percent.

When Jimmy Carter took office in January 1977, 7.4 percent of the work force was unemployed. Carter responded with an ambitious spending program and called for the Federal Reserve (the Fed) to expand the money supply. Within two years inflation had climbed to 13.3 percent.

With inflation getting out of hand, the Federal Reserve Board announced in 1979 that it would fight inflation by restraining the growth of the money supply. Unemployment increased, and interest rates rose to their highest levels in the nation's history. By November 1982 unemployment hit 10.8 percent, the highest since 1940. One out of every five American workers went some time without a job.

Along with high interest rates, the Carter administration adopted another weapon in the battle against stagflation: deregulation. Convinced that regulators too often protected the industries they were supposed to oversee, the Carter administration deregulated air and surface transportation and the savings and loan industry.

The effects of deregulation are still hotly contested. Rural towns suffered cutbacks of bus, rail, and air service. Truckers and rail workers lost the economic benefits of regulation. Travelers complained about rising air fares and congested airports. Cable TV viewers resented rising rates. Champions of deregulation argued that the policy increased competition, stimulated new investment, and forced inefficient firms either to become more efficient or shut down.

A New American Role in the World

In his inaugural address in 1961 John Kennedy stated that America would "pay any price, bear any burden, meet any hardship, support any friend or oppose any foe to assure the survival and the success of liberty." But by 1973, in the wake of the Vietnam War, American foreign policymakers regarded Kennedy's stirring pledge as unrealistic.

The Vietnam War offered a lesson about the limits of American power. It underscored the need to distinguish between vital national interests and peripheral interests, and to balance America's military commitments with its available resources. Above all, the Vietnam War appeared to illustrate the dangers of obsessive anticommunism. Such a policy failed to recognize that the world was becoming more complex, that power blocs were shifting, and that the interests of Communist countries and the United States could sometimes overlap. Too often, American policy seemed to have driven nationalists and reformers into Communist hands and to have led the United States to support corrupt, unpopular authoritarian regimes. The great challenge facing American foreign policymakers was how to preserve the nation's international prestige and influence in the face of declining defense budgets and mounting congressional opposition to direct overseas intervention.

Détente

As president, Richard Nixon radically redefined America's relationship with its two foremost adversaries, China and the Soviet Union. In a remarkable turnabout from his record of staunch anticommunism, he opened relations with China and began strategic arms limitation talks with the Soviet Union. The goal of *détente* (the easing of tensions between nations), was to continue to resist and deter Soviet adventurism while striving for "more constructive relations" with the Communist world.

Nixon and Henry Kissinger believed that it was necessary to curb the arms race, improve great-power relationships, and learn to coexist with Communist regimes. The Nixon administration sought to use the Chinese and Soviet need for western trade and technology as a way to extract foreign policy concessions.

Recognizing that one of the legacies of Vietnam was a reluctance on the part of the American public to risk overseas interventions, Nixon and Kissinger also sought to build up regional powers that shared American strategic interests, most notably China, Iran, and Saudi Arabia.

By the late 1970s an increasing number of Americans believed that the Soviet hard-liners viewed détente as a mere tactic to lull the West into relaxing its vigilance. Soviet Communist party chief Leonid Brezhnev reinforced this view, boasting of gains that his country had made at the United States's expense—in Vietnam, Angola, Cambodia, Ethiopia, and Laos.

An alarming Soviet arms buildup contributed to the sense that détente was not working. By 1975, the Soviet Union had 50 percent more intercontinental ballistic missiles (ICBMs) than the United States, three times as many army personnel, three times as many attack submarines, and four times as many tanks. The United States continued to have a powerful strategic deterrent, holding a 9,000 to 3,200 advantage in deliverable nuclear bombs and warheads. But the arms gap between the countries was narrowing.

Foreign Policy Triumphs

In the Middle East Carter achieved his greatest diplomatic success by negotiating peace between Egypt and Israel. Since the founding of Israel in 1948, Egypt's foreign policy had been built around destroying the Jewish state. In 1977 Anwar el-Sadat, the practical and farsighted leader of Egypt, decided to seek peace with Israel. It was an act of rare political courage, for Sadat risked alienating Egypt from the rest of the Arab world without a firm commitment for a peace treaty with Israel.

Although both countries wanted peace, major obstacles had to be overcome. Sadat wanted Israel to retreat from the West Bank of the Jordan River and from the Golan Heights (which it had taken from Jordan in the 1967 war), recognize the Palestine Liberation Organization (PLO), provide a homeland for the Palestinians, relinquish its unilateral hold on the city of Jerusalem, and return the Sinai to Egypt. Such conditions were unacceptable to Israeli Prime Minister Menachem Begin, who refused to consider recognition of the PLO or the return of the West Bank. By the end of 1977 Sadat's peace mission had run aground.

Jimmy Carter broke the deadlock by inviting both men to Camp David, the presidential retreat in Maryland, for face-to-face talks. For two weeks in September 1978 they hammered out peace accords. Although several important issues were left unresolved, Begin did agree to return the

Sinai to Egypt. In return, Egypt promised to recognize Israel, and as a result became a staunch U.S. ally. For Carter it was a proud moment. Unfortunately, the Camp David accords were denounced by the rest of the Arab Middle East, and in 1981 Sadat paid for his vision with his life when anti-Israeli Egyptian soldiers assassinated him.

In 1978 Carter also pushed the Panama Canal Treaty through the Senate, which provided for the return of the Canal Zone to Panama and improved the image of the United States in Latin America. One year later he extended diplomatic recognition to the People's Republic of China. Carter's successes in the international arena, however, would soon be overshadowed by the greatest challenge of his presidency—the Iran hostage crisis.

No Islands of Stability

One of the tragic aspects of American foreign policy is that the United States historically has supported many countries that hold power through murder, torture, and other violations of human rights, practices which are an affront to basic American values. During the presidency of Jimmy Carter, the United States began to show a growing regard for the human rights practices of its allies. Carter was convinced that American foreign policy should embody the country's basic moral beliefs. In 1977 Congress began to require reports on human rights conditions in countries receiving American aid.

Of the nations accused of practicing torture, one of the most frequently cited was Iran. Estimates of the number of political prisoners in

Jimmy Carter's greatest triumph as president came with the signing of the Camp David accords between Egypt and Israel.

Iran ranged from 25,000 to 100,000. It was widely believed that most of them had been tortured by SAVAK, the secret police.

Since the end of World War II, Iran had been a valuable friend of the United States in the troubled Middle East. In 1953 the CIA had worked to ensure the power of the young shah, Mohammad Reza Pahlavi. During the next 25 years, the shah often repaid the debt. He allowed the United States to establish electronic listening posts in northern Iran along the border of the Soviet Union, and during the 1973–1974 Arab oil embargo the shah continued to sell oil to the United States. The shah also bought arms from the United States, which helped ease the American balance-of-payments problem. Few world leaders were more loyal to the United States.

Like his predecessors, Carter was willing to overlook the shah's violations of human rights. To demonstrate American support, Carter visited Iran in late December 1977. He applauded Iran as "an island of stability in one of the most troubled areas of the world" and praised the shah as a great leader who had won "the respect and the admiration and love" of his people.

The shah was indeed popular among wealthy Iranians, but in the slums of Teheran and in rural, poverty-stricken villages, there was little respect, admiration, or love for his regime. Led by a fundamentalist Islamic clergy and emboldened by want, the masses of Iranians turned against the shah and his westernization policies.

In the early fall of 1978 the revolutionary surge in Iran gained force. The shah, who had once seemed so powerful and secure, was paralyzed by indecision, alternating between ruthless suppression and attempts to liberalize his regime. In Washington, Carter also vacillated, uncertain whether to stand firmly behind the shah or to cut his losses and prepare to deal with a new government in Iran.

In January 1979, the shah fled to Egypt. Exiled religious leader Ayatollah Ruholla Khomeini returned to Iran, preaching the doctrine that the United States was the "Great Satan" behind the shah. Relations between the United States and the new Iranian government were terrible, but Iranian officials warned that they would become infinitely worse if the shah were granted asylum. Nevertheless, Carter permitted the shah to enter the United States for treatment of lymphoma. The reaction in Iran was severe.

On November 4, 1979, Iranian supporters of Khomeini invaded the American embassy in Teheran and captured 66 Americans, 13 of whom were freed several weeks later. The rest were held hostage for 444 days and were the objects of intense political interest and media coverage.

Carter was helpless. Because Iran was not a stable country in any recognizable sense, its government was not susceptible to pressure. Iran's demands—the return of the shah to Iran and admission of U.S. guilt in supporting the shah—were unacceptable. Carter devoted far too much attention to the almost insoluble problem. The hostages stayed in the public spotlight in part because Carter kept them there.

Carter's foreign policy problems mounted in December 1979, when the Soviet Union sent tanks into Afghanistan. In response, the Carter administration embargoed grain and high-technology exports to the Soviet Union and boycotted the 1980 Olympics in Moscow. (The Soviet Union gradually withdrew its troops a decade later.)

As public disapproval of the president's handling of the Iran crisis increased, some Carter advisers advocated the use of force to free the hostages. At first, Carter disagreed, but eventually he authorized a rescue attempt. It failed, and Carter's position became even worse. Negotiations finally brought the hostages' release, but in a final humiliation for Carter, the hostages were held until minutes after Ronald Reagan, Carter's successor, had taken the oath of office as president.

When Carter left office in January 1981 many Americans judged his presidency a failure. Instead of being remembered for the good he accom-

After 444 days the Iranian hostage crisis ended, but not before it had virtually paralyzed Carter's administration and destroyed his chances for reelection.

plished for the Middle East at Camp David, he was remembered for what he failed to accomplish. The Iranian hostage crisis had become emblematic of a perception that America's role in the world had declined.

The Reagan Revolution

The traumatic events of the 1970s—Watergate, stagflation, the energy crisis, the decline of American industy, the defeat of South Vietnam, and the Iranian hostage crisis—produced a severe loss of confidence among the American people. Americans were deeply troubled by the relative loss of American strength in the world; the decline of productivity and innovation in American industry; and the dramatic growth of lobbies and special-interest groups that seemed to have paralyzed the legislative process. Many worried that too much power had been stripped from the presidency, that political parties were so weakened and Congress so splintered that it was impossible to enact a coherent legislative program.

Ronald Reagan capitalized on the public's frustration. When he ran for the presidency against Carter in 1980, he asked Americans, "Are you better off than you were four years ago?" With annual inflation at 18 percent, the answer was a resounding "No." Reagan won a landslide victory, carrying 43 states and almost 51 percent of the popular vote compared to Carter's 41 percent. In addition, the Democrats lost the Senate for the first time since 1954.

The Gipper

When he was elected president in 1980, Ronald Reagan was already well known to the American people as a movie actor and television announcer. He had risen to celebrity status from extremely modest beginnings. Born in 1911, Reagan, the son of a shoe salesman, grew up in a succession of small Illinois towns. After a stint as a sportscaster at a radio station in Des Moines, Reagan landed a Hollywood screen test in 1937. He went on to make 50 films, most of them B movies. Often remembered for his performance in *Knute Rockne, All American* (1940), Reagan played George Gipp, the Notre Dame halfback, whose dying words were "win one for the gipper." After World War II he served as president of the Screen Actors Guild, and in 1954 he turned to television, hosting "GE Theater" and "Death Valley Days."

In politics, he started out as a liberal, staunchly supporting Franklin D. Roosevelt and the New Deal. As head of the Screen Actors Guild, however, he became concerned about Communist infiltration of the labor movement in Hollywood. Reagan was catapulted into the national political spotlight in 1964 when he gave an emotional speech in support of Republican nominee Barry Goldwater, denouncing big government, foreign aid, welfare, urban renewal, and high taxes. Two years later, he successfully ran for governor of California, promising to cut state spending and crack down on student protesters.

In the 1980 presidential campaign Reagan drew strong support from white southerners, suburban Roman Catholics, evangelical Christians, and particularly the New Right, a confederation of disparate political and religious groups bound together by their concern over what they considered the erosion of values in America.

Reaganomics

When President Reagan took office he promised to rebuild the nation's defenses, restore economic growth, and trim the size of the federal government by limiting its role in welfare, education, and housing. He pledged to end exorbitant union contracts to make American goods competitive again, to cut taxes drastically to stimulate investment and purchasing power, and to decontrol businesses strangled by federal regulation. Even though his policies trimmed little from the size of the federal government, failed to make American goods competitive in the world market, and led to increased consolidation rather than competition—many Americans believed that he had improved the country's economic situation.

Reagan blamed the nation's economic ills on declining capital investment and a tax structure biased against work and productive investment. To stimulate the economy, he persuaded Congress to slash tax rates. In 1981 he pushed a bill through Congress cutting taxes 5 percent in 1981 and 10 percent in 1982 and 1983. In 1986 the administration pushed through another tax bill, which substantially reduced tax rates on the wealthiest Americans to 28 percent, while closing a variety of tax loopholes.

In August 1981 Reagan dealt a devastating blow to organized labor by firing 15,000 striking air-traffic controllers. Union leaders condemned the firings, but in an antiunion atmosphere most Americans backed Reagan. His popularity ratings soared.

To strengthen the nation's defenses, the Reagan administration doubled the defense budget, to more than $330 billion by 1987. Reagan believed that a militarily strong America would not have been humiliated by Iran and would have discouraged Soviet adventurism.

Reagan expanded the Carter administration's efforts to decontrol and deregulate the economy. Congress deregulated the banking and natural gas industries and lifted ceilings on interest rates. Federal price controls on airfares were lifted as well. The Environmental Protection Agency relaxed its interpretation of the Clean Air Act; and the Department of the Interior opened up large areas of the federal domain, including offshore oil fields, to private development.

The results of deregulation were mixed. Bank interest rates became more competitive, but smaller banks found it difficult to hold their own against larger institutions. Natural gas prices increased, but so did production, easing some of the country's dependence on foreign fuel. Airfares on high-traffic routes between major cities dropped dramatically, but fares for short, low-traffic flights skyrocketed. Most critics agreed, however, that deregulation had restored some short-term competition to the marketplace. Yet in the long term, competition also led to increased business failures and consolidation.

Reagan's laissez-faire principles could also be seen in his administration's approach to social programs. Convinced that federal welfare programs promoted laziness, promiscuity, and moral decay, Reagan limited benefits to those he considered the "truly needy." His administration cut spending on a variety of social welfare programs, including Aid to Families with Dependent Children; food stamps; child nutrition; job training for young people; programs to prevent child abuse; and mental health services. The Reagan administration also eliminated welfare assistance for the working poor, and reduced federal subsidies for child-care services for low-income families. A symbol of Reagan social service cuts was an attempt by the Agriculture Department in 1981 to allow ketchup to be counted as a vegetable in school lunches.

Reagan left office with the economy in the midst of its longest post-World War II expansion. The economy was growing faster, with less inflation, than at any time since the mid-1960s. Adjusted for inflation, disposable personal income per person rose 20 percent after 1980. Inflation fell from 13 percent in 1981 to less than 4 percent annually. Unemployment was down to around 5 percent.

Critics, however, charged that Reagan had only created the illusion of prosperity. They denounced the massive federal budget deficit, which increased $1.5 trillion during the Reagan presidency, three times the debt accumulated by all 39 of Reagan's presidential predecessors. They decried the growing income gap between rich and poor, as well as the expensive consequences of reduced government regulation, such as cleaning up federal nuclear weapons facilities, and, especially, bailing out the nation's savings and loans industry.

The Celebration of Wealth

In 1981, the year Ronald Reagan was inaugurated as president, ABC television introduced the smash hit "Dynasty," a show celebrating glamour and greed. It was, in the eyes of many social commentators, an appropriate beginning for the 1980s—a decade of selfishness and an anything-goes attitude.

Wall Street enthuasistically took part in the new celebration of wealth, as the Reagan years witnessed a corporate merger and takeover boom of unprecedented proportions. By using low-grade, risky "junk bonds" to finance corporate acquisitions, corporate raiders such as Michael Milken of Drexel, Burnham, Lambert purchased and then dismantled companies for huge profits. In 1987, Milken earned $550 million by financing acquisitions.

During the 1980s, 100,000 Americans became millionaires every year. The average annual earnings of the bottom 20 percent, however, fell from $9,376 to $8,800. In addition, many of the new jobs created during the Reagan years were in the low-wage service industries.

By the early 1990s, there were signs that the time had come to pay for the financial excesses of the 1980s. Following a 508-point fall in the Dow Jones industrial average on October 19, 1987—a 22.6 percent plunge in stock values—many Wall Street stock brokerage firms began to lay off employees, cutbacks which continued despite the market's recovery. In 1989 Milken was indicted on charges of criminal racketeering and securities fraud. The next year Drexel, Burnham Lambert agreed to pay a fine of $650 million and filed for bankruptcy. Wall Street speculator Ivan Boesky was fined $100 million for insider trading and sentenced to jail. Those Americans who had fostered in the ambition, greed, and excesses of the eighties seemed to be getting their comeuppance.

The Reagan Doctrine

During the early years of the Reagan presidency, Cold War tensions between the Soviet Union and the United States intensified. Reagan entered office deeply suspicious of the Soviet Union. Reagan described the Soviet Union as "an evil empire" and called for a space-based missile defense system, derided by critics as "Star Wars."

Reagan and his advisers tended to view every regional conflict through a Cold War lens. Nowhere was this more true than in the Western Hemisphere, where he was determined to prevent Communist takeovers. In October 1983 Prime Minister Maurice Bishop of Grenada, a small island nation in the Caribbean, was assassinated and a more radical Marxist government took power. Soviet money and Cuban troops came to Grenada, and when they began constructing an airfield capable of landing large military aircraft, the Reagan administration decided to remove the Communists and restore a pro-American regime. On October 25 U.S. troops invaded Grenada, killed or captured 750 Cuban soldiers, and established a new government. The invasion sent a clear message throughout the region that the Reagan administration would not tolerate communism in its hemisphere.

In his 1985 state of the union address President Reagan pledged his support for anti-Communist revolutions in what would become known as the "Reagan Doctrine." In Afghanistan the United States was already providing aid to anti-Soviet freedom fighters, ultimately helping to force Soviet troops to withdraw. It was in Nicaragua, however, that the doctrine received its most controversial application.

In 1979 Nicaraguans revolted against the corrupt Somoza regime. A new junta took power, dominated by young Marxists known as Sandinistas. The Sandinistas insisted that they favored free elections, nonalign-

U.S. Involvement in Central America and the Caribbean

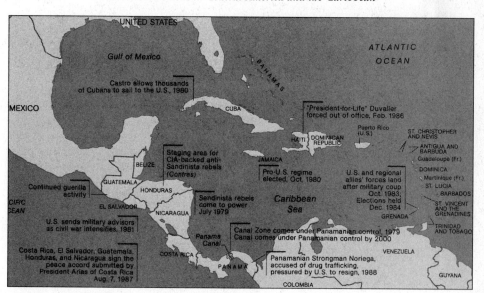

ment, and a mixed economy, but once in power they postponed elections, forced opposition leaders into exile, and turned to the Soviet bloc for arms and advisers. For the Reagan administration, Nicaragua looked "like another Cuba," a Communist state that threatened the security of its Central American neighbors.

In his first months in office President Reagan approved covert training of anti-Sandinista rebels (called "contras"). While the contras waged war on the Sandinistas from camps in Honduras, the CIA provided assistance. In 1984 Congress ordered an end to all covert aid to the contras.

The Reagan administration circumvented Congress by soliciting contributions for the contras from private individuals and from foreign governments seeking U.S. favor. The president also permitted the sale of arms to Iran, with profits diverted to the contras. The arms sale and transfer of funds to the contras were handled surreptitiously through the CIA intelligence network, apparently with the full support of CIA director William Casey. Exposure of the Iran-Contra affair in late 1986 provoked a major congressional investigation. The scandal seriously weakened the influence of the president.

The American preoccupation with Nicaragua began to subside in 1987, after President Oscar Arias Sanches of Costa Rica proposed a regional peace plan. In national elections in 1990 the Nicaraguan opposition routed the Sandinistas, bringing an end to ten turbulent years of Sandinista rule.

A Remarkable Ideological Turnaround

In 1982, 75-year-old Soviet party leader Leonid Brezhnev died. His regime had been marked by growing stagnation, corruption, and a huge military buildup. Initially, the post-Brezhnev era seemed to offer little change in U.S.- Soviet relations. KGB leader Yuri Andropov succeeded Brezhnev, but died after only 15 months in power. He was replaced by another Brezhnev loyalist, Konstantin Chernenko, who died just a year later. In 1985 Soviet party leadership passed to Mikhail S. Gorbachev, a 54-year-old agricultural specialist with little formal experience in foreign affairs who pledged to continue the policies of his predecessors.

Within weeks, however, Gorbachev called for sweeping political liberalization—*glasnost*—and economic reform—*perestroika*. He allowed wider freedom of press, assembly, travel, and religion. He persuaded the Communist party leadership to end its monopoly on power; created the Soviet Union's first working legislature; allowed the first nationwide competitive elections in 1989; and freed hundreds of political prisoners. In an effort to boost the sagging Soviet economy, he legalized small private business cooperatives, relaxed laws prohibiting land ownership, and approved foreign investment within the Soviet Union.

In foreign affairs Gorbachev completely reshaped world politics. He cut the Soviet defense budget, withdrew Soviet troops from Afghanistan and Eastern Europe, allowed a unified Germany to become a member of NATO, and agreed with the United States to destroy short-range and medium-range nuclear weapons. Most dramatically, Gorbachev actively promoted the democratization of former satellite nations in Eastern Europe. For his accomplishments in defusing Cold War tensions, he was awarded the 1990 Nobel Peace Prize.

The Reagan Revolution in Perspective

In the presidential election of 1984 Ronald Reagan and Vice President George Bush won in a landslide over Walter Mondale and Geraldine Ferraro, the first woman nominated for vice president on a major party ticket. Although Reagan's second term was plagued by the Iran-contra scandal, he left office after eight years more popular than he arrived. He could claim the distinction of being the first president to serve two full terms since Dwight Eisenhower.

Ronald Reagan could also point to an extraordinary string of accomplishments. He dampened inflation, restored public confidence in government, and presided over the beginning of the end of the Cold War. He doubled the defense budget, named the first woman to the Supreme Court, launched a strong economic boom, and created a heightened sense of national unity. In addition, his supporters said that he restored vigor to the national economy and psyche, rebuilt America's military might, regained the nation's place as the world's preeminent power, restored American patriotism, and championed traditional family values.

On the other hand, his detractors criticized him for a reckless use of military power, and for circumventing Congress in foreign affairs. They accused Reagan of fostering greed and intolerance, and they charged that his administration, in its zeal to cut waste from government, ripped the social safety net and skimped on the government's regulatory functions. The administration, they further charged, was insensitive on racial issues.

Reagan's detractors were particularly concerned about his economic legacy. During the Reagan years the national debt tripled, from $909 billion to almost $2.9 trillion (the interest alone amounted to 14 percent of the federal budget) soaking up savings, causing interest rates to rise, and forcing the federal government to shift more and more responsibilities onto the states. Corporate and individual debt also soared. During the early 1990s the American people consumed $1 trillion more goods and services than they produced. The United States also became the world's biggest debtor nation, as a result of a weak dollar, a low level of exports, and the need to borrow abroad to finance budget deficits.

The Bush Presidency

In the 1988 presidential campaign the Republican candidate, Vice President George Bush, was said to have the best résumé in Washington. Winning the Distinguished Service Cross during World War II, Bush had made a fortune in the Texas oil business, and then went to Washington where he served as a Congressman, ambassador to the United Nations, envoy to China, and director of the CIA. His Democratic opponent, Massachusetts governor Michael Dukakis, was a serious, hardworking son of Greek immigrants.

Mudslinging and personal invective are nothing new in American politics, but the 1988 campaign was unusually vacuous and cynical. Real differences between the candidates were submerged in a battle over character, abortion, prison furloughs, school prayer, and patriotism. The campaign dramatized a development that had been reshaping American politics since the late 1960s: the growing power of media consultants and pollsters, who marketed candidates by emphasizing imagery and symbolism. At the end of a race that saw both candidates use negative campaigning, Bush was elected the forty-first president of the United States, with 56 percent of the popular vote.

A Kinder, Gentler Nation

In his inaugural address, Bush signaled a departure from the avarice and greed of the Reagan era by calling for a "new engagement in the lives of others." He promised to be more of a "hands on" administrator than his predecessor, and he committed his presidency to creating a "kinder, gentler" nation, more sensitive and caring to the poor and disadvantaged.

During his first years in office President Bush and the Democratic-controlled Congress addressed many issues ignored during the Reagan years. For the first time in eight years, the minimum wage was raised from $3.35 to $4.25 an hour. Congress amended federal air pollution laws in order to reduce noxious emissions and acid rain. For the first time since 1971, Congress considered child-care legislation, and ultimately voted to provide subsidies to low-income families to defray the costs of child care. In other actions, Congress prohibited job discrimination against the disabled, required nutrition labeling on processed foods, and expanded immigration into the United States.

In two areas critics accused President Bush of reneging on his promise of a "kinder, gentler" nation. He vetoed a new civil rights bill bolstering protections for minorities and women against job discrimination, on the grounds that it would lead to quotas, and he also vetoed a bill that would have provided up to six months of unpaid family leave for workers with newly born or adopted children or emergencies. In November 1991, however, Bush signed a compromise Civil Rights Act, which made it easier for workers to win antidiscrimination lawsuits.

Economic Policy

Many Americans believed that the end of the Cold War would bring a huge peace dividend, which could be used to reduce the federal budget deficit and fund domestic social programs. Soon after Bush took office, however, Americans learned that much of the peace dividend would have to be spent to clean up nuclear wastes produced at federal facilities and to bail out the nation's troubled savings and loan industry.

The roots of the savings and loan crisis were planted during the presidency of Jimmy Carter, when high inflation and high interest rates threatened to bankrupt savings institutions, which could not compete with other financial institutions permitted to pay high interest rates. A 1980 law lifted limits on the interest rates that savings institutions could pay and allowed them to make a limited amount of investments in commercial real estate. In 1982 and 1983 Congress broadened the banking industry's capacity to make unsecured commercial loans and investments in commercial real estate.

The savings and loan industry's problems began in the mid-1980s, when falling oil prices led to a collapse of land values, especially in the Southwest, creating huge losses for institutions that had invested in real estate. By the end of the decade these institutions began to fail in large numbers. The mounting bills for the savings and loan bailout propelled President Bush in 1990 to violate his 1988 "no new taxes" campaign pledge.

Foreign Policy

The first important foreign policy act of the Bush administration was an invasion of Panama, which the Pentagon called Operation Just Cause. The origins of the conflict stretched back to 1987 when a high Panamanian military official accused strong-man General Manuel Antonio Noriega of committing fraud in the 1984 presidential election and of drug trafficking. Violent street demonstrations broke out in Panama, as angry Panamanians called for Noriega's overthrow. Noriega responded by declaring a state of emergency. The crisis escalated when two Florida grand juries indicted the general on charges that he protected and assisted the Colombian drug cartel.

U.S.-Panamanian relations deteriorated further when Noriega voided results of the 1989 presidential election and sent paramilitary forces into the streets of Panama City where they beat up opposition candidates. Conflict grew imminent when Noriega declared his country in a "state of war" against the United States. A day later four unarmed American military personnel were fired on at a roadblock by Panamanian troops, and one American was killed. Bush dispatched a force of 10,000 troops to safeguard the lives of Americans and protect the integrity of the Panama Canal treaties. Between 300 and 800 Panamanian civilians and military personnel died during the invasion; there were 23 American casualties. Noriega was forced out of power and deported to the United States to stand trial for drug trafficking.

Collapse of Communism

For 40 years Communist party leaders in Eastern Europe had ruled confidently. Although each year their countries fell further behind the West, they remained secure in the knowledge that the Soviet Union, backed by the Red Army, would always send in the tanks when the forces for change became too great. But they had not bargained on a liberal Soviet leader like Mikhail Gorbachev.

As Gorbachev moved toward reform within the Soviet Union and détente with the West, he pushed the conservative regimes of Eastern Europe outside his protective umbrella. By the end of 1989 the Berlin Wall had been smashed and across Eastern Europe citizens took to the streets, overthrowing 40 years of Communist rule. Like a series of falling dominos, Communist parties in Poland, East Germany, Hungary, Czechoslovakia, Romania, and Bulgaria fell from power.

Gorbachev, who had wanted to reform communism, may not have anticipated the swift swing toward democracy in Eastern Europe. Nor had he fully foreseen the impact that democracy in Eastern Europe would have on the Soviet Union. By 1990 leaders of several Soviet republics began to demand independence or greater autonomy within the Soviet Union.

Gorbachev had to balance the growing demand for radical political change within the Soviet Union with the demand by Communist hardliners that he contain the new democratic currents and turn back the clock. Faced with dangerous political opposition from the right and the left and with economic failure throughout the Soviet Union, Gorbachev tried to satisfy everyone and in the process satisfied no one.

For nearly three decades the Berlin Wall was the most visible symbol of the Cold War and of the division between East and West. The most dramatic incident marking the end of the Cold War was the destruction of the Wall in November 1989.

In 1990, following the example of eastern Europe, the three Baltic states of Lithuania, Latvia, and Estonia announced their independence and other Soviet republics demanded greater sovereigny. Nine of the 15 Soviet republics agreed to sign a new union treaty, granting far greater freedom and autonomy to individual republics. But in August 1991, before the treaty could be signed, conservative communists tried to oust Gorbachev in a coup d'etat. Boris Yeltsin, the President of the Russian Republic and his supporters defeated the coup, which undermined support for the Communist party. Gorbachev fell from power. The Soviet Union ended its existence in December 1991, when Russia and most other republics formed the Commonwealth of Independent States.

The Persian Gulf War

At 2 A.M., August 2, 1990, 80,000 Iraqi troops invaded and occupied Kuwait, a small, oil-rich emirate on the Persian Gulf, touching off the first major international crisis of the post-Cold War era. Iraq's leader, Saddam Hussein, justified the invasion on the grounds that Kuwait, which he accused of intentionally depressing world oil prices, was a historic part of Iraq.

Iraq's invasion caught the United States off guard. The Hussein regime was a brutal military dictatorship that ruled by secret police and used poison gas against Iranians, Kurds, and Shiite Moslems. During the 1970s and 1980s the United States—and Britain, France, the Soviet Union, West Germany—sold Iraq an awesome arsenal that included missiles, tanks, and the equipment needed to produce biological, chemical, and nuclear weapons. During Baghdad's eight-year-long war with Iran, the United States, which opposed the growth of Muslim fundamentalist extremism, tilted toward Iraq.

On August 6, 1990, President Bush dramatically declared, "This aggression will not stand." With Iraqi forces poised near the Saudi Arabian border, the Bush administration dispatched 180,000 troops to protect the Saudi kingdom. In a sharp departure from American foreign policy during the Reagan presidency, Bush also organized an international coalition against Iraq, convincing Turkey and Syria to close Iraqi oil pipelines, winning Soviet support for an arms embargo, and establishing a multinational army to protect Saudi Arabia. In the United Nations the administration succeeded in persuading the Security Council to adopt a series of resolutions condemning the Iraqi invasion, demanding restoration of the Kuwaiti government, and imposing an economic blockade.

Bush's decision to resist Iraqi aggression reflected the president's assessment of vital national interests. Iraq's invasion gave Saddam Hussein direct control over a significant portion of the world's oil supply. It disrupted the Middle East balance of power and placed Saudi Arabia and the Persian Gulf emirates in jeopardy. Iraq's 545,000-man army threatened the security of such valuable U.S. allies as Egypt and Israel.

In November 1990, the crisis took a dramatic turn. President Bush doubled the size of American forces deployed in the Persian Gulf, a sign that the administration was prepared to eject Iraq from Kuwait by force. The president went to the United Nations for a resolution permitting the use of force against Iraq if it did not withdraw by January 15, 1991. After a heated debate, Congress also gave the president authority to wage war.

President Bush's decision to liberate Kuwait was an enormous political and military gamble. The Iraqi army, the world's fourth largest, was equipped with Exocet missiles, top-of-the-line Soviet T-72 tanks, and long-range artillery capable of firing nerve gas. But after a month of allied bombing, the coalition forces had achieved air supremacy and destroyed thousands of Iraqi tanks and artillery pieces, supply routes and communications lines, command-and-control bunkers, and limited Iraq's ability to produce nuclear, chemical, and biological weapons. Iraqi troop morale suffered so badly under the bombing that an estimated 30 percent of Baghdad's forces deserted before the ground campaign started.

The allied ground campaign relied on deception, mobility, and overwhelming air superiority to defeat a larger Iraqi army. The allied strategy was to mislead the Iraqis into believing that the allied attack would occur along the Kuwaiti coastline and Kuwait's border with Saudi Arabia. Meanwhile, General H. Norman Schwarzkopf, American commander of the coalition forces, shifted more than 300,000 American, British, and French troops into western Saudia Arabia, allowing them to strike deep into Iraq. Only 100 hours after the ground campaign started, the war ended. Saddam Hussein remained in power, but his ability to control events in the region was dramatically curtailed.

Major Action in the Persian Gulf

The Persian Gulf conflict was the most popular U.S. war since World War II, restoring American confidence in its position as the world's sole superpower and helping to exorcise the ghost of Vietnam that had haunted American foreign policy debates for nearly two decades. The doubt, drift, and demoralization that began with the Vietnam War and the Watergate scandal appeared to have ended.

Enter Bill Clinton

In the Persian Gulf War, Bush acted from clear, unequivocal principles. Convinced that it was necessary to humiliate Saddam Hussein and prove that America would resist aggression, Bush demonstrated that a determined and skillful president has the power to move a reluctant nation to support his policies.

In domestic affairs, on the other hand, Bush's leadership was less decisive. On such issues as taxes, abortion, and civil rights, he adopted a flexible, pragmatic approach that led some critics to describe him as a political chameleon. Unlike Ronald Reagan, who brought a series of fixed philosophical principles to domestic issues, Bush appeared less interested in domestic affairs and more willing to renege on his pledge not to raise taxes.

Bush's failure to alter the downward slide of the American economy played the crucial role in the 1992 presidential election. In a bitter three-way contest, marked by intense assaults on the candidates' records and characters, Arkansas Governor Bill Clinton defeated George Bush and Texas businessman Ross Perot to become the first Democratic president in 12 years. President Bush, whose popularity soared to 90 percent following the Persian Gulf War, received only 38 percent of the popular vote, to Clinton's 43 percent and Perot's 19 percent.

The central issue in the election was the nation's sluggish economy. During the Bush presidency fewer new jobs were created than in any other presidential term since World War II. Unemployment reached the highest level in eight years; personal incomes stagnated; businesses failed in record numbers; the federal debt surpassed $4 trillion; and medical care absorbed 15 percent of the nation's output, while a quarter of the population lacked health insurance. Poverty rose to the highest rate in over two decades—a fact dramatically underscored by the outbreak of the deadliest riot in America's history, in Los Angeles in April 1992.

President Clinton pledged a "new covenant" for America: a new approach to government between the unfettered free market championed by the Republicans and the welfare state economics that the Democratic party had represented in the past. Promising to focus like a laser beam on he economy, he strove to reduce the federal budget deficit by raising taxes on the wealthiest Americans and on gasoline and cutting government spending. To create jobs, he sought to stimulate world trade. In late 1993 he convinced Congress to pass the North American Free Trade Agreement (NAFTA), eliminating tariff barriers between Canada, Mexico, and the United States, and also completed negotiations on the General Agreement on Trade and Tariffs (GATT), reducing global trading barriers.

Clinton committed his administration to ending twelve years of "legislative gridlock" and "social neglect." To aid working parents, he signed parental leave legislation, allowing parents to take unpaid job leaves during family emergencies. To combat violent crime, he persuaded Congress to enact a waiting period for handgun purchases and a ban on the sale of assault weapons. He also revised policies that had excluded homosexuals from the military and pledged to eliminate "welfare as we know it," by replacing welfare dependency with programs emphasizing education and job training. The centerpiece of Clinton's legislative agenda was a program of universal health care coverage—the largest federal social welfare initiative since Social Security during the Great Depression—to guarantee lifelong care to the millions of Americans without health insurance.

In foreign policy, his administration witnessed the end of apartheid in South Africa and the replacement of white rule with a multiracial democracy, as well as the Israeli transfer of control over the Gaza Strip and portions of the West Bank to the Palestine Liberation Organization. The Clinton administration also ended a longstanding U.S. trade embargo with Vietnam.

Conclusion

As the twentieth century draws to a close, America's ideals of democracy and personal freedom are ascendant across the world. From Tiananmen Square—where Chinese students erected a goddess of liberty modeled on the Statue of Liberty—to the Philippines, popular protests and demonstrations have called for "government of the people, by the people, and for the people." In Eastern Europe, the former Soviet Union, and across Latin America, people demand free speech, freedom of religion, freedom of the press, and free markets.

Yet paradoxically, as American ideals and values flourish abroad, Americans are anxious about their economy and their country's future. Many are angry, expressing cynical contempt toward their government. Many fear that American competitiveness and inventiveness are declining. Other nations, such as Japan and Germany, save more and

Chronology of Key Events

1971	Nixon authorizes establishment of "plumbers" unit
1972	Watergate burglars arrested; President Nixon takes part in summit in China; President Nixon reelected
1973	Senate Watergate hearings begin; Spiro Agnew resigns
1974	House Judiciary Committee adopts three articles of impeachment against President Nixon; Nixon resigns; Ford becomes thirty-eighth president; Federal Campaign Reform Act
1976	Jimmy Carter elected thirty-ninth president
1978	President Carter mediates Egyptian-Israeli peace settlement; Iranian revolution begins
1979	United States recognizes China; Iranian militants seize American hostages; Soviet Union invades Afghanistan; Somoza regime in Nicaragua overthrown
1980	Ronald Reagan elected fortieth president
1981	American hostages released from Iran; Reagan approves covert training of anti-Sandinista contras; Reagan tax cuts are approved
1982	Congress deregulates banking industry and lifts controls on air fares
1983	Reagan proposes "Star Wars" missile defense system: United States topples Communist government of Grenada
1985	United States begins secret arms-for-hostages negotiations with Iran; Mikhail Gorbachev becomes Soviet leader
1986	Profits from Iranian arms sales are diverted to Nicaraguan contras
1987	Iran-Contra hearings; stock market plunges
1988	George Bush elected forty-first president
1989	Communist regimes collapse in Eastern Europe
1990	Iraqi troops invade Kuwait
1991	Persian Gulf War; independence for Soviet republics
1992	Bill Clinton elected forty-second president

invest more than the United States, and their economies have been growing faster. Except for a few areas of trade—such as high-tech products, financial services, and aircraft—foreign countries dominate the most technologically advanced fields, such as consumer electronics, luxury automobiles, and machine tools. No longer does the United States possess the world's highest level of per capita income. Particularly troubling are the national debt and federal deficit, which stand at record levels.

Americans also worry about crime, the state of their central cities, and the quality of health and education in their society. The level of crime and violence in the United States is the highest in the industrialized world, as are America's rates of drug use, juvenile delinquency, teenage pregnancy, and teen suicide.

At the end of World War II many commentators referred to the twentieth century as the "American century." Today the United States remains the mightiest, most productive nation in the world, a model of freedom and pluralism that people across the globe still strive to emulate. The great question to be asked as the century comes to an end is whether Americans have the will to solve the many problems that confront their cities, their schools, and their physical environment.

Suggestions for Further Reading

Informative surveys of recent American life include Michael Barone, *Our Country* (1990); Peter N. Carroll, *It Seemed Like Nothing Happened: The Tragedy and Promise of the 1970s* (1990); Kim McQuaid, *The Anxious Years* (1989).

On Watergate and its consequences, consult Stanley I. Kutler, *The Wars of Watergate* (1990); Theodore White, *Breach of Faith* (1975). For more on the Republican presidencies in the 1970s, see James Reichley, *Conservatives in an Age of Change* (1981); Edward L. and Frederick H. Schapsmeier, *Gerald R. Ford's Date with Destiny* (1989).

The Carter presidency is examined in James A. Bill, *The Eagle and the Lion* (1988); Charles O. Jones, *The Trustee Presidency* (1988); Gaddis Smith, *Morality, Reason and Power: American Diplomacy in the Carter Years* (1986). See also Carter's memoir, *Keeping Faith* (1982). For a study of the oil crisis, consult Daniel Yergin, *The Prize* (1990).

For analyses of Reagan and the Reagan years see Sidney Blumenthal, *Our Long National Daydream* (1988); Paul Boyer, ed., *Reagan as President* (1990);

Lou Cannon, *President Reagan: The Role of a Lifetime* (1991); Robert Dallek, *Ronald Reagan: The Politics of Symbolism* (1984); Theodore Draper, *A Very Thin Line: The Iran-Contra Affairs* (1991); Haynes Johnson, *Sleepwalking Through History: America in the Reagan Years* (1991); Garry Wills, *Reagan's America* (1987). Aspects of the post-Reagan era are examined in Kevin Buckley, *Panama: The Whole Story* (1991); Lawrence J. White, *The S&L Debacle* (1991); Bob Woodward, *The Commanders* (1991).

Appendix

The Declaration of Independence
The Constitution of the United States of America
Amendments to the Constitution
Presidential Elections, 1789–1992
Presidential Administrations
Supreme Court Justices
Admission of States to the Union

The Declaration of Independence

When in the Course of human events, it becomes necessary for one people to dissolve the political bands which have connected them with another, and to assume among the Powers of the earth, the separate and equal station to which the Laws of Nature and of Nature's God entitle them, a decent respect to the opinions of mankind requires that they should declare the causes which impel them to the separation.

We hold these truths to be self-evident, that all men are created equal, that they are endowed by their Creator with certain unalienable Rights, that among these are Life, Liberty and the pursuit of Happiness. That to secure these rights, Governments are instituted among Men, deriving their just powers from the consent of the governed. That whenever any Form of Government becomes destructive of these ends, it is the Right of the People to alter or to abolish it, and to institute new Government, laying its foundation on such principles and organizing its powers in such form, as to them shall seem most likely to effect their Safety and Happiness. Prudence, indeed, will dictate that Governments long established should not be changed for light and transient causes; and accordingly all experience hath shown, that mankind are more disposed to suffer, while evils are sufferable, than to right themselves by abolishing the forms to which they are accustomed. But when a long train of abuses and usurpations, pursuing invariably the same Object evinces a design to reduce them under absolute Despotism, it is their right, it is their duty, to throw off such Government, and to provide new Guards for their future security.—Such has been the patient sufferance of these Colonies; and such is now the necessity which constrains them to alter their former Systems of Government. The history of the present King of Great Britain is a history of repeated injuries and usurpations, all having in direct object the establishment of an absolute Tyranny over these States. To prove this, let Facts be submitted to a candid world.

He has refused his Assent to Laws, the most wholesome and necessary for the public good.

He has forbidden his Governors to pass Laws of immediate and pressing importance, unless suspended in their operation till his Assent should be obtained; and when so suspended, he has utterly neglected to attend to them.

He has refused to pass other Laws for the accommodation of large districts of people, unless those people would relinquish the right of Representation in the Legislature, a right inestimable to them and formidable to tyrants only.

He has called together legislative bodies at places unusual, uncomfortable, and distant from the depository of their Public Records, for the sole purpose of fatiguing them into compliance with his measures.

He has dissolved Representative Houses repeatedly, for opposing with manly firmness his invasions on the rights of the people.

He has refused for a long time, after such dissolutions, to cause others to be elected; whereby the Legislative Powers, incapable of Annihilation, have returned to the People at large for their exercise; the State remaining in the mean time exposed to all the dangers of invasion from without, and convulsions within.

He has endeavoured to prevent the population of these States; for that purpose obstructing the Laws of Naturalization of Foreigners; refusing to pass others to encourage their migration hither, and raising the conditions of new Appropriations of Lands.

He has obstructed the Administration of Justice, by refusing his Assent to Laws for establishing Judiciary Powers.

He has made Judges dependent on his Will alone, for the tenure of their offices, and the amount and payment of their salaries.

He has erected a multitude of New Offices, and sent hither swarms of Officers to harass our People, and eat out their substance.

He has kept among us, in times of peace, Standing Armies without the Consent of our legislature.

He has affected to render the Military independent of and superior to the Civil Power.

He has combined with others to subject us to a jurisdiction foreign to our constitution, and unacknowledged by our laws; giving his Assent to their acts of pretended legislation:

For quartering large bodies of armed troops among us;

For protecting them, by a mock Trial, from Punishment for any Murders which they should commit on the Inhabitants of these States;

For cutting off our Trade with all parts of the world;

For imposing taxes on us without our Consent;

For depriving us in many cases, of the benefits of Trial by Jury;

For transporting us beyond Seas to be tried for pretended offences;

For abolishing the free System of English Laws in a neighbouring Province, establishing therein an Arbitrary government, and enlarging its Boundaries so as to render it at once an example and fit instrument for introducing the same absolute rule into these Colonies;

For taking away our Charters, abolishing our most valuable Laws, and altering fundamentally the Forms of our Governments;

For suspending our own Legislature, and declaring themselves invested with Power to legislate for us in all cases whatsoever.

He has abdicated Government here, by declaring us out of his Protection and waging War against us.

He has plundered our seas, ravaged our Coasts, burnt our towns, and destroyed the lives of our people.

He is at this time transporting large armies of foreign mercenaries to compleat the works of death, desolation and tyranny, already begun with circumstances of Cruelty & perfidy scarcely paralleled in the most barbarous ages, and totally unworthy the Head of a civilized nation.

He has constrained our fellow Citizens taken Captive on the high Seas to bear Arms against their Country, to become the executioners of their friends and Brethren, or to fall themselves by their Hands.

He has excited domestic insurrections amongst us, and has endeavoured to bring on the inhabitants of our frontiers, the merciless Indian Savages, whose known rule of warfare, is an undistinguished destruction of all ages, sexes and conditions.

In every stage of these Oppressions We have Petitioned for Redress in the most humble terms: Our repeated Petitions have been answered only by repeated injury. A Prince, whose character is thus marked by every act which may define a Tyrant, is unfit to be the ruler of a free People.

Nor have We been wanting in attention to our British brethren. We have warned them from time to time of attempts by their legislature to extend an unwarrantable jurisdiction over us. We have reminded them of the circumstances of our emigration and settlement here. We have appealed to their native justice and magnanimity, and we have conjured them by the ties of our common kindred to disavow these usurpations, which, would inevitably interrupt our connections and correspondence. They too have been deaf to the voice of justice and of consanguinity. We must, therefore, acquiesce in the necessity, which denounces our Separation, and hold them, as we hold the rest of mankind, Enemies in War, in Peace Friends.

We, therefore, the Representatives of the united States of America, in General Congress, Assembled, appealing to the Supreme Judge of the world for the rectitude of our intentions, do, in the Name, and by Authority of the good People of these Colonies, solemnly publish and declare, That these United Colonies are, and of Right ought to be Free and Independent States; that they are Absolved from all Allegiance to the British Crown, and that all political connection between them and the State of Great Britain, is and ought to be totally dissolved; and that as Free and Independent States, they have full Power to levy War, conclude Peace, contract Alliances, establish Commerce, and to do all other Acts and Things which Independent States may of right do. And for the support of this Declaration, with a firm reliance on the Protection of Divine

Providence, we mutually pledge to each other our Lives, our Fortunes and our sacred Honor.

John Hancock,
Josiah Bartlett, Wm Whipple, Saml Adams, John Adams, Robt Treat Paine, Elbridge Gerry, Steph. Hopkins, William Ellery, Roger Sherman, Samel Huntington, Wm Williams, Oliver Wolcott, Matthew Thornton, Wm Floyd, Phil Livingston, Frans Lewis, Lewis Morris, Richd Stockton, Jno Witherspoon, Fras Hopkinson, John Hart, Abra Clark, Robt Morris, Benjamin Rush, Benja Franklin, John Morton, Geo Clymer, Jas Smith, Geo. Taylor, James Wilson, Geo. Ross, Caesar Rodney, Geo Read, Thos M:Kean, Samuel Chase, Wm Paca, Thos Stone, Charles Carroll of Carrollton, George Wythe, Richard Henry Lee, Th. Jefferson, Benja Harrison, Thos Nelson, Jr., Francis Lightfoot Lee, Carter Braxton, Wm Hooper, Joseph Hewes, John Penn, Edward Rutledge, Thos Heyward, Junr., Thomas Lynch, Junor., Arthur Middleton, Button Gwinnett, Lyman Hall, Geo Walton.

The Constitution of the United States of America

W̶e the people of the United States, in Order to form a more perfect Union, establish Justice, insure domestic Tranquility, provide for the common defence, promote the general Welfare, and secure the Blessings of Liberty to ourselves and our Posterity, do ordain and establish this CONSTITUTION for the United States of America.

Article I

Section 1.

All legislative Powers herein granted shall be vested in a Congress of the United States, which shall consist of a Senate and House of Representatives.

Section 2.

The House of Representatives shall be composed of Members chosen every second Year by the People of the several States, and the Electors in each State shall have the Qualifications requisite for Electors of the most numerous Branch of the State Legislature.

No Person shall be a Representative who shall not have attained to the Age of twenty-five Years, and been seven Years a Citizen of the United States, and who shall not, when elected, be an Inhabitant of that State in which he shall be chosen.

Representatives and direct Taxes shall be apportioned among the several States which may be included within this Union, according to their respective Numbers, which shall be determined by adding to the whole Number of free

Persons, including those bound to Service for a Term of Years, and excluding Indians not taxed, three fifths of all other Persons. The actual Enumeration shall be made within three Years after the first Meeting of the Congress of the United States, and within every subsequent Term of ten Years, in such Manner as they shall by Law direct. The Number of Representatives shall not exceed one for every thirty Thousand, but each State shall have at Least one Representative; and until such enumeration shall be made, the State of New Hampshire shall be entitled to chuse three, Massachusetts eight, Rhode-Island and Providence Plantations one, Connecticut five, New-York six, New Jersey four, Pennsylvania eight, Delaware one, Maryland six, Virginia ten, North Carolina five, South Carolina five, and Georgia three.

When vacancies happen in the Representation from any State, the Executive Authority thereof shall issue Writs of Election to fill such Vacancies.

The House of Representatives shall chuse their Speaker and other Officers; and shall have the sole Power of Impeachment.

Section 3.

The Senate of the United States shall be composed of two Senators from each State, chosen by the Legislature thereof, for six Years; and each Senator shall have one Vote.

Immediately after they shall be assembled in Consequence of the first Election, they shall be divided as equally as may be into three Classes. The Seats of the Senators of the first Class shall be vacated at the Expiration of the second Year, of the second Class at the Expiration of the fourth Year, and of the third Class at the Expiration of the sixth Year, so that one-third may be chosen every second Year; and if Vacancies happen by Resignation, or otherwise, during the Recess of the Legislature of any State, the Executive thereof may make temporary Appointments until the next Meeting of the Legislature, which shall then fill such Vacancies.

No Person shall be a Senator who shall not have attained to the Age of thirty Years, and been nine Years a Citizen of the United States, and who shall not, when elected, be an Inhabitant of that State in which he shall be chosen.

The Vice President of the United States shall be President of the Senate, but shall have no vote, unless they be equally divided.

The Senate shall chuse their other Officers, and also a President pro tempore, in the absence of the Vice President, or when he shall exercise the Office of the President of the United States.

The Senate shall have the sole Power to try all Impeachments. When sitting for that purpose, they shall be on Oath or Affirmation. When the President of the United States is tried, the Chief Justice shall preside: And no person shall be convicted without the Concurrence of two thirds of the Members present.

Judgment in Cases of Impeachment shall not extend further than to removal from Office, and disqualification to hold and enjoy any Office of honor, Trust, or Profit under the United States: but the Party convicted shall nevertheless be liable and subject to Indictment, Trial, Judgment, and Punishment, according to Law.

Section 4.

The Times, Places and Manner of holding Elections for Senators and Representatives, shall be prescribed in each state by the Legislature thereof; but the Congress may at any time by Law make or alter such Regulations, except as to the Places of Chusing Senators.

The Congress shall assemble at least once in every Year, and such Meeting shall be on the first Monday in December, unless they shall by Law appoint a different Day.

Section 5.

Each House shall be the Judge of the Elections, Returns and Qualifications of its own Members, and a Majority of each shall constitute a Quorum to do Business; but a smaller number may adjourn from day to day, and may be authorized to compel the Attendance of absent Members, in such Manner, and under such Penalties, as each House may provide.

Each House may determine the Rules of its Proceedings, punish its Members for disorderly Behavior, and, with the Concurrence of two thirds, expel a Member.

Each House shall keep a Journal of its Proceedings, and from time to time publish the same, excepting such Parts as may in their Judgment require Secrecy; and the Yeas and Nays of the Members of either House on any question shall, at the Desire of one fifth of those Present, be entered on the Journal.

Neither House, during the Session of Congress, shall, without the Consent of the other, adjourn for more than three days, nor to any other Place than that in which the two Houses shall be sitting.

Section 6.

The Senators and Representatives shall receive a Compensation for their Services, to be ascertained by Law, and paid out of the Treasury of the United States. They shall in all Cases, except Treason, Felony, and Breach of the Peace, be privileged from arrest during their Attendance at the Session of their respective Houses, and in going to and returning from the same; and for any Speech or Debate in either House, they shall not be questioned in any other Place.

No Senator or Representative shall, during the Time for which he was elected, be appointed to any civil Office under the Authority of the United States, which shall have been created, or the Emoluments whereof shall have been increased, during such time; and no Person holding any Office under the United States shall be a Member of either House during his continuance in Office.

Section 7.

All Bills for raising Revenue shall originate in the House of Representatives; but the Senate may propose or concur with Amendments as on other bills.

Every Bill which shall have passed the House of Representatives and the Senate, shall, before it become a Law, be presented to the President of the United States; If he approve he shall sign it, but if not he shall return it, with his Objections, to that House in which it shall have originated, who shall enter the Objections at large on their Journal, and proceed to reconsider it. If after such Reconsideration two thirds of that House shall agree to pass the bill, it shall be sent, together with the objections, to the other House, by which it shall likewise be reconsidered, and if approved by two thirds of that House, it shall become a Law. But in all such Cases the Votes of both Houses shall be determined by Yeas and Nays, and the Names of the Persons voting for and against the Bill shall be entered on the Journal of each House respectively. If any Bill shall not be returned by the President within ten Days (Sundays excepted) after it shall have been presented to him, the Same shall be a Law, in like Manner as if he had signed it, unless the Congress by their Adjournment prevent its Return, in which Case it shall not be a Law.

Every Order, Resolution, or Vote to which the Concurrence of the Senate and House of Representatives may be necessary (except on a question of Adjournment) shall be presented to the President of the United States; and before the Same shall take Effect, shall be approved by him, or being disapproved by him, shall be repassed by two thirds of the Senate and House of Representatives, according to the Rules and Limitations prescribed in the Case of a Bill.

Section 8.

The Congress shall have Power To lay and collect Taxes, Duties, Imposts and Excises, to pay the Debts and provide for the common Defence and general Welfare of the United States; but all Duties, Imposts and Excises shall be uniform throughout the United States;

To borrow money on the credit of the United States;

To regulate Commerce with foreign Nations, and among the several States, and with the Indian Tribes;

To establish an uniform Rule of Naturalization, and uniform Laws on the subject of Bankruptcies throughout the United States;

To coin Money, regulate the Value thereof, and of foreign Coin, and fix the Standard of Weights and Measures;

To provide for the Punishment of counterfeiting the Securities and current Coin of the United States;

To establish Post Offices and post Roads;

To promote the Progress of Science and useful Arts, by securing for limited Times to Authors and Inventors the exclusive Right to their respective Writings and Discoveries;

To constitute Tribunals inferior to the Supreme Court;

To define and punish Piracies and Felonies committed on the high Seas, and Offences against the Law of Nations;

To declare War, grant Letters of Marque and Reprisal, and make Rules concerning Captures on Land and Water;

To raise and support Armies, but no Appropriation of Money to that Use shall be for a longer Term than two Years;

To provide and maintain a Navy:

To make Rules for the Government and Regulation of the land and naval forces;

To provide for calling forth the Militia to execute the Laws of the Union, suppress Insurrections and repel Invasions;

To provide for organizing, arming, and disciplining the Militia, and for governing such Part of them as may be employed in the Service of the United States, reserving to the States respectively, the Appointment of the Officers, and the Authority of training the Militia according to the discipline prescribed by Congress;

To exercise exclusive Legislation in all Cases whatsoever, over such District (not exceeding ten Miles square) as may, by Cession of particular States, and the acceptance of Congress, become the Seat of Government of the United States, and to exercise like Authority over all Places purchased by the Consent of the Legislature of the State in which the Same shall be, for the Erection of Forts, Magazines, Arsenals, dock-Yards, and other needful Buildings;—And

To make all Laws which shall be necessary and proper for carrying into Execution the foregoing Powers, and all other Powers vested by this Constitution in the government of the United States, or in any Department or Officer thereof.

Section 9.

The Migration or Importation of such Persons as any of the States now existing shall think proper to admit, shall not be prohibited by the Congress prior to the Year one thousand eight hundred and eight, but a tax or duty may be imposed on such Importation, not exceeding ten dollars for each Person.

The privilege of the Writ of Habeas Corpus shall not be suspended, unless when in Cases of Rebellion or Invasion the public Safety may require it.

No Bill of Attainder or ex post facto Law shall be passed.

No capitation, or other direct, Tax shall be laid unless in Proportion to the Census or Enumeration herein before directed to be taken.

No Tax or Duty shall be laid on Articles exported from any State.

No Preference shall be given by any Regulation of Revenue to the Ports of one State over those of another: nor shall Vessels bound to, or from, one State, be obliged to enter, clear, or pay Duties in another.

No Money shall be drawn from the Treasury, but in Consequence of Appropriations made by Law; and a regular Statement and Account of the Receipts and Expenditures of all public Money shall be published from time to time.

No Title of Nobility shall be granted by the United States: And no Person holding any Office of Profit or Trust under them, shall, without the Consent of the Congress, accept of any present, Emolument, Office, or Title, of any kind whatever, from any King, Prince, or foreign State.

Section 10.

No State shall enter into any Treaty, Alliance, or Confederation; grant Letters of Marque and Reprisal; coin Money; emit Bills of Credit; make any Thing but gold and silver Coin a Tender in Payment of Debts; pass any Bill of Attainder, ex post facto Law, or Law impairing the Obligation of Contracts, or grant any Title of Nobility.

No State shall, without the Consent of the Congress, lay any Imposts or Duties on Imports or Exports, except what may be absolutely necessary for executing its inspection Laws: and the net Produce of all Duties and Imposts, laid by any State on Imports or Exports, shall be for the Use of the Treasury of the United States; and all such Laws shall be subject to the Revision and Control of the Congress.

No State shall, without the Consent of Congress, lay any duty of Tonnage, keep Troops, or Ships of War in time of Peace, enter into any Agreement or Compact with another State, or with a foreign Power, or engage in War, unless actually invaded, or in such imminent Danger as will not admit of delay.

Article II

Section 1.

The executive Power shall be vested in a President of the United States of America. He shall hold his Office during the Term of four years, and, together with the Vice President, chosen for the same Term, be elected, as follows:

Each State shall appoint, in such Manner as the Legislature thereof may direct, a Number of Electors, equal to the whole Number of Senators and Representatives to which the State may be entitled in the Congress; but no Senator or Representative, or Person holding an Office of Trust or Profit under the United States, shall be appointed an Elector.

The Electors shall meet in their respective States, and vote by Ballot for two persons, of whom one at least shall not be an Inhabitant of the same State with themselves. And they shall make a List of all the Persons voted for, and of the Number of Votes for each; which List they shall sign and certify, and transmit sealed to the Seat of the Government of the United States, directed to the President of the Senate. The President of the Senate shall, in the Presence of the Senate and House of Representatives, open all the Certificates, and the Votes shall then be counted. The Person having the greatest Number of Votes shall be the President, if such Number be a Majority of the whole Number of Electors appointed; and if there be more than one who have such Majority, and have an equal Number of Votes, then the House of Representatives shall immediately chuse by Ballot one of them for President; and if no Person have a Majority, then from the five highest on the List the said House shall in like Manner chuse the President. But in chusing the President, the votes shall be taken by States, the Representation from each State having one Vote; a quorum for this Purpose shall consist of a Member or Members from two-thirds of the States, and a Majority of all the States shall be necessary to a Choice. In every Case, after the Choice of the President, the Person having the greatest Number of Votes of the Electors shall be the Vice President. But if there should remain two or more who have equal votes, the Senate shall chuse from them by Ballot the Vice President.

The Congress may determine the time of chusing the Electors, and the Day on which they shall give their Votes; which Day shall be the same throughout the United States.

No person except a natural-born Citizen, or a Citizen of the United States, at the time of the Adoption of this Constitution, shall be eligible to the Office of President; neither shall any Person be eligible to that Office who shall not have attained to the Age of thirty-five years, and been fourteen Years a Resident within the United States.

In Case of the Removal of the President from Office, or of his Death, Resignation, or Inability to discharge the Powers and Duties of the said Office, the same shall devolve on the Vice President, and the Congress may by Law provide for the Case of Removal, Death, Resignation, or Inability, both of the President and Vice President, declaring what Officer shall then act as President, and such Officer shall act accordingly, until the disability be removed, or a President shall be elected.

The President shall, at stated Times, receive for his Services a Compensation, which shall neither be increased nor diminished during the Period for which he shall have been elected, and he shall not receive within that Period any other Emolument from the United States, or any of them.

Before he enter on the execution of his Office, he shall take the following Oath or Affirmation:—"I do solemnly swear (or affirm) that I will faithfully execute the Office of President of the United States, and will, to the best of my Ability, preserve, protect, and defend the Constitution of the United States."

Section 2.

The President shall be Commander in Chief of the Army and Navy of the United States, and of the Militia of the several States, when called into the actual Service of the United States; he may require the Opinion, in writing, of the principal Officer in each of the executive Departments, upon any subject relating to the Duties of their respective Offices, and he shall have Power to Grant Reprieves and Pardons for Offences against the United States, except in Cases of Impeachment.

He shall have Power, by and with the Advice and Consent of the Senate, to make Treaties, provided two thirds of the Senators present concur; and he shall nominate, and by and with the Advice and Consent of the Senate, shall appoint Ambassadors, other public Ministers and Consuls, Judges of the supreme Court, and all other Officers of the United States, whose Appointments are not herein otherwise provided for, and which shall be established by Law: but the Congress may by Law vest the Appointment of such inferior Officers, as they think proper, in the President alone, in the Courts of Law, or in the Heads of Departments.

The President shall have Power to fill up all Vacancies that may happen during the Recess of the Senate, by granting Commissions which shall expire at the End of their next Session.

Section 3.

He shall from time to time give to the Congress Information of the State of the Union, and recommend to their Consideration such Measures as he shall judge necessary and expedient; he may, on extraordinary occasions, convene both Houses, or either of them, and in Case of Disagreement between them, with respect to the Time of Adjournment, he may adjourn them to such Time as he shall think proper; he shall receive Ambassadors and other public Ministers; he shall take Care that the Laws be faithfully executed, and shall Commission all the Officers of the United States.

Section 4.

The President, Vice President and all civil Officers of the United States, shall be removed from Office on Impeachment for, and Conviction of, Treason, Bribery, or other high Crimes and Misdemeanors.

Article III

Section 1.

The judicial Power of the United States, shall be vested in one supreme Court, and in such inferior Courts as the Congress may from time to time ordain and establish. The Judges, both of the supreme and inferior Courts, shall hold their Offices during good Behaviour, and shall, at stated Times, receive for their Services, a Compensation, which shall not be diminished during their Continuance in Office.

Section 2.

The judicial Power shall extend to all Cases, in Law and Equity, arising under this Constitution, the Laws of the United States, and treaties made, or which shall be made, under their Authority;—to all Cases affecting ambassadors, other public ministers and consuls;—to all cases of admiralty and maritime

Jurisdiction;—to Controversies to which the United States shall be a Party;—to Controversies between two or more States;—between a State and Citizens of another State;—between Citizens of different States,—between Citizens of the same State claiming Lands under Grants of different States, and between a State, or the Citizens thereof, and foreign States, Citizens or Subjects.

In all Cases affecting Ambassadors, other public Ministers and Consuls, and those in which a State shall be Party, the supreme Court shall have original Jurisdiction. In all the other Cases before mentioned, the supreme Court shall have appellate Jurisdiction, both as to Law and Fact, with such Exceptions, and under such Regulations as the Congress shall make.

The trial of all Crimes, except in Cases of Impeachment, shall be by Jury; and such Trial shall be held in the State where the said Crimes shall have been committed; but when not committed within any State, the Trial shall be at such Place or Places as the Congress may by Law have directed.

Section 3.

Treason against the United States, shall consist only in levying War against them, or in adhering to their Enemies, giving them Aid and Comfort. No Person shall be convicted of Treason unless on the testimony of two Witnesses to the same overt Act, or on Confession in open Court.

The Congress shall have power to declare the Punishment of Treason, but no Attainder of Treason shall work Corruption of Blood, or Forfeiture except during the Life of the Person attained.

Article IV

Section 1.

Full Faith and Credit shall be given in each State to the public Acts, Records, and judicial Proceedings of every other State. And the Congress may by general Laws prescribe the Manner in which such Acts, Records and Proceedings shall be proved, and the Effect thereof.

Section 2.

The Citizens of each State shall be entitled to all Privileges and Immunities of Citizens in the several States.

A Person charged in any State with Treason, Felony, or other Crime, who shall flee from Justice, and be found in another State, shall on demand of the executive Authority of the State from which he fled, be delivered up, to be removed to the State having Jurisdiction of the crime.

No Person held to Service or Labour in one State, under the Laws thereof, escaping into another, shall, in Consequence of any Law or Regulation therein, be discharged from such Service or Labour, but shall be delivered up on Claim of the Party to whom such Service or Labour may be due.

Section 3.

New States may be admitted by the Congress into this Union; but no new State shall be formed or erected within the Jurisdiction of any other State; nor any State be formed by the Junction of two or more States, or parts of States, without the Consent of the Legislatures of the States concerned as well as of the Congress.

The Congress shall have Power to dispose of and make all needful Rules and Regulations respecting the Territory or other Property belonging to the United States; and nothing in this Constitution shall be so construed as to Prejudice any Claims of the United States, or of any particular State.

Section 4.

The United States shall guarantee to every State in this Union a Republican Form of Government, and shall protect each of them against Invasion; and on Application of the Legislature, or the Executive (when the Legislature cannot be convened) against domestic Violence.

Article V

The Congress, whenever two-thirds of both Houses shall deem it necessary, shall propose Amendments to this Constitution, or, on the Application of the Legislatures of two-thirds of the several States, shall call a Convention for proposing Amendments, which, in either Case, shall be valid to all Intents and Purposes, as part of this Constitution, when ratified by the Legislatures of three-fourths of the several States, or by Conventions in three-fourths thereof, as the one or the other Mode of Ratification may be proposed by the Congress; Provided that no Amendment which may be made prior to the Year One thousand eight hundred and eight shall in any Manner affect the first and fourth Clauses in the Ninth Section of the first Article; and that no State, without its Consent, shall be deprived of its equal Suffrage in the Senate.

Article VI

All Debts contracted and Engagements entered into, before the Adoption of this Constitution, shall be as valid against the United States under this Constitution, as under the Confederation.

This Constitution, and the Laws of the United States which shall be made in Pursuance thereof; and all Treaties made, or which shall be made, under the

Authority of the United States, shall be the supreme Law of the Land; and the Judges in every State shall be bound thereby, any Thing in the Constitution or Laws of any State to the Contrary notwithstanding.

The Senators and Representatives before mentioned, and the Members of the several State Legislatures, and all executive and judicial Officers, both of the United States and of the several States, shall be bound by Oath or Affirmation to support this Constitution; but no religious Test shall ever be required as a qualification to any Office or public Trust under the United States.

Article VII

The ratification of the conventions of nine States shall be sufficient for the establishment of this Constitution between the States so ratifying the same.

Done in Convention by the unanimous consent of the States present, the seventeenth day of September in the year of our Lord one thousand seven hundred and eighty-seven and of the Independence of the United States of America the twelfth. In witness whereof we have hereunto subscribed our names.

George Washington,
President and Deputy from Virginia

New Hampshire
John Langdon
Nicholas Gilman

Massachusetts
Nathaniel Gorham
Rufus King

Connecticut
William S. Johnson
Roger Sherman

New York
Alexander Hamilton

New Jersey
William Livingston
David Brearley
William Paterson
Jonathan Dayton

Pennsylvania
Benjamin Franklin
Thomas Mifflin
Robert Morris
George Clymer
Thomas Fitzsimons
Jared Ingersoll
James Wilson
Gouverneur Morris

Delaware
George Read
Gunning Bedford, Jr.
John Dickinson
Richard Bassett
Jacob Broom

Maryland
James McHenry
Daniel of St. Thomas
  Jenifer
Daniel Carroll

Virginia
John Blair
James Madison, Jr.

North Carolina
William Blount
Richard Dobbs Spraight
Hu Williamson

South Carolina
J. Rutledge
Charles C. Pinckney
Pierce Butler

Georgia
William Few
Abraham Baldwin

Amendments to the Constitution

*A*rticles in Addition to, and Amendment of, the Constitution of the United States of America, Proposed by Congress, and Ratified by the Legislatures of the Several States, Pursuant to the Fifth Article of the Original Constitution.

Amendment I [1791]

Congress shall make no law respecting an establishment of religion, or prohibiting the free exercise thereof; or abridging the freedom of speech, or of the press; or the right of the people peaceably to assemble, and to petition the Government for a redress of grievances.

Amendment II [1791]

A well regulated Militia, being necessary to the security of a free State, the right of the people to keep and bear Arms shall not be infringed.

Amendment III [1791]

No Soldier shall, in time of peace, be quartered in any house, without the consent of the Owner, nor in time of war, but in a manner to be prescribed by law.

Amendment IV [1791]

The right of the people to be secure in their persons, houses, papers, and effects, against unreasonable searches and seizures, shall not be violated, and no Warrants shall issue, but upon probable cause, supported by Oath or affirmation, and particularly describing the place to be searched, and the persons or things to be seized.

Amendment V [1791]

No person shall be held to answer for a capital or otherwise infamous crime, unless on a presentment or indictment of a Grand Jury, except in cases arising in the land or naval forces, or in the Militia, when in actual service in time of War or public danger; nor shall any person be subject for the same offence to be twice put in jeopardy of life or limb; nor shall be compelled in any criminal case to be a witness against himself, nor be deprived of life, liberty, or property, without due process of law; nor shall private property be taken for public use, without just compensation.

Amendment VI [1791]

In all criminal prosecutions, the accused shall enjoy the right to a speedy and public trial, by an impartial jury of the State and district wherein the crime shall have been committed, which district shall have been previously ascertained by law, and to be informed of the nature and cause of the accusation; to be confronted with the witnesses against him; to have compulsory process for obtaining witnesses in his favor, and to have the Assistance of Counsel for his defence.

Amendment VII [1791]

In suits at common law, where the value in controversy shall exceed twenty dollars, the right of trial by jury shall be preserved, and no fact tried by a jury, shall be otherwise reexamined in any Court of the United States, than according to the rules of the common law.

Amendment VIII [1791]

Excessive bail shall not be required, nor excessive fines imposed, nor cruel and unusual punishments inflicted.

Amendment IX [1791]

The enumeration in the Constitution, of certain rights, shall not be construed to deny or disparage others retained by the people.

Amendment X [1791]

The powers not delegated to the United States by the Constitution, nor prohibited by it to the States, are reserved to the States respectively, or to the people.

Amendment XI [1798]

The Judicial power of the United States shall not be construed to extend to any suit in law or equity, commenced or prosecuted against one of the United States by Citizens of another State, or by Citizens or Subjects of any Foreign State.

Amendment XII [1804]

The Electors shall meet in their respective States and vote by ballot for President and Vice-President, one of whom, at least, shall not be an inhabitant of the same State with themselves; they shall name in their ballots the person voted for as President, and in distinct ballots the person voted for as Vice-President, and they shall make distinct lists of all persons voted for as President, and of all persons voted for as Vice-President, and of the number of votes for each, which lists they shall sign and certify, and transmit sealed to the seat of the government of the United States, directed to the President of the Senate;—The President of the Senate shall, in the presence of the Senate and House of Representatives, open all the certificates and the votes shall then be counted;—The person having the greatest number of votes for President, shall be the President, if such number be a majority of the whole number of Electors appointed; and if no person have such majority, then from the persons having the highest numbers not exceeding three on the list of those voted for as President, the House of Representatives shall choose immediately, by ballot, the President. But in choosing the President, the votes shall be taken by states, the representation from each state having one vote; a quorum for this purpose shall consist of a member or members from two-thirds of the states, and a majority of all the states shall be necessary to a choice. And if the House of Representatives shall not choose a President whenever the right of choice shall devolve upon them, before the fourth day of March next following, then the Vice-President shall act as President, as in the case of the death or other constitutional disability of the President.—The person having the greatest number of votes as Vice-President, shall be the Vice-President, if such number be a majority of the whole number of Electors appointed, and if no person have a majority, then from the two highest numbers on the list, the Senate shall choose the Vice-President; a quorum for the purpose shall consist of two-thirds of the whole number of Senators, and a majority of the whole number shall be necessary to a choice. But no person constitutionally ineligible to the office of President shall be eligible to that of Vice-President of the United States.

Amendment XIII [1865]

Section 1.

Neither slavery nor involuntary servitude, except as a punishment for crime whereof the party shall have been duly convicted, shall exist within the United States, or any place subject to their jurisdiction.

Section 2.

Congress shall have power to enforce this article by appropriate legislation.

Amendment XIV [1868]

Section 1.

All persons born or naturalized in the United States, and subject to the jurisdiction thereof, are citizens of the United States and of the State wherein they reside. No State shall make or enforce any law which shall abridge the privileges or immunities of citizens of the United States; nor shall any State deprive any person of life, liberty, or property, without due process of law; nor deny to any person within its jurisdiction the equal protection of the laws.

Section 2.

Representatives shall be apportioned among the several States according to their respective numbers, counting the whole number of persons in each State, excluding Indians not taxed. But when the right to vote at any election for the choice of electors for President and Vice-President of the United States, Representatives in Congress, the Executive and Judicial officers of a State, or the members of the Legislature thereof, is denied to any of the male inhabitants of such State, being twenty-one years of age, and citizens of the United States, or in any way abridged, except for participation in rebellion, or other crime, the basis of representation therein shall be reduced in the proportion which the number of such male citizens shall bear to the whole number of male citizens twenty-one years of age in such State.

Section 3.

No person shall be a Senator or Representative in Congress, or elector of President and Vice-President, or hold any office, civil or military, under the United States, or under any State, who, having previously taken an oath, as a member of Congress, or as an officer of the United States, or as a member of any State legislature, or as an executive or judicial officer of any State, to support the

Constitution of the United States, shall have engaged in insurrection or rebellion against the same, or given aid or comfort to the enemies thereof. But Congress may by a vote of two-thirds of each House, remove such disability.

Section 4.

The validity of the public debt of the United States, authorized by law, including debts incurred for payment of pensions and bounties for services in suppressing insurrection or rebellion, shall not be questioned. But neither the United States nor any State shall assume or pay any debt or obligation incurred in aid of insurrection or rebellion against the United States, or any claim for the loss or emancipation of any slave; but all such debts, obligations, and claims shall be held illegal and void.

Section 5.

The Congress shall have the power to enforce, by appropriate legislation, the provisions of this article.

Amendment XV [1870]

Section 1.

The right of citizens of the United States to vote shall not be denied or abridged by the United States or by any State on account of race, color, or previous condition of servitude—

Section 2.

The Congress shall have power to enforce this article by appropriate legislation.

Amendment XVI [1913]

The Congress shall have power to lay and collect taxes on incomes, from whatever source derived, without apportionment among the several States, and without regard to any census or enumeration.

Amendment XVII [1913]

The Senate of the United States shall be composed of two Senators from each State, elected by the people thereof, for six years; and each Senator shall have one vote. The electors in each State shall have the qualifications requisite for electors of the most numerous branch of the State legislatures.

When vacancies happen in the representation of any State in the Senate, the executive authority of such State shall issue writs of election to fill such vacancies: *Provided,* That the legislature of any State may empower the executive thereof to make temporary appointments until the people fill the vacancies by election as the legislature may direct.

This amendment shall not be so construed as to affect the election or term of any Senator chosen before it becomes valid as part of the Constitution.

Amendment XVIII [1919]

Section 1.

After one year from the ratification of this article the manufacture, sale, or transportation of intoxicating liquors within, the importation thereof into, or the exportation thereof from the United States and all territory subject to the jurisdiction thereof for beverage purposes is hereby prohibited.

Section 2.

The Congress and the several States shall have concurrent power to enforce this article by appropriate legislation.

Section 3.

This article shall be inoperative unless it shall have been ratified as an amendment to the Constitution by the legislatures of the several States, as provided in the Constitution, within seven years from the date of the submission hereof to the States by the Congress.

Amendment XIX [1920]

The right of citizens of the United States to vote shall not be denied or abridged by the United States or by any State on account of sex.

Congress shall have power to enforce this article by appropriate legislation.

Amendment XX [1933]

Section 1.

The terms of the President and Vice-President shall end at noon on the 20th day of January, and the terms of Senators and Representatives at noon on the 3d day of January, of the years in which such terms would have ended if this article had not been ratified; and the terms of their successors shall then begin.

Section 2.

The Congress shall assemble at least once in every year, and such meeting shall begin at noon on the 3d day of January, unless they shall by law appoint a different day.

Section 3.

If, at the time fixed for the beginning of the term of the President, the President elect shall have died, the Vice-President elect shall become President. If a President shall not have been chosen before the time fixed for the beginning of his term, or if the President elect shall have failed to qualify, then the Vice President elect shall act as President until a President shall have qualified; and the Congress may by law provide for the case wherein neither a President elect nor a Vice-President elect shall have qualified, declaring who shall then act as President, or the manner in which one who is to act shall be selected, and such person shall act accordingly until a President or Vice-President shall have qualified.

Section 4.

The Congress may by law provide for the case of the death of any of the persons from whom the House of Representatives may choose a President when ever the right of choice shall have devolved upon them and for the case of the death of any of the persons from whom the Senate may choose a Vice-President whenever the right of choice shall have devolved upon them.

Section 5.

Sections 1 and 2 shall take effect on 15th day of October following the ratification of article.

Section 6.

This article shall be inoperative unless it shall have been ratified as an amendment to the Constitution by the legislatures of three-fourths of the several States within seven years from the date of its submission.

Amendment XXI [1933]

Section 1.

The eighteenth article of amendment to the Constitution of the United States is hereby repealed.

Section 2.

The transportation or importation into any State, Territory, or possession of the United States for delivery or use therein of intoxicating liquors, in violation of the laws thereof, is hereby prohibited.

Section 3.

This article shall be inoperative unless it shall have been ratified as an amendment to the Constitution by conventions in the several States, as provided in the Constitution, within seven years from the date of the submission hereof to the States by the Congress.

Amendment XXII [1951]

No person shall be elected to the office of the President more than twice, and no person who has held the office of President, or acted as President, for more than two years of a term to which some other person was elected President shall be elected to the office of the President more than once.

But this Article shall not apply to any person holding the office of President when this Article was proposed by the Congress, and shall not prevent any person who may be holding the office of President, or acting as President, during the term within which this Article becomes operative from holding the office of President or acting as President during the remainder of such term.

Amendment XXIII [1961]

Section 1.

The District constituting the seat of Government of the United States shall appoint in such manner as the Congress may direct:

A number of electors of President and Vice President equal to the whole number of Senators and Representatives in Congress to which the District would be entitled if it were a State, but in no event more than the least populous State; they shall be in addition to those appointed by the States, but they shall be considered, for the purposes of the election of President and Vice President, to be electors appointed by a State; and they shall meet in the District and perform such duties as provided by the twelfth article of amendment.

Section 2.

The Congress shall have power to enforce this article by appropriate legislation.

Amendment XXIV [1964]

Section 1.

The right of citizens of the United States to vote in any primary or other election for President or Vice President, for electors for President or Vice President, or for Senator or Representative in Congress, shall not be denied or abridged by the United States or any State by reason of failure to pay any poll tax or other tax.

Section 2.

The Congress shall have the power to enforce this article by appropriate legislation.

Amendment XXV [1967]

Section 1.

In case of the removal of the President from office or his death or resignation, the Vice President shall become President.

Section 2.

Whenever there is a vacancy in the office of the Vice President, the President shall nominate a Vice President who shall take the office upon confirmation by a majority vote of both houses of Congress.

Section 3.

Whenever the President transmits to the President pro tempore of the Senate and the Speaker of the House of Representatives his written declaration that he is unable to discharge the powers and duties of his office, and until he transmits to them a written declaration to the contrary, such powers and duties shall be discharged by the Vice President as Acting President.

Section 4.

Whenever the Vice President and a majority of either the principal officers of the executive departments, or of such other body as Congress may by law provide, transmit to the President pro tempore of the Senate and the Speaker of the House of Representatives their written declaration that the President is unable to discharge the powers and duties of his office, the Vice President shall immediately assume the powers and duties of the office as Acting President.

Thereafter, when the President transmits to the President pro tempore of the Senate and the Speaker of the House of Representatives his written declaration that no inability exists, he shall resume the powers and duties of his office unless the Vice President and a majority of either the principal officers of the executive departments, or of such other body as Congress may by law provide, transmit within four days to the President pro tempore of the Senate and the Speaker of the House of Representatives their written declaration that the President is unable to discharge the powers and duties of his office. Thereupon Congress shall decide the issue, assembling within 48 hours for that purpose if not in session. If the Congress, within 21 days after receipt of the latter written declaration, or, if Congress is not in session, within 21 days after Congress is required to assemble, determines by two-thirds vote of both houses that the President is unable to discharge the powers and duties of his office, the Vice President shall continue to discharge the same as Acting President; otherwise, the President shall resume the powers and duties of his office.

Amendment XXVI [1971]

Section 1.

The right of citizens of the United States, who are 18 years of age or older, to vote shall not be denied or abridged by the United States or any state on account of age.

Section 2.

The Congress shall have the power to enforce this article by appropriate legislation.

[Amendment XXVII] [1992]

No law varying the compensation for the services of the Senators and Representatives shall take effect, until an election of Representatives shall have intervened.

Presidential Elections, 1789–1992

Year	Candidates	Party	Popular Vote*	Electoral Vote**
1789	**George Washington**			69
	John Adams			34
	Others			35
1792	**George Washington**			132
	John Adams			77
	George Clinton			50
	Others			5
1796	**John Adams**	Federalist		71
	Thomas Jefferson	Democratic Republican		68
	Thomas Pinckney	Federalist		59
	Aaron Burr	Democratic Republican		30
	Others			48
1800	**Thomas Jefferson**	Democratic Republican		73
	Aaron Burr	Democratic Republican		73
	John Adams	Federalist		65
	Charles C. Pinckney	Federalist		64
1804	**Thomas Jefferson**	Democratic Republican		162
	Charles C. Pinckney	Federalist		14

Year	Candidates	Party	Popular Vote*	Electoral Vote**
1808	**James Madison**	Democratic Republican		122
	Charles C. Pinckney	Federalist		47
	George Clinton	Independent Republican		6
1812	**James Madison**	Democratic Republican		128
	DeWitt Clinton	Federalist		89
1816	**James Monroe**	Democratic Republican		183
	Rufus King	Federalist		34
1820	**James Monroe**	Democratic Republican		231
	John Quincy Adams	Independent Republican		1
1824	**John Quincy Adams**	Democratic Republican	108,704 (30.5%)	84
	Andrew Jackson	Democratic Republican	153,544 (43.1%)	99
	Henry Clay	Democratic Republican	47,136 (13.2%)	37
	William H. Crawford	Democratic Republican	46,618 (13.1%)	41
1828	**Andrew Jackson**	Democratic	647,231 (56.0%)	178
	John Quincy Adams	National Republican	509,097 (44.0%)	83
1832	**Andrew Jackson**	Democratic	687,502 (55.0%)	219
	Henry Clay	National Republican	530,189 (42.4%)	49
	William Wirt	Anti-Masonic		7
	John Floyd	National Republican	33,108 (2.6%)	11
1836	**Martin Van Buren**	Democratic	761,549 (50.9%)	170
	William H. Harrison	Whig	549,567 (36.7%)	73
	Hugh L. White	Whig	145,396 (9.7%)	26
	Daniel Webster	Whig	41,287 (2.7%)	14

* Because only the leading candidates are listed, popular vote percentages do not always total 100.

** The elections of 1800 and 1824, in which no candidate received an electoral vote majority, were decided in the House of Representatives.

(continues)

Year	Candidates	Party	Popular Vote*	Electoral Vote**
1840	**William H. Harrison** **(John Tyler, 1841)**	Whig	1,275,017 (53.1%)	234
	Martin Van Buren	Democratic	1,128,702 (46.9%)	60
1844	**James K. Polk**	Democratic	1,337,243 (49.6%)	170
	Henry Clay	Whig	1,299,068 (48.1%)	105
	James G. Birney	Liberty	62,300 (2.3%)	
1848	**Zachary Taylor** **(Millard Fillmore, 1850)**	Whig	1,360,101 (47.4%)	163
	Lewis Cass	Democratic	1,220,544 (42.5%)	127
	Martin Van Buren	Free Soil	291,263 (10.1%)	
1852	**Franklin Pierce**	Democratic	1,601,474 (50.9%)	254
	Winfield Scott	Whig	1,386,578 (44.1%)	42
1856	**James Buchanan**	Democratic	1,838,169 (45.4%)	174
	John C. Frémont	Republican	1,335,264 (33.0%)	114
	Millard Fillmore	American	874,534 (21.6%)	8
1860	**Abraham Lincoln**	Republican	1,865,593 (39.8%)	180
	Stephen A. Douglas	Democratic	1,382,713 (29.5%)	12
	John C. Breckinridge	Democratic	848,356 (18.1%)	72
	John Bell	Constitutional Union	592,906 (12.6%)	39
1864	**Abraham Lincoln** **(Andrew Johnson, 1865)**	Republican	2,206,938 (55.0%)	212
	George B. McClellan	Democratic	1,803,787 (45.0%)	21
1868	**Ulysses S. Grant**	Republican	3,013,421 (52.7%)	214
	Horatio Seymour	Democratic	2,706,829 (47.3%)	80

Year	Candidates	Party	Popular Vote*	Electoral Vote**
1872	**Ulysses S. Grant**	Republican	3,596,745 (55.6%)	286
	Horace Greeley	Democratic	2,843,446 (43.9%)	66
1876	**Rutherford B. Hayes**	Republican	4,036,572 (48.0%)	185
	Samuel J. Tilden	Democratic	4,284,020 (51.0%)	184
1880	**James A. Garfield**	Republican	4,449,053 (48.3%)	214
	(**Chester A. Arthur**, 1881)			
	Winfield S. Hancock	Democratic	4,442,035 (48.2%)	155
	James B. Weaver	Greenback Labor	308,578 (3.4%)	
1884	**Grover Cleveland**	Democratic	4,874,986 (48.5%)	219
	James G. Blaine	Republican	4,851,981 (48.2%)	182
	Benjamin F. Butler	Greenback Labor	175,370 (1.8%)	
1888	**Benjamin Harrison**	Republican	5,444,337 (47.8%)	233
	Grover Cleveland	Democratic	5,540,050 (48.6%)	168
1892	**Grover Cleveland**	Democratic	5,554,414 (46.0%)	277
	Benjamin Harrison	Republican	5,190,802 (43.0%)	145
	James B. Weaver	People's	1,027,329 (8.5%)	22
1896	**William McKinley**	Republican	7,035,638 (50.8%)	271
	William Jennings Bryan	Democratic; Populist	6,467,946 (46.7%)	176
1900	**William McKinley**	Republican	7,219,530 (51.7%)	292
	(**Theodore Roosevelt**, 1901)			
	William Jennings Bryan	Democratic; Populist	6,356,734 (45.5%)	155

(continues)

* Because only the leading candidates are listed, popular vote percentages do not always total 100.
** The elections of 1800 and 1824, in which no candidate received an electoral vote majority, were decided in the House of Representatives.

Year	Candidates	Party	Popular Vote*	Electoral Vote**
1904	**Theodore Roosevelt**	Republican	7,628,834 (56.4%)	336
	Alton B. Parker	Democratic	5,084,401 (37.6%)	140
	Eugene V. Debs	Socialist	402,460 (3.0%)	
1908	**William H. Taft**	Republican	7,679,006 (51.6%)	321
	William Jennings Bryan	Democratic	6,409,106 (43.1%)	162
	Eugene V. Debs	Socialist	420,820 (2.8%)	
1912	**Woodrow Wilson**	Democratic	6,286,820 (41.8%)	435
	Theodore Roosevelt	Progressive	4,126,020 (27.4%)	88
	William H. Taft	Republican	3,483,922 (23.2%)	8
	Eugene V. Debs	Socialist	897,011 (6.0%)	
1916	**Woodrow Wilson**	Democratic	9,129,606 (49.3%)	277
	Charles E. Hughes	Republican	8,538,221 (46.1%)	254
1920	**Warren G. Harding** (Calvin Coolidge, 1923)	Republican	16,152,200 (61.0%)	404
	James M. Cox	Democratic	9,147,353 (34.6%)	127
	Eugene V. Debs	Socialist	919,799 (3.5%)	
1924	**Calvin Coolidge**	Republican	15,725,016 (54.1%)	382
	John W. Davis	Democratic	8,385,586 (28.8%)	136
	Robert M. La Follette	Progressive	4,822,856 (16.6%)	13
1928	**Herbert C. Hoover**	Republican	21,392,190 (58.2%)	444
	Alfred E. Smith	Democratic	15,016,443 (40.8%)	87
1932	**Franklin D. Roosevelt**	Democratic	22,809,638 (57.3%)	472
	Herbert C. Hoover	Republican	15,758,901 (39.6%)	59
	Norman Thomas	Socialist	881,951 (2.2%)	

Year	Candidates	Party	Popular Vote*	Electoral Vote**
1936	**Franklin D. Roosevelt**	Democratic	27,751,612 (60.7%)	523
	Alfred M. Landon	Republican	16,681,913 (36.4%)	8
	William Lemke	Union	891,858 (1.9%)	
1940	**Franklin D. Roosevelt**	Democratic	27,243,466 (54.7%)	449
	Wendell L. Willkie	Republican	22,304,755 (44.8%)	82
1944	**Franklin D. Roosevelt**	Democratic	25,602,505 (52.8%)	432
	(Harry S Truman, 1945)			
	Thomas E. Dewey	Republican	22,006,278 (44.5%)	99
1948	**Harry S Truman**	Democratic	24,105,812 (49.5%)	303
	Thomas E. Dewey	Republican	21,970,065 (45.1%)	189
	J. Strom Thurmond	States' Rights	1,169,063 (2.4%)	39
	Henry A. Wallace	Progressive	1,157,172 (2.4%)	
1952	**Dwight D. Eisenhower**	Republican	33,936,234 (55.2%)	442
	Adlai E. Stevenson	Democratic	27,314,992 (44.5%)	89
1956	**Dwight D. Eisenhower**	Republican	35,590,472 (57.4%)	457
	Adlai E. Stevenson	Democratic	26,022,752 (42.0%)	73
1960	**John F. Kennedy**	Democratic	34,227,096 (49.9%)	303
	(Lyndon B. Johnson, 1963)			
	Richard M. Nixon	Republican	34,108,546 (49.6%)	219
1964	**Lyndon B. Johnson**	Democratic	43,126,233 (61.1%)	486
	Barry M. Goldwater	Republican	27,174,989 (38.5%)	52

(continues)

* Because only the leading candidates are listed, popular vote percentages do not always total 100.

** The elections of 1800 and 1824, in which no candidate received an electoral vote majority, were decided in the House of Representatives.

Year	Candidates	Party	Popular Vote*	Electoral Vote**
1968	**Richard M. Nixon**	Republican	31,783,783 (43.4%)	301
	Hubert H. Humphrey	Democratic	31,271,839 (42.7%)	191
	George C. Wallace	Amer. Independent	9,899,557 (13.5%)	46
1972	**Richard M. Nixon**	Republican	45,767,218 (60.6%)	520
	(Gerald R. Ford, 1974)			
	George S. McGovern	Democratic	28,357,668 (37.5%)	17
1976	**Jimmy Carter**	Democratic	40,828,657 (50.6%)	297
	Gerald R. Ford	Republican	39,145,520 (48.4%)	241
1980	**Ronald Reagan**	Republican	43,899,248 (51%)	489
	Jimmy Carter	Democratic	36,481,435 (41%)	49
	John B. Anderson	Independent	5,719,437 (6%)	
1984	**Ronald Reagan**	Republican	54,455,075 (59%)	525
	Walter F. Mondale	Democratic	37,577,185 (41%)	13
1988	**George Bush**	Republican	48,881,221 (54%)	426
	Michael Dukakis	Democratic	41,805,422 (46%)	111
1992	**Bill Clinton**	Democratic	43,728,375 (43%)	370
	George Bush	Republican	38,167,416 (38%)	168
	H. Ross Perot	Independent	19,237,247 (19%)	

* Because only the leading candidates are listed, popular vote percentages do not always total 100.

** The elections of 1800 and 1824, in which no candidate received an electoral vote majority, were decided in the House of Representatives.

Presidential Administrations

Washington, 1789–1797

Vice-President	John Adams	1789–1797
Secretary of State	Thomas Jefferson	1789–1793
	Edmund Randolph	1794–1795
	Timothy Pickering	1795–1797
Secretary of War	Henry Knox	1789–1794
	Timothy Pickering	1795–1796
	James McHenry	1796–1797
Secretary of Treasury	Alexander Hamilton	1789–1795
	Oliver Wolcott, Jr.	1795–1797
Postmaster General	Samuel Osgood	1789–1791
	Timothy Pickering	1791–1794
	Joseph Habersham	1795–1797
Attorney General	Edmund Randolph	1789–1793
	William Bradford	1794–1795
	Charles Lee	1795–1797

John Adams, 1797–1801

Vice-President	Thomas Jefferson	1797–1801
Secretary of State	Timothy Pickering	1797–1800
	John Marshall	1800–1801
Secretary of War	James McHenry	1797–1800
	Samuel Dexter	1800–1801
Secretary of Treasury	Oliver Wolcott, Jr.	1797–1800
	Samuel Dexter	1800–1801
Postmaster General	Joseph Habersham	1797–1801
Attorney General	Charles Lee	1797–1801
Secretary of Navy	Benjamin Stoddert	1798–1801

Jefferson, 1801–1809

Vice-President	Aaron Burr	1801–1805
	George Clinton	1805–1809

(continues)

Secretary of State	James Madison	1801–1809
Secretary of War	Henry Dearborn	1801–1809
Secretary of Treasury	Samuel Dexter	1801
	Albert Gallatin	1801–1809
Postmaster General	Joseph Habersham	1801
	Gideon Granger	1801–1809
Attorney General	Levi Lincoln	1801–1805
	Robert Smith	1805
	John C. Breckinridge	1805–1806
	Caesar A. Rodney	1807–1809
Secretary of Navy	Robert Smith	1801–1809

Madison, 1809–1817

Vice-President	George Clinton	1809–1813
	Elbridge Gerry	1813–1817
Secretary of State	Robert Smith	1809–1811
	James Monroe	1811–1817
Secretary of War	William Eustis	1809–1812
	John Armstrong	1813–1814
	James Monroe	1814–1815
	William H. Crawford	1815–1817
Secretary of Treasury	Albert Gallatin	1809–1813
	George W. Campbell	1814
	Alexander J. Dallas	1814–1816
	William H. Crawford	1816–1817
Postmaster General	Gideon Granger	1809–1814
	Return J. Meigs, Jr.	1814–1817
Attorney General	Caesar A. Rodney	1809–1811
	William Pinkney	1811–1814
	Richard Rush	1814–1817
Secretary of Navy	Paul Hamilton	1809–1813
	William Jones	1813–1814
	Benjamin W. Crowninshield	1814–1817

Monroe, 1817–1825

Vice-President	Daniel D. Tompkins	1817–1825
Secretary of State	John Quincy Adams	1817–1825
Secretary of War	George Graham	1817
	John C. Calhoun	1817–1825
Secretary of Treasury	William H. Crawford	1817–1825
Postmaster General	Return J. Meigs, Jr.	1817–1823
	John McLean	1823–1825
Attorney General	Richard Rush	1817
	William Wirt	1817–1825
Secretary of Navy	Benjamin W. Crowninshield	1817–1818
	Smith Thompson	1818–1823
	Samuel L. Southard	1823–1825

John Quincy Adams, 1825–1829

Vice-President	John C. Calhoun	1825–1829
Secretary of State	Henry Clay	1825–1829
Secretary of War	James Barbour	1825–1828
	Peter B. Porter	1828–1829
Secretary of Treasury	Richard Rush	1825–1829
Postmaster General	John McLean	1825–1829
Attorney General	William Wirt	1825–1829
Secretary of Navy	Samuel L. Southard	1825–1829

Jackson, 1829–1837

Vice-President	John C. Calhoun	1829–1832
	Martin Van Buren	1833–1837
Secretary of State	Martin Van Buren	1829–1831
	Edward Livingston	1831–1833
	Louis McLane	1833–1834
	John Forsyth	1834–1837
Secretary of War	John H. Eaton	1829–1831
	Lewis Cass	1831–1837
	Benjamin Butler	1837
Secretary of Treasury	Samuel D. Ingham	1829–1831
	Louis McLane	1831–1833
	William J. Duane	1833
	Roger B. Taney	1833–1834
	Levi Woodbury	1834–1837
Postmaster General	William T. Barry	1829–1835
	Amos Kendall	1835–1837
Attorney General	John M. Berrien	1829–1831
	Roger B. Taney	1831–1833
	Benjamin F. Butler	1833–1837
Secretary of Navy	John Branch	1829–1831
	Levi Woodbury	1831–1834
	Mahlon Dickerson	1834–1837

Van Buren, 1837–1841

Vice-President	Richard M. Johnson	1837–1841
Secretary of State	John Forsyth	1837–1841
Secretary of War	Joel R. Poinsett	1837–1841
Secretary of Treasury	Levi Woodbury	1837–1841
Postmaster General	Amos Kendall	1837–1840
	John M. Niles	1840–1841
Attorney General	Benjamin F. Butler	1837–1838
	Felix Grundy	1838–1840
	Henry D. Gilpin	1840–1841
Secretary of Navy	Mahlon Dickerson	1837–1838
	James K. Paulding	1838–1841

(continues)

William Harrison, 1841

Vice-President	John Tyler	1841
Secretary of State	Daniel Webster	1841
Secretary of War	John Bell	1841
Secretary of Treasury	Thomas Ewing	1841
Postmaster General	Francis Granger	1841
Attorney General	John J. Crittenden	1841
Secretary of Navy	George E. Badger	1841

Tyler, 1841–1845

Vice-President	None	
Secretary of State	Daniel Webster	1841–1843
	Hugh S. Legare	1843
	Abel P. Upshur	1843–1844
	John C. Calhoun	1844–1845
Secretary of War	John Bell	1841
	John C. Spencer	1841–1843
	John M. Porter	1843–1844
	William Wilkins	1844–1845
Secretary of Treasury	Thomas Ewing	1841
	Walter Forward	1841–1843
	John C. Spencer	1843–1844
	George M. Bibb	1844–1845
Postmaster General	Francis Granger	1841
	Charles A. Wickliffe	1841
Attorney General	John J. Crittenden	1841
	Hugh S. Legaré	1841–1843
	John Nelson	1843–1845
Secretary of Navy	George Badger	1841
	Abel P. Upshur	1841
	David Henshaw	1843–1844
	Thomas W. Gilmer	1844
	John Y. Mason	1844–1845

Polk, 1845–1849

Vice-President	George M. Dallas	1845–1849
Secretary of State	James Buchanan	1845–1849
Secretary of War	William L. Marcy	1845–1849
Secretary of Treasury	Robert J. Walker	1845–1849
Postmaster General	Cave Johnson	1845–1849
Attorney General	John Y. Mason	1845–1846
	Nathan Clifford	1846–1848
	Isaac Toucey	1848–1849
Secretary of Navy	George Bancroft	1845–1846
	John Y. Mason	1846–1849

Taylor, 1849–1850

Vice-President	Millard Fillmore	1849–1850
Secretary of State	John M. Clayton	1849–1850
Secretary of War	George W. Crawford	1849–1850
Secretary of Treasury	William M. Meredith	1849–1850
Postmaster General	Jacob Collamer	1849–1850
Attorney General	Reverdy Johnson	1849–1850
Secretary of Navy	William Preston	1849–1850
Secretary of Interior	Thomas Ewing	1849–1850

Fillmore, 1850–1853

Vice-President	None	
Secretary of State	Daniel Webster	1850–1852
	Edward Everett	1852–1853
Secretary of War	Charles M. Conrad	1850–1853
Secretary of Treasury	Thomas Corwin	1850–1853
Postmaster General	Nathan K. Hall	1850–1852
	Sam D. Hubbard	1852–1853
Attorney General	John J. Crittenden	1850–1853
Secretary of Navy	William A. Graham	1850–1852
	John P. Kennedy	1852–1853
Secretary of Interior	Thomas M. T. McKennan	1850
	Alexander H. H. Stuart	1850–1853

Pierce, 1853–1857

Vice-President	William R. King	1853
Secretary of State	William L. Marcy	1853–1857
Secretary of War	Jefferson Davis	1853–1857
Secretary of Treasury	James Guthrie	1853–1857
Postmaster General	James Campbell	1853–1857
Attorney General	Caleb Cushing	1853–1857
Secretary of Navy	James C. Dobbins	1853–1857
Secretary of Interior	Robert McClelland	1853–1857

Buchanan, 1857–1861

Vice-President	John C. Breckinridge	1857–1861
Secretary of State	Lewis Cass	1857–1860
	Jeremiah S. Black	1860–1861
Secretary of War	John B. Floyd	1857–1861
	Joseph Holt	1861
Secretary of Treasury	Howell Cobb	1857–1860
	Philip F. Thomas	1860–1861

(continues)

Postmaster General	John A. Dix	1861
	Aaron V. Brown	1857–1859
	Joseph Holt	1859–1861
	Horatio King	1861
Attorney General	Jeremiah S. Black	1857–1860
	Edwin M. Stanton	1860–1861
Secretary of Navy	Isaac Toucey	1857–1861
Secretary of Interior	Jacob Thompson	1857–1861
	Caleb B. Smith	1861–1863
	John P. Usher	1863–1865

Lincoln, 1861–1865

Vice-President	Hannibal Hamlin	1861–1865
	Andrew Johnson	1865
Secretary of State	William H. Seward	1861–1865
Secretary of War	Simon Cameron	1861–1862
	Edwin M. Stanton	1862–1865
Secretary of Treasury	Samuel P. Chase	1861–1864
	William P. Fessenden	1864–1865
	Hugh McCulloch	1865
Postmaster General	Horatio King	1861
	Montgomery Blair	1861–1864
	William Dennison	1864–1865
Attorney General	Edward Bates	1861–1864
	James Speed	1864–1865
Secretary of Navy	Gideon Welles	1861–1865

Andrew Johnson, 1865–1869

Vice-President	None	
Secretary of State	William H. Seward	1865–1869
Secretary of War	Edwin M. Stanton	1865–1867
	Ulysses S. Grant	1867–1868
	John M. Schofield	1868–1869
Secretary of Treasury	Hugh McCulloch	1865–1869
Postmaster General	William Dennison	1865–1866
	Alexander W. Randall	1866–1869
Attorney General	James Speed	1865–1866
	Henry Stanbery	1866–1868
	William M. Evarts	1868–1869
Secretary of Navy	Gideon Welles	1865–1869
Secretary of Interior	John P. Usher	1865
	James Harlan	1865–1866
	Orville H. Browning	1866–1869

Grant, 1869–1877

Vice-President	Schuyler Colfax	1869–1873
	Henry Wilson	1873–1875
Secretary of State	Elihu B. Washburne	1869
	Hamilton Fish	1869–1877

Secretary of War	John A. Rawlins	1869
	William T. Sherman	1869
	William W. Belknap	1869–1876
	Alphonso Taft	1876
	James D. Cameron	1876–1877
Secretary of Treasury	George S. Boutwell	1869–1873
	William A. Richardson	1873–1874
	Benjamin H. Bristow	1874–1876
	Lot M. Morrill	1876–1877
Postmaster General	John A. J. Creswell	1869–1874
	James W. Marshall	1874
	Marshall Jewell	1874–1876
	James N. Tyner	1876–1877
Attorney General	Ebenezer R. Hoar	1869–1870
	Amos T. Ackerman	1870–1871
	G. H. Williams	1871–1875
	Edwards Pierrepont	1875–1876
	Alphonso Taft	1876–1877
Secretary of Navy	Adolph E. Borie	1869
	George Robeson	1869–1877
Secretary of Interior	Jacob D. Cox	1869–1870
	Columbus Delano	1870–1875
	Zachariah Chandler	1875–1877

Hayes, 1877–1881

Vice-President	William A. Wheeler	1877–1881
Secretary of State	William B. Evarts	1877–1881
Secretary of War	George W. McCrary	1877–1879
	Alexander Ramsey	1879–1881
Secretary of Treasury	John Sherman	1877–1881
Postmaster General	David M. Key	1877–1880
	Horace Maynard	1880–1881
Attorney General	Charles Devens	1877–1881
Secretary of Navy	Richard W. Thompson	1877–1880
	Nathan Goff, Jr.	1881
Secretary of Interior	Carl Schurz	1877–1881

Garfield, 1881

Vice-President	Chester A. Arthur	1881
Secretary of State	James G. Blaine	1881
Secretary of War	Robert T. Lincoln	1881
Secretary of Treasury	William Windom	1881
Postmaster General	Thomas L. James	1881
Attorney General	Wayne MacVeagh	1881

(continues)

Secretary of Navy	William H. Hunt	1881
Secretary of Interior	Samuel J. Kirkwood	1881

Arthur, 1881–1885

Vice-President	None	
Secretary of State	Frederick T. Frelinghuysen	1881–1885
Secretary of War	Robert T. Lincoln	1881–1885
Secretary of Treasury	Charles J. Folger	1881–1884
	Walter Q. Gresham	1884
	Hugh McCulloch	1884–1885
Postmaster General	Timothy O. Howe	1881–1883
	Walter Q. Gresham	1883–1884
	Frank Hatton	1884–1885
Attorney General	Benjamin H. Brewster	1881–1885
Secretary of Navy	William H. Hunt	1881–1882
	William E. Chandler	1882–1885
Secretary of Interior	Samuel J. Kirkwood	1881–1882
	Henry M. Teller	1882–1885

Cleveland, 1885–1889

Vice-President	Thomas A. Hendricks	1885
Secretary of State	Thomas F. Bayard	1885–1889
Secretary of War	William C. Endicott	1885–1889
Secretary of Treasury	Daniel Manning	1885–1887
	Charles S. Fairchild	1887–1889
Postmaster General	William F. Vilas	1885–1888
	Don M. Dickinson	1888–1889
Attorney General	Augustus H. Garland	1885–1889
Secretary of Navy	William C. Whitney	1885–1889
Secretary of Interior	Lucius Q. C. Lamar	1885–1888
	William F. Vilas	1888–1889
Secretary of Agriculture	Norman J. Colman	1889

Benjamin Harrison, 1889–1893

Vice-President	Levi P. Morton	1889–1893
Secretary of State	James G. Blaine	1889–1892
	John W. Foster	1892–1893
Secretary of War	Redfield Proctor	1889–1891
	Stephen B. Elkins	1891–1893
Secretary of Treasury	William Windom	1889–1891
	Charles Foster	1891–1893
Postmaster General	John Wanamaker	1889–1893
Attorney General	William H. H. Miller	1889–1891
Secretary of Navy	Benjamin F. Tracy	1889–1893
Secretary of Interior	John W. Noble	1889–1893
Secretary of Agriculture	Jeremiah M. Rusk	1889–1893

Cleveland, 1893–1897

Vice-President	Adlai E. Stevenson	1893–1897
Secretary of State	Walter Q. Gresham	1893–1895
	Richard Olney	1895–1897
Secretary of War	Daniel S. Lamont	1893–1897
Secretary of Treasury	John G. Carlisle	1893–1897
Postmaster General	Wilson S. Bissell	1893–1895
	William L. Wilson	1895–1897
Attorney General	Richard Olney	1893–1895
	Judson Harmon	1895–1897
Secretary of Navy	Hilary A. Herbert	1893–1897
Secretary of Interior	Hoke Smith	1893–1896
	David R. Francis	1896–1897
Secretary of Agriculture	Julius Sterling Morton	1893–1897

McKinley, 1897–1901

Vice-President	Garret Hobart	1897–1899
	Theodore Roosevelt	1901
Secretary of State	John Sherman	1897–1898
	William R. Day	1898
	John M. Hay	1898–1901
Secretary of War	Russell A. Alger	1897–1899
	Elihu Root	1899–1901
Secretary of Treasury	Lyman J. Gage	1897–1901
Postmaster General	James A. Gary	1897–1898
	Charles E. Smith	1898–1901
Attorney General	Joseph McKenna	1897–1898
	John W. Griggs	1898–1901
	Philander C. Knox	1901
Secretary of Navy	John D. Long	1897–1901
Secretary of Interior	Cornelius N. Bliss	1897–1899
	Ethan A. Hitchcock	1899–1901
Secretary of Agriculture	James Wilson	1897–1901

Theodore Roosevelt, 1901–1909

Vice-President	Charles Warren Fairbanks	1905–1909
Secretary of State	John M. Hay	1901–1905
	Elihu Root	1905–1909
	Robert Bacon	1909
Secretary of War	Elihu Root	1901–1904
	William Howard Taft	1904–1908
	Luke E. Wright	1908–1909

(continues)

Secretary of Treasury	Lyman J. Gage	1901–1902
	Leslie M. Shaw	1902–1907
	George B. Cortelyou	1907–1909
Postmaster General	Charles Emory Smith	1901–1902
	Henry C. Payne	1902–1904
	Robert J. Wynne	1904–1905
	George B. Cortelyou	1905–1907
	George von L. Meyer	1907–1909
Attorney General	Philander C. Knox	1901–1904
	William H. Moody	1904–1906
	Charles J. Bonaparte	1906–1909
Secretary of Navy	John D. Long	1901–1902
	William H. Moody	1902–1904
	Paul Morton	1904–1905
	Charles J. Bonaparte	1905–1906
	Victor H. Metcalf	1906–1908
	Truman H. Newberry	1908–1909
Secretary of Interior	Ethan A. Hitchcock	1901–1907
	James R. Garfield	1907–1909
Secretary of Agriculture	James Wilson	1901–1909
Secretary of Labor and Commerce	George B. Cortelyou	1903–1904
	Victor H. Metcalf	1904–1906
	Oscar S. Straus	1906–1909

Taft, 1909–1913

Vice-President	James S. Sherman	1909–1912
Secretary of State	Philander C. Knox	1909–1913
Secretary of War	Jacob M. Dickinson	1909–1911
	Henry L. Stimson	1911–1913
Secretary of Treasury	Franklin MacVeagh	1909–1913
Postmaster General	Frank H. Hitchcock	1909–1913
Attorney General	George W. Wickersham	1909–1913
Secretary of Navy	George von L. Meyer	1909–1913
Secretary of Interior	Richard A. Ballinger	1909–1911
	Walter Lowrie Fisher	1911–1913
Secretary of Agriculture	James Wilson	1909–1913
Secretary of Labor and Commerce	Oscar S. Straus	1909
	Charles Nagel	1909–1913

Wilson, 1913–1921

Vice-President	Thomas R. Marshall	1913–1921
Secretary of State	William Jennings Bryan	1913–1915
	Robert Lansing	1915–1920
	Bainbridge Colby	1920–1921
Secretary of War	Lindley M. Garrison	1913–1916

Office	Name	Dates
Secretary of War	Newton D. Baker	1916–1921
Secretary of Treasury	William Gilbert McAdoo	1913–1918
	Carter Glass	1918–1920
	David F. Houston	1920–1921
Postmaster General	Albert Sidney Burleson	1913–1921
Attorney General	James Clark McReynolds	1913–1914
	Thomas Watt Gregory	1914–1919
	A. Mitchell Palmer	1919–1921
Secretary of Navy	Josephus Daniels	1913–1921
Secretary of Interior	Franklin Knight Lane	1913–1920
	John Barton Payne	1920–1921
Secretary of Agriculture	David F. Houston	1913–1920
	Edwin T. Meredith	1920–1921
Secretary of Commerce	William C. Redfield	1913–1919
Secretary of Labor	William Bauchop Wilson	1913–1921

Harding, 1921–1923

Office	Name	Dates
Vice-President	Calvin Coolidge	1921–1923
Secretary of State	Charles Evans Hughes	1921–1923
Secretary of War	John W. Weeks	1921–1923
Secretary of Treasury	Andrew W. Mellon	1921–1923
Postmaster General	Will H. Hays	1921–1922
	Hubert Work	1922–1923
	Harry S. New	1923
Attorney General	Harry M. Daugherty	1921–1923
Secretary of Navy	Edwin Denby	1921–1923
Secretary of Interior	Albert B. Fall	1921–1923
	Hubert Work	1923
Secretary of Agriculture	Henry C. Wallace	1921–1923
Secretary of Commerce	Herbert C. Hoover	1921–1923
Secretary of Labor	James J. Davis	1921–1923

Coolidge, 1923–1929

Office	Name	Dates
Vice-President	Charles G. Dawes	1925–1929
Secretary of State	Charles Evans Hughes	1923–1925
	Frank B. Kellogg	1925–1929
Secretary of War	John W. Weeks	1923–1925
	Dwight F. Davis	1925–1929
Secretary of Treasury	Andrew W. Mellon	1923–1929

(continues)

Postmaster General	Harry S. New	1923–1929
Attorney General	Harry M. Daugherty	1923–1924
	Harlan Fiske Stone	1924–1925
	John G. Sargent	1925–1929
Secretary of Navy	Edwin Derby	1923–1924
	Curtis D. Wilbur	1924–1929
Secretary of Interior	Hubert Work	1923–1928
	Roy O. West	1928–1929
Secretary of Agriculture	Henry C. Wallace	1923–1924
	Howard M. Gore	1924–1925
	William M. Jardine	1925–1929
Secretary of Commerce	Herbert C. Hoover	1923–1928
	William F. Whiting	1928–1929
Secretary of Labor	James J. Davis	1923–1929

Hoover, 1929–1933

Vice-President	Charles Curtis	1929–1933
Secretary of State	Henry L. Stimson	1929–1933
Secretary of War	James W. Good	1929
	Patrick J. Hurley	1929–1933
Secretary of Treasury	Andrew W. Mellon	1929–1932
	Ogden L. Mills	1932–1933
Postmaster General	Walter F. Brown	1929–1933
Attorney General	William D. Mitchell	1929–1933
Secretary of Navy	Charles F. Adams	1929–1933
Secretary of Interior	Ray L. Wilbur	1929–1933
Secretary of Agriculture	Arthur M. Hyde	1929–1933
Secretary of Commerce	Robert P. Lamont	1929–1932
	Roy D. Chapin	1932–1933
Secretary of Labor	James J. Davis	1929–1930
	William N. Doak	1930–1933

Franklin D. Roosevelt, 1933–1945

Vice-President	John Nance Garner	1933–1941
	Henry A. Wallace	1941–1945
	Harry S Truman	1945
Secretary of State	Cordell Hull	1933–1944
	Edward R. Stettinius, Jr.	1944–1945
Secretary of War	George H. Dern	1933–1936
	Henry A. Woodring	1936–1940
	Henry L. Stimson	1940–1945
Secretary of Treasury	William H. Woodin	1933–1934
	Henry Morgenthau, Jr.	1934–1945
Postmaster General	James A. Farley	1933–1940
	Frank C. Walker	1940–1945

Attorney General	Homer S. Cummings	1933–1939
	Frank Murphy	1939–1940
	Robert H. Jackson	1940–1941
	Francis Biddle	1941–1945
Secretary of Navy	Claude A. Swanson	1933–1940
	Charles Edison	1940
	Frank Knox	1940–1944
	James V. Forrestal	1944–1945
Secretary of Interior	Harold L. Ickes	1933–1945
Secretary of Agriculture	Henry A. Wallace	1933–1940
	Claude R. Wickard	1940–1945
Secretary of Commerce	Daniel C. Roper	1933–1939
	Harry L. Hopkins	1939–1940
	Jesse H. Jones	1940–1945
	Henry A. Wallace	1945
Secretary of Labor	Frances Perkins	1933–1945

Truman, 1945–1953

Vice-President	Alben W. Barkley	1949–1953
Secretary of State	Edward R. Stettinius, Jr.	1945
	James F. Byrnes	1945–1947
	George C. Marshall	1947–1949
	Dean G. Acheson	1949–1953
Secretary of War	Robert P. Patterson	1945–1947
	Kenneth C. Royall	1947
Secretary of Treasury	Fred M. Vinson	1945–1946
	John W. Snyder	1946–1953
Postmaster General	Frank C. Walker	1945
	Robert E. Hannegan	1945–1947
	Jesse M. Donaldson	1947–1953
Attorney General	Tom C. Clark	1945–1949
	J. Howard McGrath	1949–1952
	James P. McGranery	1952–1953
Secretary of Navy	James V. Forrestal	1945–1947
Secretary of Interior	Harold L. Ickes	1945–1946
	Julius A. Krug	1946–1949
	Oscar L. Chapman	1949–1953
Secretary of Agriculture	Clinton P. Anderson	1945–1948
	Charles F. Brannan	1948–1953
Secretary of Commerce	Henry A. Wallace	1945–1946
	W. Averell Harriman	1946–1948
	Charles W. Sawyer	1948–1953
Secretary of Labor	Lewis B. Schwellenbach	1945–1948
	Maurice J. Tobin	1948–1953
Secretary of Defense	James V. Forrestal	1947–1949
	Louis A. Johnson	1949–1950
	George C. Marshall	1950–1951
	Robert A. Lovett	1951–1953

(continues)

Eisenhower, 1953–1961

Office	Name	Years
Vice-President	Richard M. Nixon	1953–1961
Secretary of State	John Foster Dulles	1953–1959
	Christian A. Herter	1959–1961
Secretary of Treasury	George M. Humphrey	1953–1957
	Robert B. Anderson	1957–1961
Postmaster General	Arthur E. Summerfield	1953–1961
Attorney General	Herbert Brownell, Jr.	1953–1958
	William P. Rogers	1958–1961
Secretary of Interior	Douglas McKay	1953–1956
	Fred A. Seaton	1956–1961
Secretary of Agriculture	Ezra Taft Benson	1953–1961
Secretary of Commerce	Sinclair Weeks	1953–1958
	Lewis L. Strauss	1958–1959
	Frederick H. Mueller	1959–1961
Secretary of Labor	Martin P. Durkin	1953
	James P. Mitchell	1953–1961
Secretary of Defense	Charles E. Wilson	1953–1957
	Neil H. McElroy	1957–1959
	Thomas S. Gates, Jr.	1959–1961
Secretary of Health, Education, and Welfare	Oveta Culp Hobby	1953–1955
	Marion B. Folsom	1955–1958
	Arthur S. Flemming	1958–1961

Kennedy, 1961–1963

Vice-President	Lyndon B. Johnson	1961–1963
Secretary of State	Dean Rusk	1961–1963
Secretary of Treasury	C. Douglas Dillon	1961–1963
Postmaster General	J. Edward Day	1961–1963
	John A. Gronouski	1963
Attorney General	Robert F. Kennedy	1961–1963
Secretary of Interior	Stewart L. Udall	1961–1963
Secretary of Agriculture	Orville L. Freeman	1961–1963
Secretary of Commerce	Luther H. Hodges	1961–1963
Secretary of Labor	Arthur J. Goldberg	1961–1962
	W. Willard Wirtz	1962–1963
Secretary of Defense	Robert S. McNamara	1961–1963
Secretary of Health, Education, and Welfare	Abraham A. Ribicoff	1961–1962
	Anthony J. Celebrezze	1962–1963

Lyndon Johnson, 1963–1969

Office	Name	Years
Vice-President	Hubert H. Humphrey	1965–1969
Secretary of State	Dean Rusk	1963–1969
Secretary of Treasury	C. Douglas Dillon	1963–1965
	Henry H. Fowler	1965–1969

Postmaster General	John A. Gronouski	1963–1965
	Lawrence F. O'Brien	1965–1968
	Marvin Watson	1968–1969
Attorney General	Robert F. Kennedy	1963–1964
	Nicholas Katzenbach	1965–1966
	Ramsey Clark	1967–1969
Secretary of Interior	Stewart L. Udall	1963–1969
Secretary of Agriculture	Orville L. Freeman	1963–1969
Secretary of Commerce	Luther H. Hodges	1963–1964
	John T. Connor	1964–1967
	Alexander B. Trowbridge	1967–1968
	Cyrus R. Smith	1968–1969
Secretary of Labor	W. Willard Wirtz	1963–1969
Secretary of Defense	Robert F. McNamara	1963–1968
	Clark Clifford	1968–1969
Secretary of Health, Education, and Welfare	Anthony J. Celebrezze	1963–1965
	John W. Gardner	1965–1968
	Wilbur J. Cohen	1968–1969
Secretary of Housing and Urban Development	Robert C. Weaver	1966–1969
	Robert C. Wood	1969
Secretary of Transportation	Alan S. Boyd	1967–1969

Nixon, 1969–1974

Vice-President	Spiro T. Agnew	1969–1973
	Gerald R. Ford	1973–1974
Secretary of State	William P. Rogers	1969–1973
	Henry A. Kissinger	1973–1974
Secretary of Treasury	David M. Kennedy	1969–1970
	John B. Connally	1971–1972
	George P. Shultz	1972–1974
	William E. Simon	1974
Postmaster General	Winton M. Blount	1969–1971
Attorney General	John N. Mitchell	1969–1972
	Richard G. Kleindienst	1972–1973
	Elliot L. Richardson	1973
	William B. Saxbe	1973–1974
Secretary of Interior	Walter J. Hickel	1969–1970
	Rogers Morton	1971–1974
Secretary of Agriculture	Clifford M. Hardin	1969–1971
	Earl L. Butz	1971–1974
Secretary of Commerce	Maurice H. Stans	1969–1972
	Peter G. Peterson	1972–1973
	Frederick B. Dent	1973–1974
Secretary of Labor	George P. Shultz	1969–1970
	James D. Hodgson	1970–1973
	Peter J. Brennan	1973–1974

(continues)

Secretary of Defense	Melvin R. Laird — 1969–1973
	Elliot L. Richardson — 1973
	James R. Schlesinger — 1973–1974
Secretary of Health, Education, and Welfare	Robert H. Finch — 1969–1970
	Elliot L. Richardson — 1970–1973
	Caspar W. Weinberger — 1973–1974
Secretary of Housing and Urban Development	George W. Romney — 1969–1973
	James T. Lynn — 1973–1974
Secretary of Transportation	John A. Volpe — 1969–1973
	Claude S. Brinegar — 1973–1974

Ford, 1974–1977

Vice-President	Nelson A. Rockefeller — 1974–1977
Secretary of State	Henry A. Kissinger — 1974–1977
Secretary of Treasury	William E. Simon — 1974–1977
Attorney General	William B. Saxbe — 1974–1975
	Edward H. Levi — 1975–1977
Secretary of Interior	Rogers C. B. Morton — 1974–1975
	Stanley K. Hathaway — 1975
	Thomas S. Kleppe — 1975–1977
Secretary of Agriculture	Earl L. Butz — 1974–1976
	John A. Knebel — 1976–1977
Secretary of Commerce	Frederick B. Dent — 1974–1975
	Rogers C. B. Morton — 1975–1976
	Elliot L. Richardson — 1976–1977
Secretary of Labor	Peter J. Brennan — 1974–1975
	John T. Dunlop — 1975–1976
	W. J. Usery, Jr. — 1976–1977
Secretary of Defense	James R. Schlesinger — 1974–1975
	Donald H. Rumsfeld — 1975–1977
Secretary of Health, Education, and Welfare	Caspar W. Weinberger — 1974–1975
	F. David Mathews — 1975–1977
Secretary of Housing and Urban Development	James T. Lynn — 1974–1975
	Carla Anderson Hills — 1975–1977
Secretary of Transportation	Claude S. Brinegar — 1974–1975
	William T. Coleman, Jr. — 1974–1977

Carter, 1977–1981

Vice-President	Walter F. Mondale — 1977–1981
Secretary of State	Cyrus R. Vance — 1977–1980
	Edmund S. Muskie — 1980–1981
Secretary of Treasury	W. Michael Blumenthal — 1977–1979
	G. William Miller — 1979–1981

Office	Name	Years
Attorney General	Griffin B. Bell	1977–1979
	Benjamin R. Civiletti	1979–1981
Secretary of Interior	Cecil D. Andrus	1977–1981
Secretary of Agriculture	Robert Bergland	1977–1981
Secretary of Commerce	Juanita M. Kreps	1977–1979
	Philip M. Klutznick	1979–1981
Secretary of Labor	F. Ray Marshall	1977–1981
Secretary of Defense	Harold Brown	1977–1981
Secretary of Health, Education, and Welfare	Joseph A. Califano, Jr.	1977–1979
	Patricia Roberts Harris	1979
Secretary of Health and Human Services	Patricia Roberts Harris	1979–1981
Secretary of Housing and Urban Development	Patricia Roberts Harris	1977–1979
	Moon Landrieu	1979–1981
Secretary of Transportation	Brock Adams	1977–1979
	Neil E. Goldschmidt	1979–1981
Secretary of Energy	James R. Schlesinger, Jr.	1977–1979
	Charles W. Duncan, Jr.	1979–1981
Secretary of Education	Shirley M. Hufstedler	1979–1981

Reagan, 1981–1989

Office	Name	Years
Vice-President	George Bush	1981–1989
Secretary of State	Alexander M. Haig, Jr.	1981–1982
	George P. Shultz	1982–1989
Secretary of Treasury	Donald T. Regan	1981–1985
	James A. Baker, III	1985–1988
	Nicholas F. Brady	1988–1989
Attorney General	William French Smith	1981–1985
	Edwin A. Meese, III	1985–1988
	Richard Thornburgh	1988–1989
Secretary of Interior	James C. Watt	1981–1983
	William P. Clarke, Jr.	1983–1985
	Donald P. Hodel	1985–1989
Secretary of Agriculture	John R. Block	1981–1986
	Richard Lyng	1986–1989
Secretary of Commerce	Malcolm Baldrige	1981–1987
	C. William Verity, Jr.	1987–1989
Secretary of Labor	Raymond J. Donovan	1981–1985
	William E. Brock	1985–1987
	Ann D. McLaughlin	1987–1989
Secretary of Defense	Caspar W. Weinberger	1981–1987
	Frank C. Carlucci	1987–1989

(continues)

Secretary of Health and Human Services	Richard S. Schweiker	1981–1983
	Margaret M. Heckler	1983–1985
	Otis R. Bowen	1985–1989
Secretary of Housing and Urban Development	Samuel R. Pierce, Jr.	1981–1989
Secretary of Transportation	Andrew L. Lewis, Jr.	1981–1983
	Elizabeth Hanford Dole	1983–1987
	James H. Burnley	1987–1989
Secretary of Energy	James B. Edwards	1981–1982
	Donald P. Hodel	1982–1985
	John S. Herrington	1985–1989
Secretary of Education	Terrel H. Bell	1981–1985
	William J. Bennett	1985–1988
	Lauro F. Cavazos	1988–1989

Bush, 1989–1993

Vice President	J. Danforth Quayle	1989–1993
Secretary of State	James A. Baker III	1989–1992
Secretary of Treasury	Nicholas Brady	1989–1993
Attorney General	Richard Thornburgh	1989–1991
	William P. Barr	1991–1993
Secretary of Interior	Manuel Lujan	1989–1993
Secretary of Agriculture	Clayton K. Yeutter	1989–1991
	Edward Madigan	1991–1993
Secretary of Commerce	Robert Mosbacher	1989–1992
	Barbara Franklin	1992–1993
Secretary of Labor	Elizabeth Hanford Dole	1989–1991
	Lynn Martin	1991–1993
Secretary of Defense	Richard Cheney	1989–1993
Secretary of Health and Human Services	Louis W. Sullivan	1989–1993
Secretary of Education	Lauro F. Cavazos	1989–1991
	Lamar Alexander	1991–1993
Secretary of Housing and Urban Development	Jack F. Kemp	1989–1993
Secretary of Transportation	Samuel K. Skinner	1989–1992
	Andrew H. Card Jr.	1992–1993
Secretary of Energy	James D. Watkins	1989–1993
Secretary of Veterans Affairs	Edward J. Derwinski	1989–1993

Clinton, 1993–

Vice President	Albert Gore	1993–
Secretary of State	Warren Christopher	1993–
Secretary of Treasury	Lloyd Bentsen	1993–
Attorney General	Janet Reno	1993–

Secretary of Interior	Bruce Babbitt	1993–
Secretary of Agriculture	Michael Espy	1993–
Secretary of Commerce	Ronald Brown	1993–
Secretary of Labor	Robert B. Reich	1993–
Secretary of Defense	Les Aspin	1993–1994
	William Perry	1994–
Secretary of Health and Human Services	Donna Shalala	1993–

Secretary of Housing and Urban Development	Henry G. Cisneros	1993–
Secretary of Education	Richard W. Riley	1993–
Secretary of Transportation	Federico Peña	1993–
Secretary of Energy	Hazel R. O'Leary	1993–
Secretary of Veterans Affairs	Edward J. Derwinski	1993–

Supreme Court Justices

Chief Justices in italics.

	Term of Service	Years of Service
John Jay	1789–1795	5
John Rutledge	1789–1791	1
William Cushing	1789–1810	20
James Wilson	1789–1798	8
John Blair	1789–1796	6
Robert H. Harrison	1789–1790	—
James Iredell	1790–1799	9
Thomas Johnson	1791–1793	1
William Paterson	1793–1806	13
*John Rutledge**	1795	—
Samuel Chase	1796–1811	15

	Term of Service	Years of Service
Oliver Ellsworth	1796–1800	4
Bushrod Washington	1798–1829	31
Alfred Moore	1799–1804	4
John Marshall	1801–1835	34
William Johnson	1804–1834	30
H. Brockholst Livingston	1806–1823	16
Thomas Todd	1807–1826	18
Joseph Story	1811–1845	33
Gabriel Duval	1811–1835	24
Smith Thompson	1823–1843	20
Robert Trimble	1826–1828	2

	Term of Service	Years of Service
John McLean	1829–1861	32
Henry Baldwin	1830–1844	14
James M. Wayne	1835–1867	32
Roger B. Taney	1836–1864	28
Philip P. Barbour	1836–1841	4
John Catron	1837–1865	28
John McKinley	1837–1852	15
Peter V. Daniel	1841–1860	19
Samuel Nelson	1845–1872	27
Levi Woodbury	1845–1851	5
Robert C. Grier	1846–1870	23
Benjamin R. Curtis	1851–1857	6
John A. Campbell	1853–1861	8
Nathan Clifford	1858–1881	23
Noah H. Swayne	1862–1881	18
Samuel F. Miller	1862–1890	28
David Davis	1862–1877	14
Stephen J. Field	1863–1897	34
Salmon P. Chase	1864–1873	8

*Never confirmed as Chief Justice

	Term of Service	Years of Service
William Strong	1870–1880	10
Joseph P. Bradley	1870–1892	22
Ward Hunt	1873–1882	9
Morrison R. Waite	1874–1888	14
John M. Harlan	1877–1911	34
William B. Woods	1880–1887	7
Stanley Matthews	1881–1889	7
Horace Gray	1882–1902	20
Samuel Blatchford	1882–1893	11
Lucius Q. C. Lamar	1888–1893	5
Melville W. Fuller	1888–1910	21
David J. Brewer	1890–1910	20
Henry B. Brown	1890–1906	16
George Shiras, Jr.	1892–1903	10
Howell E. Jackson	1893–1895	2
Edward D. White	1894–1910	16
Rufus W. Peckham	1895–1909	14
Joseph McKenna	1898–1925	26
Oliver W. Holmes, Jr.	1902–1932	30
William R. Day	1903–1922	19

(continues)

Name	Term of Service	Years of Service
William H. Moody	1906–1910	3
Horace H. Lurton	1910–1914	4
Charles E. Hughes	1910–1916	5
Willis Van Devanter	1911–1937	26
Joseph R. Lamar	1911–1916	5
Edward D. White	1910–1921	11
Mahlon Pitney	1912–1922	10
James C. McReynolds	1914–1941	26
Louis D. Brandeis	1916–1939	22
John H. Clarke	1916–1922	6
William H. Taft	1921–1930	8
George Sutherland	1922–1938	15
Pierce Butler	1922–1939	16
Edward T. Sanford	1923–1930	7
Harlan F. Stone	1925–1941	16
Charles E. Hughes	1930–1941	11
Owen J. Roberts	1930–1945	15
Benjamin N. Cardozo	1932–1938	6
Hugo L. Black	1937–1971	34
Stanley F. Reed	1938–1957	19
Felix Frankfurter	1939–1962	23
William O. Douglas	1939–1975	36
Frank Murphy	1940–1949	9
Harlan F. Stone	1941–1946	5
James F. Byrnes	1941–1942	1
Robert H. Jackson	1941–1954	13
Wiley B. Rutledge	1943–1949	6
Harold H. Burton	1945–1958	13
Fred M. Vinson	1946–1953	7
Tom C. Clark	1949–1967	18
Sherman Minton	1949–1956	7
Earl Warren	1953–1969	16
John Marshall Harlan	1955–1971	16
William J. Brennan, Jr.	1956–1990	34
Charles E. Whittaker	1957–1962	5
Potter Stewart	1958–1981	23
Byron R. White	1962–	—
Arthur J. Goldberg	1962–1965	3
Abe Fortas	1965–1969	4
Thurgood Marshall	1967–1991	24

	Term of Service	Years of Service
Warren E. Burger	1969–1986	18
Harry A. Blackmun	1970–1994	24
Lewis F. Powell, Jr.	1971–1987	15
*William H. Rehnquist****	1971–	—
John P. Stevens III	1975–	—
Sandra Day O'Connor	1981–	—
Antonin Scalia	1986–	—
Anthony M. Kennedy	1988–	—
David H. Souter	1990–	—
Clarence Thomas	1991–	—
Ruth Bader Ginsburg	1993–	—
Stephen Breyer	1994–	—

*Never confirmed as Chief Justice.
**Chief Justice from 1986 on.

Admission of States to the Union

State	Date of Admission
1. Delaware	December 7, 1787
2. Pennsylvania	December 12, 1787
3. New Jersey	December 18, 1787
4. Georgia	January 2, 1788
5. Connecticut	January 9, 1788
6. Massachusetts	February 6, 1788
7. Maryland	April 28, 1788
8. South Carolina	May 23, 1788
9. New Hampshire	June 21, 1788
10. Virginia	June 25, 1788
11. New York	July 26, 1788
12. North Carolina	November 21, 1789
13. Rhode Island	May 29, 1790
14. Vermont	March 4, 1791
15. Kentucky	June 1, 1792
16. Tennessee	June 1, 1796
17. Ohio	March 1, 1803
18. Louisiana	April 30, 1812
19. Indiana	December 11, 1816
20. Mississippi	December 10, 1817
21. Illinois	December 3, 1818
22. Alabama	December 14, 1819
23. Maine	March 15, 1820

State	Date of Admission
24. Missouri	August 10, 1821
25. Arkansas	June 15, 1836
26. Michigan	January 26, 1837
27. Florida	March 3, 1845
28. Texas	December 29, 1845
29. Iowa	December 28, 1846
30. Wisconsin	May 29, 1848
31. California	September 9, 1850
32. Minnesota	May 11, 1858
33. Oregon	February 14, 1859
34. Kansas	January 29, 1861
35. West Virginia	June 20, 1863
36. Nevada	October 31, 1864
37. Nebraska	March 1, 1867
38. Colorado	August 1, 1876
39. North Dakota	November 2, 1889
40. South Dakota	November 2, 1889
41. Montana	November 8, 1889
42. Washington	November 11, 1889
43. Idaho	July 3, 1890
44. Wyoming	July 10, 1890
45. Utah	January 4, 1896
46. Oklahoma	November 16, 1907
47. New Mexico	January 6, 1912
48. Arizona	February 14, 1912
49. Alaska	January 3, 1959
50. Hawaii	August 21, 1959

Credits

Index

AAA. *See* Agriculture Adjustment Act (AAA)

Abolition. *See* Antislavery movement

Abortion, 795–796

Acheson, Dean, 704–705, 712

Activism, 774–776
  of college students, 789–790

Act of Religious Toleration (1649), 31–32

Act of Supremacy, 16

Adams, John, 101, 110, 129, 174
  mission to France, 143
  negotiations with France, 174–175
  presidency of, 174
  and presidential election of 1796, 173
  and presidential election of 1800, 176–178

Adams, John Quincy, 203–204, 210, 228–229
  and foreign policy, 231
  presidency of, 230–231
  and Texas annexation, 317

Adams, Samuel, 79–80, 87, 93, 97, 99,
    101–102, 109–110, 138, 156

Adamson Act, 569, 575

Adams-Onis Treaty of 1819, 210

Addams, Jane, 557–558, 586

*Adder's Den or Secrets of the Great Conspiracy to
    Overthrow Liberty in America, The* (John
    Smith Dye), 334–335

Administration of Justice Act, 100

Adventures of Huckleberry Finn, The (Mark
    Twain), 484

Affirmative action, 795

AFL. *See* American Federation of Labor

African American nationalism, 781–784

African Americans. *See also* Blacks
  in abolition movement, 263
  education of, 405
    in early 19th century, 257

Emancipation Proclamation and, 378

enlistment in Civil War, 378–379

free. *See* Free blacks

freed. *See* Freed slaves

in government, 786

in industrial work force, in 19th century, 423

leaders, in Reconstruction, 402

legal rights over, controversy over, 353

New Deal and, 655–656

overseas colonization, 259–260, 263

problems of, 774

religion and, 405
  in Revolutionary period, 150

social justice movement in early 20th
  century and, 559–560

status of
  in 1960s, 750, 774
  in World War I, 594–596

suffrage for, 397–399

urban growth and, 612–613

World War II and, 678–679

African Methodist Episcopal Church, 150

African slave trade, 45–48
  in English colonies, 28

African tradition, in slave religion, 297

Agnew, Spiro, 763, 806

Agrarian revolts, in 19th century. *See* Grangers;
    Populist party

Agricultural Adjustment Act (AAA), 648
  effects on African Americans, 656
  effects on Mexican Americans, 656
  and Supreme Court, 658

Agriculture, 277. *See also* Farming
  commercialization of, 279–280
  in early 19th century, 211
    innovation in, 216

Native American, 4
in New South, 441
in South, 287–289
in 18th century
in Chesapeake region, 45
in New England, 44
in 19th century, 422, 436–440
Aguinaldo, Emilio, 546–547
AIM. *See* American Indian Movement (AIM)
Alabama
admission to Union, 207
secession of, 363
Alamo, 316
Alaska
prehistoric inhabitants of, 4
purchase of, 528
Albany, 23
Albany Plan of Union, 73–74, 102
Albany Regency, 229
Alcatraz, Native American occupation of, 800
Alcohol consumption, moral reform campaign
against, 253–255
Aldrich, Nelson W., 566
Alger, Horatio, 425–426
Alien Act, 175–176
Alien Enemies Act, 176
Allen, Richard, 150
Altgeld, John P., 519
AMA. *See* American Medical Association
Amalgamated Association of Iron and Steel
Workers, 518
Amateurism, in sports, 492
America
discovery of, 4–7
prehistoric inhabitants of, 4
American Anti-Slavery Society, 262
American Colonization Society, 259–260
American empire, in 1900, 546f
American exceptionalism, 529–530
American Federation of Labor (AFL), 455,
467–469, 589–590
and women, 616
American Indian Movement (AIM), 801
American Medical Association, 557–558
American Missionary Association, 389, 405
American party. *See* Know-Nothing Party
American Peace Commission, 601
American Philosophical Society, 68
American Protective Association, 561
American Railway Union, 518–519

American Society for the Promotion of
Temperance, 254
American System, 204, 231–232
American Woman Suffrage Association, 398,
506
"Amos and Andy," 624
Anaconda Plan, 369
Anarchism, 599
Ancient Order of Hibernians, 463
Anderson, Robert, 364, 383
Andropov, Yuri, 824
Andros, Sir Edmund, 62
Anglican (English) Church, 16–17
Animal magnetism, 273
Anthony, Susan B., 398, 506
Anti-Comintern Pact, 667
Antietam, battle of, 359–360, 371, 377
Antifederalists, 155
arguments of, 156
Anti-Masonic party, 228
Antinomianism, 37–38
Anti-Saloon League, 558
Antislavery movement, 260–261, 340
division in, 262–264
opposition to, 261–262
and politics, 262
radical, 262–263
rise of, 259–262
in South, 290–291
violence in, 354–355
Antitrust legislation, of late 19th century, 511
Apache Indians, 312, 409
Apocalypse Now, 768
Appeal to the Colored Citizens of the World
(David Walker), 260
Arapaho Indians, 6
conflict with settlers, 410
Arbella, 35
Architecture, urban, in 19th century, 476–477
Arkansas, secession of, 365
Armory Show (New York City), 486
Army, reduction of, in 19th century, 527–528
Army-McCarthy hearings, 712
Army Nurses Corps, 677
Army of Northern Virginia, 359, 370. *See also*
Confederacy
Army of the Potomac, 359, 370. *See also* Union
Arnold, Benedict, 112, 123, 126, 128
Art
in mid-19th century, 268–273

and urban landscape, in 19th century, 485–486

Arthur, Chester A., 508

Articles of Confederation, 138
  ratification of, 139

Artisan system of labor, disruption of, 280–281

Art Project, 651

ARU. *See* American Railway Union

Ashcan painters, 485–486

Asian markets, American ambitions for, in 19th century, 531–532

Assembly, freedom of. *See* Freedom of assembly

Assembly lines, 433–434

Astor, John Jacob, 318

Atahualpa, 12

Atlanta, capture of, 382

Atlantic Charter, 670

Atomic bomb, 674, 690, 699–700
  espionage and, 710
  in Hiroshima, 691
  Soviet Union and, 703

Attacks, Crispus, 95

Auburn Prison, NY, 256

Audiencias, 13

Austin, Moses, 314

Austin, Stephen, 314–315

Automobile industry
  and economic growth, 810
  during 1920s, 622

AWSA. *See* American Woman Suffrage Association

Axis Powers, 681

Aztecs, 5, 12

Babcock, Orville, 525–526

Baby and Child Care (Benjamin Spock), 738

Baby boom, 677–678

Back to Bataan, 677

Bacon, Nathaniel, 60–61

Bacon's Rebellion, 61

Baer, George F., 552

Baez, Buenaventura, 525–526

Baez, Joan, 791

Balboa, Vasco Núñez de, 12

Ball, George, 758

Ballinger, Richard A., 566

Baltimore, 535

Baltimore and Ohio Railroad strike of 1877, 463–464

Banking
  in early 19th century, 205–206, 241–243

in 19th century, 432
  Van Buren presidency and, 245

Banking crisis
  crash of 1929 and, 631–632
  in Great Depression, 643–644

Banking reform, in 1913, 568

Bank of the United States, 165–166
  second
    constitutionality of, 208
    establishment of, 206–207
    Jackson's war against, 241–243
    money policies, 218–219
    support for, 204–205

Barbados, slavery in, 47

Barbary pirates, 188

Barnett, Ross, 777

Barrow, Bennet H., 295

Bartholdi, Frederic Auguste, 447

Baruch, Bernard M., 589

Baseball
  as national pastime, 488–490
  segregation in, 492

Batista, Fulgencio, 730

Battle of Midway, 688

Battle of the Bulge, 685, 687

Bay of Pigs invasion, 750–751

Bear Flag Rebellion, 324–325

Beat Generation, 740–741

Beauregard, P. G. T., 364, 367, 372

Becknell, William, 308

Beckwourth, Jim, 308

Beecher, Catharine, 265

Begin, Menachem, 815–816

Bell, Alexander Graham, 420

Bell, John, 362

Bellamy, Edward, 555

Bennett, James Gordon, 272

Benton, Thomas Hart, 239

Bering Straits, land bridge, 4

Berkeley, Sir William, 60

Berkeley Free Speech Movement, 790

Berkman, Alexander, 518

Berlin airlift, 703

Berlin Wall, tearing down of, 828

Bernard, Francis, 87

Bernstein, Carl, and Watergate, 806

Bessemer steelmaking process, 421

Bethune, Mary McLeod, 656

Beveridge, Albert J., 533

Bibb, Henry, 297

Biddle, Nicholas, 242

Bidwell, John, 312
Bierstadt, Albert, 272, 485
Big business
    power of, 434–435
    rise of, in 19th century, 429–435
Big stick diplomacy, 570–572
Bilingual education programs, 799
Bill of Rights, 162
Birds of passage, immigrants as, 450–451
Birmingham, AL, resistance to desegregation in,
    777–779
Birney, James G., 262
Birth control, during the 1920s, 610–611
Birthrate
    in early 19th century, 264–265
    in 1950s, 793
    in World War II, 677–678
Bishop, Maurice, assassination of, 822–823
Bismarck, Otto von, 534
Bissell, George, 419
Blackboard Jungle, 714
Black Codes, 394–395
Black Hawk War, 237–238
Black Hills Indian reservation, gold
    discovery in, 411
Black Legend, 15
Blacklisting, 713–714
Blackmun, Harry, 788
Black Muslims, 781–782
Black Panthers, 783
Black power, 783–784
Black Republicans, 401–404
Blacks. *See also* African Americans;
        Free blacks; Slaves
    in Continental Army, 120
    discrimination against. *See also* Racism;
        Segregation
    in late 19th century, 512
    influence on modern American music,
        486–488
    legal status of, in English colonies, 28
    migration from rural South to urban North,
        in 19th century, 475
    voting rights, in early 19th century, 227
Blaine, James G., 504, 508–509
Bland-Allison Act of 1878, 507, 511
Bleeding Kansas, 346–348
Bleeding Sumner, 346–348
Board of Customs Commissioners, 93
Board of Trade and Plantations, 65

Boesky, Ivan, 822
Bonus Army, 642–643
Book of Mormon, 320
Boone, Daniel, 146
Booth, John Wilkes, 384
Bootlegging, 617–618
Borden, Abby, 472–473
Borden, Andrew, 472–473
Borden, Emma, 472
Borden, Hannah, 282
Borden, Lizzie, 472–473, 473*f*
Bork, Robert, 806
Boston Manufacturing Company, 202
Boston Massacre, 94–95
Boston Tea Party, 99
Boulder Dam, 663
Bourne, Randolph, 581–582, 599, 603
Bowie, Jim, 316
Boxer Rebellion, 548
Boxing, popularity of, in 19th century, 490–491
Boy Scouts of America, 561
Braddock, Edward, 74
Bradford, William, 3, 33
Bradley, Mamie, 721
Brandeis, Louis D., 556, 569
Brant, Joseph (Thayendanegea), 122
Breckinridge, John C., 362
Breed's Hill, 112
Brer Rabbit tales, 298
Brezhnev, Leonid, 766, 815, 824
Briand, Aristide, 665
Britain. *See* Great Britain
Brook Farm community, 267
Brooks, Preston, 347–348
Brown, James, 784
Brown, John
    death of, 354
    raid on Harpers Ferry, 354–355
    raid on Pottawatomie Creek, 348
Brown, Norman O., 790
Brown v. *Board of Education of Topeka,*
    720, 733, 774
Bryan, William Jennings, 566, 618
    anti-imperialism, 545–547
    "Cross of Gold" speech, 499
    as presidential candidate, 499–501, 520
Bryant, Roy, 720–721
Buchanan, James
    in presidential election of 1856, 349
    and slavery, 349–351

Budapest, uprising in, 727
Buell, Don Carlos, 369
Buffalo, 409, 411
Bull Moose party, 566–567
Bull Run
   battle of, 367–368
   second battle of, 371
Bunau-Varilla, Philippe, 571
Bunker Hill, battle of, 112
Bureau of Corporations, 565
Burger, Warren, 788, 796
Burgoyne, John, 109, 121, 123
Burns, Anthony, 340
Burnside, Ambrose E., 359, 379
Burr, Aaron, 173, 181, 190
Burroughs, Edgar Rice, 624
Bush, George, 826–827
   domestic policies of, 832
   foreign policy of, 827–828
   and Persian Gulf War, 829–832
   in presidential election of 1988, 826
   in presidential election of 1992, 832
Bushy Run, Pennsylvania, 83
Business, aid to, in 19th century, 427
Busing, 785
Butler, Andrew, 347

Cable cars, 475
Cabot, John. *See* Caboto, Giovanni
Caboto, Giovanni, 15
Cahokia, IL, temple mounds in, 5
Calhoun, John C., 194, 204, 205*f*, 207, 210,
   228–229, 232, 239–240, 317, 329, 338
   and secession, 363
Calhoun, William J., 540
California
   acquisition by United States, 323–324
   application for statehood, as free state,
      335–336
   effects of gold rush on, 330–331
Calvert, Cecilius, 31
Calvert, George, 31
Calvert family, 64
Calvin, John, 17
Cambodia, invasion of, 763–764
Camelot, Kennedy administration as, 749–750
Canada
   French empire in, 23
   patriot attempts to seize, 112
Canadian-United States border, Webster-
   Ashburton Treaty on, 317–318

Canal building, in early 19th century, 212–213
Canning, George, 210
Cannon, Uncle Joe, 566
Capital
   Northern, in 19th century, 442
   South's lack of, in 19th century, 442
Capital formation, in 19th century, 428–429
Capital punishment, reform efforts against, 256
Capone, Al, 617
Cardoza, Francis, 402
Carmichael, Stokely, 783
Carnegie, Andrew, 375, 417–419, 421, 425,
      432, 432*f*, 518, 545, 554
Carnegie Steel Company, 417
Carney, William H., 378
Carolinas, 32
Carpetbaggers, 400, 403
Carranza, Venustiano, 573
Carter, Jimmy, 809–810
   and deregulation, 813–814
   and human rights, 816–818
   and inflation, 813
   and Iran hostage crisis, 817–818
   and Middle East relations, 815–816
   and Panama Canal Treaty, 816
Cartier, Jacques, 16
Casey, William, 824
Cass, Lewis, 338
Castro, Fidel, 730, 750, 791
Catcher in the Rye (J. D. Salinger), 790
Catherine of Aragon, 16
Catholic Church
   in New Spain, 14–15
   parochial schools of, 257
   and slavery, 48
Catholics, bias against, 257, 341–342
Cato's Letters, 97
Catt, Carrie Chapman, 559
Cattle barons, 437
Cavalier, stereotype of, 286–287
Cavelier, René-Robert, 71
CCC. *See* Civilian Conservation Corps (CCC)
Census, 1790, 160–161
Central Intelligence Agency (CIA), 725,
      729–730
   involvement in Nicaragua, 824
   limitation of power by Congress, 809
   and Watergate, 805
Central Pacific Railroad, 446
Central Park (New York City), 493
Chamber of Commerce, 561

Chambers, Whittaker, 695–696, 697*f*
Chamoun, Camille, 730
Champlain, Samuel de, 23
Chancellorsville, battle of, 379–380
Chaney, James, 783
Chang Kai-shek. *See* Jiang Jieshi
Channing, William Ellery, 252
Chaplin, Charlie, 625
Charles I (King of England), 31–32, 34
Charles II (King of England), 32, 56, 58
Charles River Bridge v. *Warren Bridge,* 244
Charleston, SC, 32
   planned slave revolt in, 298–299
Chase, Salmon P., 346, 375
Chase, Samuel, 187
Chatham, Earl of, 92
Chattanooga, TN, capture of, 381
Chávez, César, 799
Chernenko, Konstantin, 824
Cherokee Indians, 6, 125
   adaptation to change, 236
   removal westward, 237
Cherokee Nation v. *Georgia,* 237
Chesapeake, 192
Chesapeake Bay, 128
Chesapeake Bay region
   hazards of, for colonists, 40
   migrants to, sex ratios among, 40
   population of, in seventeenth century, 40
   settlements, in 1650, 22*f*
   stabilizing life in, 45
   tobacco production in, 55–56, 60
Cheyenne Indians, 311–312, 409
   conflict with settlers, 410
Chicago, 19th-century, 478
Chickamauga, battle of, 381
Chickasaws, 6
Child care, 677
Child Health Improvement and Protection Act
   (1968), 786
Child labor, 284
Child labor laws, 563, 569, 574
Children
   in Chesapeake region, 41
   in Puritan New England, 40
Chile, confrontation with, in late 19th century,
   535
China, Open Door policy with, 547–548
China Lobby, 704
Chinese Exclusion Act of 1882, 447, 456, 512

Chinese immigrants, in 19th century
   characteristics of, 446–447
   and nativism, 455–456
   and railroad construction, 446
Chinooks, 6
Chivington, J. M., 410
Choctaw Indians, 5–6
   removal westward, 237
Chou En-lai, 766
Christianity, in slave religion, 297–298
Church, Frederick, 272
Churchill, Winston, 670, 681, 684–687,
   699–700
Church of England, 16–17, 33–34
CIA. *See* Central Intelligence Agency
CIO. *See* Congress of Industrial
   Organizations (CIO)
Cisneros, Henry, 800
Cities, in 19th century
   architecture in, 476–477
   crime in, 478
   culture of, 482–488
   ethnic neighborhoods, 477
   growth of
      early, 216–217
      problems with, 217, 478–480
   housing in, 478–479
   nightlife in, 482–483
   parks in, 493
   private *versus* public, 480–482
   segregation in, 477–478
   sewage and water problems in, 217, 479–480
   transformation of, 474–475
   transportation technology in, 475–476
City College of New York (CCNY), sports
   scandal in, 715
"Civil Disobedience" (Henry David Thoreau),
   270
Civil disobedience, in antislavery movement, 262
Civilian Conservation Corps (CCC), 649–650
   African Americans and, 656
   Mexican Americans and, 656–657
   Native Americans and, 657
Civil Rights Act (1866), 395
Civil Rights Act (1964), 779, 786, 797–798
   Title VII of, 794–795
Civil Rights movement, 731–736, 774–803
   backlash to, 787–788
   Kennedy and, 750
   Selma-Montgomery march, 781

spread to north, 784–785
student participation in, 790
Civil Service Commission, 508
Civil War, 359–384. *See also* Confederacy;
    North; South; Union
  1861-1862, 368*f*
  1863-1865, 379–383, 380*f*
  beginning of, 364
  casualties in, 360, 367–368, 372, 378–382
  cause of, 361
  effects of, 388–390
  end of, 383
  enthusiasm for, 364–365, 367
  morale during, 373–379
  Peninsula campaign of, 367
  post-war conditions, 388–392
  in West, 371–372
Civil Works Administration (CWA), 649
Clark, James, 780–781
Clark, William, 189, 306
Clarke, Edward Young, 619–620
Clay, Henry, 194, 204, 205*f,* 210, 220,
    229–232, 240–242, 262, 338–339
Clayton Antitrust Act, 568, 574
Clemenceau, Georges, 601–603
Clemens, Samuel Langhorne, 484
Clermont, 212, 213*f*
Cleveland, Grover, 447, 499, 502, 517
  first presidency of, 508–511
  and foreign policy, 536–538, 540
Clinton, Bill
  accomplishments of, 833
  election of 1992, 832
Clinton, DeWitt, 213
Clinton, Henry, 109, 124–125, 128
Clinton's Ditch, 213
Coal industry, 419
Coal miners' strike
  in 1902, 552–553
  of 1870s, 463
Cobb, Ty, 625
Cocaine abuse, in 19th century, 495
Coercive Acts, 99–101
Coinage Act of 1873, 507
Cold Harbor, battle of, 382
Cold War, 698–716, 730–731, 750, 766
  effects of, 702, 710–716
  origins of, 698
  Reagan presidency and, 822–823
  Vietnam and, 753

Cole, Thomas, 272
Colfax, Schuyler, 408
Colleges, reform in, 258
Collier, John, 657
Columbian exchange, 24
Columbus, Christopher, 8, 13*f*
  expeditions to America, 9–10
Comanche Indians, 312
Comic book industry, 714
Commerce, and expansionism, in 19th century,
    530–532
Committee for the Reelection of the President
    (CREEP), 805
Committee on Public Information (CPI),
    591–593
Commodity Credit Corporation, 648
Common Sense (Thomas Paine), 113–114
Commonwealth of Independent States, 829
Commonwealth v. *Hunt,* 282
Communal ideal, 791
Communication revolution, during 1920s,
    623–624
Communications, innovations, in 19th
    century, 420
Communism, 695–697, 702, 746
  in China, 703–704
  collapse of, in Eastern Europe, 828
  and Red Scare after World War I, 599
  in Vietnam, 746, 755
Competition, control of, by big business,
    429–432
Compromise of 1850, 338–339
Compromise of 1877, 412–413
Compromise Tariff (1832), 338
Concentration camps, 680
Concord, Massachusetts, 109–110
Coney Island, 493
Confederacy, 363
  aid from Europe, 373
  conscription act, 374
  constitution of, 363
  readmission to Union, 391. *See also*
    Reconstruction
  shortages in, 373–374
Confederate States of America. *See* Confederacy
Congregational church, 38
Congregationalism, 145
Congress
  and labor, 675
  in late 19th century, 502, 505

powers of, 396, 808–809
and reconstruction, 395–399
role in foreign policy, in 19th century,
526–528
and World War II, 668–669
Congressional Budget Office, 809
Congressional election
of 1808, 193
of 1846, 327
of 1854, 346
of 1862, 377
of 1866, 396
of 1890, 516
of 1918, 601
of 1946, 700, 708
Congressional Government (Woodrow Wilson),
568
Congressional Medal of Honor, 378
Congress of Industrial Organizations (CIO), 653
Congress of Racial Equality (CORE),
679, 776, 783
Conkling, Roscoe, 504
Connecticut, as Puritan colony, 38
Connor, Eugene "Bull," 778
Conscription
in Confederacy, 374
of slaves, 382
in Union, 379
Conscription Act (1863), 379
Conservationism, in Roosevelt era, 565, 575
Constitution. *See also specific amendment*
and Civil War, 391
framers of, 151
framing of, 151–155
ratification of, 155–157
Constitutional Convention, 150–151
Constitutional Union party, 362
Consumer culture, during 1920s, 621–622
Consumerism, 738
Containment policy, 702–707
and Berlin, 703
Continental Army, 111, 119–120, 125–126
treatment of, 141
uprisings against Congress, 141–142
Continental Association, 102
Continental Congress, 122
First, 101, 109
Second, 110
Continentals, 107
Continental System, 192
Conwell, Russell, 425

Coode, John, 63
Coolidge, Calvin, 626
biography of, 628
election of 1924, 627
Cooper, James Fenimore
The Pioneers, 269
The Spy, 269
Copper industry, 419
CORE. *See* Congress of Racial Equality
(CORE)
Cornwallis, Charles Lord, 125–128
Coronado, Francisco Vásquez de, 12
Corporal punishment, 255–256
in schools, 257
Corporation, modern, rise of, 427–429
Corruption
of Gilded Age, 505
in presidential election of 1876, 412
Cortés, Hernando, 12
Corwin, Thomas, 327
Cotton gin, 215–216, 277
Cotton industry, in early 19th century, 216
Cotton States Exposition of 1895, 440
Coughlin, Father Charles, 651–652, 655
Council for the Indies, 13–14
Council of Economic Advisors, 707
Counterculture, 791–792
Countryside, transformation of, 280
Coverture, doctrine of, 42
Cow towns, 436
Cox, Archibald, 806
Cox, James M., 605
Coxey, Jacob S., 519
CPI. *See* Committee on Public Information
(CPI)
Crane, Stephen, 485
Crawford, William, 229–230
Crédit Mobilier scandal, 408
Creek Indians, 5–6
removal westward, 237
Creel, George W., 591
CREEP. *See* Committee for the Reelection of
the President (CREEP)
Creole populations, 299–300
Crime
in early 19th century, 251
reform ideas about, 255–257
"Crime Against Kansas, The" (Charles
Sumner), 347–348
Crittenden, John J., 363
Croatoan Indians, 19

Crockett, Jim, 316
Cromwell, Oliver, 32
Crusade for Justice, 799
Crusades, 8
Crystal City, TX, voter registration campaign in, 798–799
Cuba, 10
    attempted acquisition of, 343
    Bay of Pigs invasion of, 750–751
    Castro takeover in, 730
    independence of, 544–545
    in Spanish-American War, 543
    U.S. intervention in, 730
Cuban missile crisis, 751
Cuban Revolution, of 1895, 539–542
Cultural growth, during Great Depression, 651
Culture
    in early 19th century, 268–273
    popular
        in early 19th century, 272–273
        in 1890s, 538
Currency Act of 1764, 84–85
Currency issues, in late 19th century, 507, 511
Curtis Act of 1898, 458
Custer, George A., 411
CWA. *See* Civil Works Administration (CWA)
Czolgosz, Leon, 455, 564

Dana, Richard Henry, Jr., *Two Years Before the Mast*, 272–273
Dare, Virginia, 19
Darrow, Clarence, 618
Dartmouth, 99
Dartmouth College, charter of, 208–209
Dartmouth v. *Woodward*, 208
Daugherty, Harry, 627
Davis, Jefferson, 361, 363, 366–367, 380, 382
Davis, John W., 627
Davis, Richard H., 543
Dawes, Charles, 667
Dawes, Henry, 458
Dawes Act, 512
Dawes Plan, 667
Dawes Severalty Act of 1887, 458, 657
Days of Rage, 790
D-day, 685
Dean, John, 806
Debs, Eugene V., 519, 567, 586, 593
Debt, imprisonment for, reform efforts against, 256–257
Decatur, Stephen, 209

Declaration of Colonial Rights and Grievances, 101
Declaration of Independence, 114–115
    influence on reformers, 252
    painting of (Trumbull), 272
Declaration of Sentiments, 266
Declaratory Act, 91–92
Declension, in New England, 44–45
de Gaulle, Charles, 681–682
Deism, 69
de Lacome, Enrique Dupuy, 540
Delaware River, crossing, by George Washington, 118
DeMille, Cecil B., 625
Democratic party, 341, 346
    after Civil War, 391–392
    and Communism, 710–711
    and election of 1846, 327
    and election of 1860, 361–362
    and election of 1876, 412–413
    and election of 1896, 499–501
    and election of 1968, 761–762
    instability of, 336
    in late 19th century, 502–506
    and progressivism, 567
    and Reconstruction, 406–407
    split into North and South factions, 335
    in 19th century, 224
    and white supremacy, 403
Dempsey, Jack, 625
Dennis, David, 783
Department of Commerce and Labor, 565
Department of Housing and Urban Development, 786
Department stores, in 19th century, 483
Depression
    of 1783, 142
    of 1819–1822, 218, 229
    of 1837, 243
    of 1873, 408–409
    of 1893, 501
    Great. *See* Great Depression
    of 1870s, 463
    of 1890s, 517–519
    19th-century, 531–532
Deregulation
    and inflation, 813–814
    during Reagan presidency, 821
Desegregation, 776–777
    of armed services, 732
    of schools, 733–734

Desert Land Act of 1877, 437
Deslondes, Charles, 298
Détente, 814–815
Dewey, George, 543
Dewey, John, 556, 588
Dewey, Thomas E., 676, 703
Dewson, Molly, 657
Dialectic of Sex, The (Shulamith Firestone), 796
Dias, Bartholomeu, 9
Diaz, Porfirio, 572–573
Dickens, Charles, 212
Dickinson, John, 93, 110–111, 114, 138,
    150–151
Diddley, Bo, 739
Diem, Ngo Dinh, 753
Dien Bien Phu, siege of, 753
Dingley Tariff of 1897, 521
Dinwiddie, Robert, 73
Direct democracy, 562
Disease(s)
    European
        carried to New World, 2–3
        Native Americans and, 10–12, 24
    in Mexican American War, 327
    in pioneering of West, 313
    in 19th century, 479
Disestablishment, 145
Disney, Walt, 714
Divorce
    in early 19th century, 264, 266
    in Puritan society, 42
Dix, Dorothea, 258
Dixiecrats. *See* States' Rights Democratic
    Party (Dixiecrats)
Dole, Sanford B., 537
Dollar diplomacy, 572
Dominican Republic, American expansionist
    efforts in, 525–526
Dominion of New England, 62
Domino theory, 755
Doniphan, A. W., 325
Donner, George, 304
Donner party, 304
Douglas, Stephen A., 338–339
    debates with Lincoln, 352–354
    and presidential election of 1860, 362
    and slavery, 344–346
Douglass, Frederick, 263, 264*f,* 378, 389, 398
Dove, Arthur, 486
Dr. Jekyll and Mr. Hyde (Robert Louis
    Stevenson), 495

Drake, Edwin L., 419
Drake, Francis, 17
Dred Scott decision, 350–351, 391
    in Lincoln-Douglas debates, 353
Dreiser, Theodore, 484–486
Dresden, bombing of, 685
Drug abuse, in 19th century, 494–495
Drug use
    in counterculture, 791–792
    in Vietnam War, 767
Dry farming, 439–440
Du Bois, W.E.B., 402, 560, 577, 594
Dukakis, Michael, 826
Duke, James B., 441
Dulles, John Foster, 724–726, 728
Dunmore, Lord, 112, 114
Dustan, Hannah, 53
Dutch, settlements in New York, 23
Dutch West India Company, 23
Dye, John Smith, *The Adder's Den or Secrets of
    the Great Conspiracy to Overthrow Liberty
    in America,* 334–335
Dylan, Bob, 791

Eakins, Thomas, 485
Eastern State Penitentiary, PA, 256
East India Company, 99
Eastman, George, 420
Eaton, John H., 240
Eaton, Peggy, 240
Economic class, emergence of, 67
Economic expansion, in 19th century,
    416–444. *See also* Big business;
    Industrialization
Economic growth
    in early 19th century, 211–217
    and election of 1992, 832
    since the 1970's, 810
Economic Opportunity Act (1964), 786
Economic policy, of Eisenhower, 725
Economy. *See also* Depression; Panic
    after World War II, 707–708
    in World War II, 673–675
Edison, Thomas, 421, 421*f*
Edison General Electric Company, 421
Education
    compulsory school attendance laws, 257
    of freed slaves, 389–390
    in pre-Civil War South, 289
    and progressivism, 563
    public, after Civil War, 404

Educational opportunity, struggle for, 257–258
Educational Opportunity Act (1968), 786
Edwards, Jonathan, 69
EEOC. *See* Equal Employment Opportunity Commission (EEOC)
Ehrlichman, John, 763
Eighteenth Amendment
  passage of, 594
  repeal of, 617
Eisenhower, Dwight David, 687, 722–723, 727
  and Civil Rights movement, 732–734
  foreign policy of, 725–731
  presidency of, 723–725
  in 1952 presidential election, 722
  and Third World, 728–730
  and Vietnam, 753
  and World War II, 684–685
Electricity, 215, 421
  and transformation of cities, in 19th century, 482
Elementary and Secondary Schools Act (1965), 786
Elevated railways, 476
Elizabeth I (Queen of England), 17–19, 21
Elkins Act of 1903, 565
Ellison, William, 300
Emancipation, proposals for, 260–261
Emancipation Proclamation, 361, 374, 376–377
  reactions to, 377–379
Emancipation proclamation of 1775, 112–113
Embargo, under Thomas Jefferson, 192–194
Emergency Banking Relief Bill, 644
Emergency Quota Act, 457
Emerson, Ralph Waldo, 268–270, 330, 354
  "Nature," 270
  "Self-Reliance," 270
Employment Act (1946), 707
Empresarios, 314
Enclosure movement, 18
Encomenderos, 14
Encomienda system, 14
Enemy aliens, in World War II, 679–680
Enforcement Acts, 406–407
Enlightenment, 68–71
Enlightenment philosophy, influence on reformers, 252
Enola Gay, 691
Entail, abolition of, 145
Entertainment, in late 19th and early 20th century

commercialization, 488
  popular, 488–495
Equal Employment Opportunity Commission (EEOC), 794–795
Equal Opportunity Commission, 780
Equal Pay Act (1963), 794, 797
Equal Rights Amendment (ERA), 795, 797
Equiano, Olaudah, 46
Era of Good Feelings, 203
Ericson, Leif, 7
Eric the Red, 7
Erie Canal, 212
Escobedo v. *Illinois,* 787
Espionage Act of 1917, 593
Essay Concerning Human Understanding (1690) (John Locke), 68
Ethiopian regiment, 113
Ethnicity, and party loyalty, in late 19th century, 503
Europe
  aid to, 701–702
  and Confederacy, 373
Europeans, first known contacts with North America, 7
Evangelical revivalism, 252–253
Evans, Oliver, 215
Evers, Medgar, 779
Executive Order 11375, 795
Executive privilege, 172
Exeter, New Hampshire, 38
Expansionism
  Seward's role in, 528
  in 19th century, 525–526, 533
Ex Parte Merryman, 375–376
Experiments and Observations on Electricity (Benjamin Franklin), 68

Factionalism, political, growth in 19th century, 218–221
Factory system, 281–282
Fair Deal, 709–710
Fair Employment Practices Commission (FEPC), 678
Fair Housing Act (1968), 786
Falaba, bombing by German submarines, 585
Fall, Albert B., 627
Fallen Timbers, battle of, 170
Family economy, 459–460
Family life
  in Chesapeake region, 41

in Puritan New England, 40
  of slaves, 48–49
Family planning, during 1920s, 610–611
Fannin, James, 316
Farm Credit Administration, 648
Farmers
  crash of 1929 and, 631
  in late 19th century
    economic problems, 513–514
    political agenda, 515–516
    revolt, 513–517
Farmers' Alliance, 515–516
Farming. *See also* Agriculture
  during Great Depression, 647–648
  in 19th century, 438–440
Farm Security Agency (FSA), 651
Farragut, David G., 369
"Father Knows Best," 736–738
Faubus, Orval, 734
FDIC. *See* Federal Deposit Insurance
    Corporation
Federal Bureau of Investigation, 599
  and Civil Rights movement, 750
Federal Deposit Insurance Corporation
    (FDIC), 644
Federal Election Commission, 808
Federal Employee Loyalty Program, 710–711
Federal Farm Loan Act, 569
Federal Highway Act of 1916, 624
Federal Housing Authority (FHA), effects
    on African Americans, 655–656
Federalist Papers, The (Madison, Hamilton,
    and Jay), 155
Federalist party, 182, 185, 194, 228
  and Northern Confederacy, 189–190
  and presidential election of 1796, 173
  and presidential election of 1800, 177
Federalists, 155, 203
  arguments of, 155–156
Federal Reserve Act, 568
Federal Reserve Board, 568, 575
  and crash of 1929, 630
  and inflation, 813
Federal Reserve System, 568, 575
Federal Trade Commission, 568, 574
Federal Writers Project, 651
Female Eunuch, The (Germaine Greer), 796
Feminine Mystique, The (Betty Friedan), 793
Feminist movement, 774, 792–798
  origins of, 264–266
  radical, 795–796

Ferdinand of Aragon, 9–10
Ferguson, Patrick, 126
Ferraro, Geraldine, 798, 825
Fetchit, Stepin, 625
FHA. *See* Federal Housing Authority (FHA)
Field, Marshall, 483
Fifteenth Amendment, 388, 398–399
Fifties, images of, 736–741
"Fifty-four forty or fight," 319
54th Massachusetts Infantry, 378
Fillmore, Millard, 339
  and Know-Nothing party, 342
  in presidential election of 1856, 349
Financial program, of early U.S.
    government, 163–167
  protests of, 170
Finney, Charles Grandison, 253
Firestone, Shulamith, *The Dialectic of Sex,* 796
First Continental Congress, 101, 109
First Hundred Days, of Franklin Roosevelt's
    presidency, 643–652
Fish, Hamilton, 532
Fiske, John, 530
Fisk University, 405
Fitzgerald, F. Scott, 623
Fitzhugh, George, 290
Five Points, New York City, 255*f*
Five-Power Naval Treaty, 664
Flappers, 615
Flathead Indians, 312
Fletcher v. *Peck,* 208
Flint, Alvin, Jr., 359–360, 360*f*
Florida
  annexation of, 209–210
  secession of, 363
Foch, Ferdinand, 597
Folklore, of slaves, 298
Folliard, Edward T., 695
Food Administration, during World War I, 589
Force Act, 240
Ford, Gerald, 806–807, 809–810
  and inflation, 813
Ford, Henry, 622
Fordney-McCumber Tariff of 1922, 632
Foreign policy, 163
  of Bush, 827–828
  of Eisenhower, 725–731
  of Lincoln, 374
  of Nixon, 814–815
  in 19th century
    aggression in, 533–538

Congressional role in, 526–528
and spirit of American greatness, 528–533
Foreign service, 526–527
Formalism, challenges to, in early 20th century, 555–556
Fort McHenry, 197
Fort Necessity, 73–74
Fort Schuyler, siege of, 122
Fort Sumter, 364, 383–384
Fort Wagner, assault on, 378
Foster, Stephen, 273
Fourier, Charles, 267
Four-Party Treaty, 664
Fourteen Points, 600–601
Fourteenth Amendment, 388, 428, 441
  adoption of, 396
  ratification of, 397
  and women, 398
Fox Indians, in Black Hawk War, 237–238
Fragging, 767
  definition of, 761
France
  in American Revolution, 108, 121, 123, 125
  Canadian colony and exploration, 23–34
  claims to North America, 15–16
  exploration of New World, 11*f*
  trade warfare with Britain, 192
  Treaty of Versailles and, 601–602
  undeclared naval war with, in 1790s, 174–175
  in World War II, 667, 669, 681–682
Franciscans, in Spanish settlement of Southwest, 310
Francis I (King of France), 15
Frank, Leo, 454–455
Franklin, Benjamin, 54, 68, 73, 92, 101, 129
  and antislavery movement, 148
  and Constitution, 151, 153
  delegation to Paris, 121
Franz Ferdinand (Archduke), 582
Free blacks, 299–300
  and Fugitive Slave Law, 340
  in Revolutionary period, 150
Freedmen's Bureau, 389–390, 395–396, 399–400, 405
Freedom dues, 29
Freedom of assembly, 162
  in state constitutions, 145
Freedom of Information Act, 773, 809
Freedom of religion, 162
  English colonists' goal of, 32–39

in Revolutionary period, 144–145
Freedom of speech, 162
  in state constitutions, 145
Freedom of the press, 162
  in state constitutions, 145
Freedom riders, 776
Freed slaves, 387
  after emancipation, 389, 400
  land for, 390
  legal status of, 390–391
  treatment in South, 394–395
Free enterprise, 426
Freemasons, 228
Freemen, in Massachusetts Bay Colony, 36
Free silver movement, 499
Free Soil party, 262, 329–330
  in Kansas, 351
  and Kansas-Nebraska Act, 345
Frémont, John C., 325
  and Civil War, 376
  in presidential election of 1856, 349
  "The Pathfinder," 307
French and Indian War, 74
French Revolution, effects on U.S., 168–169
Freud, Sigmund, 614–615
Frick, Henry, 518
Friedan, Betty, 738, 792–793, 795
  The Feminine Mystique, 793
Fries, John, 176
Fries Rebellion, 176
FSA. *See* Farm Security Agency (FSA)
Fuel Administration, during World War I, 589
Fuentes, Albert, 799
Fugitive Slave Law (1850), 263, 339–341
Fulton, Robert, 212, 215
Furs, trade in, 23–24, 307–308

Gage, Thomas, 100, 109, 112, 117
Gag Rule, 245
Gallatin, Albert, 207
Gallaudet, Thomas Hopkins, 258–259
Galloway, Joseph, 101–102
Gálvez, Bernardo de, 128
Gama, Vasco da, 9
Gang system, of slave labor, 294
Gardoqui, Diego de, 143
Garfield, James A., 507–508
Garrison, William Lloyd, 260–263
Garvey, Marcus, 613
Gaspée, 98

Gates, Horatio, 123, 125, 142
GATT. *See* General Agreement on Trade and
   Tariffs (GATT)
Genacet, Edmond, 169–170
Genacet affair, effects on party feeling, 169–170
General Agreement on Trade and Tariffs
   (GATT), 833
General Court, in Massachusetts Bay Colony, 36
General Intelligence Division, 599
General Motors Corporation, 773
Gentlemen-planter, in Chesapeake region,
   44, 46*f*
George, Henry, 555
George II (King of England), 72
George III (King of England), 81, 91, 96, 100,
   103, 109, 111, 115–116
Georgia, secession of, 363
Germain, George, 116, 124
Germany
   alliance with Japan, 667
   bombing of, 685
   confrontation with, over Samoa, 534–535
   defeat of, 597–598
   division of, 699
   invasions in Europe, 667, 669
   role in American Revolution, 117
   after World War I, 666–667
   in World War II, 683–684
     public opinion of, 676
Gerrish, Abigail, 41*f*
Gettysburg, battle of, 380–381
Ghost Dance, 457
G.I. Bill, 676
Gibbons v. *Ogden,* 209
Gideon v. *Wainwright,* 787
Gilbert, Humphrey, 19
Gilded Age
   corruption of, 505
   government in, 506–513
   politics of, 501–502, 504–505
Gillespie, Archibald H., 323
Ginsberg, Allen, 741
   "Howl," 741
Glackens, W. J., 486
Glasnost, 824
Glass-Steagall Banking Act of 1933, 644
Glorious Revolution, 61–64
Godey's Lady Book, 265
Godkin, E. L., 545
"Go Down Moses," 298

Going after Cacciato (Tim O'Brien), 768
Gold Democrats, 499
Golden Gate Bridge, 663
Goldman, Emma, 586
Gold rush, 330–331, 418–419
Gold standard, 499, 521–522
Goldwater, Barry, 755, 820
Gompers, Samuel, 455, 468*f,* 468–469, 545
Gonzales, Rodolfo "Corky," 799
Goodman, Andrew, 783
Goodman, Paul, 790
Good Neighbor Policy, 665
Gorbachev, Mikhail S., 824–825, 828
Gordon, Thomas, 97
Gosiute Indians, 312
Gospel of Wealth, and industrialization,
   424–426
Government, American
   formation of, 136–138
   forms of, debate over, 136
   in Gilded Age, 506–513
   machinery of, establishment of, 162
   problems of, in 1790s, 161
   putting into operation, 161–167
   right to petition, 162
Grady, Henry W., 440–441
Grand Alliance, 681–683
Grandfather clauses, 520
Grange, Harold, 625
Granger laws, 509
Grangers, 509, 515, 531–532
Grant, Ulysses S., 322, 366, 372*f*
   and Civil War, 371–372, 381–382
   expansionist efforts, 525–526
   presidency of, 407–408
   in presidential election of 1868, 397
   in presidential election of 1872, 408
   and Reconstruction, 406–407
Grass-roots activism, 773
Great American Desert, 306–307
Great Awakening, 69–71
Great Bridge, battle of, 113
Great Britain
   claims to North America, 15
   claims to Pacific Northwest, 318–319
   and Confederacy, 373–374
   confrontation with, over Venezuelan
     boundary, 537–538
   exploration of New World, 11*f*
   as naval power, 18

population growth, in sixteenth century, 18
Protestant Reformation in, 16–17
relations with America, in post-Revolutionary period, 170–171
trade warfare with France, 192
trade with America, in post-Revolutionary period, 142–143
and Treaty of Versailles, 601
wars with European nations, during American Revolution, 124
westward expansion, 18–19
after World War II, 700
in World War II, 669–670, 681, 683
Great Compromise, on Constitution, 153
Great Crash, 629–633
Great Depression, 638–640, 668
effect on Germany, 667
onset of, 632–633
prices during, 645*t*
Great Migration
to New England, 35
during World War I, 595–596
Great Plains, misconceptions about, 306
Great Serpent Mound, 5
Great Society, 756, 785–787
Great Strike of 1877, 463–464
Great Train Robbery, The, 493–494
Great War. *See* World War I
Greece, struggle against Communism in, 700–701
Greeley, Horace, 408
Greenback money, 408
Greenback party, 507
Greene, Nathanael, 126–128
Greer, Germaine, *The Female Eunuch,* 796
Grenada, invasion of, 822–823
Grenville, George, 83–86, 91, 97
Grey, Zane, 624–625
Griggs v. *Duke Power Company,* 796
Grimké, Angelina, 266
Grimké, Sarah, 266
Letters on the Equality of the Sexes and the Condition of Women, 266
Guadalcanal Diary, 677
Guam, 688–689
American acquisition of, 544
Guatemala, CIA coup d'état in, 730
Guerrilla warfare
in Cuban revolution of 1895, 539
in Philippine revolt, 547

Guilford Courthouse, battle for, 127
Guiteau, Charles, 508
Gulf of Tonkin Resolution, 756
Gutenberg, Johannes, 8
Guthrie, Woody, 637–638

Hacendados, 14
Haciendas, 14
Haight-Ashbury, 791–792
Haldeman, H. R., 763
Hale, Sarah J., 265
Half-Breeds (Republicans), 504, 507
Half-Way Covenant, 44
Halleck, Henry Wager, 369, 372
Hamilton, Alexander, 150–151, 163, 171, 175, 181, 190
The Federalist Papers, 155
financial program of, 163–167
and presidential election of 1796, 173
Hamiltonians, 167
birth of, 168
Hancock, John, 93, 109
Hancock, Winfield Scott, 508
Hannah's Cowpens, 126
Harding, Warren G., 626–627
and bootlegging, 617
in presidential election of 1920, 605
Harlem Renaissance, 614
Harpers Ferry, Brown's raid on, 354–355
Harrington, Michael, 790
Harrison, Benjamin, 505, 511–512
and foreign policy, 535–536
second presidency of, 517
Harrison, William Henry, 195, 224, 317
presidential candidacy in 1836, 245–246
Harrison Anti-Narcotic Act of 1914, 495
Harte, Bret, 483–484
Hartley, Marsden, 486
Harvard College, founding of, 36
Hat Act of 1732, 65
Hatch Act of 1887, 440
Hawaii
annexation of, 535–537
revolution in, 535–537
Hawkins, John, 17
Hawley-Smoot Tariff of 1930, 632
Hawthorne, Nathaniel, 270–271
The Scarlet Letter, 271
Hay, John, 533, 544, 571
Open Door policy with China, 547–548

Hay-Bunau-Varilla Treaty, 571
Hayden, Tom, 789
Hayes, Rutherford B., 464
  and "Money Question," 506–507
  in presidential election of 1876, 412–413
Hay-Herrán Treaty, 570–571
Haymarket Square riot of 1886, 464–466,
    465*f*, 532
Hayne, Robert Y., 239
Haywood, "Big Bill," 586
Headrights, 30
Hearst, William Randolph, 539–540, 654
Hemingway, Ernest, 623
Hennessy, David, 453
Henri, Robert, 485–486
Henry, Patrick, 90, 101, 148, 156
Henry the Navigator (Prince of Portugal), 9
Henry VII (King of England), 15
Henry VIII (King of England), 16–17
Hepburn Act of 1906, 565, 574
Herrera, José, 323
Hesse-Cassel, role in American Revolution, 117
Hessians, 117–118, 123
Hester Street, New York City, 456*f*
Hidalgo y Costilla, Miguel, 310
Higginson, Thomas W., 378
Higher Education Act (1965), 786
Highway system, 723–724
Hill, James J., 565
Hillsborough, Lord, 93
Hippies, 791–792
Hiroshima, bombing of, 691
Hispanic America, 309–310
Hispanic settlers, in Texas, treatment of, 316
Hispaniola, 10, 12
Hiss, Alger, 695–696, 697*f*
Hitler, Adolf, 666–667, 668*f*, 669, 687
Ho Chi Minh, 745–747, 752, 791
Ho Chi Minh Trail, bombing of, 763
Holland
  aid during War for Independence, 108
  exploration of New World, 11*f*
Hollywood. *See also* Movies
  investigations of Communism in, 713–714
Hollywood Ten, 713
Holmes, Oliver Wendell, 556, 599
Homer, Winslow, 485
Homestead Act (1862), 375, 437–438
Homestead strike of 1892, 518, 538
Hood, James Walker, 402
Hooker, Joseph "Fighting Joe," 379–380

Hooker, Thomas, 38
Hoover, Herbert, 626, 629, 666
  in election of 1928, 628–629
  in election of 1932, 642–643
  Great Depression and, 638–640
  and Latin America, 665
  in World War I, 589
Hoover, J. Edgar, 599, 714–715
Hopi Indians, 6, 312, 409
Hopkins, Harry, 649
Horses, 24, 311–312
Hotels, grand, in 19th century, 483
Hours, for industrial workers, in late 19th and
    early 20th century, 460–461
Household industries, 280
House Judiciary Committee, and
    Watergate, 807
House of Burgesses, 30
House of Trade, Spanish, 13
House Un-American Activities Committee
    (HUAC), 696
  and Hollywood, 713–714
Housing
  in early 19th century, 211
  urban, in 19th century, 478–479
Houston, Sam, 315–316
Howard University, 405
Howe, Samuel Gridley, 258–259
Howe, William, 109, 117–118, 121–124
Howells, William Dean, 484
"Howl" (Allen Ginsberg), 741
How the Other Half Lives (Jacob Riis), 454
Hudson, Henry, 23
Hudson Bay Company, 318
Hudson River school, 272
Huerta, Victoriano, 573
Hughes, Charles Evans, 569, 586, 664
Hughes, Langston, 614
Huguenots, 17
Huitzilopochtli (Aztec war god), 5
Hulbert, William A., 490
Hull, Cordell, 665, 671–672
Hull House, 558
Human rights, 816–818
  in Revolutionary period, 144–150
Humphrey, Hubert, 762
Hussein, Saddam, 830–831
Hutchinson, Anne, 37–38
Hutchinson, Thomas, 73, 79–80, 86, 88, 97,
    99–100
Hyde Amendment, 797

ICC. *See* Interstate Commerce Commission
Ickes, Harold, 656
IECP. *See* Indian Emergency Conservation
    Program (IECP)
"I have a dream..." (Martin Luther King, Jr.),
    779–780
Illinois, admission to Union, 207
"I Love Lucy," 794
Immigrants
    bachelor subculture, in late 19th and early
        20th century, 488
    employment of, 282, 284–285
    hostility toward, in 19th century, 453–457
    in industrial work force, in 19th century,
        423, 445–470
    in late 19th century, 503–504
    literacy tests for, 456
    permanent, 450–453
    and temperance reform, 254–255
    temporary (birds of passage), 450–451
    voting rights, in early 19th century, 227
Immigration
    1840-1860, 284–285, 285f
    in late 19th and early 20th century,
        445–453, 449f
        restrictions on, 456–457
    limitation on, in late 19th century, 512
    new, source of, 449f, 449–450
    old, source of, 448–450, 449f
    opposition to, 341–342
    during 1920s, 619
    in 18th century, 66
    and urbanization, in 19th century, 474–475
Immigration policy, in early 20th century, 561
Immigration Reform and Control
    Act (1986), 799
Imperialism, American, in late 19th century,
    545–546
Implied powers, doctrine of, 165–166
Import duties, in financing of Revolutionary
    War, 141
Impressment, 192
Incas, 12
Income, during Great Depression, 640–641
Income tax, 568
    first, 518
Indentured servant(s), 28
    in Chesapeake region, 43
Indentured servitude, 29–30, 41
    and family life, 43
Independence, debate over, in individual
    colonies, 113–115

Indiana, admission to Union, 207
Indian Emergency Conservation Program
    (IECP), 657
Indian Historical Society, 801
Indian New Deal, 657
Indian Peace Commission, 410
Indian policy
    of Jackson's presidency, 236–238
    of Jefferson's presidency, 236
Indian Reorganization Act, 657
Indians, 9. *See also* Native Americans
Indulgences, 16
Industrialists, in 19th century
    power of, 464–466
    as robber barons, 466
Industrialization
    Civil War and, 375
    in early 19th century, 214–216
    mechanization and, 461
    in 19th century, factors contributing to,
        424–429
    and urbanization, in 19th century, 474–475
    and worker discontent, 462
Industrial revolution, 279
Industrial Workers of the World (IWW), 599
    during World War I, 589–590
Industrial work force
    in late 19th and early 20th century, 445–470
        African Americans in, 423
        immigrants in, 423, 445–470
        population increase and, 422–423
    in 19th century, 422–423
Industry
    consolidation of, in 19th century, 429–435
    and Hamilton's financial program, 166–167
    Jefferson and, 167
Inflation, 810–811
    after World War I, 599
    in World War II, 674–675
Influence of Sea Power upon History, The (Alfred
    Thayer Mahan), 532–533
Inquisition, 9
Insanity defense, 256
Interstate commerce
    federal power over, 209
    regulation, 509
Interstate Commerce Act of 1887, 509–510
Interstate Commerce Commission, 426, 509,
    565–566, 574
Invasion of the Body Snatchers, 738
Inventions, in 19th century, 215, 420–421
Iran

CIA coup d'état in, 729–730
and human rights violations, 816–818
Iran-Contra affair, 824
Iran hostage crisis, 817–818
Irish-Americans, and boxing, in 19th
century, 491
Irish immigrants, and early labor violence, 463
Irish potato blight, 284–285
Irish Rebellion, 584
Iron Act of 1750, 65
Iroquois Indians, 7, 23
Iroquois nation, 60–61, 122–123
Irving, Washington, 268
Isabella of Castile, 9–10
Island-hopping, 688–689
Isolationism, 664–665
in 19th century, 527
and World War II, 668–670
Italian city-states, 8
Italian immigrants, in 19th century, 450–451
Italy, and Treaty of Versailles, 602
Iwo Jima, conquest of, 689
IWW. *See* Industrial Workers of the
World (IWW)

Jackson, Andrew, 197, 229–230, 235*f*
assassination attempt on, 256
as champion of people, 233–245
election to presidency, 232–233
expedition against Seminole Indians, 210
and Indian policy, 236–238
judicial appointments, 244
legacy of, 244–245
and Texas annexation, 317
war against second Bank of the United
States, 241–243
Jackson, Thomas J. "Stonewall," 322, 367, 380
Jackson State University, demonstration against
Vietnam War, 764
James, William, 556
James I (King of England), 21, 29, 31, 34
James II (King of England), 56
Jamestown, 21–23
Japan
alliance with Germany, 667
invasions of Asia, 666, 671
relations with, in early 20th century, 570
and Treaty of Versailles, 602
in World War II, 666–672, 683, 687–691
public opinion of, 676
surrender of, 691

Japanese Americans, in World War II, 679–680
Jaworski, Leon, 806
Jay, John, 101, 129, 143, 163, 171
The Federalist Papers, 155
Jay Treaty, 171–172, 174
Jazz, 487–488
Jefferson, Thomas, 114, 138, 163, 176–177,
182–183, 188–189, 192, 219, 277, 306
and Declaration of Independence, 144
and freedom of religion, 145
and Hamilton's financial program, 165, 167
ideology of, 182–185
Notes on the State of Virginia, 148
and presidential election of 1796, 173
and presidential election of 1800, 176–178
and slavery, 148
Jeffersonians, 167, 172
birth of, 168
Jenney, William LeBaron, 477
Jeremiads, 44
Jesuits, in Spanish settlement of Southwest, 310
Jewish immigrants
and nativism, 457
in 19th century, 451–453
Jewish refugees, in World War II, 680
Jiang Jieshi, 703–704
Jim Crow laws, 492, 520, 720, 731–732, 775
challenges to, 732–733
Jingoism, in 1890s, 538
John I (King of Portugal), 9
Johnson, Andrew, 393, 394*f,* 528
impeachment of, 397
and presidential election of 1864, 382
and Reconstruction, 393–397
Johnson, Hugh, 646
Johnson, Lyndon Baines, 755, 760
and Civil Rights movement, 780, 785
and 1964 election, 755–756
and Great Society, 785–787
and inflation, 811
and Vietnam War, 755–760
Johnson, Tom L., 562
Johnston, Albert Sidney, 366, 372
Johnston, Joseph E., 366, 370, 381
Joint Committee on Reconstruction, 395
Joint-stock trading companies, 21
Jones, John Paul, 128
Jones, Samuel "Golden Rule," 562
Joplin, Scott, 487
Joseph (Chief of Nez Percé), 410
Joseph, William, 63

Judicial review, 187
Judiciary, 185–187. *See also* Supreme Court
  in early 19th century, 214, 227
  in late 19th century, 502
Judiciary Act of 1789, 186
Judiciary Act of 1801, 185
Julian, George, 399
Jungle, The (Upton Sinclair), 557, 565

Kaiser, Henry J., 663–664
Kaiser Steel, 677
Kansas
  admission into Union, 351
  slavery controversy in, 346–348
  territorial elections of 1855, 347
Kansas-Nebraska Act (1854), 344–345
Karankawa Indians, 312
Kaufman, Irving R., 711
Kearny, Stephen, 324
Keating-Owen Child Labor Act, 569
Keaton, Buster, 625
Kellogg, Frank B., 665
Kendall, Amos, 233
Kennan, George, 701–702
Kennedy, John Fitzgerald
  assassination of, 750–751, 754
  and Civil Rights movement, 776, 779
  debates with Nixon, 747–748
  presidency of, 748–750
  and Vietnam, 754–756
  and women's liberation movement, 794
Kennedy, Robert, 750
  assassination of, 761
  in 1968 presidential campaign, 761
Kent State University, demonstration against
  Vietnam War, 764
Kerouac, Jack, 741
Key, Francis Scott, 197
Khomeini, Ayatollah Ruholla, and Iran hostage
  crisis, 817–818
Khrushchev, Nikita, 726–727, 731, 751
King, Martin Luther, Jr., 735, 775,
  779–780, 783
  assassination of, 785
  in Birmingham protests, 777
  "I have a dream...," 779–780
  "Letter from Birmingham Jail," 777
  Malcolm X and, 782
  philosophy of, 735–736, 775, 778
King George's War, 72

King Philip. *See* Metacomet
King Philip's War, 38–39
Kings Mountain, South Carolina, 126
King William's War, 71
Kinsey, Alfred C., 615
Kiowa Indians, 312
Kipling, Rudyard, 478
Kissinger, Henry, 763, 766
  and China, 815
  and Soviet Union, 814–815
  and Vietnam War, 765–767
Know-Nothing party, 341–343
Knox, Henry, 163
Knox, John, 17
Knox, Philander C., 552
Korean prisoner of war controversy, 715–716
Korean War, 704–707, 706*f*
Ku Klux Klan, 406–407, 619–621, 720
Kuwait, invasion of, 829–830

Labor
  new conception of, 281
  protests, 282
  in 19th century, organized and unorganized,
    466–469
  unskilled, problems of, 284
Laborers
  discontent with industrialization, 462
  hierarchy of, in late 19th and early 20th
    century, 460
Labor legislation, of progressivism, 574–575.
  See also Child labor laws
Labor unions. *See* Unionism
Labor unrest
  after World War I, 598–600
  after World War II, 708–709
  in World War II, 675
Ladies' Magazine, 265
LaFarge, John, 485
La Follette, Robert, 566, 627–628
La Guardia, Fiorello, 670
Laissez-faire economics
  challenges to, in early 20th century, 555–556
  theory and practice of, 426–427
Lake Champlain, 111–112
Lake Erie, battle of, 196
Land claims, ceded by states, 139, 140*f*
Land grants
  to Native Americans, 458
  in 19th century, 427

and western expansion, 437
Landon, Alfred M., 654–655
Land policy, federal, in early 19th century, 207, 238
Land reform, 283
Land sales, in early 19th century, 207, 238–239
La Raza Unida, 799
Las Casas, Bartolomé de, 14
Latin America, 665
    American ambitions for, in 19th century, 531–532
    American interventions in, in early 20th century, 570–573
Laud, William, 34
Lawrence, KS, sack of, 347
Lawrence, Richard, 256
Lawrence, William, 425
Lawson, Ernest, 486
Lazarus, Emma, 447
League of Nations, 600, 603–606, 664, 666–668
Leary, Timothy, 791
Lease, Mary E., 513
Leaves of Grass (Walt Whitman), 271
Lebanon, U.S. intervention in, 730
Lecompton constitution, 351
Lee, Richard Henry, 114, 156
Lee, Robert E., 322, 354, 371*f*
    and Civil War, 359, 365–368, 380–382
Legal system, in early 19th century, 214
"Legend of Sleepy Hollow, The" (Washington Irving), 268
Leisler, Jacob, 62, 64
Leisure, during 1920s, 624–625
Lend-lease aid, 670–671
Lenin, V. I., 791
Lenorson, Samuel, 53
Leopard, 192
"Letter from Birmingham Jail" (Martin Luther King, Jr.), 777
Letters from a Farmer in Pennsylvania (John Dickinson), 93
Letters on the Equality of the Sexes and the Condition of Women (Sarah Grimké), 266
Levitt, William, 732
Lewis, John L., 653, 708
Lewis, Meriwether, 189, 306
Lewis, Sinclair, 623
Lewis and Clark expedition, 189, 306–307

Lexington, 110
Liberal Republican party, 408
Liberation movements, 792–801
Liberator, The, 260, 327
Liberia, 259
Liberty party, 262
Liliuokalani (Queen of Hawaii), 536–537
Lincoln, Abraham, 346, 352–353, 367, 376
    assassination of, 384, 393
    and Civil War, 361, 367–370
    debates with Douglas, 352–354
    and Emancipation Proclamation, 376–378
    Gettysburg address, 381
    inaugural address, 364
    and John Brown, 355
    and Mexican War, 327
    presidency of, 374
    and presidential election of 1860, 361–362
    and presidential election of 1864, 382
    and presidential powers, 375–376
    and Reconstruction, 384, 392–393
    and secession, 362–364
Lincoln, Benjamin, 125
Lincoln-Douglas debates, 352–354
Lindbergh, Charles, 624
Linoleum, 420
Literacy tests, for immigrants, 456
Literature
    in early 19th century, 270–271
    in late 19th century, 483–485
Little Bighorn, 411
Little Richard, 739
Little Rock, AR, desegregation crisis in, 734
Livingston, Robert, 189
Lloyd George, David, 601, 603
Locke, John, 68
Lodge, Henry Cabot, 512, 533, 601, 604
Lodge Election Bill, 512
Lonely Crowd, The (David Riesman), 738–739
Long, Huey, 651–652, 655
Long, Stephen J., 306
Longfellow, Henry Wadsworth, 269
Looking Backward (Edward Bellamy), 555
Lost Generation, 622–623
Louisiana
    admission to Union, 207
    secession of, 363
Louisiana Purchase, 188–189
Louis XIV (King of France), 71
Louis XVI (King of France), 123

L'Ouverture, Toussaint, 189
Lovejoy, Elijah P., 262
Lowell, Francis Cabot, 202
Lowell, James Russell, 324
Loyalists, 102
LSD, 791–792
Lucas, Eliza, 53
Lucas, George, 53–54
Luce, Henry, 704
Luks, George, 485–486
Lumber barons, 437
Lusitania, bombing of by German
    submarines, 585
Luther, Martin, 16
Lutheranism, 16
Lynching, 519

MacArthur, Douglas, 688, 691, 705–707
    and Bonus Army, 643
    invasion of Philippines, 689
Macfadden, Bernard, 538
Mackintosh, Ebenezer, 87–88, 99
Macon's Bill No. 2, 193
Macy, Rowland H., 483
Madison, James, 150, 176, 186, 193,
    203–204, 207
    and bank controversy, 165
    and Constitution, 151–153
    The Federalist Papers, 155–156
Mafia, 453
Magazines
    confessional, 625
    in early 19th century, 272
Maggie: A Girl of the Streets (Stephen
    Crane), 485
Mahan, Alfred Thayer, 532–533
Maine, 38
    admission to Union, 220
Maine, 541
Makino, Nobuaki, 602
Malcolm X, 781–783
Management techniques, in 19th century, 433
Manassas
    battle of, 367–368
    second battle of, 371
Manhattan Island, 23
Manhattan Project, 674, 690
    spies in, 710
Manifest Destiny, 314–321
Mann, Horace, 257

Mann-Elkins Act of 1910, 566
Manpower Development and Training Act
    (1964), 786
Manufacturing, in early 19th century, 206, 211
    innovation in, 215
Manufacturing industry, American *vs.*
    foreign, 812
Mao Zedong, 703, 752, 791
Mapp v. *Ohio,* 787
Marbury, William, 186
Marbury v. *Madison,* 186, 208
March on Washington, of 1894, 519
Marcuse, Herbert, 790
Marcy, William, 236
Marin, John, 486
Marion, Francis, 126
Marriage
    in Puritan society, 42–43
    of slaves, 48–49, 296–297
    in World War II, 678
Married Women's Property Laws, 266
Marshall, George C., 701, 723
Marshall, James W., 30
Marshall, John, 186–187, 191, 208, 244
Marshall, Thurgood, 786
Marshall Plan, 701–702
Martin, Joseph Plumb, 107–108, 130, 139
Martin v. *Hunter's Lessee,* 208
Marx, Karl, 791
Mary II (Queen of England), 62, 64
Maryland
    population of, in seventeenth century, 40
    settlement of, 31–32
    slavery in, 28, 47
    stabilizing life in, 45
    state constitution of, 137
Mason, James M., 374
Mason-Dixon line, 277–279
Massachusetts
    government of, 36
    hivings out from, 38
Massachusetts Bay Colony, 33–34
    commercialism in, 43–49
Massachusetts Government Act, 100
Massachusetts Land Bank, 79
Mass marketing, 433–434
Mass markets, rise of, 422–423
Mass production, 215, 433–434
Mayas, 5
Mayflower, 33

Mayflower Compact, 33
McCarthy, Eugene, 760–761
McCarthy, Joseph, 711–713
McClellan, George B., 322, 359, 369–370
  and presidential election of 1864, 382
McCord, James, 805
McCoy, Joseph G., 436
McCulloch v. *Maryland,* 208
McDowell, Irwin, 367
McGovern, George, 767
McGuffey Readers, 425
McKinley, William, 499, 501, 520
  assassination of, 455, 564
  and foreign policy, 540–542, 545–547
McKinley Tariff, 511–512, 517, 536
McParlan, James, 463
Meade, George C., 327, 380
Meat Inspection Act, 565, 575
Meat packing industry, 422, 433–434
Mechanization, and industrialization, 461
Medicaid Act (1968), 786
Medicare, 786
Mediterranean trade, 8
Meetinghouses, in Massachusetts Bay
  Colony, 36
Melville, Herman, 271, 314, 326
  Moby Dick, 271
Mencken, H. L., 479, 623
Men's suffrage, in early 19th century, 225–227
Mentally ill, treatment of, 258
Mental testing, 597
Mercantilism, 54–56
Merchants, in eighteenth century New
  England, 44
Meredith, James, 777
Mesmerism, 273
Metacomet, 38–39
Mexican American liberation, 798–800
Mexican Americans
  activism in 1960s, 774
  in government, 799–800
  New Deal and, 656–657
  problems of, 799
  World War II and, 679
Mexican War, 321–331, 326*f*
  causes of, 322
  declaration of, 324
  enthusiasm for, 325–327
  opposition to, 326–327
  peace settlement of, 328
  significance of, 328–329

Mexican War for Independence, 310
Mexico
  and American settlement of Texas, 314–316
  relations with, in early 20th century, 572–573
Micmacs, 6
Middle class, in 19th century, 433
Middle East oil embargo, 811–812
Midway Islands, acquisition of, 528
Mier y Terán, Manuel de, 315
Milam, J. W., 720–721
Miles, Nelson A., 544
Military
  reduction of, in 19th century, 527–528
  in 1970s, 815
Military-industrial complex, 731
Military Reconstruction Act (1867), 396–397
Milken, Michael, 822
Millett, Kate, *Sexual Politics,* 796
Mills, C. Wright, 790
Mineral wealth, 418–420
Mining
  in 19th century, 419
  and western expansion, 436–437
Minorities, wages for, in late 19th and early
  20th century, 460
Minority rights. *See also specific minority*
  in late 19th century, 512–513
  in 1890s, 519–520
  and social justice movement in early 20th
  century, 559–560
Minstrel shows, 273
Minutemen, 110
Miss America pageant, protests of, 796
Missionaries
  in Philippines, 545
  in 19th century, 530
Missionary diplomacy, 572–573
Mission system, 310
Mississippi
  admission to Union, 207
  secession of, 363
Mississippi Plan, 519
Mississippi River, 188–189
Missouri, admission to Union, 220
Missouri Compromise, 219–221, 336,
  344, 350
Mitchell, John, 552
Moby Dick (Herman Melville), 271
Model Cities Act (1966), 786
Model Cities program, 787
Modernists, 486

Modern Republicanism, 723–724
Modern Woman: The Lost Sex, 738
Mohawk Indians, 122
Mohicans, 6
Molasses Act of 1733, 65, 84
Molly Maguires, 463
Molotov, V. M., 698
Monetary policy, in late 19th century, 507
Monroe, James, 189, 203, 209, 228
  and Indian policy, 236–237
Monroe Doctrine, 210–211, 527, 537
  Roosevelt Corollary to, 572, 665
Montezuma II, 12
Montgomery, AL, bus boycott in, 735–736
Montgomery, Bernard, 684
Montgomery, Richard, 112
Montreal, siege of, 111
Moore's Creek Bridge, battle of, 114
Morgan, Daniel, 126
Morgan, J. P., 417–418, 421, 429, 432,
  518, 565
Morgan, J. P., Jr., 599
Morganthau, Henry, 658
Mormons
  images of, 320–321
  migration to West, 319–321
  persecution of, 320
Morrill Land Grant Act of 1862, 375, 439
Morrill Tariff, 427
Morris, Gouverneur, 141, 151
Morris, Robert, 141–142, 151
Morse, Samuel F. B., 215
Motion picture industry, development
  of, 493–494
Mott, Lucretia, 266
Mound Builders (Adena and Hopewell
  peoples), 5
Mountain men, 307–308
Mount Holyoke, 258
Movies. *See also* Hollywood
  images of Communism, 697, 714
  images of suburbia, 738–739
  images of World War I, 591–592
  images of World War II, 676–677
  images of youth, 714
  in 1920s, 625
Ms., 796
Muckrakers, 557
Mugwumps, 504, 508
Muhammad, Elijah, 781

Muller v. *Oregon,* 556
Mumford, Lewis, 738
Munn v. *Illinois,* 509
Murray, John (Lord Dunmore), 112, 114
Museums, in 19th century, 493
Music
  in counterculture, 791–792
  modern American, 486–488
  in 1950s, 739–740
Mussolini, Benito, 667, 668*f*
My Lai Massacre, 760–761

NAACP. *See* National Association for the
  Advancement of Colored People
Nader, Ralph, 772–774
  Unsafe at Any Speed, 773
NAFTA. *See* North American Free Trade
  Agreement (NAFTA)
Napoleon Bonaparte, 189, 192
Narcotic abuse, in 19th century, 494–495
Narragansett Indians, 37–38
Narváez, Pánfilo de, 12
NASA. *See* National Aeronautics and Space
  Administration (NASA)
Nashville (USS), 571
Nasser, Gamal Abdel, 727
Natchez, 5
National Labor Relations Act, effects on
  Mexican Americans, 657
National Aeronautics and Space Administration
  (NASA), 728
National American Woman Suffrage
  Association, 506, 559
National Anti-Cigarette League, 618
National Association for the Advancement of
  Colored People, 560, 576, 595, 613, 679,
  732–733
National Association of Manufacturers, 561
National Birth Control League, 561
National Child Labor Committee, 563
National Civic Federation, 561
National Collegiate Athletic Association, 561
National Congress of American Indians
  (NCAI), 800–801
National Conservation Congress, 565
National Consumers League, 558
National Day of Mourning, 800
National debt, in 1790, 164
National Defense Education Act (1958), 728
National Emigration Convention, 263

National Indian Youth Council, 801
National Industrial Recovery Act (NIRA),
    646–647, 653
Nationalism
    in early 19th century
        in foreign affairs, 209–211
        growth of, 202–211
        judicial, 208–209
    in 1890s, 538
National Labor Relations Act, 653
National Labor Relations Board (NLRB), 653
National Labor Union, 466–467
National Organization for Women
    (NOW), 795
National Origins Act of 1924, 447, 457, 619
National Recovery Administration
    (NRA), 646–647, 658
    effects on African Americans, 655
National Road, 207
National Security Council Paper Number 68
    (NSC-68), 704
National System of Interstate and Defense
    Highways Act (1956), 724
National Trades' Union, 282
National Traffic and Motor Vehicle Safety Act,
    773
National Urban League, 613
National Woman's party, 559, 594
National Woman Suffrage Association,
    398, 506
National Youth Administration (NYA)
    African Americans and, 656
    Native Americans and, 657
Nation-states, support of explorations, 8–10
Native American power movement, 800–801
Native American Rights Fund, 801
Native Americans
    activism in 1960s, 774
    as adversaries, 24
    athletic skills of, 7
    conflict with settlers, 410–411
    contact with Europeans, consequences
        of, 2–4
    decline in population, in 1840s and 50s, 312
    destruction of, 24
    Eastern Woodland, 6–7
    enslavement of, by Spanish, 14
    and explorers of West, 307
    first, 4–5
    Great Plains tribes, 311
    languages of, 6

life-styles of, 6
nativism and, 457–458
origins of, 4
population, in 15th century, 6
problems of, 800
on ranchos, 310
relations with France, 71
religious values of, 6
social organization of, 6–7
and Spanish settlers, 310
treatment of, in early 19th century, 236–238
tribal organization of, 7
warfare of, 7
in West, 311–312
and westward expansion, 409–411
women, social status of, 7
Nativism, 341–342
    and Native Americans, 457–458
    racial, 454
    in 19th century, 453–458
    and violence, 455–457
NATO. *See* North Atlantic Treaty
    Organization (NATO)
Naturalism, in 19th-century literature,
    484–485
Naturalization Act, 175
Natural resources, 419–420
"Nature" (Ralph Waldo Emerson), 270
Navaho Indians, 409
Navigation Acts of 1651, 1660, 1663, and
    1673, 55–57
Navy
    rebuilding of, in late 19th century, 532–533
    reduction of, in 19th century, 527–528
Navy Nurses Corps, 677
NAWSA. *See* National American Woman
    Suffrage Association
Nazi-Comintern Pact, 669
NCAI. *See* National Congress of American
    Indians
Neo-Hamiltonianism, 203–206
Neutrality, during World War I, 583
Neutrality laws, 669
New Amsterdam, siege of, 56–57
Newburgh Conspiracy, 141–142
New Deal, 574, 643–646, 675
    African Americans and, 655–656
    Mexican Americans and, 656–657
    Native Americans and, 657
    second. *See* Second New Deal
    women and, 657

New England
  hazards of, for colonists, 40
  population of, in seventeenth century, 39–40
  religious dissenters in, 32–39
New England Emigrant Aid Company, 346
New England Non-Resistance Society, 262
New Freedom, 567
New Frontier, 749
New Hampshire, 38
New Harmony, IN, 267
New Jersey, state constitution of, and
    women, 137
New Jersey Plan, for Constitution, 153
Newlands Reclamation Act, 565
New Left, 789–791
  and counterculture, 791–792
New Look, 725
New Mexico, acquisition by United States,
    323–324
New Nationalism, 567
New Netherland, 23, 56–57
New Orleans, LA
  capture of (1862), 369
  influence on modern American
    music, 486–488
  public schools, integration in, 404
  slave march on, 298
New Panama Canal Company, 570
New South, 440–442
New Spain, 10–12
Newspapers
  in 1790, 160
  in early 19th century, 272
  and Mexican War, 321–322, 327
New York, 56
  campaign for, in American Revolution,
    117–118
New York City, crime in, 251, 255*f*
New York *Herald,* 272
New York Journal, 539–540
New York *Sun,* 272
New York World, 539–540
New York Yacht Club, 491
Nez Percé Indians, 312
Nguyen Van Thieu, 763
Niagara Movement, 560
Nicaragua, during Reagan presidency, 824
Nicholson, Francis, 62
Nimitz, Chester, 688–689
Nine-Power Treaty, 664

Nineteenth Amendment, 616
  passage of, 594
NIRA. *See* National Industrial Recovery Act
Nixon, Richard M., 696, 710, 762
  and Civil Rights movement, 787–788
  debates with Kennedy, 747–748
  foreign policy of, 814–815
  and inflation, 813
  and power of presidential office, 808
  presidency of, 762–763
  in 1968 presidential election, 762
  in 1972 presidential election, 766–767
  and Vietnam War, 763–767
  visit to China, 766
  and Watergate, 805–807
NLRB. *See* National Labor Relations Board
NLU. *See* National Labor Union
Noble and Holy Order of the Knights of
    Labor, 466–467
Non-Intercourse Act, 193
Noriega, Manuel Antonio, 827–828
Norris, Frank, 423, 483
Norris, George, 566, 628
North. *See also* Civil War; Union
  advantages and disadvantages of, 366
  culture of, pre-Civil War, 277–278
  effects of Reconstruction on, 407–409
  financing of Civil War, 375
  industrialization in, 279–286
  prosperity in, 375
  slavery in, 277
  social stratification in, 285–286
North, Lord Frederick, 96–101, 103–104,
    116, 129
North American Free Trade Agreement
    (NAFTA), 833
North American League for Immigrants, 561
North Atlantic Treaty Organization
    (NATO), 703
North Carolina
  Reconstruction in, 394
  secession of, 365
  settlement of, 32
Northern Confederacy, 189–190
Northern Securities Company, 565
Northrup, Solomon, 294
North-South Compromise, for
    Constitution, 154
North Star, The, 263
Northwest Ordinance (1787), 146

and slavery, 154
Northwest Passage, search for, 19, 23
Notes on the State of Virginia (Thomas
    Jefferson), 148
NOW. *See* National Organization for Women
    (NOW)
Noyes, John Humphrey, 268
NRA. *See* National Recovery
    Administration (NRA)
Nuclear Test Ban Treaty (1963), 755
Nuclear weapons, 725
Nullification, principle of, 232, 239–240
NWSA. *See* National Woman Suffrage
    Association
NYA. *See* National Youth Administration
    (NYA)
Nye, Gerald P., 668–669

Oberlin College, 258
O'Brien, Tim, *Going after Cacciato,* 768
Occupational Health and Safety Act, 773
Ochs, Phil, 791
O'Connor, Sandra Day, 798
Office of Economic Opportunity, 787
Office of Facts and Figures, 676
Office of Price Administration (OPA), 674,
    707–708
Office of Scientific Research and Development
    (OSRD), 674
Oglethorpe, James, 72
Ohio region, settlement in, 146
Oil embargo, and inflation, 811–812
Oil industry, consolidation, in 19th
    century, 431
Oil refining, 422
O'Keeffe, Georgia, 486
Okinawa, conquest of, 689
Olive Branch petition of 1775, 111
Oliver, Andrew, 87, 97, 104
Oliver, Peter, 87–88
Olmsted, Frederick Law, 493
Olney, Richard, 519, 537
Olympic Games, 492
Omnibuses, 475
Oneida Community, 268
OPA. *See* Office of Price Administration
OPEC. *See* Organization of Petroleum
    Exporting Countries
Opechancanough, 30–31
Open Door policy, 664, 671
    with China, 547–548

Operation Linebacker II, 767
Operation Overlord, 685
Operation Rolling Thunder, 758
Order of the Star-Spangled Banner, 342
Orders in Council, 83, 192
Oregon, dispute with Britain over,
    318–319, 319*f*
Oregon Trail, 309
Oregon Trail, The (Francis Parkman), 272–273
Organization of Afro-Americans, 782
Organization of Petroleum Exporting Countries
    (OPEC), 810
Orlando, Vittorio, 602
Osgood, Samuel, 163
OSRD. *See* Office of Scientific Research and
    Development
Ostend Manifesto, 343
O'Sullivan, John L., 314
Oswald, Lee Harvey, 751
Otis, James, Jr., 87
Owen, Robert, 267

Pacific Railway Act (1862), 375
Pacific region, American ambitions for, in 19th
    century, 531–532
Pago Pago, 534–535
Pahlavi, Mohammad Reza, 729, 817
Paine, Thomas, 113–114, 119, 138
Paiute Indians, 312
Paleo-Indians, 4
Palestine Liberation Organization (PLO), 815
Palmer, A. Mitchell, 599
Panama
    invasion of, 827–828
    Republic of, 571
Panama Canal, 570–571
Panama Canal Treaty, 816
Panay, bombing of, 666
Panic
    of 1819, 218–219, 229
    of 1837, 243, 283
    of 1873, 408–409, 507
    of 1893, 517–518
Paper money, issued during Revolutionary
    War, 140
Paranoid style, 713–716
Paredes y Arrillaga, Mariano, 323
Parker, Alton B., 565
Parker, Dorothy, 614
Parkman, Francis, *The Oregon Trail,* 272–273
Parks, Rosa, 735

Parks, urban, 492–493
Parliament
    taxation by, 85
    trade acts of, 65, 84
Participatory democracy, 789
Party politics, in early 19th century, 228–233
Party system
    birth of, 167–172
    disintegration of, 341–346
Paternalism, in slavery, 291
Paterson, William, 153
Patronage, political
    spoils system of, in 1870s, 508
    in 19th century, 501, 504
Patrons of Husbandry, 509, 514–515
Patton, George, 685
Patuxets, 2
Paul, Alice, 559, 594
Pawnee Indians, 6, 409
Payne-Aldrich Tariff, 566
Pearl Harbor, 671–673
Pendleton Act of 1883, 508
Penitentiaries, 256
Penn, William, 58
Pennsylvania
    emancipation laws in, 148
    First Frame of Government of, 58
    state constitution of, 137
People's Republic of China
    and Korean War, 705–706
    relationship with United States, during
        Nixon presidency, 814–815
    U.S. recognition of, 704, 766
    and Vietnam, 752, 765–766
Pequots, 38
Perestroika, 824
Perkins, Francis, 657
Perot, Ross, and presidential election of
    1992, 832
Perry, Matthew, 343
Pershing, John J., 573, 596, 598
Persian Gulf War, 829–832
Petroleum industry, rise of, 419–420
Phagan, Mary, 454–455
Phalanxes, 267
Philadelphia, siege of, 121
Philadelphia Centennial Exposition, 420
Philip II (King of Spain), 17–18
Philippines
    American acquisition of, 544–546

independence, war for, 546–547
    invasion of, 689
    in Spanish-American War, 542–544
Philips, Sam, 739–740
Phips, Sir William, 64
Phrenology, 273
Pickering, John, 187
Pierce, Franklin, 349
    and Kansas controversy, 347
    and Kansas-Nebraska Act, 344
    presidency of, 343
Pike, Zebulon, 306
Pilgrims, 2–3, 24
    in New England, 32–39
Pinchot, Gifford, 565–566
Pinckney, Charles C., 191
Pinckney, Thomas, 173, 387
Pinckney's Treaty, 172
Pine Ridge Reservation, confrontation at,
    in 1890, 457
Pinkerton agency, 463
Pioneers, 312–313
    in early 19th century, 206–208
    life on trail, 313
    motivation of, 313
Pioneers, The (James Fenimore Cooper), 269
Piracy, 188
Pitt, William, 74, 92
Pittsburgh, growth of, in 19th century, 217
Pittsburgh Landing, battle of, 372
Pizarro, Francisco, 12
Plains Indians, 24, 311–312, 387, 409
Plantation legend, 287–288
Plate fleets, Spanish, 13
Platt Amendment, 545, 570, 665
Plessy v. *Ferguson*, 441, 520, 563, 732
PLO. *See* Palestine Liberation Organization
Plymouth Colony, 2–3, 37
Plymouth Plantation, 33
Pocahontas, 30
Poe, Edgar Allen, 271
Pokanoket Indians, 2
Poland, in Cold War, 698
Polish immigrants, in 19th century, 451
Political democratization, in early 19th
    century, 225–228
Political polarization, factors affecting, 168–170
Politics, deferential, breakdown of, 227–228
Polk, James Knox
    and Mexican War, 323–324

and presidential election of 1844, 317, 319
  and slavery, 329
Pollution, urban, in 19th century, 479
Polo, Marco, 8
Polygamy, 321
Ponce de León, Juan, 12
Pontiac, 83
Popé, 15
Pope, John, 371
Pope Alexander VI, 10
Pope Clement VII, 16
Popular sovereignty, 338, 344–345, 350
Population
  1790 census, 160–161
  in early 19th century, 211
  urban, growth of, in 19th century, 216–217
Population increase
  and industrial work force, 422–423
  in 18th century, 66
Populist party, 516–517, 520, 531–532
Porter, Edwin S., 493
Port Huron Statement (1962), 789
Portsmouth, RI, 38
Portugal
  explorations and conquests, fifteenth and
    sixteenth century, 10–12
  Far Eastern empire of, 9
  15th century, 9
Portugese, in slave trade, 45–46
Potsdam Conference, 689–690
Potsdam Declaration, 690
Poverty
  in early America, 145
  effects of World War II on, 679
  urban, in 19th century, 217
Powderly, Terence V., 466–467
Powell, Lewis, 788
Powers, Francis Gary, 731
Powhatan, 21–22, 30
Pragmatism, doctrine of, 556
Prendergast, Maurice, 485–486
Preparedness program, for World War I, 586
Presbyterian church, 17
Presidency
  defining role of, 162–163
  in late 19th century, 502
  powers of, 396–397, 808–809
    in Constitution, 154
    and Lincoln, 375–376
    and Nixon, 808

President, election of, Constitutional
    provision for, 154
Presidential election
  of 1796, 173
  of 1800, 176–178
  of 1804, 191
  of 1808, 193
  of 1824, 229–230
  of 1828, 232–233
  of 1832, 242
  of 1836, 243, 245
  of 1840, 224–225, 246
  of 1844, 317–319
  of 1848, 247, 330
  of 1852, 247, 343
  of 1856, 342, 349
  of 1860, 361–362, 363*t*
  of 1864, 382
  of 1868, 397–398
  of 1872, 408
  of 1876, 412*t*, 412–413
  of 1880, 507–508
  of 1884, 508–509
  of 1888, 505, 510–511
  of 1892, 517
  of 1896, 499–501, 520–522
  of 1900, 547, 554
  of 1904, 565
  of 1908, 565
  of 1912, 566–567, 577
  of 1916, 569, 586
  of 1920, 605–606, 642
  of 1928, 628–629
  of 1932, 641–643
  of 1936, 654–655
  of 1940, 670
  of 1944, 676
  of 1948, 703, 709
  of 1952, 722–723
  of 1960, 747–748, 779
  of 1964, 755–756, 758
  of 1968, 760–762, 787
  of 1972, 755–756, 766–767, 806
  of 1984, 825
  of 1988, 826
  of 1992, 832
Presidential pardons, after Civil War, 394
President's Commission of Civil Rights, 732
President's Commission on the Status of
    Women, 794

Presley, Elvis, 739–740
Press, freedom of. *See* Freedom of the press
Preston, Thomas, 95–96
Primogeniture, abolition of, 145
Princeton, NJ, and American Revolution, 118
Private city, in 19th century, 481–482
Proclamation of 1763, 83–84
Progress and Poverty (Henry George), 555
Progressive party, 566–567, 627–628
Progressivism
  accomplishments and failures of, 573–577
  international, 569–573
  moral, under Wilson, 568–569
  national, 564–569
  origins and appeal of, 553–557
  quiet, under Taft, 566–567
  state, 562–564
  and urban reform, 561–562, 573–574
  and voices for changes, 555–557
  winners and losers under, 575–577
Progressivists
  activism of, 557–564
  heterogeneity of, 557
Prohibition, 575, 617–618
  early seeds of, 512
  in Maine (1851), 254
  repeal of, 617
  during World War I, 593–594
Prohibitionism, 558
  and progressivism, 563
Property rights, 144, 399
Prosser, Gabriel, 298
Protestant ethic, 252
Protestant Reformation, 16–17, 34
Protestant Wind, 18
Providence, RI, 37
Pseudoscience, 273
  and slavery, 290
Public schools, 257
Public virtue, 136
Public Works Administration (PWA), 647
  effects on Native Americans, 657
Pueblo Indians, 312
  challenge to Spanish rule, 15
Pueblos, 6
Puerto Rico, American acquisition of, 544
Pulitzer, Joseph, 540
Pullman strike of 1894, 518–519, 532, 538
Punch, John, 28
Pure Food and Drugs Act, 565, 575

Puritans, 17, 24, 32, 56, 58
  in England, 33–34
  family life of, 40
  in New England, 32–39
  patriarchal values of, 42
PWA. *See* Public Works Administration

Quakers, 58–59
Quartering Act of 1765, 100
Quebec, 23
Quebec Act of 1774, 100–101
Quebec City, 1775 patriot attack on, 112
Queen Anne's War, 72
"Queen for a Day," 792
Quota systems, 788

Race relations
  in New South, 441–442
  and progressivism, 576–577
  in 1890s, 519–520
Racial discrimination
  in late 19th century, 512
  during 1920s, 612–614
Racial justice
  current state of, 788
  struggle for, 774–792
Racial prejudice, and Social Darwinism, 530
Racial separatism, 783
Racial violence, of 1890s, 519–520
Racism, 273, 731–734, 774, 785. *See
  also* Segregation
  and Emancipation Proclamation, 377
  in military, in Spanish-American War, 542
  and Native Americans, 409–411
  and Reconstruction, 399, 401–402
  in Revolutionary period, 148–149
  and slavery, 289–290
  during World War II, 676, 678–679
Radical Republicans, 391–392
Radical revolutionaries, 136–138
  beliefs of, 136
Radio, during 1920s, 623–624
Railroad Administration, during World
  War I, 589
Railroads
  early, 213
  in early 19th century, growth, 213–214
  in late 19th century, regulation, 509
  pools, in 19th century, 430–431
  regulation of, 565, 574

in 19th century
  and agriculture, 440
  consolidation, 430
  control of competition, 430
  expansion, 420, 423–424
  management, 433
  rebates, 430–431
  subsidies, 427
  transcontinental, 446
  and western expansion, 436–438
Railroad strike, of 1877, 463–464
Raleigh, Walter, 19
Rambo: First Blood II, 768
Ranching, western, in 19th century, 436–438
Ranchos, 310
Randolph, A. Philip, 613
Randolph, Edmund, 163
Rankin, Jeannette, 562
Rationalism, 68
Rationing, in World War II, 674
REA. *See* Rural Electrification
  Administration (REA)
Reader's Digest, 794
Reagan, Ronald, 819–820, 825–826
  in presidential election of 1980, 819
  in presidential election of 1984, 825
  and social welfare programs, 821
Reagan Doctrine, 823–824
Reaganomics, 820–821
Realism
  in 19th-century art, 485
  in 19th-century literature, 484
Rebel Without a Cause, 714–715, 790
Reconstruction, 388–414
  congressional, 392–393, 395–399
  decline of, reasons for, 409, 411–413
  effects on blacks, 404–405
  effects on whites, 406
  end of, 506
  in North, 407–409
  in North Carolina, 394
  presidential, 392–395
  radical, 396–397
  resistance to, 406–407
  social programs in, 404
  in South, 399–407
Reconstruction Finance Corporation
  (RFC), 639
Red Scare, 710–713
  after World War I, 598–600

Reed, Margaret, 305*f*
Reed, Walter, 479
Reform
  moral, 253–255
  radical, 259–268
  social, 255–259
Reformatories, 256
Reform Darwinists, 556
Reform impulse, 251–253
  effects of Civil War on, 275
  sources of, 251–252
Regionalism, and party loyalty, in late 19th
  century, 503
Rehnquist, William, 788, 796
Religion
  and antislavery movement, 290
  and expansionism, in 19th century, 530
  freedom of. *See* Freedom of religion
    in Pennsylvania, 58
  and Gospel of Wealth, 425
  influence on reformers, 252
  and nativism, 454
  and party loyalty, in late 19th century, 504
  of slaves, 297–298
Religious liberalism, 252
Religious toleration, 37
Renaissance, 8
Rendezvous system, 307
Republicanism, ideals of, 136
Republican motherhood, 147
Republican party, 342
  adoption of Federalist policies, in early
    19th century, 203–204
  ascendancy, in late 19th and early 20th
    century, 520
  and big business, 511–512
  after Civil War, 391–392
  creation of, 344–345
  Dred Scott decision and, 350
  in early 19th century, 228–233
  economic platform, in 19th
    century, 426–427
  and election of 1854, 346
  and election of 1860, 362
  and election of 1862, 377
  and election of 1866, 396
  and election of 1876, 412–413
  and election of 1896, 499–501
  Jeffersonian, 181, 190, 194, 203
    and presidential election of 1796, 173

and presidential election of 1800, 177
in late 19th century, 502–505
and progressivism, 566
and Reconstruction, 403–404
Research, in World War II, 674
Reservation system, 411
and Native Americans, 457–458
Resumption Act (1875), 408
Reuther, Walter, 653
Revels, Hiram, 402
Revenue Act (1764), 84
Revenue Act (1942), 675
Revere, Paul, 102
Revolutionary War, 108–130
British military buildup for, 116–117
financing
contention over, 139–141
foreign aid in, 140
start of, 110
RFC. *See* Reconstruction Finance
Corporation (RFC)
Rhode Island, declaration of independence
of, 114
Richardson, Elliot, 806
Richmond, VA
and Civil War, 367, 374
slave march on, 298
Riesman, David, *The Lonely Crowd,* 738–739
Right to life movement, 796–797
Riis, Jacob, 454
Riots
New York draft (1863), 379
1964-1968 race riots, 784–785
Ripley, George, 267
"Rip Van Winkle" (Washington Irving), 268
Ritchie, Thomas, 233
Roads, in early 19th century, 211–214
Roanoak Indians, 19
Roanoke, lost colony of, 19–20
Roanoke Island, natives of, 19, 20*f*
Robber barons, 466
Robinson, Jackie, 492
Rochambeau, comte de, 128
Rock and roll, 739–740
Rockefeller, John D., 375, 422, 425, 431,
431*f,* 599
Rockingham, Marquis of, 91–92
Rocky Mountain Fur Company, 307
Roe v. *Wade,* 795–796
Rogers, William, 762–763

Rogue River Indians, 312
Rolfe, John, 23, 29–31
Rome-Berlin Axis, 666–668
Rommel, Erwin "Desert Fox," 683
Roosevelt, Eleanor, 657, 794
Roosevelt, Franklin Delano, 641–642, 687
and fireside chats, 644
First Hundred Days, 643–652
and Great Depression, 640
and labor, 675
and Latin America, 665
legislation enacted during first hundred days
of presidency, 650*t*
and New Deal, 643–646
and New York governor election
of 1928, 642
and presidential election of 1932, 641
and presidential election of 1936, 654–655
and presidential election of 1940, 670
and presidential election of 1944, 676
Second Hundred Days, 653–654
and Vietnam, 752
and World War II, 668–671, 673, 679,
683–684, 686–687
Roosevelt, Theodore, 410, 533, 538, 543, 557,
576, 597
and coal miners' strike of 1902, 552–553
and foreign policy, 570–572
and Progressive party, 566–567
as reformer, 564–566
Roosevelt Corollary, to Monroe Doctrine, 665
Roosevelt Corollary to Monroe Doctrine, 572
Rosenberg, Julius and Ethel, 710–711
Rosie the Riveter, 677
Rotary Club, 561
Roundheads, 32
Ruckleshaus, William, 806
Rum industry, and Molasses Act of 1733, 65
Rural Electrification Administration
(REA), 648
Rush-Bagot Agreement, 209
Rushin, Thomas Jefferson, 359, 360*f*
Rusk, Dean, 751
Russian Revolution, 587
Russo-Japanese War, 570
Ruth, Herman "Babe," 625

Sacco, Nicola, 619
Sacco-Vanzetti trial, 619
Sachems, 7

el-Sadat, Anwar, and Middle East peace, 815–816
St. Lawrence River, 16
St. Leger, Barry, 122
Salem witch trials, 63–64
Salinger, J. D., *Catcher in the Rye,* 790
Samoa, confrontation with Germans in, 534–535
Samoset, 2
Sanger, Margaret, 610–611
San Salvador, 9
    Columbus's landing on, 13*f*
Santa Anna, Antonio López de, 315–316, 328
Santa Clara County v. *The Southern Pacific Railroad,* 428
Santa Fe Trail, 308–309
Santo Domingo, American expansionist efforts in, 525
Saratoga, 123
Sauk Indians, in Black Hawk War, 237–238
SAVAK, and human rights violations, 817
Savings and loan crisis, 827
Savio, Mario, 790
Scalawags, 400
Scarlet Letter, The (Nathaniel Hawthorne), 271
Schafly, Phyllis, 797
Schechter v. *United States,* 652–653
Schools. *See also* Education
    in Massachusetts Bay Colony, 36
Schurz, Carl, 388
Schwab, Charles, 417
Schwarzkopf, H. Norman, 831
Schwerner, Michael, 783
Science, in early 19th century, 273
Scientific agriculture, 439
Scopes, John, 618
Scopes "Monkey" Trial, 618–619
Scott, Dred, 350
Scott, Winfield, 247, 325, 327, 366, 369–370
Scrooby Manor, 33
SDS. *See* Students for a Democratic Society
Sea dogs, 17
Secession, 189–190
    of South, 336–337, 361–365
    rationale for, 363
Second Continental Congress, 110
Second Great Awakening, 252–253
Second Hundred Days, of Franklin Roosevelt's presidency, 653–654

Second New Deal, 652–655
Sectionalism, growth in 19th century, 218–221
Sedition Act (1798), 176
Sedition Act (1918), 593
Segregation, 404, 520, 731–732, 785. *See also* Desegregation
    in New South, 441–442
    and progressivism, 563
    in sports, 492
    struggle against, 775–779
    in 19th-century cities, 477–478
    during World War II, 678
Segretti, Donald, 805
Selective Service Act (1917), 597
"Self-Reliance" (Ralph Waldo Emerson), 270
Seminole Indians, 6, 238
    Jackson's expedition against, 210
Senate, direct election of, 562, 573
Senate Watergate Committee, 806
Seneca Falls convention, 266
Separate but equal doctrine, 732–733
Separatists, 33
Sequoyah, 236
Seven Days, battle of, 370
Seven Pines, battle of, 370
1785 Ordinance, 146
1784 Ordinance, 146
Seventeenth Amendment, 562
Seven Years' War, 74, 80–81, 120
Sewall, Arthur, 520
Seward, William H., 339, 346, 362, 364, 374, 528, 532
Sex discrimination, 796–797
Sexual patterns
    in Chesapeake colonies, 43
    in Puritan New England, 43
Sexual Politics (Kate Millett), 796
Sexual revolution, of 1920s, 615–616
Shafter, William R., 543–544
Shakers, 267, 274
Shakespeare, Joseph, 453
Shamans, 6
Shame of the Cities, The (Lincoln Steffens), 557
Sharecropping, 405
Shasta Indians, 312
Shaw, Robert Gould, 378
Shays, Daniel, 143
Shays' Rebellion, 143–144
Shelley v. *Kraemer,* 732
Sheridan, Philip, 388

Sherman, William Tecumseh, 322, 366, 390
  march across Georgia, 383
  march to Atlanta, 381–382
Sherman Antitrust Act, 511, 552, 565
Sherman Silver Purchase Act, 511, 518
Shiloh, battle of, 372
Shinn, Everett, 486
Shippen, Nancy, 133–134, 134*f*
Shipping, during trade wars between France
    and Great Britain, 192
Shipping Board, during World War I, 589
Sicilian immigrants, 453
Sierra Leone, 259
Sigourney, Lydia, 272
Simmons, William Joseph, 619
Sinclair, Upton, 557, 565
Sioux Indians, 311, 409
  conflict with settlers, 410
  and Wounded Knee, 457
Sirhan, Sirhan B., 761
Sister Carrie (Theodore Drieser), 485
Sit-ins, 679, 775
Sitting Bull, 411, 457
Sixteenth Amendment, 568
Skyscrapers, 477
Slater, Samuel, 281
Slave insurrections, 241
Slave labor, 294–295
Slave ownership, prevalence of, 287, 289
Slave rebellions, in Stono River area of South
    Carolina, 49
Slavery, 259, 288, 292–300
  beginnings of, 45–46
  and Civil War, 361
  codes for, 291
  conspiracy theories of, 334–335
  and Constitution, 153–154
  controversy over, in Kansas, 346–348
  decline of, 336–337
    in 1790s, 277
  effects of cotton gin on, 277
  effects of Mexican War on, 329–330
  effects on Southern economy, 288–289
  in English North America, 28, 47–49
  expansion in West, controversy over,
    225–241
  and Great Britain, 373
  Jefferson and, 183
  Lincoln-Douglas debates over, 352–354
  and Missouri Compromise, 219–221

  in New Spain, 14–15
  political debate over, 329–330
    renewal of, 345–346
  and presidential election of 1860, 361–362
  prohibition in Mexico, 315
  resistance to, 298–299
  in Revolutionary period, 147–150
  Southern defense of, 289–290
Slaves. *See also* Freed slaves
  African, 14–15
  concentration of, in 1860, 337*f*
  in Continental Army, 120
  cultural expression of, 297–298
  diet of, 295
  emancipation of, by Lord Dunmore, 112–113
  family life of, 48–49, 296–297
  infant mortality among, 295
  legal status of, 292–294
  lodging of, 296
  material conditions of, 295–296
  motivation of, 294–295
  Native Americans as, 14
  regulation of, 291, 293–294
  religion of, 297–298
  southern, 48
Slavic immigrants, in 19th century, 451
Slidell, John, 323, 374
Sloan, John D., 485–486
Sloat, John D., 324
Slums, 255*f*
Smallpox, in 19th century, 479
Smith, Adam, 426
Smith, Alfred, 628
Smith, Francis, 109
Smith, Jedediah, 307
Smith, John, 22
Smith, Joseph, 320–321
Smith-Connally Act, 675
Snake Indians, 312
SNCC. *See* Student Nonviolent Coordinating
    Committee
Snyder Act of 1924, 458
Social Bands, 347
Social change, in Revolutionary period, 144–150
Social Darwinism, 530
  challenges to, in early 20th century, 555–556
  and industrialization, 424–426
Social Gospel movement, 556–557
Socialism, in early 20th century, 562
Social issues, in late 19th century, 512–513

Socialist Labor party, 519
Social justice movement, in early 20th
    century, 558–560
Social Security, 709
Social Security Act (1935), 653–654
    effects on Mexican Americans, 657
Social unrest, after World War I, 598–600
Social welfare programs, during Reagan
    presidency, 821
Soil Conservation Service, 648
Sons of Liberty, 88
Sons of the South, 347
Soto, Hernando de, 12
Souls of Black Folk, The (W.E.B. Du Bois), 560
Sousa, John Philip, 538
South, 286–292. *See also* Civil War;
    Confederacy
   advantages and disadvantages of, 366
   antislavery movement in, 290–291
   antislavery movements and, 290
   blockade of coastline, 369, 373–374
   culture of, pre-Civil War, 277–278
   distinctive identity of, 289–290
   economy of
     modernization in 19th century, 440–442
     and slavery, 288–289
   and expansion of slavery into West, 336–337
   images of, pre-Civil War, 287
   involvement in federal government, after
     Civil War, 394
   progressivism in, 563
   social stratification in, 287, 289
Southampton County, VA, slave revolt in, 299
South Carolina
   and nullification, 240–241
   secession of, 363
   settlement of, 32
Southern colonies, English settlers in, 32
Southern nationalism, 291–292
South Improvement Company, 431
Soviet military, in 1970s, 815
Soviet Union, 668
   arms limitation talks with, 766
   and Cold War, 698–699
   containment policy for, 702–707
   and Germany, 699
   relationship with United States, during
     Nixon presidency, 814–815
   and Vietnam, 752, 765–766
   in World War II, 670–671, 682–683,
     686–687, 691

Space race, 728
Spain
   aid during War for Independence, 108
   exploration of New World, 11*f*
   explorations and conquests, fifteenth and six-
     teenth century, 10–12
   15th-century, 9
   relations with, in post-Revolutionary
     period, 172
   settlements in America, 309–310
   unification of, 9
Spanish, in slave trade, 46
Spanish-American War, 534, 542–544
Spanish Armada, 18
Spanish *conquistadores,* 10–12
Spanish empire, construction of, 12–15
Spanish settlers, in sixteenth century, 14
Specie Circular of 1836, 242–243
Specie Resumption Act, 507
Speech, freedom of. *See* Freedom of speech
Spencer, Herbert, 425, 530
Spies, August, 465–466
Spiritualism, 273
Spirituals, 298
Spock, Benjamin, *Baby and Child Care,* 738
Spoils system, 235–236
Sports, 714–715
   college, scandals in, 715
   during 1920s, 625
   in 19th century
     amateurism in, 492
     exclusive, 491–492
     popular, 488–491
     segregation in, 492
   women in, 492
Spotsylvania Court House, battle of, 382
Sputnik, 728
Spy, The (James Fenimore Cooper), 269
Squanto, 2–3, 3*f*
Square Deal, 565
Squatter sovereignty, 338
Stagecoach, 212
Stagflation, 812–814
   definition of, 813
Stalin, Joseph, 682–683, 695, 697–698, 726
   and Cold War, 700
   and World War II, 684–687
Stalwart Republicans, 504, 507
Stamp Act Congress, 90
Stamp Act of 1765, 85, 87–88
   intercolonial boycott in response to, 90–91

repeal of, 91

Standard of living, for industrial workers, in late 19th and early 20th century, 459–461

Standard Oil, 431, 557, 574

Stanton, Edwin M., 378, 397

Stanton, Elizabeth Cady, 266, 398, 506

"Stars and Stripes Forever" (John Philip Sousa), 538

Star-Spangled Banner, 197

State Department, in 19th century, 526–527

State governments, establishment of, 136–138

Statehood, for territories, 146

States' rights, 391

States' Rights Democratic Party (Dixiecrats), 709

Statue of Liberty, 447

Statute of Religious Freedom (Virginia), 145

Stay laws, 229

Steam engine, 215

Steamship, 212, 215

Steel industry, in 19th century, 417–419, 421–422, 432

Steffens, Lincoln, 557

Steinem, Gloria, 796

Steuben, Friedrich von, 123

Stevens, Thaddeus, 392, 411

Stevenson, Adlai, 722

Stevenson, Robert Louis, 495

Stieglitz, Alfred, 486

Stimson, Henry, 666

Stimson Doctrine, 666

Stock Market, crash of 1929, 629–633

Stockton, Robert F., 325

Stone, Lucy, 398

Stono uprising, 49

Stony Mountains, 306

Storyville, 487

Stowe, Harriet Beecher, 265, 271
    Uncle Tom's Cabin, 340–341

Strategic Arms Limitation Treaty (SALT I), 766

Strikes
    of 1880s, 467
    in 19th century, 462, 532
    and violence, 518–519
    in 19th century, 463–464

Strong, Josiah, 530

Stroyer, Jacob, 296–297

Student Nonviolent Coordinating Committee (SNCC), 775, 783

Students for a Democratic Society (SDS), 761, 789–790

Stuyvesant, Peter, 56

Submarine warfare, 584–585

Suburban values, criticism of, 738–739

Suburbia, 736–738
    rise of, during 1920s, 624

Subways, 476

Suez Canal, seizure of, 727

Suffolk Resolves, 102

Suffrage
    for African Americans, 397–399
    for women. *See* Women's suffrage

Sugar Act of 1764, 84, 86

Sullivan, Bridget, 472–473

Sullivan, John L., 123, 491–492, 538

Sullivan, Louis Henri, 477

Sumner, Charles, 392, 411, 525–526
    "The Crime Against Kansas," 347–348

Sumner, William Graham, 425

Supreme Court, 185
    and Agricultural Adjustment Act, 658
    in early 19th century, 208–209
    Jackson's appointments to, 244
    and National Recovery Act, 658
    and New Deal, 658

Sussex, bombing of by German submarines, 585

Sutter, John A., 30

Swann v. *Charlotte-Mecklenburg Board of Education,* 785

Sweden, exploration of New World, 11*f*

Swift, Gustavus, 422, 434

Swift, Henry, 87–88

Taft, Robert, 708

Taft, William Howard, 490, 547, 566–567, 626
    and foreign policy, 572

Taft Commission, 547

Taft-Hartley Act, 708

Talleyrand, Charles Maurice de, 174

Tallmadge, James, 219

Tammany Hall, 561

Taney, Roger B., 244

Taney, Roger Brooke, 350, 375

Tappan, Arthur, 262

Tappan, Lewis, 262

Tarbell, Ida, 557

Tariff of 1828, 240

Tariff of 1832, 240

Tariff of Abominations, 232
Tariffs, protective, 218–219, 231–232, 329. *See also specific tariffs*
    division over, in late 19th century, 510, 518
    in early 19th century, 204, 206–207
    and Hamilton's financial program, 166–167
    and Jackson's presidency, 240
    and presidential election of 1860, 362
    in Taft administration, 566
    in 19th century, 427
Task system, of slave labor, 294
Taverns, in Massachusetts Bay Colony, 36
Taxes, in Massachusetts Bay Colony, 36
Taxi Driver, 768
Taylor, Frederick W., 434
Taylor, Zachary, 247, 327, 339
    and Compromise of 1850, 339
    and Mexican War, 323–325
    in presidential election of 1848, 330
Tea Act of 1773, 98
Teapot Dome scandal, 627
Technology
    advances in, in 19th century, 420–422
    and agriculture, in 19th century, 439–440
    innovation in, in early 19th century, 215
Teheran Conference, 684–685
Telegraph, 215, 420
Telephone, 420–421
Television
    and civil rights struggle, 750
    and Kennedy-Nixon debates, 747–748
    and McCarthy hearings, 712
    and racism, 734
    in 1950s, 736–738
Teller Amendment, 542, 544
Temperance reform, 253–255
Temperance Society of the Methodist Episcopal Church, 558
Temple Mound Builders (Mississippian peoples), 5
Tenements, in 19th century, 478–479
Tennessee, secession of, 365
Tennessee Valley Authority (TVA), 648
Tenochtitlán, 5, 12
Ten percent plan, 392–393
Tenure of Office Act, 397
Tet Offensive, 759
Texas
    American settlement in, 314–316
        Mexican conditions on, 314–315
    annexation of, 316–317

    and Mexican War, 322–323
    economic growth in, 316
    population growth in, 316
    secession of, 363
Texas Revolution, 315–316
Textile industry
    in early 19th century, 202
    innovation in, in early 19th century, 216
    in New South, 441
Textile manufacturers, competition among, 282
Thanksgiving, first, 3
Thayendanegea (Joseph Brant), 122
Theatre Project, 651
Third Reich, 667
Third World, nationalist movements in, 728–730
Thirteenth Amendment, 398
    ratification of, 389, 394
Thoreau, Henry David, 270
Thorpe, Jim, 492
Ticonderoga, 111, 122
Tijerina, Reies Lopez, 799
Tilden, Samuel J., 412
Till, Emmett, 720–721
Tillman, "Pitchfork Ben," 515
Timber Culture Act of 1873, 437
Tinian, 688–689
Tituba, 63
Tobacco, 23–24, 29, 32
    and mercantile economy, 55–56, 60
    in New South, 441
    prohibition of, 617–618
Tojo, Hideki, 672
Toll roads, 212
Toltecs, 5
Toombs, Robert, 336
Toomer, Jean, 614
Tories, 102
Townsend, Francis, 651–652, 655
Townshend, Charles, 92–93, 97
Trade
    with Britain, in Revolutionary period, 142–143
    British intervention in, in post-Revolutionary period, 170–171
    and expansionism, in 19th century, 530–532
    with France, 192–193
        during American Revolution, 108, 121, 123
    with Great Britain, 192–193
Trade checks, 441

Traders, 307

Trail of Tears, 237

Transcendentalism, 269–270

Transportation
  in early 19th century, 207, 211–214
  mass, in 19th century, 475–476
  in 19th century, 420

Trappers, 307

Travis, Joseph, 299

Travis, William, 316

Treaty of Alliance, 123

Treaty of Amity and Commerce of 1778, 123

Treaty of Guadalupe Hidalgo, 329

Treaty of Paris of 1899, 545–546

Treaty of San Lorenzo, 172

Treaty of Tordesillas, 10, 15

Treaty of Utrecht (1713), 72

Treaty of Versailles, 600–606, 666
  ratification of, 603–604

Trenchard, John, 97

Trent, interception of, 374

Trenton, New Jersey, and American
    Revolution, 118

Trial by jury, 145, 162

Triangle Sirtwaist Company fire, 563

Trist, Nicholas, 329

Trolleys, 475–476

Trotter, William Monroe, 560

Truman, Harry S., 676, 687, 689–691,
    703, 707
  and Cold War, 697–700, 710–711
  and Korean War, 705–707
  and labor unions, 708
  and presidential election of 1948, 709
  and Vietnam, 752

Truman Doctrine, 700–702

Trumbull, John, 272

Trust-busting, 565–566. *See also* Sherman
    Antitrust Act

Trusts, 417, 431

Tubman, Harriet, 263, 264*f*

Turkey, struggle against Communism in,
    700–701

Turner, Nat, 299

Turnpikes, construction, in early 19th
    century, 212

Tuskegee Normal and Industrial Institute, 440

TVA. *See* Tennessee Valley Authority (TVA)

Twain, Mark, 484, 545
  on baseball, 488–489

Twelfth Amendment, 230

Twenty-Fourth Amendment, 781

Two Years Before the Mast (Richard Henry
    Dana, Jr.), 272–273

Tyler, Elizabeth, 619–620

Tyler, John, 246
  and slavery, 317

UAW. *See* United Automobile Workers

UMW. *See* United Mine Workers

Un-American Activities Committee. *See* House
    Un-American Activities Committee

Uncle Tom's Cabin (Harriet Beecher Stowe),
    340–341

Underground railroad, 263

Underwood Tariff, 568, 574

Unemployment
  during Great Depression, 639–640
  and inflation, 813

UNIA. *See* Universal Negro Improvement
    Association

Union
  morale in, 379
  naval superiority, 373–374
  offensive in West, 371–372
  strategy of, 368–369
  Virginia campaign, 382

Unionism. *See also* Strikes
  in late 19th century, 518–519
  rise of, 282–284
  in 19th century, 466–469

Union Pacific Railroad, 446

Unitarianism, 252

United Automobile Workers (UAW), during
    Great Depression, 653

United Mine Workers, 552, 574
  strike of 1946, 708

United Nations, and Persian Gulf War, 830

United States Military Academy at West Point,
    cheating scandal in, 715

United States Steel Corporation, 418

United States v. *E. C. Knight Co.,* 511, 565

Universal Negro Improvement Association
    (UNIA), 613–614

Universities, youth movement against, 789–790

University of California at Berkeley,
    protests at, 790

University of Mississippi at Oxford,
    desegregation in, 777

University of South Carolina,
    integration in, 404

Unsafe at Any Speed (Ralph Nader), 773

Urban growth, during 1920s, 612–613
Urbanization
  and industrialization, in 19th
    century, 474–475
  in late 19th and early 20th century, 471–497
  in 19th century, 422–423
Urban reformers, of early 20th century,
    561–562, 573–574
U-2 spy flights, 731
Utopian communities, 266–268

Vaca, Cabeza de, 12
Valley Forge, 107, 119–120
Van Buren, Martin, 224, 227–229, 233, 330
  presidency of, 243, 245
Vandenberg, Arthur, 700
Vanderbilt, Cornelius, 430
Van Devanter, Willis, 658
Vanguard, 728, 729*f*
Vanzetti, Bartholomew, 619
Vassar College, 265
Venezuela, boundary dispute, in 1890s,
    537–538
Verrazzano, Giovanni da, 15–16
Vesey, Denmark, 241, 298–299
Vespucci, Amerigo, 10
Viceroys, Spanish, 13–14
Vicksburg, siege of, 381
Victorianism, 473–474, 495
Vietnam
  division into North and South, 753
  philosophy of, 746
  struggle for independence, 746, 752
Vietnamization, 763–765
Vietnam War, 752–769, 757*f*
  beginnings of, 752–754
  bombings of Christmas 1972, 767
  effects of, 768–769
    on soldiers, 760
  end of, 763–767
  escalation of, 758–760
  and inflation, 811
  and limits of American power, 814
  protests of, 763–764, 790
  public opinion of, 759–761
  student opposition to, 790
  surrender of South Vietnam, 767
  U.S. troop levels in, 765*f*
  veterans of, 767–768
Vigilantism, 599

Vikings, first known contacts with North
    America, 7
Villa, Pancho, 573
Vinland, 7
Violence
  labor, in 19th century, 463–464
  and nativism, 455–457
Virginia
  charter of, 1618, 30
  founding of, 20–23
  migrants to, 29
  population of, in seventeenth century, 40
  secession of, 365
  slavery in, 47
  stabilizing life in, 45
  tobacco in, 29
Virginia colony, government of, 31
Virginia Company, 21–23, 29, 31
Virginia Plan, for Constitution, 152–153
Virginia Resolutions of 1765, 90
Visual art
  in early 19th century, 272
  and urban landscape, in 19th century,
    485–486
Volstead Act, 594
Voting rights
  African American struggle for, 780–781
  expansion of, in early 19th century, 225–227
  qualification tests for, 781
Voting Rights Act (1965), 781, 787

Wabash v. *Illinois,* 509
WAC. *See* Women's Army Corps (WAC)
Wade-Davis Bill, 392–393
Wage controls, 675
Wages, for industrial workers, in late 19th and
    early 20th century, 459–461
Wagner, Robert F., 653
Wagner Act, 658. *See also* National Labor
    Relations Act
Walker, David, *Appeal to the Colored Citizens of
    the World,* 260
Walker, William, 292
Walker Tariff, 329
Wallace, George C., 762
  and Civil Rights movement, 777
Wallace, Henry, 648
Wall Street, during Reagan presidency, 822
Wampanoag Indians, National Day of
    Mourning, 800

Wanamaker, John, 483
War bonds, 675
War for American Independence. *See* American
    Revolution
War guilt clause, 603, 666
War Hawks, 194, 204
War Industries Bond (WIB), 588–589
War Labor Board (WLB), 589, 675
Warmouth, Henry C., 404
Warner, Susan, *The Wide, Wide World,* 272
War of 1812, 194–199
    effects of, 198–199
War on Poverty, 786
War Powers Act (1973), 768–769, 808–809
War Production Board (WPB), 673
War Refugee Board, 680
War Relocation Authority, 680
Warren, Earl, 788
Warren, Joseph, 102, 109
Warsaw Pact, 727
War Trade Board, during World War I, 589
Washington, Booker T., 440, 560, 576,
    576*f,* 613
    "Atlanta Compromise" speech, 440
Washington, DC
    burning of, 196–197
    and Civil War, 367
Washington, George, 73, 76, 101, 107, 111,
    119–120, 123, 151, 175, 183
    and Constitution, 154–155
    Farewell Address, 228, 527
    and French Revolution, 169
    and Newburgh Conspiracy, 141–142
    retirement of, 167, 172
    and role of president, 162–163
    and slavery, 148
Watergate, 805–807
Water transportation, in early 19th century,
    212–213
Watson, Tom, 517, 520–521
Watts riot, 784–785
WAVES. *See* Women Accepted for Voluntary
    Emergency Service
Wayne, Anthony, 170–171
WBA. *See* Workingmen's Benevolent
    Association
Wealth
    concentration of, in 19th century, 435
    distribution of, in early America, 145–146
Wealth of Nations, The (Adam Smith), 426
Weathermen, 790

Weaver, James B., 516
Weber, Max, 486
Webster, Daniel, 204–205, 239, 241, 327
    and Compromise of 1850, 338–339
    presidential candidacy in 1836, 245
Webster-Ashburton Treaty, 317–318
Weed, Thurlow, 227–228
Weld, Theodore, 261
Welfare capitalism, 664
Welfare programs, during Great Depression,
    648–651
Welles, Gideon, 369
Wertham, Frederic, 714
Wesley, John, 69
West
    economic modernization, in 19th century,
        436–440
    exploration of, 146, 305–309
    ignorance about, 305–306
    Indian migrations to, under Jackson,
        236–238
    popular conception of, 306
    and propertyless poor, in 18th century,
        145–146
    settlement of, 312–313
    trailblazing in, 308*f,* 308–309
Westinghouse, George, 420–421
Westmoreland, William, General, 759
Westward expansion, 387
    in early 19th century, 206–208
    and Native Americans, 409–411
Weyler y Nicolau, Valeriano, 539–540
Wheatley, Phillis, 133–135, 135*f*
Wheelwright, John, 38
Whig party, 341
    collapse of, 335, 343–345
    composition of, 246–247
    in election of 1846, 327
    instability of, 336
    and Mexican War, 327
    rise of, 245–246
    in 19th century, 224
Whiskey Rebellion, 170
White, Hugh Lawson, 245
White, John, 19, 20*f*
Whitefield, George, 69–70
White man's burden, 530
White supremacy, 441
Whitman, Walt, 271
    Leaves of Grass, 271
Whitney, Eli, 215–216, 277

Whitten, John C., 721
WIB. *See* War Industries Bond
Wide, Wide World, The (Susan Warner), 272
Wilderness, battle of, 381–382
Wilderness Road, 146
Wild One, The, 714
Wild West, 437
Wilkinson, James, 190–191
Willard, Samuel, 42
William III (King of England), 62, 64
Williams, Eugene, 598
Williams, Roger, 37, 145
Willkie, Wendell, 670
Wilmot, David, 329, 338
Wilmot Proviso, 329
Wilson, Edith, 604
Wilson, Woodrow, 567, 669
    declaration of neutrality, 583
    and foreign policy, 572–573
    Fourteen Points, 600–601
    meeting with Ho Chi Minh, 764
    and moral progressivism, 568–569
    preparedness program for World War 1, 586
    and presidential election of 1916, 586
    and race relations, 577
    and Treaty of Versailles, 603–604
    and World War I, 597–598
Wilson-Gorman Tariff, 518, 539
Winthrop, John, 34–38, 68
Winthrop, John IV, 68
Witch trials, in New England, 63–64
WLB. *See* War Labor Board
Woman's Christian Temperance Union, 558
Women
    in antislavery movement, 266
    and Civil War, 383
    in Continental Army, 120
    discrimination against, legal, 794
    economic status of, 794
    educational opportunities of, 265
        in early 19th century, 257–258
    education of, in Revolutionary period, 147
    employment of
        in early 19th century, 265
        in mills and factories, 281–282
        after World War II, 708–709
    in evangelical revivalism, 253
    in government, 793–794
    laborers, protection of, 563, 574–575
    New Deal and, 657

and New Jersey state constitution, 137
    in pioneering of West, 313
    and politics, in late 19th century, 505–506
    in progressive reform, 558–559
    role in Puritan society, 42
    in slavery, treatment of, 297
    in sports, 492
    status of
        among Chesapeake colonies, 43
        in early 19th century, 264–265
        in pre-Civil War South, 288
        in Revolutionary period, 133–135, 147
        in 1950s, 737–738, 792–793
    in textile industry, in early 19th century, 202
    voting rights, in early 19th century, 227
    wages for, in late 19th and early 20th
        century, 460
    working conditions of, in late 19th and early
        20th century, 460–461
    World War II and, 677–678
Women Accepted for Voluntary Emergency
    Service (WAVES), 677
Women's Army Corps (WAC), 677
Women's Division of Democratic
    Committee, 657
Women's liberation movement, 792–798
    impact of, 798
Women's Loyal League, 398
Women's suffrage, 398, 505–506, 559, 562
    during World War I, 594
Wood, Leonard, 544
Woodstock Music Festival, 792
Woodward, Bob, and Watergate, 806
Woolen Act of 1699, 65
Worcester v. *Georgia,* 237
Work-day, ten-hour, 283–284
Workingmen's Benevolent Association, 463
Working Men's parties, 282
Workman's Compensation Act, 569
Workmen's compensation, 563, 574–575
Works Progress Administration (WPA),
    650–651
    effects on African Americans, 656
    effects on Mexican Americans, 656–657
    effects on Native Americans, 657
World Court, 664
World's Columbian Exposition, 420
World War I
    declaration of war, 587–588
    preparedness program for, 586

World War II, 663, 669–693
  coming of, 666–673
  declaration of, 673
  economic mobilization in, 673–674
  end of, 691
  in Europe, 681–687, 682*f*
  in Pacific, 683, 687–691, 688*f*
  public opinion on, 676–677
  social changes during, 677–680
Wounded Knee
  battle of, 457
  occupation by Native Americans, 801
WPA. *See* Works Progress Administration
WPB. *See* War Production Board
Wright, Carroll D., 459
Wright, Harry, 490
Wright, Mose, 720–721

Xenophobia, during 1920s, 619
XYZ affair, 174–175

Yachting, 491
Yalta Conference, 686–687, 696
Yancey, William L., 361
Yankee, stereotype of, 286–287
Yellow fever, in 19th century, 479
Yellow journalism, 539–542
Yeltsin, Boris, 829
Yom Kippur War, 811
Yorktown, siege of, 128
Young, Brigham, 321
Young America, 343
Youth
  images in 1950s, 714–716
  protest in 1950s, 739–740
  revolt in 1960s, 789–792

Zimmerman, Arthur, 587
Zimmerman telegram, 587
Zuñi Indians, 6, 312, 409